*THE GREAT TERROR*

## By the Same Author

**History and Politics**

Power and Policy in the USSR

Common Sense about Russia

Courage of Genius: The Pasternak Affair

Russia after Khrushchev

The Great Terror

The Nation Killers

Where Marx Went Wrong

V. I. Lenin

Kolyma: The Arctic Death Camps

Present Danger: Towards a Foreign Policy

We and They: Civic and Despotic Cultures

What to Do When the Russians Come (with Jon Manchip White)

Inside Stalin's Secret Police: NKVD Politics 1936–39

The Harvest of Sorrow

Stalin and the Kirov Murder

Tyrants and Typewriters

**Poetry**

Poems

Between Mars and Venus

Arias from a Love Opera

Coming Across

Forays

New and Collected Poems

**Verse Translation**

Aleksandr Solzhenitsyn's *Prussian Nights*

**Fiction**

A World of Difference

The Egyptologists (with Kingsley Amis)

**Criticism**

The Abomination of Moab

# THE GREAT TERROR

## A REASSESSMENT

ROBERT CONQUEST

NEW YORK  OXFORD    OXFORD UNIVERSITY PRESS

Oxford University Press

Oxford   New York   Toronto
Delhi   Bombay   Calcutta   Madras   Karachi
Petaling Jaya   Singapore   Hong Kong   Tokyo
Nairobi   Dar es Salaam   Cape Town
Melbourne   Auckland

and associated companies in
Berlin   Ibadan

First published in 1990 by Oxford University Press, Inc.,
200 Madison Avenue, New York, New York 10016

First issued as an Oxford University Press paperback, 1991

Oxford is a registered trademark of Oxford University Press

Library of Congress Cataloging-in-Publication Data
Conquest, Robert.
The great terror: a reassessment / Robert Conquest.
p.   cm.   Includes bibliographic references.
1. Terrorism—Soviet Union.
2. Soviet Union—Politics and government—1936–1953.
3. Kommunisticheskaia partiia Sovetskogo Soiuza—Purges.
4. Stalin, Joseph, 1879–1953.  I. Title.
DK267.C649   1990   947.084'2—dc20   89-37810

ISBN 0-19-505580-2
ISBN 0-19-507132-8 (PBK.)

2 4 6 8 10 9 7 5 3 1

Printed in the United States of America

*To Helena Alexandrovna*
*and my other friends in the Soviet Union*
*who showed that even these events*
*did not destroy the spirit of the people*

# PREFACE

It is a particularly appropriate moment to put before the public a reassessment of the Great Terror, which raged in the Soviet Union in the 1930s.

First, we now have enough information to establish almost everything past dispute. Second, the Terror is, in the immediate present of the 1990s, a political and human issue in the USSR. That is to say, it is on the most striking, the most critical, and the most important agenda of the world today.

My book *The Great Terror* was written twenty years ago (though a certain amount of additional material went into editions published in the early 1970s). The brief period of Khrushchevite revelation had provided enough new evidence, in conjunction with the mass of earlier unofficial reports, to give the history of the period in considerable and mutually confirmatory detail. However, there was much that remained deduction, and there were occasional gaps, or inadequately verified probabilities, which precluded certainty.

During the years since then, *The Great Terror* remained the only full historical account of the period—as, indeed, it does to this day. It was received as such not only in the West but also in most circles in the Soviet Union. I seldom met a Soviet official or academic (or émigré) who had not read it in English, or in a Russian edition published in Florence, or in *samizdat;* nor did any of them question its general accuracy, even if able to correct or amend a few details.

*Moscow News* lately noted that the overseas Russian edition had "come by unofficial channels to the Soviet Union, and quickly circulated amongst the intelligentsia, and was valued by them as one of the most significant of foreign researches into Soviet history."[1] And finally it was serialized in the Soviet literary–political periodical *Neva* in 1989–1990, marking adequate confirmation of the book's status. But not merely its status as a work of history: *Neva*'s editor-in-chief (who is also a People's Deputy), while describing it as "far the most serious" research on the period, added that *Neva* "strives to promote the creation of the rule of law and a deepening of democracy in our society. We consider that the work of R. Conquest develops just this idea."[2]

But *The Great Terror* has been out of print for a number of years, and much new material has meanwhile accumulated: first in the *samizdat* writings of the late 1970s and early 1980s, and then, from 1987 on, in a mass of new evidence in Soviet publications of the *glasnost* period.

*The Great Terror* still had to rely to a large extent on émigré, defector, and other unofficial material. As with the writing of ancient history, it was a matter of balancing and assessing incomplete, partial, and uneven material—and not, as with the writing of modern Western history, the deployment, in addition to these, of adequate and credible official archives. Some information was, of course, available from Soviet official sources of the period, but all the main facts had been falsified or suppressed on a grand scale; and the Khrushchevite contribution, though of great importance, was far from exhaustive or decisive.

I printed in *The Great Terror* a long bibliographical note, in which I explained why and to what extent I accepted (not always in every detail) Nicolaevsky, Orlov, Barmine, Krivitsky, Weissberg, and other material published in the West. Since such accounts have now been overwhelmingly confirmed in recent Soviet publications, it has not been thought necessary to print such a note in the present book, for it appears in the period when *glasnost* has confirmed the general accuracy of such testimony and put the long-suppressed facts of the Terror beyond serious controversy. It is true that this has not yet, as I write, been done systematically, but rather in series of scattered articles. But these have accumulated sufficiently to make a full reappraisal of the Great Terror both useful and necessary. This is especially true of specific events like the Tukhachevsky Trial, the 1937 "February–March plenum," the fate of Yezhov, the developments in late 1936, and similar important phenomena.

Yet, while the new material extends our knowledge, it confirms the general soundness of the account given in *The Great Terror*. And while in this resassessment I have thus been able to give a greatly enhanced account of these years, I have not made any changes for their own sake.

In the preparation of this book, my thanks are due above all to Professor Stephen F. Cohen and Dr. Mikhail Bernstam; to Nancy Lane, for endless help and encouragement; to Irene Pavitt, for her editorial skills; to Kate Mosse; to Delano DuGarm, for irreplaceable research and other assistance; to Semyon Lyandres; to Susan Rupp; once more to Amy Desai, for her ever-admirable secretarial work; to the John Olin Program for the Study of the Soviet Union and Eastern Europe at the Hoover Institution; and, as always, to my wife.

*Stanford*                                                                                                   R.C.
*January 1990*

# CONTENTS

# BOOK I

# *THE PURGE BEGINS*

*This fear that millions of people find insurmountable,
this fear written up in crimson letters over the leaden
sky of Moscow—this terrible fear of the state . . .*
Vasily Grossman

# THE ROOTS
# OF TERROR

*The remedy invented by Lenin and Trotsky, the general suppression of democracy, is worse than the evil it was supposed to cure.*

Rosa Luxemburg

## LENIN'S PARTY

The Great Terror of 1936 to 1938 did not come out of the blue. Like any other historical phenomenon, it had its roots in the past. It would no doubt be misleading to argue that it followed inevitably from the nature of Soviet society and of the Communist Party. It was itself a means of enforcing violent change upon that society and that party. But all the same, it could not have been launched except against the extraordinarily idiosyncratic background of Bolshevik rule; and its special characteristics, some of them hardly credible to foreign minds, derive from a specific tradition. The dominating ideas of the Stalin period, the evolution of the oppositionists, the very confessions in the great show trials, can hardly be followed without considering not so much the whole Soviet past as the development of the Party, the consolidation of the dictatorship, the movements of faction, the rise of individuals, and the emergence of extreme economic policies.

After his first stroke on 26 May 1922, Lenin, cut off to a certain degree from the immediacies of political life, contemplated the unexpected defects which had arisen in the revolution he had made.

He had already remarked, to the delegates to the Party's Xth Congress in March 1921, "We have failed to convince the broad masses." He had felt obliged to excuse the low quality of many Party members: "No profound and popular movement in all history has taken place without its share of filth, without adventurers and rogues, without boastful and noisy elements. . . . A ruling party inevitably attracts careerists."[1] He had noted that the Soviet State had "many bureaucratic deformities," speaking of "that same Russian apparatus . . . borrowed from Tsardom and only just covered with a Soviet veneer." And just before his stroke he had noted "the prevalence of personal spite and malice" in the committees charged with purging the Party.[2]

Soon after his recovery from this first stroke, he was remarking, "We are living in a sea of illegality,"[3] and observing, "The Communist kernel lacks general culture"; the culture of the middle classes in Russia was "inconsiderable, wretched, but in any case greater than that of our responsible Communists."[4] In the autumn he was criticizing carelessness and parasitism, and invented special phrases for the boasts and lies of the Communists: "Com-boasts and Com-lies."

In his absence, his subordinates were acting more unacceptably than ever. His criticisms had hitherto been occasional reservations uttered in the intervals of busy political and governmental activity. Now they became his main preoccupation. He found that Stalin, to whom as General Secretary he had entrusted the Party machine in 1921, was hounding the Party in Georgia. Stalin's emissary, Ordzhonikidze, had even struck the Georgian Communist leader Kabanidze. Lenin favored a policy of conciliation in Georgia, where the population was solidly anti-Bolshevik and had only just lost its independence to a Red Army assault. He took strong issue with Stalin.

It was at this time that he wrote his "Testament." In it he made it clear that in his view Stalin was, after Trotsky, "the most able" leader of the Central Committee; and he criticized him, not as he did Trotsky (for "too far-reaching self-confidence and a disposition to be too much attracted by the purely administrative side of affairs"), but only for having "concentrated an enormous power in his hands" which he was uncertain Stalin would always know how to use with "sufficient caution." A few days later, after Stalin had used obscene language and made threats to Lenin's wife, Krupskaya, in connection with Lenin's intervention in the Georgian affair, Lenin added a postscript to the Testament recommending Stalin's removal from the General Secretaryship on the grounds of his rudeness and capriciousness—as being incompatible, however, only with that particular office. On the whole, the reservations made about Trotsky must seem more serious when it comes to politics proper, and his "ability" to be an administrative executant rather more than a potential leader in his own right. It is only fair to add that it was to Trotsky that Lenin turned for support in his last attempts to influence policy; but Trotsky failed to carry out Lenin's wishes.

The Testament was concerned to avoid a split between Trotsky and Stalin. The solution proposed—an increase in the size of the Central Committee—was futile. In his last articles Lenin went on to attack "bureaucratic misrule and wilfulness," spoke of the condition of the State machine as "repugnant," and concluded gloomily, "We lack sufficient civilization to enable us to pass straight on to Socialism although we have the political requisites."

"The political requisites . . ."—but these were precisely the activity of the Party and governmental leadership which he was condemning in practice. Over the past years he had personally lauched the system of rule by a centralized Party against—if necessary—all other social forces. He had created the Bolsheviks, the new type of party, centralized and disciplined, in the first place. He had preserved its identity in 1917, when before his arrival from exile the Bolshevik leaders had aligned themselves on a course of conciliation with the rest of the Revolution. There seems little doubt that without him, the Social Democrats would have reunited and would have taken the normal position of such a movement in the State. Instead, he had kept the Bolsheviks intact, and then sought and won sole power—again against much resistance from his own followers.

It is clear from the reports of the meeting of the Central Committee nine days before the October Revolution in 1917 that the idea of the rising was "not popular," that "the masses received our call with bewilderment." Even the reports from most of the garrisons were tepid. The seizure of power was, in fact, an almost purely military operation, carried out by a small number of Red Guards, only partly from the factories, and a rather larger group of Bolshevized soldiery. The working masses were neutral.

Then, and in the Civil War which followed, by daring and discipline a few thousand comrades* imposed themselves on Russia, against the various representatives of all political and social trends, and with the certain prospect of joint annihilation if they failed. The "Old Bolsheviks" among them had the prestige of the underground years, and the evident far-sightedness which had led them to form such a party gave them a special cachet: the *myth* of the Party, and the source of its leading cadres right up to the mid-1930s, was the underground struggle. But the vital force which forged in those concerned an overruling Party solidarity was the Civil War, the fight for power. It transformed the new mass Party into a hardened and experienced machine in which loyalty to the organization came before any other consideration.

When the Civil War ended, the Mensheviks and Socialist Revolutionaries quickly began to gain ground. The rank and file of the trade unions turned away from the Bolsheviks. And as the failure of the first attempt to impose strict State control of the economy became obvious, Lenin began to realize that to continue on those lines would lead to ruin. He determined on the economic retreat which was to be the New Economic Policy. But with this admission that the Bolsheviks had been wrong, the way was open for the moderate parties, to which the workers were already turning, to claim political power.

At the Xth Party Congress, in May 1921, Radek, with rather more frankness than Lenin, dotted the *i*'s by explaining that if the Mensheviks were left at liberty, now that the Communists had adopted their policy, they would demand political power, while to concede freedom to the Socialist Revolutionaries when the "enormous mass" of the peasants was opposed to the Communists would be suicide.[5] Both had now to be either fully legalized or completely suppressed. The latter course was naturally chosen. The Menshevik Party, which had operated under enormous disadvantages but had not been completely illegalized, was finally crushed. The Socialist Revolutionaries followed, receiving the death blow at a trial of their leaders in 1922.

Within the Communist Party itself, centers of discontent, to some degree linked with the workers' feelings, had built up: the Democratic Centralists, led by Sapronov, and the Workers' Opposition, led by Shlyapnikov. The former stood for at least freedom of discussion within the Party, and both opposed the increasing bureaucratization—though as so often with Communist opposition, Lenin was able to ask Shlyapnikov and his supporters why they had not been such keen opponents of Party bureaucracy when they themselves held Cabinet posts.

At the Xth Party Congress, Lenin had suddenly introduced two resolutions forbidding the formation of such groups, or "factions," within the Party. From

---

*The effective central core of the Party at the time of the October Revolution is estimated at 5,000 to 10,000, a third of whom were intellectuals (D. J. Dallin, cited in Boris Souvarine, *Stalin* [London, 1949], p. 317).

then on, the Secret Police took on the suppression of the even more radical opposition groups which refused to disband. But its chief, Dzerzhinsky, found that even many loyal Party members regarded those who belonged to such groups as comrades and refused to testify against them. He went to the Politburo to obtain an official decision that it was the duty of every Party member to denounce other Party members who were engaged in agitation against the leadership. Trotsky pointed out that of course it was an "elementary" obligation for members to denounce hostile elements in Party branches.

The illegal "Workers' Truth" group started issuing, at the end of 1922, proclamations attacking the "new bourgeoisie," speaking of "the gulf between the Party and the workers," of "implacable exploitation." The class, they added, which was supposed to be exercising its dictatorship was "in fact deprived of the most elementary political rights."[6] And in fact the Party, which had crushed opposition parties and had openly denied the rights of the nonproletarian majority in the name of the proletarian class struggle, was now on the brink of a breach of its last meaningful link to a loyalty outside itself.

When the Constituent Assembly, with its large anti-Bolshevik majority, was dispersed by force in January 1918 almost as soon as it met, Lenin had openly proclaimed that the "workers" would not submit to a "peasant" majority.

But as early as 1919 he found it necessary to remark that "we recognize neither freedom, nor equality, nor *labor democracy* [my italics] if they are opposed to the interests of the emancipation of labor from the oppression of capital."[7] In general, the working class itself began to be regarded as unreliable. Lenin insisted that "revolutionary violence" was also essential "against the faltering and unrestrained elements of the toiling masses themselves."[8] The right-wing Communist Ryazanov chided him. If the proletariat was weighed down with unreliable elements, he asked, "on whom will we lean?"[9]

The answer was to be—on the Party alone. Early in 1921 it had become obvious that the workers opposed the Party. Karl Radek, addressing the War College cadets, put the case clearly:

> The Party is the politically conscious vanguard of the working class. We are now at a point where the workers, at the end of their endurance, refuse any longer to follow a vanguard which leads them to battle and sacrifice. . . . Ought we to yield to the clamors of workingmen who have reached the limit of their patience but who do not understand their true interests as we do? Their state of mind is at present frankly reactionary. But the Party has decided that we must not yield, that we must impose our will to victory on our exhausted and dispirited followers.[10]

The crisis came in February 1921, when a wave of strikes and demonstrations swept Petrograd, and culminated in the revolt in March of the Kronstadt naval base.

Kronstadt saw the Party aligned finally against the people. Even the Democratic Centralists and the Workers' Opposition threw themselves into the battle against the sailors and workers. When it came to the point, Party loyalty revealed itself as the overriding motive.

War was openly waged on the *idea* of libertarian radical socialism, on proletarian democracy. On the other side there remained only the idea of the Party.

The Party, cut off from its social justification, now rested on dogma alone. It had become, in the most classical way, an example of a sect, a fanaticism. It assumed that popular, or proletarian, support could be dispensed with and that mere integrity of motive would be adequate, would justify everything in the long run.

Thus the Party's mystique developed as the Party became conscious of its isolation. At first, it had "represented" the Russian proletariat. Even when that proletariat showed signs of flagging, the Party still "represented" it as an outpost of a world proletariat with whose organizations it would shortly merge when the World Revolution or the European Revolution was completed. Only when the revolutions in the West failed to mature was the Party left quite evidently representing no one, or not many, in the actual world. It now felt that it represented not so much the Russian proletariat as it existed, but the future and real interests of that proletariat. Its justification came no longer from the politics of actuality, but from the politics of prophecy. From within itself, from the ideas in the minds of its leading members, stemmed the sources of its loyalty and solidarity.

Moreover, Lenin had established within the Party all the seeds of a centralized bureaucratic attitude. The Secretariat, long before Stalin took it over, was transferring Party officials for political reasons. Sapronov had noted that local Party committees were being transformed into appointed bodies, and he put the question firmly to Lenin: "Who will appoint the Central Committee? Perhaps things will not reach that stage, but if they did, the Revolution will have been gambled away." [11]

In destroying the "democratic" tendency within the Communist Party, Lenin in effect threw the game to the manipulators of the Party machine. Henceforward, the apparatus was to be first the most powerful and later the only force within the Party. The answer to the question "Who will rule Russia?" became simply "Who will win a faction fight confined to a narrow section of the leadership?" Candidates for power had already shown their hands. As Lenin lay in the twilight of the long decline from his last stroke, striving to correct all this, they were already at grips in the first round of the struggle which was to culminate in the Great Purge.

## STALIN CRUSHES THE LEFT

> *When one of the factions is extinguished, the remainder subdivideth.*
> FRANCIS BACON

It was in the Politburo that the decisive confrontations took place. Over the following years Trotsky, Zinoviev, Kamenev, Bukharin, Rykov, and Tomsky were to meet death at the hands of the only survivor, Stalin. At the time, such a denouement seemed unlikely.

Trotsky was the first and, on the face of it, the most dangerous of Stalin's opponents. On him Stalin was to concentrate, over the years, the whole power of his immense capacity for political malice. The personal roots of the Great Purge extend back to the earliest period of Soviet rule, when the most bitter of the various bitter rivalries which possessed Stalin was centered on the man who seemed, at least to the superficial observer, the main claimant to the Lenin succession, but who, for that reason, roused the united hostility of the remainder of the top leadership.

Trotsky's revolutionary record, from the time he had returned from abroad to become President of the St. Petersburg Soviet during the 1905 Revolution, was outstanding. His fame was European. In the Party, however, he was not as strong as his repute suggested. Right up to 1917, he had stayed clear of Lenin's tightly organized Bolshevik group and operated, with a few sympathizers, as an independent revolutionary, though in some ways closer to the Mensheviks. His own group had merged with the Bolsheviks in June 1917, and he had played a decisive role in the seizure of power in November of that year. But he was regarded as an outsider by most of the Old Bolsheviks. And at the same time, he was lacking in the experience of intrigue which they had picked up in the long and obscure inner-Party struggles in which he had tried to operate as a conciliator. They also thought of him as arrogant. The respect he won by his gifts and intellect was wrung from them reluctantly. Although he had a number of devoted adherents, on the whole he repelled as much as he attracted. With Lenin's partial support, he was undoubtedly the second man in the Party and State. With Lenin dead, he became vulnerable. But in spite of the weakness of his position, it had its strength. He had powerful backing, not only from many able Bolsheviks, but also from the students and younger Communists. The "Left" associated with Trotsky had opposed Lenin on the great issues of the early 1920s. By the New Economic Policy, Lenin had saved the country from collapse, and at the same time had kept the Party's grip on power, but at the expense of large concessions to "capitalism": the rich peasant proprietor and the profiteering "NEP-man" flourished. All this was repulsive, even sinful, to the purists. They were often not particularly devoted to Trotsky in person, but rather held to the views—dogmatic or principled, depending on how one looks at it—which Trotsky had come to personify in the early 1920s, as Bukharin had in 1918. When Stalin himself went "Left" in 1928, most of them ceased to support Trotsky in his opposition.

This group included Pyatakov, one of the six men named by Lenin in his Testament; Lenin saw him, with Bukharin, as the ablest of the younger men. Pyatakov, a tall dignified man with a long, straight beard and a high domed forehead, had started his political career as an anarchist, becoming a Bolshevik in 1910. During the Civil War, his brother had been shot by the Whites in the Ukraine, and he had only just escaped the same fate. His modesty and lack of personal ambition were admired as much as his ability.

Other leading "Trotskyites" were Krestinsky, member of the first Politburo and original senior Secretary of the Central Committee until the Left were removed from administrative power by Lenin; Rakovsky, the handsome Bulgarian veteran who had virtually founded the Balkan revolutionary movement; Preobrazhensky, the great theorist of the creation of industry on the basis of squeezing the funds out of the peasantry, who has been described as the true leader of the Left in 1923 and 1924;[12] and Radek, ugly and intelligent, who had come to the Bolsheviks from Rosa Luxemburg's Polish Social Democratic Party and had also worked in the German Socialist Left. He had operated with great daring and skill in the revolutionary Berlin of 1919, where he had been imprisoned. But his element was very much that of underground intrigue and the political gamble, and as an able journalist, sharp and satirical. His image in the Party was that of an erratic, unreliable, and cynical talker rather than a serious politician.

Trotsky was, however, quite isolated in the Politburo itself. His greatest strength was his control of the War Commissariat. An old Trotskyite later took the view that Trotsky could have won in 1923 if he had held his base in the army and personally appealed to the Party workers in the great towns. Trotsky did not do so (this observer felt) because his victory would then have meant a sure split in the Central Committee, and he hoped to secure it by negotiation.[13]

But this was the wrong arena. Trotsky's weaknesses as a politician were demonstrated:

> . . . the great intellectual, the great administrator, the great orator lacked one quality essential—at any rate in the conditions of the Russian Revolution—to the great political leader. Trotsky could fire masses of men to acclaim and follow him. But he had no talent for leadership among equals. He could not establish his authority among colleagues by the modest arts of persuasion or by sympathetic attention to the views of men of lesser intellectual calibre than himself. He did not suffer fools, and he was accused of being unable to brook rivals.[14]

His hold on Party workers was dependent on great gestures and great speeches. A listener remarks:

> But as soon as he [Trotsky] had finished he left the hall. There was no personal contact in the corridors. This aloofness, I believe, may partly explain Trotsky's inability as well as his unwillingness to build a large personal following among the rank and file of the Party. Against the intrigues of Party leaders, which were soon to multiply, Trotsky fought only with the weapons he knew how to use: his pen and his oratory. And even these weapons he took up only when it was too late.[15]

Above all, Trotsky's self-dramatization, his conviction that he would triumph by mere personal superiority, without having to condescend to unspectacular political actions, was fatal. A devastating comment from an experienced revolutionary sums it up: "Trotsky, an excellent speaker, brilliant stylist and skilled polemicist, a man cultured and of excellent intelligence, was deficient in only one quality: a sense of reality."[16]

Stalin left the fiercest attacks on Trotsky to his allies. He insistently preached moderation. When Zinoviev and Kamenev urged the expulsion of Trotsky from the Party, he opposed it. He said that no one could possibly "conceive of the work of the Political Bureau . . . without the most active participation of Comrade Trotsky."[17] But his actions were far more effective than his allies' words. His Secretariat organized the dispersal of Trotsky's leading supporters. Rakovsky was sent to the Soviet Legation in London, Krestinsky on a diplomatic mission to Germany, others to similar exile. By these and similar means, Trotsky was isolated and outmaneuvered with little trouble. His views, which had already been in conflict with those of Lenin, were officially condemned, and by 1925 it was possible to remove him from the War Commissariat.

Stalin now turned on his erstwhile allies Zinoviev and Kamenev. Only to a lesser degree than Trotsky himself they were to be pivotal to the Great Purge.

It is hard to find anyone who writes of Zinoviev in other than a hostile fashion. He seems to have impressed oppositionists and Stalinists, Communists and non-Communists, as a vain, incompetent, insolent, and cowardly nonentity. Except for Stalin himself, he is the only Bolshevik leader who cannot be called an intellectual. But, at the same time, he had no political sense either. He had no understanding of economic problems. He was a very effective orator, but his speeches lacked substance and were only temporarily effective in rousing mass audiences. And yet this was the man who was for a time the leading figure in the Soviet State just before and after Lenin's death. He owed his position simply to the fact that he had been one of the most useful amanuenses and hangers-on of Lenin (often a poor judge of men) during the period from 1909 to 1917—in fact, his closest collaborator and pupil. Just before, and for some time after, the October Revolution, he often opposed what he thought to be the risks in Lenin's policies, on occasion resigning his posts. But he always came back with apologies. And from 1918 on, he had again followed Lenin loyally.

Lenin is said to have complained, "He copies my faults";[18] nevertheless, he had forgiven him his weakness in 1917, and relied on him heavily in important posts. He had also said that Zinoviev was bold when danger was past.[19] "Panic personified" was Sverdlov's comment.[20] Yet Zinoviev had worked in the underground until joining Lenin abroad in 1908, and his conduct in opposition to Stalin (including long spells in jail), though neither firm nor reasonable, was not pure cowardice. With all his faults, he did at least make a serious bid for power, which is more than can be said for either Trotsky or Bukharin. He built up his Leningrad fief, and he and Kamenev exerted all their capacities to defeat Stalin. But perhaps the best thing to be said in Zinoviev's favor is that Kamenev, a more reputable figure, worked loyally with him for many years, and in fact right up to the time of their execution.

Like Stalin, Kamenev had lived in Tbilisi as a boy, and had gone from the Tbilisi Gymnasium to be a law student in Moscow. He was again in Tbilisi, representing the Party, in the early years of the century, when Stalin was barely known. He had been in the Butyrka jail when a student. After his underground work, he had stayed abroad between 1908 and 1914 as Lenin's closest collaborator after Zinoviev. He did not follow Lenin quite so closely as Zinoviev did, but worked for compromise with the Mensheviks and later, in Russia, dissociated himself from Lenin's defeatism in the First World War. After the February Revolution in 1917, he came back from exile in Siberia with Stalin, and they launched a program of support for the Provisional Government. When Lenin returned and insisted on a more revolutionary attitude, Kamenev alone continued to resist this view. In October 1917 he joined Zinoviev in opposing the seizure of power, attracting Lenin's violent, though temporary, rage. From 1918 on, he stuck to the Party line. He was not ambitious and was always inclined to moderation. In any case, he had neither the will power nor the judgment to compete adequately in the new phase.

Zinoviev and Kamenev had no truly outstanding adherents, but their following nevertheless included men like Lashevich (Vice Commissar for War, who was later to die before the Purges), G. E. Evdokimov (Secretary of the Central Committee), and a number of other powerful figures. Moreover, Zinoviev still controlled the Leningrad Party, and it voted solidly against Stalin's majority. There was thus the curious sight of the organizations of the Party "representing" the workers of Leningrad and of Moscow respectively passing *unanimously* resolutions condemning each other. "What," Trotsky asked ironically, "was the social explanation?"[21]

Once again, Stalin was able to appear the moderate. He represented Zinoviev and Kamenev as wanting to destroy the majority. In passages which were to require much amendment in later editions of his *Works,* he asked, "You demand Bukharin's blood? We won't give you his blood." And again: "The Party was to be led without Rykov, without Kalinin, without Tomsky, without Molotov, without Bukharin. . . . The Party cannot be led without the aid of those comrades I have just named."[22]

Defeated, Zinoviev and Kamenev, who had been particularly strong against Trotsky, now turned to him for support, forming "the United Opposition." This involved their accepting the left-wing line on economic policy, and it automatically ranged against them the followers of Lenin's line, in particular Bukharin and his supporters. By 1926, as Souvarine remarks, Trotsky had "more or less already handed Stalin the dictatorship by his lack of foresight, his tactic of patient waiting broken by sudden and inconsequent reactions, and his mistaken calculations," but his final mistake was the forming of this bloc with Zinoviev and Kamenev, "men devoid of character or credit who had nothing concrete to offer to offset the disrepute they brought with them."[23] Trotsky did not understand what the Party now was or the nature of the problem he faced.

In April 1926, Evdokimov, the only Zinovievite on the Secretariat, was removed. In July, Zinoviev was expelled from the Politburo, being replaced by the Stalinist Rudzutak; and in October, Trotsky and Kamenev were expelled in turn. In October, the opposition submitted. Zinoviev, Kamenev, Trotsky, Pyatakov, Sokolnikov, and Evdokimov denounced their own offenses,[24] a most striking precedent for the long series of self-denunciations by the oppositionists.

In 1927, the Trotsky–Zinoviev bloc made one last effort. Defeated and isolated in the ruling councils of the Party, they thought to appeal to the "Party masses" and the workers. (This was a measure of their lack of contact with reality: the masses were now wholly alienated.) In the autumn came the setting up of an illegal Trotskyite printing press, and illegal demonstrations in Moscow and Leningrad. Mrachkovsky, Preobrazhensky, and Serebryakov accepted responsibility for the print shop. They were all immediately expelled from the Party, and Mrachkovsky was arrested. Stalin gave the whole thing a most sinister air by representing the GPU provocateur who had exposed the opposition printing in an entirely false role as "a former Wrangel officer." Opposition demonstrations on 7 November were a fiasco. The only result was that on 14 November Trotsky and Zinoviev were expelled from the Party, and Kamenev, Rakovsky, Smilga, and Evdokimov from the Central Committee. Their followers everywhere were also ejected. Zinoviev and his followers recanted. Trotsky's, for the moment, stood firm. The effective number of Trotskyites and Zinovievites is easy to deduce: 2,500 oppositionists recanted after the 1927 Congress, and 1,500 were expelled. The leading Trotskyites were sent into exile. In January 1928, Trotsky was deported to Alma-Ata. Rakovsky, Pyatakov, Preobrazhensky, and others of the Left followed him to other places in the Siberian and Asian periphery.

On 16 December 1928 Trotsky refused to abjure political activity. In spite of efforts by Bukharin, together with Tomsky and Rykov, with the support, apparently, of the moderate Stalinist Kuibyshev, the Politburo agreed to his expulsion from the USSR. He was arrested on 22 January 1929 and expelled to Turkey.

## STALIN'S MEN

As his rivals fell one by one, Stalin was promoting a following with different qualities. Not one of them had any status as a theoretician, though most were capable of putting a line to a Party Congress in the conventional Marxist phrasing, which to some degree disguised this disability. Few of them had great seniority in the Party. But they were all Old Bolsheviks, and their characteristics were doggedness and a willingness to work at the dull detail of administration.

They included men of ability, if not of brilliance. It was natural that Molotov, Russia's best bureaucrat, should gravitate to Stalin's side. He had been one of the first leaders in Petrograd when the underground Bolsheviks emerged in 1917, and before that he had edited *Pravda*. He had become a candidate member of the Politburo in 1921. In 1922 he was joined in that capacity by the administrative tough V. V. Kuibyshev. But it was not until January 1926 that a further intake of Stalin's men took place: Voroshilov, his creature since the Civil War, became a full member; and Yan Rudzutak, a Latvian who typified the *durs* of the old underground, and G. I. Petrovsky, formerly a member of the Duma and latterly an executive of Stalinist policy, came in as candidates.

Later in 1926 Rudzutak was promoted to the full membership lost by Zinoviev, and the candidates were reinforced by five more Stalinists, including the Georgian "Sergo" Ordzhonikidze, who had been a member of the Central Committee even before the war; Sergei Kirov, appointed to head the Leningrad Party on the rout of the Zinovievites; Lazar Kaganovich; and Anastas Mikoyan. Ordzhonikidze, whom Lenin had proposed to expel from the Party for two years for his brutality to the Georgian Communists in 1922, was a *feldsher*, or medical orderly. Uneducated, except in Party matters, he gave foreigners the impression of being genial but sly. He seems to have intrigued with Zinoviev in 1925 and with Bukharin in 1928 and then let each of them down.[25]

Ordzhonikidze's vacillations, though, appear to have been due to weakness rather than ill will. He was apparently willing to accept Zinoviev and Kamenev back into the Party in 1927 on better terms than Stalin granted, describing them as men "who have brought a good deal of benefit to our Party,"[26] and he expressly dissociated himself from some of the more extreme charges against Trotsky.[27] He was reasonably popular in the Party, and in the years to come was to be to some extent a moderating influence.

Kirov had joined the Party at the age of eighteen in Tomsk in 1904. Arrested or deported four times under Tsarism, he was leader of the Bolshevik organization at Vladikavkaz in the Caucasus—a typical minor but high testing post for the underground militant—during the February 1917 Revolution. He, too, was lacking in some of the worst Stalinist characteristics. He, too, was fairly popular in the Party. He was Russian, as Stalin was not. He was also, alone among the Stalinists, a very effective orator. Although Kirov unflinchingly enforced Stalin's collectivization and industrialization policies, he does not seem to have had that streak of malice which characterized Stalin and his closest associates. Although ruthless, he was neither vicious nor servile. A foreign Communist who had dealings with him says that his Leningrad office had no air of revolutionary enthusiasm, and he himself "by his remarks and methods, reminded me of the cultured high officials of the Austrian administration I had known at Brunn."[28]

Such men as Kirov and Ordzhonikidze, Rudzutak and Kuibyshev, whose fates were to be important cruxes in the Great Purge, were supporters and allies of Stalin rather than real devotees. They did not see the logical tendencies of Stalin's political attitude or penetrate the obscure potentialities of his personality. The same seems to apply to such men as Vlas Chubar, who joined the Politburo as a candidate member in November 1926, and S. V. Kossior, who came in in the following year—both of them Bolsheviks since 1907 and of worker origin.

There was a story in the early 1930s of Stalin telling Yagoda that he preferred people to support him from fear rather than from conviction, because convictions could change.[29] When it came to the point, he could not rely on these men to support him through everything. He was to deal with them just as ruthlessly as with the oppositionists, reminding one of Cosimo de' Medici's remark that "we are nowhere commanded to forgive our friends."

The truest Stalinist of these promotions of the 1920s was Lazar Kaganovich. He was brought in by Stalin in 1922 as leader of the "Organization and Instruction" Section of the Central Committee under the Secretariat. He was raised to the Central Committee and to the Secretariat at the XIIIth Congress in 1924. Thenceforward, he undertook Stalin's most important assignments—as First Secretary in the Ukraine from 1925 to 1928, being withdrawn as part of the concessions Stalin then felt worth making; as First Secretary in the Moscow Party organization from 1930 to 1935; and as administrator of the key Agricultural Department of the Central Committee in 1933.

Kaganovich, though to some degree shallow in his appreciation of problems, was a brilliant administrator. A clear mind and a powerful will went with a total lack of the restraints of humanity. If we have used the word *ruthless* as generally descriptive of Kirov, for Kaganovich it must be taken quite literally—there was no ruth, no pity, at all in his make-up.

In the Purge, he took the extreme line that the Party's interest justified everything. Fixing him "with his steely blue eyes," he told an industrial official that as the Party was cleansing itself there were bound to be occasional mistakes: "When the forest is cut down the chips fly." He added that a Bolshevik must be ready to sacrifice himself for the Party: "Yes, ready to sacrifice not only his life but his self-respect and sensitivity."[30] His public speeches, too, are full of appeals for ruthlessness and self-sacrifice. When he himself was removed, in rather easier circumstances, in 1957, he telephoned the victor and begged not to be shot. It is not difficult to conclude that we have here a bully and a coward.

We may also note here the rise of future Politburo members. Andrei Zhdanov, First Secretary of the important Nizhni-Novgorod (later Gorky) province, was typical of the younger Stalinist generation. In him we find an ideological fanaticism much more dominant than in most of his generation. To him is due one of the few benefits of the Stalin epoch as compared with the 1920s—the reestablishment of an educational system which, though narrow and sycophantic, at least restored in the nonpolitical subjects the rigor and effectiveness of Russian education, which had deteriorated in the experimental interlude. Georgi Malenkov, an equally ruthless and intelligent young man, worked in the Party apparatus. His mind ran less in the channels of ideological conviction and political fanaticism than in the skills and details of political maneuver, the apparatus and its personalities. Lavrenti Beria, a former OGPU operative, was appointed by Stalin in 1931 to head the Party organization in Transcaucasia, against the objections of local leaders. These four were to combine some political capacity with satisfactory ruthlessness and to rise high in the State. Their roles in the Purge were particularly murderous.

One view commonly held at the time was that the essential struggle of the early 1930s was waged between the Stalinist "moderates" and men of the Kaganovich type, for "priority of influence over Stalin." In fact, Stalin himself was occasionally giving in with apparent good grace to hostile majorities while leaving Kaganovich and company the task of overtly putting the extreme case. As a result, the moderates seem to have thought that Stalin might have been induced to accept compromise and make shift with less than autocratic power. This mistake weakened them, as it had weakened all the previous opponents of Stalin.

There seems, indeed, no doubt that Kaganovich and others identified with terrorism did their best to dissuade Stalin from any policy of relaxation. For the Party would have forgiven Stalin, but a change in line would certainly have led to the fall of this cabal. That Stalin needed their encouragement is a more dubious proposition: his suspicions and ambitions were so strong as not to be notably affected by the efforts of these advisers. Khrushchev probably had the hierarchy of influence right when he commented, "Arbitrary behavior by one person encouraged and permitted arbitrariness in others."[31]

Apart from the true politicians operating the overt machinery of Party and State, Stalin began from the 1920s to build up a personal group of agents, chosen for their lack of scruple and totally dependent on and devoted to himself. There is a Russian proverb, "Out of filth you can make a prince," which, Trotsky says, Stalin was fond of quoting.[32] These men were truly disgusting characters by any standards, a cadre which had abandoned all normal political or even Communist standards and which may be regarded as in effect a personal group of hatchet men, ready for any violence or falsification at the orders of their leader. At the same time, the political mechanism—containing comparatively reputable figures—continued to exist and was held to the front, just as Al Capone's rule over Cicero was fronted for by civic officials, and employed the usual quota of economic and administrative cadres.

The "bloodthirsty dwarf" Yezhov—he was only about five feet tall—joined the Party in March 1917. Stalin found him in provincial posts and brought him into the Secretariat. He became a member of the Central Committee in 1927. An old Communist remarks, "In the whole of my long life I have never seen a more repellent personality than Yezhov's."[33] He was reminded of one of those slum children whose favorite occupation was to tie paraffin-soaked paper to a cat's tail and set fire to it—and this was long before Yezhov had shown his full potential. On one view, Yezhov was merely a typical apparatchik: if so, the level implied is deplorable. A recent Soviet account speaks of his "low moral qualities" and "sadistic inclinations"; "women working in the NKVD were frightened of meeting him even in the corridors"; he "lacked any trace of conscience or moral principles." [34]

The intelligence of Yezhov himself has universally been described as low. But that is not to say that he, and the others, did not have adequate organizational and "political" capacities. Such have been found also in leading gangsters, who have, indeed, also been known to nourish a sense of allegiance to the mystique of an organization in much the same way as Yezhov and his colleagues. For such men, the Party was indeed *cosa nostra*—"our thing."

Another such character, even closer to Stalin, was his secretary Poskrebyshev—bald, slightly humpbacked, heavily pockmarked. He was accustomed to speak quietly, but in the coarsest possible language, and gave a general impression of being almost totally uneducated. As head of the "Special Sector" of the Central Committee for many years, he was Stalin's closest confidant until 1952.

Similar men, who were to play important roles in the Terror, were Mekhlis and Shchadenko, who destroyed the Army; Shkiryatov, Yezhov's chief Purge assistant; and a dozen others of lesser note.

A last figure, more important than most, was Andrei Vyshinsky. Educated, intelligent, cowardly, and servile, he had been a Menshevik until 1921 and had joined the Bolshevik Party only after it established itself as victor. He was thus vulnerable to pressures and threats, and soon sought the protection of the faction best able to provide it. He made a quasi-academic career for himself in the Faculty of Law at Moscow University, and rapidly became its Rector on the intervention of the Party apparatus. Later he was a high official in the Commissariat for Education and was deeply involved in the purge of the academic world.

Vyshinsky was originally only on the fringe of the Purges, like a gangland lawyer. He was despised, and often openly snubbed, by the police and Party operatives. He was to survive them, after a career of unrelieved falsification and slander. He struck the present writer, who spoke with him in the last years of his life when he was Foreign Minister, as both physically and spiritually a creature who gave life to the worn image of a "rat in human form."

Machiavelli mentions several instances of actual criminals rising to control the State—Agathocles of Syracuse, for example. Georgian Communists used to refer to Stalin as a *kinto,* the old Tiflis equivalent of the Neapolitian *lazzaroni.* This tendency in his character is most clearly seen in his selection of followers. In the 1937 Trial, Vyshinsky was to say of the oppositionists, "This gang of murderers, incendiaries and bandits can only be compared with the medieval *camorra* which united the Italian nobility, vagabonds and brigands." [35] There is a sense in which this analysis is not inappropriate to the victors.

## DEFEAT OF THE RIGHT

With the promotion of his own allies into the Politburo, Stalin had a clear potential majority. There remained one further group to defeat: the Rightists Bukharin, Rykov, and Tomsky, with whom he had hitherto allied himself.

The Bolsheviks had taken power in a country which was not, even in their own theory, ready for their "proletarian" and "socialist" rule. For the first few years, it was maintained that though this was true, they had broken capitalist sway in a "weak link" and revolutions would soon follow in the Western world. Meanwhile, the Bolsheviks should maintain their advanced position in the hope, or rather certainty, of support from revolutions in, as Lenin put it, Berlin and London. This view lasted after the end of Lenin's active political life. As late as 1923, the attempted coup in Germany was expected to regularize the situation.

When this failed, Stalin's theory of Socialism in One Country was propounded. It had the obvious advantage that the alternative of giving up power, or even sharing power, on theoretical grounds was naturally unattractive to those who now held all the positions of power.

The new idea was, then, to "socialize" the country from above. If this had to be done without international assistance, then the Party must face the problem. Its very raison d'être was to socialize. The alternative was to adjust to the reality of a party ruling a country not suited to its ideas—that is, to face facts, to accept the economic situation and abandon the rigors of dogma. It was clear that the new system could only be achieved by force, and if established could only be kept in existence by the further and constant application of force. Above all, it was clear that the peasantry, the vast majority of the population, had accepted the Communists precisely to the extent that (under the New Economic Policy) they did not socialize the countryside.

Such a compromise was feasible. Feasible, but not possible—in the sense that the Party's whole raison d'être was "socialism." Its ideological mind-set was unsuited to reality, but was also prevented from adjusting to it by organizational principle. "Democratic centralism" by now meant that "Party discipline" involved the acceptance of a "Party line" determined by the victors of struggle within the Politburo. Those who counseled a longer patient interim in which the peasantry would be persuaded of the advantages of a socialized agriculture were seen as cowards. Stalin's problems were to rid himself of such Rightists, but also to win the leading party stratum. It was the latter who, at this time, provided him with effective support.

Zinoviev and Trotsky were no sooner defeated than Stalin turned against the Right. Its most influential leader was Nikolai Bukharin. He had been described by Lenin as "the favorite of the Party." But Lenin had earlier referred to him as "(1) credulous toward gossip and (2) devilishly *unstable* in politics."[36] He was much the most intellectual of the Bolsheviks, and had an intense interest in theory (being, in Lenin's peculiar formulation, "a most valuable and most eminent Party theoretician" who nevertheless did not properly understand Marxism). In 1917 Lenin had thought of Sverdlov and Bukharin as the natural successors if he and Trotsky were killed.[37]

But in the following year, Bukharin had led the "Left Communists" in opposition to the Brest-Litovsk Treaty, in a struggle that at one time reached the point of tentative plans for Lenin's overthrow. He had worked with the "Left" tendency until 1921, when he had suddenly become the strongest supporter of the NEP, a line he was to maintain until his fall.

Deutscher describes Bukharin as combining "angularity of intellect" with "artistic sensitivity and impulsiveness, a delicacy of character, and a gay, at times almost schoolboyish, sense of humour."[38] He was also possessed from time to time by a soggy, tearful romanticism—even about the Secret Police. Trotsky speaks of "his behaving in his customary manner, half hysterically, half childishly."[39]

His main associate was Alexei Rykov, Lenin's successor as Premier, who had worked in the underground top leadership since it first stabilized, but who had consistently tended to compromise with the Mensheviks. With Bukharin and Rykov stood the striking figure of Tomsky, leader of the trade unions, the only worker in the Politburo. He had led one of the earliest of all Soviets, that in Reval, in the 1905 revolution, and had been one of the three representatives of underground organizations at the conference of Bolshevik leaders in Paris in 1909.

Bukharin's Right won men like Uglanov, successor to Kamenev as leader of the Moscow Party; and around Bukharin in particular there grew up a group of younger men, mainly intellectuals, who were perhaps the best minds in the Party in the early 1930s. During the attack on the Left, Stalin strongly censured the idea of "fantastic plans for industry without reckoning up our reserves" and rebuked "people who look on the mass of laboring peasants as . . . an object to be exploited for the benefit of industry."[40] But he now began to take a different line, adopting the left-wing policy in its most rigorous form.

On 11 July 1928 Bukharin had a secret meeting with Kamenev, organized by Sokolnikov. Kamenev made a résumé of the conversation which finally leaked and was published abroad. Bukharin had finally seen, as he said, that the political divergences between his own right-wing faction and the left-wing faction of Zinoviev and Kamenev were as nothing compared with the total divergence of principle which separated them all from Stalin. It was not a question of ideas, since Stalin did not have any: "He changes his theories according to the need he has of getting rid of somebody at such-and-such a moment." Stalin had concluded that the advance to socialism would meet more and more popular resistance. Bukharin commented, "That will mean a police State, but nothing will stop Stalin." On the peasant issue Bukharin added in true Party style, "The kulaks can be hunted down at will, but we must conciliate the middle peasants."

Bukharin's appeal to the disgraced Kamenev was the poorest possible tactics. Not only was Kamenev no use, and the news of the approach to him highly damaging to Bukharin, but the real forces of the Left were beginning to be reconciled to the Party line, now that it had evidently swung their way; Pyatakov capitulated as early as February 1928. By mid-1929, Krestinsky, Radek, and most of the other "Trotskyites" had petitioned for readmission to the Party. Of the leaders, Rakovsky alone held out (until 1934). An observer remarks that Communists who had become involved in the opposition and needed to redeem their past faults were "particularly ruthless."[41]

Towards the end of 1928, Bukharin, Rykov, and Tomsky put in their resignations, in anger at Stalin's steady undermining of their positions. It was too soon for Stalin, and he immediately made his usual verbal concessions, passed a Politburo resolution compromising with the Right, and thus obtained "unanimity." Thereafter, the attack on the Rightist deviation went on as before but without any naming of the leaders.

In January 1929, Bukharin submitted a declaration to the Politburo protesting against plans to squeeze the peasantry and strongly criticizing the absence of intra-

Party democracy. It included the remarks "We are against one-man decisions of questions of Party leadership. We are against control by a collective being replaced by control by a person, even though an authoritative one." This, it was charged, was "direct slander of the Party, direct slander of Comrade Stalin, against whom they try to advance accusations of attempting the single-handed direction of our Party."[42]

Stalin's success in organizational detail now bore fruit. The Rightists were supported in the Central Committee by a mere handful of members.[43] That body, meeting in April 1929, condemned the right wing's views, removed Bukharin from his editorship of *Pravda* and chairmanship of the Comintern, and dismissed Tomsky from the trade union leadership. As Kaganovich was to say of the trade unions: "The greater part of the leadership . . . has been replaced. It could be said that this was a violation of proletarian democracy, but, comrades, it has long been known that for us Bolsheviks democracy is no fetish. . . ."[44]

In April, too, the principles of crash industrialization and of collectivization were adopted at the XVIth Party Conference. After their views had been condemned, the Rightists submitted. On 26 November 1929 they published a very general recantation of their views on "a series of political and tactical questions." Bukharin now lost his Politburo post.

Stalin's political problem was not yet solved. Although he had beaten the Right, there was no true guarantee against a revival of its fortunes. But with the launching of the Party into the bitter adventure of sudden collectivization, the effect on any wavering section might be calculated to be a swing to more solidarity. The effect on the Leftists, already opposed to Bukharin's views, would be further to disarm their complaints against Stalin's policies and to make them start thinking of the old Party loyalty in the presence of the enemy. As for the just-defeated Rightists, how could they rock the boat during the crisis?

Whenever the Party had been unpopular, this sort of solidarity had been demonstrated. At Kronstadt, all the oppositionists—even the Workers' Opposition—had rallied to the leadership for the critical period.

The last serious pretense that persuasion, or even economic pressure, was to be the method of enforcing the Party will on the peasantry had disappeared. Pure force, a frontal assault, was the chosen method. Without any serious preparation or planning on the economic side, the Party was launched into a civil war in the rural areas. It was the first great crisis of the Stalin regime, and it marks the beginning of a whole new era of terror.

On 5 January 1930 the Central Committee issued a decision, switching from the original plan of collectivizing 20 percent of the sown area during the Five-Year Plan to the *complete* collectivization of the more important regions by the autumn of 1930 or at the very latest the autumn of 1931, and in other areas by the autumn of 1931 or at the very latest the autumn of 1932.[45] In one way or another, everything got out of hand, and in a few weeks the Party had been carried to the brink of disaster. Between January and March 1930, the number of peasant holdings brought into the collective farms increased from 4 million to 14 million. Over half the total peasant households had been collectivized in five months. And in the countryside the peasants fought back with "the sawed-off shotgun, the axe, the dagger, the knife."[46] At the same time, they destroyed their livestock rather than let it fall into the hands of the State.

Kalinin, Ordzhonikidze, and other members of the Politburo visited the provinces and seem to have reported realistically about the disaster. But Stalin is said not to have bothered to obtain Politburo permission for his key article "Dizziness with Success," published in *Pravda* on 2 March 1930.[47] The article put most of the blame on excesses committed by local Party workers, and this, it is said, came as a shock to local enthusiasts. It was followed on 14 March by a condemnation of "distortions" of the Party line in the application of compulsion to the peasantry—which, the statement said, was a Leftist deviation which could only help to strengthen right-wing elements in the Party. Bauman, who had replaced Uglanov as First Secretary in Moscow and candidate member of the Politburo, was now made a scapegoat on charges of Left deviation, removed from his post, and sent to a lesser position in Central Asia.[48]

Defeat had been accepted. The peasants left the kolkhozes. Stalin's policy lay in ruins.

In any other political system, this would have been the moment for the opposition to stand forward. They had been proved right. And support for the Rightist leadership sprang up spontaneously in Party branches all over the country. Among the people as a whole, they were of course stronger still. But to this vast potential support, Bukharin, Tomsky, and Rykov gave no lead. On the contrary, they went out of their way to say that to come out against "the Party," especially with the support of peasants, was unthinkable. So Stalin's policy defeat was accompanied by a political victory. Tomsky was removed from the Politburo in July 1930, and Rykov in December. Henceforth, it was purely Stalinist.

The Rightist leaders privately regarded Stalin's leadership as catastrophic and hoped for his fall, but advised their closest adherents to wait in patience for a change in the Party mood. Bukharin favored working up a general support of the idea of a change without any direct organized struggle for the time being. He is described as having counseled the younger oppositionists to rely on the masses, who must sooner or later realize the fatal consequences of the Stalin line.[49] Patience would be necessary. So he accepted defeat in the vague hope of some improvement later on.

The Trotskyists voiced a similar hope for a change. Ivan Smirnov, a "capitulator," now considered, "In view of the incapacity of the present leadership to get out of the economic and political deadlock, the conviction about the need to change the leadership of the Party is growing."[50]

Stalin, though retreating, had not given up his plans for collectivization. He now proposed to bring it into being over a longer period—by means just as inhuman but not so ill-prepared. Everywhere in the countryside, the Party, faced with a hostile peasantry, regrouped and prepared further desperate action.

By a far better prepared combination of ruthlessness and economic measures, the almost complete collectivization of the bulk of the country was again attained by the end of 1932.

The peasants remaining in the villages were now subjected to demands for amounts of grain which they were unable to produce. In 1932 and 1933, the

Ukraine, the North Caucasus, and the Lower Volga suffered a terrible famine. There was enough grain, but it was taken away to the last kilogram. As recent Soviet accounts put it, "this famine was organized by Stalin quite consciously and according to plan."[51]

The main weight of the assault was against the Ukraine, and the (then) Ukrainian-speaking areas of the Kuban, in the North Caucasus. It was combined with a devastating attack on the Ukrainian intelligentsia and the Ukrainian Party itself. In fact, the campaign may be said to resemble the "laying waste" of hostile subject territories practiced by Jenghiz Khan and other figures of the past.

But it was not until 1988 that, on this as on other aspects of Stalinism, full accounting of the impact, the method, and the motives appeared in Soviet publications. The deaths in the terror-famine cannot have been lower than 6 to 7 million. The death toll among the peasantry over the whole period 1930 to 1933 is given in the recent Soviet literature as around 10 million—higher than the dead of all the belligerents put together in the First World War. That is, it was all on a scale as large as that of the subsequent "Great Terror." These events are not the subject of this book, except insofar as they are a part of the preparation for the full scale Stalinist regime. (The present writer has in fact dealt with the 1930–1933 terror in *The Harvest of Sorrow;* indeed, in a sense, the two books form a sequence on Stalinism in the 1930s.)

There seems little doubt that the main issue was simply crushing the peasantry, and the Ukrainians, at any cost. One high official told a Ukrainian who later defected that the 1933 harvest "was a test of our strength and their endurance. It took a famine to show them who is master here. It has cost millions of lives, but the collective farm system is here to stay. We have won the war."[52] In fact, we find that mass terror was now already in existence in the countryside, and thousands of police and Party officials had received the most ruthless operational experience.

On the other front, that of crash industrialization, a similar atmosphere of discipline prevailed. The great steelworks went up among ramshackle barracks packed with ill-fed workers. But in this field there was economic achievement. It was not that presaged by the plans or claimed by the propaganda authorities. The idea of smoothly planned progress was quite inapplicable.

Even in theory, the idea of plan fulfillment gave way to a race for the maximum. "Over-fulfillment" was the target, and awards went to the director who produced 120 percent of his quota. But if he did so, how did he get the raw materials? They must, of course, have been obtained at the expense of some other industry. The method, in fact, is not strictly speaking that of a planned economy; it is, rather, that of a competitive expansion without regard to allocation of resources or to the necessity of the goods produced. This system gave rise to enormous dislocations.

Even admitting the basic validity of the crash programs, the Party had not by 1930 had time to prepare adequate technical and managerial staffs or to educate the workers and peasants. Hence, everything had to be handled on the basis of myth and coercion rather than rationality and cooperation. The new proletariat was "alienated" even more thoroughly than the old. In October 1930, the first decree was issued forbidding the free movement of labor, followed two months later by one that forbade factories to employ people who had left their previous place of work without permission. At the same time, unemployment relief was abolished on the grounds that "there was no more unemployment." In January 1931 came the first law introducing prison sentences for violation of labor discipline—confined for the time being to railwaymen. February brought the compulsory Labor Books for all industrial and transport workers. In March, punitive measures against negligence were announced, followed by a decree holding workers responsible for damage done to instruments or materials. Preferential rations for "shock brigades" were introduced, and in 1932 the then very short food supplies were put under the direct control of the factory managers through the introduction of a kind of truck-system for allocation by results. July 1932 saw the abrogation of Article 37 of the 1922 Labor Code, under which the transfer of a worker from one enterprise to another could be effected only with his consent. On 7 August 1932 the death penalty was introduced for theft of State or collective property—a law which was immediately applied on a large scale. From November 1932, a single day's unauthorized absence from work became punishable by instant dismissal. Finally, on 27 December 1932, came the reintroduction of the internal passport, denounced by Lenin as one of the worst stigmata of Tsarist backwardness and despotism.

The trade union system became simply an appendage of the State. Tomsky's view that "it is impossible simultaneously to manage production on a commercial basis and to express and defend the workers' economic interests" and that "first wages must be raised, and only then can we expect a rise in productivity" were publicly rejected at the IXth Trade Union Congress in April 1932, and his successor Shvernik put forward instead, as "the trade unions' most important task," the mass introduction of "piecework on the basis of . . . norms"—that is, the rigid payment-by-result which was to be the instrument of sweating the worker over the following decades.

However, the workers did not, on the whole, die. Industrial advances were made. The system of coercion, which became institutionalized at a less desperate level, worked in the sense that industry grew. It is clear that other methods could have produced much greater advance at far less human cost. But there were tangible results, and the Party could feel that the policy had proved successful.

Stalin's other evident political objective had also been attained. In the struggle with the people, there was no room for neutrality. Loyalty could be called for from the Party membership on a war basis. He could demand absolute solidarity and use all rigor in stamping out weakness. The atmosphere of civil war resembled that of the foreign wars which autocrats have launched, throughout history, to enable them to silence the voices of criticism, to eliminate waverers. It was, once again, a question of "My party right or wrong." The oppositionists made no move. The Menshevik Abramovitch is not being unfair when he says, "The famine evoked no reaction on the part of Trotsky, who found time and space to write of the 'dreadful persecution' of his own partisans in Russia and to denounce Stalin for the latter's falsification of Trotsky's biography. The 'proletarian humanist' Bukharin and the tempestuous Rykov likewise remained silent."[53]

Bukharin was, however, beginning to understand that "rapid socialization," involving as it was bound to so much ruthlessness, dehumanized the ruling party. During the Revolution, he said privately, he had seen

> things that I would not want even my enemies to see. Yet 1919 cannot even be compared with what happened between 1930 and 1932. In 1919 we were fighting for our lives. We executed people, but we also risked our lives in the process. In the later period, however, we were conducting a mass annihilation of completely defenseless men, together with their wives and children.[54]

But he was even more concerned with the effect on the Party. Many Communists had been severely shaken. Some had committed suicide; others had gone mad. In his view, the worst result of the terror and famine in the country was not so much the sufferings of the peasantry, horrible though these were. It was the "deep changes in the psychological outlook of those Communists who participated in this campaign, and instead of going mad, became professional bureaucrats for whom terror was henceforth a normal method of administration, and obedience to any order from above a high virtue." He spoke of a "real dehumanization of the people working in the Soviet apparatus."[55]

He and his friends nevertheless remained silent, awaiting a moment when Stalin, at last realized to be a unsuitable leader of State and Party, would somehow be removed from power. They had misunderstood the nature of this last problem.

# STALIN
# PREPARES

*Resolv'd to ruin or to rule the state.*
Dryden

It was while he was securing his victory in the countryside that Stalin made the first moves toward the new style of terror which was to typify the period of the Great Purge.

While the opposition leaders thrashed about ineffectively in the quicksands of their own preconceptions, lesser figures in the Party were bolder and less confused. Three movements against Stalin came in the period 1930 to 1933. The first, in 1930, was led by men hitherto his followers: Syrtsov, whom he had just raised to be candidate member of the Politburo (in Bauman's place) and Chairman of the RSFSR Council of People's Commissars, and Lominadze, also a member of the Central Committee. They had obtained some sort of support from various local Party Secretaries (among them the Komsomol leader Shatskin and Kartvelishvili, First Secretary of the Transcaucasian Party) for an attempt to limit Stalin's powers.[1] They objected both to authoritarian rule in the Party and State and to the dangerous economic policies. They seem to have circulated a memoir criticizing the regime for economic adventurism, stifling the initiative of the workers, and bullying treatment of the people by the Party. Lominadze had referred to the "lordly feudal attitude to the needs of the peasants."[2] Syrtsov had described the new industrial giants, like the Stalingrad Tractor Plant, as so much eyewash.[3]

Stalin learned of the plans of this group before they could complete their preparations, and they were expelled in December 1930. Lominadze committed suicide in 1935; all the others concerned were to perish in the Purges.

And now we come to a case crucial to the Terror—that of Ryutin. Throughout the ensuing years, this was named as the original conspiracy; all the main oppositionists in turn were accused of participating in the Ryutin "plot," on the basis of what came to be called the "Ryutin Platform." Ryutin, with the help of Slepkov and other young Bukharinites, produced a long theoretical and political document, of which, according to Soviet articles as late as 1988, no copy remained in existence. In 1989, it seems to have been rediscovered, and a summary was printed; it consisted of thirteen chapters, four of them attacking Stalin.[4] It is believed to have run to 200 pages, and according to reports later reaching the

West the key sentence was "The Right wing has proved correct in the economic field, and Trotsky in his criticism of the regime in the Party."[5] It censured Bukharin, Rykov, and Tomsky for their capitulation. It proposed an economic retreat, the reduction of investment in industry, and the liberation of the peasants by freedom to quit the kolkhozes. As a first step in the restoration of democracy in the Party, it urged the immediate readmission of all those expelled, including Trotsky.

It was even more notable for its severe condemnation of Stalin personally. Its fifty pages devoted to this theme called forcefully for his removal from the leadership. It described Stalin as "the evil genius of the Russian Revolution, who, motivated by a personal desire for power and revenge, brought the Revolution to the verge of ruin."[6] Ryutin saw, far more clearly than his seniors in the opposition, that there was no possibility of controlling Stalin. It was a question either of submission or of revolt.

Ryutin was expelled from the Party in September 1930, and arrested six weeks later. However, on 17 January 1931 the OGPU Collegium acquitted him of criminal intent, and he was released and later restored to Party membership, with a warning.[7]

In June 1932, Ryutin and a group of minor officials wrote an "Appeal to All Members of the All-Union Communist Party (bolshevik)" in the name of an "All Union Conference of the Union of Marxist-Leninists." This much shorter document has lately been printed in Moscow, where Ryutin is now regarded as a model figure in the struggle against Stalinism. It speaks even more urgently of the destruction of the countryside, the collapse of genuine planning, the imposition of lawlessness and terror on Party and country alike under "dishonest, cunning, unprincipled people ready on the leadership's orders to change their opinions ten times, careerists, flatterers and lackeys." The arts had been crushed, the press reduced "in the hands of Stalin and his clique to a monstrous factory of lies." Above all, it stated, "Stalin and his clique will not and cannot voluntarily give up their positions, so they must be removed by force." It added that this should be done "as soon as possible."[8]

The Appeal was first shown to Slepkov and the rest of the former "young Bukharinite" group, one of whom, Yan Sten, showed it to Zinoviev and Kamenev. And other ex-oppositionists like Ter-Vaganyan, Mrachkovsky, and Uglanov also saw it.

Stalin interpreted the Appeal as a call for his assassination. In the Bukharin–Rykov Trial in 1938, it was to be spoken of at length as "registering the transition to the tactics of overthrowing the Soviet power by force; the essential points of the Ryutin platform were a palace coup, terrorism. . . ."[9] We may take it that such a remark, put into the mouth of the accused by the authorities, shows Stalin's attitudes to the Ryutin case—that he regarded it as the occasion for starting to accuse the opposition of capital crimes.

On 23 September 1932, Ryutin was again expelled from the Party and arrested. Stalin seems to have hoped that the OGPU might shoot Ryutin without involving the political authorities. But it referred the question to the Politburo. There Kirov is said to have spoken "with particular force against recourse to the death penalty. Moreover, he succeeded in winning over the Politburo in this view."[10] Another account says that in addition to Kirov, Ordzhonikidze, Kuibyshev, Kossior, Kalinin, and Rudzutak spoke against Stalin, who was only supported by Kaganovich. Even Molotov and Andreyev seem to have wavered.[11]

Such a division of views was first officially confirmed (in connection with a lesser figure who happened to have been rehabilitated) by a Soviet article of the Khrushchev period. It represents Stalin attempting at this time to purge the Armenian Communist Nazaretyan, but being unable to do so because Ordzhonikidze defended him and Stalin knew that "Kirov and Kuibyshev would also speak out in the Politburo on the same lines."[12] For the first time, in fact, Stalin was faced with powerful opposition from his own allies.

Like so much of the history of the period, this definite identification of a bloc of "moderate" Stalinists thwarting the leader's will was thus first reported by credible and respectable unofficial sources as long ago as the late 1930s, was substantially confirmed in the 1960s, and was rejected by some Western writers on the subject until the late 1980s! It has now been clearly and fully stated in the Soviet press of the glasnost period.[13]

Ryutin's would have been the first such execution within the ranks of the old Party.* It was particularly unacceptable, in any case, to start applying such measures (even though the OGPU is said to have already concocted a story about a plot at the Military Academy to go with the Platform).[14] The old Party loyalty, whatever its bad side, not merely had involved the submission of intra-Party oppositions to the will of the majority, but also had defended at least the skins of the oppressed Party minorities. Lenin could work amicably with Zinoviev and Kamenev, although he had for a time denounced them as traitors when they attacked the plan for the armed uprising in October 1917. Bukharin could later admit his talk in 1918 of arresting Lenin and changing the Government, without thereby forfeiting Party esteem. Now it emerged that Stalin's new Stalinist Politburo would not automatically accept his decisions when they contradicted such deep-set Party traditions.

It is certain that the defeat rankled. In each of the Great Trials of 1936, 1937, and 1938, the accused confessed to complicity in the Ryutin plot, which marked, they said, the first coming together of all the oppositions on a terrorist basis. It was precisely four years after the exposure of Ryutin that Stalin significantly remarked that "the OGPU is four years behind" in unmasking Trotskyites. The four years from September 1932 to September 1936 were, in fact, for him a period in which he set himself the task of breaking resistance to the physical destruction of his Party enemies.

The first lesson he seems to have drawn was that he could not easily obtain his followers' consent to execution of Party members for purely political offenses. The attempt to read an assassination program into the Ryutin Platform was too unreal. A genuine assassination might prove a better theme.

At the same time, he saw among his own adherents men whose resistance could not easily be broken, and for whose removal it was difficult to find any political excuse. Over the next two years, he was to put these two thoughts together and find a logical solution—the assassination of Kirov.

---

*Blyumkin (the ex-Socialist Revolutionary who had shot the German Ambassador in 1918) had been executed as a secret envoy of Trotsky in 1929, but that was a rather different matter.

A joint session of the Central Committee and the Central Control Commission took place from 28 September to 2 October 1932. (Zinoviev, Kamenev, and others had already been called before the Presidium of the Control Commission; Zinoviev and Kamenev had expressed regret, but Uglanov is reported "accusing his accusers.") The Ryutin group were now expelled from the Party "as degenerates who have become enemies of Communism and the Soviet regime, as traitors to the Party and to the working class, who, under the flag of a spurious 'Marxism-Leninism,' have attempted to create a bourgeois-kulak organization for the restoration of capitalism and particularly kulakdom in the USSR."[15] Ryutin was sentenced to ten years' imprisonment, and twenty-nine others to lesser terms.[16]

The plenum passed another resolution "immediately expelling from the Party all who knew of the existence of this counterrevolutionary group, and in particular had read the counterrevolutionary documents and not informed the CCC and CC of the All Union Communist Party (bolshevik), as concealed enemies of the Party and the working class." It was signed "Stalin."[17] Zinoviev and Kamenev, thus again expelled from the Party, were deported to the Urals. Soon afterward, Ivan Smirnov, who on his readmission to the Party had become head of the Gorky Automobile Works, was rearrested and sentenced to ten years in jail, going to the "isolator" at Suzdal. Smilga received five years, and with Mrachkovsky was sent to Verkhne-Uralsk.

A resolution on a more general purging of the Party was passed by a plenum of the Central Committee on 12 January 1933. More than 800,000 members were expelled during the year, and another 340,000 in 1934.

The method of the Party purge was in itself an encouragement to informers, lickspittles, and conscienceless careerists. The local Purge commissions, in the presence of the entire local membership, would examine each member about every detail of his political and personal past. Intervention from the audience was welcomed. In theory, all this was a sign of Party democracy and comradely frankness. In practice, it attracted—and of course increasingly so as conditions got worse—first the inflation of true though pettifogging points from the past, such as distant relationship or acquaintance with former White Army officers, and finally simple invention or misrepresentation.

At the January 1933 plenum, too, the last of the new cycle of plots was exposed. The distinguished Old Bolshevik A. P. Smirnov, Party member since 1896 and formerly member of the Central Committee's "Orgburo," was charged with two other Old Bolsheviks, Eismont and Tolmachev (members since 1907 and 1904, respectively), with forming an anti-Party group.

A. P. Smirnov's group is said to have had contact with Old Bolshevik workers, mainly in the trade unions, in Moscow, Leningrad, and other cities. Realizing that no legal methods could break Stalin's grip, they had to a large degree gone underground, with a view to organizing for a struggle. Their program seems to have covered the revision of the unbalanced industrial schemes, the dissolution of most of the kolkhozes, the subjection of the OGPU to Party control, and the independence of the trade unions. Above all, they had discussed the removal of Stalin. When taxed at the plenum Eismont said, "Yes, there were such conversations among us. A. P. Smirnov started them." Unlike Ryutin and his friends, none of the three had had any connection with the Trotskyite or Rightist oppositions. The exposure of this plot was described in the Khrushchev era as "the beginning of reprisals against the old Leninist cadres."[18]

In his speech on the matter, Stalin significantly remarked, "Of course, only enemies could say that to remove Stalin would not affect matters."[19]

Again, an attempt to have the oppositionists shot seems to have been made and blocked. It appears that Kirov, Ordzhonikidze, and Kuibyshev again played the main role in opposing the death penalty. Kalinin and Kossior supported them; Andreyev, Voroshilov, and, to some degree, Molotov took a vacillating position, and once again only Kaganovich supported Stalin to the end.[20]

The top Rightists had refused to have anything to do with Smirnov's plans. And even in the published Resolution on this group, it is only alleged that Rykov, Tomsky, and V. V. Shmidt had "stood aside from the struggle with anti-Party elements and even maintained relations with Smirnov and Eismont, thus in fact encouraging them in their anti-Party activities."

At the plenum, Bukharin, not implicated even to this extent, made a speech typical of the extravagant and insincere tone which was now conventional in ex-oppositionist statements, demanding "the severe punishment of A. P. Smirnov's grouping"; and he spoke of his own earlier "Right-opportunist, absolutely wrong general political line," of his "guilt before the Party, its leadership, before the Central Committee of the Party, before the working class and the country," mentioning Tomsky and Rykov as his "former companions in the leadership of the Right opposition."[21]

Eismont and Tolmachev were expelled from the Party, and A. P. Smirnov from the Central Committee.

The views of A. P. Smirnov and his followers mark an important crux. For we find veteran senior officials who had never been associated with any opposition speaking not merely of a policy change, but specifically of Stalin's removal, and it was soon to be apparent that such an idea was widely held.

Neither the Ryutin group nor the A. P. Smirnov group had any serious chance of success. The significance of the cases was, rather, in the opposition offered to Stalin by his own supporters in the Politburo on the issue of executing the conspirators. The revulsion of Kirov, Ordzhonikidze, and the others against the proposal was clearly quite genuine. The extraordinary strength of the idea of Party solidarity is nowhere better shown.

It is here that the true *dvoeverye*—double belief—of the Party "moderates" lay. It explains, as nothing else can, the horrified resistance of many who had cheerfully massacred the Whites, and at least uncomplainingly starved and slaughtered the peasantry, to the execution of prominent Party members, to "shedding the blood of Bolsheviks." It reflects a double standard of morality comparable to the attitude of sensitive and intelligent men in the ancient world to slaves or of the French nobility of the eighteenth century to the lower classes. Non-Party people were hardly more taken into account, even by the better Old Bolsheviks, than slaves were by Plato. They were, in effect, non-men. One is reminded of a famous scene in *Salammbô* when Hamilcar discovers, but is not quite able to grasp, that a slave is capable of sorrow at the proposed death of his son. For it is not, indeed, wholly impossible to maintain humanist virtues within a limited circle and at the same time to treat outsiders with indifference or brutality.

A view of the Purges which requires us to sympathize with the loyal Party victim while withholding our sympathy from such men as those who suffered in the Shakhty Case is unlikely to be accepted very widely. It is, indeed, defensible, but only from a narrow and rigorist Party viewpoint. It may perhaps be argued, from the opposite viewpoint, that those at least of the Party victims who had themselves committed or connived at similar repressions against non-Party figures are entitled not to a greater, but to a considerably smaller, meed of sympathy for their own later sufferings.

All the apparatus of oppression under which they themselves were to suffer was already in existence. They had raised no objection to its employment so long as the animus of the State was directed against men and women they too believed to be enemies of the Party. If Bukharin in the Politburo had spoken up against the Shakhty Trial, if Trotsky in exile had denounced the Menshevik Trial—if they had even objected not to the injustice as such, but merely to the blemish on the reputation of the Party and State—the oppositionists would have been on solider ground.

We are perhaps in danger of romanticizing the better actions of some of these men. When Isaac Deutscher—or even Arthur Koestler—puts the fate of the oppositionists in a tragic light, we should nevertheless recall that they themselves in their time had thought nothing, as Bukharin himself said at his trial, of killing political opponents on a large scale and for no other reason but to establish the power of their own Party against popular resistance. They had, moreover, at least not effectively protested against the trials in which non-Party people were convicted on patently falsified evidence. Few of them had stood for anything resembling democracy even within the Party (and it is notable that those few, men like Sapronov, never came to public trial).

All the same, even avoiding the romanticizing of revolution (a habit to which the British, who do not have to go through revolutions themselves, are perhaps particularly prone), we need not fall into denying any virtue to men some of whose actions may appear to us to be dubious. For this would be to lay down criteria as narrow in their way as those of the Stalinists themselves. Joseph Goebbels was one of the most unpleasant characters in Europe; yet it does not seem amiss to grant him a certain admiration for his courage and clearheadedness in the last days of the Third Reich, particularly in comparison with the cowardly and stupid intrigues of most of his colleagues.

In fact, courage and clearheadedness are admirable in themselves. And if they do not rank high among the moral virtues, we can see in some of the Soviet oppositionists something rather better. It is true that those who did not confess, and were shot secretly, demonstrated not merely a higher courage, but a better sense of values. In them, however touched by the demands of Party and revolutionary loyalty, loyalty to the truth and the idea of a more humane regime prevailed. But even among those who confessed, we can often see the struggle between Party habits and the old impulses to justice which had originally, in many cases at least, been one of the motives for joining the Party.

If the oppositionists were not spotless, it is at least true of their conduct during the Civil War that to have acted

> right or wrong
> Within that furious age

was different from planning the cold-blooded Terror shortly to be launched. Even the attempt to save Ryutin by those who had just decimated the Ukraine, absurd though it may appear to logical Stalinist and logical humanist alike, perhaps indicates not merely a wish to preserve privilege, but also a residuum of humane feeling.

There is, after all, a moral difference between some restraint and none. Although indulgence in terrorist action against any section of the population may corrupt the entire personality, as it clearly had done in the cases of Yezhov and others, the contrary is also true: the preservation of more or less humanist attitudes, even if only in a limited field, may, when the particular motives for terror against others have lapsed, spread out again and rehumanize the rest.

Over the next few years, Stalin was to burn out the last roots of humanism. There was no longer to be a section of the community reserved from the operation of arbitrary rule. And, in itself, this was not unwelcome to the non–Party members. We often find in the prison and concentration-camp literature accounts of ordinary victims being cheered up at the sight of some notorious persecutor from the NKVD or the Party machine appearing in the same cell or barrack.

For the general objection to the Terror is not that it was to strike at the Party members as well as at the population, but that the sufferings of the population itself under it increased immeasurably. The true crux of the Ryutin dispute resides less in preserving the privileged sanctuary of Party membership than in the fact that it was the issue on which Stalin was to fight the battle with his own colleagues to decide if the country was or was not to submit unreservedly to his single will. In an oligarchical system, there is at lowest always the possibility of some members of the ruling elite taking moderate views, or at least acting as a brake on their more repressive fellows. In an autocracy, the question depends entirely on the will of one man. There have been comparatively mild autocrats. But Stalin was not one of them.

In this period when Stalin was the effective binding power of the State, the pressures he met penetrated his personal life as well. On 8 November 1932 his wife, Nadezhda Alliluyeva, committed suicide. But neither personal loss nor public crisis broke his will. And this was widely understood as the decisive factor in the terrible struggle just concluded. He had met wavering and refused it countenance. We are told that "in 1932 Stalin was adamant against the proposal to surrender the positions already gained." [22] An official of the period comments,

> Loyalty to Stalin at the time of which I am writing [1932] was based principally on the conviction that there was no one to take his place, that any change of leadership would be extremely dangerous, and that the country must continue in its present course, since to stop now or attempt a retreat would mean the loss of everything. [23]

Even a Trotskyite could comment, "If it were not for that so-and-so . . . everything would have fallen into pieces by now. It is he who keeps everything together. . . ." [24]

By the beginning of 1933, many circles in the Party previously unconvinced about the possibility of success began to alter their attitude and to accept that Stalin had in fact won through. As Kamenev was made to remark at his trial in 1936, "Our banking on the insuperability of the difficulties which the country was experiencing, on the state of crisis of its economy, on the collapse of the economic policy of the Party leadership had obviously failed by the second half of 1932."[25] The "victory" did not amount to the creation of an efficient industry and agriculture. But the Party, which had staked its existence on winning the battle against the peasantry, had succeeded in crushing them, and a collective farm system was now firmly established.

By early summer, a certain relaxation took place in all fields. In May 1933, a decrease of peasant deportations to a figure of 12,000 households a year was ordered by a secret circular signed by Stalin and Molotov.[26] In the same month, Zinoviev and Kamenev were brought back from Siberia to make another confession of error. *Pravda* published a piece by Kamenev, condemning his own mistakes and calling on the oppositionists to cease any resistance.[27]

The former theological students among them—and there were always a surprising number of these in the Party, from Stalin and Mikoyan down to men like Chernov—might have remembered the scenes which took place after the Council of Nicaea, when one of the more extreme Arians remarked to a colleague who had surrendered, "Thou hast subscribed to escape banishment, but within the year thou shalt be as I am." But it is also true that even the opposition was often won over by the victory of Stalin's line and the successes gained, at whatever cost, in industry.

Moreover, the rise of Nazism in Germany was a strong shock. Stalin had played on a quite implausible war scare in the late 1920s, trapping Trotsky in particular into implying that even in war he would oppose the leadership—a sure formula for accusations of "traitor." But no serious figure had been shaken by the maneuver. Now Rakovsky and Sosnovsky, the last leading oppositionists in exile, finally made their peace with the regime, giving the war danger as their main motive. Rakovsky, who earlier seems to have been badly hurt in an attempt to escape, had pointed out that even Lenin had expressed qualms about the power of the Party, and that since his death it had become ten times more powerful. Getting to the heart of the dispute, he had said, "We have always based ourselves on the revolutionary initiative of the masses and not on the apparatus." He had added that no more faith could be placed in "enlightened bureaucracy" than in "the enlightened despotism of the seventeenth century."[28] But now he was persuaded. He was welcomed back by Kaganovich in person.[29] It was plain that an air of general reconciliation was prevalent.

Radek had long since become a shameless adulator of Stalin, detested by the less venal oppositionists. He pleased Stalin greatly by an article purporting to be a lecture delivered in 1967 at the School of Interplanetary Communications, on the fiftieth anniversary of the October Revolution. At this date (now far behind us) the World Revolution had evidently triumphed and looked back on Stalin as its most brilliant architect. Radek was put up early in 1934 to distinguish between the old oppositionists who merely lacked "proper understanding and will" and the "alien" Trotsky—a striking token of peace with the Zinovievs and Bukharins.[30] (Trotsky himself had been meanwhile writing that the slogan "Down with Stalin" was wrong[31] and that "at the present moment, the overthrow of the bureaucracy would surely serve counter-revolutionary forces.")[32]

If Stalin's special talents had been vital during the crisis, he now no longer seemed quite so essential to the Party's survival. But if it had been impossible to remove Stalin at a time when the Party and the regime were engaged in a desperate struggle, it now became difficult for a different reason: he was the victor, the man who had won against all the odds. His prestige was higher than ever.

It began to be hoped not so much that Stalin would be removed, as that he would take a more moderate line, lead a movement of reconciliation, adjust to the Party's desire to enjoy the fruits of victory in comparative peace. He might be expected to retain the leadership but to let many of his powers devolve. Alternatively, he might be given a more senior, but less powerful post. "In seasons of great peril, 'Tis good that one bear sway"; but when the danger is past, more constitutional ways return.

Stalin, Khrushchev later told the world, had not been to a farm since 1928; for him, the collectivization operation was a desk-bound one. Those who had to carry it out in the field had a more shaking time. With all the ruthlessness with which men like Kossior put through the Stalin policies, there seems no doubt that their nerves were strained and they felt something of the battle exhaustion which affected the entire organization in the field.

Now the worst tensions had somewhat slackened. The Party machine everywhere was firmly in the hands of operators who had shown their devotion to Stalin's policies. If Stalin wanted only this—political victory and the enforcement of his plans—he had won. It was now only necessary to consolidate—to consolidate, and perhaps to relax, to reestablish the Party's links with the people, and to reconcile the embittered elements in the Party itself.

Such were the ideas which seem to have entered the minds of many of the new Stalinist leadership. But they did not enter Stalin's. His aim remained, as is now clear, unchallenged power. So far, he had brutalized the Party, but he had not enslaved it. The men he had brought to the top were already adequately crude and ruthless, but they were not all vicious and servile. And even the hard-won brutality might peter out if reconciliation were practiced, if terror became thought of as not an institutionalized necessity, but only a temporary recourse.

For the moment, however, the new "unity" of the Party was celebrated. In January 1934 its XVIIth Congress, the "Congress of Victors," assembled. The 1,966 delegates (of whom 1,108 were to be shot over the next few years)[33] listened to the unanimously enthusiastic speakers.

Stalin himself set the theme:

> Whereas at the XVth Congress it was still necessary to prove the correctness of the Party line and to fight certain anti-Leninist groupings, and at the XVIth Congress, to finish off the last supporters of these groupings, at the present Congress there is nothing to prove and, it seems, nobody to beat.[34]

Former oppositionists were allowed to speak: Zinoviev, Kamenev, Bukharin, Rykov, Tomsky, Preobrazhensky, Pyatakov, Radek, and Lominadze. It is usually said that they were received respectfully, and it is true that on the whole there

was much less bitterness expressed against them than at the previous Congress.*
The line they took was one of complete Stalinist orthodoxy, replete with compliments to the General Secretary and abuse of his enemies.

Kamenev said that the first wave of anti-Party opposition had been Trotskyism; the second, the right wing; and went on:

> The third was not even a wave, but a wavelet; this was the ideology of the most rabid
> kulak scum, the ideology of the Ryutinites. . . . It would have been absurd to fight
> them by theoretical means, by ideological exposure. Other, more tangible weapons
> were needed, and these were brought to bear against the members of this group and
> their accomplices and protectors alike.[35]

We have spoken of the miscalculation, as it turned out, in the oppositionist
line of abject repentance, now repeated. The oppositionists' basic error was that
they did not understand Stalin. If he had been less determined and unprincipled,
they might have succeeded. Doubtless Zinoviev had little chance of returning to
power. But the Rightists, at least, were not in a bad tactical position. During the
extreme crisis of 1930, they had not rocked the boat, and, as a result, the crisis
had been overcome by methods which represented at least to some slight degree
of concession to their views. Their admission of their faults to the Congress was
received in much better part than had been the case on previous similar occasions.
At the same time, there was everywhere hope that the worst strain was over, that
the terrible efforts and sufferings of the first Five-Year Plan and of the collectivization drive could now be forgotten. The second Five-Year Plan pointed to a
rather more moderate approach to the economy.

All these circumstances were favorable for the Right. They were most unfavorable to Stalin. The mood, in fact, was one of intra-Party reconciliation, and of
an attempt to rebuild the bridges between the Party and the people. And such a
formulation seems to have been the conscious line of thought of Kirov and others.[36]

Between sessions, delegates discussed in this context the whole question of
Stalin's leadership. A *Pravda* account of the Khrushchev period remarks that Stalin was already "deviating further and further from Leninist norms," becoming
"more and more isolated" and "abusing his position"; the "abnormal situation"
in connection with this "alarmed many Communists"; some delegates to the Congress got the idea that the time had come to transfer Stalin from the post of
General Secretary to other work. This could not but have reached Stalin; "he
knew that the old Leninist cadres of the Party would be a decisive hindrance to
the further strengthening of his position and the concentration in his own hands of
even greater power."[37] The *Pravda* article immediately goes on, without logical
connection, but with obvious implications, to speak of "that splendid Leninist
S. M. Kirov," whom it describes as "the favorite of the Party" and whose speech
to the Congress is reported as arousing great enthusiasm. This story of a plan—or

---

*Pyatakov's speech was welcomed by "prolonged applause." Zinoviev and Bukharin were not
interrupted and gained "applause." Radek and Kamenev were interrupted, but applauded. Rykov and
Tomsky were interrupted and not applauded. But even these last were comparatively well received.

at any rate of conversations—on the desirability of transferring Stalin was repeated in a 1964 life of Kirov.[38]

Thus "the old Leninist cadres," including that "splendid Leninist" Kirov, were planning to limit Stalin's power; their intention was to relax the dictatorship and effect a reconciliation with the opposition; and Stalin, having found out their plans, saw them as a "decisive hindrance" to his own desire to extend his power. Politically, in 1934, it looked as though Stalin was not indeed beaten, but on the point of being blocked in his drive for unlimited authority. And this may have been a sound view, within the limits of politics proper.

Such was the state of our knowledge when *The Great Terror* was written. A fuller story has now emerged. Some delegates indeed discussed installing Kirov as General Secretary. He refused, on the grounds that this would call the Party's policies into question. Stalin learned of it, but Kirov told him that he himself was to blame because of the "drastic" way he did things. Moreover, at the voting for membership of the Central Committee, between 150 and 300 votes seem to have been cast against Stalin—though in the official count this was reduced to 3 (with 4 against Kirov). All this, as a recent Soviet article puts it, left Stalin with "hostility and a will to revenge against the whole congress, and of course Kirov personally."[39]

It had taken years of maneuver to defeat the old oppositionists. The new men who had blocked Stalin were neither so vulnerable nor so naive. Yet to allow the situation to stabilize while the oppositionists were still alive, and while men like Kirov were gaining popularity in the Party, must have seemed a dangerous policy to Stalin. Sooner or later he might have to face the emergence of a more moderate alternative leadership.

But what action was open to him? These trends could only be contained by force. Stalin had manned the machinery of terror with his own men. But it was necessary that the highest Party organs should approve his using it, and they had refused. To create a situation in which they could be panicked or bullied into consent—such was Stalin's problem.

For the moment nothing was done on either side. A Central Committee was elected, consisting almost solely of Stalinist veterans of the intra-Party struggle, but including Pyatakov among its full members and Sokolnikov, Bukharin, Rykov, and Tomsky among its candidates. Of the 139 members and candidate members now elected, 99 (that is, more than 70 percent) were to die violent deaths over the next five years—and eight others later on."[40]

The leading organs elected by the new Central Committee reflected a stalemate. The Politburo was no more satisfactory to Stalin than the one which had blocked him over the Ryutin issue in 1932. And, in particular, this time Kirov was elected not only to the Politburo, but to the Secretariat as well, where he joined Stalin, Kaganovich, and Stalin's equally sinister protégé Zhdanov.

The Central Control Commission which had failed Stalin in 1932 was reduced in status and lost its remnant of independence from the political leadership; Kaganovich became its head. But Rudzutak was brought back to the Politburo, though with reduced seniority. He had been a full Politburo member before taking up the CCC post. Now he was the junior candidate member. This was the only change in the Politburo apart from the addition to candidate membership of Pavel Postyshev, "tall and thin as a lath, with a grating bass voice. No fool . . . but careless of others' feelings,"[41] Stalin's latest and toughest emissary in the Ukrainian campaign.

The leading Party organs elected by the Congress were not to be the only bodies to play important roles in the forthcoming period. While the overt political struggle of the past decade had been going on, more sinister developments were taking place in what might be called the technical side of despotic rule. The Secret Police, founded in 1917, had become a large and highly organized body, and had gained great experience in arbitrary arrest, repression, and violence. None of the oppositionists had objected to it; Bukharin in particular had been effusively enthusiastic about its role.

In July 1934 the OGPU was abolished, or rather subsumed into a new All-Union NKVD. The thin-faced terror veteran Genrikh Yagoda was placed at the head of the new organization. His First Deputy was an old adherent and friend of Stalin, Ya. D. Agranov, who had been in charge of the brutal "investigation" of the Kronstadt rebels.[42]

The new body was to be efficiently deployed over the following years. Its increasingly privileged and powerful officers were to make its emblem—a serpent being struck down by a sword—prevail everywhere against the hammer and sickle of the Party membership. From Politburo members down, no one was to be exempt from their attentions. They themselves were to remain under the careful control of the supreme political authority, Stalin. In addition to police organization proper, a number of key measures date from this period. After the announcement in January 1933 of the forthcoming purge of the Party, a central Purge Commission was formed (on 29 April) which included Yezhov and M. F. Shkiryatov.

It is at this time, too, that what was to be, in many respects, the most important body of all came to the surface: the "Special Sector" of the Central Committee,[43] headed by Poskrebyshev. It was in effect Stalin's private secretariat, the immediate organ for carrying out his will. It has been compared with Nicholas I's Personal Chancellery of His Imperial Majesty. All sensitive issues were effectively handled through this channel—for example, the assassination of Trotsky.[44]

In connection with this personal secretariat, a special State Security Committee appears to have been organized; the main figures are believed to have been Poskrebyshev, Shkiryatov, Agranov, and Yezhov, at that time head of the Records and Assignment Department of the Central Committee.[45] Shkiryatov's key role is implied in an official description of his being "representative of the Central Control Commission to the Politburo and the Orgburo."[46]

On 20 June 1933 a Prosecutor-Generalship of the USSR was established. Andrei Vyshinsky, though at first ranking only as First Deputy Prosecutor-General, was the most important figure. Links with the OGPU, the "legality and regularity" of whose acts the Prosecutors were supposed to check, were provided for.

Another major element in the Stalinist State had already emerged: the show trial. In 1922, a trial expressly designed by Lenin to crush the Social Revolutionary Party had been presided over, ironically enough, by Pyatakov. Although there was an important element of falsification, in that many of the supposed prisoners were agents provocateurs, the genuine Social Revolutionaries were given reasonable freedom of defense. And death sentences (much to Lenin's anger) were abandoned under heavy pressure from the Socialist parties of Western Europe. In 1928 came the first trial in a newer mode—that of the Shakhty engineers, presided over by Vyshinsky. This was the first testing ground of the more recent technique of founding a case on false confessions extracted by terror. Over the following years came three similar great set pieces: the so-called Industrial Party of 1930, the Mensheviks in 1931, and the Metro-Vic engineers in 1933. The oppositionists, including Trotsky in exile, made no public objection to these horrible farces.

Thus a positive machinery of despotism had been created outside of and independent of the official political organs. Everywhere, in fact, the potential mechanisms for further terror were in existence, and manned for Stalin not by allies who might balk, but by accomplices who could be relied on against enemies, or friends, inside or outside the Party.

Meanwhile, the official leadership retained its power. The Stalinist writer Alexander Fadeyev commented on the Politburo, "They are bound together by the manly, principled, iron, gay friendship of the *bogatyrs*." [47] Half were to meet death or disgrace in the next four years. Kirov was the first to go.

There is little in his past record to suggest that he could have been a major leader. Even if Stalin had dropped dead, the Politburo contained men at least equally forceful, and more experienced, who would not willingly have submitted to Kirov. Pyatakov's opinion was that if Stalin went, Kaganovich would be able to take over. Even granted the defeat of the entire Stalinist wing, we have no ground for any certainty that Kirov could have coped with his seniors among the "moderates." But meanwhile, he seems to have presented the most awkward immediate problem from Stalin's point of view.

Kirov was the best orator the Party had produced since Trotsky. And the concern he had shown, now that the Stalinist victory was complete, for the welfare of the Leningrad workers was beginning to gain him a certain amount of personal popularity. In the Party itself, this popularity was genuine and unqualified. But the most significant thing was the fact that Kirov controlled a definite source of power—the Leningrad organization. When the Leningrad delegates demonstratively led the applause for Kirov at the XVIIth Congress, it may have reminded Stalin of the similar support given by an earlier Leningrad Party generation to Zinoviev.

Throughout Stalin's career this powerful fief was viewed as a seedbed of rebellion—from his removal of Zinoviev in 1926 to his slaughter of the third generation of Leningrad Communists in 1950. And it is true that in the great northern metropolis, no longer—since 1918—the country's capital, a certain alienation from the great mass of the hinterland was still present. Russia's "window on Europe" had always been a sort of advanced outpost. Its citizens thought of themselves as far ahead, even dangerously far, of the rest of the country in civilization and the arts of the West. In this youngest of the great cities of Europe—founded, indeed, after New York, Baltimore, Boston, and Philadelphia—Kirov was truly showing signs of a certain independence.

It was not easily possibly for Stalin to attack Kirov for deviationism. He had never belonged to the oppositions and had fought them firmly. But he had been generous to them in defeat. The NKVD had already turned up the fact that a number of minor oppositionists or former oppositionists were working quite freely in Leningrad. Officials taxed with permitting this were able to say that Kirov had personally ordered it. In particular, encouraging the cultural life of the city, he had allowed many of them to take posts in publishing and other similar activities. He had also worked in Leningrad in reasonable concord with Party veterans who were not strictly speaking oppositionists, but whose views tended well to the right of the Party line. If he and his Politburo colleagues with similar views had come to power, their standing was scarcely great enough to enable them to rule the Party without appealing to the old oppositionists and effecting a reconciliation with at least the right wing. One could perhaps envision a situation in which Kirov, Ordzhonikidze, and Kuibyshev sat in the Politburo with Bukharin and Pyatakov, and even Kamenev, on a moderate program.

Meanwhile, Kirov had used his position in Leningrad in other ways unwelcome to Moscow. He was in dispute with the Stalinist members of the Politburo on various issues. On the matter of the food supply to the Leningrad workers, he and Stalin had an exchange of sharp words, witnessed by Khrushchev.[48]

Kirov's election to the Secretariat seems to have been made with a view to his transfer to Moscow, where he would be under Stalin's eye. In August, Stalin asked Kirov down to Sochi, where he was holidaying with Zhdanov. Here they discussed the proposed transfer, and Stalin eventually had to settle for Kirov's agreement to come to Moscow ''at the end of the second Five-Year Plan''—that is, in 1938. But Stalin clearly believed that the political issues before him must be settled one way or another in the immediate future.[49]

It must have been about this time that Stalin took the most extraordinary decision of his career. It was that the best way of ensuring his political supremacy and dealing with his old comrade—Secretary of the Central Committee, member of the Politburo, First Secretary of the Leningrad Party organization—was murder.

# THE KIROV
# MURDER

*That many men were undone by not going deep enough in roguery;
as in gaming any man may be a loser who doth not play the whole
game.*

Henry Fielding

Late in the afternoon of 1 December 1934, the young assassin Leonid Nikolayev
entered the Smolny, headquarters of the Communist Party in Leningrad. The few
hours of the city's thin winter daylight were over, and it was quite dark. The
lights of the former aristocratic girls' school, from which Lenin had organized the
"ten days that shook the world," shone out over its colonnade and gardens, and
eastward up the icy Neva. The outer guard examined Nikolayev's pass, which
was in order, and let him in without trouble. In the interior, the guard posts were
unmanned, and Nikolayev wandered down the ornate passages until he found the
third-floor corridor on to which Sergei Kirov's office opened. He waited patiently
outside.

Kirov was at home preparing a report on the November plenum of the Central
Committee, from which he had just returned. He was to deliver it to the *aktiv* of
the Leningrad Party in the Tavride Palace that evening, and was not expected at
the Smolny. However, he arrived there at about 4:00 P.M., and after speaking to
his trusted aide, Leningrad's Second Secretary Mikhail Chudov, and others, he
walked on towards his own office just after 4:30.[1] Nikolayev moved from a corner, shot him in the back with a Nagan revolver, and then collapsed beside him.

At the sound of the shot, Party officials came running along the corridor.
They were astonished at the absence of guards. Even Kirov's chief bodyguard,
Borisov, who according to standing instructions should have been with him, was
nowhere to be seen, though he had accompanied Kirov as far as the Smolny's
front door.

This killing has every right to be called the crime of the century. Over the
next four years, hundreds of Soviet citizens, including the most prominent political leaders of the Revolution, were shot for direct responsibility for the assassination, and literally millions of others went to their deaths for complicity in one
or another part of the vast conspiracy which allegedly lay behind it. Kirov's death,
in fact, was the keystone of the entire edifice of terror and suffering by which
Stalin secured his grip on the Soviet peoples.

For a full account, based on the current state of our knowledge, readers are referred to my *Stalin and the Kirov Murder,* published early in 1989. The new information available since I wrote of the murder in *The Great Terror* validates the story then given in all points of substance, and I have had to amend it, there and here, only as to certain details.

Fairly sound accounts of the murder had been available in the West for many years. They lacked confirmation—indeed, they were hotly rejected—by Soviet sources. No full story of the Kirov murder has even now appeared in the Soviet Union; but strong hints have been given, details have been confirmed or amended, and statements have appeared which are incompatible with any version but the one long since published in the West by certain of Stalin's enemies, and often previously rejected even here as coming from biased sources and, in any case, being beyond reasonable belief.

The truth is, indeed, beyond reasonable belief.

The first official Soviet line, accepted by many in the West, was that Niko-layev was a Zinovievite indirectly inspired by Zinoviev and Kamenev. Then, in 1936, the fallen leaders were accused of being directly involved, of having or-dered the killing. Finally, in 1938, the Soviet view took the form it was to keep until 1956: Zinoviev and Kamenev, together with Trotsky, had ordered the assas-sination. It had been facilitated by Yagoda, head of the NKVD, who, as a Rightist under Yenukidze's instructions, had ordered Zaporozhets—the second-in-command of the Leningrad NKVD—to remove all obstacles to the assassin.

This change of line, which contained elements of truth, was evidently de-signed to mask or neutralize the real version, which began to circulate in the NKVD within weeks of the crime—that Nikolayev was an individual assassin, and Stalin had arranged his opportunity. There is no real doubt that it is the correct explanation; we can now reconstruct the details.

The problem Stalin faced in 1934 admitted of no political solution entirely satisfactory to him. But he saw one way out. It was extremely unorthodox. It shows more clearly than anything else the completeness of his lack of moral or other inhibitions. To kill Kirov would remove the immediate obstacle, and at the same time create an atmosphere of violence in which the enemies on to whom he shifted the blame for the murder could be wiped out without the sort of arguments he had encountered over Ryutin.

Stalin seems to have been impressed by the 30 June 1934 Purge in Nazi Germany. But he did not himself proceed in the same way. The one principle firmly established in the Nazi Party, that the will of the leader is the highest law, had no equivalent in the Communist Party. Even when, later on, Stalin was in practice able to destroy his critics at least as freely as Hitler, it was always either done in the form of some sort of trial accompanied by some sort of justification or carried out in complete secrecy. The only case in which Stalin struck with a simulacrum of the urgency of Hitler's June Purge was when he destroyed the generals in June 1937. It is true that Hitler really had some fear of Roehm and the S.A. as a rival power center, against which no other method could be risked, and something of the same sort of argument seemed at least plausible as regards the Soviet High Command. (Stalin could have learned another point from Hitler's June Purge, though there is no reason to suppose him incapable of discovering the same tactics for himself. When destroying one group of enemies, it is helpful to throw in, and accuse of the same plot, a variety of other hostile figures in no way connected with them.)*

During the Zinoviev Trial, the planning of the Kirov murder was said to have taken place in the summer of 1934.[2] Of course, the form in which this was put was untrue, but the date was do doubt thought plausible because it was around this time that Stalin himself, as we have suggested, had actually started to organize the murder. It was in August that he had spoken with Kirov about his future, and in the interim Kirov was in Central Asia, only returning to Leningrad on 1 October.[3] By that time the plot was already in preparation.

According to one account, Stalin's original plan involved replacing Filip Medved, the head of the Leningrad NKVD, with his own crony E. G. Evdokimov, the old Secret Policeman of Shakhty fame, who was on cool terms with the rest of the NKVD officers. However, this transfer was blocked by Kirov,[4] who protested against such moves being made without the permission of the Leningrad Provincial Committee, and it had to be countermanded.

Stalin could only approach Yagoda. But, even as a second choice, it is an extraordinary idea that the head of the NKVD could be approached with an order to procure the death of a Politburo member. One plausible explanation would be that Stalin had some special hold over him. This would be quite in accord with Stalin's style. There are a number of cases in which Stalin seems to have secured support by blackmail of this type (for example, Voroshilov, whose conduct in 1928 convinced Bukharin that this was true in his case). The rumor in Russia was that Stalin had discovered some discreditable incident in Yagoda's pre-Revolutionary career, involving acting in some way for the Tsarist police. In the NKVD, it was said that in 1930 Yagoda's then deputy Trilisser made an investigation of Yagoda's past and found that he had almost entirely falsified his pre-Revolutionary record. When Trilisser reported this to Stalin, Stalin merely censured and dismissed Trilisser. But Stalin was in fact glad to have the information, and to keep on as effective head of the police a man he had something against.[5]

Yagoda selected a suitable NKVD man in Leningrad. This was Medved's assistant Ivan Zaporozhets. Zaporozhets would naturally not accept such an assignment just at Yagoda's orders, so he had to receive instructions from Stalin. For the junior man in particular (in Yagoda's case, ambition must have played a more important role) the idea of Party discipline must already have been corrupted into something unrecognizable.

When Yagoda himself came to trial with the "Bloc of Rights and Trotskyites" in 1938, he testified that he had been instructed by Yenukidze "to assist in the murder of Kirov." Although he objected, he said, "Yenukidze insisted." If anyone in Soviet political life was totally unqualified to insist on anything, it was Yenukidze, a far less powerful figure than Yagoda himself. If we were to substitute for him the name of a man who was in a position to insist, we should not have to look far. Yagoda went on, "Owing to this, I was compelled to instruct Zaporozhets, who occupied the post of Assistant Chief of the Regional Adminis-

---

*There are earlier assassinations in Russia's own history which may also have inspired Stalin; for example, the killing of Prime Minister Stolypin in 1911 by an assassin who seems to have acted with the approval and connivance of the Tsarist Secret Police, which objected to Stolypin's policies.

tration of the People's Commissariat of Internal Affairs, not to place any obstacles in the way of the terrorist act against Kirov."[6]

During Yagoda's cross-examination things did not go smoothly. Without giving anything away, he yet managed to imply that there was something fishy about the whole business. Asked what methods he used in the other alleged murders, he answered, "In any case not such as . . . described here," and when questioned as to whether he would confirm his own testimony at the preliminary investigation, said, "It is exaggerated, but that does not matter." When it came to the Kirov murder itself, the following exchange was particularly odd:

> *Yagoda:* I gave instructions . . .
>
> *Vyshinsky:* To whom?
>
> *Yagoda:* To Zaporozhets in Leningrad. That is not quite how it was.
>
> *Vyshinsky:* We shall speak about that later. What I want now is to elucidate the part played by Rykov and Bukharin in this villainous act.
>
> *Yagoda:* I gave instructions to Zaporozhets. When Nikolayev was detained . . .
>
> *Vyshinsky:* In whose briefcase . . .
>
> *Yagoda:* There was a revolver and a diary. And he released him.
>
> *Vyshinsky:* And you approved of this?
>
> *Yagoda:* I just took note of the fact.
>
> *Vyshinsky:* And then you gave instructions not to place obstacles in the way of the murder of Sergei Mironovich Kirov?
>
> *Yagoda:* Yes, I did. . . . It was not like that.
>
> *Vyshinsky:* In a somewhat different form?
>
> *Yagoda:* It was not like that, but it is not important.[7]

In Leningrad, Zaporozhets looked around for a method and found in the files a report on a disillusioned and embittered young Communist—Nikolayev. Nikolayev had told a friend that he intended to assassinate some Party figure as a protest. The friend had reported him. Through the friend, Zaporozhets got into contact with Nikolayev and saw that he was provided with a pistol. In addition, Zaporozhets got the friend to persuade Nikolayev to select Kirov as his victim.[8]

Zaporozhets's next task was to steer his gunman to the heavily guarded Kirov. As so often in real life, his plans did not run smoothly. The revolver had been got to Nikolayev. He was worked up to assassination pitch. But his attempts to get into the Smolny did not at first succeed. He was arrested twice in that neighborhood. The first time, "a month and a half before the killing"—that is, within a couple of weeks of Kirov's return from Kazakhstan—he was "not even searched." The second time, only a few days before his successful attempt, he got as far as the outer guard in the Smolny. There the guard found on him "a revolver and a chart of the route Kirov usually took" (according to Yagoda at the 1938 Trial) or "a notebook and a revolver" (according to the evidence of Yagoda's secretary Bulanov on the same occasion); in any case, "arms were found on him. But upon Zaporozhets's instructions he was released on both occasions" (as Khrushchev was to put it in his speech to the XXIInd Party Congress in 1961).

It says a good deal for Nikolayev's nerve that he brought himself to make his last, and successful, attempt.

Zaporozhets had gone on holiday, leaving the affair in the hands of accomplices, not yet (1989) identified. Apart from instructions to the outer guard to let Nikolayev through unsearched, the arrangements included the "temporary" abandonment of the internal guard posts on each floor. They also managed to detain Kirov's bodyguard, Borisov. And finally, after all the earlier muddles, Stalin's plan succeeded, and his colleague lay dead in the Smolny corridors. But there was still much to do.

When the news reached Moscow, it was announced to the accompaniment of a strong expression of grief and comradeship for the dead man by Stalin and the Politburo. Stalin, with Voroshilov, Molotov, and Zhdanov,[9] left for Leningrad the same evening to "conduct the inquiry." Yagoda, Agranov, and other leading NKVD men accompanied them.

Stalin and his entourage took over an entire floor of the Smolny. But before the investigation, there were political moves to be made.

An official speaker remarked at the XXIInd Party Congress in 1961:

> On the day of the murder (which at that time had not yet been investigated, of course), upon Stalin's instructions from Leningrad, a law was adopted on an accelerated, simplified and conclusive examination of political cases. This was immediately followed by a wave of arrests and political trials. It is as if they had been waiting for this pretext in order, by deceiving the Party, to launch anti-Leninist, anti-Party methods of struggle to maintain a leading position in the Party and State.[10]

(It is difficult to see how Stalin could have given instructions from Leningrad on the day of the murder. He traveled by train, and Leningrad and Moscow are 400 miles apart by rail. He could scarcely have arrived earlier than "the crack of dawn on 2 December"—the time given by a Soviet source.[11] The decree is indeed dated 1 December. Stalin doubtless put it in hand before he left and telephoned after arriving in Leningrad to have it signed by the State authorities and issued.)

The decree, decided on without consultation in the Politburo,[12] was to be a Charter of Terror over the following years. It ran:

1. Investigative agencies are directed to speed up the cases of those accused of the preparation or execution of acts of terror.

2. Judicial organs are directed not to hold up the execution of death sentences pertaining to crimes of this category in order to consider the possibility of pardon, because the Presidium of the Central Executive Committee of the USSR does not consider as possible the receiving of petitions of this sort.

3. The organs of the Commissariat of Internal Affairs are directed to execute the death sentence against criminals of the above-mentioned category immediately after the passage of sentences.

This was published the following day, and the Politburo, presented with a *fait accompli,* approved it "casually" the day after that.[13] This was the first exercise in Stalin's new technique, by which the state of emergency was used to justify personal, and technically unconstitutional, action. In the circumstances any attempt at disapproval would have been extremely difficult. And thus even what poor guarantees Soviet law gave to "enemies of the State" were destroyed. On 10 December new Articles 466 to 470 of the Code of Criminal Procedure of the RSFSR were enacted to bring it into line. We are told that the extrajudicial bodies set up at this period were instituted on the basis of a draft by Kaganovich.[14]

Stalin then turned to the inquiry. He at once discovered various snags. First, Borisov, whose devotion to Kirov was well known, had become suspicious. This was dealt with at once. On 2 December "an accident occurred to the automobile which took Borisov to the Smolny. Borisov was killed in the accident, and in this way they got rid of a dangerous witness" (Bulanov's evidence in the 1938 Trial). This was, much later, interestingly expanded by Khrushchev:

> When the chief of Kirov's bodyguard was being taken for questioning—and he was to be questioned by Stalin, Molotov, and Voroshilov—the car, as its driver said afterward, was involved in an accident deliberately arranged by those who were taking the man to the interrogation. They said that he died as a result of the accident, even though he was actually killed by those who accompanied him.
>
> In this way, the man who guarded Kirov was killed. Later, those who killed him were shot. This was no accident but a carefully planned crime. Who could have done this? A thorough investigation is now being made into the circumstances of this complicated affair. It transpires that the driver of the car in which the chief of Kirov's bodyguard was being taken for questioning is alive. He has said that an NKVD operative sat with him in the cab during the drive. They went in a lorry. It is, of course, very strange why a lorry was used to take the man for questioning, as if no other vehicle could be found for the purpose. Evidently, everything had been planned in advance and in detail. Two other NKVD operatives were in the back of the lorry, together with Kirov's chief bodyguard.
>
> The driver continued his story. When they were driving through one street, the man sitting next to him suddenly took the steering wheel from his hands and steered the car directly at a house. The driver regained control of the wheel and steered the car, and it only hit the wall of the house sideways. He was told later that Kirov's chief bodyguard lost his life in this accident. Why did he die when no other person in the car suffered? Why were both officials of the People's Commissariat for Internal Affairs, escorting Kirov's chief bodyguard, later shot? This means that someone wanted to have them liquidated and to remove all traces.[15]

Why did Stalin dispose of Borisov in such a roundabout way? It seems that in view of Borisov's known loyalty to Kirov, to have him shot or "disappear" as an accomplice of Nikolayev's would have aroused instant incredulity in the Leningrad Party organization. It was not until 1938, when such considerations no longer applied, that Borisov was alleged to have been an accomplice.[16]

And here we may note that the Khrushchevite version of the Kirov affair, with all its air of throwing fresh light, did not produce any *facts* incompatible with Stalin's own final version. As we see, on the murder of Borisov, the essentials had emerged as to the 1938 Trial. Almost every detail of Yagoda's and Zaporozhets's involvement was given at that trial. Why, then, we may ask, did Khrushchev produce the same material—with insubstantial additional detail—as though it amounted to a great revelation? The answer clearly is that he meant to *imply* something further. And this method of dealing with the case—of implication—is the one that was pursued in the Soviet Union from 1956 to 1964.

In his Secret Speech of February 1956, Khrushchev said, "It must be asserted that to this day the circumstances surrounding Kirov's murder hide many things which are inexplicable and mysterious and demand the most careful examination.'' This was said in the context of an attack on Stalin. But nothing was made explicit. At the XXIInd Party Congress in October 1961 Khrushchev said, this time in public: ''Great efforts are still needed to find out who was really to blame for his death. The more deeply we study the materials connected with Kirov's death, the more questions arise. . . . A thorough inquiry is now being made into the circumstances of this complicated case.'' The same cautious line was taken by other speakers. But the ''inquiry'' was slow to produce results. And in a *Pravda* article of 7 February 1964, the hint was conveyed by remarking that Kirov represented an obstacle to Stalin's ambitions and going on immediately to add: ''Less than a year had passed after the XVIIth Congress when a criminal hand cut short life of Kirov. . . . This was a premeditated and carefully prepared crime the circumstances of which, as N. S. Khrushchev declared at the XXIInd Congress, have not yet been fully cleared up.''

Short of actually saying that Stalin was responsible, an announcement which still seemed to stick in the Soviet throat, it would hardly be possible to make the point more clearly. If we still had to find out who was really to ''blame,'' then obviously the case against the previously blamed—Zinoviev and Kamenev, and later the Rightists—was no longer sustained. Only one major suspect remained. Stalin's daughter, writing in 1963, rightly speaks of ''transparent hints'' then being given in Russia that her father was responsible. And there is no doubt that they were so intended and so taken.*[17] But it was not until 1988 that Yagoda was officially implicated and Stalin often, though not yet officially, named as mainly responsible. The latest Soviet account concludes, ''Stalin's participation in the murder is extremely probable, though there is no documentary confirmation''; or, as Khrushchev put it in a section of his memoirs which remained unpublished until mid-1989, ''Yagoda could only have acted on secret orders from Stalin.''[18]

With Borisov liquidated, Stalin was left with the major problem—Nikolayev.

Leonid Nikolayev had, indeed, been a dupe of Stalin, Yagoda, and Zaporozhets. But he had also acted on his own beliefs. He has, naturally, been treated in a hostile fashion by every generation of Soviet and of oppositionist commentators, including the present one. And his act, far from bringing any benefit to Russia, was made the excuse for worse tyranny than ever. For these and other reasons, it is not easy to get a clear idea of the thirty-year-old tyrannicide.

Like many revolutionaries, he seems to have been something of a misfit. He had fought in the Civil War as a teenager, and afterward had been unable to make a successful career amid an increasingly bureaucratic society.

A Party member since 1920, he had not been known as an oppositionist, and, indeed, seems to have been very hostile to Trotskyism.

Nikolayev had been out of work since March 1934, when he seems to have attacked a decision sending him to work outside the city, which he believed to be a piece of bureaucratic intrigue.[19] He had been expelled from the Party for this

---

*Stalin's similar complicity in the murder of the Yiddish actor-producer Solomon Mikhoels in Minsk in 1948 now seems well established. Described at the time as an accident, it was admitted in the Khrushchev era to have been the work of the MGB (*Sovetskaya Byelorossiya,* 13 January 1963; Svetlana Alliluyeva, *Only One Year* [London, 1969], p. 190).

breach of discipline,[20] but his membership had been restored two months later on his making a declaration of repentance.[21]

After the crime, he had been interrogated by local men before the Moscow delegation arrived, and through some slip had realized that the NKVD had been using him. When he was brought before Stalin, he said so flatly and was removed. Even if he could be tortured into temporary submission, it was out of the question to produce him in open court.

Ordering Agranov to follow up the "Zinovievite" line as best he could, Stalin returned to Moscow and for the moment satisfied himself with other measures to intensify the atmosphere of terror.

Back in the capital, Kirov's body lay in state. The highest in the land mounted guard over it in the Hall of Columns. When Stalin saw the corpse, the Soviet press noted, he appeared so overcome by emotion that he went forward and kissed it on the cheek. It would be interesting to speculate on his feelings at that moment.

It is a trifle ironic that Zinoviev, too, had just expressed his sorrow over Kirov's death, in an obituary rejected by *Pravda,* and that at the 1936 Trial Vyshinsky was to speak of it in these terms: "The miscreant, the murderer, mourns over his victim! Has anything like it ever occurred before? What can one say, what words can one use fully to describe the utter baseness and loathsomeness of this: Sacrilege! Perfidy! Duplicity! Cunning!"[22]

On 4 December it was announced that Medved had been dismissed (and replaced by Agranov) and that he and seven of his subordinates would be brought before a court for their failure to protect Kirov; Zaporozhets's name was not among them. A long list of those arrested in connection with the case in Moscow and Leningrad, all "White Guards," was given at the same time. Within a few days, "trials" of these, under the new decree, were announced. In Leningrad, the Stalinist judge I. O. Matulevich chaired a circuit court of the Military Collegium which, on 5 December, sentenced thirty-seven named "White Guards" to death for "preparation and organization of terrorist acts against officials of the Soviet regime," and in Moscow a similar session under the even more notorious V. V. Ulrikh did the same for thirty-three others.[23]

On 13 December, Ulrikh went down to Kiev to preside over the sentencing to death of twenty-eight Ukrainians. They too were charged with "organizing acts of terror against officials of the Soviet Government," and it was also said that most of them had been "apprehended with revolvers and hand grenades."[24] In this Ukrainian case we chance to know more about those concerned than we do about the victims in Leningrad and Moscow. Although the accused in all three cases were charged with having, in their majority, crossed the frontier from abroad for their terrorist purposes, we find that these Ukrainians were almost all well-known writers and cultural and social workers. Apart from one minor diplomat, and a poet who had visited Germany, they had been living in the Ukraine for years.[25] There was later a brief attack on one of them, the deaf poet Vlyzko.[26]

These official executions were supplemented by scores of others performed with less formality. Throughout the country, a great wave of arrests swept in thousands of those listed in the NKVD records as in one way or another politically suspect. The period of comparative relaxation was now at an end.

The last great assassination and attempted assassination had been in August

1918, when Socialist Revolutionaries killed Uritsky and wounded Lenin. Following that, Sverdlov had issued a hysterical call for "merciless mass terror," adding that there was no doubt that the assassins would turn out to be "hirelings of the English and French." In the event, hundreds of prisoners were shot as reprisals. Few Bolsheviks (apart from the brave Olminsky) made any protest. Now that a similar case had arisen, how could they object to the slaughter of a few score "White Guards" from Leningrad and elsewhere?

There was one typical distinction between the two terrors. Stalin implied that the victims of his terror decree were actually associated with the crime, while in Lenin's time those shot had quite frankly been no more than class hostages.

Amid this orgy of shootings, the Soviet press was launched into one of those campaigns replete with calls for vigilance and ruthlessness towards the hidden enemy which were to appear at intervals throughout Stalin's life. An atmosphere was created, in fact, in which no voice of even comparative reason or moderation could raise itself. The mutual denunciation sessions in which Communists fought for their Party membership, and indeed for their lives, by panicky and sycophantic accusations against their own accusers had died down to some considerable extent since 1933; they now revived. The "moderate" line toward the rank-and-file opposition was reversed. Thousands who had been readmitted to the Party were expelled.

In December 1934 a secret letter from the Central Committee, entitled "Lessons of the Events Connected with the Evil Murder of Comrade Kirov," was sent to all Party Committees. It amounted to a call to them to hunt down, expel, and arrest all former oppositionists who remained in the Party organizations and was followed by a storm of indiscriminate denunciations. At this early phase in the Purge, however, some discrimination was still shown in the action taken on these. Friendship with an exposed "Trotskyite" usually received a severe reprimand rather than expulsion: "only a few years later," Merle Fainsod comments, "such mild punishment would come to be regarded not merely as extreme liberalism, but as clear indication of the complicity of the judges in counter-revolutionary activity."[27] Throughout the month the press attacked Trotskyites discovered in various parts of the Union, censured Party organizations for "rotten liberalism," and called for vigilance. Mass deportations to Siberia and the Arctic took place. Within a few months 30,000 to 40,000 Leningraders had already been taken.[28]

A typical case from the times, of which dozens might be related, was that of the writer Alexander G. Lebedenko, who was arrested in Leningrad in January 1935 and exiled. One and a half years later—that is, in mid-1937—he was sentenced without trial or investigation, by decision of an NKVD Troika, to twenty years' isolation, and was released after the XXth Congress in 1956.[29]

Meanwhile, Agranov had been working on the Zinoviev connection. He established a connection between Nikolayev and the men who had been leading figures in the Leningrad Komsomol during Zinoviev's ascendancy in the city. The most prominent was I. I. Kotolynov, former member of the Central Committee of the Komsomol. It had been Kotolynov who had boldly protested at the Stalinist bully boys who were then taking over the youth organization, saying of them, "They have the mentality—if he is not a Stalinist, put on the screws, let him have it, chase him so hard that he won't open his mouth again."[30] He had, in fact, been a real oppositionist, and one against whom a real grudge persisted. Right through the Purge, this was to be a bad combination.

Agranov found that Kotolynov and some others of this group had met for discussion in 1934 because the local Party Institute was talking of producing a history of the Leningrad Komsomol. These meetings, encouraged by Kirov, were quite open and under Party control, but unorthodox views had been expressed. Agranov built this up into a "conspiracy." Nine other men who had been present, including another former member of the Komsomol Central Committee, Rumyantsev, were arrested. They were under arrest, or some of them were, by 6 December.[31] "Severe" interrogation methods were employed.

Even so, most of the young oppositionists refused to capitulate. This method of dealing with Party members was new, and they could not have had the feeling of hopelessness which later set in in similar circumstances. On the contrary, the whole thing must have seemed a dangerous and horrible lunacy of the interrogators, which might be overruled at any moment. By 12–13 December,[32] Agranov nevertheless had one or two confessions ready. These connected the former oppositionist Komsomols of Leningrad with Kamenev and Zinoviev, who had met their former supporters once or twice in an innocent way.[33] Agranov's report to Stalin represented this as Kamenev and Zinoviev going back on their various promises to "disarm" politically and in effect as a sort of conspiracy.

When this report came before the Politburo, in "an atmosphere of extreme tension,"[34] the majority still supported the liberalization envisaged by Kirov. Stalin accepted this warmly, but added that it should be amended at one point: since the opposition had failed to disarm, the Party should in self-defense undertake a check of all former Trotskyites and Zinovievites. This was agreed to with some hesitation, and as to the assassination itself, it was to be left to the investigating authorities.[35]

Before the middle of the month, G. E. Evdokimov, former Secretary of the Central Committee, Bakayev, who had been Zinoviev's head of the Leningrad GPU, and others were arrested. Zinoviev then drafted a letter to Yagoda saying that he was disturbed by these arrests and asking to be summoned so that he could establish that he had no connection with the murder. Kamenev dissuaded him from sending it.[36]

On 16 December, Pauker, Head of the Operations Department of the NKVD, and Bulanov, Yagoda's personal assistant, arrested Kamenev, and at the same time Molchanov, Head of the Secret Political Department, and Volovich, Deputy Head of the Operations Department,* pulled in Zinoviev.[37] It says something for the respect which leading Old Bolshevik oppositionists even then commanded in the Party that the routine "search" was dispensed with.[38]

For the first four or five days after the murder, the press had been full of the demands of workers' meetings for revenge, accounts of Kirov's life, descriptions of his lying in state and his funeral, listings of executed "White Guard" terrorists, and so on. Then came, for a week or ten days, a curious pause. But now, on 17

---

*All four NKVD officers were later themselves to be denounced and shot as conspirators— Pauker and Volovich as German spies in addition.

December, the Moscow Committee of the Party passed a resolution to the effect that "loathsome, hateful agents of the class enemy, foul dregs of the former Zinoviev anti-Party group, have torn Comrade Kirov from our midst," the first public reference to the alleged political feelings behind the murder.[39] The Leningrad Committee, which had just "elected" Andrei Zhdanov as Kirov's replacement (on 16 December), passed a resolution in almost identical terms.

As yet, no NKVD announcement had *directly* blamed the assassination on anyone but Nikolayev. The "White Guards" had been vaguely charged with "terrorism." On 21 December, it was at last officially stated that Kirov had been murdered by a "Leningrad Center," headed by Kotolynov, and consisting of him, Nikolayev, and six others—all of them categorized as former members of the Zinoviev opposition who had "at various times been expelled from the Party," though mostly restored to membership after statements of solidarity with the Party Line.[40] Six other accomplices were also implicated.

On the following day, a list was given for the first time of the arrested Zinovievite leaders, with a decision on the conduct of their cases.

There were distinguished names among them: Zinoviev and Kamenev, formerly members of the Politburo; G. E. Evdokimov, formerly member of the Secretariat; other former members and candidate members of the Central Committee—Zalutsky, who had formed with Molotov and Shlyapnikov the first Bolshevik Committee in Petrograd after the February Revolution; Fedorov; Kuklin; Safarov.[41] For the moment, a partial accusation went forward. Regarding seven of those arrested, including Zinoviev, Kamenev, Zalutsky, and Safarov, it was announced that the NKVD, "lacking sufficient data for bringing them before a court," would take them before a Special Board, with a view to sending them into administrative exile. With the others, headed by Bakayev, "further investigation" would take place. It was a typical Stalin move—suitable for gradually getting his colleagues and the Party used to the idea of Zinoviev's guilt, and at the same time complicated and confusing enough to mask or blur his real intent.

Of the fifteen now mentioned, ten were to appear in the first Zinoviev–Kamenev Trial the following month, together with nine not previously named.

On 27 December the formal accusation against the Nikolayev "group" was published. Now fourteen in number, they had allegedly been working since August, keeping a watch on Kirov's flat and office, and deducing his usual movements. "Witnesses" were mentioned—Nikolayev's wife, Milda Draule; his brother; and others. The conspirators were accused of having planned to kill Stalin, Molotov, and Kaganovich in addition to Kirov. And Nikolayev was also said to have been passing anti-Soviet material to an unspecified foreign consul, who later turned out to be the Latvian Bisseneks, though the NKVD is said to have originally favored his Finnish colleague.[42] The already executed "White Guards" were vaguely worked in through connections Nikolayev was said to have formed with "Denikinists."

"Documentary evidence" was mentioned, including a diary of Nikolayev's and statements he had prepared. Apparently these showed clearly that he had no accomplices. It could not be totally suppressed at this stage, as too many uninitiated investigators and others seem to have seen it. So the official account, mentioning the diary, says that it was a forgery designed to give the impression that there was no conspiracy, but only a protest against the "unjust treatment of individuals," [43] or, as a later and fuller version has it:

> The accused Nikolayev prepared several documents (a diary, declarations addressed to various institutions, etc.) in which he tried to represent his crime as a personal manifestation of despair and discontent arising from the aggravation of his material situation and a protest against the unjust attitude of certain members of the Government toward a living person. [44]

Three volumes of testimony are cited, each of them at least 200 pages long, including various confessions. [45] From all this it might have been expected that the prosecution could have held an open trial. It did not do so. On 28 and 29 December, a court presided over by the ubiquitous Ulrikh sat behind closed doors.

For the more important of Nikolayev's alleged accomplices seem still to have refused to confess in spite of severe interrogation. [46] There were rumors, to put it no higher, that fellow prisoners had seen Kotolynov at the time of his interrogation, badly scarred and beaten. [47] But he and the other Zinovievite ex-Komsomols are said to have resisted to the end. The published announcement of their "trial" reported the conspirators as saying that their motive for killing Kirov was to replace the leadership with Zinoviev and Kamenev. [48] Nikolayev and all the others were sentenced to death and executed on 29 December.

The result so far was not entirely satisfactory to Stalin. The Party would still scarcely have accepted a direct incrimination of Zinoviev and Kamenev simply on trust, without the assassin being produced to testify to it in public. Moreover, after the first shock of Kirov's death had died down, a strong element in the Politburo and elsewhere continued to put out Kirov's own line of reconciliation and relaxation.

Negotiations were afoot with the imprisoned opposition leaders to get them to assume the entire guilt for reasons of Party discipline, but these were unproductive. On the other hand, they began to feel that it was in their own interests to do all they could to discourage terrorism, which could only lead to worse repressions against themselves and their followers. So they finally agreed to accept "moral responsibility" for the murder—in that the assassin could conceivably have been encouraged to his act by their political attitudes.

On 15 and 16 January, Zinoviev, Kamenev, Evdokimov, Bakayev, Kuklin, and fourteen others were brought to trial in Leningrad as the "Moscow Center." Ulrikh again presided, and Vyshinsky prosecuted. The line taken was that, knowing the terrorist inclination of Kotolynov's "Leningrad Center," those now accused had given it political encouragement.

The new trial was not, however, reported fully. Only a three-quarter-page summary appeared in the press, with a few quotations from the evidence of Zinoviev and others admitting their partial guilt. The group was said to have been "exposed" by Bakayev and by Safarov, who was not on trial. [49] Bakayev, who had been under interrogation for over a month, seems to have made the fullest confession. Zinoviev was reported as saying in court, "The former activity of the former opposition could not, by the force of objective circumstances, but stimulate the degeneration of those criminals." [50]

He took full responsibility for those he had misled, and summed up by re-marking that

> the task that I see confronting me on this subject is to repent fully, frankly and sincerely, before the court of the working class, for what I understand to be a mistake and a crime, and to say it in such a way that it should all end, once and for all, for this group.[51]

But though this general acceptance of the moral responsibility of the opposi-tion was made, charges of more sinister involvement were rejected. Kamenev expressed his lack of trust in the ''witness'' Safarov; he also stated flatly that he did not know of the existence of the ''Moscow Center,'' of which it now turned out he was an active member, though insofar as it existed he took responsibility for it.[52] Zinoviev, too, said that many of those in the dock were unknown to him,[53] and added that he learned of Kotolynov's role only from the indictment in the ''Leningrad Center'' Case.[54] In spite of the partial surrender of the opposition-ists, it is clear that their stand was not fully satisfactory to Stalin and that a public trial would not have been a success.

On 16 January 1935 Zinoviev was sentenced to ten years' imprisonment, Evdokimov to eight, Bakayev to eight, and Kamenev to five. The other sentences ranged from ten years to five. At the same time, it was announced that the NKVD Special Board had sentenced forty-nine people, including Zalutsky, to ''confine-ment to concentration camps for a period of four to five years,'' while twenty-nine others, including Safarov, had been sentenced to exile. The length of the sentences was in any case to prove unimportant, as there is no known instance of any of these figures, major or minor, ever being released. Two days after the trial (18 January 1935) a further secret circular on vigilance was issued by the Central Committee—an official call to all branches to start rooting out ''enemies'' which significantly condemned lack of vigilance as ''a re-echoing of the Right devia-tion.''[55] A fresh wave of arrests, running into tens of thousands, now struck all the former opposition and other suspects at local levels.

There was still one batch of prisoners from the Kirov Case left to be dealt with—the Leningrad NKVD leadership, whose forthcoming trial had been an-nounced on 4 December. On 23 January they finally came before a court under, as ever, Ulrikh. Instead of the nine originally charged, there were now twelve—and Zaporozhets was among them. Medved and Zaporozhets were charged with failure to observe the basic requirements of State security, in that ''having re-ceived information about the preparations for the attempt on S. M. Kirov . . . they failed to take the necessary measures to prevent the assassination . . . al-though they had every possible means of arresting it.''

The sentences were extremely light. One official, Baltsevich, got ten years for—in addition to the main charge—unspecified wrongful acts during the inves-tigation. Medved got three years, and the others either two or three. The sentences were specifically to be served in a *kontslager* (concentration camp), a word soon to fall into disuse.

These sentences struck observant NKVD officers as totally out of proportion to the charges, especially as those sentenced for mere ''negligence'' got two years, and those for ''criminal negligence'' (apart from Baltsevich) three years—only one year more! Stalin's natural reaction to a criminal failure to guard against a genuine assassination attempt—of the sort which might strike him next—would have been the exemplary execution of all the NKVD defaulters; in fact, they could scarcely have avoided a charge of complicity in the actual crime. But the whole thing became even odder and more sinister when it was discovered that Medved and Zaporozhets were being treated as though the sentences were little more than a tedious formality.

As was later said at the 1938 Trial, Yagoda displayed "exceptional and unusual solicitude" towards them. He had "entrusted the care of the families of Zaporozhets and Medved" to his personal secretary, Bulanov; he had "sent them for detention to the camp in an unusual way—not in the car for prisoners, but in a special through car. Before sending them, he had Zaporozhets and Medved brought to see him."[56]

This is, of course, impossible to conceive as a personal initiative of Yagoda's. A higher protection was being provided. Moreover, NKVD officers learned that Pauker and Shanin (Head of the NKVD Transport Department) were sending records and radio sets to Zaporozhets in exile—contrary to the strict Stalinist rule of instantly breaking even with one's best friend, once arrested.[57]

After the various odd circumstances of the whole Kirov Case, it was this above all which convinced many officials that Stalin had approved, if not arranged, the Kirov killing. The true story gradually filtered through the NKVD apparatus. Even then it was recounted with great reserve. Both Orlov and Krivitsky were told, as the former puts it, "The whole affair is so dangerous that it is healthier not to know too much about it."[58]

A prisoner from the White Sea Canal camps reports that Medved appeared at the headquarters of the camp complex, arriving by train in a special compartment and being put up by the head of the project, Rappaport, in his own house, where he gave a party for him. Medved was wearing an NKVD uniform without the insignia of his rank. He then went on, in the same style, to Solovetsk.[59]

When the ice of the Okhotsk Sea made the move possible, Medved, Zaporozhets, and all the others we can trace were sent to Kolyma, where they were technically prisoners, but in fact given high posts—Zaporozhets as head of the road-building administration in the Kolyma complex.[60]

As to the final fate of these NKVD exiles, Khrushchev was to remark twenty years later: "After the murder of Kirov, top functionaries of the Leningrad NKVD were given very light sentences, but in 1937 they were shot. We can assume that they were shot in order to cover the traces of the organizers of Kirov's killing."[61]

Khrushchev's point is fairly taken, but it is too crudely put. No doubt, in a general way, Stalin favored silencing those who knew his secrets. In fact, during the Zinoviev–Kamenev Trial of 1936, the accused are represented as planning, "after their seizure of power, to put Bakayev in charge of the NKVD with a view to 'covering up traces' by killing all officials who might have knowledge of the plot, and also so that the conspiratorial group could destroy its own activists, its own terrorist gunmen." As the conspiracy was simply an invention of Stalin's with evidence faked to suit, this shows that he thought it natural to shoot NKVD men and others who knew too much.

But Stalin could scarcely liquidate everyone who knew of, or suspected, his crimes. It was not practical politics to execute Yagoda's subordinates until there had been time for all sorts of leaks. If it comes to that, several men who were in possession of some of Stalin's worst secrets—like Shkiryatov, Poskrebyshev, Vyshinsky, Beria, and Mekhlis—survived until 1953 to 1955, while Kaganovich is still alive.

It is true that in 1937 a great purge swept the NKVD in Kolyma. Once it was decided to expose Yagoda's part in the Kirov murder, and to tell the whole story of the NKVD involvement, it was time to sacrifice all concerned. At the 1938 Trial, Zaporozhets's role was plainly described, and it was announced that he had not appeared in court because he was being made the "subject of separate proceedings." This seems to confirm that he was then still alive but that, if such was the case, he would not long remain so.

With the January 1935 trial of the Leningrad NKVD chiefs, the Kirov Case was wound up—for the time being. The old Zinoviev oppositionists were all in prison. Leningrad had been taken from independent hands and put under Stalin's devoted satrap, Zhdanov. A terror expressed mainly in mass deportations, but partly in mass executions, had struck the city and—to a lesser extent—the country as a whole. Among the victims brought to book in this aftermath, Nikolayev's wife, Milda Draule, together with Olga Draule (her sister) and another relative, were tried by the Military Collegium and were shot on 10 March 1935.[62]

The murder of Kirov was indeed the key moment in Stalin's road to absolute power and extreme terror. Eugenia Ginzburg starts her *Journey into the Whirlwind* with the sentence "The year 1937 began, to all intents and purposes, at the end of 1934—to be exact, on the first of December." As a recent Soviet article puts it, "It marked a turning point": prior to 1 December there was a chance of better things and the scales of history trembled, but "Stalin threw Nikolayev's smoking gun into the scales."[63] Another, in a more formal analysis, agrees, while adding that of course this does not mean that Stalin's action was unpremeditated or that he was now to carry out his whole program immediately.[64] In fact, much remained to be done to crush his opponents entirely and to overcome the resistance of his less enthusiastic allies. The *coup de grâce* had not been given. And meanwhile hostility to his actions was once again arising in the lower levels of the Party.

In the Komsomol, for example, there was surprisingly frank resistance to Stalinism as late as 1935. The Secret Archive[65] from Smolensk province reveals the extent of this feeling. In a Komsomol discussion on the Kirov assassination, one member is quoted as saying, "When Kirov was killed they allowed free trade in bread; when Stalin is killed, all the kolkhozes will be divided up." A Komsomol school director, serving as a propagandist, declared, "Lenin wrote in his will that Stalin could not serve as leader of the Party." Another teacher accused Stalin of having transformed the Party into a gendarmerie over the people. A nine-year-old Pioneer was reported to have shouted, "Down with Soviet Power! When I grow up, I am going to kill Stalin." An eleven-year-old schoolboy was overheard saying, "Under Lenin we lived well, but under Stalin we live badly." And a sixteen-year-old student was said to have declared, "They killed Kirov; now let them kill Stalin." There were even occasional expressions of sympathy for the opposition. A worker Komsomol was quoted as saying, "They have slandered Zinoviev enough; he did a great deal for the Revolution." A Komsomol propagandist in answer to a question denied that Zinoviev had had any hand in the Kirov affair and described him as an "honored leader and cultivated man." An instructor of a district Komsomol committee "came out in open support of the views of Zinoviev."

In fact, there was much to do before a situation satisfactory to Stalin could be established.

# ARCHITECT
# OF TERROR

*A Prince must possess the nature of both beast and man.*
Machiavelli

The events of December 1934 and January 1935, so horrible, but above all so extraordinary, lead to the question of the mind behind them. The nature of the whole Purge depends in the last analysis on the personal and political drives of Stalin.

If we have put off any consideration of his personality until after we have seen him in characteristic action, it is because we can recount what he did (and, later, describe the results of the State he brought into being) more easily than we can describe him as an individual. He was not one of those figures whose real intentions were ever openly declared, or whose real motives can readily be deduced. If Stalin's personal drives were the motive force of the Purge, it is also true that his ability to conceal his real nature was the rock on which all resistance to the Purge foundered. His opponents could not believe that he would either wish to, or be able to, do what he did.

Stalin was now fifty-five. Until the age of thirty-seven he had been a not particularly prominent member of a small revolutionary party whose prospects of coming to power in his lifetime even Lenin had doubted as late as 1916.

When the Revolution came, Stalin appeared to be outshone by many glittering contemporaries. The time since had been spent in ceaseless political maneuver. As a result, he had defeated in turn every rival, and had now been for five years the undisputed head of State and Party; he had lately had his methods put to the severest test in the collectivization campaign and, against all prediction, had won through. This had not proved enough for him. Contrary to all that Marx had thought, we shall find in the Soviet Union of the Stalin epoch a situation in which the economic and social forces were not creating the method of rule. On the contrary, the central factor was ideas in the mind of the ruler impelling him to action very often against the natural trend of such forces. An idealist conception of history was for once correct. For Stalin created a machine capable of taking on the social forces and defeating them, and infused it with his will. Society was reconstructed according to his formulas. It failed to reconstruct him.

As the physicist Alexander Weissberg, himself a victim of the Great Purges, points out, a Marxist view of history—and, one might say, any sociological interpretation of politics—has its validity restricted "to systems which allow of the application of the statistical conception,"[1] just as with the other true sciences. When a society is so organized that the will of one man, or a small group, is the most powerful of the political and social forces, such explanations must give way, at least to a very considerable degree, to a more psychological style.

And so we are driven to an examination of the individual Joseph Stalin. But, as Arthur Koestler remarks:

> What went on in No. 1's brain? . . . What went on in the inflated grey whorls? One knew everything about the far-away spiral nebulae, but about them nothing. That was probably the reason that history was more of an oracle than a science. Perhaps later, much later, it would be taught by means of tables of statistics, supplemented by such anatomical sections. The teacher would draw on the blackboard an algebraic formula representing the conditions of life of the masses of a particular nation at a particular period: 'Here, citizens, you see the objective factors which conditioned this historical process'. And, pointing with his ruler to a grey foggy landscape between the second and third lobes of No. 1's brain: 'Now here you see the subjective reflection of these factors. It was this which in the second quarter of the twentieth century led to the triumph of the totalitarian principle in the East of Europe'. Until this stage was reached, politics would remain bloody dilettantism, mere superstition and black magic. . . .[2]

Stalin's head "had a solid peasant look about it,"[3] but his face was pockmarked and his teeth were uneven. His eyes were dark brown with a tinge of hazel. He had a stiff left arm and shoulder, the result of an accident when he was about ten. His torso was short and narrow, and his arms were too long.* Like many ambition-driven men he was very short, only about five feet, three inches. He raised himself an inch or so by specially built shoes, and at the May Day and 7 November parades stood on a wooden slab which gave him another inch or two. Bukharin said:

> It even makes him miserable that he cannot convince everyone, including himself, that he is a taller man than anybody else. That is his misfortune; it may be his most human trait and perhaps his only human trait; his reaction to his 'misfortune' is not human—it is almost devilish; he cannot help taking revenge for it on others, but especially those who are in some way better or more gifted than he is. . . .[4]

Such psychological science as we have would turn also to Stalin's childhood. W. H. Auden wrote of the origins of another dictatorship:

> Accurate scholarship can
> Unearth the whole offence . . .

and not only in the history of a country, but in the early life of a dictator:

*By the time of the Second World War, when many Western observers first saw him, he had changed. He had developed quite a large paunch; his hair had become very thin; and his face was now white with ruddy cheeks. This coloration was common in high Soviet circles, where it was known as "Kremlin complexion" and attributed to working through the night in its offices.

Find what occured at Linz . . .

But it seems doubtful if it will ever be possible really to trace what occurred at Gori, where Stalin was born and grew up, in anything like the detail implied. In any case, the necessary type of research, the free questioning of relatives and contemporaries and others in the area, has not been possible; even if it were soon to become so, it is by now presumably too late. Not that any definitive and generally accepted psychological study of the formation even of Hitler has emerged either; *a fortiori,* on the little and dubious evidence before us in Stalin's case, it would seem best not to venture even the sketchiest reconstruction.

There are, anyhow, probably few historians today who would care to deduce the essentials of a personality from a few secondhand reports about a long-past childhood. With Stalin, moreover, the bare facts are in dispute. His father was, according to some accounts, a worthless drunkard; according to others, this was not so. The biographers are faced with pursuing the matter, but in the circumstances we may be excused. This is a pity, in a way, for if it were possible to describe with rigor a set of childhood conditions likely to produce a Stalin, worldwide legislation to prevent their recurrence would be a laudable enterprise.

Legends clung even about his birth. Georgians, anxious for the reputation of their country, represented him as really of Tatar or Ossetian origin.[5] In the period of his greatness, there was a story that he was the illegitimate son of a Georgian prince.[6] Other putative fathers include the explorer Przhevalsky and, more plausibly, a local merchant. At any rate, his accepted father was a peasant cobbler (who treated him either well or badly—for as early as this, discord descends on the accounts). His father died when he was eleven, leaving a hard-working and strong-minded mother to bring up the boy. When nearly fifteen, Stalin left the Gori elementary school for the Theological Seminary at Tbilisi, being expelled, or removed for health reasons, when he was nineteen.

This was in 1899. He had already joined the Party circles in which he was to pass the remainder of his life, and by 1901 had given up all other activity to become a professional revolutionary.

His early life in the Social Democratic organizations in the Caucasus is still a very obscure subject. The Trotskyite line, that he was unimportant and inactive, is clearly exaggerated. The hagiological stories which appeared in the 1930s and 1940s representing Stalin as a "Lenin of the Caucasus" are even more baseless. But he seems at least to have been elected a member of the Executive of the All-Caucasus Federation of the Social Democratic Party in 1903. The whole early history of the Bolsheviks in Transcaucasia has been thoroughly obfuscated by a series of historians. The main point is that Bolshevism never struck root in Georgia, and most of those who later became Bolsheviks were little more than occasionally mutinous hangers-on of the large and efficient Menshevik organization.[7]

When, after the failure of the 1905 Revolution, Lenin started to rely on bank robbery as a source of funds for the Party, Stalin was involved in organizing raids on banks in the Caucasus, though he never directly took part in them. At this time, these "expropriations" were being widely condemned in the European and the Russian Social Democratic movement, and Trotsky, among others, was pointing to the demoralization involved. Even Lenin saw this to some degree, and attempted to bring the "fighting squads" under strict control and to eliminate the semibandit elements which had got into them. But Stalin seems to have had no qualms of any sort. However, after his rise to power, nothing was ever said about this activity.

Whatever Lenin's tactical qualms, this ruthlessness appealed to him, and in 1912 Stalin was co-opted on to the Central Committee of the Party. Thenceforward, in Siberian exile or at the center of power, he remained a high though unobtrusive figure in the Bolshevik leadership. In Lenin's last days, his estimate of the "wonderful Georgian" changed. He said of him, "This cook's dishes will be too peppery." Trotsky tells us, plausibly enough, that Lenin admired Stalin for "his firmness and his direct mind," but finally saw through "his ignorance . . . his very narrow political horizon, and his exceptional moral coarseness and unscrupulousness."[8] It was on grounds of personal unpleasantness—not of political unreliability—that he urged Stalin's removal, not from positions of power, but from the particular post of General Secretary. Only at the very last—too late—did Lenin plan Stalin's ruin.

At about the same time, Stalin is reported as saying to Kamenev and Dzerzhinsky, "To choose one's victims, to prepare one's plans minutely, to slake an implacable vengeance, and then to go to bed . . . there is nothing sweeter in the world."[9]

This often quoted story is entirely in accord with Stalin's practice, but it is perhaps a little unlikely that he would have spoken in quite these terms in front of possible, and not yet forewarned, rivals. His opponents, on the whole, only realized his implacability too late. But it is unnecessary today to labor the point of Stalin's unscrupulousness or yet the extreme vindictiveness of his nature.

The Stalin method of argument, long prevalent in the Soviet Union, can be traced as early as his first articles in 1905. Its particular marks are expressions like "as is well known" (kak izvestno), used in lieu of proof to give weight to some highly controversial assertion, and "it is not accidental" (ne sluchayno), used to assert a connection between two events when no evidence, and no likelihood, of such a connection exists. These and similar expressions became the staple of Soviet speeches in Stalin's time, and after.

Such phrases are extraordinarily illustrative and significant. A statement like "As is well known, Trotskyites are Nazi agents" is difficult to object to in an authoritarian State, while the idea that nothing is accidental, a strictly paranoid formulation, makes it possible to construe every fault and weakness as part of a conscious plot.

This attitude accords with Stalin's notoriously suspicious nature. Khrushchev tells us:

> . . . Stalin was a very distrustful man, sickly suspicious; we knew this from our work with him. He could look at a man and say: "Why are your eyes so shifty today?" or "Why are you turning so much today and avoiding looking me directly in the eyes?" The sickly suspicion created in him a general distrust even toward eminent Party workers whom he had known for years. Everywhere and in everything he saw "enemies," "double-dealers" and "spies."[10]

A result of this attitude was that he almost never let down his guard. In politics, particularly in those of the sharpest style, this was to prove an excellent tactical principle.

We cannot know how far Stalin really cherished the principles he professed. Khrushchev, in his Secret Speech of February 1956, concluded a series of appalling revelations of terror by remarking of them that

> Stalin was convinced that it was necessary for the defense of the interests of the working class against the plotting of the enemies and against the attack of the imperialist camp. He saw this from the position of the working class, the interests of the working people, the interests of the victory of Socialism and Communism. We cannot say that these were the deeds of a giddy despot. He considered that this should be done in the interests of the Party, of the working masses, in the name of defense of the revolution's gains. In this lies the whole tragedy.

Most people would not perhaps regard it as the *whole* tragedy. But, more to our point, there is no way of telling what Stalin's true motivation was. The fact that to all appearances he took the view attributed to him by Khrushchev does not prove that he held it sincerely. Whether he consciously thought of the state of things he created and found good as the Socialism taught in his youth, or whether he saw it as an autocracy suitable to his own aims and to Russian reality, we cannot say.

A Soviet Air Force expert who had attended a number of meetings with the top Soviet leadership in connection with plans for an intercontinental rocket mentions Stalin saying that the project would make it "easier for us to talk to the great shopkeeper Harry Truman and keep him pinned down where we want him," but then turning to him with a curious remark: "You see, we live in an insane epoch." [11]

None of the Soviet leaders of the time was ever reported as expressing in private anything but a straightforward and cynically put desire to crush the West. This philosophical comment certainly goes deeper. Whether it represents Stalin's real thinking and self-justification, or is a sign of that sensitivity to the attitude of others occasionally reported of him, cannot be guessed.

When Litvinov was discarded in 1947, he used to meet regularly with his old friend Surits, another of the rare survivors of the old Soviet diplomatic service. They frequently discussed Stalin. They both agreed that he was a great man in many ways. But he was unpredictable. And he was stubborn, refusing to consider facts which did not correspond to his wishes. He imagined, they thought, that he was serving the people. But he did not know the people and did not wish to know them, preferring the abstract idea "the People," made up to his own liking. [12]

For what it is worth, the evidence seems to be that Stalin really believed that the abolition of incomes from capital was the sole necessary principle of social morality, excusing any other action whatever. Djilas's summary is perhaps correct: "All in all, Stalin was a monster who, while adhering to abstract, absolute and fundamentally utopian ideas, in practice had no criterion but success—and this meant violence, and physical and spiritual extermination." [13]

Except for the priceless, though limited, light thrown on it by Stalin's daughter's books, the more personal side of his character must remain to a large degree enigmatic.

But it seems that the human moments, few as they were, arose in connection with his wives. When the first, Ekaterina Svanidze, died, a friend who went to the cemetery with him says that he remarked, ". . . this creature softened my stony heart. She is dead and with her died my last warm feelings for all human beings."[14]

His second wife, Nadezhda Alliluyeva, held to the old revolutionary ideas. She is said to have become horrified with what she had learned of the sufferings of the collectivization campaign. She seems to have obtained most of her information from students at a course she had been allowed to take, and they were arrested as soon as Stalin found out.

Her suicide on 9 November 1932 took place as the result of the last series of violent quarrels with her husband, whom she accused of "butchering the people." All early accounts agree that Stalin lost his temper with her and cursed her in front of his friends (though this is somewhat toned down in the version later given to his daughter).[15] For if Nadezhda, following Ekaterina, touched him in a comparatively soft spot, it was not as soft as all that, and remarkable only in comparison with his usual conduct. She left him a letter which "wasn't purely personal: it was partly political as well."[16] We are told that this made him think—and, of course, rightly—that he had enemies everywhere, and that it much exacerbated his suspiciousness. Stalin seems to have been deeply affected by Nadezhda's death. He felt it for the rest of his life, blaming it on "enemies" (and on Michael Arlen, whose book *The Green Hat* she had been reading at the time).[17]

Nadezhda's brother, the Old Bolshevik Paul Alliluyev, was Political Commissar of the Armored Forces. After a time, he was put under special surveillance. Later he told an old acquaintance that he was being kept away from Stalin and had had his Kremlin pass taken from him. It was clear to him that Yagoda and Pauker had suggested that he might be personally dangerous to Stalin in revenging his sister. He was removed from his post in 1937 and given a minor job in the Soviet Trade Delegation in Paris.[18] The causes of his early death in 1937 have been variously interpreted, but his wife was later given ten years for allegedly poisoning him.[19]

An interesting family sidelight arises too in Stalin's attitude toward his younger son, Vasili. With his elder son, Yakov, by his first wife, he was always on poor terms, occasionally subjecting him to minor persecutions. The feeling was mutual. With Vasili, Nadezhda Alliluyeva's son, his attitude was quite different. The young man is described with contempt and detestation by all who came in contact with him. He was a stupid bully, a semiliterate drunkard, "a beastly pampered schoolboy let out into the world for the first time."[20] In spite of a very poor record at the Kachinsky Flying School, where he received special tuition, he was passed into the Soviet Air Force without a single bad mark, and by the time he was twenty-nine was already a Lieutenant General. In his intemperate outbursts, he invariably traded on his father's name.[21]

But Stalin finally removed Vasili from his command for drunken incompetence. And it does not seem that he ever intervened directly to advance his career. It was rather that his subordinates did not dare to do other than recommend the young man enthusiastically in spite of his lack of qualifications. All the same, there seems to be a faint echo here of Napoleonic vulgarities. H. G. Wells writes of Napoleon's relation to the French Revolution:

> And now we come to one of the most illuminating figures in modern history, the figure of an adventurer and a wrecker, whose story seems to display with an extraordinary vividness the universal subtle conflict of egoism, vanity and personality with the weaker, wider claims of the common good. Against this background of confusion and stress . . . this stormy and tremendous dawn, appears this dark little archaic personage hard, compact, capable, unscrupulous, imitative and neatly vulgar.[22]

Many people have felt something of the same about the squat, vulgar figure of Stalin against the tremendous dawn of the Russian Revolution. But, in the first place, Wells is more than a little unfair to Napoleon. His political, as well as military, talents were considerable. Doubtless the Emperor vulgarized the Revolution, but it had already vulgarized itself.

No doubt all revolutions are doomed to vulgarization. But the idealization of the first glories of the new regime often contains a large element of vulgar sentimentalism, and the change to vulgar cynicism may constitute only a comparative deflation. Both Napoleon and Stalin, however that may be, established their rule largely, though not entirely, by to some degree replacing the motivation of general ideas by that of careerism and personal loyalty.

Napoleon was, of course, a vain man. Stalin's vanity has also been much remarked on. But it did not, at least until his last years, run to palatial ostentation. Until the Second World War, he dressed with traditional Bolshevik modesty in a plain brown military coat and dark trousers stuffed into leather boots. He lived unpretentiously in a small house in the Kremlin, formerly part of the Tsar's servants' quarters. Ownership and money as such played no part in his life. In the 1930s, his official salary was about 1,000 rubles a month—in purchasing power, perhaps $40. One of his secretaries accepted and dealt with this small sum, paying the superintendent of the Kremlin a modest rent for his apartment, and dealing with his Party dues, his payment for his holiday, and so on. He owned nothing but had immediate right to everything, like the Dalai Lama or the Mikado in the old days. His country villa at Borovikha and his seaside Government Summer House No. 7 at Sochi were "State property."[23]

With all this personal simplicity, Stalin's reputation for envious emulation arose early among his colleagues. When the Order of the Red Banner began to be awarded in the Civil War, and was to be given to Trotsky, Kamenev proposed that Stalin should receive it too. Kalinin, the new Head of State, asked in surprise, "For what?" Bukharin intervened: "Can't you understand? This is Lenin's idea. Stalin cannot live unless he has what someone else has. He will never forgive it."[24]

In the final stages of the "cult of personality," he was built up with the most astonishing adulation as a genius not only in politics, but also in strategy, the sciences, style, philosophy, and almost every field. His picture looked down from every hoarding; his bust was carried by Soviet alpinists to the top of every Soviet peak. He was elevated to be, with Marx, Engels, and Lenin, the fourth of the great political geniuses of the epoch. The histories were, of course, rewritten to make his role in the Revolution a decisive one. Khrushchev describes him inserting in a draft of his own *Short Biography* the following passage: "Although he performed his task as leader of the Party and the people with consummate skill and enjoyed the unreserved support of the entire Soviet people, Stalin never allowed his work to be marred by the slightest hint of vanity, conceit or self-adulation."

Khrushchev goes on to say:

> In the draft of his book appeared the following sentence: "Stalin is the Lenin of today." This sentence appeared to Stalin to be too weak, so, in his own handwriting, he changed it to read: "Stalin is the worthy continuer of Lenin's work, or, as it is said in our Party, Stalin is the Lenin of today." You see how well it is said, not by the nation but by Stalin himself.
>
> . . . I will cite one more insertion made by Stalin concerning the theme of the Stalinist military genius. "The advanced Soviet science of war received further development," he writes, "at Comrade Stalin's hands. Comrade Stalin elaborated the theory of the permanently operating factors that decide the issue of wars, of active defense and the laws of counter-offensive and offensive, of the cooperation of all services and arms in modern warfare, of the role of big tank masses and air forces in modern war, and of the artillery as the most formidable of the armed services. At the various stages of the war Stalin's genius found the correct solutions that took account of all the circumstances of the situation."
>
> And further, writes Stalin: "Stalin's military mastership was displayed both in defense and offense. Comrade Stalin's genius enabled him to divine the enemy's plans and defeat them. The battles in which Comrade Stalin directed the Soviet armies are brilliant examples of operational military skill."[25]

It can be argued, though, that precisely because his claim to leadership was shakily based, it had to be exaggerated and made unchallengeable. Lenin, whose dominance in the Party was genuine and accepted, had had no need of such methods. For Stalin they were, in part at least, the necessary cement of autocracy. One shrewd Soviet diplomat in the 1930s writes, "Anyone who imagines that Stalin believes this praise, or laps it up in a mood of egotistical willingness to be deceived, is sadly mistaken. Stalin is not deluded by it. He regards it as useful to his power. He also enjoys humiliating these intellectuals. . . ."[26]

To discuss Stalin's character and beliefs is not to estimate his abilities. There have been two main views of these. On the first, he was an infallible genius, a "Coryphaeus of science," an inspired leader of the human race, and so forth. On the second, he was a mediocrity. The first view, taken (during Stalin's lifetime) by Professor Bernal, Khrushchev, and others, has been submitted to enough destructive criticism, and we need hardly deal with it. The view that he was a nonentity who reached the top by luck and low cunning still has influence. It is true that most of those who hold it would concede that he was also a monster. But they would grant him few other active qualities.

The Menshevik historian Sukhanov, soon to be his victim, described him in 1917 as making no more impression than a gray blur. Trotsky called him "the most outstanding mediocrity in our Party."[27] And Khrushchev later said, in his Secret Speech of 1956, "I shall probably not be sinning against the truth when I say that ninety-nine percent of the persons present here heard and knew very little about Stalin before 1924.'' He had, in fact, made little impression on the talkative politicians of the Party at that time. Thus there was some basis for the judgment of Trotsky and his successors. But on the whole it was a shallow one, as later events bore out. The qualities Stalin lacked and Trotsky possessed were not the essentials for political greatness. And Lenin alone among the Bolshevik leaders had recognized Stalin's ability.

It is early yet to look at his career objectively, with his technique of despotism simply ''considered as a fine art.'' Nevertheless, we can avoid dismissing with the negative estimate of his unsuccessful rivals and their intellectual heirs the brilliant politician who was able to produce such vast and horrible effects.

Stalin had a good average grasp of Marxism, and though his adaptations of that flexible doctrine to suit his purposes were not so elaborate or so elastic as the similar interpretations of his rivals and predecessors, they were adequate to his career. His lack of the true theoretician's mind was noted by many, and he seems to have resented it.

Bukharin told Kamenev in July 1928 that Stalin was ''eaten up with the vain desire to become a well-known theoretician. He feels that it is the only thing he lacks.'' The old Marxist scholar Ryazanov once interrupted Stalin when he was theorizing: ''Stop it, Koba, don't make a fool of yourself. Everybody knows that theory is not exactly your field.'' Nevertheless, as Isaac Deutscher rightly comments, his great theoretical departure—''socialism in one country''—however crude and even un-Marxist a notion, was a powerful and appealing idea.[28]

Deutscher says that ''the interest of practitioners of Stalin's type in matters of philosophy and theory was strictly limited. . . . The semi-intelligentsia from whom socialism recruited some of its middle cadres enjoyed Marxism as a mental labor-saving device.'' But this view exaggerated Stalin's philosophical clumsiness. Or rather, perhaps, it overrates the more philosophical Bolsheviks, such as Lenin, with whom Deutscher goes on to compare him. Lenin's only venture into philosophy proper—*Materialism and Empirio-Criticism*—is his least impressive work. Stalin's brief summary of Marxism, which appears in Chapter 4 of the *"Short Course" History of the All-Union Communist Party,* is, in an unpretentious way, as clear and able an account as there is. Georg Lukács, the veteran Communist theoretician (who in the 1950s showed some revulsion from Stalinism), commented, ''Since we have to do with a popular work written for the masses, no one could find fault with Stalin for reducing the quite subtle and complex arguments of the classics on this theme to a few definitions enumerated in schematic text book form.''[29]

With the exception of Zinoviev, Stalin was the only non-''intellectual'' in Lenin's leadership. But his knowledge of more truly relevant matters was not small. Djilas tells us that ''Stalin had considerable knowledge of political history only, especially Russian, and he had an uncommonly good memory. Stalin really did not need any more than this for his role.''[30]

In 1863, Bismarck reminded the Prussian Chamber that ''politics is not an exact science.'' It would have been a truism to every previous generation, and he was perhaps provoked into giving the idea such definite expression by the rise of the new rationalism in historical science, of the claims to rigor of the social and political professors. Among the Russian Communists of the post-Revolutionary period, this tendency had reached its fullest development. They were political scientists; they were using the methods of the political science devised by Marx, the Darwin of society. Everything was discussed in theoretical terms.

Unfortunately, the theories were not correct, and the claim to scientific rigor was, to say the least, premature. Even if their formulations had been closer to the definitiveness claimed for them, it is still perhaps doubtful if such leaders would have prevailed in actual politics: professors of ballistics do not necessarily make good baseball players. As it was, the more intuitive Stalin, less able to analyze and plan his moves in theoretical terms, had a fuller operational grasp of reality.

As his daughter remarks, in spirit Stalin was completely Russianized. He had not learned Russian until he was eight or nine, and always spoke it with an accent. But he spoke it well, and his conversation was often rich and vivid in a coarse way. Although not well educated, he was widely read in the Russian classics—in particular, the satirists Shchedrin and Gogol. He had also read when young a number of foreign authors in Russian translation—in particular, Victor Hugo— and popular works on Darwinism and social and economic matters. Gendarmerie reports on the Tiflis Theological Seminary in the last part of the nineteenth century mention the reading by students of "seditious" literature of this sort, and Stalin's name appears in the seminary bad-conduct book a number of times for the discovery of such works from the local "Cheap Library," showing that he was engaged in absorbing this sort of self-education.[31]

His style of writing was unsubtle, and here again his opponents sneered at him. Djilas associates it, and its crudeness, with the backward nature of revolutionary Russia: "it contains simplicities from the writings of the church fathers, not so much the result of his religious youth, as the result of the fact that this was the way of expression under primitive conditions." Djilas adds elsewhere that "his style was colorless and monotonous, but its oversimplified logic and dogmatism were convincing to the conformists and to common people."[32] But there is more to it than that. Clear and plain arguments are appealing not only to "common" minds. A Soviet official writes, "It was precisely his lack of brilliance, his plainness, which inclined us to believe what he said."[33]

Stalin is often described as having a curious effect of sullenness, but he could be charming enough, and had "a rough humor, self-assured but not entirely without subtlety and depth."[34] In this he contrasts with the humorlessness of Lenin, and of Trotsky too. It seems doubtful that he would have had the same sort of success in a more experienced political community, but in the political circumstances in which Stalin found himself he proved a master. Tactically, he far outshone his rivals. Bukharin commented of him that he was a master of "dosing"— of giving the right dose at the right time. It is a measure of Bukharin's own comparative ineptitude that he seems to have thought of this as an insult. In fact, it is a sound compliment to one of Stalin's greatest strengths.

He won his position by devious maneuver. It is notable that from 1924 to 1934, there were none of the abrupt coups which mark the post-Stalin period. Stalin would attack and discredit a man, then appear to reach a compromise, leaving his opponent weakened but not destroyed. Bit by bit his opponents' positions were undermined, and they were removed one by one from the leadership.

Lenin saw this side of Stalin's political methods. When he was working to defeat Stalin on the Georgian issue in the last days of his active life, he told his secretary not to show Kamenev the notes he had prepared for Trotsky, or they would leak to Stalin, in which case "Stalin would make a rotten compromise in order then to deceive."[35] And this indeed Stalin did in the months following Lenin's death, exhibiting, as Gibbon says of Alaric, "an artful moderation, which contributed to the success of his designs."

It was because Stalin never committed himself irretrievably until he felt certain of success that his opponents were so often put into a dilemma. They were never sure how far he was intending to go. And they could—and did—frequently delude themselves into thinking that he had submitted to the will of the Politburo majority, and would henceforth be possible to work with. Even when he was pressing forward hard to the terrorist solution of the question of the oppositionists, they were able to feel that this was partly due to the influence of Kaganovich and others, whom Stalin might well be induced to abandon if suitable arguments were produced. It is notable that few of the alternative solutions seriously put forward from 1930 onward envisaged the total removal of Stalin from positions of power, which alone could have saved the situation.

Thus in a manner almost unprecedented in history, he continued his "coup d'état by inches," culminating in a vast slaughter, while *still* giving an air of moderation. Through his silences and unprovocative talk, he not merely deceived many foreigners, but even in Russia itself, at the height of the Purge, was to some degree able to avoid popular blame.

A friend who had contact in the higher circles in both Stalin's Russia and Rákosi's Hungary remarks that Rákosi was indeed much the more educated and in a sense more intelligent man. But he laid himself open in the most unnecessary way. The most important example was that during the period of the Rajk Trial in 1949, he made a speech saying that he had spent sleepless nights until he himself had unraveled all the threads of the conspiracy. When Rajk was rehabilitated, this was a deadly weapon against Rákosi. But quite apart from that, it meant that even at the time he personally was blamed by the people and the Party for all malpractices in connection with his purge.[36] Stalin, who never said a word more than was necessary, would not have dreamed of making so crude a revelation. It was his triumph that the Great Purge was very largely blamed on Yezhov, the Head of the NKVD. "Not only I but very many others thought the evil came from the small man they called 'the Stalinist Commissar.' The people christened those years the 'Yezhovschchina' [Yezhov Times]," remarks Ilya Ehrenburg. Ehrenburg also tells of meeting Pasternak in the Lavrushensky Lane on a snowy night. Pasternak raised his hands to the dark sky and exclaimed, "If only someone would tell Stalin about it!"[37] Meyerhold, too, remarked, "They conceal it from Stalin."[38]

In fact, the opposite was true. The cartoonist Boris Efimov describes his brother Mikhail Koltsov telling him of a conversation with Mekhlis, who explained how the arrests were taking place. Mekhlis showed him, in confidence, "a few words in red pencil addressed to Yezhov and Mekhlis, laconically ordering the arrest of certain officials." There were, Koltsov noted, "people still at liberty and at work, who had in fact already been condemned and . . . annihilated by one stroke of this red pencil. Yezhov was left with merely the technical details— working up the cases and producing the orders for arrest."[39]

Stalin's achievement is in general so extraordinary that we can hardly dismiss him as simply a colorless, mediocre type with a certain talent for terror and intrigue. He was, indeed, in some ways a very reserved man. It is said that even in his younger days if beaten in an argument, he would show no emotion, but just smile sarcastically. His former secretary penetratingly remarks, "He possessed in a high degree the gift for silence, and in this respect he was unique in a country where everybody talks far too much."[40] His ambitions, and even his talents, were not clear to most of his rivals and colleagues.

Because he did not elucidate and elaborate his views and plans, it was thought that he did not have any—a typical mistake of the garrulous intellectual. "His expression," an observer writes, "tells nothing of what he feels."[41] A Soviet writer speaks of "the expression which he had carefully devised for himself over the years as a fixture and which Comrade Stalin, as he had long been in the habit of calling himself in his thoughts and sometimes aloud, in the third person, had to assume in the presence of these people."[42] He would listen quietly at meetings of the Politburo, or to distinguished visitors, puffing at his Dunhill pipe and doodling aimlessly—his secretaries Poskrebyshev and Dvinsky write that his pads were sometimes covered with the phrase "Lenin-teacher-friend," but the last foreigner to visit him, in February 1953, noted that he was doodling wolves.

All early accounts agree that one of Stalin's characteristics was "laziness" or "indolence," which Bukharin impressed on Trotsky as Stalin's "most striking quality."[43] Trotsky remarked that Stalin "never did any serious work" but was always "busy with his intrigues." Another way of putting this is that Stalin paid the necessary attention to the detail of political maneuver. In his words, "Never refuse to do the little things, for from the little things are built the big."[44] One may also be reminded of a remark by a former German Commander-in-Chief, Colonel-General Baron Kurt von Hammerstein-Equord, about his officers:

> I divide my officers into four classes. . . . The man who is clever and industrious is suited to high staff appointments; use can be made of the man who is stupid and lazy; the man who is clever and lazy is fitted for the highest command, he has the nerve to deal with all situations; but the man who is stupid and industrious is a danger and must be dismissed immediately.

In the political struggle, Stalin's great characteristic was precisely "nerve." He had complete determination and considerable patience, together with an extraordinary ability to apply and to relax pressure at the right moment, which carried him through a series of critical situations, until his final victory.

At the center of Stalin's superiority over his competitors was certainly his intense will, just as Napoleon ranked what he called "moral fortitude" higher in a general than genius or experience. When Milovan Djilas said to Stalin during the Yugoslav–Soviet discussions in Moscow during the war that the Serbian politician Gavrilović was "a shrewd man," Stalin commented, as though to himself, "Yes, there are politicians who think shrewdness is the main thing in politics. . . ."[45] His was a will power taken to a logical extreme. There is something nonhuman about his almost total lack of normal restraints upon it.

He is said to have been a constant reader of Machiavelli, as indeed is reasonable enough. In Chapter 15 of *The Prince,* he would find the simple advice that rulers should in no case practice villainies which might lose them the State, but must nevertheless, if it comes to the worst, "not flinch from being blamed for vices which are necessary for safeguarding the State," making whatever effort is feasible to "escape the evil reputation" involved. Or, again, in Chapter 18, Machiavelli recommends the appearance of mercy, faithfulness, and so forth, while noting that the Prince "and especially a new Prince, must often act in a fashion contrary to those virtues."

When the great film director Eisenstein produced his film on Ivan the Terrible, Stalin objected to his attitude. He had been inclined to treat Ivan, in the way most people have, as a ruthless and paranoid terrorist. Stalin told Eisenstein and the actor N. K. Cherkasov that, on the contrary, Ivan had been a great and wise ruler who had protected the country from the infiltration of foreign influence and had tried to bring about the unification of Russia. "J. V. Stalin also remarked on the progressive role played by the Oprichnina [Ivan's Secret Police]"; Stalin's criticism of Ivan was limited to his having "failed to liquidate the five remaining great feudal families." On that point, Stalin added humorously, "There God stood in Ivan's way"—since Ivan, after liquidating one family, would repent for a year "when he should have been acting with increasing decisiveness." *

Stalin also understood how to destroy his enemies' political reputations. He could have learned in certain respects from another totalitarian leader whom he to some extent admired. Hitler gives a recipe for the whole tenor of the Purges:

> The art of leadership, as displayed by really great popular leaders in all ages, consists in consolidating the attention of the people against a single adversary. . . . The leader of genius must have the ability to make different opponents appear as if they belonged to the one category; for weak and wavering natures among a leader's following may easily begin to be dubious about the justice of their own cause if they have to face different enemies. . . . Where there are various enemies . . . it will be necessary to block them all together as forming one solid front, so that the mass of followers in a popular movement may see only one common enemy against whom they have to fight. Such uniformity intensifies their belief in their own cause and strengthens their feeling of hostility towards the opponent.[46]

But Stalin was deeper and more complex than Hitler. His view of humanity was cynical, and if he, too, turned to anti-Semitism, it was as a matter of policy rather than dogma. We can see traces of this later anti-Semitism, or rather anti-Semitic demagogy, as early as 1907, when he was remarking, in the small underground paper he then controlled at Baku, "Somebody among the Bolsheviks remarked jokingly that since the Mensheviks were the faction of the Jews and the Bolsheviks that of the native Russians, it would be a good thing to have a pogrom in the Party."[47]

The Yiddish writers shot in August 1952 were accused of the *political* offense of wishing to set up a secessionist state in the Crimea—a charge faintly linked with reality through the fact that a proposal had indeed arisen in the Jewish Anti-Fascist Committee, after the war, to resettle Jews in the then-desolate penin-

---

*Cherkasov gives an account of this conversation in *Zapiski sovetskogo aktera* (Moscow, 1953), pp. 380–82. This book was passed for publication while Stalin was still alive, and (we are told in the Soviet historical journal *Voprosy istorii,* no. 8 [1956]) he raised no objections.

sula. In the Doctors' Plot of 1952–1953, a majority of those accused were Jews, but some were not. The Jewish element was publicly emphasized, but it was under the guise of a link with "Zionism," just as in the campaign leading up to it, Jewish literary men were called "cosmopolitans" ("cosmopolitans . . . that long-nosed lot," a bureaucrat comments in one of Avram Tertz's stories). When critics in the West pointed out the undoubted anti-Semitic element in the alleged "Plot," there were still people to come forward and say that, no, Gentiles were being accused too, and that Zionism was, after all, more or less implicitly anti-Soviet. For, as we shall see, Stalin's policies in strictly political matters were never elaborated clearly in such a fashion that they could be refuted. There was never any complete certainty in an individual case about what his disposition would be.

This enigmatic attitude misled even experienced and clever people. Lion Feuchtwanger (Ehrenburg remarks), a passionate defender of the Jews, could never believe that Stalin persecuted Jews—just as Romain Rolland, devoted to freedom in the arts, was easily deceived by Stalin on the absence of freedom in Soviet literature.[48]

The "anti-Semitism," thus disguised, was in accord with Stalin's general exploitation of prejudices and of the gullibility and pliability of men in general. In a broader sense, this was doubtless at the root of Stalin's acceptance of the theories of the physiologist Pavlov (who loathed the Soviet regime). Moreover, he interpreted Pavlov in the crudest way as applying to human beings, sponsoring an attack on the view that Pavlov had dealt with the elementary nervous process of animals only and that in the case of man it was necessary to take into account the phenomenon of "resistance to the formation of conditioned reflexes."[49]

But the dull, cool, calculating effect given cumulatively through Stalin's long career, the air of a great glacier moving slowly and by the easiest path to overwhelm some Alpine valley, is only part of the picture. At various times—and especially in his early career—the calm of his general manner was broken, and expression given to the driving emotions that possessed him.

In Lenin's time, if offended, Stalin would sulk and stay away from meetings for days.[50] Lenin noted of him that he often acted out of anger or spite and that "spite in general plays the very worst role in politics." He also noted Stalin's hastiness and his tendency to solve everything by administrative impulse. At the time of Lenin's death, he had nearly ruined himself by this "capriciousness" and needed all his skill to retrieve the situation.

Nor, later, was his terrorism wholly rational. He "practiced brutal violence, not only toward everything that opposed him but also toward that which seemed, to his capricious and despotic character, contrary to his concepts."[51] As George Kennan has remarked, to Stalin's "darkly mistrustful mind no political issue was ever without its personal implications."[52] His daughter takes it as central to his character that "once he had cast someone he had known a long time out of his heart, once he had mentally relegated that someone to the ranks of his enemies, it was impossible even to talk to him about that person any more."[53] There can be no doubt that Stalin pursued his grudges implacably, even after many years. But, of course, this cannot be more than a partial motive for the killings he ordered. For these involved friends as well as enemies, and men he hardly knew as much as personal rivals. Men who had injured him did not survive the Terror. And nor, of course, did men whom he himself had injured, like Bauman.

Nevertheless, when Khrushchev represents Stalin as a capricious tyrant, this is not necessarily incompatible with a basic rationale. It is true that anyone Stalin had a personal grudge against was almost automatically included on the death list, but even a long life of quarrelsome intrigue could not provide anything like the required number of victims from that source alone. To obtain the terror effect, after all those who really had stood in his way or annoyed him had been dealt with, the quota could just as efficiently be made up by caprice as by any other method.

Stalin's Terror, in fact, begins to show a more rational pattern if it is considered as a statistical matter, a mass phenomenon, rather than in terms of individuals. The absence of strict categories of victims, such as a Trotsky might have listed, maintained the circumspect deviousness of the Purge and avoided presenting any clear-cut target to critics. The effect of terror is produced, he may have argued, when a given proportion of a group has been seized and shot. The remainder will be cowed into uncomplaining obedience. And it does not much matter, from this point of view, which of them have been selected as victims, particularly if all or almost all are innocent.

Ilya Ehrenburg, as late as 1964, still asked himself why some were shot and some spared. Why Litvinov was never in serious trouble (though kept away from active work for years), while all the diplomats associated with him were eliminated; why Pasternak, independent and unyielding, survived, while Koltsov, anxious to do everything required of him, was liquidated; why the biologist Vavilov perished, and the even more independent-minded Kapitsa remained in favor.[54]

Whatever the "statistical" rationale, the way Stalin's caprice operated is a useful sidelight on his character. A British writer of great political experience noted in the 1940s, "It seemed almost . . . as if Stalin simultaneously demanded and hated the sycophancy of absolute obedience."[55] This was confirmed and elaborated in a more recent Soviet account by the novelist Konstantin Simonov, who had much direct contact with the high Soviet leadership. In his *Soldiers Are Made, Not Born,* Stalin receives a letter from a general during the war asking for the release of a colleague, whose Civil War services he recounts:

> Serpilin's recalling of past efforts had failed to touch Stalin. It was the directness of the letter that had interested him. In his ruthless character side by side with a despotic demand for total subservience, which was the rule with him, there lay the need to come across exceptions—which was the obverse side of the same rule. At times he evinced something akin to flashes of interest in people who were capable of taking risks, of expressing opinions which ran counter to his own opinions, whether genuine or assumed. Knowing himself, he knew the degree of this risk and was all the more capable of setting store by it. Sometimes, that is! Because it was far more frequently the other way around and this was where the risk lay.

Stalin gives Serpilin an interview, which goes fairly well:

> Still, on his way out, Serpilin considered that his fate had already been finally settled during his conversation with Stalin. But in actual fact it had been settled not while

they had been talking but a moment ago when Stalin had silently looked at his back as he left. That was the way he often finally decided people's fate, looking at them not in the eyes but from behind as they left.[56]

With certain categories, Stalin seems to have had different standards. His former Georgian rivals and friends were mostly shot, like their Russian counterparts. But whereas Stalin showed nothing but contempt for most of his victims, the execution of his Georgian Old Bolshevik brother-in-law Alyosha Svanidze in 1942, on charges of being a Nazi agent, brought out a different attitude:

> Before the execution, Svanidze was told that Stalin had said that if he asked for forgiveness he would be pardoned. When Stalin's words were repeated to Svanidze, he asked: "What am I supposed to ask forgiveness for? I have committeed no crime." He was shot. After Svanidze's death, Stalin said: "See how proud he is: he died without asking forgiveness."[57]

An even more extraordinary example is that of another Georgian, S. I. Kavtaradze. He had been Chairman of the Council of People's Commissars in Georgia from 1921 to 1922, and had fallen with the rest of the Georgian leadership during Stalin's clash with them before and after Lenin's death. He was expelled from the Party as a Trotskyite in 1927, and was among those not readmitted during the following years. He was arrested and sentenced in connection with the Ryutin affair, and is reported in Maryinsk and Kolyma labor camps in 1936, thoroughly disillusioned.[58] In 1940, he was still in camp. One day the commandant called him, and he was sent off to Moscow. Much to his surprise, instead of being shot, he was taken directly in his prison clothes to see Stalin, who greeted him affably, asking him where he had been all these years. He was at once rehabilitated, and sent to the Commissariat of Foreign Affairs, where he shortly became Assistant People's Commissar. After the war, he was Ambassador to Romania for a time. In his biography, as given in various Soviet reference books, a bare mention is made of the thirteen-year gap in his Party membership between December 1927 and December 1940![59] This is a clear and conscious example of Stalin indulging a caprice.

Of his leading opponents in post-Revolutionary Georgia, while he had Mdivani shot, he made a remarkable exception to the Purge in sparing Philip Makharadze. Makharadze, though publicly censured for various errors in the particularly sensitive field of Georgian Party history,[60] remained Chairman of the Presidium of the Georgian Supreme Soviet until he died, in good odor, in 1943. His survival is very peculiar—unless, indeed, we regard the reprieve as amounting to no more than four years' imminent expectation of arrest, and see in it a particularly subtle piece of revenge.

What may be a curious remnant of Caucasian chivalry can be seen in one of Stalin's more general omissions from the Purge lists. He had no objection to killing or imprisoning women—in fact, "wife" is mentioned as a normal category for execution (see p. 235). But within the inner Party itself, there is a curious survival of Old Bolshevik women. Krupskaya, Lenin's widow, is in a sense a special case, though she had been strong in the opposition to Stalin in the 1920s and had given him personal offense. But it would not by any means be beyond

Stalin's powers or beyond the usual scope of his malice to prove that Lenin's wife had betrayed her husband.

But there are many other cases of Old Bolshevik women surviving. Elena Stasova lasted right through the Stalin epoch. L. A. Fotieva, Lenin's secretary, who must also have known a good deal about what was one of Stalin's most sensitive points—the quarrel with Lenin in his last days—was also spared. So was K. I. Nikolayeva, the only woman full member of the 1934 Central Committee apart from Krupskaya, who was one of the few who was carried over into the Committee elected in 1939, and she was an ex-Zinovievite at that. Another case was R. S. Zemlyachka, member of the 1904 Central Committee. A brutal terrorist, she had been Béla Kun's chief colleague in the great slaughter in the Crimea in 1920, to which Lenin himself had objected. She survived, while Kun went to the execution cellars. Alexandra Kollontai, the star of the Workers' Opposition, had been married to Dybenko and had lived with Shlyapnikov. On top of all this, after her acceptance of the Stalin line she remained as Ambassador (to Sweden), a profession which was anyhow almost invariably fatal. Yet she survived the Stalin epoch unscathed, *en poste*.

Psychologists might make something about this trait of Stalin's. In any case, it is a comparatively human characteristic and one perhaps harking back to Caucasia as much as the blood feud does. Another ''category'' to be spared has no such obvious source: the former Bolshevik members of the Duma (including Grigori Petrovsky, who was under the direct threat in 1939) all survived.

But when all is said, we are still peering into the glooms of an extreme reticence. A shrewd Soviet official, who was impressed by Stalin's patience and also by his capriciousness, comments, ''That rare combination is the principal key to his character.''[61] Doubtless this is a sound view, yet it only takes us into the outskirts of a full understanding.

Even as to his political aims, he never spoke his mind. That he knew in general what he was doing cannot be doubted. It is much more difficult, as we have seen, to tell how far he had made his aims explicit even in his own mind, and how far ahead he looked during a given crisis. What he had, politically speaking, was less definite than a planned control of developments. It was, rather, the feel of events, the flow. In this he was unsurpassed among his contemporaries.

We do not need to posit a conscious long-term plan to say that in a general way the drive for power was Stalin's strongest and most obvious motivation. There have been men, like Cromwell, whose paths to supreme power were truly accidental, who neither planned nor particularly wished for the result. This is quite certainly not true of Stalin.

Bukharin said plainly, ''At any given moment he will change his theories in order to get rid of someone.''[62] But politically speaking, this shows a basic consistency. The one fundamental drive that can be found throughout is the strengthening of his own position. To this, for practical purposes, all else was subordinate. It led him to absolute power. As Machiavelli points out, though the actual seizure of power is difficult in despotic States, once seized, it is comparatively easy to hold. And Stalin seized it and held it.

Over the next four years, he carried out a revolution which completely transformed the Party and the whole of society. Far more than the Bolshevik Revolution itself, this period marks the major gulf between modern Russia and the past. It was also the deepest trauma of all those which had shaken the population in the turbulent decades since 1905. It is true that only against the peculiar background of the Soviet past, and the extraordinary traditions of the All-Union Communist Party, could so radical a turn be put through. The totalitarian machinery, already in existence, was the fulcrum without which the world could not be moved. But the revolution of the Purges still remains, however we judge it, above all Stalin's personal achievement. If his character is to some degree impenetrable to direct investigation, we shall see it adequately displayed in his actions over the following years, and in the State he thus created and found good.

# OLD BOLSHEVIKS CONFESS

*"In what did his fascism show itself?"*
*"His fascism showed itself when he said that in a situation like the*
*present we must resort to the use of every possible means."*

Exchange between Vyshinsky and Zinoviev at the August 1936 Trial

The six months following the Medved–Zaporozhets Trial is one of the most obscure periods of the Purge. It starts with the death, in circumstances which are
still unknown, of another member of the Politburo, and ends with another trial,
of which even the charges were only made public in 1989, of Kamenev and others. But the pattern is clear, and much of the detail can now be reconstructed.

After the first wave of terror following the Kirov murder, the "moderate"
faction in the Politburo continued to urge the policy of relaxation. It could, after
all, equally well be argued that the assassination was the sign of tensions which
might best be dealt with by a more popular policy, as the opposite, that it indicated the need for further terror.

In the Politburo, Valerian Kuibyshev, Head of the State Planning Commission (Gosplan), is believed to have been particularly active along Kirov's line,
and is said to have opposed the January Zinoviev–Kamenev Trial.[1] Outside, the
influence of Maxim Gorky and of Lenin's widow, Nadezhda Krupskaya, was of
importance. The Society of Old Bolsheviks, which had long acted as a sort of
Party conscience, strongly opposed the idea of death sentences for the opposition.
Among Stalin's immediate entourage, Abel Yenukidze, who was Secretary of the
Central Executive Committee and (among other duties) responsible for the administration of the Kremlin, urged the same view.

Yenukidze was the first target of Stalin's counter-measures. As if to emphasize the connection, he was required on 16 January 1935, the very day Zinoviev
and his adherents were sentenced, to perform a significant though minor act of
self-denunciation—on the always thorny theme of the origins of Georgian Bolshevism. In a half-page of *Pravda,* he wrote of his errors in articles in the encyclo-
pedias and elsewhere, where he had attributed too big a role to himself.[2] This
marked the beginning of his rapid decline.

The next great blow to moderation was the death of Kuibyshev on 26 January. Most of his subordinates in Gosplan, including his deputy, Professor Osad-
chy, had been purged for opposing ill-prepared crash programs in the first years
of the decade. Although Kuibyshev's death was at first described as being from

natural causes, it was later to be alleged that he was murdered by willful medical mistreatment on the orders of Yagoda. It is still difficult to be certain about the Kuibyshev case. Common sense gets us nowhere. There are, in fact, two different "commonsensical" ways of looking at it. The first would say that what appears to be a natural death should be taken as such if there is no absolutely firm evidence to the contrary. After all, Kuibyshev had to be ill in the first place if he was being treated medically; people do die naturally, and we should not strain to fit every death into a preconceived pattern. The other view is that Kuibyshev had, as is now officially said, been one of three Politburo members who had blocked Stalin; that of this group one had been shot just before Kuibyshev's death and the other was to perish later of a faked heart attack; and that, moreover, Stalin was making moves against other advocates of moderation, such as Gorky and Yenukidze, at precisely this time. Against a member of the Politburo, at once more dangerous and less vulnerable, what sanction was left except the one that had succeeded with Kirov? At any rate a certain amount of suspicion seems reasonable when we consider that *all* the other nine Politburo members (and ten ex-Politburo members) to die in the years 1934 to 1940 were victims of Stalin; that *all* those of his own supporters who opposed him on the Purge perished; and, perhaps most important, that the others of his own Politburo supporters who died before 1938 were disposed of by him, but in ways not easily attributable to his own actions.

Kuibyshev was photographed at a meeting of the Council of People's Commissars on 22 January.[3] On 26 January, his death was announced—of heart disease. The signatories to the medical bulletin included Kaminsky, Khodorovsky, and Levin, all of whom were to sign the certificate of Ordzhonikidze's equally sudden death from the same cause, which is known to be a fake.

Kuibyshev seems to have had a bad heart, and to have been under treatment at least since August 1934. An attack of tonsillitis and an operation weakened him still further. But he was not at this stage particularly ill, and was still at work within an hour or two of his death.[4]

The account of his death given at the Bukharin Trial was that he had some sort of angina pectoris attack while at his office at the Council of People's Commissars, was allowed to go home unaccompanied, and climbed to his flat on the third floor. There chanced to be a maid at home who telephoned his secretary and the doctor on duty, but by the time they arrived Kuibyshev was dead.[5]

It was alleged that it was the purposely incorrect treatment which had been given him which caused his death, and that the doctors should anyhow have insisted on his being in bed.[6] The doctors (and Kuibyshev's secretary Maximov) were later accused of working under Yagoda's orders. They were rehabilitated in 1988, and are thus clearly innocent. If Kuibyshev did not die naturally, he was killed in some other way than that stated—perhaps by another member of the Council of People's Commissars dropping in from a nearby office with a glass of non-medicine. If so, it is possible that the true facts were known only to a few now dead, and that they are no longer available even to investigators in Russia. However, the most recent Soviet references stress his heart condition.

Among those actively opposed to the persecution of oppositionists throughout this period, another of the most forceful was Maxim Gorky. Moreover, his great ambition was to assist in a reconciliation between the Party and the intelligentsia—to lead the Soviet regime, of which he had originally disapproved, into the socialist humanism he believed it capable of. It was partly for this reason that he had compromised himself by returning from Italy in 1928 and defending the regime against its external critics.

Gorky is said to have personally worked to reconcile Stalin with Kamenev and to have apparently succeeded in doing this early in 1934,[7] even securing a friendly personal meeting. Kamenev was given a job in the Akademia publishing house.

Gorky is said to have at first been greatly enraged against the supposedly anti-Party assassins of Kirov, but soon to have reverted, as far as general policy went, to his "liberal" position. Stalin's resentment at his stand was expressed by the appearance, for the first time, of articles highly critical of him. For example, one by the writer Panferov in *Pravda* of 28 January 1935. However, Gorky continued in his efforts to reconcile Stalin with the oppositionists. So did Krupskaya, who had been Kamenev's and Zinoviev's main ally in 1924.

Krupskaya, up to a point, represented a moral threat to Stalin's plans. But unlike Gorky, she was a Party member and subject to that same Party discipline which had led her to acquiesce in the suppression of her husband's Testament. Her sympathies with the Zinovievite opposition over the years had been common knowledge in the Party. By now she had as a result lost most of the prestige she had once enjoyed on the higher levels, even though her name was still useful with the Party masses. The exact methods by which Stalin silenced her are unknown. He is said to have once remarked that if she did not stop criticizing him, the Party would proclaim that not she, but the Old Bolshevik Elena Stasova, was Lenin's widow: "Yes," he added sternly, "the Party can do anything!"[8]

This story (from Orlov) has, not unnaturally, often been doubted; but it was confirmed by Khrushchev in his memoirs, where he says that Stalin "used to tell his inner circle that there was some doubt whether Nadezhda Konstantinovna was really Lenin's widow, and that if the situation continued much longer we would begin to express our doubts in public. He said that if necessary we would proclaim another woman Lenin's widow."[9] He named the replacement, of whom Khrushchev says only that she was a solid and respected party member who was still alive as he dictated the memoirs. Stasova, or possibly Lenin's secretary Fotieva, seems the only plausible candidate.

In any case, there was little Krupskaya could do. It was not difficult to keep foreigners away from her, to surround her with NKVD men, and at the same time to call on her to obey the Party's orders—a situation quite different from that of Gorky. It is said that she was in fear for her life in her last few years.

On 1 February 1935, a plenum of the Central Committee elected Mikoyan and Chubar to the posts on the Politburo left vacant by the deaths of Kirov and Kuibyshev, and promoted Zhdanov and Eikhe to candidate membership. To the extent that Mikoyan, at least, was to support the extreme Stalinist line throughout the Purge period (as, of course, was Zhdanov among the candidate members), this was a gain for Stalin. But he was not yet ready wholly to overwhelm the "moderates" in the leading policy bodies.

In the key organizational posts in the Party and Purge machinery, it was another matter. Nikolai Yezhov, a tested and ruthless operator, became a member of the Secretariat, and on 23 February was appointed in addition to the key post of Head of the Party Control Commission.[10] Another prominent young Stalinist, Kaganovich's protégé Nikita Khrushchev, was made First Secretary of the Moscow Party organization a few days later.[11] Andrei Vyshinsky had been made Prosecutor-General by June. And by 8 July 1935 Georgi Malenkov was Yezhov's chief deputy as Assistant Director of the Cadres Department of the Central Committee.[12]

Thus by mid-1935, Stalin had men of his personal selection, who were to prove themselves complete devotees of the Purge, in control of Leningrad and Moscow, and in the Transcaucasus, where Beria ruled; in the Control Commission and the key departments of the Party Secretariat; and in the Prosecutor-Generalship; and if the leadership of the NKVD was later to prove unsatisfactory to him, it was at least totally under his control.

In the formal organs of Party power, the Central Committee and the Politburo, he had not yet achieved the same total grip. Many of the provincial committees were still headed by men who dragged their feet. And the Ukraine was under the control of the same style of leadership which it had been necessary to remove in Leningrad by an assassin's bullet. But a firm basis for attack on these old cadres had been established.

A quiet purge of the ex-oppositionists now in jail continued. The leading ex-Trotskyite, Ivar Smilga, arrested on 1 January 1935, was secretly sentenced on 26 March 1935 to imprisonment in the Verkhne-Uralsk isolator (later, apparently on 10 January 1937, to death) by the Military Collegium.[13]

In March and April 1935 came a secret trial of the "Moscow Counter-Revolutionary Organization–'Workers' Opposition' Group." A. G. Shlyapnikov, Lenin's chief representative in Russia during the First World War, had headed the intra-Party Workers' Opposition, which had opposed the bureaucracy until Lenin banned such groupings in 1921. He spent his later years sometimes free, sometimes in jail, sometimes in exile in the Arctic, or working on the Lower Volga Shipping Line. Like Smilga, he was rearrested on 1 January 1935. Shlyapnikov, his chief henchman S. P. Medvedev, and thirteen others were now sentenced by the Special Board to various terms of imprisonment, though worse faced them later.[14] Shlyapnikov's wife was sent to labor camp.[15]

The same piecemeal progress was being made, during this outwardly quiet period, in thought control and in the Party purge. A circular of 7 March 1935 ordered the removal from libraries of all the works of Trotsky, Zinoviev, and Kamenev. Another, dated 21 June, extended the list to include Preobrazhensky and others.[16]

A secret letter dated 19 May 1935 from the Central Committee called for the special investigation of "enemies of the Party and the working class" who had remained within the Party. On 27 June, a special (and evidently typical) Central Committee resolution on the Western province censured the local officials in charge of the Party purge for insufficient vigilance.

In the Smolensk *rayon,* 455 out of 4,100 members examined were expelled, after 700 oral and 200 written denunciations.[17] One member was denounced for having admitted that he had in his possession "a platform of the Trotskyites." A professor had given a favorable character reference to a Trotskyite and now "never expressed his attitude toward the Trotskyite counter-revolution." A group of worker members of the Party wrote denouncing their local leadership for refusing to listen to denunciations. Typical of remarks at Party meetings were such attacks as "There is information that Smolov is married to the daughter of the merchant Kovalev, and that the Party organizer of the second group of the Institute is the son of a person who was given a strict reprimand."[18] By 1 August, as a report signed by Yezhov and Malenkov noted, 23 percent of the Party cards in this representative area had been withdrawn or held pending investigation.[19]

Even more striking were some of the changes in Soviet law. A decree of 30 March made the illegal carrying of a knife punishable by five years' imprisonment. A decree of 9 June, later incorporated into the Criminal Code (Article 58 [i.a, i.b, i.c]), was a much more startling departure, exemplifying in full the style of the Stalin epoch. It provided the death penalty for flight abroad by both civil and military; in the case of the military, members of the family aware of the intended offense were subject to up to ten years' imprisonment, while (the real novelty) those who knew nothing whatever about it—"the remaining adult members of the traitor's family, and those living with him or dependent on him at the time"—were made liable to a five-year exile.

A Soviet law book, justifying this, speaks approvingly of

> the application of special measures in respect of the adult members of the family of a serviceman-traitor in the event of the latter's flight or escape across the frontier in those cases where the adult member of the family in no way contributed to the act of treachery that was being prepared or executed and did not even know of it. . . . The political significance of it consists in the strengthening of the overall preventive action of the criminal law for the purpose of averting so heinous a felony as the action of a serviceman in crossing or flying across the frontier, as the result of which the guilty party cannot himself be subjected to punishment.[20]

In fact, we have a crude and frank institution of the hostage system—a sign of the way Stalin was thinking in other cases as well.*

More extraordinary still, and just as relevant to Stalin's general plans, was the decree of 7 April 1935 extending all penalties, including death, down to twelve-year-old children.[21]

This decree was noted in the West, where it made very bad anti-Soviet propaganda. Many people wondered why Stalin had made such a law public. Even if he meant to shoot children, this could be done without publicity. Indeed, an NKVD veteran tells how the *bezprizorniye*—homeless orphans of the wars and famines—had been reduced by indiscriminate shooting two or three years earlier.[22]

Stalin's motives, as it turned out, were centered elsewhere. He could now threaten oppositionists quite "legally" with the death of their children as accomplices if they did not carry out his wishes. The mere fact of his accepting the disadvantages of publicizing the law gave it a sinister seriousness.

Why the age limit of twelve was chosen is uncertain. Presumably, there were oppositionists whose children were just within that limit. On the other hand, it might be suggested that Stalin had a rough precedent to which the opposition had

---

*This was extended during the war to provide for "the punishment of relatives of those who had been taken prisoner" (Svetlana Alliluyeva, *Twenty Letters to a Friend* [London, 1967], p. 196).

made no objection. The youngest member of the Tsar's family, executed in the cellar at Ekaterinburg on 16 July 1918, was the Tsarevich Alexis, aged thirteen.

As to the precise timing, while it is true that Stalin often showed great foresight in his maneuvers, it seems that we must associate this decree with another case that was just coming up.

Almost nothing was published on the matter. But in effect, it was an attempt to link the opposition with an alleged plot against the life of Stalin in the library of the Central Executive Committee, by a young woman.[23] Starting in January 1935, there were scores of arrests: eventually, according to a recent Soviet account, 110 in all. Nine cleaners, a porter, a twenty-year-old telephone girl, eighteen librarians, six persons working in the Secretariat of the Presidium of the Central Executive Committee, sixteen from the Kremlin Commandant's administration, and other army men. In fact, there were two main "terrorist groups," one in the library, the other in the Commandant's headquarters, linked by the fact that one of the librarians was the sister of the leading victim from the *Komendatura;* and a "White Guard" counter-revolutionary group of five, all from non-Kremlin jobs, was thrown in for good measure.

The rest had various personal connections with the Kremlin accused, though they also included Trotsky's son Sergei Sedov, and five of Kamenev's relatives, his ex-wife, Tatiana Glebova, among them.[24]

For once again, Stalin determined to involve the opposition. Kamenev had a brother, the painter Nikolai Rosenfeld, whose Armenian ex-wife, Nina, worked in the Kremlin library. The case was first referred to in Soviet articles in 1988 and 1989, which describe it as the "Kremlin Affair." Rosenfeld, after interrogation, implicated Kamenev. Others giving such evidence (though not charged) included Pikel, Zinoviev's secretary; the prominent Zinovievite S. M. Zaks-Gladnev; and Zinoviev himself.[25] Yezhov, as Chairman of the Control Commission, demanded the death penalty. Opposition remained strong. Gorky was particularly outspoken.

Yenukidze's job as Secretary of the Central Executive Committee included general supervision of the Kremlin. It was easy to accuse him of negligence in the plot formed in the old palace. Moreover, he had long been giving a certain amount of protection to minor nonpolitical survivors from the pre-Revolutionary classes—with, of course, Stalin's concurrence. This, too, was now turned against him. He seems to have been removed from his posts as early as March, with the promise of an important position in the Caucasus, which never materialized.

Another prominent Kremlin figure and confidant of Yenukidze also went. The Latvian Peterson, who had commanded Trotsky's train[26]—the celebrated mobile G.H.Q. of the Civil War—was Commandant of the Kremlin. He was not arrested, but was transferred in September 1935 to a post in the Kiev Military District, which he held until 1937, when he was liquidated.[27] He was later (in 1938) to be named as one of the military conspirators who had been thinking in terms of a Kremlin coup, having allegedly been selected for the purpose by Yenukidze.[28]

Yenukidze was not the only Party veteran who had experienced qualms at the fierceness of the assault on the opposition. The Society of Old Bolsheviks, and the equally distinguished Society of Former Political Prisoners, had been collecting signatures in influential circles for a petition to the Politburo against the death penalty for the opposition.[29] This was now treated as factional activity. On 25 May, a brief decree by the Central Committee abolished the Society of Old Bolsheviks and appointed, to deal with its dissolution, a commission headed by Shkiryatov and consisting mainly of Stalin's young adherents, including Malenkov.[30]

The Society had its own publishing house, which printed the memoirs of its members and certain theoretical works. It was almost impossible that these, particularly the memoirs, should not have been offensive to the new regime. In fact, Stalin was, as usual, combining a political move with the settlement of a personal grudge. Starting at the end of July, *Pravda* itself prominently serialized an example of what was now to be the only right sort of record of the Party's past, a "History" of pre-Revolutionary Bolshevism in the Caucasus by Beria, which is simply Stalinist hagiography. The facts had previously been distorted, with hostile intent, it was said, by Yenukidze and Orakhelashvili. They had not given due prominence to Stalin, though in their time their works had appeared to strain facts in his favor rather than not: standards of adulation were changing.

Yenukidze's fall has been attributed entirely to Stalin's desire to inflate his own role in the history of Caucasian Bolsheviks, and the responsibility put on "the notorious falsifier of Party history, the provocateur and adventurist, Beria."[31] Beria's role and the whole question of these memoirs can only have been secondary, and this sort of interpretation anyhow takes too superficial a view of Stalin's motives. But still, this concern with suppressing and transforming the past certainly played its part. In fact, Old Bolshevik memoirs now ceased to be published. Kossior, who had evidently thought of writing some, was told by Petrovsky that Stalin was opposed to this.[32]

Early in June, Yenukidze was politically outlawed. He was denounced, in one of the main items of the agenda at a Central Committee meeting held on 5 to 7 June, for "political and personal dissoluteness."[33] Yezhov reported on his errors, and the former Secretary of the Central Executive Committee was expelled from the Central Committee and from the Party.* Over the following weeks, the papers printed violent attacks on him by Stalin's young Party Secretaries in Leningrad and Moscow, Zhdanov and Khrushchev. He was accused of taking "enemies" under his wing—"former princes, ministers, courtiers, Trotskyites, etc . . . a counter-revolutionary nest"[34]—and in general of "rotten liberalism."

These "former princes" and so on seem to have been represented by a quasi-aristocratic woman who tended the Kremlin antiques[35] and who was now inflated into an agent of the class enemy. In one account, the girl alleged to have plotted against Stalin's life was a countess.[36] In any case, the link with the case boiling up in the Kremlin is undoubted. Yenukidze was not put on trial at this time, being presumably charged with negligence only. But he seems to have been under arrest not later than early 1937.[37]

The next blow was at the Society of Former Political Prisoners, which was dissolved on 25 June, in the same way as the Society of Old Bolsheviks had been.

---

*He was replaced by Akulov, who had been serving as Prosecutor-General. It was now that Vyshinsky received that post.

A commission headed by Yezhov was appointed to deal with its effects. A number of its members who had been especially closely involved in the campaign for clemency were already, or were shortly to be, under arrest.

If the old revolutionaries had been offering a certain resistance, the main revulsion from Stalin and his new line was to be found in the very youngest generation of Communists. As we have seen, openly seditious remarks were noted in their ranks by the NKVD. More threatening still, the Kirov murder inspired various groups to talk of, and even to plan, in an amateurish fashion which was no match for the police of the new regime, the killing of Stalin. Either way, such circles were now invariably arrested and shot. But the Komsomol as a whole also needed thorough purging. Its reorganization, with a view to eliminating "enemies of the Party," was announced at the end of June.[38]

In general, Stalin's moves over the past six months had strengthened his position in obvious ways. Even so, they had not broken down the resistance to a death sentence on Kamenev. It was clear that that could only be done by a massive purge of the Stalinist moderates. And for this, the ground had not yet been adequately prepared. For the moment, Stalin abandoned the project.

And so, on 27 July, Kamenev was sentenced, at a secret trial by the Military Collegium of the "Kremlin Case," to ten years' imprisonment under Article 58 (viii) of the Criminal Code, dealing with terrorist actions against Soviet officials.[39] Two of his fellow accused, A. I. Sinelobov, Secretary for Assignments to the Kremlin Commandant, and M. K. Chernyavsky, head of a sector in the Intelligence Administration of the Red Army, were sentenced to death. The two Rosenfelds and six others got ten years' imprisonment, and another nineteen various shorter terms. Of those so sentenced, fourteen, including Kamenev, pleaded not guilty; ten pleaded guilty only to "anti-Soviet" talk; and six, including the two Rosenfelds, guilty to terrorist intentions against Stalin.

In addition, the NKVD Special Board sentenced eighty more to imprisonment (forty-two) or exile (thirty-seven), though Olga Kameneva, Party member since 1902, was only forbidden to live in Moscow or Leningrad for five years. Sergei Sedov was among those sent to labor camp for five years.[40] All concerned have lately been rehabilitated.

The heavy pressure exerted by Stalin over the summer had to some degree advanced his plans for a purge. The dissolution of the Society uniting the Old Bolsheviks, the campaign against the "rotten liberalism" of Yenukidze, and the fresh sentence on Kamenev had taken things a step further. Nevertheless, the going had been hard, and it had been impossible to produce a public trial or even a death sentence for Kamenev. Further and more thorough preparation was evidently necessary. The next months were spent in consolidating the gains achieved and laying the groundwork for an NKVD set piece to crush the opposition.

## THE NKVD PREPARES A TRIAL

From the point of view of the purges, the period from July 1935 to August 1936 was to all outward appearances something of an idyllic interlude. In the sense that nations without any history are the happiest, it seemed a greatly improved time.

There were no deaths of Politburo members, no trials of important oppositionists, no removals of leading political figures. The harvest, too, was reasonably good.

A plenum of the Central Committee held in December 1935 passed a long resolution on checking Party documents, which was later to be the organizational basis of the Purge at the grass roots. But in itself, it appeared harmless. Moreover, it was announced at the same time that the purge of the Party ordered in 1933 was now complete.

The draft of a new Constitution had been occupying the minds of Bukharin and Radek, as the active members of a Commission set up for the purpose in February 1935.[41] It was ready in June 1936, and Bukharin, in particular, thought of it as a document which would make it impossible for the people any longer to be "pushed aside."[42]

It was indeed a model document, giving, for example, guarantees of freedom from arbitrary arrest (Article 127), the inviolability of the home and secrecy of correspondence (Article 128), and indeed freedom of speech, of the press, of meetings, and of demonstrations (Article 125). That Bukharin, who was mainly responsible for it, thought that it might be implemented shows that even he now imagined that a genuine relaxation was taking place.

Bukharin's view of the Communists at this time was "They are all good people, ready for any sacrifice. If they are acting badly now, it is not because they are bad, but because the situation is bad. They must be persuaded that the country is not against them, but only that a change of policy is necessary." He had come around to the view that Bolshevism needed humanizing, and had looked to the intellectuals—in particular, Ivan Pavlov and Gorky—to help him. Pavlov, the great physiologist, was strongly opposed to the Communists. When Bukharin's name was put up for election to the Academy of Sciences in the mid-1920s, Pavlov spoke against him as "a person who is up to his knees in blood." Eventually, however, the two men had become friendly. Pavlov himself was indeed now dead. But Bukharin is even quoted as wanting the intelligentsia to put up candidates under the New Constitution as a sort of "second party,"[43] not to oppose the regime, but to give constructive criticism.

In reality, Stalin had simply changed his tactics. Under the calm façade, there was furious activity. He had ready all the ingredients which he was to bring together into the set pieces of the Great Purge. First, he had developed direct control of the Secret Police and had set up other mechanisms of power responsible to himself alone and capable, given careful tactics, of overcoming the official hierarchy of Party and State. Second, the tradition of faked trials for political purposes had been established and not objected to in the Party, whose tradition of maintaining flat untruths for political purposes was in any case of still longer standing. Third, the former oppositionists had, under the particular pressures available in Communist life, already been induced to make admissions of error which they did not sincerely believe to be correct, in what they took to be the Party's interest. Fourth, his operatives were accustomed to the use of torture, blackmail, and falsification—if as yet mainly on non-Party figures.

If his technical arrangements were complete, the same was evidently not so of his political preparations. It was still quite possible that he might have met with formidable opposition if he had set about the problem in the same way again. He chose a different method. The case was to be prepared in secret—not too difficult a matter, as the doomed Zinovievites and Trotskyites were already under arrest. It would take its course during the summer vacation, and in the absence of Stalin in particular. The death sentences would not be mentioned until they were pronounced, and even then every indication would be given that they would be commuted. But they would, on the contrary, be carried out without discussion.

When Stalin was retreating on the question of a death sentence for Kamenev, he was taking the first steps to gain the same result by his alternative method. A group of Komsomol students in the town of Gorky, said to have planned an attempt on Stalin, was one of many arrested at this time. They had not actually done anything beyond discussion, but already even this made the death penalty a foregone conclusion. This group was confessing to the plots to kill Stalin by early November 1935, though without implicating any of the Zinovievite or other accused of the August 1936 Trial.[44] The trial routine was about to be gone through when the case was held for "further investigation," under instructions from the Secretariat.[45]

The NKVD selected this particular group because it had a ready-made way of linking the students with Trotsky, and hence of building a political conspiracy around them. The link was through one of its own men, Valentin Olberg.

Olberg was a former agent of the Foreign Department of the NKVD, and had worked in Berlin as a secret informer among the Trotskyites. In 1930, he had attempted to get a post as Trotsky's secretary, one of the first of the many NKVD attempts to penetrate Trotsky's ménage (which ended in success in 1940). Since 1935, Olberg had been working for the NKVD Secret Political Department, exposing Trotskyite tendencies in the important Gorky Pedagogical Institute, where the students in question worked: his appointment had been opposed by the local Party officials, in particular Yelin, Head of the Provincial Committee's Propaganda and Education Section, since Olberg lacked qualifications and was a foreigner. Yelin, moreover, rightly complained that his documents seemed forged, and appealed to the Central Committee; but Yezhov then personally imposed Olberg.

By the beginning of 1936, the NKVD had made a good beginning in extending the scope of this Komsomol plot. Olberg and some professors at the Institute were arrested. Olberg, interrogated on 25 to 28 January, denied all the charges. Eventually, he is reported ordered as a matter of Party and police discipline to confess to being a link between the Gorky group and Trotsky. He was told that this was simply an NKVD assignment, and that whatever the verdict of the court he would be freed and given a post in the Far East. He then signed whatever was required of him.[46] This was, in brief, that he had been sent by Trotsky to arrange the assassination of Stalin, recruiting professors and students to make the attempt when they went to Moscow for the 1936 May Day Parade.

The processing of the Olberg case was not straightforward, and took time. Yelin, who knew too much, was executed without trial,[47] though he was to be mentioned several times during the public hearings. Olberg's brother, P. Olberg, was implicated, and his evidence was to be quoted in court, though he was not produced. Other accused included the Head of the Pedagogical Institute, I. K. Fedotov. He confessed, but perhaps did not seem reliable enough to present in public, for he was not brought to trial. Nelidov, a teacher of chemistry who was required as the hypothetical maker of bombs, was not a Communist and, in spite of violent pressure by one of the most vicious of the interrogators, the younger Kedrov, was not broken.

But by late February 1936, Olberg's story had been worked up into a usable version,[48] and the NKVD definitely selected it as the basis of the "plot."

The Head of the Secret Political Department, G. A. Molchanov, now held a conference of about forty NKVD executive officers. He told them that a vast conspiracy had been uncovered and that they would all be released from their ordinary duties and set to investigating it. The Politburo regarded the evidence as absolutely trustworthy, and the task was therefore simply to discover the details. The question of any accused being not guilty did not arise.[49]

The officers at once realized that the whole business was a frame-up, since they themselves were the men who had for years been in charge of supervision of the oppositionists, and they had detected no such activity. Moreover, if such a plot had come into being without their discovering it, they would clearly have been reprimanded at the very least. How little Stalin himself must have believed in the existence of any real plots was shown by the mere fact of his withdrawing so many of the most experienced officers from all the active departments of the Secret Police into what he knew to be an investigative farce.

In the NKVD as it was now, Stalin had a powerful and experienced instrument. At its head stood Yagoda. His deputy in security matters was Stalin's crony Agranov, who had finished his special operations at Leningrad and handed over that city to the dreadful Zakovsky, who is said to have boasted that if he had Karl Marx to interrogate he would soon make him confess that he was an agent of Bismarck.

The Secret Police machine proper was concentrated in the NKVD's Chief Administration of State Security. This consisted of a highly organized array of departments, skilled in the ways of their trade, and practiced in all modes of investigation, interrogation, and falsification. Almost all its leading officers had been with it for a decade, and had coped with the great cases of the late 1920s and early 1930s. (The NKVD controlled, in addition to this Secret Police machine, the "militia" [ordinary police], the frontier guards, its own internal troop formations, the fire service, and the labor camps, whose main administration, Gulag, under Matvei Berman, was already receiving a vast number of assorted purgees.)

Yagoda and Agranov themselves, and Yezhov representing the Central Committee, played a prominent part in the organization of the trial, and Stalin personally conducted the key conferences. Under them, the Secret Political Department was technically responsible for the whole operation, though it now had at its disposal the services of a number of officers from the other departments of State Security, including their chiefs.

The *Secret Political Department,* which had been the kernel of the Cheka from the beginning,[50] was still the key center of Secret Police operations. That is, it had the overall responsibility of supervising all the country's organizations and carrying on the political struggle against all hostile political elements. It was headed by G. A. Molchanov, an unscrupulous careerist, and his deputy, G. S. Lyushkov.

The *Economic Department* had security responsibility for all industry and agriculture (except for transport, dealt with by the Transport Department). In Soviet conditions, this gave it a role as weighty, in a general way, as that of the Secret Political Department, and it had had the main responsibility for trials such as the Shakhty, which, though in a general sense political, were centered on economic crimes. Its Head, L. G. Mironov, was a man with an extraordinary memory, which was to be of great use in composing and mastering the details of the first two trials. At the same time as he ran his vast department, he acted as assistant to Yagoda in the whole of the State Security side of the NKVD. He is described as a conscientious Party man who was depressed by the prosecution of the Old Bolsheviks.[51] Previous cases that he had organized, and which do not seem to have depressed him similarly, included the "Industrial Party" and the Metro-Vic Trials—cases, with all their political importance, definable as "economic." The Zinoviev Trial had no economic component. Nevertheless, Mironov was given an important role.

The *Operative Department* was responsible for guarding leading personnel and installations and investigating terrorist acts against them. Its main concern at this time was the protection of Stalin. Its Head, K. V. Pauker, or his deputy, A. I. Volovich, was almost continually with him except when he was actually in his heavily guarded offices, and L. I. Chertok, one of their chief subordinates, also spent much time organizing his local defense.

Pauker was a sort of evil buffoon. He had been a barber and valet to opera stars in Budapest, and had himself a turn for comic acting. Taken prisoner by the Russians in 1916, he had become one of the group of Communists which emerged from that milieu. An ignorant and uneducated man without any political convictions, he was recruited to the Cheka, like so many other foreigners in those days, to work on searches and arrests. He rose by becoming a personal attendant again, this time to Menzhinsky, who came to rely on him and finally appointed him head of the Kremlin bodyguard and chief of the Operative Department. He was on close terms with Stalin, who even allowed him to shave him.[52]

The *Special Department* in general covered the armed forces. Its Head was M. I. Gay.

The *Foreign Department* dealt with espionage and terror abroad. Its Head, A. A. Slutsky, was a sly intriguer who played an important role in the major interrogations. His deputies were Boris Berman and M. Shpigelglas.

The *Transport Department*, under A. M. Shanin, was the only one not deeply involved, having its hands full with Kaganovich's endless purges on the railways.

There was a good deal of flexibility in these arrangements. Postings between departments were fairly frequent. And reorganization involving the transfer of lesser matters between the departments was also quite common.

Such was the order of battle of the shock troops of repression that Stalin was now launching on the helpless prisoners in the Lubyanka.

They were assisted by another organization: the Prosecutor's Office. This had not been centralized on an All-Union basis until 1933, when it became one of the most centralized bodies in the USSR, having all its legal agencies completely and uniformly subordinate to the Prosecutor-General in Moscow, who was now Vyshinsky. He announced his operative principle—that any discrepancies between the commands of the law and those of the Revolution "must be solved only by the subordination of the formal commands of law to those of Party policy." [53] His chief assistant was G. Roginsky, a fanatic who was to defend mass liquidation even after he himself had been purged and sent to a penal camp.

By the end of February, the testimony of Olberg and others was satisfactory. One of those confessing, I. I. Trusov, had some of Trotsky's archives from the 1920s; Stalin now proposed to the Politburo that Yezhov should examine these and that "the NKVD should question the accused together with Comrade Yezhov." From now on, Yezhov plays a major role in the investigation. [54]

A former oppositionist, Isak Reingold, Chairman of the Cotton Syndicate, had been arrested as a Trotskyite in January or February. He was a friend of Sokolnikov's and was connected with Kamenev. A strong man, still only thirty-eight, he proved hard to break. He was interrogated for three weeks, often for periods of forty-eight hours at a time without sleep or food, by Chertok. The order to arrest his family was given in his presence. Finally, he was handed a death sentence and told it would be carried out automatically if he did not testify at once. He still refused to do so, but said that he would sign anything if so instructed by the Party. Yagoda refused to accept these terms, and the interrogation dragged on. Finally, Yezhov intervened and personally ordered Reingold in the name of the Central Committee to provide the evidence required. [55]

The confessions had been obtained with some difficulty. Stalin is said to have brought about 300 former oppositionists from prisons and isolators [56] for the NKVD to test for suitability as accused. By May, about fifteen suitable confessions had been obtained, and more were coming in.

In mid-May, Stalin held a conference with a number of the leading NKVD officials, and ordered the NKVD to produce further links with Trotsky. Molchanov, much to the anger of the Foreign Department, nominated two more NKVD agents, who had been working as its representatives in the German Communist Party and in the Comintern, Fritz David and Berman-Yurin. [57] They were arrested in June [58] and had no choice but to accept their instructions. They, too, claimed that they had each visited Trotsky and received orders from him to kill Stalin.

Two more figures, Moissei Lurye, a scientist, and Nathan Lurye, a surgeon, whose conduct in court led even Western journalists to suspect them of being agents provocateurs, are also reported by fellow prisoners, in on different charges, as scarcely bothering to conceal this. [59] They, too, were supposed to be Trotskyite terrorists. With their evidence, a mass of material was now accumulating.

## "THE TROTSKYITE–ZINOVIEVITE CENTER"

In March, Yagoda had reported to Stalin on "the liquidation of the Trotskyite underground and the exposure of the terrorist groups." On 31 March, Stalin instructed Yagoda and Vyshinsky to submit a concrete proposal on the trial of these Trotskyites, of whom they shortly gave eighty-two names. By April, the leading Trotskyites accused—I. N. Smirnov, Mrachkovsky, and Ter-Vaganyan—were under interrogation. [60]

As was later pointed out, the "Center" contained "not . . . a single one of the old political leaders" from the Trotskyite side. [61] Smirnov, Mrachkovsky, and

Ter-Vaganyan were all, however, men of repute in the Party. (Trotsky's Army Inspector-General, the heroic giant Muralov, had been arrested on 17 April, and it was doubtless intended to use him too; but he held out until December, and this plan had to be postponed.)

Smirnov alone had been a member of the Central Committee, but he at least was a most distinguished Old Bolshevik. A factory worker, he had been an active revolutionary from the age of seventeen, and had often been arrested.[62] He had spent many years in Tsarist prisons and in Arctic exile. He had fought in the 1905 Revolution, and in the Civil War had led the Fifth Red Army to its victory over Kolchak. Known as "the Lenin of Siberia," he had ruled there for some years after the Revolution.

Smirnov had been proposed as the leading Secretary of the Party in 1922, just before the job went to Stalin.[63] After being exiled with the other Trotskyites in 1927, he had recanted but, during the Ryutin period, had spoken approvingly of the proposals to remove Stalin and had been in jail ever since. Stalin thus had a particular grudge against him.

Perhaps it was this that led Stalin to insist on his inclusion in the "Center" in spite of the physical impossibility of his having participated in anything of the kind. For, as even Agranov is said to have tentatively objected, there would be some difficulty in making the charge plausible, since Smirnov had been held in jail throughout the period of the alleged plot. Stalin "gave Agranov a sullen look and said, 'Don't be afraid, that's all.' "[63]

Mrachkovsky had also fought in Siberia. He had run Trotsky's underground printing press in 1927, and had been the first oppositionist to be arrested. He was regarded as simply a "fighter." He had been in jail since 1933. Ter-Vaganyan, an intellectual Armenian described as both honest and unambitious, had fought with great distinction in the Revolution and Civil War, and afterward had reverted to ideology and journalism. He, too, had been in exile in Kazakhstan since 1933.

A fourth Trotskyite was thrown in for some good measure—Dreitzer, the former head of Trotsky's bodyguard and prominent in the 1927 demonstrations. He was not accused of being a member of the "Center," but rather as the head organizer of assassin groups.

The first examinations of the leading prisoners were a total failure. Smirnov had gone on hunger strike for thirteen days on 8 May, and on 20 May was still replying, "I deny that; again I deny; I deny." Ter-Vaganyan also twice undertook hunger strikes and wrote to Stalin that he had decided on suicide.[65] Mrachkovsky's key interrogation is said to have lasted ninety hours, without result, though Stalin rang up at intervals to inquire how things were going.[66]

So far the case was entirely Trotskyite. Stalin now ordered the implication of the Zinovievites. Yagoda was later to be accused of rejecting the evidence against them, and Agranov (or so he was to say when attacking Yagoda and Molchanov in 1937) went behind his back to the Moscow Provincial NKVD. He and Yezhov composed the full plan of the "United"—that is Trotskyite and Zinovievite—Center, and with A. P. Radzivilovsky and other leading figures in the Moscow NKVD he obtained the necessary confessions. Radzivilovsky wrote later that "extraordinarily difficult work for three weeks on Dreitzer and Pikel" was needed before they gave testimony. Although Yagoda at first rejected it, Agranov said that it was only thus that the investigation was put on the right track. Richard

Pikel, formerly Zinoviev's secretary, had already given evidence in the "Kremlin Affair." A writer and playwright who had served in the Civil War, he became more cooperative when transferred to the central NKVD, where a number of the leading figures were old friends of his. They promised him his life, an offer later confirmed by Yagoda.[67]

It was only in late June or early July that Zinoviev and his leading supporters were brought to Moscow from their isolators.[68] At first Zinoviev made "obdurate denials."[69] Bakayev made "persistent denials."[70] In general, all the genuine oppositionists refused to confess and pointed out that they had been in prison or exile in the remotest parts of the country during most of the period, and under close NKVD supervision during the rest of it. Molchanov then gave the interrogators to understand that earlier orders about not using unlawful means of interrogation were not to be taken too seriously.[71]

The interrogation of Zinoviev and Kamenev was put in charge of the most senior officials: Agranov, Molchanov, and Mironov. Zinoviev was ill at the time with a liver ailment, and the routine interrogation was postponed.[72] He had once again written to the Politburo vaguely accepting "responsibility" for the assassination of Kirov. This was returned with an insistence on "greater sincerity."[73]

With Kamenev, the attempt was made to secure a confession by ordinary interrogative methods. Mironov conducted it. But Kamenev resisted him in spite of all his efforts, exposing Reingold at a "confrontation" and in general standing firm.

Mironov reported to Stalin that Kamenev was refusing to confess, and later gave an account of the conversation to a close acquaintance:

"You think that Kamenev may not confess?" asked Stalin, his eyes slyly screwed up.

"I don't know," Mironov answered. "He doesn't yield to persuasion."

"You don't know?" inquired Stalin with marked surprise, staring at Mironov. "Do you know how much our state weighs, with all the factories, machines, the army, with all the armaments and the navy?"

Mironov and all those present looked at Stalin with surprise.

"Think it over and tell me," demanded Stalin. Mironov smiled, believing that Stalin was getting ready to crack a joke. But Stalin did not intend to jest. He looked at Mironov quite in earnest. "I am asking you, how much does all that weigh?" he insisted.

Mironov was confused. He waited, still hoping Stalin would turn everything into a joke, but Stalin kept staring at him and waited for an answer. Mironov shrugged his shoulders and, like a schoolboy undergoing an examination, said in an irresolute voice, "Nobody can know that, Yosif Vissarionovich. It is in the realm of astronomical figures."

"Well, and can one man withstand the pressure of that astronomical weight?" asked Stalin sternly.

"No," answered Mironov.

"Now then, don't tell me any more that Kamenev, or this or that prisoner, is able to withstand that pressure. Don't come to report to me," said Stalin to Mironov, "until you have in this briefcase the confession of Kamenev!"[74]

The transfer of Kamenev's case to the third-rate bully Chertok also produced no results, though the usual pressures of sleeplessness, semistarvation, and general bullying must have begun to wear him down.[75]

## THE DEATH OF GORKY

Stalin planned to carry through the execution of the oppositionists regardless of possible revulsion in the Party. For, as ever, he was prepared to deal with this by his usual combination of hardness and maneuver. The only figure who could not be handled in this fashion and who, if alive, would be difficult to silence, was Maxim Gorky, who "remained until his death the only person whom Stalin was compelled to take into consideration, to some extent at least."[76] It is possible that had he lived, the August Trial might have had a different denouement. He had become ill on 31 May,[77] and died on 18 June.

When Gorky had opposed the October Revolution in 1917, Stalin had attacked him in a tone more venomous than any other Bolshevik's. He had even said (quite falsely), in an assault on an article of Gorky's entitled "I Cannot Keep Silent," that Gorky and his type had "kept silent" when landlords and capitalists were attacking the peasantry and the proletariat, that they reproached only the Revolution and not the counter-revolution. Gorky's work had of course been one long blast at the ruling classes, and he had been associated with the Social Democrats from the start. Stalin went on to write that the Revolution was quite prepared to throw away "great names," including Gorky's, if necessary.

Gorky's own views were by no means lacking in pugnacity. He several times remarked that if "the enemy" did not surrender "he must be destroyed." Nevertheless, he had protected both Pilnyak and Zamyatin during the outcry against those writers in 1930—and this alone must have been very galling to Stalin, particularly in the case of Pilnyak (see p. 298). And since then, more significantly still to our point, he had intervened strongly in favor of the policy of reconciliation and been an outspoken opponent of the earlier attempts to destroy Kamenev and Zinoviev.

His mere existence was a factor strengthening the morale of Kamenev and others in their ordeal. His voice, they could be sure, would be raised against the new persecution of them, as soon as this became publicly known. To some degree, knowledge of this must have fortified their resistance. By the same token, his death at this particular time must have been a moral blow and must have made Stalin's task easier.

As with Kuibyshev, we have a case of a death at a time very convenient to Stalin. Most deaths at times convenient to Stalin were so for the obvious reason.

The doctors attending Gorky were later to be accused of murdering him on Yagoda's orders. When we come to the Bukharin Trial of 1938, at which this charge was made, we shall consider the evidence (see p. 388). Meanwhile, we may note that the current trial was held as soon after the necessary confessions as was feasible, and, moreover, seems to have been dated to suit the absence on holiday of some of the Politburo. If Gorky had hung on for even a few months, he would certainly have represented an impediment to Stalin's plans. The indefinite postponement of the trial would have been at the least awkward, and time would have been given for the mustering of opposition in the Central Committee. To have proceeded with the trial and *not* executed the oppositionists would have been contrary to Stalin's whole plan. But to have carried this out regardless would, with Gorky alive, have had disadvantages. A powerful voice would have supported and heartened the already restless elements in the leadership; and while it might have been possible, it would not have been easy to silence the writer.

All such considerations are merely logical, and prove nothing. But Stalin was, in his way, a logical man. He was not averse to having people murdered, and his respect for literature was not such as to prevent his disposing of many other Russian writers of repute. We shall consider this suspicion later.

## ZINOVIEV SURRENDERS

It now seemed suitable for Stalin to make a direct political approach to Zinoviev and Kamenev. Yezhov gave them what were represented as the Politburo's instructions, to "disarm in a manner that will preclude any hope on your part of raising your head against the Party ever again." The alternative was a trial by military court behind closed doors and the execution of the entire opposition, including the thousands in the camps.

Zinoviev refused, and a similar attempt on Kamenev was also unsuccessful, though Yezhov this time directly threatened that Kamenev's son would be shot if he did not give in.

A tighter interrogative routine was then inflicted on them. Yagoda had the heat put on in the cells, though the weather was now hot. Zinoviev's physical condition was very bad, and Kamenev was beginning to weaken under the threats to his son, whose arrest was finally ordered in his presence. In July, Zinoviev, after an all-night interrogation, asked to speak to Kamenev, and when they had discussed the matter they agreed to go on trial on condition that Stalin would confirm his promises to them, of executing neither themselves nor their followers, in the presence of the whole Politburo.

This was accepted. However, when they were taken to the alleged Politburo meeting, only Stalin, Voroshilov, and Yezhov were present. Stalin explained that they formed a "commission" of the Politburo authorized to hear the case.[78]

This appeal to the Politburo and Stalin's partial evasion of it present some interesting points. Both appeal and evasion suggest that there were still some men in the Politburo who might have been relied on to try to have its guarantees respected. In fact, it is curious that as late as the execution of Rudzutak in 1938, some attempt at a similar appeal is suggested when we are told that "he was not even called before the Central Committee Political Bureau because Stalin did not want to talk to him."[79]

Although shaken by the absence of the other Politburo members, the prisoners, after some argument, finally accepted Stalin's terms, which guaranteed their lives, the lives of their supporters, and the liberty of their families. (A member of Zinoviev's family told Krivitsky that one reason for capitulation was "to save his family,"[80] and in Kamenev's case the same is obviously true—and can be seen in his final plea.)

With the surrender of Zinoviev and Kamenev, the game was in Stalin's hands. The trial was on. The lesser political figures were expendable at a pinch, and in any case no stronger argument could be put to them than the willingness of their seniors to go along with the trial and accept Stalin's promises.

Kamenev's own confession was under way on 13 July (and presumably Zinoviev's too). Bakayev was confessing by 17 July; Dreitser, by 23 July.[81] Mrachkovsky was confessing by 20 July, and on 21 July he had a "confrontation" with Smirnov. There are two slightly different accounts of this.[82] One of them, evidently based on the official record, has these old friends quarreling because of what Smirnov regarded as Mrachkovsky's weakness in surrendering. The other shows them as still on good terms at the end. In any case, Mrachkovsky made some such remark as "Why, Ivan Nikitich, you want to get out of a sordid bloody business with a clean shirt?" And Smirnov's firm comment was "invention and slander!"[83]

In spite of Smirnov's recalcitrance, the political preparation for the case could now go forward. On 14 January 1936 there had been a ruling from the Central Committee that all members should turn in their Party documents for new ones, with a view to screening unworthy members. Now, on 29 July, a top-secret letter of the Central Committee was sent out to Provincial, Territory, Republican, City, and District Committees. It quoted confessions, some of them dated as late as 25 July, by Zinoviev, Kamenev, Mrachkovsky, Bakaev, Pikel, Dreitzer, Berman-Yurin, N. Lurye, M. Lurye, and Reingold—but not Smirnov—among those who were to appear in court, together with Karev, Motorin, Esterman, Kuklin, and others to be implicated but not produced. The picture presented was of a detailed array of assassinations planned by the Trotskyite–Zinovievite bloc, to be carried out by numbers of named accomplices, and in particular the Kirov murder. In some respects, it gave a fuller account than that of the official publication of the trial itself.[84] The letter also pointed out that several of those now under arrest had, in spite of all previous measures, managed to keep their Party cards, though "all boundaries have been obliterated" between "spies, *provocateurs,* White Guards, *kulaks"* and "the Trotskyites and Zinovievites." It called for a renewal of "revolutionary vigilance," and asserted firmly the main duty of the Party membership in the forthcoming period: "The inalienable quality of every Bolshevik under present conditions should be the ability to recognize an enemy of the Party, no matter how well he may be masked."[85]

On receiving the circular, local officials began a further round of feverish delation. The First Secretary of Kozelsk *rayon,* for example, wrote to the Provincial Committee denouncing not only local inhabitants, but also people he had met in previous posts and now thought suspicious, commenting in each case, "It is possible that up to this time he has not been unmasked."[86]

This was, in fact, the political preparation of the Party branches throughout the country for the campaign about to be launched, in connection with the Zinoviev Trial, against all the enemies of the General Secretary. As one result, even longer lists of anti-Soviet elements than those already in existence were compiled everywhere, and the mass Purge began to get under way.

Meanwhile Smirnov, incriminated in the Secret Letter, was still giving trouble. A Soviet periodical has lately printed excerpts from Smirnov's NKVD interrogations. He denied that his alleged "organization" existed. When told that he had sent out directives through his mother when in prison in 1935, he replied, "A lie." He admitted that he had (evidently in 1932) received a letter from Trotsky, and had answered it. Trotsky had written about the rise of Fascism, and Smirnov had written back about the situation in the Soviet Union, and nothing more.[87]

Further pressure was brought on Smirnov through his former wife, Aleksandra Safonova, also implicated. She was brought to a "confrontation" with him in Gay's office, where she pleaded with him to go to trial. Since Kamenev and Zinoviev had already confessed, she is also said to have argued, it would be best for him to stick with them and go to public trial, in which case there would be no question of shooting them.[88] Safonova had accepted the argument that the opposition must "disarm" when Yezhov, as Secretary of the Central Committee, had told her that her evidence was needed by the Party, and she followed instructions. She now said that in 1930 and 1931 Smirnov, Ter-Vaganyan, Mrachkovsky, and she had formed a "Trotskyite Center" with terrorist aims; that Trotsky had sent directives with that purpose; and that Smirnov had spoken in their home of the need to kill Stalin.

Smirnov replied, as before, that he had met Trotsky's son in Berlin and had exchanged letters with Trotsky, but that there had never been any terrorist plans, and that no "Center" ever existed.

Safonova then said, "You, Ivan Nikitich, want to hide in the bushes. You don't want to disarm." Smirnov answered, "Oh, Shura, Shura. I want to die at peace."[89]

Smirnov seems also to have been "confronted" with Zinoviev, who said he was confessing and argued in favor of Smirnov doing so too. Zinoviev said that he really believed that his admissions would open the way to his returning to the Party, and that Stalin—whom he referred to by his old Party nickname of Koba—was at present the focus of the Party's will, and would come to a compromise with the opposition, since in practice he could not do without the "Lenin guard" in the long run. Smirnov replied that, on the contrary, it was obvious that the Politburo wanted the physical annihilation of the opposition; otherwise there was no point in the case.[90]

The interrogator told Smirnov that it was useless for him to resist, as there were plenty of witnesses against him. And, moreover, it was not only Smirnov but his family too that would suffer—as the assassin Nikolayev's had suffered. Smirnov knew nothing of the arrest of his family and took this simply to be a disgusting threat by the interrogator. But shortly afterward, on his way to an interrogation, he saw his daughter Olga at the other end of the corridor, held by two guards. She is reported later in prison. (Her mother, Smirnov's wife Varvara, was sent to a women's camp at Kotlas and was shot in the camp in April or May 1938, during a mass execution of 1,300 undesirables. However, his former wife, Safonova, who had testified against him, remained alive but imprisoned, until 1958, when she described her testimony as "ninety percent lies.")[91]

Under all these pressures, Smirnov finally gave way, but he would only consent to make a partial confession. This would not have been accepted from anyone else, but time was getting short and Stalin wanted Smirnov in the trial at all costs. Smirnov also managed to have Safonova removed from the list of defendants, and she only appeared as a "witness." All this rankled with Stalin, and Yagoda and Mironov were later charged with having shielded Smirnov.[92] By 5 August,* Smir-

---

*These dates are those given sporadically in the indictment, in the evidence of the trial, and in the Secret Letter of the Central Committee.

nov was well into his confession. Even now, a final decision on who would appear in the trial had not been taken. On 7 August, Vyshinsky presented a formal indictment of twelve named accused. Stalin corrected some of the phraseology, and added ''Lurye'' twice, upon which the two Luryes were included. The revised indictment, presented to Stalin on 10 August, thus had fourteen names. He then added those of Ter-Vaganyan and Evdokimov. Neither had been mentioned in the Secret Letter of 29 July; Evdokimov had not even been questioned about the case: he is said to have been treated with particular brutality, in view, doubtless, of the short notice.[93] On 11 August, the official orders for holding the trial were given by the Central Executive Committee, and the final indictment is dated 14 August. On the same day, Ter-Vaganyan, who had vaguely admitted the existence of the ''Center'' on 16 July, was making a full confession.

The last confessions were eased, and the earlier ones fortified, on 11 August by a decree which (going back, to some extent, on that of 1 December 1934) reestablished public hearings and the use of lawyers, and allowed appeals from the accused for three days after the sentence.[94] The timing of this decree is decisive. While clearly intended to strengthen the accused's hope that a reprieve would be granted, it was also designed, of course, to put the same idea about among the apprehensive Party membership. These included some of the interrogators themselves. It seems that reassurances that no death sentences would be carried out were believed by, for example, Boris Berman, and that this led him to quite sincere advice to Ter-Vaganyan that the best course open to him was to surrender.[95] And with the publication of the indictment on 15 August, it was at last necessary to take such measures as would best put the case over to the Party as a whole. The preparatory work had been done in great secrecy. There was no preliminary discussion in the Politburo. ''The trial came as a complete surprise not only for the rank and file of Party workers but also to members of the Central Committee and some members of the Politburo,'' in the sense that they were only informed about it when the Secret Letter of 29 July reached them.[96]

To objectors in the current leadership, Stalin now had a simple answer: the matter was in the hands of the Prosecutor and the court. It was they who were so keen on legality, after all. They must let justice take its course. And the 11 August decree was a considerable reassurance.

Opposition to the trial would in any case have been very difficult to organize once confessions had been obtained. But Stalin played safe by springing it on the country when he himself was on holiday, and many of the rest of the leadership were also scattered around the country. Molotov and Kalinin, for example, are said to have gone on holiday in ignorance of the forthcoming massacre.[97]

Whether this is true of Molotov in quite this form seems dubious. However that may be, there now came a startling proof that Stalin was discontented with him.

In the Party when the Secret Letter arrived, and among the public when the indictment came out, a sensation was caused by the omission from the list of those the conspirators were planning to kill of one important Soviet leader—Molotov. Stalin, Ordzhonikidze, Voroshilov, Kaganovich, Kossior, Postyshev, and Zhdanov were named (the last three specifically as the targets of local terrorist branches in the Ukraine and Leningrad), but not the Soviet Premier. Right through the trial, the confessions gave the same listing, and it was repeated in Vyshinsky's final speech for the prosecution. In Soviet conditions this was taken to mean, and without any doubt at all really meant, that Molotov was in disfavor. An NKVD defector account says that Stalin crossed Molotov's name out of the early evidence (where it had naturally been included) with his own hand, and that Yagoda then instructed the interrogators not to bring it in again.[98] This story must be substantially true. Without a personal decision of Stalin's, Molotov could not have been omitted.

There seem grounds for supposing that Molotov had in some way dragged his feet about the plan to destroy the Old Bolsheviks. And the episode lends at least some credence to the reports that in the discussions about the Ryutin Case in 1932 he had not wholeheartedly supported Stalin in calling for extreme measures. Thus from around May 1936 until the end of the trial in August, Molotov faced elimination. He went on his holiday under careful NKVD supervision.[99]

Some weeks after the Zinoviev Trial, he seems to have returned to favor. His name *was* included as a target of the conspirators in the 1937 and 1938 Trials—even though this raised the anomaly that the later batches of conspirators had allegedly plotted with Zinoviev and Kamenev for this purpose, but Zinoviev and Kamenev had inexplicably omitted to confess it.

Stalin's pressure had brought Molotov to heel. Henceforth, there were no reports of anything but enthusiastic complicity on his part in the Great Purge. Why Stalin saved him cannot be more than guessed at. He was, of course (or was to be after Ordzhonikidze's removal), the only Old Bolshevik of any repute at all among Stalin's ruling group.

Meanwhile, it was impossible for Molotov, or anyone else, to interfere with the trial, through they could hope that it would end merely with prison sentences.

## THE TRIAL BEGINS

At ten minutes after midday on 19 August 1936, the trial opened before a session of the Military Collegium of the Supreme Court in the little October Hall of the Trade Union House—chosen in preference to the huge Hall of Columns, which had been the scene of earlier show trials. A large, high, bright room, decorated rather floridly in the Russian nineteenth-century style with white Corinthian columns and light blue walls, it had formerly been one of the ballrooms of what was then the Nobles' Club. In this small hall there was room for no more than 150-odd Soviet citizens and 30-odd foreign journalists and diplomats. The foreign audience was crucial to the show. Unanimously hostile criticism might have prevented further performances. Too many of these privileged witnesses allowed themselves to be taken in by an improbable plot and incredible details. The Soviet spectators were all selected by the NKVD and were, in fact, mainly NKVD clerks and officials.[100] Many officials of the Central Committee and the Government were not able to get in. Nor were relatives of the accused.[101]

We are told of a later trial (Bukharin's) that "the first five rows were occupied by members of the NKVD."[102] At such trials, we hear, the NKVD officers responsible for the accused sat "in front of" them.[103] This apparently means facing them closely, in the first row of the audience—we are definitely told this of one later accused.[104] This crowd is reported to have been under instructions to raise a commotion at a given signal, which might be necessary if any untoward outbreak from one of the prisoners took place.[105]

The court commandant, in uniform tunic and breeches, and wearing the magenta hatband and collar tabs of the NKVD, called the court to order. Everyone stood, and the judges took their seats. Presiding was Ulrikh, a fat man, with dewlaps like a bloodhound and little pig eyes. His shaven head rose to a point. His neck bulged over the collar of his uniform. His voice was soft and oily. He had much experience in political cases.

On his right was another veteran of these trials, Matulevich, who had presided over the mass slaughter of the Leningrad "White Guards" in December 1934. On his left was a figure of great interest to Westerners, the unimpressive, thin-faced Divisional Military Jurist I. I. Nikitchenko. Ten years later, he was to appear on the Supreme Allied Tribunal at Nuremberg, with the most distinguished judges of Britain, America, and France, to preside over the trial of Goering and others.* He represented a judicial tradition so different from that of the rest of the Tribunal that his mere presence may be thought to have made a mockery of those proceedings.

One important respect in which Soviet justice differed from that practiced by his future colleagues in Nuremberg was that sentences had been prepared beforehand by nonjudicial authorities. "The vicious practice was condoned of having the NKVD prepare lists of persons whose cases were under jurisdiction of the Military Collegium and whose sentences were prepared in advance. Yezhov would send these lists to Stalin personally for his approval of the proposed punishment. . . . He approved these lists."[106] It was even the case that "Kaganovich, before court sittings on various cases had come to an end, would personally edit the draft sentences and arbitrarily insert charges that suited him, such as allegations that acts of terrorism had been planned against his person,"[107] while Molotov is described as personally changing a sentence on a "wife of an enemy of the people" from imprisonment to death when the list when through his hands.[108] In the case now before Nikitchenko and his colleagues, there is no reason to doubt that the sentences were part of the original script, and had been imposed by the General Secretary himself.†

Three large and healthy NKVD soldiers, with rifles and fixed bayonets, escorted the prisoners to the dock, behind a low wooden bar along the right-hand wall of the courtroom, and took up positions guarding them. The accused had gained a little weight and caught up on their sleep in the few days past. But they still looked pale and worn.

Just before the trial, Yagoda and Yezhov had a conference with Zinoviev, Kamenev, Evdokimov, Bakayev, Mrachkovsky, and Ter-Vaganyan. Yezhov repeated Stalin's assurance that their lives would be spared, and also warned them

---

*He is also mentioned by General A. V. Gorbatov as presiding in 1939 over the four- or five-minute farce which sentenced him to fifteen years' imprisonment. He died in good odor in 1967 (*Years Off My Life* [London, 1964], pp. 117–18).

†Just as the Czechoslovak investigation of the Slansky Trial made in 1968 established that "the individual sentences had been settled beforehand by the Political Secretariat" (*Nova mysl*, no. 7 [10 July 1968]).

that a single attempt at "treachery" would be regarded as implicating the whole group.[109]

Now they sat, ill at ease among the agents provocateurs scattered among them and separating them. The practice of trying a group of important political prisoners with various second-rate crooks (or alleged crooks), as though they formed one group, is an old technique. At the trial of Danton and the Moderates on 13 and 14 Germinal, he and his four closest followers were mingled in with men accused as thieves and common spies, and each was carefully linked with the others by joint accusations. The Soviet press was doing just such a job. An angry and violent campaign filled the papers in which, meanwhile, other and contrary themes were appearing—in particular, almost daily photographs of a series of airmen, like those of the astronauts a generation later. These were men like Chkalov, who with his crew flew a new Soviet plane on a round tour of the country to the Far East and back, and Kokkinaki, who produced a series of altitude records. They were photographed with Stalin and others, being received in the Politburo, being awarded Orders, and simply on their own. Through them, an air of youth and progress, of the triumph of the young Stalinist generation, was projected at the same time as the forces of darkness represented by the Old Bolsheviks were being dissipated.

At the side of the room, opposite the doomed representatives of anti-Stalinism, Vyshinsky sat at a small table, with his trim gray moustache and hair, neatly dressed in stiff white collar and well-cut dark suit.

Ulrikh went through the formalities of identification and asked if there were objections to the court and if the accused wanted defending lawyers. The answer to both questions was a unanimous negative. The secretary of the court then read the indictment. This based itself on the trial of January 1935, at which, it said, Zinoviev and his colleagues had concealed their direct responsibility for the Kirov murder. The since-revealed circumstances showed that they and the Trotskyites, who had practiced terrorism earlier still, had formed a united bloc at the end of 1932. The bloc had been joined also by the Lominadze group. They had received instructions, through special agents, from Trotsky. In fulfilling them, they had organized terrorist groups which had "prepared a number of practical measures" for the assassination of Stalin, Voroshilov, Kaganovich, Kirov, Ordzhonikidze, Zhdanov, Kossior, Postyshev, and others;[110] one of these terrorist groups had actually murdered Kirov. They had no program other than murder.

Trotsky had sent written instructions to Dreitzer, who had passed them to Mrachkovsky, to assassinate Stalin and Voroshilov. The five junior accused, together with Holtzman, had been personally sent by Trotsky or his son Sedov to assist in these acts. Olberg, in addition, had contacts with the Gestapo. All the accused had fully admitted their guilt, with the exception of I. N. Smirnov, whose full guilt was, however, proved by the confessions of the other accused. He had made only a partial confession: of belonging to the "United Center" and being personally connected with Trotsky up to the time of his arrest in 1933; and of having received, in 1932, instructions from Trotsky to organize terror. He had denied, however, taking part in terroristic activities.

The indictment concluded by mentioning various names of accused who were to be tried separately: "The cases of Gertik, Grinberg, Y. Gaven, Karev, Kuzmichev, Konstant, Matorin, Paul Olberg, Radin, Safonova, Faivilovich, D. Shmidt and Esterman, in view of the fact that investigation is still proceeding, have been set aside for separate trial.''[111] Matorin, who had been Zinoviev's private secretary, was elsewhere said to be still under investigation with a view to later trial ''in connection with another case.''[112] None of them was ever to come to public trial, and in most cases we know nothing whatever of their fate.

After the reading of the indictment, the accused pleaded guilty on all counts, with the exception of Smirnov and Holtzman. Smirnov admitted to having belonged to the ''Center'' and to having received terrorist instructions from Trotsky, but again denied participation in preparing or executing terrorist acts. Holtzman, too, though admitting having brought terrorist instructions from Trotsky, denied himself participating in terrorism. After a fifteen-minute recess, *Mrachkovsky* was called upon to testify.

Under Vyshinsky's questioning, he recounted the formation of the ''Center'' and the planning of terrorism under instructions from Trotsky and his son Sedov, partly passed through Smirnov and partly by a letter from Trotsky in invisible ink sent to him through Dreitzer. Under Smirnov there had been formed a Trotskyite group consisting of himself (Mrachkovsky), Ter-Vaganyan, and Safonova. Dreitzer joined them, and they had a number of lesser agents.[113]

When Mrachkovsky implicated Smirnov in direct terrorist activity, Smirnov several times denied the evidence, and there were warm wrangles between him and Vyshinsky. Zinoviev, called on to confirm the story, added that the murder of Kirov had been a joint enterprise involving both Zinovievites and Trotskyites, including Smirnov. Kamenev also confirmed this. The joint terror network was thus sketched out right at the start of the trial. For good measure, Mrachkovsky also implicated Lominadze (who had committed suicide the previous year),[114] and a Red Army group of assassins headed by Divisional Commander Dmitri Shmidt. This latter charge was to be of far-reaching significance.

Mrachkovsky was followed by *Evdokimov,* who said he had deceived the court in January 1935. He then explained how he, Bakayev, Zinoviev, and Kamenev had organized the Kirov assassination. The plan had been to get Stalin at the same time: ''. . . Bakayev warned Nikolayev and his accomplices that they must wait for Zinoviev's signal,'' said Evdokimov, ''that they must fire simultaneously with the shots to be fired in Moscow and Kiev.''[115] (Mrachkovsky had been quoted in the indictment as having said at the preliminary examination that ''Stalin was to be killed first,'' but in any case Kirov was not supposed to precede the General Secretary to the grave.) Evdokimov for the first time involved the Old Bolshevik Grigori Sokolnikov, former candidate member of the Politburo and still a candidate member of the Central Committee.

In the course of Evdokimov's evidence, Smirnov, once more implicated, again denied the testimony.

At the evening session, *Dreitzer* recounted his connections with Sedov and his organization of two other terrorist groups for killing Stalin and Voroshilov, respectively. As to Smirnov, ''Trotsky's deputy in the U.S.S.R.,'' Dreitzer remarked harshly, ''There could be no acting on one's own, no orchestra without a conductor among us. I am surprised at the assertions of Smirnov, who, according to his words, both knew and did not know, spoke and did not speak, acted and did not act. This is not true!"[116] Smirnov again denied the evidence, and said he had not discussed terrorism with Dreitzer. Zinoviev was again called to confirm Smirnov's role, and did so at length.

*Reingold,* who followed, extended the conspiracy further, speaking of negotiations with Rykov, Bukharin, and Tomsky, and mentioning yet two more terrorist groups, headed by the "Rightists" Slepkov and Eismont. He went on to tell of a plan of Zinoviev and Kamenev to put Bakayev in charge of the NKVD on their coming to power so that he could kill all police officials who "might be in possession of the threads of the controversy," and also "all the direct perpetrators of the terroristic acts"—an interesting sign, as we have noted, of the way Stalin's mind was working.

*Bakayev,* who followed, confessed to having organized the Kirov murder and planned that of Stalin:

*Vyshinsky:* Did you take a number of practical measures to carry out these instructions, namely, to organize several attempts on the life of Comrade Stalin, which failed through no fault of yours?

*Bakayev:* That is so.[117]

But he introduced a note of reservation, of a type to be found in later cases, when he said that the other plots now attributed to the accused he had learned of for the first time when he read the indictment.[118] He also had some lesser reservations, saying, for example, that he did not go to Leningrad to meet Vladimir Levin (one of the Nikolayev "group") for terrorist reasons.[119] These minor denials could count for nothing against the major admissions. Nevertheless, they can still perhaps be treated as slight and pathetic signals that the evidence was not to be relied on.

*Pikel* came next. He had agreed, he said, to take part in an attempt on Stalin's life. He mentioned a tragedy of 1933, when Zinoviev's secretary, Bogdan, had committed suicide as a protest against the Party purge then going on. A new interpretation was now imposed on this, through Pikel's mouth. Bogdan had indeed "left a note making it appear that he was a victim of the Party cleansing," but in fact he had been ordered by Bakayev either to attempt Stalin's life or to commit suicide. Even this extravagant tale roused no incredulity from some of those present in the press box.

Pikel had been away in Spitzbergen; as a member of the Union of Soviet Writers, he had been on assignment to do some work on the Soviet mining concession there. This was represented as an attempt to keep clear in order to avoid discovery.[120] Thus when a man was away, this proved that he was a terrorist trying to escape discovery, and when he came back (as Pikel did), he was a terrorist resuming work—in this case further attempts on the lives of Kaganovich, Voroshilov, and others.

Next morning, 20 August, *Kamenev* gave his evidence. He spoke at first with a certain dignity, but as the cross-questioning went on, this began to collapse. He made an almost complete confession, repudiating only the idea that the plotters had intended to cover the traces of their crimes by physically exterminating NKVD men and others who might know about them. About Smirnov's denials, he said, "It is ridiculous wriggling, which only creates a comical impression." [121]

In Reingold's evidence, Sokolnikov had been named as a full member of the "Center." [122] However, Kamenev now put it slightly differently:

> *Kamenev:* . . . Among the leaders of the conspiracy another person may be named who in point of fact was one of the leaders, but who, in view of the special plans we made in regard to him, was not drawn into the practical work. I refer to Sokolnikov.
>
> *Vyshinsky:* Who was a member of the Centre, but whose part was kept a strict secret?
>
> *Kamenev:* Yes. Knowing that we might be discovered, we designated a small group to continue our terroristic activities. For this purpose we designated Sokolnikov. It seemed to us that on the side of the Trotskyites this role could be successfully performed by Serebryakov and Radek.

He also extended the conspiracy to include the former Workers' Opposition group of Shlyapnikov.

On the involvement of the Rightists he said:

> In 1932, 1933 and 1934 I personally maintained relations with Tomsky and Bukharin and sounded their political sentiments. They sympathized with us. When I asked Tomsky about Rykov's frame of mind, he replied: 'Rykov thinks the same as I do.' In reply to my question as to what Bukharin thought he said: 'Bukharin thinks the same as I do, but is pursuing somewhat different tactics: he does not agree with the line of the Party, but is pursuing tactics of persistently enrooting himself in the Party and winning the personal confidence of the leadership.' [123]

This was not a complete incrimination, in theory at least, but it could hardly be regarded as meaning anything other than an intention by Stalin to bring Bukharin and his associates into dock.

A "witness," Professor Yakovlev, was next produced, to corroborate the testimony. Kamenev, he said, had put him in charge of a terrorist group at the Academy of Sciences. [124]

*Zinoviev* was now called on for his evidence-in-chief. He appeared cowed. The formerly eloquent orator was hardly able to speak. He looked puffy and gray, and gasped asthmatically. His confession was complete, involving him not only in the Zinovievite terrorist groups, but also with M. Lurye, allegedly sent by Trotsky. He invoked Tomsky's name unambiguously, and also named Smilga, the veteran member of Lenin's Central Committee who had led the Baltic Fleet in the seizure of power. He asserted that he was in constant communication with Smirnov, [125] adding:

> . . . In this situation I had meetings with Smirnov who has accused me here of frequently telling untruths. Yes, I often told untruths. I started doing that from the moment I began fighting the Bolshevik Party. In so far as Smirnov took the road of fighting the Party, he too is telling untruths. But it seems, the difference between him and myself is that I have decided firmly and irrevocably to tell at this last moment the truth, whereas he, it seems, has adopted a different decision. [126]

Next came—as witness only—Smirnov's former wife, Safonova. She said that Smirnov had transmitted Trotsky's instructions on terrorism and strongly supported them. Smirnov firmly denied both assertions, but others of the accused backed her up. Vyshinsky then questioned Smirnov:

*Vyshinsky:* What were your relations with Safonova?

*Smirnov:* Good.

*Vyshinsky:* And more?

*Smirnov:* We were intimately related.

*Vyshinsky:* You were husband and wife?

*Smirnov:* Yes.

*Vyshinsky:* No personal grudges between you?

*Smirnov:* No.[127]

At the afternoon session, *Smirnov* was the first to be questioned. He continued with his partial confession. He had passed on Trotsky's and Sedov's ideas about terrorism; but he had not shared them, and he had done nothing else:

I admit that I belonged to the underground Trotskyite organization, joined the *bloc,* joined the centre of this *bloc,* met Sedov in Berlin in 1931, listened to his opinion on terrorism and passed this opinion on to Moscow. I admit that I received Trotsky's instructions on terrorism from Gaven and, although not in agreement with them, I communicated them to the Zinovievites through Ter-Vaganyan.[128]

*Vyshinsky:* (ironically) When did you leave the Centre?

*Smirnov:* I did not intend to resign; there was nothing to resign from.

*Vyshinsky:* Did the Centre exist?

*Smirnov:* What sort of Centre . . . ?

*Vyshinsky:* Mrachkovsky, did the Centre exist?

*Mrachkovsky:* Yes.

*Vyshinsky:* Zinoviev, did the Centre exist?

*Zinoviev:* Yes.

*Vyshinsky:* Evdokimov, did the Centre exist?

*Evdokimov:* Yes.

*Vyshinsky:* Bakayev, did the Centre exist?

*Bakayev:* Yes.

*Vyshinsky:* How, then, Smirnov, can you take the liberty to maintain that no centre existed?[129]

Smirnov again said that no meetings of such a Center had taken place, and again three of the other members of it were made to bear him down. After the evidence of the others that it was he who had been head of the Trotskyite side of the conspiracy, he turned to them sardonically and said, "You want a leader? Well, take me!"[130]

Even Vyshinsky commented that this was said "in rather a jocular way."[131]

Smirnov's partial confession was a rather difficult position to maintain, but on the whole he succeeded in confusing the issue. When the contradictions in his stance became awkward, he simply did not answer the questions.

*Olberg,* next, told of his long membership in the German Trotskyite organization, through which he had met Sedov and by means of a forged Honduran passport had got to Russia. He gave no explanation of how, with a tourist visa on a Central American passport, he had got a job at the Gorky Pedagogical Institute; but there he had organized the terrorist act to be committed in Moscow on May Day 1936. Olberg's plan to assassinate Stalin failed because he had been arrested. A peculiar item in Vyshinsky's closing speech (not given in the compressed English version) was a piece of material evidence involving Olberg. This was the visiting card of Wladimir Tukalevsky, Director of the Slavic Library of the Czechoslovak Ministry of Foreign Affairs. (Tukalevsky wrote in the Prague press that Olberg had indeed done work in the library at various dates from 1933 to the spring of 1935.) The visiting card, Vyshinsky said, had on it "the letters 'P' and 'F' and the date '1936,' which served as a code or password previously agreed on between Olberg and Tukalevsky." This was supposedly discovered in Stalinabad, where Olberg had earlier worked in the Pedagogical Institute. What it was supposed to prove is unclear, and its omission in the English version is understandable.[132] Olberg was one of those of whom it was noted even at the time that his evidence was given in an almost jaunty fashion: Fritz David and the two Luryes made the same mistake. Several observers at once concluded that they were agents provocateurs.

Following Olberg, *Berman-Yurin* gave evidence that Trotsky had personally sent him to shoot Stalin at a Comintern plenum. He gave a very detailed account of meetings with Trotsky and his entourage in Copenhagen in November 1932. This evidence had been constructed by the NKVD as follows. Jack Soble, the Soviet spy whose career only ended with his arrest in 1957 in New York, had infiltrated Trotsky's circle in 1931. He met him for the last time in Copenhagen in December 1932 when Trotsky had been admitted there on a short lecture tour. Soble then lost Trotsky's confidence. But his account of Trotsky's moves in Copenhagen, as transmitted to the NKVD, was edited to form the basis of Berman-Yurin's evidence.[133]

Berman-Yurin concluded by saying that he had been unable to get a ticket for the XIIIth plenum at the Comintern, and so could not shoot Stalin after all.

Ever since the publication of the indictment, the Soviet press had been violently demanding the death penalty. Resolutions from all over the country came in and were printed. Workers in the Kiev Red Flag Factory and the Stalingrad Dzerzhinsky Tractor Works, Kazakh kolkhozes and Leningrad Party organizations, calling for the shooting of the accused, day by day made an overwhelming build-up. Now, on the morning of 21 August, *Pravda* carried something new. There were still dozens of mass resolutions, and the usual hack verses by the poetaster Demyan Bedny, with the title "No Mercy." But, in addition, there were manifestos from Rakovsky, Rykov, and Pyatakov, which showed another aspect of Party discipline. They, too, all demanded the death penalty. Rakovsky's was headed "No Pity." Rykov insisted that no mercy be shown to Zinoviev. The tone of all may be judged from Pyatakov's contribution, which said:

One cannot find the words fully to express one's indignation and disgust. These people have lost the last semblance of humanity. They must be destroyed like carrion which is polluting the pure, bracing air of the land of the Soviets; dangerous carrion which may cause the death of our leaders, and has already caused the death of one of the best people in our land—that wonderful comrade and leader S. M. Kirov. . . . Many of us, including myself, by our heedlessness, our complacency and lack of vigilance toward those around us, unconsciously helped these bandits to commit their black deeds.

. . . It is a good thing that the People's Commissariat of Internal Affairs had exposed this gang.

. . . It is a good thing that it can be exterminated.

. . . Honor and glory to the workers of People's Commissariat of Internal Affairs.[134]

Under these mounting pressures, the accused continued with their evidence. For 21 August, the last day of testimony, only one leading figure—Ter-Vaganyan—remained. Otherwise, there were three more "assassins" and Trotsky's alleged emissary, Holtzman.

*Holtzman,* a genuine ex-Trotskyite of junior rank, was a personal friend of Smirnov's. His evidence turned out to be highly unsatisfactory to the prosecution, on two grounds.

First, no doubt under the influence of Smirnov's example, he had already reverted from the complete confession the indictment had attributed to him to a refusal to admit that he was implicated in terrorism. He now said flatly that though he had passed it on, he (like Smirnov) "did not share" Trotsky's point of view about the necessity of terror. Vyshinsky was only able to get him to admit that he had remained a member of the Trotskyite organization, and alleged that this amounted to the same thing.

The second point was different. Holtzman confessed that he had met Sedov in Copenhagen. In that city, he had arranged to "put up at the Hotel Bristol" and to meet him there. "I went to the hotel straight from the station and in the lounge met Sedov."

When Holtzman's testimony was published, Trotsky declared it false, and immediately published a demand that the court ask Holtzman on what sort of passport and in what name he had entered Denmark—a point which could be checked with the Danish immigration authorities. This was a matter that had not been prepared, and naturally the court paid no attention to it. But soon after the trial ended, the organ of the Danish Social Democratic Party pointed out that Copenhagen's Hotel Bristol had been demolished in 1917.[135] Soviet propaganda had some difficulty with this point and belatedly settled for a story that Holtzman had met Sedov at a Café Bristol, which was near a hotel of a different name at which he was staying, a version inconsistent with the original testimony. There was, in addition, convincing evidence that Sedov had been taking examinations at the Technische Hochschule in Berlin at the time when (in 1932) he was supposed to have been in Copenhagen.[136]

The "Hotel Bristol" error is said to have arisen as follows. Yezhov decided that the alleged meeting should take place in a hotel, and asked Molchanov to provide a name. Molchanov referred to the Travel Section of the Foreign Department of the NKVD. To cover the inquiry, he asked the names of several hotels in Oslo as well as Copenhagen, ostensibly needed for a group of prominent Soviet visitors. Molchanov's secretary jotted down the lists telephoned to him, and in typing them out accidentally put the Oslo hotels under the heading "Copenhagen."[137]

The prosecution case made much of better-established contacts between Smirnov, Holtzman, the absent Gaven, Sedov, and others in the early 1930s, and the establishment of a "bloc" between them and the Trotskyists. These contacts had indeed taken place, and in the old sense of the coming together of factions in the prewar party (like the "August bloc") the Trotskyists certainly thought that an opposition bloc had been established. When the accused were so charged, however, the Trotskyites in exile denied the whole story, apparently on the supposition that this would help the accused and discredit the trial.

And, given the incredibility of much of the other evidence, their calculation was reasonably correct. The result has been that the Trotskyite view has been widely accepted. We need merely note that these agreements, such as they were, between exiles and those still in the Soviet Union were political, with a view to a possible revival of the opposition. Conspiratorial from the NKVD point of view, they had no "terrorist" content whatever.[138]

The two Luryes followed Holtzman. Their relationship is uncertain; they were not brothers. They had worked together. *Nathan Lurye,* the surgeon, confessed to having been sent by the Trotskyites abroad to make an attempt on Voroshilov's life. He had worked on assassinating Voroshilov from September 1932 to the spring of 1933, with two accomplices, and "frequently went to Frunze Street and to the adjacent street armed with revolvers."[139]

> *President:* So that you would have committed the terroristic act had a favorable moment offered itself? Why did you not succeed in doing so?
>
> *N. Lurye:* We saw Voroshilov's car going down Frunze Street. It was travelling too fast. It was hopeless firing at the fast-running car. We decided that it was useless.[140]

N. Lurye was then sent to Chelyabinsk, where he tried to meet Kaganovich and Ordzhonikidze when they visited the city. The plan, a simple one, was as follows. In Ordzhonikidze's case, Moissei Lurye instructed Nathan Lurye "to take the opportunity of a possible visit to the Chelyabinsk Tractor Works by Comrade Ordzhonikidze to commit a terrorist act against him." N. Lurye "tried to meet" both leaders, but "he failed to carry out his intention."

This unpromising assassin was then transferred to Leningrad, where he was put in touch with "Zeidel's terrorist group" (one of the miscellaneous assassin groups named throughout the trial; Zeidel was a historian). Here N. Lurye's instructions were to assassinate Zhdanov. He planned to do this at the 1 May demonstration. Ulrikh established in detail the type of revolver (a medium-sized Browning), but as Lurye made no use of it, this point lost some of its significance:

*President:* Why did you fail to carry out the attempt on the life of Zhdanov?

*N. Lurye:* We marched by too far away.[141]

He had now been involved in "assassination attempts" on four leading figures, and no overt action of any sort had been taken—comparing most unfavorably with the efficiency of the killers of Kirov.

*Moissei Lurye*'s evidence was of the same type. He also had instructions from Trotsky, through the German Communist oppositionist leaders Ruth Fischer and Maslow, and had met Zinoviev too. He had prepared his namesake for his various attempts.

*Ter-Vaganyan* appeared next. He implicated a new group, the Georgian deviationists, who had been terrorists, "as is well known," since 1928. This implied Mdivani and his followers, but the only person Ter-Vaganyan named was Okudzhava. He had also conducted the negotiations with his close friend Lominadze and with the Trotskyite historians Zeidel and Friedland.

Ter-Vaganyan also implicated Smirnov, who again put his denials in the record, though eventually conceding that one disputed meeting "may have taken place."

The last accused, *Fritz David,* gave evidence of having been sent by Trotsky and Sedov and having attempted to carry out "two concrete plans to assassinate Stalin," both of which failed, one because Stalin did not attend the meeting of the Comintern Executive Committee chosen as the occasion for action, and the other because, at the Comintern Congress, David had been unable to get near enough. Sedov had (not surprisingly) been furious when he earned of these hitches. Not a single one of all the terrorists sent into the Soviet Union at such trouble and expense had even slightly inconvenienced, let alone killed, any of the Stalin leadership. In spite of this, Vyshinsky remarked that "the Trotskyites operated with greater determination and energy than the Zinovievites"![142]

Dreitzer was recalled at the end of the evening session on 21 August to implicate Corps Commander Vitovt Putna (see Chapter 7), who had "ostensibly left the Trotskyites" but had actually carried instructions from Trotsky to Dreitzer for transmission to Smirnov. Smirnov here again intervened to deny that Putna was a Trotskyite, but Pikel, Reingold, and Bakayev confirmed it.

This concluded the evidence, but the published record of the case consists only of excerpts from the full record. Other allegations, doubtless also made at the trial itself, are contained in the Secret Letter of the Central Committee of 29 July 1936, mentioned above. There we read, in addition to the plotters in Gorky, of a group in the Ukraine confessing in December 1935 of plotting to kill Kossior and Postyshev (though without implicating the August 1936 accused), and also of planning robberies to obtain funds to support this venture; of various other conspirators not named in the trial report, one (under the leadership of I. S. Esterman) seeking the assassination of Kaganovich, others that of Voroshilov; and of the "nests" of Trotskyites in "a number of scientific-research institutes," the Academy of Sciences, and other organizations in Moscow, Leningrad, Kiev, and Minsk.

At the end of the 21 August session, Vyshinsky issued the following statement:

At preceding sessions some of the accused (Kamenev, Zinoviev and Reingold) in their testimony referred to Tomsky, Bukharin, Rykov, Uglanov, Radek, Pyatakov,* Serebryakov and Sokolnikov as being to a greater or lesser degree involved in the criminal counter-revolutionary activities for which the accused in the present case are being tried. I consider it necessary to inform the court that yesterday I gave orders to institute an investigation of these statements of the accused in regard to Tomsky, Rykov, Bukharin, Uglanov, Radek and Pyatakov, and that in accordance with the results of this investigation the office of the State Attorney will institute legal proceedings in this matter. In regard to Serebryakov and Sokolnikov, the investigating authorities are already in possession of material convicting these persons of counter-revolutionary crimes, and, in view of this, criminal proceedings are being instituted against Sokolnikov and Serebryakov.[143]

On 22 August, this announcement was printed, together with a prompt demand by a workers' meeting at the Dynamo Factory that these charges be "pitilessly investigated."

Immediately after reading Vyshinsky's announcement, Tomsky committed suicide in his dacha at Bolshevo. (He left a letter to Stalin denying the charges.)[144] The Central Committee, of which he was a candidate member, next day denounced his suicide, attributing it (truly enough) to his having been incriminated.

The morning of 22 August was devoted to Vyshinsky's speech for the prosecution. First he laid the theoretical basis of the trials, of the whole Purge: "Three years ago Comrade Stalin not only foretold the inevitable resistance of elements hostile to the cause of socialism, but also foretold the possibility of the revival of Trotskyite counter-revolutionary groups. This trial has fully and distinctly proved the great wisdom of this forecast."[145]

After an attack on Trotsky, he took the court at length through the history of Zinoviev's and Kamenev's various recantations and promises. He then gave great prominence to the Kirov murder:

These mad dogs of capitalism tried to tear limb from limb the best of the best of our Soviet land. They killed one of the men of the revolution who was most dear to us, that admirable and wonderful man, bright and joyous as the smile on his lips was always bright and joyous, as our new life is bright and joyous. They killed our Kirov; they wounded us close to our very heart. They thought they could sow confusion and consternation in our ranks.[146]

Vyshinsky took some time to deal with Smirnov's "wrigglings" (and, in passing, condemned Holtzman for having "adopted the same position as Smirnov"); Smirnov had "stubbornly denied that he took any part in the terroristic activities of the Trotskyite-Zinovievite centre."[147] His guilt was, however, established by the other confessions. One awkward point was dealt with thus:

I know that in his defence Smirnov will argue that he had left the centre. Smirnov will say: 'I did not do anything, I was in prison.' A naive assertion! Smirnov was in prison from 1 January 1933, but we know that while in prison Smirnov organized contacts with his Trotskyites, for a code was discovered by means of which Smirnov,

---

*For some reason, no evidence implicating Pyatakov is given in the printed version of the court proceedings. In fact, Reingold had incriminated him.

while in prison, communicated with his companions outside. This proves that communication existed and Smirnov cannot deny this.[148]

In fact, no evidence of any sort on this point had been, or ever was to be, produced.

Vyshinsky, in passing, dealt with an unfortunate idea which had evidently gained popularity:

> The comparison with the period of the Narodnaya Volya [People's Will] terrorism is shameless. Filled with respect for the memory of those who in the times of the Narodnaya Volya sincerely and honestly, although employing, it is true, their own special, but always irreproachable, methods, fought against the tsarist autocracy for liberty—I emphatically reject this sacrilegious parallel.[149]

He concluded with the appeal, "I demand that these dogs gone mad should be shot—every one of them!"

The evening session of 22 August and the two sessions of 23 August saw the last pleas of the accused.

They spoke in the same order as they had given their evidence. Mrachkovsky started by telling of his background, a worker, son and grandson of workers, a revolutionary, son and grandson of revolutionaries, who had suffered his first arrest when thirteen years old.

"And here," he went on in a bitter and ironic tone, "I stand before you as a counter-revolutionary!" The judges and Prosecutor looked apprehensive, but all was well. For a moment Mrachkovsky was overcome. He struck his hand on the bar of the dock and regained his self-control,[150] going on to explain that he had only mentioned his past so that everyone should "remember that not only a general, not only a prince or nobleman can become a counter-revolutionary; workers or those who spring from the working class, like myself, can also become counter-revolutionaries."[151] He ended by saying that he was a traitor who should be shot.

Most of the other pleas were simple self-condemnations; the accused described themselves as "dregs" undeserving of mercy. But an occasional wrong note was struck, as when Evdokimov said—surely not without meaning—"Who will believe a single word of ours?"[152]

When Kamenev had finished his plea, and had already sat down, he rose again and said that he would like to say something to his two children, whom he had no other means of addressing. One was an Air Force pilot; the other, a boy. Kamenev said that he wanted to tell them, "No matter what my sentence will be, I in advance consider it just. Don't look back. Go forward. Together with Soviet people, follow Stalin." He then sat down again and rested his face in his hands. Others present were shaken, and even the judges are said to have lost their stony expressions for an instant.[153]

Zinoviev made a satisfactory definition of the whole inadmissibility of opposition to Stalin: "My defective Bolshevism became transformed into anti-Bolshevism, and through Trotskyism I arrived at Fascism. Trotskyism is a variety of Fascism, and Zinovievism is a variety of Trotskyism. . . ."[154] But he ended that worse than any punishment was the idea that "my name will be associated with the names of those who stood beside me. On my right hand Olberg, on my left—

Nathan Lurye. . . . ''[155] And this remark is, in an important sense, incompatible with the idea of the trial: for on the face of the evidence, how was Zinoviev better than the two he named?

Smirnov again denied any direct implication in any terrorist activity. However, he denounced Trotsky, though in comparatively mild terms, as an enemy "on the other side of the barricade."

When Fritz David had finished, the court withdrew to consider the verdict. Yagoda had it ready for them in the Council Chamber. But a decent interval was allowed to pass, and at 2:30 the following morning the court reassembled and found all concerned guilty on all counts. They were all sentenced to death.

As Ulrikh finished reading the verdict, one of the Luryes shrieked hysterically, "Long live the cause of Marx, Engels, Lenin and Stalin!" Then the prisoners were taken out, to the police wagons that were to return them to the Lubyanka.

## TO THE EXECUTION CELLARS

As soon as the trial was over, the defect in the bargain Zinoviev and Kamenev had struck with Stalin became apparent. Having carried out their side of it, they no longer possessed any sanction to make him do the same with his.

Under the new law, seventy-two hours' grace was allowed for the accused to put in their petitions for pardon. Some of these may have been put in and rejected, though Smirnov, at least, seems not to have made an appeal. In any case, the announcement of their execution was made only twenty-four hours after the verdict.

Various accounts of the actual execution have filtered out. They are of course based on unconfirmable NKVD reports.

Zinoviev was unwell and feverish. He was told he was to be transferred to another cell. But when he saw the guards, he at once understood. All accounts agree that he collapsed, yelling in a high-pitched voice a desperate appeal to Stalin to keep his word. He gave the impression of hysteria, but this is probably not fair, as his voice was always very piercing when he was excited, and he was perhaps trying to make a last speech. He was, in addition, still suffering from heart and liver trouble, so that some sort of collapse is understandable. It is said that the NKVD lieutenant in charge, fearing the effect of this scene if prolonged along the corridor and down into the cellar, hustled him into a nearby cell and shot him there and then, later receiving an award for his presence of mind.[156]

When Kamenev was called from his cell to execution, he made no complaint and appeared stunned. He was not killed by the first shot, and the NKVD lieutenant in charge became hysterical and kicked the executioner with a cry of "finish him off." Smirnov was calm and courageous. He is reported as saying, "We deserve this for our unworthy attitude at the trial."[157]

Recent Soviet publications tell us of the fate of some others incriminated in the trial. Gaven, the main link to Trotsky, apparently gave evidence against Smirnov,[158] and so may be presumed to have confessed. His nonappearance at the trial may have been due to illness. He was carried out to be shot on a stretcher on 4 October.[159] The leading Zinovievite, G. F. Fedorov, brought from the Chelyabinsk isolator on 4 September, was shot on 5 October, the day after Gaven. And this may indicate a broader secret trial—though others implicated survived a little longer.[160]

We can trace the fate of a few of the relatives of the accused, apart from Smirnov's, with whom we have already dealt. Evdokimov's son was shot.[161] Kamenev's wife had been arrested on 19 March 1935 and sentenced to exile by the Special Board. She was retried in January 1938 and shot in the autumn of 1941. As for the sons Kamenev had tried to save, the elder, Alexander, was arrested in August 1936, sentenced in May 1937, and shot in July 1939; the younger was sent to an NKVD children's home, and his name was changed to Glebov.[162] Zinoviev's sister, F. A. Radomislskaya, a doctor, is reported in the Vorkuta camps and was shot there later. Three other sisters were sent to labor camp, together with two nephews, a niece, a brother-in-law, and a cousin. Three brothers and another nephew were shot. Zinoviev's son Stefan, for whom he had made a special appeal to Stalin, was also shot in 1937, as were Bakayev's wife and Ter-Vaganyan's brother.[163] Dreitzer's wife, Sonia, was also sent to Vorkuta, and is also reported shot there.[164] Olberg's wife, Betty, was sent to labor camp. In prison, very ill and thin, she had made an attempt to commit suicide by throwing herself over some banisters. She was sent back to Germany with the Communists handed over to the Gestapo by Stalin in 1940.[165]

The executions took place when many Party leaders were on holiday. Stalin himself had left for the Caucasus, and only a quorum of the formal State body, the Central Executive Committee, was available to hear appeals, which their general instructions were to reject unless ordered to the contrary by the Politburo. Yezhov had remained in Moscow to see that nothing could interfere with the processes Stalin had set in motion.[166] Nothing did.

## THE CREDIBILITY OF THE TRIAL

The trial had on the whole been a success for Stalin. The Communists and the Soviet people could make no overt objection to his version. And the outside world, whose representatives he had allowed in to authenticate it, as it were, was at least inclined not to reject it outright, from the start, as a fabrication. There was very considerable uneasiness about the confessions. But even if they had been obtained by unwarrantable methods, that did not in itself prove that they were untrue. In fact, the one phenomenon which was difficult to reconcile with the complete innocence of the accused was precisely their confessions. Thus to a considerable degree, the confession method justified itself politically.

The case itself must come as something of an anticlimax to us today, who know the falsehood of the charges and something of the ways in which the whole thing was prepared. At the time, to the world, and to the Party itself, it appeared differently—as a terrible public event. The allegations were examined in detail. They were found convincing by various British lawyers, Western journalists, and so forth, and were thought incredible by others. As so often, this appears to be a case in which alleged facts were accepted or rejected in accordance with preconceived opinion. Most people felt either that it was incredible that old revolutionaries should commit such actions, or that it was incredible that a Socialist State should make false accusations. But neither position is really tenable. It was by no means absolutely inconceivable that the opposition might have planned the assassination of the political leadership. There are various reasons for thinking it was out of character and contrary to their previous views, but that is a much weaker argument.

Some Western commentators, applying "commonsensical" criteria to the situation, argued that the oppositionists should logically have seen that the removal of Stalin was the only way of securing their own lives and a tolerable future, from their point of view, for the Party and the State. So it was, yet history gives many examples of inadequate common sense.

But in any case, it seems perfectly clear that the opposition, up to the actual execution of the Zinoviev–Kamenev group, never expected that Stalin would really kill off the old leadership. The whole of their maneuvers up to that point had been designed to keep themselves alive and, if possible, in the Party, until such time as Stalin's failures and excesses would swing Party feeling back in their favor and give them another chance. After the first executions, no oppositionists of any standing were in a position to attempt assassination whether they thought it suitable or not. The only people with any chance of getting rid of the General Secretary were those close to him.

It seems certain that Stalin himself was really afraid of assassination. He must have known that the leading oppositionists could scarcely organize such plots, so closely did he have them watched. But at a lower level in the Party, there were thousands and thousands of potential enemies. Individual assassination was indeed contrary to established Marxist principles. In fact, Zinoviev had been supposed to be banking on this idea. Reingold remarked: "Zinoviev told me . . . 'When under examination the main thing is persistently to deny any connection with the organization. If accused of terroristic activities, you must emphatically deny it and argue that terror is incompatible with the views of Bolsheviks-Marxists.' " Nikolayev, the assassin of Kirov, had been a dupe; but, himself a Communist, he had shot down a Party leader with a quite clear idea of what he was doing. That others should refrain on Marxist principle from individual terror was not a certain hope. Desperation had already, for example, driven the Bulgarian Communist Party to the bomb outrage in Sofia Cathedral in 1925.*

Again, the selective assassination of NKVD defectors and of other political enemies in the West was soon to become routine. And Stalin himself—an Old Communist too!—had organized the killing of Kirov. In the circumstances, we may agree with the idea that after all assassinations by Zinoviev and Kamenev *were* possible, that Reingold *could* have been telling the truth when he deposed: "In 1932, Zinoviev, at Kamenev's apartment, in the presence of a number of members of the united Trotskyite-Zinovievite Centre argued in favor of resorting

---

*At the time, it is true, the Communists denied responsibility and claimed that they had been framed by their enemies. Georgi Dimitrov, at the Reichstag Trial, said, "This incident was not organized by the Bulgarian Communist Party . . . that act of provocation, the blowing up of Sofia Cathedral, was actually organized by the Bulgarian police" (*Selected Articles* [London, 1951], pp. 22–23). However, in a speech in 1948, he admitted and criticized "the desperate actions of the leaders of the Party's military organization culminating in the attempt at Sofia Cathedral" (p. 203).

to terror as follows: although terror is incompatible with Marxism, at the present moment these considerations must be abandoned. . . .''[167]

Moreover, some of the ideas placed in the mouths of Zinoviev and Kamenev were plausible. It was quite reasonable to suppose that if Stalin had been assassinated, as a result of the leadership struggle that would ensue, ''negotiations would be opened with us.'' As Kamenev said, ''Even with Stalin we, by our policy of double-dealing, had obtained, after all, forgiveness of our mistakes by the Party and had been taken back into its ranks.''[168] And it was also plausible that they had anticipated the rehabilitation of Trotsky as a later result.

But to support either view of the case, there was very little genuine reference to the facts. Yet at this level, the only one worth a sensible examination, the outward semblance of an established plot could easily be shown to rest on absurdities and contradictions. For its composition, as in later cases, bears many marks of crudity. It seems that these are not attributable to Molchanov and Yagoda, but to Stalin himself, who personally insisted, for example, on the inclusion of Smirnov.

In spite of the inconsistencies and incredibilities, *Pravda,* on 4 September 1937, was able to give prominence to a statement by ''the English jurist Pritt'' from the London *News Chronicle* on the complete propriety and authenticity of the trial. And this was one case among many.

But Zinoviev and Kamenev had been in exile or prison for most of the period of the active plot. Mrachkovsky had been in exile in Kazakhstan. Smirnov had been in a prison cell since 1 January 1933. Vyshinsky had spoken of ways in which ''even those not at liberty'' had been able to take part in the plot. But no evidence had been produced of their methods of liaison. It might have been thought that even observers like Pritt would have found it odd that a conspiracy directed from outside the country should, when one of its members was actually in prison in a distant area, have continued to pass instructions through him, rather than use alternative channels—of which, the evidence implied, they had a profusion.

A further striking point is the proportion between the number of assassinations planned and those carried out. Two separate plans to kill Stalin at the meeting of the Communist International had been made, another to shoot Voroshilov, a third to assassinate Kaganovich and Ordzhonikidze, and many others simply decided on in principle.

No reference was made during the trial to some of the previous trials in connection with the Kirov assassination. The action of NKVD officers in Leningrad was not referred to. The allegation about the Latvian Consul was not mentioned.

No documentary evidence (except Olberg's Honduran passport and Tukalevski's visiting card) was produced. The failure of the prosecution to produce documents should have struck observers as particularly odd. For in the arrest of underground Bolsheviks, the Tsarist police repeatedly discovered documents—without which, indeed, it is difficult to see how an underground could operate. When the February 1917 Revolution opened up the police archives, hundreds of secret Party documents were found in them, including letters written by Lenin himself. And the underground Bolsheviks of that time were at least as skilled in conspiracy as the men Stalin now arrested; indeed (as Orlov points out), "They were the *same men.*"

Again, prominent conspirators and witness were simply missing. Sokolnikov was clearly a relevant and important witness. But he was not called. Nor were Bukharin, or Tomsky, or Rykov—or any of the newly implicated. Among the Zinovievites who were not called but who had appeared at previous trials were Gertik, one of the main links with the "Leningrad Center," which had allegedly assassinated Kirov,[169] and Karev, who was supposed to have been personally instructed by Zinoviev and by Bakayev to prepare the Kirov murder with others of the Leningrad assassination group,[170] with which Faivilovich was also a contact man.[171] (Kuklin, actually named as a full member of the "Center," seems to have died in the interim.)[172]

But meanwhile, questions of evidence, of logic, were not decisive. The prestige of the "Socialist State" was high. There was little choice between accepting the trial at its face value and branding Stalin as a vulgar murderer, and his regime as a tyranny founded on falsehood. The truth could be deduced, but it could not be proved. Few cared to hear it, given the more evident menace of Fascism.

In the Soviet Union itself, things were different. Few, perhaps, credited the confessions. But fewer still could even hint their doubts.

A week after the execution of Zinoviev and his fellow defendants, Stalin ordered Yagoda to select and shoot 5,000 of the oppositionists then in camps.[173] At this time, the last privileges were withdrawn from political prisoners in camps. In March 1937, some rights were temporarily restored. But a few months later, another mass execution was ordered. The brick factory at Vorkuta became notorious as the center of the operation.[174] The victims included Trotsky's son Sergei Sedov. In March 1938, the Armenian Sokrates Gevorkian and twenty other former Leftists were executed near their camp. From then until the end of 1938, groups of forty or so were executed there once or twice a week. Children under twelve alone were spared.[175]

There are reports of a last hunger strike by the oppositionists before they were separated, resulting in many deaths and, eventually, the disappearance of all concerned.[176] Roy Medvedev tells us that of several thousand Old Bolsheviks who returned to Moscow after rehabilitation in 1956 and 1957, he was "only able to find two former Trotskyists and one former Zinovievist."[177]

# THE PROBLEM
# OF CONFESSION

*He lies like an eyewitness.*
Russian Saying

When, at 1:45 P.M. on 19 August 1936, Mrachkovsky started to confess in public to a series of appalling crimes, it marked the beginning of a series of events which shook and astonished the entire world. Mrachkovsky was a former worker and an Old Bolshevik, a member of the Party since 1905. He had actually been born in prison, where, in 1888, his mother was serving a sentence for revolutionary activity. His father, a worker like himself, was a revolutionary too, and became a Bolshevik when that party was organized. Even his grandfather, also a worker, had belonged to one of the first Marxist groupings, the Southern Russian Workers' Union.

Mrachkovsky himself had come to prominence by leading a rising in the Urals. He had fought in Siberia in the Civil War, and had been wounded several times. He had later been one of the boldest of Trotsky's followers, and had been the first to be arrested when, in 1927, he organized the Trotskyites' short-lived underground printing press.

He was, in fact, a real epitome of revolutionary boldness, born and bred to resistance. He now stood up and complaisantly confessed to active membership in a plot to murder the Soviet leadership. Over the next few days, half a dozen other Old Bolsheviks followed suit, including leaders known the world over. Lastly, they made final pleas, condemning themselves for "contemptible treachery" (Kamenev), speaking of themselves as "the dregs of the land" (Pikel), "not only murderers but fascist murderers" (Holtzman). Several expressly said that their crimes were too foul to let them ask for clemency; Mrachkovsky described himself as "a traitor who should be shot."

Twice in the next two years the same scene was to be repeated, always to the bafflement of commentators, friendly or hostile. The impression of unanimous surrender was not, indeed, entirely a correct one. Two of the 1936 accused (Smirnov and Holtzman) hedged considerably in their admissions, but this was hardly noticed among the self-abasement of so many others, including the two major figures, Zinoviev and Kamenev.

And similarly, the minor hitches and qualifications of later trials passed barely noticed. Krestinsky withdrew his confession on the first day of the 1938 Trial, and only reaffirmed it after a night in the hands of the investigators. Bukharin refused to confess to some of the major charges, such as that of having planned to kill Lenin. Radek, admitting that he was a treacherous liar, took occasion to point out that the case rested entirely on his evidence.

But such points were on the whole lost in the picture as it appeared in gross: everyone had confessed; the Old Bolsheviks had publicly avowed disgraceful plans and actions. The whole business almost passed belief. Were the confessions true? How had they been obtained? What did it all signify? We are told that the confessions were as little believed in Russia as abroad, "or even less," but that the average Soviet citizen who had not been in jail found them as puzzling as foreigners did.[1]

It was curiously argued, not only by Vyshinsky, but also in the West, that the accused confessed owing to the weight of evidence against them, that they had "no choice." Apart from the fact that there was no evidence against them *except* their confessions and those of others, this does not accord with common experience. People, especially on capital charges, plead not guilty even if there is a great deal of evidence against them. In the past, Communists had frequently denied facts. But in any case, it was not only confession which was so strange, but also repentance—the acceptance of the prosecution's view that the acts confessed to were appalling crimes. If Zinoviev and Kamenev had really concluded that the way out of Russia's difficulties was the assassination of Stalin, this would be to say that experienced politicians had made a definite political decision suited, as they thought, to the circumstances. It would not be a decision they felt guilty about. Their natural line of reasoning—as with the terrorists of the People's Will— would have been, if the facts were admitted, to defend their plans and actions. The complete acceptance of the opinion of their accusers was the real and crowning implausibility of the whole affair.

## THE PARTY MIND

The problem of these confessions is really a double one. We have to consider the technical means, the physical and psychological pressures by which false public confessions could be secured. And this is a question that applies to non-Party as well as to Party victims.

But in the surrender and self-abasement of at least some of the revolutionaries, a further element enters. Their surrender was not a single and exceptional act in their careers, but the culmination of a whole series of submissions to the Party made in terms they knew to be "objectively" false. And this attitude is a key to Stalin's victory going far beyond the trials themselves, largely accounting as it does for the extraordinary and disastrous failure of the successive Party elements who objected to his rule to take any effective action to block him.

In Soviet circumstances, where all factions had long been united in imposing the principle of the one-party State and the practice of crushing all alternative and independent political enterprise by police methods, the responsibility for saving the country and the people from Stalin rested squarely on his leading opponents within the Party.

They had abdicated that responsibility. The Party mystique led them to submission to the Party leadership, however packed the Congresses and Committees which produced it. They could see no political possibilities outside the Party. Even when they had been expelled, they thought of nothing but a return at any price.

The leading oppositionists—with the exception of Trotsky himself—had made a basic tactical error. Their constant avowals of political sin, their admissions that Stalin was, after all, right, were based on the idea that it was correct to "crawl in the dust," suffer any humiliation, to remain in or return to the Party. In this way, they thought, when Stalin's policies came to grief, they themselves would be there, available as the alternative leadership which the Party must then seek.

In the first place, the policy was too abjectly cunning. The constant avowals and humiliations ate into the morale of rank-and-file oppositionists, and wore away their reputations, perhaps irretrievably. But the basic miscalculation was on an even more crucial point. The members of an alternative government have at least got to be alive. It is certainly true that some of the oppositionists—Kamenev, for instance—did not underestimate Stalin's desire to crush them at all costs. But they did not believe that it would be politically possible for him to face the Party with the execution of its veteran leaders. They underestimated not his ruthlessness, but his determination, cunning, and unscrupulousness. When he had finished, there was no such thing as a living ex-member of the Politburo, with the single exception of Grigori Petrovsky, working on sufferance as a museum administrator.

Their view of history made it hard for them to conceive that the proletarian Party could simply be converted by intrigue or any other method into an apparatus of personal dictatorship. And if they did not understand the unappeasable drive to power in Stalin's mentality or the fact that with the simplicity of genius he was prepared to undertake actions contrary to the "laws of history" and to do what had never been done before, they also did not understand his methods. That a modern, a Marxist, State could be subverted by intrigue and maneuvers in the political organs, this they had at least begun to grasp. It did not occur to them that their opponent could use the methods of a common criminal, could procure assassination, and could frame others for his own crime. A rank-and-file oppositionist commented (of Rykov), "To spend twenty years with Stalin in an illegal Party, to be with him during the decisive days of the Revolution, to sit at the same table in the Politburo for ten years after the Revolution and still fail to know Stalin is really the end."[2]

There were two great preconditions for the Purge. First, the personal drives and abilities of its prime mover, Stalin; and second, the context, the political context, in which he operated. We have traced the changes which had come over the Party after the Civil War and the trauma of Kronstadt. Since then, the final silencing of debate and the extravagantly bitter test of the "Second Civil War," against the peasantry, had put it on the anvil. Under these new strokes, an ever greater premium was put on ruthlessness and will, but at the same time the idea of the Party itself as an object of devotion and of its membership as an elite brotherhood had strengthened yet further.

For his opponents as well as his supporters, Stalin's leadership was thus the authentic—or at least the only—representative of the "Party." While Lenin had always been prepared to split a party if he had felt the majority to be wrong, the oppositionists were now hamstrung by an abstract loyalty. Just as most of the German generals were later to be reduced to impotence by their oath of loyalty to a man who would not himself have thought twice about breaking his word, so the Rightists were brought to ruin by a similar intellectual and moral muddle.

In 1935, Bukharin, who had just been denouncing Stalin's "insane ambition," was asked why, in that case, the oppositionists had surrendered to him, and he replied, "with considerable emotion": "You don't understand, it is not like that at all. It is not him we trust but the man in whom the Party has reposed its confidence. It just so happened that he has become a sort of symbol of the Party. . . ."[3]

Bukharin's faith in the Party, as the incarnation of history, was seen again in 1936, a year before his own arrest, when he remarked to the Menshevik Nicolaevsky:

> It is difficult for us to live. And you, for example could not accustom yourself to it. Even for some of us, with our experience during these decades, it is often impossible. But one is saved by a faith that development is always going forward. It is like a stream that is running to the shore. If one leans out of the stream, one is ejected completely. (Here Bukharin made a scissor-like gesture with his two fingers.) The stream goes through the most difficult places. But it still goes forward in the direction in which it must. And the people grow, become stronger in it, and they build a new society.[4]

This view is admittedly an act of faith, of pure theoretical anticipation. Stalin held in effect that his personal rule was essential on precisely the same grounds. The moral distinction between the two attitudes is not a very clear one. The whole general ethic had been expressed most plainly by Trotsky in 1924:

> None of us desires or is able to dispute the will of the Party. Clearly, the Party is always right. . . . We can only be right with and by the Party, for history has provided no other way of being in the right. The English have a saying, 'My country, right or wrong'; whether it is in the right or in the wrong, it is my country. We have much better historical justification in saying, whether it is right or wrong in certain individual cases, it is my party. . . . And if the Party adopts a decision which one or other of us thinks unjust, he will say, just or unjust, it is my party, and I shall support the consequences of the decision to the end.[5]

And this, as we shall see, is absolutely cardinal in explaining not so much Stalin's rise to power, as the almost total failure to oppose him *after* his aims and methods had declared themselves.

A very revealing account of the attitude of an old oppositionist to the already Stalinized Party—more revealing than official statements, since it was made in the heat of the moment in private—had been given in a series of remarks made by Pyatakov in 1928 to a former Menshevik friend, N. V. Volsky. Pyatakov had just "capitulated"[6] and, meeting the Menshevik in Paris, provoked him by a suggestion that he lacked courage. Volsky replied warmly that Pyatakov's capitulation a couple of months after his expulsion from the Party in 1927, and repudiation of the views that he had held right up until then, showed a real lack of moral courage.

Pyatakov, in an excited and emotional manner, replied with a long harangue. Lenin, he said, had become a tired and sick man towards the end of his life:

> The real Lenin was the man who had had the courage to make a proletarian revolution first, and then to set about creating the objective conditions theoretically necessary as a preliminary to such a revolution. What was the October Revolution, what indeed is the Communist Party, but a miracle? No Menshevik could ever understand what it meant to be a member of such a Party.[7]

Pyatakov's "miracle" was a reasonable description from the Marxist point of view of what the Party, as he thought, was attempting to do. For it was contrary to the natural "Laws of Society" as propounded by Marx: instead of socialism arising as the result of the conquest of political power by a Party representing a large proletarian majority in a country already thoroughly industrialized, the Communist Party in the Soviet Union was (in theory) attempting to create by mere will power and organization the industry and the proletariat which should in principle have preceded it. Instead of economics determining politics, politics was determining economics.

> 'According to Lenin', Pyatakov added, 'the Communist Party is based on the principle of coercion which doesn't recognize any limitations or inhibitions. And the central idea of this principle of boundless coercion is not coercion by itself but the absence of any limitation whatsoever—moral, political and even physical, as far as that goes. Such a Party is capable of achieving miracles and doing things which no other collective of men could achieve. . . . A real Communist . . . that is, a man who was raised in the Party and had absorbed its spirit deeply enough becomes himself in a way a miracle man'.[8]

From this attitude, significant conclusions followed:

> 'For such a Party a true Bolshevik will readily cast out from his mind ideas in which he has believed for years. A true Bolshevik has submerged his personality in the collectivity, "the Party", to such an extent that he can make the necessary effort to break away from his own opinions and convictions, and can honestly agree with the Party—that is the test of a true Bolshevik'.
> There could be no life for him (Pyatakov continued) outside the ranks of the Party, and he would be ready to believe that black was white, and white was black, if the Party required it. In order to become one with this great Party he would fuse himself with it, abandon his own personality, so that there was no particle left inside him which was not at one with the Party, did not belong to it.[9]

This idea of all morality and all truth being comprehended in the Party is extraordinarily illuminating when we come to consider the humiliations Pyatakov and others were to accept in the Party's name. For this evaporation of objective standards, though it did not affect all members of the old Party, was widespread. Many had by the end of the 1920s become quite disillusioned with the idea that the workers, let alone the peasants, could play any part in a country like Russia. By 1930, a foreign Communist noted among his students in Leningrad that they thought it entirely natural for the masses to be mere instruments under both Fascism and Communism—the moral distinction being simply one of the respective leaders' intentions.[10] One Trotskyite remarked that there was much to be said for

Stalin: "No doubt Trotsky would have done it with more go and with less brutality, and we, who are more cultured than Stalin's men, would have been at the top. But one should be able to rise above these ambitions. . . ."[11]

Even those who did not go to Pyatakov's self-immolating lengths no longer felt capable of the intellectual and moral effort of making a break and starting afresh:

> They were all tired men. The higher you got in the hierarchy, the more tired they were. I have nowhere seen such exhausted men as among the higher strata of Soviet politicians, among the Old Bolshevik guard. It was not only the effect of overwork, nervous strain and apprehension. It was the past that was telling on them, the years of conspiracy, prison and exile; the years of the famine and the Civil War; and sticking to the rules of a game that demanded that at every moment a man's whole life should be at stake. They were indeed 'dead men on furlough', as Lenin had called them. Nothing could frighten them any more, nothing surprise them. They had given all they had. History had squeezed them out to the last drop, had burnt them out to the last spiritual calorie; yet they were still glowing in cold devotion, like phosphorescent corpses.[12]

Even the brave Budu Mdivani is quoted as saying, "I belong to the opposition, that is clear. But if there is going to be a final break . . . I prefer to return to the Party I helped create. I no longer have the strength to begin creating a new party." [13] As a psychological hurdle, the fresh start was too high. The oppositionists fell back into submission, surrender.

This loyalty to "the Party" has an element of unreality about it. The original Party of 1917 had been decimated by the expulsion of thousands of oppositionists. By the end of 1930, only Stalin, of the original leadership, remained in the Politburo. His nominees, from the ranks of the new men, controlled the elements of power. The Party itself, diluted by the great influxes of the 1920s, had changed in the style of its membership and now contained a rank and file who had regularly, so far at least, acted as reliable voting fodder for the secretaries imposed by Stalin's Secretariat.

On the face of it, the opposition could well have argued that Stalin's control of, and claim to represent, the Party was based on no higher sanction than success in packing the Party Congresses, that in fact he had no real claim to be regarded as the genuine succession. But the oppositionists themselves had used similar methods in their day, and had never criticized them until a more skilled operator turned the weapon against them.

In 1923, Stalin was already able to attack such arguments from his opponents by pointing out that appeals for democracy came oddly from people like Byeloborodov and Rosengolts, who had ruled Rostov and the Donets Basin, respectively, in the most authoritarian fashion.[14] Even more to the point, in 1924 Shlyapnikov ironically remarked that Trotsky and his followers had all supported the action taken against the Workers' Opposition at the Xth Party Congress in 1921, so that their claims to stand for Party democracy were hypocritical.[15] Kamenev denounced Party democracy in this struggle with Trotsky in revealing terms:

> For if they say today, let us have democracy in the Party, tomorrow they will say, let us have democracy in the trade unions; the day after tomorrow, workers who do not

belong to the Party may well say: give us democracy too . . . and surely then the myriads of peasants could not be prevented from asking for democracy.[16]

A year later he was asserting, "We object to the Secretariat, uniting policy and organization in itself, being placed above the political organism." It was too late. And the Stalinists were able to comment tellingly, as when Mikoyan said, "While Zinoviev is in the majority he is for iron discipline. . . . When he is in the minority . . . he is against it."[17]

When Stalin proceeded to the further step of arresting those responsible for the Trotskyite underground printing press, headed by Mrachkovsky, in 1927, he was again able to refute opposition objections, remarking: "They say that such things are unknown of the Party. This is not true. What about the Myasnikov group? And the Workers' Truth group? Does not everyone know that Comrades Trotsky, Zinoviev and Kamenev themselves supported the arrest of the members of these groups?"[18] Mere truth is a common casualty in all types of political systems, but in nontotalitarian parties this never becomes an overt and overriding principle, remaining sporadic and occasional, and discrediting its authors when exposed. Among the Communists, it was consciously and systematically accepted.

It was ironically enough Trotsky who had publicly denied the existence of Lenin's Testament. When Stalin attacked Kamenev in 1926 for having sent a telegram of congratulations to the Grand Duke Michael at the time of the February 1917 Revolution, Kamenev pointed out that Lenin had personally signed a denial of this. Stalin retorted quite matter-of-factly that Lenin had, in the interests of the Party, knowingly stated a falsehood.[19] At the XIVth Congress in 1925, Krupskaya appealed, as a member of the defeated faction, to objective truth. Bukharin retorted: "N. K. Krupskaya says truth is that which corresponds to reality, each can read and listen, and answer for himself. But what about the Party? Disappeared, as in the magic picture!"[20]

Also going back to the earliest days of the Party was the tradition that the best method of winning political argument was to smear the opponent by every conceivable means. Lenin once said to Angelica Balabanoff, "Everything that is done in the proletarian cause is honest." The great Italian Socialist leader Serrati, though sympathetic to the Communists, had tried to prevent their splitting his movement to suit their strategies, and had been attacked in terms to which Balabanoff, at that time Secretary of the Comintern, had objected. After Serrati's death, it was Zinoviev who explained the Leninist tactics to her: "We have fought and slandered him because of his great merits. It would not have been possible to alienate the masses [from him] without resorting to these means."[21] It was natural, then, that the oppositionists should be required to cast filth on their own motives and ideas.

At the XVth Party Congress in December 1927, Kamenev argued that the denunciation of their own views then required of the opposition would be meaningless. He explained the dilemma. They now had no choice but either to constitute a second party, which would be ruinous for the Revolution and "lead to political degeneration," or to make "a complete and thorough surrender to the Party." He and Zinoviev had decided on the latter, taking the view that "nothing could be done outside of and despite the Party." They would obey, but he pleaded that they should not be obliged to denounce views that they had obviously held just a few weeks earlier. None, he said, had previously made such a demand. (Though, in fact, Zinoviev had made exactly the same demand of Trotsky in 1924!)

Stalin did not accept Zinoviev's and Kamenev's recantation. They were trapped. They could hardly go back on what they had already said. Finally, they accepted the terms of the victor, denouncing their own views on 18 December as "wrong and anti-Leninist." Bukharin told them they were lucky to have made their minds up in time, as this was "the last moment available to them."

Again denounced, expelled from the Party, and sent into exile in 1932, Zinoviev and Kamenev were readmitted in 1933 on similar but yet more abject self-abasement. Zinoviev wrote to the Central Committee:

> I ask you to believe that I am speaking the truth and nothing but the truth. I ask you to restore me to the ranks of the Party and to give me an opportunity of working for the common cause. I give my word as a revolutionary that I will be the most devoted member of the Party, and will do all I possibly can at least to some extent to atone for my guilt before the Party and its Central Committee.[22]

And soon afterward, he was allowed to publish an article in *Pravda* condemning the opposition and praising Stalin's victories.[23]

In crawling as he did,* Zinoviev was acting logically from the point of view of Party ethics. He believed that any humiliation could be undergone for the purpose of remaining in the Party, where he might, in the future, play a useful role. But such logic was in any case to prove inapplicable. And meanwhile, the long process of deception and apology was corrupting the oppositionists. As a close observer commented:

> It must be admitted that from the point of view of political morals, the conduct of the majority of the oppositionists was by no means of high quality. To be sure, the conditions prevailing in the Party are intolerable. To be loyal, to do every single thing that is demanded of us is almost impossible: to do so would mean to become an informer, to run to the Central Control Commission with reports on every utterance of opposition picked up more or less accidentally, and on every oppositionist document one comes across. A party which expects such things from its members cannot be expected to be regarded as a free association of persons of like views, united for a common purpose. We are all obliged to lie: it is impossible to manage otherwise. Nevertheless, there are limits which should not be exceeded even in lying. Unfortunately, the oppositionists, and particularly their leaders, often went beyond these limits.
>
> . . . To plead for pardon has become a common phenomenon, on the supposition that the party in power being "my party," the rules which applied in the Tsarist days are no longer valid. One hears this argument everywhere. At the same time, it is considered quite proper to consistently deceive "my party," since the party does

---

*We should note, incidentally, that some of the earlier crop of capitulations by "Trotskyites" had been much less abject than those of Zinoviev. Muralov had never made any declaration against the opposition. Ivan Smirnov's "capitulation" had been in rather noncommittal terms, and when he met Sedov in Berlin, they had been friendly. Trotsky recognized that Serebryakov's capitulation, too, was "more dignified than some."

not fight its intellectual opponents by trying to convince them, but by the use of force. This has given rise to a special type of morality, which allows one to accept any condition, to sign any undertakings, with the premeditated intention not to observe them.[24]

This attitude had a very demoralizing effect. The border between treachery and compromise became very vague. At the same time, Stalinists could point out that it was impossible to believe the opposition precisely because of their idea that telling lies was permissible.

Zinoviev and Kamenev had been expelled for the third time in 1934, on suspicion of politically inspiring Nikolayev in the murder of Kirov. And in January 1935, as we have seen, they had once again declared their political guilt, this time accepting it in a form which was already a partial plea of guilty before the criminal law.

Their successive surrenders had never been voluntary, in the sense that they would have preferred to avoid them. But they had accepted them, under pressure, as unavoidable moves in the political and moral conditions of the one-party system to which they adhered. They had abandoned in turn each of their objections—to falsification, to undemocratic procedures, to insincere retractions, to arrest. They had chosen to do so in order to remain in the Party, or to gain readmission after they had been expelled. The Rightist Slepkov is reported by a Soviet writer as being brought back from a political isolator and supplying the names of over 150 accomplices, on the grounds, "We must disarm! We must go on our knees to the Party."[25]

A thoughtful Soviet analysis which appeared recently notes that Ryutin (and later Raskolnikov) flatly denied the legitimacy of the Stalin regime, but that most of the victims of the trials were "paralyzed" by feeling themselves to be "within the system personified by Stalin." Even in his "last letter" (see p. 395), Bukharin merely says that he has not opposed the Party line for eight years, and has no quarrel with Stalin.[26] In the case of the prominent Communists accused at the great show trials of 1936, 1937, and 1938, there is no doubt that the rational, or rationalized, component in their motives included this idea of service to the Party. This theme has been most strikingly and persuasively developed in Arthur Koestler's *Darkness at Noon,* and is often taken as *the* explanation of the public confessions—though Koestler himself makes no such claim and, on the contrary, remarks:

> Some were silenced by physical fear, like Hare-lip; some hoped to save their heads; others at least to save their wives or sons from the clutches of the Gletkins. The best of them kept silent in order to do a last service to the Party, by letting themselves be sacrificed as scapegoats—and, besides, even the best had each an Arlova on his conscience.[27]

Koestler's last point—that the oppositionists felt they had lost the right to judge Stalin—is confirmed in various reports. A non-Communist prisoner notes how "nearly every supporter of the regime, before falling a victim to it, has in his time been involved by it in actions which have conflicted with his political conscience."[28] And he agrees with Koestler on the main issue:

It is true that the interrogation methods, particularly when applied for months or years, are capable of breaking the strongest will. But the decisive factor is something else. It is that the majority of convinced Communists must at all costs preserve their faith in the Soviet Union. To renounce it would be beyond their powers. For great moral strength is required in certain circumstances to renounce one's long-standing, deep-rooted convictions, even when these turn out to be untenable.[29]

Koestler's account is in fact extremely well founded on the facts. For instance, when he describes an attempt to break Rubashov's morale by dragging a badly tortured prisoner past his cell to execution, he can base this firmly on the evidence.[30] Briefly summarized, Rubashov's surrender is based on a feeling that his own past actions have deprived him of the right to judge Stalin's, coupled with a feeling of loyalty to the Party and its conception of history; and it is largely a conscious process—the pressure of the interrogation, toothache, and so on merely intensifying his reflection leading up to the decision. In fact, he is shown in court as resisting the temptation not to confess. They key thought in his confession is formulated thus:

'I know', Rubashov went on, 'that my aberration, if carried into effect would have been a mortal danger to the Revolution. Every opposition at the critical turning-points of history, carries in itself the germ of a split in the Party, and hence the germ of civil war. Humanitarian weakness and liberal democracy, when the masses are not mature, is suicide for the Revolution. And yet my oppositional attitude was based on a craving for just these methods—in appearance so desirable, actually so deadly. On a demand for a liberal reform of the dictatorship, for a broader democracy, for the abolition of the Terror, and a loosening of the rigid organization of the Party. I admit that these demands, in the present situation, are objectively harmful and therefore counter-revolutionary in character. . . .'[31]

We have here, though in more extreme form, that extravagant identification with Party which is to be found in Bukharin's private utterances before his arrest and in Pyatakov's 1928 outburst. Bukharin was to say publicly in his last plea,

For three months I refused to say anything. Then I began to testify. Why? Because while I was in prison I made a revaluation of my entire past. For when you ask yourself: 'If you must die, what are you dying for?'—an absolutely black vacuity suddenly rises before you with startling vividness. There was nothing to die for, if one wanted to die unrepented. . . . And when you ask yourself, 'Very well, suppose you do not die; suppose by some miracle you remain alive, again what for?' Isolated from everybody, an enemy of the people, an inhuman position, completely isolated from everything that constitutes the essence of life.[32]

Koestler does not, as we have noted, put forward his account as a general theory of the motivation of confessions. He is simply giving an account of one presumable mechanism: and it is clear from much that has been written since that what he describes, or something like it, was genuinely involved in certain cases.

These considerations did not apply to all Party members. Ryutin and his associates were clearly prepared to remove Stalin. And similarly with the confessions. Ivan Smirnov was only induced to make his partial and derisory confession on the grounds that without it he would be shot in secret and his name dragged in the mud by those who had already decided to confess, and by the promise to spare his former wife and his family,[33] while his presence would to some extent check the smears of the Prosecutor. Even so, he is said to have gone to his death remarking that he and the other defendants had behaved despicably.[34]

And what greater contrast could there be between Pyatakov's words and those reported of Ter-Vaganyan:

> But in order to sign the testimony which is demanded of me, I must be sure first that it is really needed in the interests of the Party and the Revolution. . . .
>
> . . . You suggest that I do not think and rely blindly on the Central Committee, because the Central Committee sees everything more clearly than I. But the trouble is that by my very nature I am unable to stop thinking. And when I do think, I come to the inescapable conclusion that the assertions that the oldest Bolsheviks have turned into a gang of murderers will bring incalculable harm not only to our country and the Party, but to the cause of Socialism all over the world. . . .
>
> . . . If now the new program of the Central Committee deems it necessary to discredit Bolshevism and its founders, then I don't agree with that program and I no longer consider myself bound by Party discipline. And besides, I am already expelled from the Party, and for that reason alone I am not obliged to submit to Party discipline.[35]

When he was finally persuaded that there was no point in resisting while Zinoviev and Kamenev, greatly senior figures, were going to smear the Party anyhow, and he was advised by the interrogator Boris Berman, with whom he had become friendly, that he might just as well save his own life this way, he gave in. Berman remarked that in this way he hoped, after years had passed, to see Ter-Vaganyan rehabilitated and given an important post. Ter-Vaganyan is said to have replied,

> I have not the slightest desire to be in a high post. If my party, for which I lived, and for which I was ready to die any minute, forced me to sign this, then I don't want to be in the Party. Today I envy the most ignorant non-Party man.[36]

And yet Ter-Vaganyan was one of those who gave in. We can be sure that similar views, even more strongly held, determined the attitudes of men who could not be broken. Kuklin is reported in prison as saying that "all was lost" as far as the Party and the Revolution were concerned, and a new start would be necessary.[37]

The argument that Party-style thinking, the idea of Party discipline, is *the* main explanation for the public confessions has one obvious objection. This logic, if it existed, was as formally true at the moment of arrest as it was later. We have seen how Safonova took it to be her Party duty to confess and to try to persuade Smirnov to confess. Similarly with other recent Soviet accounts. For example, one such tells, as illustrative, of another old Party member: "The interrogator asked him whether he considered himself a Bolshevik and, receiving an affirmative answer, continued: 'Well, the Party demands that you, as a Bolshevik, confess that you are an English spy.' To this the former member of the Supreme Court replied: 'If the party demands it, I confess.' "[38] Yet in most cases the accused resisted for a longer or shorter period. Why was the idea of Party discipline convincing to Muralov in December 1936, when for eight months previously he had found it unconvincing? Why did Bukharin resist for three months?

Bukharin, indeed, gave an answer at his trial: cut off and exposed, removed from the Party, with nothing to live for, he started a reexamination of his thoughts, a reevaluation which led him to surrender. If it comes to that, Boguslavsky went through the whole process in eight days, during which "owing to my arrest, I recovered my balance and I was able to bring my still largely, if not utterly, criminal ideas in order"[39]—which, though expressed suitably to the trial, amounts to the same thing.

Thus it is not the case that good Communists automatically obeyed when told "The Party needs your evidence"; they did so after a varying length of imprisonment and interrogation. Even Bukharin himself (who is supposed to have been the main follower of this line) did not after all produce a confession wholly in accord with the prosecution's wishes, but chose to speak in such a way that anyone of any sense could see that the charges were false. And we have already noted that when Kaganovich, one of the keenest supporters of the Purge, himself fell from power, he omitted to suggest that the Party's image would be best served by bringing him to trial and blackening him as a spy, terrorist, and saboteur and shooting him amid public execration. On the contrary, he rang up Khrushchev and begged him "not to allow them to deal with me as they dealt with people under Stalin"[40]—a grave dereliction from the point of view of service to the Party. Clearly, without denying that in many cases the idea of being useful to the Party was a component of the intellectual and psychological conditions of surrender, we can at least say that it took effect in combination with a good many other pressures.

It is obvious enough that the oppositionists did not expect just fair treatment and political persuasion. Tomsky's suicide the day he heard of the charges against him is enough to show that, and his was not the only one. The political argument about service to the Party can, in fact, be seen as a component in some cases (but not all) of a larger system of physical, intellectual, and moral pressures. In a case like Kamenev's, where the argument about the Party's interests was combined with exhausting interrogation, heat, lack of food, threats to his family, and promises of his life, we can hardly expect to decide which played the most important part.

For having gone into the habits of mind of the oppositionists who confessed, there are two major qualifications to add. First, as we have seen, not all the Communists held the ideas of Party unity and of self-abasement in the way that Zinoviev and Kamenev, Bukharin and Pyatakov did; and from them it was often impossible to obtain public confessions. We are told that Syrtsov (interrogated by the dreadful Vlodzimirsky) "signed nothing" and that the same was true of Uglanov, Preobrazhensky, Shlyapnikov, Smilga, and others.[41] And, second, public confessions were produced from non-Communists: the doctors in the 1938 Trial, most of the Polish underground leaders in 1945, the Bulgarian Protestant pastors in 1949. The motivations just described were of primary importance in the whole great cycle of party submission to Stalin, but in the trials themselves they were neither necessary nor sufficient causes of the particular surrender involved in public confession. In a number of the most important cases, they predisposed the leading accused to giving in to the pressures put on them, and they provided the rationale of the confessions made. But it was by the merely technical action of the NKVD interrogation system that these and other predisposing factors were brought to the full fruition of the scenes in the October Hall.

## TORTURE

When it came to explaining how the confessions had been obtained, the first thought of hostile critics was torture. Indeed, Khrushchev was to remark in 1956,

> How is it possible that a person confesses to crimes which he has not committed? Only in one way—because of application of physical methods of pressuring him, tortures, bringing him to a state of unconsciousness, depriving him of his judgment, taking away his human dignity. In this manner were "confessions" acquired.[42]

The interrogation of the accused in the 1938 Trial was started with a laconic memo from NKVD Deputy People's Commissar Frinovsky: "I authorize transfer to the Lefortovo. Beating permitted."[43] And it is clear that Krestinsky, for example, was severely tortured.[44]

Physical torture had, of course, been in use since the early days of the regime. There are many reports of police brutality in the early 1930s: in Rostov, prisoners were hit in the stomach with a sandbag; this was sometimes fatal. A doctor would certify that a prisoner who had died of it had suffered from a malign tumor.[45] Another interrogation method was the *stoika*. It consisted of standing a prisoner against a wall on tiptoe and making him hold that position for several hours. A day or two of this was said to be enough to break almost anyone.[46]

Other "improvised" torture methods included the "swallow," which involved tying the hands and feet behind the back and hoisting the victim into the air.[47] One prisoner describes having her fingers slammed in a door.[48] Beating up was usual. Interrogators sometimes had to hand over prisoners to special heavily built thugs known to the prisoners as "boxers," who would carry this out.[49] Nor was this done only with peasants and socially hostile elements: a colonel, later restored to the Party, reports being badly beaten up by the NKVD in 1935.[50] There are many accounts of women being beaten.[51] In general, the provincial interrogators were the more brutal. A Red Army Choir accordionist had both legs broken at Khabarovsk;[52] toenails were torn out at Baku; genitals beaten at Ashkhabad.[53]

All this was, in a sense, "unofficial." In most prisons, physical torture remained so. Needles, pincers, and so on are sporadically reported, and more specialized implements seem to have been in use at the Lefortovo.[54] But on the whole, some appearance of spontaneity was maintained. Feet and fingers were stamped on. Broken-off chair legs were the usual weapon for beatings, which were sometimes distinguished from "torture." But as one very experienced prisoner says, this distinction was rather absurd when a man came back after such a beating with broken ribs, urinating blood for a week, or with a permanently injured spine and unable to walk.[55]

Physical torture, though not uncommon, had been contrary to regulations until 1937. Then it suddenly became the usual method of interrogation, at least in the bulk of cases at the lower level. The time of the Zinoviev Trial saw the first official, though secret, permission to use "any method" put out on 29 July 1936.[56] Early in the following year, an authorization from the "Central Committee"— that is, Stalin—was given to the NKVD. It was only on 20 January 1939 that a coded telegram formally confirming the system was circulated to the secretaries of Provincial Committees and Republican Central Committees of the Party, and the heads of NKVD organizations:

> The Party Central Committee explains that application of methods of physical pressure in NKVD practice is permissible from 1937 on, in accordance with permission of the Party Central Committee. . . . It is known that all bourgeois intelligence services use methods of physical influence against the representatives of the socialist proletariat and that they use them in their most scandalous forms. The question arises as to why the socialist intelligence service should be more humanitarian against the mad agents of the bourgeoisie, against the deadly enemies of the working class and of the collective farm workers. The Party Central Committee considers that physical pressure should still be used obligatorily, as an exception applicable to known and obstinate enemies of the people, as a method both justifiable and appropriate.[57]

This instruction has all the signs of being written by Stalin himself. He was, in fact, a great believer in "physical methods." Khrushchev tells of his orders to "beat, beat and beat again" the accused in the 1952 Doctors' Plot. A recent Soviet article quotes from the archives a written note of his to Yezhov, when the old Bolshevik Beloborodov was giving unsatisfactory testimony: "Can't this gentleman be made to tell of his dirty deeds? Where is he—in a prison or a hotel?"[58]

A Soviet general describes his fate under this system:

> I accidentally found out that my fiend of an interrogator's name was Stolbunsky. I don't know where he is now. If he is still alive I hope he will read these lines and feel my contempt for him, not only now but when I was in his hands. But I think he knew this well enough. Apart from him, two brawny torturers took part in the interrogation. Even now my ears ring with the sound of Stolbunsky's evil voice hissing "You'll sign, you'll sign!" as I was carried out, weak and covered in blood. I withstood the torture during the second bout of interrogation, but when the third started, how I longed to be able to die![59]

He adds that every one of his cell mates had confessed to imaginary crimes: "Some had done this after physical coercion and others after having been terrified by accounts of the tortures used." Another report, by an Old Bolshevik, says that only 4 of the 400-odd cell mates he met in prison had failed to confess; and the critic Ivanov-Razumnik similarly writes that in his years in jail in Moscow and Leningrad only 12 of his 1,000-odd cell mates had held out.[60] In most cases, the threat of further torture was enough to prevent retraction.

Various forms of humiliation were often especially effective on men weakened by torture. An army officer who withstood beating finally broke when the interrogator pushed his head into a spittoon brimful of spittle. Another gave way when an interrogator urinated on his head—an interrogation practice which according to reports became traditional.[61]

Moreover, when it came to those tried in open court, "the defendants were warned that the tortures would be continued after the trial if they did not give the necessary testimony."[62] The presence of their interrogators, who sat in front of them in court, would reinforce this.[63]

And, of course, confessions obtained by torture were useful in bringing pressure to bear on other victims. When Bukharin's first wife, Nadezhda Lukina, was interrogated, her brother Mikhail was among the members of the family who were tortured to give evidence against the others and her. A recent Soviet article gives a horrifying account of his withdrawing his evidence, and then, after further interrogation, confirming it again. The article quotes another former prisoner, a woman who, asking "How could a brother give evidence against a sister?" answered that a Comintern worker in her cell came back from interrogation one day, complaining bitterly that a close comrade had incriminated her; the examiners had shown her the testimony in his own handwriting. Soon afterward, she returned from a further session. This time she cried, "How could I? How could I? Today I had a confrontation with him and I saw not a man, but live raw meat."[64]

Yet in spite of Khrushchev's comment, torture is not a complete explanation when it comes to the public confessions of the oppositionists. We should record its extent, and its overwhelmingly powerful effects throughout the period. But critics were right in saying that torture alone could probably not have produced the public self-humiliation of a whole series of Stalin's enemies, when returned to health and given a platform.

We shall see, in fact, that some accused withdrew in closed court confessions obtained by torture. Others "insisted even in the preliminary investigation or in court that their statements charging violations of socialist legality be entered in the examination record."[65]

## THE "CONVEYOR"

When there was time, the basic NKVD method for obtaining confessions and breaking the accused man was the "conveyor"—continual interrogation by relays of police for hours and days on end. As with many phenomena of the Stalin period, it has the advantage that it could not easily be condemned by any simple principle. Clearly, it amounted to unfair pressure after a certain time and to actual physical torture later still, but when? No absolutely precise answer could be given.

But at any rate, after even twelve hours, it is extremely uncomfortable. After a day, it becomes very hard. And after two or three days, the victim is actually physically poisoned by fatigue. It was "as painful as any torture."[66] In fact, we are told, though some prisoners had been known to resist torture, it was almost unheard of for the conveyor not to succeed if kept up long enough. One week is reported as enough to break almost anybody.[67] A description by a Soviet woman writer who experienced it speaks of seven days without sleep or food, the seventh standing up—ending in physical collapse. This was followed by a five-day interrogation of a milder type, in which she was allowed three hours' rest in her cell, though sleep was still forbidden.[68]

The conveyor and torture were not, of course, mutually exclusive. Recent Soviet accounts describe the actions of V. Boyarsky, still alive and in a post in a scientific commission. In the late 1930s, he served as interrogator in Northern Ossetia, where he "falsified accusations against 103 people, of whom 51 were shot and the remainder sent to camps, where most of them died.'' On one occasion, he interrogated a woman schoolteacher, Fatimat Agnayeva, for eight days—and then had her hung by her hair to a bracket on the wall, where she died.[69]

There is nothing new about the conveyor method. It was used on witches in Scotland. The philosopher Campanella, who withstood all other tortures during his interrogation in the sixteenth century, succumbed to lack of sleep. Hallucinations occur. Flies buzz about. Smoke seems to rise before the prisoner's eyes, and so on.

Beck and Godin report a case in which interrogation lasted without any break for eleven days, during the last four of which the prisoner had to stand. Towards the end of even lesser periods, prisoners collapsed about every twenty minutes and had to be brought round with cold water or slaps.[70] Sitting on a stool for fourteen hours is, according to one victim, more painful than standing against a wall, where you can at least shift your weight from one foot to the other. The groin swells, and violent pains set in.

In Weissberg's account of his interrogation, he mentions that on one occasion he was questioned for eighteen hours, and then left locked in the washroom, where the floor was under water.[71] He was, however, able to lie down on a footrack. After fourteen hours, he was called out for a brief interrogation and sent back to find that the rack had been removed, so that he had to stand in an inch or so of water for forty hours, until the next interrogation. Later, he was beaten up, under the new practice, but was then returned to the conveyor. A ''technical improvement'' had been made in that the seat had been taken out of the chair, and it was extremely painful, even briefly.[72]

There are very few accounts of successful resistance to the conveyor. One is of a fifty-five-year-old anarchist, Eisenberg, who on being called a counter-revolutionary refused to answer any more questions. Beating up had no effect on him, and he survived a conveyor lasting for thirty-one days—an extraordinary record. Examination by a doctor showed that though he was physically very sound, there was something abnormal about his imperviousness to pain. He is supposed to have been sent to a lunatic asylum.[73] Weissberg himself held out for seven days, helped by a brief interruption, but finally confessed. After a day's rest, he withdrew the confession. Interrogation started again. This time he gave way on the fourth day, having already told the examiners that every confession he made he would withdraw when he recovered. The third conveyor session ended on the fifth day without his signing a fresh confession, though by now the interrogators had two ''documents.''

And here we have the defect of the ''conveyor.'' Although it was almost always successful, and usually in two to three days, it has no essential advantage over torture proper (with which it was often combined), since the confessions it produced could be withdrawn.

## THE LONG INTERROGATION

The interrogation system which broke down many prisoners to the extent of maintaining their confessions at public trial was conceived on rather different lines. It aimed at a more gradual, but more complete, destruction of the will to resist.

With intellectuals and politicians, the process often lasted a long time—some (with interruptions) up to two and a half years. The average is thought to have been about four or five months.[74]

Throughout the period the prisoner was kept with inadequate sleep, in cells either too hot or (most usually) too cold, on insufficient though attractively prepared food. The Spanish Communist general El Campesino speaks of three and a half ounces of black bread and some soup "served beautifully and tastily" twice a day,[75] with results such as scurvy, which must be taken as planned. Physical exhaustion produces increased liability to psychological disorders, a well-established phenomenon noted in the Second World War in, for example, boats' crews who had drifted for a long time; even persons whose stability was such that they were not likely to break down under the most difficult situations frequently then succumbed.

Interrogation usually took place at night and with the accused just roused—often only fifteen minutes after going to sleep. The glaring lights at the interrogation had a disorientating effect. There was a continual emphasis on the absolute powerlessness of the victim. The interrogators—or so it usually seemed—could go on indefinitely. Thus the struggle seemed a losing one. The continual repetition of a series of questions is also invariably reported to disorient both semantically and as regards the recollection or interpretation of facts. And there was a total lack of privacy.

A Pole, Z. Stypulkowski, who experienced the whole process in 1945 describes it:

> . . . Cold, hunger, the bright light and especially sleeplessness. The cold is not terrific. But when the victim is weakened by hunger and by sleeplessness, then the six or seven degrees above freezing point make him tremble all the time. During the night I had only one blanket.
> . . . After two or three weeks, I was in a semi-conscious state. After fifty or sixty interrogations with cold and hunger and almost no sleep, a man becomes like an automaton—his eyes are bright, his legs swollen, his hands trembling. In this state he is often convinced he is guilty.[76]

He estimated that most of his fellow accused had reached this condition between the fortieth and seventieth interrogations. International considerations made it necessary to bring the Polish underground leaders to trial before Stypulkowski (alone among the accused) was ready to confess. We have also had the evidence of men who made a full confession: Artur London[77] and, more revealingly, Evzen Loebl, sentenced to life imprisonment in the Czechoslovak Slansky Trial in 1952.

Loebl mentions other prisoners being beaten, having their genitals crushed, being put into ice-cold water, and having their heads wrapped in wet cold cloth, which, when it dried, shrank and caused "unbearable pain." But (unlike London) he was not tortured himself and confirms that torture was inadequate for the preparation of the victim of a set-piece trial, when "the whole of the person had to be 'broken.' " He describes having to be on his feet eighteen hours a day, sixteen of which were devoted to interrogation. During the six-hour sleep period, the warder pounded on the door every ten minutes, upon which he had to jump to attention and report, "Detainee No. 1473 reports: strength one detainee, everything in order." He was, that is, "awakened thirty or forty times a night." If the banging did not wake him, a kick from the warder would. After two or three weeks, his feet were swollen and every inch of his body ached at the slightest touch; even washing became a torture. He says that the worst pain came in his legs when he lay down. He was taken six or seven times to what he was led to believe would be his execution; he did not mind it at the time, but the reaction afterwards affected him badly. Like others in various Eastern European trials, he is convinced that he was given drugs. But if so, this was a late refinement and does not appear in reports of prewar interrogations in Russia. (Loebl notes, incidentally, that the doctor's brutality was even greater than that of the interrogators.) He finally reached the stage where it did not occur to him to repudiate his confession. Having confessed, he was allowed books, adequate food, and rest, but he had (as he puts it) been deprived of his ego: "I was quite a normal person—only I was no longer a person."[78]

A manual for NKVD workers was written on orders from Yezhov by three of the most notorious inquisitors—Vlodzimirsky, Ushakov, and Shvartsman—and approved by Beria after Yezhov's fall. It contained no overt call for torture; but a few quotations from it, given recently in the Soviet press, are worth recording:

> . . . investigations at the NKVD are carried out according to the Code of Criminal Procedure. But the grounds for initiating a criminal case are somewhat broader.

> . . . the accused must not be allowed to get the better of you. . . . During the investigation the accused must be kept strictly in line.

> . . . Failure to confirm the evidence [already obtained] is indicative of poor work by the interrogators.[79]

There is no doubt that not only nonpolitical defendants, but even strong political opponents can be broken by the "Yezhov method." In this connection the statements of the Bulgarian Protestant pastors in their February 1949 Trial are the most relevant, since no one could possibly argue that loyalty to Party or creed induced them. In their confessions, they all remarked that they now saw Communist rule of their country "in a new light." In their final pleas, Pastor Naumov thanked the police for their "kindness and consideration" and said, "I have sinned against my people and against the whole world. This is my resurrection"; Pastor Diapkov was in tears as he admitted his guilt and said, "Do not make of me a useless martyr by giving me the death sentence. Help me to become a useful citizen and a hero of the Fatherland Front"; Pastor Bezlov, who had earlier stated that he had read 12,000 pages of Marxist literature while in prison and that this had entirely changed his outlook, declared, "I have now an intellectual appreciation of what the new life means and I want to play my part in it."*

In his speech to the United Nations General Assembly on 26 October 1953, Dr. Mayo drew attention to the parallel between the similar treatment of the American prisoners of war in Korea to obtain confessions of "germ warfare" and

---

*The factual side of the confessions, as so often, contained impossibilities—as when the Head of the Congregationalist Church mentioned meetings with a British Vice Consul over a long period when the man concerned had not been in the country.

the work of Pavlov in establishing conditioned reflexes in dogs. Soviet psychologists and physiologists always treated Pavlov as the basis of their work, and his method of associating stimuli to provide an automatic response accords with the reduction of prisoners to the point at which they associate survival with the single response of accepting what their captors tell them. In a human being, this involves considerable degradation. An animal's response—at least to situations which it recognizes (the only ones it can cope with)—is in principle unconditional and without discrimination. Man's higher status consists precisely in his ability to distinguish and discriminate. To put it another way, among men it is only the psychotic who gives an unconditional reaction to a stimulus.

But a man, even in this state, is not an animal. He needs at least the appearance of rational motives. In the case of Communists, as we have seen, this was ready to hand in their Party principles: a survivor of the 1949 purges in Hungary describes how Laszlo Rajk, after severe torture, regarded service to the Party as a "Golden Bridge" back to his self-respect.[80] There were other pressures.

## HOSTAGES

There is no doubt that threats to the family—the use, that is, of hostages for good behavior—was one of the most powerful of all Stalin's safeguards. It seems a general rule that with confessions by prominent figures, members of the family were in the power of the NKVD. Bukharin, Rykov, and Zinoviev all had children of whom they were very fond, whereas at least some of those tried in private, such as Karakhan, did not. Several of the accused in their final pleas referred to their children—for example, Kamenev and Rosengolts.

Engineers under arrest as early as 1930 had been threatened with reprisals against their wives and children.[81] And the decree of 7 April 1935, which extended full adult penalties down to children of twelve, was a terrible threat to those oppositionists with children. If Stalin could openly and publicly declare such an atrocity, they could be sure that he would not hesitate to apply the death penalty secretly to their own children in cases where he thought it would bring him advantage. According to Orlov, it became regular practice, on Yezhov's orders, for interrogators to have a copy of the decree on their desks.[82] We are also told that fear of reprisals was made more dramatic and emotionally effective by the display on the interrogator's desk of private belongings of members of the family.[83] Even if accepted and allowed for on the conscious level, this must have been a continual argument in the unconscious in favor of surrender.

The use of relatives as hostages, and their imprisonment or execution in other cases, was a new development in Russian history. In Tsarist times, revolutionaries never had this problem. Here again, Stalin recognized no limits. Moreover, it was not merely a matter of threats to relatives' lives: "They tortured husbands in front of wives and vice versa." Again, Roy Medvedev tells us that Kossior stood up under torture, and was only broken when his sixteen-year-old daughter was brought to the interrogation room and raped in front of him.[84]

On the other side of the coin, it was suggested, even at the time, that there was something about the confessions which was specifically Russian. The Dostoievsky-style habit of self-abasement was much spoken of. Bukharin denied that the *âme slave* had any bearing on the confessions. He was himself a more intellectual and in a sense more Westernized character than many of the leaders. But in any case, these adumbrations of national psychology are very vague and in themselves unconvincing. It is not surprising that at the time people faced with the extraordinary phenomenon of the confessions should have sought out extraordinary explanations. Nevertheless, like any other, the Russian culture has its own characteristics, affecting the attitudes of all those brought up in it. We can hardly quite exclude *some* effect of a tradition of self-immolation (even though the Russian tradition also contains famous examples of most outright defiance or authority, as with Archpriest Avvakum, who spat in the face of the Tsar).

Another powerful motive was that of self-preservation. This is a paradox which confused observers in the West, and still confuses some. By the full and sometimes abject confession of capital crimes, it appeared that the defendants were actively seeking the death sentence, which, they themselves sometimes said, they fully deserved. The reality was different. The absolutely certain way for a defendant to get himself shot was to refuse to plead guilty. He would then not go before an open court at all, but either perish under the rigors of the preliminary investigation, or be shot, like Rudzutak, after a twenty-minute closed trial. The logic of Stalin's courts was different from what is customary elsewhere. The only chance of avoiding death was to admit to everything, and to put the worst possible construction on all one's activities. It is true that even this seldom saved a man's life. But it did sometimes, for a while—as in the cases of Radek, Sokolnikov, and Rakovsky. At the August 1936 Trial, moreover, the defendants had actually been promised their lives and had reasonable expectation that the promise would be fulfilled. The same promise was evidently made to Pyatakov and others in the second trial. It must have lost a good deal of its efficacy; yet, even then, it represented the only possible hope. Besides, on the face of it, the Pyatakov situation was different. While Zinoviev and Kamenev had continued in effect to oppose the Stalin leadership, and had long since been excluded from decent Party society, Pyatakov had been of the greatest service to the dictator and had been admitted by him to his latest Central Committee. He was, in addition, under the apparently powerful protection of Ordzhonikidze. And a little hope goes a long way. Promises that confessions in court would save their lives continued to be made to various groups of accused—for example, the generals in the Tukhachevsky Case.[85]

As to Communist motives proper, the Party and the old opposition had already been smeared beyond relief. Even for a man like Sokolnikov, it may have appeared that no action he could take could affect the issue one way or the other, and that the only consideration left was to attempt to save his family. So much more admirable, then, is the sense of truth and personal courage shown by men like Ryutin, who even under the pressure of such arguments seem to have "died in silence." For when everything is said of the pressures for confession, it is remarkable how many did not give way or—if they did—were not trusted to maintain their confessions in court. Nonconfessors were a special breed. Koestler analyses his friend Alexander Weissberg:

> What enabled him to hold out where others broke down was a special mixture of just those character traits which survival in such a situation requires. A great physical and

mental resilience—that jack-in-the-box quality which allows quick recuperation and apparently endless comebacks, both physical and mental. An extraordinary presence of mind. . . . A certain thick-skinnedness and good-natured insensitivity, coupled with an almost entirely extroverted disposition—notice the absence in Dr. Weissberg's book of any contemplative passage, of any trace of religious or mystic experience which is otherwise almost inevitably present in solitary confinement. An irresponsible optimism and smug complacency in hair-raising situations; that 'it can't happen to me' attitude, which is the most reliable source of courage; and an inexhaustible sense of humour. Finally, that relentless manner of persisting in an argument and continuing it for hours, days or weeks, which I mentioned before. It drove his inquisitors nuts, as it sometimes had his friends.[86]

Similar attitudes can be seen in other known nonconfessors—for example, the Spaniard El Campesino. We can trace the tough temperaments elsewhere. In Pervouralsk, in 1938, the chief construction engineer at the Novo-Trubi Plant, who had been in prison for thirteen months, "little more than a skeleton in rags" and with patches of blood and bruises all over him, was interrogated by the local NKVD chief, Parshin. He was accused of having put wooden roofs over furnaces, which might well have caught fire. He continued to explain that though the roofs should have been made of iron, a Government order signed by Ordzhonikidze had ordered wood because of the iron shortage. To several similar questions, he answered in the same way.[87] Similar accounts are given all through the literature, though they are always treated as most exceptional; as we have noted, only about one in a hundred failed to confess.[88]

It is significant that many oppositionists who had repudiated the Bukharin view of Party discipline in the early 1930s did not come to trial. Stalin must have wanted Ryutin in the dock, but he did not get him. The same no doubt applies to Uglanov, Syrtsov, A. P. Smirnov, and the others who tried to organize resistance while the Right leaders were counseling patience. The absence in their make-ups of the Party fetishism noted in Bukharin, Zinoviev, and most of the other public confessors must be a factor. It is fairly clear that neither the pressures nor the arguments were enough to break many or, in other cases, to keep them broken. (Just as a number of prominent accused were not brought to trial with Slansky in Prague because they "would not behave in court," of fifty or sixty leading functionaries available, only fourteen were used.)[89]

According to most reports, there were several hundred candidates for the Moscow Trials, but only about seventy actually came into court. Of those named for complicity in the Zinoviev Trial, sixteen appeared at the time, three committed suicide, and seven were tried later. Forty-three others were never brought to trial and so never made public confessions. (They included men as prominent as Uglanov, Shlyapnikov, and Smilga. At least twenty-two of them must have been dropped at a fairly late stage. For the dossiers quoted from the preliminary investigation are numbered intermittently from 1 to 38.)

In the Pyatakov Trial, where dossiers ran from 1 to 36, there are nineteen missing. The leading figures have the low numbers: Pyatakov, 1; Radek, 5; Sokolnikov, 8; Drobnis, 13. Serebryakov and Muralov do not happen to be quoted; but even inserting their names, there are clearly missing volumes, and the presumption is that they existed and covered figures at this political level not brought to trial. This presumably includes those shot in secret a couple of weeks earlier, among them Ryutin and Smilga.

## THE IDEA OF CONFESSION

The question naturally arises, not only why the accused made the confessions, but also why the prosecution wanted them. In the public trials, indeed, as Radek pointed out in the dock, there was no other evidence. A case in which there was no evidence against the accused, who denied the charges, would clearly be rather a weak one by any standards.

In fact, confession is the logical thing to go for when the accused are not guilty and there is no genuine evidence. For in these circumstances, it is difficult to make people appear guilty unless they themselves admit it. And it is easier to stage-manage a trial of this sort if one can be sure that no awkward defendant is going to speak up at unpredictable intervals.

In general, moreover, in the public trials of Zinoviev and the others, the confession method can be easily accounted for. Stalin wanted not merely to kill his old opponents, but to destroy them morally and politically. It would have been difficult simply to announce the secret execution of Zinoviev. It would have been equally difficult to try him publicly, without any evidence, on charges which he could vigorously and effectively deny.

Even if confessions seem highly implausible, they may have some effect on skeptics, on the principles that there is no smoke without fire and that mud sticks. Even if the confession is disbelieved, a defendant who humbly confesses and admits that his opponents were right is to some extent discredited politically— certainly more than if, publicly, he had put up a stout fight. Even if the confession is disbelieved, it is striking demonstration of the power of the State over its opponents. It is more in accordance with totalitarian ideologies that a defendant should confess, even under duress: it is better discipline and a good example to all ranks. (Those who would not confess properly in court were sometimes provided with posthumous confessions, to keep up the standards, as with the Bulgarian Kostov in 1949.)

These are rational considerations. But it is also clear that the principle of confession in all cases, even from ordinary victims tried in secret, was insisted on. In fact, the major effort of the whole vast police organization throughout the country went into obtaining such confessions. When we read, in cases of no particular importance, and ones never to be made public, of the use of the ''conveyor'' system tying down team after team of police investigators for days on end, the impression one gets is not simply of vicious cruelty, but of insane preoccupation with a pointless formality. The accused could perfectly well, it seems, have been shot or sentenced without this frightful rigamarole.

But the extraordinary, contorted legalism of the whole operation remained to the end. It would have been possible simply to have deported thousands or millions of people on suspicion. Yet perhaps 100,000 examiners and other officials spent months interrogating and guarding prisoners who did not, during that time, even provide the State with any labor.[90] One explanation advanced in the prisons was that, apart from a hypocritical wish to preserve the façade, the absence of confessions would have made it much more difficult to find fresh inculpations.

It is also clear that the confession system, involving one single type of evidence, was easier to stereotype down the whole line of investigators than were more substantial methods of faking. When evidence of actual objects was involved, there was often trouble. In the Ukraine, a group of Socialist Revolutionaries confessed to having a secret arms cache, at the instance of an inexperienced interrogator. The first "conspirator" confessed to having put it in charge of another man. The second man, under torture, said that he had passed the weapons on to another member. They went through eleven hands until, after a discussion in his cell, the last consignee was urged to think of someone who had died whom he knew well. He could only remember his former geography master, a completely nonpolitical character who had just died, but maintained that the examiner would never believe him to have been a conspirator. He was finally persuaded that all the examiner wanted was to get rid of the arms somehow, so he made the confession as suggested, and the examiner was so delighted that he gave him a good meal and some tobacco.[91]

We may also feel that with the establishment of the confession principle in the public trials, its abandonment with lesser accused might have been taken in NKVD usage as an implied criticism of the trials. The principle had become established that a confession was the best result obtainable. Those who could obtain it were to be considered successful operatives, and a poor NKVD operative had a short life expectancy. Beyond all this, one forms the impression of a determination to break the idea of the truth, to impose on everyone the acceptance of official falsehood. In fact, over and above the rational motives for the extraction of confession, one seems to sense an almost metaphysical preference for it.

As early as 1918, Dzerzhinsky had remarked, of enemies of the Soviet Government, "When confronted with evidence, criminals in almost every case confess; and what argument can have greater weight than a criminal's own confession?"[92] Vyshinsky was the great theorist of confession. He regarded a confession, however obtained, as "in itself grounds for a conviction," and recommended prosecutors and investigators to make a practice of getting the defendant's testimony in his own handwriting, as looking more voluntary. He added, "I personally prefer a half confession in the defendant's own handwriting to a full confession in the investigator's writing," thereby, as a recent Soviet legal commentator remarks, "creating the appearance of the 'voluntary nature' of this testimony."[93] (One prisoner reports that after several days of bullying and beating to make him sign a confession which he had not read, with the interrogator showing especial rage at his obstinacy, he found himself unable to speak or use his hand, whereupon the interrogator put a pen in his fingers and signed it thus.)[94]

Vyshinsky's remark is interesting, as showing some awareness on the part of Stalin's entourage of the basic incredibility likely to attach to confessions. But as to their general desirability, we can note that Vyshinsky was not a man likely to intrude his own prejudices in a matter in which Stalin was deeply concerned. We can take it that basically the idea must have been Stalin's own. It involved endless thousands of men and women in days and months of mental and physical torment.

# BOOK II

# THE YEZHOV YEARS

*For the truth cannot be hid;*
*Somebody chose their pain,*
*What needn't have happened did.*
                    W. H. Auden

# LAST
# STAND

*Singleness of purpose became with him duplicity of action.*
Karl Marx on Ivan III

## AUTUMN MANEUVERS

The Zinoviev Trial, and particularly the executions, severely shook the "officer corps" of the Party—"those elements who, until recently, had considered themselves the sole possessors of the right to occupy themselves with politics."[1] Everything had been arranged without consulting them. Nothing could now be done about the dead. A dangerous precedent had been successfully established.

Preparations for the next round were already at hand. N. I. Muralov, former Inspector-General of the Red Army, had been arrested on 17 April 1936. He had previously been working in Western Siberia. On 5 and 6 August[2] two more ex-Trotskyites from the same area—Y. N. Drobnis and M. S. Boguslavsky—were pulled in. These were distinguished old revolutionaries of the second rank.

Drobnis, a worker, a shoemaker, an active revolutionary at the age of fifteen who had served six years in a Tsarist prison, had survived three death sentences. From one of these, when captured and wounded by the Whites during the Civil War, he had escaped by a rare chance. He had later been a Secretary of the Ukrainian Central Committee. The giant Muralov came from a poor toiling family and had joined workers' circles in 1899 and the Party in 1905.[3] He had had an extraordinary Civil War record. Boguslavsky, too, was a veteran of both the underground and the Civil War.

We have already noted the arrests of the more important figures of Sokolnikov (26 August) and Serebryakov (17 or 18 August),[4] who were under interrogation soon after. Sokolnikov was already confessing, though "vaguely," in August.[5] And as Vyshinsky had said in his statement of 21 August, Bukharin, Rykov, Pyatakov, Radek, and Uglanov were to be the subject of further investigation, with Tomsky, who had, however, escaped by suicide.

On 27 August, two days after the executions, most of the members of the Politburo* were in Moscow, including the Kiev-based Kossior and Postyshev. On

---

*Kossior, Voroshilov, Kalinin, Chubar, Kaganovich, Ordzhonikidze, Andreyev, and Postyshev (*Pravda,* 28 August 1936).

the last day of the month, Molotov returned from leave.[6] Apart from Mikoyan, the only full member not there was Stalin himself, who was still holidaying at Sochi, where he was to remain for several weeks. Yezhov, however, was in Moscow, and doubtless in touch with his superior.

Bukharin now wrote letters to the members of the Politburo and to Vyshinsky protesting his innocence, and followed them up on 1 September with a letter to Voroshilov in more personal terms, approving the executions and saying that perhaps even Tomsky had become involved with the opposition. Voroshilov answered curtly on 3 September, returning the letter and referring to Bukharin's "disgusting" attacks on the Party leadership. Bukharin then wrote to him again, defending himself at some length, but got no reply.[7]

Over the next week or so, the Party leadership discussed the cases of the newly incriminated, and the revulsion felt seems to have shown itself in opposition to further persecution. To question the guilt of Zinoviev and Kamenev, or the conduct of the case, was now impossible, for they were proven traitors. But with Bukharin and Rykov, it was different. Moreover, they were popular in the country and in the Party in a way that Zinoviev and Co. had never been. And the suicide of Tomsky had evidently been a severe shock.

On 8 September 1936, Bukharin and Rykov were brought to a "confrontation" with Sokolnikov in the presence of Kaganovich, Yezhov, and Vyshinsky. Sokolnikov repeated the charges, but said he had no direct evidence and had heard of the Rightist involvement only from Kamenev. When the guards removed Sokolnikov, Kaganovich said to Bukharin that the testimony was all lies and that Bukharin should go back to his editorial offices and work tranquilly.[8]

On 10 September, in a small paragraph at the top of page 2, *Pravda* announced that the investigation into the charges against Rykov and Bukharin was being dropped, for lack of evidence. This reversal is said to have been made "under pressure of some members of the Politburo."[9]

Politically, the exculpation is understandable. From a judicial point of view, it is fantastic. The accused in the Zinoviev Case had been sentenced to execution on their own evidence against themselves. But their evidence against Rykov and Bukharin was of exactly the same status, neither more nor less credible. It might be thought that this alone would have shown Western observers the meaninglessness of the whole trial. (Moreover, though the case against the two Rightists was suspended, it was not found necessary to make amends to their colleague Tomsky. Article 107 of the Criminal Code of the RSFSR laid down penalties for provoking suicide by moral or physical persecution. It was not applied.)

It is improbable that a majority against the Purge now existed in the Politburo. Voroshilov, Kaganovich, and probably Andreyev were by now committed to it. Molotov, too, must already have learned his lesson. At least, he was back in good odor by 21 September,[10] when an alleged attempt on his life was being put into the scenario for the next trial. And this return to favor can hardly be accounted for except on the view that he had aligned himself wholeheartedly with Stalin's plans in the September discussions.

Nevertheless, Stalin retreated as far as the two Rightists were concerned. He had, it should be noted, never committed himself finally to their arrest. He may well have intended no more at this stage than a preliminary sounding, a putting of the Bukharin problem on the agenda, as it were, in his usual devious style. In that case, it was not a question of decisive votes in the supreme body. And in his absence, his own prestige was not directly involved.

As I write in 1989, there is still some uncertainty about the plenums of the Central Committee which took place in the last half of 1936, but were never announced. For many years, the only reference to any in an official document came in evidence at a later trial referring to "one of the autumn plenums of the Central Committee of the Party," which, from the context, must have been after March 1936 and before 1937.[11] Roy Medvedev writes of "one of the plenary sessions held in the late summer or early autumn of 1936," at which the arrest of Pyatakov (and "apparently" of Sokolnikov) was sanctioned.[12]

As to "late summer," one former official has described a four-day plenum held in early September, with the Bukharin issue debated on the last day. But this is hard to reconcile with the absence of various leaders, and it shows signs of confusion with later plenums. Moreover, we are told that a plenum discussed the Bukharin issue "for the first time" in December.[13] The December plenum (described as "unofficial") was only confirmed in 1988.[14] If the other was convened in "early autumn," it was presumably in late September or October.

As for the constitutional point, this does not, after all, help us with this plenum's dating. Khrushchev remarks that the Central Committee members arrested in 1937 and 1938 were expelled from the Party illegally through gross violation of the Party statutes, since the question of their expulsion was never studied at a Central Committee plenary session. By implication, the arrests of Pyatakov and Sokolnikov, the only Central Committee member and candidate member known to have been arrested in 1936, *were* legalized. But we are now told that this was not done, as Khrushchev implies, by a plenum. Instead, the Central Committee was *polled* on 25–26 August in the case of Sokolnikov, and on 10–11 September in the case of Pyatakov.[15] The plenum, when it assembled, was presumably required to vote formal approval. It was quite a different matter, as yet, from proceeding against men like Kamenev and Zinoviev, already in jail, already expelled from the Party.

Stalin had made certain gains. The materials were in his hand for prolonging the Purge. He now had, after all, a reasonable quota for the next trial: Serebryakov and Sokolnikov, and now Radek, arrested on 22 September, and Pyatakov, who had been taken on 12 September, while Sokolnikov (though not Serebryakov) was already confessing. The failure over Bukharin and Rykov, even if Stalin had not been certain of success at the first attempt, evidently rankled. It was plain that a powerful effort, a new campaign, would be needed. In the Black Sea sunshine, he considered the next move. The Soviet press concerned itself with other matters: democracy, the triumph of Soviet aviation, the successful harvest, and massive support for the struggle of the Spanish Republic.

Like a general who transfers the weight of his offensive from a line where the going is heavy to an easier approach, Stalin shifted his attack to Yagoda.

Yagoda's position at that time remains something of a mystery. It is clear that he was involved in the preparations for the 1936 Trial from the start—though perhaps excluded from the key discussions and conversations preceding the case. He is indeed said to have "urged that the case be discussed in the Politburo."[16]

At the same time, it seems that he was himself deceived by Stalin's assurance that Zinoviev and Kamenev would not be executed.[17] He was later to be accused of shielding I. N. Smirnov—though there was an obvious motive here, in that this was advanced as an explanation for Smirnov's unsatisfactory behavior in the dock.[18] Nevertheless, it does seem that Yagoda may have made some attempt to temper the wind to the oppositionists.[19] He was to be similarly accused of ordering that Uglanov's testimony be kept "within certain limits."[20] And there are other reports of underground obstruction within the NKVD which took the form of framing questions in such a way as to protect those interrogated.[21] The most likely occasion for the development of more definite resistance on Yagoda's part would be *following* the executions. This could only have manifested itself in the discussions about the fates of Bukharin and Rykov.

We can be sure that Yezhov (who was to replace Yagoda) offered stronger resistance to clearing the Rightists. He seems to have acquiesced very reluctantly in the decision. He regarded the rehabilitation of Bukharin and Rykov as temporary, "vowing that he would yet make good the 'mistake,' "[22] and he and Agranov almost immediately started accusing Yagoda of laxness.

For the moment, Bukharin and Rykov were safe. The former continued to hold his position as editor of *Izvestiya,* and both remained candidate members of the Central Committee. It was clear that some leaders hoped that the momentum of the Purge would peter out with the forthcoming Pyatakov Case. But if Stalin could not obtain the support he needed in the highest Party bodies, he had other methods of gaining his ends. He proceeded to the coup which was to bring the Terror to its most frightful climax—the appointment of Yezhov as People's Commissar for Internal Affairs.

On 25 September, Stalin and Zhdanov sent a telegram from Sochi to Kaganovich, Molotov, "and other members of the Political Bureau":

> We deem it absolutely necessary and urgent that Comrade Yezhov be nominated to the post of People's Commissar for Internal Affairs. Yagoda had definitely proved himself to be incapable of unmasking the Trotskyite–Zinovievite bloc. The OGPU is four years behind in this matter. This is noted by all Party workers and by the majority of the representatives of the NKVD.[23]

The "four years" is significant and sinister. It was four years almost to the day since the September session of 1932 which had blocked the attempt to execute Ryutin. It has since been suggested that the phrase might refer to the four years passed after meetings and connections between Trotsky's son and Soviet sympathizers, and the alleged formation of the Trotskyite–Zinovievite bloc, in 1932. But the chief offender, I. N. Smirnov, had been arrested within weeks, and since 1934 the NKVD had been finishing off Trotskyites and Zinovievites by the score, so could hardly have been said to have fallen behind four years. The point is hardly a crucial one. But in fact it was now that Ryutin was brought back to the Lubyanka from an isolator and his interrogation began. On 4 November, he was signing a "categorical refusal" to confess to terrorism.[24] It seems certain that Stalin proposed to use him in the next show trial, but despite "illegal methods" he remained recalcitrant.

No one, of course, thought for a moment that Yagoda's removal indicated mere "incapability." It was at once noted in the Party that "it was not a question of dissatisfaction with his insufficiently active work . . . this indicated political distrust of him."[25]

The transfer of Yezhov to duties that he was already much concerned with in any case could hardly have been the occasion for members of the Politburo to oppose the General Secretary, even if Ordzhonikidze, Chubar, or Kossior might have wished this. Although the tone and the intention of the new appointment would be obvious, as a practical measure it would be hard to argue against.

The following day, Molotov carried out instructions. The shift was used to rid the Soviet Government of Rykov. Next day, the papers announced Rykov's "release," without the conventional comment that he was going to "other work"; the appointment of Yagoda to Rykov's post of People's Commissar of Communications; and Yezhov's appointment as Head of the NKVD.

On 29 September 1936 (and again on 21 October 1936) circulars were issued from the Central Committee. They called in effect for the end of unfair expulsions from the Party and a stepping-up of fair ones. They were followed by press censures of a number of local leaders for failure in one or another of these respects. On 29 September, too, a secret directive (drafted by Kaganovich, accepted by the Politburo, and signed by Stalin) called for settling with the Trotskyite–Zinovievites, including not only those arrested whose interrogation was complete, and those like Muralov, Pyatakov, and Beloborodov, whose investigation had not yet ended, but also "those who were earlier exiled."[26] That is to say, Ryutin and others who had never been Trotskyites or Zinovievites.

Yagoda handed over his office on 30 September 1936. On the same day, the announcement of M. D. Berman as Deputy Head of the NKVD was made, while Yagoda's Second Deputy, G. E. Prokofiev, was transferred with him. On 17 October, a more sinister figure still, the puffy-faced M. P. Frinovsky, was also appointed a Deputy Head of the NKVD (and on 3 November, L. N. Bel'ski). Neither Berman nor Frinovsky nor Bel'ski had been serving in the old Secret Police apparatus proper. Berman had headed the Labor Camp Administration, Gulag; Frinovsky commanded the Frontier Guards; while Bel'ski was Head of the Militia. Otherwise, the old NKVD chiefs were not yet disturbed. Even Yagoda's personal assistant remained in the NKVD for some time. Molchanov and the other departmental chiefs kept their posts, though Yezhov brought in his own men from the Central Committee apparatus to help them in their work, and to learn how to supplant them.

A team of more than twenty-five interrogators headed by Agranov started to prepare the new trial.[27] The original script for this described Pyatakov and his fellow accused simply as a "Reserve Center" which had plotted but not acted. By this means, the case was represented as less serious than that of August, and one not implying the death penalty. It was no doubt partly by this means that Stalin had gained the leadership's consent to go forward with the Pyatakov Case— which, it might be hoped, would be no more than a tidying-up of loose ends in a fairly restrained fashion.

But after the NKVD had proceeded on these lines for a few weeks, the line suddenly changed. Molchanov, in Yezhov's presence, instructed a meeting of interrogators that "a new line of investigation" was to be pursued. The accused were to be required to confess that they had plotted to seize power and had worked with the Nazis for this purpose.[28]

Stalin had not, since Radek's recantation in the 1920s, had anything to complain about from him. He had betrayed Trotsky's emissary, Blyumkin, who as a result was shot in 1929. In early September 1936, Radek wanted to remind the General Secretary of these services in exposing Trotskyites, but feared that if he himself wrote to Stalin, his message would be intercepted by the NKVD. So he had asked Bukharin to write to Stalin about it if he himself were arrested.[29] Radek was one man who had truly burned his bridges to the opposition; at the same time, he was nowhere regarded as a serious politician, and there was no question of his ever competing for even the lowest rung of power. What Stalin's motive was in bringing Radek in particular into the plot at all is obscure. It may simply be that until he could secure the arrest of the Rightists, he was rather low on big names for another trial. And Radek was at least a very well-known man.

Sokolnikov seems to have had an interview with Stalin and to have been promised his life. It is not clear why Sokolnikov believed this promise. It was, in all probability, made before the execution of Zinoviev and his followers. But Sokolnikov seems to have been convinced of its efficacy even after the executions. But in any case, he had little choice. He had a young wife and a son by a previous marriage who was in his twenties.[30]

Sokolnikov was brought to a "confrontation" with Radek immediately after the latter's arrest.[31] This did not lead to anything at once. Radek was worked on on the "conveyor" system by Kedrov and other interrogators.[32] At first he resisted stubbornly.

The sacrifice of Pyatakov is perhaps the clearest sign of Stalin's motives. He had been, it was true, an oppositionist, and an important one. But he had abandoned opposition in 1928 and had worked with complete loyalty ever since. He was regarded by the Trotskyites as a deserter. Trotsky's son Sedov, chancing to meet him on the Unter den Linden, had publicly insulted him.[33] He had not liked, but he had honestly accepted, Stalin's leadership. There was, in his case, no real question—as might have been thought of Zinoviev and Kamenev, and of Bukharin—of any desire to present an alternative leadership.

And his services to Stalin's Government were extremely valuable. His energy and intelligence, probably unrivaled in the whole leadership, had been channeled into carrying out Stalin's industrialization plans.

What was there to be said against him?

He had loyally accepted the Stalin leadership, but he would have accepted an alternative leadership if Stalin could have been overthrown; he supported him with reservations. He had been a major critic of Stalin's in the 1920s. He had made it clear that he regarded his rise to power as unfortunate. Above all, he was even now, whatever his own desires, leadership timber. Lenin had named him among the six most important figures in the Party (of them all, Stalin was to allow none but himself to survive). He had even been thought of as an alternative Prime Minister to Lenin in the "Left Communist" plans of 1918.

Ordzhonikidze, as People's Commissar for Heavy Industry, depended entirely on the genius of Pyatakov, and was generous enough to admit this. Pyatakov's was the brain and the driving force behind the Plan, creating a major industrial base against all the handicaps that resulted from Stalin's system—the wastages due to the purges of experts, the establishment of impossible prestige targets, and the suspicions and inefficiencies of administrators.

There is a report that after Pyatakov's arrest, but before its announcement, the director of a scientific institute who knew of it made a public attack on him in Ordzhonikidze's presence. Ordzhonikidze interrupted him with the remark "It is very easy to attack a man who is not there to defend himself. Wait till Yuri Leonidovich returns."[34]

But Pyatakov broke down comparatively quickly—in thirty-three days (Radek held out for two months and eighteen days, Serebryakov for three months and sixteen days, Muralov for seven months and seventeen days). We have already noted the extravagance of Pyatakov's earlier submission to "the Party." When he was incriminated in August 1936, Yezhov had told him that he was being demoted to a post in the Urals. He denied the terrorist charges (Yezhov reported), but said that he deserved demotion for not having denounced his ex-wife's connections with Trotskyites. To regain the trust of the Party, he would be willing to appear for the prosecution at a trial, and would personally offer to shoot all the accused, including his ex-wife, and announce this publicly. Yezhov said that this was absurd. Pyatakov then wrote to Stalin, denying the accusations and saying that he would die for the Party and Stalin. He was to have his wish, but not yet.[35]

## SABOTEURS IN SIBERIA

One theme already well established in Soviet mythology, that of sabotage, had not been raised in the Zinoviev Trial. It would have been difficult, in fact, to charge men who were all either in prison or cut off from major work with such acts; anybody can commit assassination, but sabotage is carried out by industrialists and engineers or, anyhow, people with access to the relevant machines. Almost all those in the group now coming to trial had held, until shortly before their arrests, posts as People's Commissars, Assistant People's Commissars, leaders of industrial complexes, engineers, and so forth. And to show that no breach in tradition was intended, they were specifically linked with the saboteurs of the earlier period.

The concept of sabotage as a political weapon is in general an absurd one. The very word, with its implications of peasants throwing clogs into machinery, is a fair description of what is almost invariably an individual and illiterate protest. The only real exception is to be found in large underground movements in occupied countries in time of war, operating with the sympathy of most of the population. In those circumstances, on the one hand, it becomes possible on a fairly wide scale; and on the other, it becomes, or at least appears to be, a genuine contribution to the defeat of the enemy. In peacetime, a small conspiracy could scarcely hope to achieve any political result whatever by such means. In any case, plotters working to remove the political leadership by terror would hardly dissipate their forces, or run the extra risk of discovery, for local and indecisive actions of this type. Nor had any previous conspiracy of the sort ever done so. The illogic of the accusations was not the sort of consideration to stop Stalin, and over the following years sabotage became the theme of a mass purge at all levels.

The official definition of sabotage was now extended, and the penalties for it were made more severe: "On 29 November 1936, Vyshinsky ordered that within a month all criminal cases of major conflagrations, accidents and output of poor-quality products be reviewed and studied with the aim of exposing a counter-revolutionary and saboteur background in them and making the guilty parties more heavily liable." [36]

In the new industrial region of the Upper Ob basin—the "Kuzbas"—almost 2,000 miles east of Moscow, a number of reconstructed Trotskyites held posts suitable to their condition. The great plants had gone up, amid a squalor for the workers—mainly deportees—which the old industrial revolutions in the capitalist West had not matched. At the same time, unrelenting pressure for results at all costs had led to the virtual abandonment of the usual sort of safety precautions. Frightful accidents were common.

On 23 September 1936 there was an explosion in the Tsentralnaya Mine at Kemerovo. Its director, Noskov, and several of his subordinates were at once arrested. His superior, Norkin, Head of the Kemerovo Combined Works Construction Trust since 1932, was arrested on 30 September.[37] For the NKVD this was a most useful line of responsibility, as Norkin was an immediate link with Drobnis and, through him, with Muralov. A whole "Trotskyite nest" in West Siberia, operating moreover under the direct orders of the Deputy People's Commissar for Heavy Industry, Pyatakov, was thus laid open to easy attack. To make it yet easier, the NKVD ordered its representative in the Kemerovo industrial area, Shestov, to accept the role of accomplice.[38]

It was thus possible to establish the idea of widespread sabotage before Pyatakov and the others came to trial. From 19 to 22 November, a great trial took place in Novosibirsk, before a court of the Military Collegium under Ulrikh, in which the accidents in the mines and factories of that city and Kemerovo were charged against Noskov and eight other defendants, including a German engineer, Stickling. In addition, the charge was now put forward that an attempt had been made to assassinate Molotov. The defendants were linked, through Drobnis and Shestov (who appeared as "witnesses"), with Muralov and Pyatakov.

At this trial there were confessions, and even documents, about an anti-Soviet printing establishment. It seems that this actually existed. The cellar where it had stood still showed signs of its presence three years later. But the whole thing had been an NKVD operation. The job had been done at night by prisoners under guard awaiting execution. As to the thousands of leaflets supposed to have been distributed, it was clear that this had not happened, since anyone caught with such a leaflet would have been arrested, and no one in Kemerovo knew of any such arrests. One local commented, "Maybe the conspirators printed them up just to provide themselves with bedtime stories." [39]

One of the accused, the German engineer Stickling, was not given a death sentence. Later, in the Gestapo prison in Lublin, he said that his confession was false, and implied that it had been obtained because the NKVD was able to black-mail him about his private life.[40]

A Soviet industrialist who was sent to Kemerovo in 1939, and actually took over the very office from which Norkin had allegedly organized his crimes, has produced an account of the background of the trial. As a prominent local figure pointed out, though the saboteurs were now dead, the accidents still went on. In any case, if engineers had really wished to make trouble, it was clear that they could have blown the whole place to pieces. Moreover, in the files there were many reports from the executed men sent by them to the Commissariat of Heavy Industry coal administration warning about the conditions which were bound to lead to accidents.[41]

But the Tsentralnaya Mine disaster was not the only one which a determined investigation could turn up in the Kuzbas. On 29 October, a Commission of Experts was sent to Kemerovo to investigate two explosions and other accidents which had taken place in the plants of the Kemerovo Combined Works Construction Trust in February, March, and April 1936. A similar body started work on a series of pit fires in the nearby Prokopyevsk coal mines—sixty of these had occurred up to the end of 1935.[42] The experts produced findings of sabotage. The material now available was sufficient by any standards to damn the West Siberian defendants.

Although this West Siberian group was to provide no less than seven out of the seventeen accused in the forthcoming trial, two other sabotage groups were also being prepared. One was headed by Rataichak, Chief of the Central Administration of the Chemical Industry in Pyatakov's Commissariat: on 22 October 1936 the Head of the Gorlovka Nitrogen Fertilizer Works, Pushin, was arrested in connection with an explosion there on 11 November 1935. He confessed at once and implicated his chief.[43] This group of saboteurs was completed by an NKVD agent, Hrasche,[44] who worked in the Foreign Division of Rataichak's Administration, and so formed a useful link with Japanese espionage and other sinister foreign forces.

More important was the third and last of the saboteur groups—that devoted to wrecking the railways. Its three leaders were Yakov Livshits, an Old Bolshevik and reformed Trotskyite, who was now Kaganovich's Deputy People's Commissar of Communications, and the lesser figures of Knyazev, Assistant Chief of the Central Traffic Department in the Commissariat, who had formerly been Head of the South Urals Railway, and Turok, Assistant Head of the Traffic Department of the Perm Railway.

Livshits's dismissal was announced on 14 November, and Knyazev was giving evidence in mid-December, later than the other main figures, so it seems that the railway theme was the last to be brought in. It implicated in particular Serebryakov, who had run the Commissariat in the 1920s, and it linked up with Boguslavsky, who was responsible for railway wrecking in the West Siberian set-up.

The charge of sabotage was a serious one. But, ironically enough, it could have been represented to the Central Committee as a sign of possible clemency. Professor Ramzin, the main "saboteur" in the "Industrial Party" Case, not only had been amnestied a couple of years after sentence and repentance, but had been restored to office and to favor, and even awarded an Order.*

Stalin is reported back in Moscow, from his holiday, at a reception for a Mongolian delegation on 4 November. With him were several members of the Polit-

---

*In the January 1937 Trial itself, there was to be a curious reflection of this attitude: an engineer formerly sentenced in connection with the Shakhty Trial, Boyarshchinov, was referred to as having become an honest Soviet engineer, killed by the conspirators because he was exposing their wrongful methods of work.

buro, including Mikoyan and, of course, Yezhov. At the 7 November Parade, all the Politburo members based in Moscow were on the stand.

The slogans for this nineteenth anniversary of the Revolution included a violent attack on the Trotskyite–Zinovievite spies. There was no reference to the Right deviation, which presumably shows that the issue was still in abeyance. But the cat-and-mouse game with Bukharin continued. At the Red Square celebrations, he and his wife were on one of the minor stands. A soldier came over with Stalin's invitation to join him on the Lenin mausoleum.[45] Soon after, Bukharin was served with an eviction order from his Kremlin apartment. Stalin telephoned, and on being told of this said angrily that the evictors must get out immediately, and they did so.[46]

And now Stalin, perhaps looking ahead from the purge of the ex-oppositionists to the completer sweep he was to make of the Party, made his first move against one of his own followers.

Postyshev had served in Kiev from 1923, becoming a Secretary of the Kiev Committee in 1924, and from 1926 to 1930 had been a member of the Ukrainian Politburo, before going to Moscow to be a Secretary of the Central Committee. He had been again intruded on the Ukrainian apparatus in January 1933 to toughen it in its difficult struggle with the peasantry and Ukrainian national feeling. Although Kossior and his group were not displaced, as much power and prestige attached to Postyshev as to his theoretical superior. In addition to his Ukrainian Second Secretaryship, he held the First Secretaryship of the Kiev Provincial Committee of the Party.

During the whole period, it became customary to give Postyshev what, on the face of it, looked like an anomalous seniority. When greetings were sent to the Soviet Government, to the Central Committee of the All-Union Communist Party, or to the Ukrainian Government, in each case only the single leading figure was named as the recipient. But when it came to the Ukrainian Central Committee, both Kossior and Postyshev were conventionally named.*

A younger and better-looking man than most of the others, with a clipped moustache and high hair swept back over his oval head, Postyshev was in fact an irreproachable Stalinist. His reputation for fair-mindedness (within the limits of the system) was fairly good. It is said that he had been among the opponents of the proposal to shoot Ryutin, and had redeemed himself in Kiev. Opposition from such a source could, as with Kirov's, have been a real threat.

Postyshev had been interpreting the Central Committee circulars on expelling Party members in the wrong fashion. He was expelling provocateurs and slanderers and retaining their victims. One of these delators was a woman called Nikolayenko, who had been particularly troublesome for a year.[47] Postyshev had expelled her from the Kiev Party organization.

Clearly, this expulsion was an action totally contrary to the whole spirit of the Purge and particularly to Central Committee decisions of 29 September and

---

*For example, in *Pravda* of 6 January 1937, a Ukrainian public report is made to all four bodies: to the Central Committee in Moscow, it simply goes to Stalin; to the Central Committee in Kiev, to both Kossior and Postyshev. All this was later to be censured as a personality cult, reflecting years of complacency on the part of Postyshev and his entourage, who as a result had "let in enemies" (*Pravda*, 29 May 1937).

21 October 1936, which may indeed have already been aimed at Postyshev. Everywhere, as the "Yezhovshchina" got going, it was precisely through the denunciation by such types that the police got their grip on the leaders of the Party organizations. It was later to be alleged that in Kiev, more than anywhere else in the Ukraine, Trotskyites had been able to gain important posts.[48] Postyshev's attitude is thus plainly established as being against this system, even before the showdown. In November, Stalin, seeking a pretext, took over the Nikolayenko case.[49] The Central Committee apparatus in Moscow, that is to say, examined her appeal against expulsion in a favorable fashion. She was later found to have the execution of "some eight thousand people" on her conscience.[50]

The New Constitution finally passed into law amid a fanfare of speeches, ovations, and a press campaign which culminated in a speech by Stalin on 27 November. He went at great length into the questions which had arisen about how best to guarantee democracy, freedom of the subject, and all the other attributes of a State fully attuned to the people's will.

Meanwhile, the issue of Bukharin and Rykov again came to the fore. Even before Yagoda's fall, the NKVD was sending Stalin the interrogation records of E. F. Kulikov and others, which implicated Bukharin, Rykov, and Tomsky. On 7 October, Tomsky's former secretary, Stankin (admitting to implication in a terrorist act planned against Stalin for November 6), gave testimony that Tomsky had told her of a "Right Counter-Revolutionary Center" consisting of "Tomsky, Bukharin, Rykov, Uglanov, [V. V.] Shmidt and Syrtsov." The former director of the Lenin Library, V. I. Nevsky, gave testimony on 23 November that Bukharin, Rykov, and Tomsky were the leaders of the counter-revolutionary Rightist organization. (In January 1937, he was to withdraw this, and at his secret trial on 25 May 1937 he said that the NKVD had insisted on his signing it in the interests of the Party.)[51]

The Central Committee plenum met on 4 to 7 December. On 4 December, Yezhov reported on "the Trotskyite and Rightist anti-Soviet organizations" and said that Bukharin and Rykov had not "laid down their arms" but had gone underground. He produced the evidence of Kulikov and others, and Bukharin and Rykov were violently denounced by Kaganovich, Molotov, and Voroshilov. Although many seem to have remained silent, and Ordzhonikidze is reported as making remarks implying distrust of Yezhov,[52] many speakers demanded the expulsion of the two Rightists from the Central Committee and the Party (all the Central Committee—including Bukharin and Rykov themselves—had been receiving confidential copies of the testimony against the two men). They strongly denied the accusations. During intervals they were brought to confrontations with Kulikov and with Pyatakov and Sosnovsky. But Stalin again temporized, and the plenum accepted his proposal "to consider the question of Rykov and Bukharin as incomplete. Further investigation to be undertaken, a decision postponed until the next plenum."[53]

It was now that many of the accused in the Pyatakov Case were beginning to confess. This may show that a reluctant compromise had been reached among the leadership about the trial. At any rate, Ordzhonikidze already seems to have obtained from Stalin a promise to spare Pyatakov's life. Comparable tactics, combined with the conveyor and the *stoika*, helped with others.[54] On 4 December,

Radek gave his first evidence. He had in the end decided to surrender if Stalin would give him the same guarantee he had given Sokolnikov. For some time Stalin refused to see him—but finally, it is said, he visited the Lubyanka and had a long talk with Radek in the presence of Yezhov. Radek then became the closest collaborator of the interrogation, and helped replan the scenario of the plot.[55] Muralov, who had held out so long, now gave in—reportedly under Radek's influence—and on the following day he too was confessing. Norkin started confessing about the same time. By January, hundreds of pages of evidence from all the defendants were in the files.

On the anniversary of the founding of the Secret Police, 20 December 1936, Stalin gave a small banquet for the heads of the NKVD. Yezhov, Frinovsky, Pauker, and others were present. Afterward, an account of what happened circulated among the NKVD. When everyone had drunk a good deal, Pauker, supported by two other officers acting the parts of warders, played for Stalin the part of Zinoviev being dragged to execution. He hung by their arms, moaning and mouthing, then fell on his knees, and, holding one of the warders by the boots, cried out, "Please, for God's sake, Comrade, call up Yosif Vissarionovich!"

Stalin roared with laughter, and Pauker gave a repeat performance. By this time, Stalin was almost helpless with laughing, and when Pauker brought in a new angle by raising his hands and crying, "Hear, Israel, our God is the only God!" Stalin choked with mirth and had to signal Pauker to stop the performance.[56]

In fact, Stalin had good reason to be pleased with his secret policemen, who had their second production almost ready to go on. He now ordered pursuit of the line on which he had been blocked in the autumn. Bukharin and Rykov were to be implicated. At the end of December 1936, Radek's evidence incriminating the Rightists in terrorism and other crimes was delivered to Bukharin, whose life now became a nightmare of denunciations and confrontations,[57] until, on 16 January 1937, his name appeared for the last time as editor of *Izvestiya*.

A number of the Rightists under arrest, including Uglanov and V. V. Shmidt, did not give evidence against Bukharin before his own arrest. Some of his junior associates, however, were testifying to his plans for a "palace coup," and their statements were sent to him.[58] Bukharin was then called in for several confrontations in the presence of the whole Politburo and Yezhov. First the prominent ex-Trotskyite Sosnovsky gave testimony that some money Bukharin had given him when he was in trouble was a conspiratorial payment.[59] Then came a confrontation with Pyatakov. Pyatakov is described as looking like a skeleton, and so weak that he could hardly stand. When he had confessed his membership in a counter-revolutionary center, implicating Bukharin, Ordzhonikidze asked him if his testimony was voluntary. He replied that it was.[60] The next confrontation was with Radek. Although pale, he was not in such a bad state as Pyatakov, and, unlike the lifelessness reported of the others, was "visibly agitated." He confessed everything, on his own behalf and Bukharin's, including a plot of theirs at *Izvestiya* to assassinate Stalin.[61] Rykov, who had earlier been sent confessions implicating him made by his secretary Ekaterina Artemenko, also had "confrontations" with Sokolnikov, Pyatakov, and others.[62] Meanwhile, with the Bukharin–Rykov group thoroughly implicated, Stalin was fully prepared to face the resistance of his own "moderates" squarely.

The intervention against Postyshev in the Nikolayenko case was made formal by a decision of the All-Union Central Committee, dated 13 January 1937 (and unpublished at the time), attacking "unsatisfactory leadership" in the Kiev Party and faults in the Ukrainian Central Committee as a whole.[63]

Postyshev expressed his resentment. As a result, Kaganovich was immediately sent to Kiev to straighten out the situation. In his capacity as Secretary of the Central Committee, he urgently convoked a plenum of the Kiev Provincial Party Committee.[64] On 16 January 1937 he had Postyshev replaced as First Secretary of the Kiev Provincial Committee, while leaving him his more important post. The official reason given was that Postyshev's duties as Second Secretary of the Ukrainian Party were too demanding to allow him to hold the Kiev post as well. This was plainly false; indeed, when Khrushchev was appointed in 1938 to be First Secretary of the Ukrainian Party, he held the Kiev post as well without any difficulty arising.

So far, this was no more than one of Stalin's typical first steps against a victim. Meanwhile, the preparations for the Pyatakov Trial were complete. First, however, the recalcitrant figures of Ryutin and others in like case were disposed of. On 10 January, he, Smilga, Zalutsky, Shatskin, and no doubt others were tried *in camera* by the Military Collegium and shot.[65]

## THE PYATAKOV TRIAL

On 23 January 1937 another gruesome little pageant assembled among the florid columns of the October Hall. It was a bitterly cold day, and the hall was dark and gloomy. Just after midday, Ulrikh and Matulevich, with Divisional Military Jurist Rychkov in Nikitchenko's old place, took their seats at the judges' bench. Vyshinsky sat at his old table on the left. The NKVD soldiers were in their winter uniforms, with long coats and muffled helmets.

The men who filed into the dock were of a different sort from those of the previous August. Then, genuine rivals had been crushed. The new accused had presented no such obvious challenge. But they were quite impressive figures. Pyatakov had never been a member of the Politburo, but as we have seen he had long been one of the most prominent and able figures in the Party. Sokolnikov, former candidate member of the Politburo, was a most serious and respected politician. Serebryakov, former Secretary of the Central Committee, was also no negligible figure. And Radek was at least a widely known public person.

The new trial did not have the immediate and obvious aims of the first. The motives remaining are plain enough. First, revenge. Most of the leading ex-Trotskyites were now destroyed. And revenge carried with it, of course, Stalin's idea of precautionary or preventive measures. A clean sweep, even if there was no more compelling reason for action by normal standards, fitted Stalin's firm belief in "Stone dead hath no fellow" and "Better safe than sorry."

Moreover, Stalin had been temporarily balked of a more important prey—Bukharin and the Rightists. The trial was thus not the one he had intended, but a pale substitute. At the same time, it kept the pot boiling. It provided continuity. And it could be, and was, used to implicate the Right once again. A minor mystery, given this motive of Stalin's, is why Uglanov was not brought into it. He had been named as subject to investigation in the announcement of 21 August. He was not among those rehabilitated in September, and yet he was not tried. It would have been greatly to Stalin's advantage to have put up so prominent a Rightist in January 1937, as a bridge to Bukharin and Co. And even though Yagoda is alleged to have protected him, there was time, on ordinary reckoning, between Yagoda's fall and the January 1937 Trial for Yezhov to prepare him. One can only presume that, as we have said, he refused to talk.

The new batch of accused were designated simply "the Anti-Soviet Trotskyite Center." No other group or faction was represented, unlike the case at the 1936 Trial of the "Trotskyite–Zinovievite Terrorist Center" or the later "Bloc of Rights and Trotskyites." The first trial had anyhow been, as we saw, unimpressive on the Trotskyite side. Radek was now put up to say,

> If you take the composition of the old centre you will find that the Trotskyites did not have a single one of the old political leaders on it. There were Smirnov, who was more of an organizer than a political leader; Mrachkovsky, a soldier and a fighting man; and Ter-Vaganyan, a propagandist.[66]

Since there were no genuine Trotskyites to hand, as there were genuine Zinovievites and genuine Rightists, the distinguished *ex*-Trotskyites had to serve.

In other ways, the new accused presented a different impression from that of their predecessors. Then, there had been a seven-man "Center," plus various hangers-on. This time, the Center consisted of only four people: Pyatakov, Radek, Serebryakov, and Sokolnikov. Radek and Sokolnikov were not accused of crimes as serious as those of the other two. Pyatakov and Serebryakov were charged with organizing three main sabotage groups (among dozens they had allegedly set up): the railway-wrecking organization headed by Livshits; the "West Siberian Anti-Soviet Trotskyite Center" at Novosibirsk, consisting of Muralov, Boguslavsky, and Drobnis, having under them a variety of industrial wreckers in the area; and the three wreckers in the chemical industry, coming directly under Pyatakov. The specializations were not complete; for example, the railway wrecker Knyazev was also a Japanese spy, while the coal wreckers of Siberia were also the organizers of the attempted assassination of all visiting Politburo members.

The indictment differed greatly from that of August 1936. Then, it had simply been a matter of terrorism. It had been remarked by Vyshinsky and in evidence that the accused had no policy except the seizure of power from Stalin. But such a policy was by no means unpopular,[67] and soon after the executions the press had started to announce that Zinoviev did have a political program after all—one involving the restoration of capitalism, which he had naturally tried to conceal.[68] Stalin was to remark:

> At the Trial in 1936, if you will remember, Kamenev and Zinoviev categorically denied that they had any kind of political platform. They had full opportunity to unfold their political platform at the Trial. Nevertheless, they did not do so, declaring

that they had no political platform whatsoever. There can be no doubt that they both lied in denying that they had a platform.[69]

This theme was strongly put in the new indictment. The accused intended to renounce industrialization and collectivization, and they relied for support in particular on the German and Japanese Governments. They proposed to make territorial concessions to Germany, to allow German capital into the country, and in case of war with Germany to carry out wrecking in industry and at the front. This had all been arranged at a meeting between Trotsky and Rudolf Hess.

Trotsky had also at least implied the desirability of defeat in war, having allegedly written to Radek: "It must be admitted that the question of power will become a practical issue for the bloc only as a result of the defeat of the U.S.S.R. in war. For this the bloc must make energetic preparations. . . ."[70]

Espionage contact had been established with the Germans and Japanese. And, as in the Zinoviev Trial, a number of terrorist groups had been organized, "in Moscow, Leningrad, Kiev, Rostov, Sochi, Novosibirsk and other towns." An attempt had actually been made on Molotov's life by involving him in a car crash at Prokopyevsk in 1934. Nor had their practical activity been limited to the preparation of terrorist acts. In addition, they had been responsible for many industrial accidents and deficiencies.

Other activities likely to prove more unpopular than assassination had been thrown in for good measure. For example, Knyazev was quoted as having confessed that "the Japanese intelligence service strongly stressed the necessity of using bacteriological means in time of war with the object of contaminating troop trains, canteens and army sanitary centres with highly virulent bacilli. . . ."*[71]

Although such accusations transferred unpleasant responsibilities to the accused, they had the disadvantage of appearing less plausible than those of 1936. Although the Zinoviev trial was full of evident falsehoods, it could at least be argued that there *might* have been a genuine case, tarted up by the NKVD. It was at least not incredible that the oppositionists might have shot Kirov, and even less so that they might have wished to shoot Stalin. The new accusations were highly unbelievable on any view. Sabotage, by Pyatakov and his subordinates, was most implausible. Moreover, it was virtually incompatible with the charges of terrorism. As we have said, a plot designed to break the Government by terrorist acts could scarcely divert its energies, and risk exposure, by a vast network of people blowing up mines and causing railway accidents, simply to weaken the economy and sow distrust of the Government.

In the economic field, if not in the political, there is nevertheless some sort of rationale in Stalin's choice of victims. For there were genuine failures which required scapegoats. Men like Livshits were shot, it might be argued, like Admiral Byng†—*pour encourager les autres*. Even this peculiar style of common sense has its limits. To shoot the best economic organizers in order to encourage the

---

* An early adumbration of the line to be used in the Korean War in the 1950s.

† One difference between Byng's situation and that of the Soviet industrialists 200 years later is that on his tomb in Southill, Bedfordshire, it was possible at once for his family to erect a monument, with the famous inscription beginning "To the Perpetual Disgrace of Public Justice . . ."

second-best to be more effective than they had been is doubtful policy. It is true that the Soviet Union finally gained a fairly competent cadre of administrators capable of working under the threat of liquidation. But there are no doubt managers who do not give their best in such circumstances, and of whose services the country was deprived.

The sabotage theme was not, of course, new. It was in the old Shakhty Trial tradition—and, indeed, it was expressly stated in evidence that the old saboteurs had linked up with the new. The Shakhty/Metro-Vic Trial technique was also revived. An immense amount of confusing technical evidence was given. As a result, the trial of the present seventeen took seven days as against the five days which had been sufficient for the Zinoviev sixteen.

The accused were this time presented in a more logical order. First, the four leaders, then the seven West Siberian terrorists and saboteurs, then the three railwaymen, and last the three from the chemical industry.

First was *Pyatakov*. His appearance was still intellectual and dignified, but he had visibly aged and was thin and pale.

He made certain limitations in his evidence. Admitting the responsibility for forming terrorist and sabotage groups, and for planning acts of terror and "diversion" to be carried out in the future, he at no time confessed to complicity in any particular act of violence, and specifically denied being in direct touch with all the plotters. After considerable revelations about the political contacts of the alleged plot, he went on to confess to the organization of sabotage. But his sabotage acts were always of the following type:

> In the Ukraine the work was carried on mainly in the coke industry by Loginov and a group of persons connected with him. Their work, in the main, consisted of starting coke ovens which were not really ready for operations, and of holding up the construction of very valuable and very important parts of the coke and chemical industry. They operated coke ovens without utilizing those very valuable by-products which are obtained in coking and thereby huge funds were rendered valueless.[72]

> . . . Maryasin carried on the wrecking work along the following lines. First of all he sank money in piling up unnecessary materials, equipment and so on. I think that by the beginning of 1936 about fifty million roubles were frozen in the form of materials. . . .
> The wrecking activities in the last period assumed new forms. Despite the fact that, after a delay of two or three years, the plant began to enter on its operation stage, Maryasin created intolerable conditions, fomented intrigues, and in a word did everything to obstruct operation.[73]

> . . . An absolutely faulty plan of development was drawn up for the war-chemical industry . . . a plan providing for a smaller output capacity and, consequently, for a larger outlay of capital than was required.[74]

> Despite the fact that our country abounds in salt and raw materials for soda, and that the process of manufacturing soda is very well known, there is a shortage of soda in the country. The construction of new soda plants was delayed.[75]

That is, the overt acts he directly admitted were ones of negligence and bad planning by subordinates—which may well have been genuine.

He bluntly denied certain incriminations:

*Vyshinsky:* Accused Pyatakov, do you agree with what Shestov said?

*Pyatakov:* Shestov perhaps talked with somebody, but not with me when he says that somebody with pencil in hand calculated the cost of the ore. There was no such conversation with me.[76]

And again:

*Vyshinsky:* Do you now recall the conversation with Rataichak about espionage?

*Pyatakov:* No, I deny it.

*Vyshinsky:* And with Loginov?

*Pyatakov:* I also deny it.

*Vyshinsky:* And that members of your organization were connected with foreign intelligence services?

*Pyatakov:* As to the fact that there were such connections, I do not deny; but that I knew about the establishment. . . .[77]

Whether the line he took was on his own initiative, as Smirnov's had been, or whether he was permitted to evade the more extreme responsibilities as part of the encouragement to him (and to Ordzhonikidze) to think that his offenses would be held to be noncapital, is unclear.

Even as to his relations with Trotsky, he made certain vague reservations, as if to cast doubt on them. For example:

*Vyshinsky:* The conversation you had with Trotsky in December 1935 and the line he gave, did you accept it as a directive or simply as something said in a conversation but not binding for you?

*Pyatakov:* Of course as a directive.

*Vyshinsky:* Hence, we can take it that you subscribed to it?

*Pyatakov:* We can take it that I carried it out.

*Vyshinsky: And* carried it out.

*Pyatakov:* Not 'and carried it out,' but 'carried it out'.

*Vyshinsky:* There is no difference in that whatever.

*Pyatakov:* There is a difference for me.

*Vyshinsky:* What is it?

*Pyatakov:* As far as action is concerned, particularly criminally liable action, there is no difference whatever.[78]

The meeting with Trotsky here referred to was the central point of the whole conspiracy. Trotsky had then laid down the entire program of the plotters—seven pages in the official *Report of Court Proceedings.*[79] The difficulty was that Trotsky was in Norway, and Pyatakov never got nearer to him than Berlin, where, in December 1935, he was conducting Soviet Government business. His absence for any length of time would have been noticed, so his evidence was that by arrangement with an agent of Trotsky's he met in the Berlin Zoo, he arranged to fly to Norway. On the morning of 12 December, he took off from the Tempelhof with a forged German passport, "landed at the airdrome in Oslo" at 3:00 P.M., drove to Trotsky's home, and there conducted the conspiratorial business (in which Trotsky revealed for the first time that he had met the Nazi leader Hess and made arrangements for cooperation in war and peace).

This story was immediately proved false. Once again Stalin, at whose personal insistence this direct involvement of Trotsky had been inserted into the script,[80] was to find the disadvantages of a foreign venue for a fabrication. On 25 January, the Norwegian paper *Aftenposten* published the information that no civil aircraft had landed at Oslo's Kjeller Airfield during the entire month of December 1935. On 29 January, the Norwegian Social Democratic *Arbeiderbladet,* after further investigation, established that no aircraft had used the field at all between September 1935 and May 1936.

Trotsky now published a demand that Pyatakov be asked the full details of his alleged flight, including the name on his passport, by which entry could have been further checked. He went on to challenge Stalin to seek his extradition in a Norwegian court, where the facts could be judicially established.

No effective cover story could be found to offset this glaring falsification. In leading Party circles, the truth soon circulated, as Raskolnikov, for example, makes clear (see p. 425).

Vyshinsky's counter, an extremely weak one, was made at the end of the trial, on 27 January:

> *Vyshinsky:* I have an application to the Court. I interested myself in this matter and asked the People's Commissariat of Foreign Affairs to make an inquiry, for I wanted to verify Pyatakov's evidence from this side too. I have received an official communication which I ask to have put in the records.
> (Reads.)
>> 'The Consular Department of the People's Commissariat of Foreign Affairs hereby informs the Prosecutor of the U.S.S.R. that according to information received by the Embassy of the U.S.S.R. in Norway the Kjeller Airdrome near Oslo receives all the year round, in accordance with international regulations, airplanes of other countries, and that the arrival and departure of airplanes is possible also in winter months.'
>
> *(To Pyatakov):* It was in December?
>
> *Pyatakov:* Exactly.[81]

Thus another agency of the Soviet Government "certified" not the fact, but merely the technical possibility, of Pyatakov's flight. It might well be thought that this debacle alone would have discredited the whole trial in foreign eyes. Anyone who may have hoped so soon found that Stalin's ideas about political gullibility were even better based than had first appeared.

*Radek,* who had been partly responsible for the script of the trial, made a brilliant showing over the morning of 24 January. While the other accused spoke flatly and drearily, he put real feeling into his evidence. He developed the post-1927 history of Trotskyism, and the complex links between those now accused and the Zinoviev group. He then listed a number of fresh terrorist bands, implicated Bukharin, spoke of the "Bonapartist" regime Trotsky intended, which would in fact be under fascist control, and added that Trotsky was already prepared to sacrifice the Ukraine and the Far East to the aggressors.

He aptly explained the belated Trotskyite call for Party democracy: "People begin to argue about democracy only when they disagree on questions of principle. When they agree they do feel the need for broad democracy, that goes without saying."[82]

In spite of his agreement to cooperate, he made several points against the indictment, in an oblique fashion. When he complained, "For nothing at all, just for the sake of Trotsky's beautiful eyes—the country was to return to capitalism,"[83] he was in effect saying that the charge of a gratuitous wish to restore capitalism for no other motive than to put Trotsky in power was an extraordinary idea, especially as regards "such men as Yakov Livshits or Serebryakov, with decades of revolutionary work behind them,"[84] whose "moral fibre" must now be "utterly broken" if they "could descend to wrecking" and "act on the instructions of the class enemy."

On the whole, Radek was a most cooperative and convincing defendant. Even so, when he had completed the main body of his evidence, Vyshinsky started to bully him, eliciting several sharp retorts, such as "You are a profound reader of human hearts, but I must nevertheless comment on my thoughts in my own words."[85] Or again:

Vyshinsky: You accepted this? And you held this conversation?

Radek: You have learned it from me, that means that I did hold it.[86]

Finally, Vyshinsky reminded him that he not only had failed to report the conspiracy, but also had refused to confess for three months, and said, "Does not that cast doubt on what you said about your vacillations and misgivings?"

Radek became irritated and snapped out the weak point in the whole case: "Yes, if you ignore the fact that you learned about the programme and about Trotsky's instructions only from me, of course, it does cast doubt on what I have said."[87]

In the course of Radek's evidence, he had been made to remark that in 1935 "Vitaly [sic] Putna came to see me with some request from Tukhachevsky."[88]

Thus Corps Commander Putna was once again implicated. More striking still was the mention of Tukhachevsky's name, even in an innocent context. Moscow was shaken by what appeared to be, conceivably, the first hint of trouble for the Marshal.

During the evening session, Radek was recalled and exculpated Tukhachevsky in a long exchange with Vyshinsky (see p. 191). The threat had nevertheless been made, and understood.

The same day, *Sokolnikov* was called. He had little to add, apart from identifying a few more terrorist groups. He had, it appeared, little direct connection with terror or sabotage, and unlike the case with Pyatakov, Vyshinsky did not put questions implying the opposite. His main contribution of substance was to make the point about the older generation of saboteurs:

*Sokolnikov:* . . . It was pointed out that former wrecking organizations among the specialists should be found.

*Vyshinsky:* Among the former wreckers of the period of the Industrial Party and the Shakhty Trial. Well then, what was your line?

*Sokolnikov:* Trotsky's line, which permitted the wrecking groups of the bloc to establish contact with these groups.[89]

*Serebryakov,* who followed, exposed a number of railway chiefs and explained that the system of railway organization prior to Kaganovich's appointment in 1935 had amounted to intentional sabotage. Otherwise, he only contributed accounts of a few more terrorist groups to the already large pool. It is uncertain if he knew that Vyshinsky had taken over his dacha.[90]

On 25 and 26 January came the questioning of the "Siberians." The evidence was mainly concerned, on the one hand, with the establishment of the links between these men and Pyatakov and the Moscow Center; and, on the other, with the detail of the ways in which they had contrived accidents and explosions.

*Drobnis* started with the usual examples of faulty planning in industry:

Needless to say, this retarded the speed and progress of construction work. It must be said that this was done rather cleverly. For example, there were plans for the main, basic buildings of the Combined Fertilizer Works, but for things like the gas mains, the steam supply pipes and so forth, which might appear of secondary importance but were really of very great importance for starting the plant on schedule, plans were not prepared in time, and of course this constant fussing in dealings with the organizations responsible for the designs led to the plan arriving much too late. . . .[91]

. . . The Kemerovo district power station was put into such a state that, if it were deemed necessary for wrecking purposes, and when the order was given, the mine could be flooded. In addition, coal was supplied that was technically unsuitable for the power station, and this led to explosions. This was done quite deliberately.[92]

He went on to the case of the Tsentralnaya Mine. He ended, but only after considerable bullying from Vyshinsky, with the confession that the plotters had hoped for as much loss of life as possible from the explosions. Although he had been in jail at the time of the disaster, he accepted responsibility.

*Shestov,* the NKVD agent, confirmed Sokolnikov on the old saboteurs. He gave a useful warning to engineers throughout the country: ". . . Although Ovsyannikov was not a member of our organization he was the sort of manager who left everything to the engineers and did not do anything himself, and he could quickly be converted into a Trotskyite."[93]

His own excavation system in Prokopyevsk had resulted in no fewer than sixty underground fires by the end of 1935.[94]

Shestov explained that it was Trotskyites rather than Government policy which was rendering the worker's life intolerable:

Instructions were issued to worry the life out of the workers. Before a worker reached his place of work, he must be made to heap two hundred curses on the heads of the pit management. Impossible conditions of work were created. Not only for Stakhanovite methods but even for normal methods.[95]

Norkin and Stroilov gave similar evidence of sabotage. *Norkin* had "planned to put the State District Power Station out of action by means of explosions. In February 1936 there were three explosions."[96] He had also been responsible for a faulty investment program.[97] When asked the motives of his confession, he contrived to hint at the truth:

> *Vyshinsky:* And why did you afterwards decide to give way?
>
> *Norkin:* Because there is a limit to everything.
>
> *Vyshinsky:* Perhaps pressure was brought to bear upon you?
>
> *Norkin:* I was questioned, exposed, there were confrontations.
>
> *Vyshinsky:* You were confronted with evidence, facts?
>
> *Norkin:* There were confrontations.[98]

*Stroilov*'s evidence is chiefly interesting for what is presumably Stalin's view of Trotsky's writings: "I said that I had read Trotsky's book, *Mein Leben*. He asked me whether I liked it, I said from the literary point of view he, as a journalist, wrote well, but because of the infinite number of 'I's' in it, I did not like it."[99]

At the end of his testimony, Vyshinsky, who had not bothered to check the Oslo airfield situation, went through a long rigmarole to establish the reality of a minor contact of Stroilov's from Berlin:

> *Vyshinsky:* I request the court to have attached to the records a statement by the Savoy Hotel: 'Foreign tourist H.V. Berg, born 1874, German subject, merchant by profession, Hotel Savoy, Room 223 (it is identical with the telephone number), December 1–15, 1930, arrived from Berlin.
>
>    'In the room occupied by Berg there was a telephone No. 8-50, ext. 223. Director of the hotel. Seal and reference number.'[100]

Immediately afterward, he was doing the same thing about an address in Berlin Stroilov had visited:

> *Vyshinsky:* I request the Court to have attached to the record this Berlin address and telephone number taken from this official publication [hands to the Court a big book in a red binding]. On page 206, against No. 8563 there is Wüster, Armstrasse, and the address of this Wüster, which is mentioned also in Stroilov's notebook.[101]

The Court acceded to both these requests, so that the *Telephone Address Directory of the German Reich,* 7th edition, Volume 2, now forms part of the dossier, which, somewhere in the purlieus of the Soviet State Archives, has been gathering dust for half a century.

Like Drobnis, *Muralov* had been in jail at the time of the Tsentralnaya explosion. But he refused to accept responsibility.

> *The President:* Did you know that at the Kemerovo coal mines the Trotskyites had gassed the pits and created absolutely intolerable conditions of work?
>
> *Muralov:* Drobnis was at the Chemical Works—these are under one trust, and the mines are under another trust.

> *The President:* I understand. I am speaking about the Kemerovo mine.
>
> *Muralov:* I did not know that there they had adopted the course of gassing the Tsentralnaya Pit, and Drobnis did not report this to me. This occurred when I was already in prison.
>
> *The President:* One of the passages in your testimony contains this sentence: 'At the Kemerovo mine the Trotskyites gassed pits and created intolerable conditions for the workers.'
>
> *Muralov:* I learned about that while I was in prison, as being a result of all the undermining Trotskyite work.[102]

His main concern, in any case, was assassination. One of the weaknesses in the whole legend came to light:

> *Vyshinsky:* But was it not said that terrorism in general produces no result if only one is killed and the others remain, and therefore it is necessary to act at one stroke?
>
> *Muralov:* Both I and Pyatakov felt that it was no use working by Socialist-Revolutionary, guerrilla methods. We must organize it so as to cause panic at one stroke. We regarded causing panic and consternation in the leading ranks of the Party as one of the means by which we would come into power.[103]

But while admitting to the preparation of attempts on Eikhe and Molotov, he warmly repudiated the accusation that Ordzhonikidze was another intended victim:

> *Muralov:* . . . About 1932 and Shestov's reference to the attempt on the life of Ordzhonikidze, I categorically declare that this belongs to the realms of Shestov's phantasy. I never gave such instructions.
>
> *Vyshinsky:* He is mixing things up?
>
> *Muralov:* I do not know whether is he mixing things up or whether he is simply letting his phantasy run away with him.[104]

Vyshinsky was so annoyed that he referred to this is his closing speech: "Muralov, who will under no circumstances agree to having the preparation of an attempt on the life of Comrade Ordzhonikidze attributed to him . . . admits that he did indeed organize a terrorist act against Comrade Molotov." And it certainly is anomalous. We can hardly see it as other than a demonstration of loyalty to, and hope of help from, Ordzhonikidze.

As to the attempt on Molotov, this is interesting as the only piece of action the terrorists had accomplished since the Kirov murder. The presumable truth of the matter was given in 1961:

> Here is still another example of Molotov's extreme cynicism. On a trip to the city of Prokopyevsk in 1934, the car in which he was riding went off the road, its right wheels landing in a ditch. None of the passengers was injured in any way. This episode subsequently provided grounds for a story about an "attempt" on Molotov's life, and a group of completely innocent people was sentenced for it. Who knew better

than Molotov that in reality there had been no such attempt? But he had not a word to say in defense of these innocent people. [105]

As explained by Muralov, the plan was for the driver to sacrifice himself by plunging Molotov to destruction:

> *Muralov:* The car was to turn into a ditch while at full speed. Under such circumstances, the car by its own momentum would overturn and get smashed, while the people . . .
>
> *Vyshinsky:* Was the attempt made to overturn the car in the ditch?
>
> *Muralov:* The attempt was made, but then the chauffeur funked and the car did not fall into the ditch. . . .
>
> *Shestov:* . . . One spot—for those who know Prokopyevsk—was near Pit No. 5 on the way to the Mine Management Office, and the second spot was between the workers' settlement and Pit No. 3. There is a gully there, not a ditch, as Muralov said, a gully, about 15 metres deep.
>
> *Vyshinsky:* A 'ditch' 15 metres deep! Who chose this spot?
>
> *Muralov:* Permit me to say something about Shestov's explanation. I will not argue with Shestov about whether it was a ditch or a gully. . . .
>
> *Vyshinsky:* Have you yourself been at the spot where this ditch is?
>
> *Muralov:* No, I have never been there.
>
> *Vyshinsky:* So you have not seen it?
>
> *Muralov:* No, but there are many gullies in Prokopyevsk, gully upon gully, hill after hill.
>
> *Vyshinsky:* If you have not seen the place you cannot argue about it.
>
> *Muralov:* I will not argue about it. [106]

Muralov's disturbing reference to the alleged ravine as a "ditch" was presumably based on definite knowledge. Vyshinsky commented in his closing speech, "But the fact remains a fact. An attempt on the life of Comrade Molotov was made. That the car overturned on the brink of the 15-metre 'ditch', as Muralov here modestly called it, is a fact." [107]

It is curious, moreover, that the only terrorist plot (apart from the Kirov murder) which actually reached the stage of any action was not committed by one of the trained and devoted Trotskyites, but by the locally recruited petty adventurer "Arnold, alias Ivanov, alias Vasilyev, alias Rask, alias Kulpenen . . ." as Vyshinsky put it. [108] Although Trotsky had "insisted . . . particularly strongly" on committing a number of terrorist acts "more or less simultaneously," only the one against Molotov had come to anything. It is true (even officially) that Molotov was only rather shaken. But still, none of the proposed victims of Prigozhin or Golubenko, or the other professional assassins, was even shaken.

And now the court found the difficulty of mixing fact with fiction. Since there really had been an accident, which it was decided to inflate into an assassination attempt, the assassin was not a picked NKVD agent provocateur but the chauffeur actually involved. This proved to be a mistake. Instead of an Olberg or a Berman-Yurin, chosen and groomed for the occasion, the court was faced with a man who was wholly unsuited to the part that chance had called on him to play.

At the evening session of 26 January, Vyshinsky came to the examination of *Arnold,* the driver who had allegedly, under orders from the Siberian conspirators, made the attempt. The whole exchange was a ludicrous interlude. Vyshinsky for once seemed to lose control of the situation.[109]

Arnold said that he had lost his nerve and only produced a slight accident. But it was perfectly clear that no conspirator could ever have expected a man of his type to sacrifice himself, as the plan allegedly intended. In fact, his final remark completely contradicted the idea that he would be dead after the accident, since he explained his motives in becoming a Trotskyite as being based on the Trotskyites' promise that when they came to power "I would not be among the last people then."

In the exchange (which goes on for thirty pages in the transcript), Vyshinsky no longer faced a more or less intellectual collaborator, but a small-time *lumpenproletarian* crook and adventurer. It took five or ten minutes to straighten out Arnold's real name from his various aliases, and even then this was not properly settled and caused further trouble later on.

Owing to the loose family life prevailing in the slums of Petrograd, he had already accumulated "three surnames by the age of seven," Vyshinsky remarked. He had wandered to Finland, then to Germany and Holland, while still in his early teens, with yet another surname, and then, during the First World War, to Norway and England. On his return, he was conscripted, but deserted and was then jailed for six months. There are pages of this sort of interrogation, and now Vyshinsky again became entangled in the names, and also in a complicated muddle about the various regiments Arnold had joined and deserted from in the war and the ranks he had held as compared with those he had gained by simply sewing a stripe on. What he said, moreover, contradicted the story he had given during the investigation. The President had to call him to order, but still little progress was made. He had managed to steal some railway passes and got to Vladivostok and, finally, under yet another name, to New York, where he joined the U.S. Army, though he could not then speak English. In America, he was jailed for five or six months— though here Vyshinsky got bogged down in a further exchange about how many times he had been jailed (apparently twice). There was also confusion about whether he had or had not joined the U.S. Army twice or never. He claimed he had got to France with the U.S. Army, and a visit to South America also comes up. He had also enrolled as a Freemason in America, and at the same time as a member of the Communist Party of the United States. Twenty-three pages of evidence contain this extraordinary farrago, in which the only incriminating point established is the Freemasonry, which Arnold had concealed from the Party. He seems finally to have got himself shipped to Russia with a group of American specialists being sent to Kemerovo, and there joined the Russian Communist Party. In West Siberia, he had been an office manager, then in charge of water transport, then in a commercial department, and then in charge of a "telephone system," in big enterprises in Kemerovo and Kuznetsk. In 1932, he finally got in touch with the Trotskyites, being recruited by Shestov. Arnold had already been dismissed from some job for anti-Soviet remarks, and Shestov had something more on him, having discovered two of his names—though to establish this latter point, Vyshinsky again became involved in a long argument about how many there were in all. The only relevant evidence is contained in about a page and a half.

This indicated that Shestov and Cherepukhin, the local Party Secretary, had ordered Arnold to have an accident with Ordzhonikidze, Eikhe, and Rukhimovich in the car. But he lost his nerve.

When Molotov came, the plan was the same. But the "ditch" had now become not a "gully," but a "bank":

> Arnold: . . . On this curve there is not a gully, as Shestov called it, but what we call an embankment, the edge of the road, about eight or ten metres deep, a drop of nearly ninety degrees. When I came to the station, Molotov, Kurganov, Secretary of the District Committee of the Party, and Gryadinsky, Chairman of the Territory Executive Committee, got into the car. . . .

However, he again funked it, and only turned just off the road when another lorry, evidently hired by the conspirators, drove at him. No one was hurt.

He was reprimanded for negligent driving, got a job in Tashkent, returned to Novosibirsk, and became assistant manager in a supply department and, finally, manager of a garage. And that was all.

After Arnold came Assistant People's Commissar of Railways *Livshits,* and the other railway plotters. This section of the trial was evidently Kaganovich's private preserve. In their final speeches, both Livshits and Knyazev were to speak of the forfeit of Kaganovich's trust as a particularly heinous side of their offenses. Livshits remarked:

> Citizen Judges! The charge advanced against me by the State Prosecutor is still further aggravated by the fact that I was raised by the Party from the ranks to a high position in state administration—to that of Assistant People's Commissar of Railways. I enjoyed the confidence of the Party, I enjoyed the confidence of Stalin's comrade-in-arms, Kaganovich.[110]

while Knyazev mourned:

> . . . I always experienced a dreadful feeling of pain when Lazar Moiseyevich [Kaganovich] said to me 'I know you as a railway worker who knows the railways both from the theoretical and from the practical side. But why do I not feel in you that wide range of activity which I have a right to demand of you?'[111]

Livshits, as a senior figure, was also involved in various assassination schemes, but the main evidence of the railway accused was of wrecking trains and conducting espionage for Japan. The extent of the "hostile" ring in the railways bears all the marks of Kaganovich's root-and-branch style. All the accused named whole lists of wreckers, pervading entire railway systems. Vyshinsky was particularly concerned to pin the killing of innocent citizens on the saboteurs:

> Vyshinsky: You do not remember if these twenty-nine Red Army men were badly mutilated?
>
> Knyazev: About fifteen were badly mutilated.

*Vyshinsky:* But what sort of serious injuries were there?

*Knyazev:* They had arms broken, heads pierced. . . .

*Vyshinsky:* Heads pierced, arms broken, ribs broken, legs broken?

*Knyazev:* Yes, that is so.

*Vyshinsky:* This happened by the grace of you and your accomplices?[112]

But the extent of the criminal ring was equally well developed, as can be seen from the list of those involved in a single act of sabotage:

*Vyshinsky:* . . . But why was such a violation of railway service regulations possible? Was it not because the administration of the station was in league with the Trotskyites?

*Knyazev:* Quite right.

*Vyshinsky:* Name these persons.

*Knyazev:* Markevich, the station master, Rykov, the acting station master, Vaganov, assistant station master, Rodionov, assistant station master, Kolesnikov, head switchman.

*Vyshinsky:* Five.

*Knyazev:* Switchman Bezgin.

*Vyshinsky:* Six.

*Knyazev:* And then there was also the permanent way manager of that section, Brodovikov.

*Vyshinsky:* Yes, and the chief of the railroad, himself.[113]

On his single line, the South Urals Railway, Knyazev now implicated a long series of accomplices, in a way which adumbrates the extraordinary scope of the purge among railwaymen throughout the Soviet lines. Leading figures at his own headquarters were supplemented by the permanent-way managers of the various sections; the traffic managers; the traffic inspectors; the heads of traction departments; locomotive foremen; depot engineers; and station masters, assistant stationmasters, drivers, switchmen. He named thirty-three men in all as the "cadres of my Trotskyite organization on the South Urals Railway."[114]

Knyazev went on to say:

From thirteen to fifteen train wrecks were organized directly by us. I remember in 1934 there were altogether about 1,500 train wrecks and accidents.

Powerful locomotives of the F.D. type were introduced in the Kurgan depot. Taking advantage of the fact that not much was known about them in this depot, the management deliberately slackened the supervision of current repairs, frequently compelled the engine-drivers to leave before repairs were completed. Almost all the water gauges were reduced to a ruinous condition. As a result of this neglect, a boiler burst in January 1936 on the Rosa–Vargashi stretch. . . .

*Vyshinsky:* . . . The train wreck on 7 February 1936, on the Yedinover–Berdyaush section, was carried out on your instructions?

*Knyazev:* Yes. . . . Railwaymen have a notion that if a rail splits no one on the road is to blame.

*Vyshinsky:* That is to say, they attribute it to objective causes?

*Knyazev:* They did not find the culprits.[115]

Last of all came the chemical criminals. The familiar charges recurred in a slightly different context. *Rataichak* made a slight attempt to defend himself:

*Rataichak:* . . . No, but I had to do that, Citizen Prosecutor, because if we had not taken this measure of precaution there was a danger that the lives of hundreds of workers might have been lost. That is why I myself directed the clearance work on the spot.

*Vyshinsky:* You directed it in such a way that 17 workers were killed and 15 wounded. Is that so?

*Rataichak:* (Remains silent.)

*Vyshinsky:* You directed the clearance operations in such a way that 17 workers were killed and 15 injured.

*Rataichak:* That is true, but it was the only thing to do.[116]

The prosecution ended with the reports of various Commissions of Expert Witnesses, who blamed all the explosions and pit fires on the accused. But Stroilov commented shrewdly that the excavating system the wreckers were accused of bringing in for their own purposes had in fact been in use for some time previously.

On 28 January at 4:00 P.M., Vyshinsky started on his speech for the prosecution:

This is the abyss of degradation!
This is the limit, the last boundary of moral and political decay!
This is the diabolical infinitude of crime![117]

These were, he exclaimed, the sentiments with which every honest man had condemned the Zinovievites. And now the cry should be raised again. For "the conversion of the Trotskyite groups into groups of diversionists and murderers operating as the instruments of foreign secret services and of General Staffs of aggressors merely crowns the struggle Trotskyism has been waging against the working class and the Party, against Lenin and Leninism, for decades."[118]

This was "not a political party. It is a gang of criminals, merely the agency of foreign intelligence services."[119] In fact, they were worse than the Whites; "they sank lower than the worst Denikinites or Kolchakites. The worst Denikinites or Kolchakites were superior to these traitors. The Denikinites, Kolchakites, Milyukovites, did not sink as low as these Trotskyite Judases. . . ."[120]

Rataichak was cited as a typical conspirator. Vyshinsky remarked, in a rather unbalanced fashion, "Whether he is a German or a Polish spy is not clear, but that he is a spy there cannot be any doubt; and as is appropriate to his profession, a liar, a swindler and a rascal."[121]

Such analyses, which may be translated as defining anti-Stalinism as criminal Fascism, naturally fitted in with Stalin's own predictions, now reinforced by Stalin's own court:

. . . Comrade Stalin's forecast has fully come true. Trotskyism has indeed become the central rallying point of all the forces hostile to socialism, the gang of mere bandits, spies and murderers who placed themselves entirely at the disposal of foreign secret services, became finally and irrevocably transformed into lackeys of capitalism, into restorers of capitalism in our country.[122]

More interesting than the direct assaults in Vyshinsky's speech were the preparations for further action. He said pointedly:

I would like to remind you of how, in the case of the united Trotskyite–Zinoviev centre, say, certain of the accused vowed, right here, in this very dock, during their last pleas, some begging, others not begging for clemency, that they had spoken the whole truth, that they had said everything, that in their hearts no opposition whatever remained against the working class, against our people, against our country. And later, when the revolting skein of monstrous crimes committed by these people became more and more unravelled, we found that at every step these people had lied and deceived when they already had one foot in the grave.

. . . I think that all these circumstances enable me to say that if there is any shortcoming in the present trial, it is not that the accused have said what they have done, but that, after all, the accused have not really told us all they have done, all the crimes they have committed against the Soviet State.[123]

The further charges to be made against Bukharin the following year were implicit in a particularly sinister passage:

*Vyshinsky:* . . . It was Pyatakov and Co. who in 1918, in a period of extreme danger for the land of Soviets, carried on negotiations with the Socialist-Revolutionaries with a view to bringing about a counter-revolutionary *coup d'état* and arresting Lenin so that Pyatakov might occupy the post of head of government, of chairman of the Council of People's Commissars. It was through the arrest of Lenin, through a *coup d'état*, that these political adventurers wanted to lay for themselves the road to power.[124]

Finally, he quoted Sokolnikov, on the essential unity of all the oppositions, based on the Ryutin program:

As for the lines of the programme, as far back as 1932 the Trotskyites, the Zinovievites and the Rights all agreed in the main on a programme which was characterized as the programme of the Rights. This was the so-called Ryutin platform; to a large extent, as far back as 1932 it expressed the programme policy common to all three groups.[125]

Further personnel for new trials had already been adumbrated. In addition to Bukharin and Rykov, Rakovsky was implicated (by Drobnis).[126] Mdivani in Georgia was now incriminated by name.[127]

The present case had, Vyshinsky pointed out, been proved with a rigor not demanded in bourgeois courts:

With the assistance of the experts, we verified the evidence of the accused, and although we know that according to the laws of certain European countries the confession of an accused person is regarded as sufficient proof of guilt and the court does not consider itself obliged to call corroborating evidence, we, however, in order to

observe strict impartiality, notwithstanding the confessions of the criminals themselves, verified their statements once again from the technical side and obtained a
categorical reply concerning the explosion of 11 November, the fires in the Prokopyevsk mine, and the fires and explosions at the Kemerovo plant. Malicious intent
was established without any possibility of doubt.[128]

Certain of the objections to the Zinoviev Trial were dealt with. For example,
on the absence of documentary proof Vyshinsky now remarked:

The accused committed the deeds attributed to them. . . . But what proof have we
in our arsenal from the point of view of judicial procedure? . . . The question can
be put this way: a conspiracy, you say, but where are the documents? . . . I am bold
enough to assert, in keeping with the fundamental requirements of the science of
criminal procedure, that in cases of conspiracy such demands cannot be put.[129]

(On this point, one of the defense lawyers, inadequately briefed, was to refer
approvingly to "documents available in the case.")[130]

The popular rage line was heavily played:

They blow up mines, they burn down workshops, they wreck trains, they mutilate
and kill hundreds of our best people, sons of our country. Eight hundred workers in
the Gorlovka Nitrate Fertilizer Works, through *Pravda,* communicated the names of
the best Stakhanovites in those works who died by the treacherous hand of the diversionists. Here is the list of these victims: Lunev—Stakhanovite, born 1902. Yudin—a
talented engineer, born 1913. Kurkin—a member of the Young Communist League,
Stakhanovite, 23 years of age. Strelnikova—girl shock brigade worker, born 1913.
Moisets—shock brigade worker, also born 1913. These were killed, over a dozen
were injured. Maximenko, a Stakhanovite who fulfilled his norm of 125 to 150 per
cent, was killed. Nemikhin—one of the best shock brigade workers—sacrificed his
ten days' leave to go down the Tsentralnaya Pit, and there somebody waited for him
and killed him. Shot-firer Yurev—one of the men who took part in the fighting against
the White Chinese—was killed. Lanin, an old miner, a participant in the Civil War,
was killed. And so on and so forth.[131]

As a result, Vyshinsky felt justified in shouting, as he perorated,

I do not stand here alone! The victims may be in their graves, but I feel that they are
standing here beside me, pointing at the dock, at you, accused, with their mutilated
arms, which have mouldered in the graves to which you sent them!

I am not the only accuser! I am joined in my accusation by the whole of our
people! I accuse these heinous criminals who deserve only one punishment—death by
shooting![132]

Unlike the defendants in the Zinoviev Trial, some of the junior accused this
time had defense counsel. These took a different view of their duties from those
in bourgeois courts. Braude started by saying, in a *locus classicus* for Stalinist
defense lawyers:

Comrade Judges, I will not conceal from you the exceptionally difficult, the unprec-
edentedly difficult position in which the Defence finds itself in this case. First of
all, Comrade Judges, the Counsel for Defence is a son of his country. He, too, is a
citizen of the great Soviet Union, and the great indignation, anger and horror which
is now felt by the whole population of our country, old and young, the feeling

which the Prosecutor so strikingly expressed in his speech, cannot but be shared by Counsel. . . .

In this case, Comrade Judges, there is no dispute about the facts. Comrade Prosecutor was quite right when he said that from all points of view, from the point of view of documents available in the case, from the point of view of the examination of the witnesses who were summoned here, and cross-examination of the accused, all this has deprived us of all possibility of disputing the evidence. All the facts have been proved, and in this sphere the Defence does not intend to enter into any controversy with the Procurator. Nor can there by any controversy with the Procurator concerning the appraisal of the political and moral aspects of the case. Here, too, the case is so clear, the political appraisal made here by the Procurator is so clear, that the Defence cannot but wholly and entirely associate itself with that part of his speech.[133]

When the "defense" had finished, the last pleas followed. Pyatakov ended his, with downcast eyes:

In a few hours you will pass your sentence. And here I stand before you in filth, crushed by my own crimes, bereft of everything through my own fault, a man who has lost his Party, who has no friends, who has lost his family, who has lost his very self.[134]

Radek's most useful contribution was to make the point that there were still "semi-Trotskyites, quarter-Trotskyites, one-eighth-Trotskyites, people who helped us, not knowing of the terrorist organization but sympathizing with us, people who from liberalism, from a Fronde against the Party, gave us this help. . . ." This was in fact a charter for disposing of any critics of the Purge, even if "seven-eighths-Stalinist."

Yet while both abject and cogent in his presentation of the charges against Trotsky and the accused, he managed to make a few two-edged remarks. He continued to dissociate himself and his co-defendants from the direct German connection:

But when I read about Olberg and asked others whether they had known of the existence of Olberg, and none of them had heard about him, it became clear to me that in addition to the cadres who had passed through his school, Trotsky was organizing agents who had passed through the school of German Fascism.[135]

And finally he repeated the fact that it was only on his word, and Pyatakov's, that the entire case was erected:

What proofs are there in support of this fact? In support of this fact there is the evidence of two people—the testimony of myself, who received the directives and the letters from Trotsky (which, unfortunately, I burned), and the testimony of Pyatakov, who spoke to Trotsky. All the testimony of the other accused rests on our testimony. If you are dealing with mere criminals and spies, on what can you base your conviction that what we have said is the truth, the firm truth?[136]

The others took the more usual line. Drobnis, Muralov, and Boguslavsky referred to their splendid records and proletarian origins. Sokolnikov spoke at length, and Serebryakov very briefly. All the politicals, though to very different degrees, attacked Trotsky in person. Arnold pleaded "weak, low political development," as well he might.

At 3:00 A.M. on 30 January, the verdict was pronounced. Death to all except Sokolnikov and Radek (as not "directly participating in the organization and execution" of the various crimes) and Arnold, who got ten years each, and Stroilov, who got eight. A story circulating in NKVD circles has it that Stalin was asked for Radek's life to be spared by Lion Feuchtwanger, as the price for his agreeing to write his book *(Moscow 1937)* justifying the trials, which Stalin was particularly anxious to have written to counter the effect of André Gide's *Retour de L'URSS*.[137] The sentence on Arnold, supposed actually to have carried out a terrorist act, contrasts extraordinarily with those of the previous failed assassins like Fritz David. It has been suggested that Stalin had been so entertained by his evidence that, when he drafted the sentences he indulged the caprice of showing special clemency.

When Radek heard the verdict, his face showed relief. He turned to his fellow accused with a shrug and a guilty smile, as though unable to explain his luck.*[138] He is said to have been later retried on a charge of suppressing evidence against Tukhachevsky and sentenced to death but reprieved. A recent official account has him "killed in jail, 19 May 1939." There have long been reports that he was murdered by a criminal prisoner, acting on orders,[139] and it is now confirmed that both he and Sokolnikov were "killed in prison by cell mates in May 1939." Stroilov and Arnold were shot in 1941.[140]

The relations of several prisoners are identified in camps or jail. Radek's daughter got eight years.[141] Drobnis's wife was seen in 1936 in the Krasnoyarsk isolator. She had become almost completely deaf as the result of treatment in the Lubyanka.[142] Muralov's brother was shot; his sixteen-year-old son was sentenced to labor camp, and died of dystrophy in Dalstroy in 1943; and a number of other relatives, including his niece Yelka, were also imprisoned.[143] Galina Serebryakova, who spent nearly twenty years in Siberia from this time, had been married to two leading victims, Serebryakov and Sokolnikov. Through all this, she retained her Party-mindedness, and after her rehabilitation spoke up warmly at writers' meetings in 1962 and 1963 against the liberalizing trends. During the early months of 1963, when heavy pressure was being put on the "liberal" writers, Khrushchev was able to point to her as an example, comparing her with Ilya Ehrenburg, who during Stalin's lifetime had praised him warmly and lived comfortably, but was now departing from Party principles.[144]

There had been a progressive increase in the incredibility of the trials. At first (1936) the Party was only asked to accept the idea that Zinoviev and Kamenev, together with some genuine Trotskyites, had plotted to murder the leadership and had in fact been responsible for Kirov's death. Although the execution of Zinoviev and the rest aroused a great revulsion, there were other factors. First of all, though it seems unlikely that many members of the Central Committee could have believed the charges literally, or taken the confessions at face value (and there were certainly rumors circulating about the true role of the NKVD in the Kirov killing), still the Zinoviev opposition had really fought Stalin by all the

---

*Which was by no means a foregone conclusion. Yezhov had given Ulrikh instructions on the sentencing on 28 January: all the accused were to be shot. Stalin must have changed his mind (as he had about the names for trial—Livshits and Turok being added at the last moment) (*Izvestiya TsK KPSS*, no. 9 [1989]).

means at its disposal, in a political fight in which almost all the present Committee had been on Stalin's side. They had compromised themselves by lying their way back into the Party, as was quite evident. And it was at least possible that the assassination of Kirov was "objectively" Zinoviev's responsibility.

As to the more obvious falsehoods of the trial itself, the Party was quite used to falsehood for Party reasons, and, if it came to that, to fake trials designed to impress the public. Stalin was, it might have been felt, getting rid of irreconcilable enemies.

None of this applied to Pyatakov and his fellow defendants. And, at the same time, the case produced all the anomalies and oddities of the previous one, in fact in an exaggerated form.

As with the Zinoviev group, it was alleged that Pyatakov and his fellow defendants had organized a vast underground of assassins. Radek referred, perhaps ironically, in his evidence to "scores of wandering terrorist groups waiting for the chance to assassinate some leader of the Party."[145] At least fourteen separate groups or individuals are named who had the task of assassinating Stalin (several of them), Kaganovich, Molotov, Voroshilov, Ordzhonikidze, Kossior, Postyshev, Eikhe, Yezhov, and Beria. Again, in spite of the protection and complicity of high officials everywhere, they had been unable to carry out any overt act, successfully or unsuccessfully, with the sole exception of the attempt to murder Molotov, and even this did not sound very professional. Indeed, the sentencing of Arnold to only ten years' imprisonment was virtually an admission that he was not a political enthusiast. Why, when the conspiracy brimmed with fanatical Trotskyites, they should have entrusted this suicide operation to such a figure was not explained.

And the plotters were not even able to assassinate Kaganovich, though several of the men closest to him in his governmental post, like Livshits, Serebryakov, and Knyazev, were members of the conspiracy.

Vyshinsky had to deal with the fact that Zinoviev and his colleagues, who had supposedly made full confessions, had (as it now appeared) concealed much of the story. He said flatly, as we saw, that they "lied and deceived when they already had one foot in the grave."[146] But in that case, while their confessions of fact might have been limited to what they could not deny, their abject expressions of guilt must have been insincere; that is, everything they said in their final speeches was retrospectively canceled. People who believed in the trials, however, had no difficulty in reconciling, or rather ignoring, these contradictory versions.

A minor anomaly is, as we have seen, that the accused now admitted that they had plotted with Zinoviev and Kamenev to kill Molotov as well as the other leaders. Zinoviev and Kamenev had not confessed to this crime, since they had not been required to do so.

Once again, important plotters were mentioned and not produced. When the Old Bolshevik Byeloborodov, who had ordered the execution of the Royal Family, was implicated in a fashion which could not be cleared up properly, Vyshinsky remarked, "So now it will be necessary to ask Byeloborodov himself?"[147] But Byeloborodov was not produced, then or ever. And the same applies, of course, to Smilga, Preobrazhensky, Uglanov, and other important links, who were simply omitted without explanation.

In addition there were, of course, the factual mistakes, and particularly the Oslo visit. Yet in a summary published in England under the sponsorship of the Anglo-Russian Parliamentary Committee, a preface by the Moscow correspondent of the *Daily Herald,* R. T. Miller, could say "They confessed because the State's collection of evidence forced them to. No other explanation fits the facts." Neil Maclean, Labour M.P. for Govan and Chairman of this committee, noted in a foreword: "Practically every foreign correspondent present at the Trial—with the exception of course of the Japanese and German—have expressed themselves as very much impressed by the weight of evidence presented by the Prosecution and the sincerity of the confessions of the accused." This is an interesting (though untrue) smear on correspondents who thought otherwise. They were clearly in the same boat as the minority of committed fascists, excluded from the company of all decent folk. (This is not the earliest or the only use of this polemical method.) Even when the trial was in progress, *Pravda* published a long article about how a British lawyer, Dudley Collard, had described it (in the *Daily Herald*) as judicially unexceptionable.[148]

On 27 January 1937, three days before the verdict was handed down, *Pravda* had printed a more suitable item: an idealized portrait of Yezhov with the information that he had been promoted to be General Commissar of State Security. In general, the press and "public" had mounted the usual violent campaign. When the verdict was announced, a crowd of 200,000 assembled in the Red Square, in a temperature of $-27°$ Celsius, to be harangued by Khrushchev and Shvernik, and to demonstrate spontaneously against the accused.[149] They carried banners demanding the immediate carrying-out of the death sentences—a demand readily acceded to by the authorities. The victims were fully rehabilitated just over fifty years later.

## THE ORDZHONIKIDZE SUICIDE

Once again, the executions shocked the inner circles of the Party. This time, Stalin had to face an immediate threat of firm opposition from a colleague who could not easily be dismissed—Sergo Ordzhonikidze. He had been double-crossed. Personally involved in the negotiations before the Pyatakov Case, he had had Stalin's assurance that Pyatakov would not be executed. According to a recent Soviet writer, Ordzhonikidze had already been shaken by the "Hotel Bristol" matter; Stalin had given him a promise to check such evidence. When Pyatakov was arrested, Stalin told Ordzhonikidze, "Pyatakov will not be executed." After the trial, Yezhov told him, "Pyatakov is alive"; Ordzhonikidze demanded a meeting with him, and this was promised. Yezhov then told him that Pyatakov was in a state of shock after the "trick played by the Norwegians." But Ordzhonikidze can hardly have been put off for long.[150] He saw in all this a fatal precedent. It became clear that he would now carry on the fight against the Purge by every means at his disposal.

One account describes his behavior when he learned of the arrest of the head of one of the big trusts under his authority. He rang up Yezhov, called him a "filthy lickspittle," and demanded the documents in the case instantly. He then phoned Stalin on the direct circuit. By this time he was trembling, and his eyes were bloodshot. He shouted, "Koba, why do you let the NKVD arrest my men without informing me?" After some reply from Stalin, he interrupted: "I demand that this authoritarianism cease! I am still a member of the Politburo! I am going to raise hell, Koba, if it's the last thing I do before I die!"[151]

As usual, Stalin was not caught unprepared. In fact, though we usually think of the dispute between the two men about Pyatakov as a matter of Stalin wanting to get rid of Pyatakov and being willing to put up with trouble from Ordzhonikidze in the process, it seems equally plausible that Stalin fully intended the destruction of Pyatakov as a blow against Ordzhonikidze too and that the destruction of Ordzhonikidze was not simply a by-product of the Pyatakov Case, but something planned from the start. (As we have suggested, it was perhaps as a political signal of some sort that at that trial Muralov, while freely admitting plans to kill Molotov and others, firmly denied any plans against Ordzhonikidze.)[152] Ordzhonikidze's elder brother, Papuliya, had already been arrested in November 1936, and was "shot after being tortured" on 9 or 10 February.[153] Stalin must therefore have been preparing to strike at his old colleague, but to have shown his hand only a short time before his final move.

Meanwhile in the Transcaucasus, NKVD operatives were working "to compel arrested people to give false testimonies against S. Ordzhonikidze." This would have been meaningless after Ordzhonikidze's death, and shows that Stalin was already preparing a dossier against his old friend. Similarly, former NKVD officers tried in November 1955 were charged with "collecting slanderous material" against him, and later of terrorist acts against members of his family and close friends in responsible posts.[154]

It is also the case that most of Ordzhonikidze's associates fell before or after his death, and that this is a reasonable indication of Stalin's feelings. Among them was Gvakharia, Ordzhonikidze's nephew, the head of the great Makeyevka iron foundry. The leaders of Soviet heavy industry followed: Gurevich (a leading figure in the metallurgical industries), Tochinsky, and many others. The top directors and industrialists, the men who had actually, under Pyatakov, created Stalin's one real achievement, disappeared.

Ordzhonikidze himself was being increasingly harassed. Police officers

arrived at Ordzhonikidze's flat with a search warrant. Humiliated and frantic with rage, Sergo spent the rest of the night trying to get through to Stalin on the telephone. As morning came he finally got through and heard the answer: "It is the sort of organ that is even liable to search my place. That is nothing extraordinary. . . ."[155]

On 17 February, he had a conversation with Stalin lasting several hours. Stalin seems to have accused him of having earlier sympathized with the kulaks and now showing weakness and not enough "real proletarian principledness."[156] He made "a last attempt to explain to Stalin, a friend of many years' standing, that dark forces were currently profiting from his pathological lifelong suspiciousness and that the Party was being deprived of its best cadres."[157] So far, the "cadres" the party was being "deprived of" were practically all oppositionists or ex-oppositionists, and Ordzhonikidze's formulation seems well suited to Pyatakov, and perhaps—in anticipation—Bukharin and Rykov. The talk of "dark forces" is quite clearly an attack on Yezhov, and perhaps Kaganovich and others as well.

Ordzhonikidze worked in his People's Commissariat until 2:00 A.M. the next day, 18 February. When he got home, he had another equally fruitless conversation with Stalin on the telephone. At 5:30 in the afternoon, he was dead.

We are now definitely told in a recent Soviet article that he died of a gunshot wound.[158]

His wife, Zinaida, rang Stalin, who soon appeared. He "didn't ask a single question, but merely expressed astonishment: 'Heavens, what a tricky illness! The chap lay down to have a rest and the result was a fit and a heart attack,' "[159] thus establishing the official view, confirmed in the medical report, which ran as follows:

> Comrade Ordzhonikidze suffered from sclerosis accompanied by serious sclerotic transformations of the cardiac muscle and cardiac vessels, and also from a chronic affection of the right kidney, the only one he possessed after the removal in 1929 of the left kidney owing to tuberculosis.
>
> For two years Ordzhonikidze, from time to time, suffered from attacks of stenocardia *(angina pectoris)* and cardiac asthma. The last such attack, which was a very serious one, occurred at the beginning of November 1936.
>
> On the morning of 18 February Ordzhonikidze made no complaint about his health, but at 17.30, while he was having his afternoon rest, he suddenly felt ill and a few minutes later died of paralysis of the heart.
>
> > G. Kaminsky, People's Commissar for Health, U.S.S.R.
> > I. Khodorovsky, Head of the Kremlin Medical-Sanitary Administration
> > L. Levin, Consultant to the Kremlin Medical-Sanitary Administration
> > S. Mets, Duty Medical Officer of the Kremlin Clinic.[160]

Of the four signatories, Kaminsky (who, we are told, was "very unwilling"[161] to sign) was shot later in the year, Khodorovsky was referred to as a plotter in the Bukharin Trial, and Levin actually appeared as a defendant at that trial and was shot afterwards. What happened to the more obscure Mets is unknown.

Curiously enough, it was never alleged against the doctors, or anyone else, that Ordzhonikidze had been a victim of a murder plot by the opposition. It is true that at Ordzhonikidze's funeral a few days later, Khrushchev was to remark,

> It was they who struck a blow to thy noble heart. Pyatakov—the spy, the murderer, the enemy of the working people—is caught red-handed, caught and condemned, crushed like a reptile by the working class, but it was his counter-revolutionary work which hastened the death of our dear Sergo.[162]

And, indeed, the authoritative article on him in the *Large Soviet Encyclopedia,* describing him as "the favorite comrade-in-arms of the great Stalin" and saying that he "died at his post as a warrior of the Lenin-Stalin Party," added that "the Trotskyite–Bukharinite degenerates of Fascism hated Ordzhonikidze with a bitter hatred. They wanted to kill Ordzhonikidze. In this the Fascist agents did not succeed. But the sabotage activity and monstrous treachery of the despicable Right–Trotskyite hirelings of Japanese–German Fascism greatly hastened the death of Ordzhonikidze."[163]

But nevertheless, no one was ever charged with murdering him. This shows a curious restraint on Stalin's part (though, of course, he may have been saving the case for one of the post-Bukharin trials which never occurred, at least in public). One of Ordzhonikidze's deputies, Vannikov, was indeed summoned by Yezhov a few days after his death, to report on "wrecking" activities by Ordzhonikidze. It looks as though there was or had been some notion of posthumously attacking him, as Tomsky and Gamarnik had been attacked after their suicides. If so, this too was not pursued.[164]

It is now no longer disputed that Stalin did in fact procure Ordzhonikidze's death. But the details are still debatable. And the way in which the original official version lost credence, first in the defector literature, and finally in the Soviet Union itself, is an interesting demonstration of the relative worth of the sources.

Soon after Ordzhonikidze's death, rumors began to come out of Russia. These varied as to detail, some saying that he had been forced to kill himself under threat of immediate arrest as a Trotskyite, others that he had actually been shot, or poisoned under the supervision of Poskrebyshev, Stalin's secretary.[165] For example, Kravchenko, in his book published a decade before Khrushchev's revelations at the XXth Party Congress, says that some believed that he committed suicide, others that he was killed.[166] But no one had any doubt that he died by violence, that his end was not "natural."

Khrushchev said in 1961 that he had believed what was said about Ordzhonikidze's heart attack, and only "much later, after the war, I learned quite by chance that he had committed suicide."[167] But we know from Soviet sources that the suicide story had circulated widely in the Party. Amirdzhanov, a "worker of the Baku Soviet"—scarcely a very senior position—was "repressed" in 1937 because when "a certain section of the Party *aktiv*" had—already—learned of the suicide story, he had passed it on to "an intimate circle of comrades."[168] It was circulating in Kazan prison by April 1937.[169] Again, we are told that Nazaretyan, "one of the first" to learn the truth about Ordzhonikidze's death, was arrested in June 1937 and had already learned it by then.[170] In the NKVD, too, rumors circulated to the same effect.[171]

In the USSR, the natural-death version remained official until in February 1956 Khrushchev remarked in his Secret Speech:

> Beria also cruelly treated the family of Comrade Ordzhonikidze. Why? Because Ordzhonikidze had tried to prevent Beria from realizing his shameful plans. Beria had cleared from his way all persons who could possibly interfere with him. Ordzhonikidze was always an opponent of Beria, which he told Stalin. Instead of examining this matter and taking appropriate steps, Stalin permitted the liquidation of Ordzhonikidze's brother and brought Ordzhonikidze himself to such a state that he was forced to shoot himself.

This account is clearly misleading. Khrushchev represents Ordzhonikidze's death as simply due to the failure of an attempt to hamper Beria, as a result of which Stalin turned against him. But at this time, Beria was in the Caucasus, and though he was certainly influential he played little part in the great affairs of state going on at Politburo level in Moscow. The interest of the 1956 version is elsewhere, in the "he was forced to shoot himself."

Indeed, Khrushchev himself, when he raised the matter for the first time in a nonsecret speech, omitted the Beria angle, which by 1961 was no longer a "must." He said:

> Comrade Ordzhonikidze saw that he could no longer work with Stalin, although previously he had been one of his closest friends . . . circumstances had become such that Ordzhonikidze could no longer work normally, and in order to avoid clashing with Stalin and sharing the responsibility for his abuse of power, he decided to take his life.[172]

This version has not since been amended or contradicted. It may be worth examining the other possibilities. There are, in effect, three stories (now that natural death has been eliminated): suicide out of despair—a voluntary act, straight murder, and suicide as the result of a threat of worse alternatives by Stalin. Khrushchev implies the first. But it seems reasonable to think that, at most, he is making the best of a forced suicide—just as, in the Kirov Case, he could not quite, in a public speech, bring himself to accuse Stalin directly of murder.

A close friend of Ordzhonikidze's widow relates that she thought he had been killed by others, and had seen men running across the lawn away from the house at the time of his death.[173] A Caucasian Party official who was in Moscow at the time says that Stalin sent several secret policemen to Ordzhonikidze, offered him the alternative of arrest or suicide, and gave him a revolver.[174] This account fits in with the fact that a dossier against Ordzhonikidze had been accumulated. It does not, of course, give any guarantee that the fatal shot was fired by Ordzhonikidze himself. In fact, there seems no real point in making him shoot himself, when the NKVD men could do that equally easily. One recent Soviet account has it that the first guard on the spot after his death noted that Ordzhonikidze's revolver had no signs of having been fired, and so reported (being soon shot himself).[175]

The stories associating Poskrebyshev with the death would be probable, in such circumstances. Ordzhonikidze could scarcely have been expected to accept a political ultimatum or, indeed, to commit suicide at all, on a threat from a lesser NKVD officer; the presence of Stalin's personal representative is a reasonable idea. Ordzhonikidze's own NKVD guards must, of course, have been given suitable orders.

There was one obvious motive for at least pretending suicide. If the doctors, or any of them, had seen the body and been told it was suicide, it is of course understandable that they could have been induced to hush up the scandal in the interests of Party and State. Kaminsky, at least, was to prove a brave critic of the new Terror over the months that were left to him; it may perhaps have been his direct connection with the Ordzhonikidze case which brought him to his moral decision. Hushed up or not, and even taking it as suicide and not murder, at his political level (as candidate member of the Central Committee) he might have guessed what a suicide in those circumstances signified. But if it had *obviously* been murder, he might well have taken a stronger line.

The decisive argument against any but a forced suicide (or murder) is different. If Ordzhonikidze had felt "unable to share responsibility," if he "did not want to play the scoundrel" as an accomplice in Stalin's plans, it is quite untrue that "the only thing to do was to depart," as a Soviet account of the 1960s has it.[176] On the contrary, the Central Committee was to meet the next day.[177] When, after a postponement, the full plenum met on 23 February, some attempt was made to block the Purge. The natural, in fact the "only" thing for Ordzhonikidze to do was to throw himself into the struggle. Suicide at this moment was pointless.

Ordzhonikidze had been asked to prepare a report for the impending Central Committee plenum. This is still in the archives, and a Soviet historian describes Ordzhonikidze's draft being returned by Stalin with coarse and hostile comments. This led to "stormy" exchanges.[178] Another recent Soviet publication suggests that Ordzhonikidze indeed planned to make a stand against the purges at the February–March plenum, hoping for the support of "Postyshev, Chubar, perhaps Kalinin."[179] But from Stalin's point of view, the opposite consideration prevailed. An opposition led by an angry Ordzhonikidze was likely to prove much more difficult to handle than one lacking his support. Voluntary suicide was pointless; but forced suicide (or murder) was logically indicated. A recent article by a Soviet historian tells us that those who saw him on the last day of his life reported him energetic, with no signs of depression, making appointments for the next day—as confirmed by his papers, still in the archives.[180]

It is not uninteresting that Vyshinsky described the death of Zinoviev's secretary, Bogdan, who had allegedly been forced to commit suicide under the terms "Kill yourself or else we will kill you," as "really murder."[181] In this sense, even accepting a forced suicide, we can in any case certainly speak of the murder of Ordzhonikidze. As I write, the question of whose hand held the gun must be left as recently put by a Soviet historian—that "Ordzhonikidze killed himself (or was shot)."[182]

On 19 February 1937,[183] the first photographs of Ordzhonikidze's corpse show, grouped around it, his wife and Stalin's own cabal: Stalin himself, Yezhov, Molotov, Zhdanov, Kaganovich, Mikoyan, and Voroshilov. They all appear overcome with comradely sorrow.

A Central Committee announcement the same day spoke of him as "an irreproachably pure and staunch Party man, a Bolshevik."[184] And Ordzhonikidze continued to be honored by Stalin, just as Kirov did. There is one curious public sign of the dictator's animus. Seven years later, in 1942, the main towns that had been named after Ordzhonikidze were quietly rechristened: Ordzhonikidzegrad (formerly Bezhitsa), Ordzhonikidze (formerly Yenakiyevo), and Sergo (formerly Kadiyevka) reverted to their earlier names, while Ordzhonikidze in the Caucasus (formerly Vladikavkaz), was given a new Ossetian name, Dzaudzhikau. Such action, in the Stalinist protocol, had hitherto invariably been a sign of disgrace (and was to be so in future under his successor as well, when the town of Molotov reverted to Perm, and so on).

As to Ordzhonikidze's relatives (though without publicity), Papuliya Ordzhonikidze's wife, Nina, was sentenced to ten years on 29 March 1938, and to death on 14 June 1938. Two other Ordzhonikidze brothers and a sister-in-law were jailed from 1939 through 1941; two other relatives were shot in 1937 and 1938; and another was imprisoned.[185] Yet no further public degradation was inflicted.

Five days after Ordzhonikidze's death, the Central Committee assembled. In the last trial of strength which now took place, his presence was to be sorely missed among the elements attempting to halt the Purge.

## THE FEBRUARY–MARCH PLENUM

The agenda of the plenum as first circulated consisted of two items:

1. The question of N. I. Bukharin and A.I. Rykov
2. Organizational questions

Bukharin had already begun to think of suicide, and several times toyed with a revolver long ago presented to him, with ammunition, by Voroshilov. Another of Bukharin's revolvers (as his wife was told in 1939 by Yezhov's secretary Ryzhova, her cell mate in the Lubyanka) had been fixed so that it could not fire, presumably by the NKVD, which would perhaps have taken the same precaution with this one.

Bukharin now went on a hunger strike.

Just before the plenum opened, on 23 February, a new agenda was circulated:

1. The question of the anti-Party action of Bukharin in connection with his declaring a hunger strike to the Plenum
2. The question of N. Bukharin and A. Rykov
3. Organizational questions [186]

Livshits's last words, as he was being led to execution, had been a cry of "What for?" Or so a story went that now circulated in the upper levels of the Party. Army Commander Yakir, a full member of the Central Committee, commented privately when he heard it that the question was a good one, as the men were quite clearly innocent. [187] This appears to have been the mood among some members of the Central Committee as the "February–March plenum" opened.

The atmosphere was extremely tense. Stalin, though, was determined finally to overcome the hesitations and qualms which had for so long held him up and forced him to mark time. The struggle at the plenum is another of the cases in which long-standing rumor was, after decades of official silence, more or less confirmed by Khrushchev in 1956 and 1961.

The session was, of course, "managed" by Stalin's men; the official *rapporteurs* were Yezhov, Zhdanov, Molotov, and Stalin himself. Formally speaking, they dealt with different subjects—Yezhov with police affairs, Zhdanov with Party organization, Molotov with the economic side, while Stalin made the political report. But in practice, all the reports centered on the Purge theme, from Yezhov's "Lessons Emerging from the Harmful Activity, Diversion and Espionage of the Japanese-German-Trotskyite Agents," [188] through Zhdanov's condemnation of wrongful methods of expelling Party members and Molotov's "report on wrecking and sabotage," [189] to Stalin's "Deficiencies of Party Work and Methods for the Liquidation of the Trotskyites and other Two-faced People."

In fact there was, in reality, only one item on the agenda—the fate of Bukharin and Rykov.

Even now, one or two old colleagues, perhaps still hoping for successful resistance at the plenum, had the courage to show their feelings. Akulov said to Bukharin, "Play the man, Nikolai Ivanovich"; Uborevich pressed his hand.[190]

When Bukharin saw Stalin, Stalin told him to apologize to the plenum for his hunger strike and assured him that he would not be expelled. Bukharin then started proceedings by making the appropriate apology, and was then once again violently attacked by Yezhov, Molotov, Kaganovich, and later Kalinin.[191]

Yezhov in his report charged Bukharin and Rykov with all the available anti-Soviet crimes: implication in the conspiracies of Zinoviev and Pyatakov, planning the return of capitalism through fascist interventionists, organizing peasant rebellions, inspiring the Ryutin Platform, and plotting the murder of Stalin and the overthrow of the Soviet Government. Kossior then attacked Bukharin for having helped draft the Ryutin document. Bukharin retorted that he had been in the Pamirs at the time to which Kossior referred, and Kossior replied, "Nevertheless we must believe Yezhov."[192] Bukharin rejected this and all the other charges, and both he and Rykov bitterly protested their innocence: "They did not take the road of repentance."[193] Every point raised against them they denied "many times."[194]

On 26 February, they made their final defense. Both again denied all the charges.

Bukharin is said to have made a strong and emotional speech, agreeing that a conspiracy existed but claiming that its leaders were Stalin and Yezhov, who were plotting to install an NKVD regime giving Stalin unlimited personal power.[195] The two men were hotly abused and shouted down with cries of "to jail!" Voroshilov cursed Bukharin. Molotov shouted that Bukharin was proving his fascist affiliations by casting doubt on earlier confessions, and thus supporting anti-Soviet propaganda.[196] Stalin interrupted him, saying that he was behaving in a manner unbecoming to a revolutionary, and he could prove his innocence in a prison cell.[197] Bukharin finally took his seat, saying that even in jail he would not change what he was saying.

The plenum appointed a commission of thirty-six members, with Mikoyan in the chair (and not voting), to report on the question.[198] Twenty spoke. Yezhov, supported by five others, proposed the expulsion of Bukharin and Rykov from the Central Committee and the Party, trial before the Military Collegium, and execution. Postyshev, supported by seven others, including Petrovsky and Kossior, proposed the same, without the application of execution. Stalin, supported by five others, proposed merely sending them to the NKVD for further investigation.[199] Stalin's proposal was eventually accepted unanimously.[200]

A subcommittee, consisting of Stalin, Molotov, Voroshilov, Kaganovich, Mikoyan, and Yezhov, then prepared a resolution. It asserted that "as a minimum" the NKVD had established that Bukharin and Rykov were aware of the counter-revolutionary activity of the Trotskyite Center, and of other Rightists of their own circle. It also accused Bukharin of slandering the NKVD. And it accepted Stalin's formulation of expulsion and handing over to the investigative organs. The resolution then passed, Bukharin and Rykov dissenting.[201] The two men were arrested on the spot and dragged off to the Lubyanka.

The search of Bukharin's apartment, unlike those of Zinoviev and Kamenev in 1934, was rigorous, including personal searches of his wife, his father, and the other occupants, though the baby's cot was not disturbed. Boris Berman, now head of an NKVD Department, supervised a group of twelve or thirteen male and female officers. When they finished, at midnight, they made a convivial supper in the Bukharins' dining room.[202]

The plenum continued, with Zhdanov's organizational report. He took the opportunity to criticize sharply the situation in Kiev under Postyshev for "incorrect leadership" and "gross breaches of the Party constitution and the principles of democratic centralism"—the main point being that the Kiev and other organizations had been resorting to co-option instead of election, and that this was extremely undemocratic.[203]

During the weeks since January, the indirect attacks on Postyshev's position had continued. On 1 February, his close supporter Karpov was denounced as "an enemy of the Party, a loathsome Trotskyite."[204] Over the following weeks, about sixty expulsions of his old nominees from the Kiev Party were announced. These lesser figures were more easily removable. They had no Old Bolshevik past, and even if their record as Stalinists was a sound one, it was not so widely known throughout the Party as to make charges against them sound unbelievable. In attacking men like Karpov, Stalin was undermining Postyshev without having the assault made directly. But at the same time, establishing the "Trotskyism" of the second- and third-rank Stalinists in the entourages of men he wished to remove, Stalin was setting up precedents which, as resistance weakened, gave him a freer and freer hand to deal with more important men with perfect records.

On 8 February came attacks on faults that had been found in the Kiev, Azov-Black Sea, and Kursk provinces.[205] On the following day, "lordly and immodest" actions that had come to light in the Party leaderships in Kiev and Rostov provinces were described.[206] The concentration on Kiev was obvious enough.*

These attacks had not so far cowed Postyshev, and he held himself ready to put his viewpoint. There seems to have been no intention of removing Stalin, but only of curbing him and getting him to abandon Yezhov and the Purge. There were precedents in Russian history, but they were not encouraging ones. The *boyar,* Prince Michael Repnin, had called on Ivan the Terrible to rid himself of his Secret Police:

> "To our misfortune, you have surrounded your
> throne with the *oprichnina.* . . .
> Perish the *oprichnina!*" he said, making the
> Sign of the Cross;
> "May he live for ever, our orthodox Tsar!
> May he rule over men as he ruled them of old!
> May he spurn, as treason, the voice of shameless
> flattery! . . ."

The declaration of loyalty to the ruler and hostility to his Secret Police was unsuccessful, and Repnin was killed, a lesson to all who undertake such half-measures.

---

*Although we may note that the Secretary of the Azov-Black Sea Committee, Malinov, and the head of his Party Organs Department were to be denounced as Trotskyite conspirators (*Pravda,* 5 June 1937).

Stalin seems to have learned of Postyshev's plan in advance. Speaking first, he anticipated and refuted the arguments to be brought against him, and made an appeal for unity and responsibility in the Communist leadership.

Postyshev then went to the platform. In his "dry, hoarse and unpleasant voice," he began to read his text. After a careful preamble, he spoke of the excesses of the Purge:

> I have philosophized that the severe years of the struggle have passed; Party members who lost their backbone broke down or joined the camp of the enemy, healthy elements fought for the Party. Those were the years of industrialization and collectivization. I never thought it possible that after this severe era had passed Karpov and people like him would find themselves in the camp of the enemy. And now, according to the testimony, it appears that Karpov was recruited in 1934 by the Trotskyites. I personally do not believe that in 1934 an honest Party member who had trod the long road of unrelenting fight against enemies, for the Party and for socialism, would now be in the camp of the enemies. I do not believe it. . . . I cannot imagine how it would be possible to travel with the Party during the difficult years and then, in 1934, join the Trotskyites. It is an odd thing. . . .[207]

Stalin, who was listening without apparent emotion, uttered a loud interjection, which made it clear to everyone that he was aware of what was going on.

This was perhaps the occasion on which Stalin turned to Postyshev and said, "What are you, actually?" to which Postyshev replied, "I am a Bolshevik, Comrade Stalin, a Bolshevik."[208] This reply, in any case, was at first represented in the Party as showing lack of respect for Stalin, and later "it was considered a harmful act and consequently resulted in Postyshev's annihilation and in his being branded without reason as an enemy of the people"[209]—an exaggerated and compressed account.

Whatever Stalin said, Postyshev (according to one version)[210] faltered from the text of his speech and later withdrew his doubts. In any case, it is clear that his forlorn hope of swaying the plenum had failed.

Yezhov made a wide-ranging report. For instance, he complained that over recent months he could not think of a case in which the economic ministries had telephoned him to express suspicions about any of their staff; on the contrary, they had tried to defend them.[211]

A resolution on Yezhov's report was accepted which repeated Stalin's formulation about the NKVD's failure under Yagoda to act four years previously— that is, against Ryutin:

> The Plenum of the Party Central Committee considers that all facts revealed during the investigation into the matter of an anti-Soviet Trotskyite center and of its followers in the provinces show that the People's Commissariat of Internal Affairs had fallen behind at least four years in the attempt to unmask these most inexorable enemies of the people. . . .[212]

Stalin severely criticized Yagoda.[213] This must have been the occasion when Yagoda turned on the applauding members and snarled that six months earlier he could have arrested the lot of them.[214]

Ordzhonikidze's report to which Stalin had objected had been supposed to cover sabotage in industry. Molotov, taking up Yezhov's point, now performed this duty, saying that 585 people had been arrested in the People's Commissariat of Heavy Industry alone, and hundreds in other ministries concerned.[215] He sneered at those who urged caution "against conjuring up all sorts of conspiracies and sabotage and espionage centers," and called on the Party to annihilate enemies of the people "hiding behind Party cards." The present-day subversives and saboteurs were especially dangerous, he said, because they "pretend to be Communists, ardent supporters of the Soviet regime."[216]

On 3 March, Stalin made his political report, and on 5 March a short "final speech" closing the plenum. These two speeches were printed in full in the press on 29 March in a version believed to differ considerably, chiefly by omission, from what he had actually said. They were later in the year sponsored in England in one volume with a slightly compressed transcript of the Pyatakov Trial. Neil Maclean, M.P., the British commentator we have already quoted, commented in a preface: "These speeches in that simple and clear style of which M. Stalin is such a master form an interesting background and commentary on the Trial. . . ." They do indeed.

Stalin's report developed the theoretical justification for the Terror. Quoting the Central Committee letters of 18 January 1935 and 29 July 1936, he propounded his view (to be denounced in the Khrushchev period) that as socialism gets stronger, the class struggle gets sharper.

He pointed out that the fact of there only being a few counter-revolutionaries should not comfort the Party: "Thousands of people are required to build a big railway bridge, but a few people are enough to blow it up. Tens and hundreds of such examples could be quoted. . . ."

But his central theme was in effect a censure of leaders who had failed in their vigilance:

Some of our leading comrades, both in the centre and locally, not only failed to discern the real countenance of these wreckers, diversionists, spies, and murderers, but proved so unconcerned, complacent and naïve, that at times they themselves assisted in promoting the agents of the foreign States to one or other responsible post.[217]

"The espionage-diversionist work of the Trotskyite agents of the Japanese–German secret police," he added,

was a complete surprise to some of our comrades. . . . Our Party comrades have not noticed that Trotskyism has ceased to be a political tendency in the working class, that from the political tendency in the working class that it was seven or eight years ago, Trotskyism has become a frenzied and unprincipled band of wreckers, diversionists, spies and murderers, acting on instructions from intelligence service organs of foreign States.[218]

He made a sinister suggestion, which was to prove a fair statement of his plans: "First of all it is necessary to suggest to our Party leaders, from cell secretaries to the secretaries of province and republic Party organizations, to select, within a certain period, two people in each case, two Party workers capable of being their real substitutes."[219]

His final speech fully implicated Bukharinites as well as Trotskyites:

Two words about wreckers, diversionists, spies, etc. I think it is clear to everybody now that the present-day wreckers and diversionists, no matter what disguise they may adopt, either Trotskyite or Bukharinite, have long ceased to be a political trend in the labour movement, that they have become transformed into a gang of professional wreckers, diversionists, spies and assassins, without principles and without ideals. Of course, these gentlemen must be ruthlessly smashed and uprooted as the enemies of the working class, as betrayers of our country. This is clear and requires no further explanation.[220]

The bulk of the speech concentrated on a different matter—the censure, in effect, of his next batch of victims. His theme was incorrect conduct, and unjustified expulsions, by leading Communists still in high positions. Then, after remarking that

we, the leaders, should not be conceited, and should understand that if we are members of the Central Committee or People's Commissars, this does not yet mean that we possess all the knowledge required to give correct leadership. The rank in itself gives neither knowledge nor experience. Still less so does the title.[221]

he went on to deal with the unfortunate case of Nikolayenko in Kiev:

Nikolayenko—is a rank and file member of the Party, she is an ordinary 'little person'. For a whole year she had signalled about a wrong situation in the Party organization in Kiev, exposing the family atmosphere, philistine approach to workers, gagging of self-criticism, high-handed action by the Trotskyite wreckers. She was shunned like a bothersome fly. At last, in order to get rid of her, they expelled her from the Party. Neither the Kiev organization nor the Central Committee of the Communist Party of the Ukraine helped her to obtain justice. It was only the intervention of the Central Committee of the Party which helped to disentangle that twisted knot. And what was revealed by an examination of the case? It was revealed that Nikolayenko was right, while the Kiev organization was wrong.[222]

and he added, of the inhuman attitude to such expulsions by some Party bureaucrats, "Only people who are essentially deeply anti-Party can have such an approach to members of the Party."[223]

With these sinister words ringing in their ears, the defeated "moderates" dispersed to their posts, where worse awaited them.

In Postyshev's old fief, a "Ukrainian Trotskyite Center" came to some sort of trial straight away—Kotsiubinsky being shot on 8 March, Golubenko on 9 March, and Musulbas on 10 March, together with O. P. Dzenis of the Ukrainian Institute of Marxism-Leninism. Their accomplice V. F. Loginov (named as a prominent Ukrainian "Trotskyite," and giving satisfactory evidence as a "witness" at the Pyatakov Trial) was held over and only executed on 11 October 1938.

On 17 March, the Ukrainian Central Committee relieved Postyshev of his post as Second Secretary.[224] He was demoted to be First Secretary in Kuibyshev province. There, though still officially retaining his rank as candidate member of the Politburo, he was to moulder, under constant criticism, for a year. The new post was supposed to be an opportunity to "correct his errors," it was later to be said,[225] with the verdict that he had failed to measure up.

In Kiev, a resolution was passed saying that as a result of Postyshev's leadership, and its "un-Bolshevik style of work" which suppressed criticism and formed a solid clique, enemies of the Party had been able to penetrate the organization and sometimes to persecute honest Communists.[226]

In the following months, the implications grew. At the Ukrainian Congress in May, Kossior attacked Postyshev. In Kiev more than anywhere, he said, Trotskyites had been able to gain important posts.[227] Other speakers upbraided those in Kiev "who had let in enemies." Over several years of complacency, the main thing had been a personality cult involving "Greetings to Postyshev!" as the restored and rehabilitated Nikolayenko smugly remarked to the uneasy delegates.[228] He had been, in fact, "intoxicated with success" because of "the noise our press made round his name."[229]

The defeat and demotion of Postyshev was only the beginning. Over the next few years, the great majority (70 percent) of the Central Committee which had just seen his final and fumbling stand was to follow Bukharin and Rykov to the death cells.

For, politically, Stalin's battle had now been won. The way was at last completely open to the total annihilation of the old oppositionists. At the same time, by his actions against Postyshev, he had made the first moves to undermining and destroying that group of his own followers who had hoped to block him.

But the main change was that the last attempt to preserve some sort of constitutional procedure had been defeated. In future, he was not to observe any such limitations. In six months, the position had changed radically. In the autumn of 1936, Stalin had had to argue and exert pressure to secure the arrest and trial even of potential rivals. Now, he could order the arrest of his closest colleagues without consulting anyone. He could strike when and where he liked, without appeal. The point at which his despotism became an absolute autocracy may be dated as the February–March plenum.

There were still steps to be taken to ensure the irrevocability of the victory. The demoralized and defeated rank and file of the Central Committee, convicted of the most capital of all crimes, ineffective disloyalty, had to be mopped up. The Purge had so far only affected a limited section of the Soviet people, among whom there remained much political indiscipline to be eradicated. And the Army remained—to all appearances wholly obedient, but tyrants have often been misled on this point, and Stalin was soon to insure himself against such a mistake.

But first, the instrument of terror needed retuning. The old NKVD of Yagoda's time was technically efficient, but in certain respects it lacked the true Stalinist spirit. In any case, its new master could not trust his predecessor's men.

In March, Yezhov ordered the departmental chiefs of the NKVD to proceed to various parts of the country on a massive inspection. Only Slutsky of the Foreign Department and—for the moment—Pauker were not so assigned. The others, leaving shortly afterward, were arrested at the first stations out of Moscow in their various directions, and brought back to prison. Two days later, the same trick was played on the deputy heads of the departments. At the same time, Yezhov changed the NKVD in all sensitive spots.[230] He had already barricaded himself in a separate wing of the NKVD building, surrounded by a formidable bodyguard and elaborate security precautions.[231]

On 18 March 1937[232] Yezhov addressed a meeting of senior officers of the NKVD in the Secret Police club room at the Lubyanka. He denounced Yagoda as a former Tsarist police spy and a thief and an embezzler, and went on to speak of "Yagoda's spies" in the NKVD. He proceeded to clean up the remaining Yagoda cadres. They were arrested in their offices by day or in their homes by night. Chertok, the bullying interrogator of Kamenev, threw himself from his twelfth-floor apartment. Other officers shot themselves, or committed suicide by jumping from their office windows.[233] Most went passively, Bulanov, arrested at the end of March, among them.[234] Three thousand of Yagoda's NKVD officers are reported executed in 1937,[235] while over the whole period about 20,000 NKVD men "fell victim."[236] Of his departmental chiefs, Molchanov, Mironov, and Shanin were to be denounced as Rightist conspirators,[237] organized as such in the OGPU in 1931 and 1932, while Pauker (who disappeared in the summer) and Gay were transmuted to spies,[238] together with Pauker's deputy Volovich. (Pauker, a Jew, was spoken of as specifically a German spy.)[239]

On 3 April it was announced that Yagoda himself had been arrested for "offenses of a criminal nature in connection with his official duties."[240] Next day, an announcement was made of a new People's Commissar and Assistant People's Commissar of Communications.[241] The transfer of the former Assistant People's Commissar G. E. Prokofiev was also published. Although he was still named as "Comrade," he was arrested shortly afterward as a Rightist and later attempted suicide in prison.[242] The wives of both men were also arrested and were sent to a camp.[243] Yagoda's dacha was taken over by Molotov.[244]

Yezhov now had his machine cleared and ready for action. At the same time, the other main element in the Purge mechanism, Vyshinsky's Prosecutor's apparatus, was being similarly renovated. A number of the old Prosecutors had attempted to maintain a semblance of legality. For example, the Assistant Chief Prosecutor of Water Transport had put in a memorandum on 26 June 1936 urging this. Similar protests were made by a number of provincial Prosecutors—for example in Bryansk, where two were arrested "for spreading false and defamatory rumors." Ninety percent of the provincial Prosecutors were removed, and many of them were arrested. "Vyshinsky carried out a mass purge in the organs of the Prosecutor's office. With his sanction, many prominent workers in the Prosecutor's Office who had tried in one way or another to mitigate repressive measures and stop the lawlessness and arbitrariness were arrested and subsequently perished."[245] As late as the beginning of 1938, the ironically titled Stalinist law journal *Socialist Legality*[246] called for further work in purging "fascist agents" among the Prosecutors.

The authorities on Soviet law who had inculcated the "formalist" attitude to legality were held to responsibility. The Deputy Commissar for Justice, the Soviet Union's leading legal theorist, E. Pashukanis, was severely criticized in January 1937[247] and shot, and in April was to be linked by Vyshinsky with Bukharin as a wrecker "who has now been exposed."[248] Another unsatisfactory Deputy Commissar for Justice, V. A. Degot, was arrested on 31 July 1937. Sent to camp, he died in 1944.[249]

By early spring, all the machinery was in good order. The old Communist police and prosecutors, ruthless as they had been, had not proved sufficiently so for the new phase. Russians who had thought that the country was already in the grip of terrorists were now to see what terror really meant.

# ASSAULT
# ON THE ARMY

*Ils sauront bientôt que nos balles*
*Sont pour nos propres généraux*
"The Internationale"

On 11 June 1937 it was announced that the flower of the Red Army Command had been charged with treason, and next day that they had been tried and executed. Unlike the victims of the political purges, there had been virtually no public build-up of feeling against the generals. For most people, in the Soviet Union and outside, the news came as a complete and shocking surprise. No details were given of the "treason." The "campaign" appearing in the papers on 12 June could hardly have the effect obtained on previous occasions by months or years of abuse. The newspapers did their best with meetings demanding the death penalty for the "foul band of spies"; there had already been time for Demyan Bedny to compose a fifty-four-line poem including the names of the generals in the rhyme scheme; and in the pages around them, factory demonstrators, the Academy of Sciences, the polar explorers on Rudolph Island, and in fact representatives of the entire community demanded the shooting of the traitors, which had, as it turned out, already taken place. On 15 June, *Pravda* published Voroshilov's report to a meeting of members of the Government and the Military Soviet of the People's Commissariat of Defense on the crimes of the soldiers. They had "admitted their treacherousness, wrecking and espionage."

The men concerned were Marshal Tukhachevsky, Deputy People's Commissar of Defense; Army Commander Yakir, commanding the Kiev Military District; Army Commander Uborevich, commanding the Byelorussian Military District; Corps Commander Eideman, Head of the civil defense organization Osoaviakhim; Army Commander Kork, Head of the Military Academy; Corps Commander Putna, lately Military Attaché in London; Corps Commander Feldman, Head of the Red Army Administration; and Corps Commander Primakov, Deputy Commander of the Leningrad Military District. In addition, Yan Gamarnik, Head of the Political Administration of the Red Army and First Deputy Commissar of Defense, whose suicide had been announced on 1 June, was implicated in the alleged conspiracy. The original communiqué said that "the above-named persons were accused of breach of military duty and oath of allegiance, treason to their country, treason against the peoples of the USSR and treason against the Workers' and Peasants' Red Army."[1]

There was some discrepancy between these charges and those given in Voroshilov's report, which associates the accused with Trotsky and charges them with "preparing the assassination of leaders of the Party and Government," as well as with espionage.[2] As we shall see, both the Trotskyite and the treason themes had been prepared over many months, and the treason at least was well "documented."

The accused were all leading members of the group around Tukhachevsky which had pioneered military rethinking through the 1930s. They had developed the ideas and to some degree the organization of an efficient, modern army.

The military leaders were still young men. They had been commanding Armies while still in their twenties. Apart from Kork, who was just fifty, those now seized were all in their forties. Even now, Tukhachevsky and Putna were forty-four; Yakir and Uborevich, only forty-one—the same age as Zhukov, who was to play an important military and political role for many years to come. Gamarnik, too, was only forty-three.

Tukhachevsky had by general recognition the finest military brain in the Army, and the strongest powers of will and nerve. He came of the minor aristocracy. During the First World War, he had served as a subaltern in the Semeonovsky Guards Regiment. He had been taken prisoner by the Germans in 1915. After five attempts to escape, he was lodged in the security fortress of Ingolstadt, the Colditz of the First World War (where his fellow inmates include young Captain de Gaulle). In 1917, he got back to Russia, where he joined the Bolsheviks. "Brilliant, quick of mind, with a streak of cruelty allied to an impetuousness which bordered on the rash, the young Red Army Commander cultivated a certain *hauteur* and an arrogance which was not calculated to ease all his friendships."[3] He was twenty-seven when, in 1920, he commanded the Armies attacking Poland, having several times saved the Communists on the Eastern Front. He later commanded at Kronstadt and against the Antonov rebellion in the Tambov region.

The Kiev and Byelorussian Military Districts, under Yakir and Uborevich, respectively, were the two largest, containing between them twenty-five of the ninety rifle divisions and twelve of the twenty-six cavalry divisions.

Yakir, brisk and young in appearance and activity, was the son of a small Jewish chemist in Kishinev. He had organized a Bolshevik band in the Ukraine when only twenty-one, and had risen within three years to command the so-called Fastov army groups against the Poles. From 1926, he had commanded the key Ukrainian Military District, under its various successive names. He was the only professional soldier who was a full member of the Central Committee.*

Uborevich, a bespectacled military intellectual, had also commanded an Army against the Poles in 1920, and had then figured in the brilliant operations which finally led to the storming of the Crimea at the end of 1920 and put an end to the Civil War. He was a candidate member of the Central Committee, the only Army one besides four Marshals† and Gamarnik's Assistant Head of the Political Administration, A. S. Bulin.

The other accused were almost equally distinguished. Kork and Eideman, too, had commanded Armies in the Civil and Polish wars. Eideman, a square-

---

*The other "military" full members were Voroshilov and Gamarnik.
†Blyukher, Budenny, Tukhachevsky, and Yegorov.

headed, mustached, sergeant-major-looking type, was in fact a Latvian writer. Putna, who had served with Tukhachevsky in the Semeonovsky Guards before the Revolution, had had lesser commands, but had held major posts in the training side of the Army in the 1920s. Feldman, of Jewish origin, was one of Tukhachevsky's closest associates.

The other main victim of Stalin's blow, Yan Gamarnik, Head of the Army Political Administration and First Deputy People's Commissar for War, was not in quite the same category. He had been engaged in controversies against the military leaders on matters of political–military organization. A typical Old Bolshevik, he had fought in very dangerous circumstances in the Ukraine in the Civil War, and had voted with the Sapronov faction at the time of its influence in the Republic.[4] But he had had no connection with the oppositionists since the mid-1920s. He had been appointed Head of the Political Administration of the Red Army in 1929. With his long, rough beard and resemblance to Dostoyevsky, he was thought of—in the Party context, it is true—as a sort of saint.

Far from their fine records being of any service to the generals, the contrary seems to apply. In 1937, one-fifth of the officer corps were still veterans of the Civil War; this included almost all the High Command. But there were many grudges outstanding from those earlier times. During the battles for Tsaritsyn, a group had formed around Voroshilov and Stalin which continually disobeyed and stood out against the orders of Trotsky as Commissar for War. A long, bloody-minded intrigue, in which Voroshilov in particular behaved extremely badly, caused perhaps the worst ill-feeling to be found even among the freely quarreling Bolshevik leadership.

Under this Tsaritsyn group had come a cavalry unit headed by Budenny, initially little better than bandits. He himself relates that Trotsky at the time spoke of them as "a horde," under "an Ataman ringleader. . . . Where he leads his gang, there they will go; for the Reds today, tomorrow for the Whites."[5] One of Budenny's commanders actually shot a commissar for protesting against the sack of Rostov. As recruits came in, the "horde" was later expanded, with Stalin's help, to be the First Cavalry Army. It had attracted efficient as well as erratic elements, and improved with organization. Its Military Council had consisted of Voroshilov, Shchadenko, and Budenny.

The First Cavalry Army was involved in the fiercest controversy of all—the argument about responsibility for the Soviet defeat in the Battle of Warsaw in 1920. As Tukhachevsky had struck north of the Polish capital with the main bulk of the Soviet forces, Yegorov and Stalin with the Southern Front, including Budenny's men, had been attacking toward Lwów. Orders to divert Budenny northward had been disregarded until too late, at best on technical excuses, at worst in a short-sighted attempt to secure local glory at the expense of the main effort. It is arguable that the Soviet forces were anyhow overextended, but the bulk of Soviet military opinion followed Tukhachevsky in feeling that Stalin, Yegorov, and Budenny had wantonly robbed the offensive of whatever chance it had. Lenin seems to have agreed, remarking, "Who on earth would want to get to Warsaw by going through Lwów?"[6] The whole matter was thrashed out in public in military lectures. There can be no doubt that it rankled bitterly with Stalin, and when he gained full control of the history books the whole episode was represented as a strategically sound drive on Lwów, sabotaged for motives of treason by Tukhachevsky and Trotsky.*

But at the time, the controversy soon began to seem minor and academic. Compared with the true political virulences then prevailing, the Army gradually became a quiet area amid the storms of Soviet political life.

In the 1920s, Communists in the armed forces were at first strongly and openly involved in the political arguments of the time. Antonov-Ovseenko, Head of the Army Political Administration, had been forthrightly Trotskyite. Lashevich, the Zinovievite Deputy Commissar for War, had actually held a more or less secret oppositionist meeting in a wood while still at his post.

But later, this sort of overt action ceased. For a time, Army Communists still entered, though more discreetly than the civilians, into the controversies of the time. Putna was among the officers signing some sort of confidential defense of the opposition in 1927.[7] Tukhachevsky had not been involved in this, or any similar move. We may make a certain distinction between the professional soldiers who became Communists, like Tukhachevsky, Kork, and Yegorov, and the Communists who became professional soldiers, like Yakir, Blyukher, and Alksnis. Even at this time, the former played little part in politics—except when military matters were directly affected, as when Tukhachevsky and Uborevich opposed Trotsky's ideas of Army organization.

But in any case, from the establishment of Stalin's primacy at the end of the 1920s, the Army Command had wholly withdrawn from the political struggle. In part, this was evidently due to the same ideas that decided Pyatakov: the leadership question was settled. What remained was the professional problem of creating a sound military force. And, conversely, Stalin had been careful not to stir up trouble among the soldiery. Just as he had "neutralized" the Ukraine by withdrawing Kaganovich in 1928, so he now left Tukhachevsky and his fellows a comparatively free hand. The Army's Communists had a high reputation in the Party. In the comparatively mild Party purge of 1929, some 5 percent of military Communists were purged, compared with 11.7 percent in the Party as a whole; in the 1933 purge, the figures were 4.3 percent and 17 percent, respectively.

It is true that an occasional officer suffered. But this was usually a special case, like that of the military academic Snesarev, formerly a Tsarist general, since rehabilitated. "In January 1930, on a charge of having participated in a counter-revolutionary monarchist officers' organization, he was arrested along with other military specialists," and at the age of sixty-five was deported to hard labor in the far north, where he died in 1937.[8]

But on the whole, the Army received more and more friendly attention, and less and less persecution. Its prestige began to be built up in a variety of ways. The principle of shared responsibility between the commander and the political commissar was abolished in March 1934, leaving the commander in full control, with the commissar simply as his political adviser. The old military ranks up to, but not including, general, were restored on 22 September 1935. The same decree gave all except junior commanders the privilege of immunity from arrest by the

---

*Stalin also put some of the blame for the Polish debacle on Smilga (John Erickson, *The Soviet High Command* [London, 1962], p. 99).

civil organs without a special authorization from the People's Commissar of Defense. At the same time, the first five Marshals of the Soviet Union were named: Tukhachevsky, Blyukher, and Yegorov of the genuine military, plus Stalin's nominees Voroshilov and Budenny.

At his trial in 1938, Bukharin was to speak vaguely of the "military men" among his fellow plotters. When Vyshinsky asked, "Which military men?" he answered, "The Right conspirators." Vyshinsky, accepting this, asked for the names in the particular context, and was given those of Tukhachevsky and Kork.[9] In his speaking of them as not simply members of the far-flung "bloc" but as actual Rightists, we can perhaps find a clue to part of the reason for Stalin's resentment of the military. They had not been Rightists in the sense that Bukharin was. But it is more than likely that they had shown Rightism, in the sense that Rudzutak, Chubar, and so on had done—that is, in failing to show enthusiasm for the increasing tempo of the purge during the final phase, from September 1936 to February 1937.

Not that we can so simply exhaust Stalin's motives. Former grudges and present nuisance value certainly played a part. But there are more general, and more powerful, considerations.

Despotism enforced by a terrorist and terrorized bureaucracy may be in a general way extremely strong. But it presents certain points of vulnerability. There is a brittleness in the strength. Even the most rigorous precautions can never entirely rule out the possibility of assassination. There is no real evidence of any serious attempt on Stalin's life. There are a few vague reports of genuine plots, usually among young Communists, discovered before they came to fruition. And there are one or two individual incidents, such as that reported during the Second World War of a soldier who shot at random at a car emerging from the Kremlin which chanced to contain Mikoyan.[10]

The other vulnerability was to a military coup. Even a few dozen determined men might conceivably have seized the Kremlin and the persons of the leadership. And in those circumstances, the type of machine Stalin built can crack very easily. Even the farcical attempt by General Malet to overthrow Napoleon in 1812, by sheer bluff, had an almost incredible measure of preliminary success. The best chance of getting rid of Stalin would have been a coup by Tukhachevsky in alliance with the surviving oppositionists, just as the best chance of blocking Hitler in 1933 would have been a coup by Schleicher backed by the Social Democratic Party.

But just as the German Social Democrats were hobbled by their notions of constitutionality (and just as, later, most of Hitler's generals were hamstrung by their formal allegiance to Hitler as Head of State), the Soviet Marshals, like the civilian oppositionists, seem to have been mesmerized by the notion that the Stalin leadership, with all its faults, had inherited the Party legitimacy.

For there is no evidence that any conspiracy really existed. Isaac Deutscher has indeed written that "all non-Stalinist versions concur in the following: the Generals did indeed plan a *coup d'état*."[11] In reality, there is virtual unanimity that this was not the case. The leading defector information (including that deriving from NKVD officers in prison who discussed the matter with cell mates who eventually came West)[12] and later Soviet revelations all agree on the nonexistence of any plot. The Nazi secret archives contain no evidence of anything of the kind. Admittedly, one cannot prove a negative, and we must not formally exclude the possibility of evidence one day turning up to show that some of the military were seriously considering action.* But it seems unlikely, to say the least. The curious thing is that the legend of a real conspiracy long persisted, though the "conspiracies" alleged at the three great political trials either were rejected from the start or have long since been seen through.

The reason, paradoxically, seems to be that this is the one case in which Stalin did not produce his evidence. From Stalin's point of view, it was the best method. If a real military plot had suddenly been discovered, immediate court-martial and execution were natural-looking reactions. They had many precedents in other countries and, indeed, in Russia. Moreover, while the likelihood of the plots hitherto exposed in court was on the face of it dubious, the seizure of power by Tukhachevsky appeared a perfectly rational and possible move. In this case, public "proofs" were not required. In a sense, this is itself a curious irony, as this is the only case in which Stalin did dispose of documentary evidence. It was, of course, faked, but it really was of German origin.

But Stalin had the wit not to publish these documents. They had not been devised solely for his benefit, and perhaps did not entirely suit his intention. And if they had been made public, it might, for all he knew, have been possible for experts to detect flaws, or even for the Germans to blow the gaff.

Thus the result of Stalin's sudden blow, and the absence of specific evidence, was that people found it easier to believe that a plot genuinely existed. As the Minister of War remarks in *Penguin Island* of the efforts of his Chief of Staff in providing reams of proofs against the accused Jewish officer,

> Proofs! Of course it is good to have proofs, but perhaps it is better to have none at all . . . the Pyrot affair, as I arranged it, left no room for criticism; there was no spot at which it could be touched. It defied assault. It was invulnerable because it was invisible. Now it gives an enormous handle for discussion.

It was not so much that people believed the precise charges. Some of these, as later developed, were incredible—in particular that Yakir and Feldman, both Jews, had really worked for Nazi Germany. What was found tolerable was simply the central thesis that the generals were plotting to use their power against Stalin.

The essence of the plot, according to evidence in the Bukharin Trial,[13] was Tukhachevsky's "favorite plan"—the seizure of the Kremlin and the killing of the leadership by a group of military men. Gamarnik had proposed also seizing the NKVD headquarters. He is represented as believing that "some military under his direct command" would obey him. He considered he had sufficient Party and political prestige in the Army and that some of the commanders, "especially the daredevils," would support him.[14]

A curious sidelight is that Gamarnik, with a choice of "daredevil" officers

---

*The same is true of vague reports that the idea of a coup occurred to some officers, in particular Feldman, but that none of the senior generals were involved. The other "military conspiracy" mentioned at the Bukharin Trial—that of Peterson, Commander of the Kremlin Guard, who intended a palace coup—is only perfunctorily linked with Tukhachevsky (*Bukharin Trial*, pp. 570, 177); but again, though not implausible, there is no evidence for it.

allegedly at his disposal, and Yakir, the fighting general, are supposed to have instructed the Chief of the Department of Savings Banks of the Ministry of Finance, Ozeryansky, to prepare a terrorist act against Yezhov.[15] This is another of those little touches which might perhaps have fortified the skepticism of Western dupes.

Various versions were planted. For example, the American Ambassador, Joseph Davies, says in his memoirs that he was told by Ambassador Troyanovsky on 7 October 1937, when he had queried the idea that Tukhachevsky would have become a German agent simply for money, that the Marshal had a mistress who was herself a German agent. This story was evidently planted elsewhere: Davies reports hearing it also from the French Ambassador on the authority of the Deuxième Bureau, which is supposed to have got it from Prague. Walter Duranty recounts a similar story. There is no reason to believe it.

As we have said, the apparent suddenness of the blow at the Army, the great air of urgency, contributed to the plausibility of Stalin's story. And this theme was put about even in the outer circle of the NKVD. A senior NKVD officer, as late as October 1937, was telling his subordinates in Spain, "That was a real conspiracy! That could be seen from the panic which spread there on the top: all the passes to the Kremlin were suddenly declared invalid; our [i.e., NKVD] troops were held in a state of alarm: as Frinovsky said, 'the whole Soviet Government hung by a thread. . . .' "[16]

To another, Frinovsky remarked that the NKVD "had uncovered a giant conspiracy—we have got them all!"[17] though this seems to have been said around 20 May, when the "uncovering" was accomplished, but three key arrests were yet to come.

This notion of a sudden secret emergency was doubtless useful in providing a panic tension in military, Party, and NKVD circles. But it was not in accord with the facts. The pressure against the Army, though little publicized, had, on the contrary, been gradual and cumulative.

It was eleven months since Stalin had in fact made the first moves against the High Command, which had now borne such fantastic fruit.

The first arrest in the series that was to lead up to the great blow at the generals had taken place on 5 July 1936, when the NKVD seized Divisional Commander Dmitri Shmidt, commanding a tank unit in the Kiev Military District, without informing or consulting his superior officer, Yakir. Yakir went to Moscow, where Yezhov showed him "material" implicating Shmidt.[18] This material presumably consisted of the confessions of Mrachkovsky, Dreitzer, and Reingold, which revealed Shmidt and his accomplice B. Kuzmichev (Chief of Staff of an Air Force unit) as having been under Mrachkovsky's instructions, through Dreitzer, to assassinate Voroshilov, in the interests of the Trotskyite element in the "Bloc."[19] In accordance with Stalin's style, Shmidt was a man against whom a particular individual grudge awaited settlement. Not only was he an ex-oppositionist, but he had give Stalin personal offense.

Shmidt, a Party member since 1915, was the son of a poor Jewish shoemaker. He had become a sailor, and then, through the Civil War, a brilliant cavalry commander in the Ukraine. During the period, all sorts of rival factions were fighting right through the area; for example, Vasily Grossman recounts that Berdichev had changed hands fourteen times. It had been occupied "by Petlyura,

Denikin, the Bolsheviks, Galicians, Poles, Tutnik's and Maroussia's bands and 'nobody's Ninth Regiment.' "[20]

Amid this chaos, Shmidt had risen to command first a regiment and then a brigade, had captured Kamenets-Podolsk, far to the west and surrounded by enemy forces, and had finally been ordered to prepare for the attempt, never in fact made, to break through Poland and Romania to help the Hungarian Soviet Republic in 1919. He had ridden into a camp of nationalist guerrillas with two aides and, after negotiations failed, engaged in a successful gunfight. In fact, he was a typical though not outstandingly gifted "natural leader" of partisans—swashbuckling, simple, frightened of nothing, a true product of the Civil War. Later, in peacetime, he had shot, but failed to kill, a senior officer who had insulted his wife, the matter being hushed up.

Between 1925 and 1937, Shmidt had become associated with the opposition, though not in any significant way. Arriving in Moscow at the time of the 1927 Congress, when the expulsion of the Trotskyites was announced, he had met Stalin coming out of the Kremlin. Shmidt, in his black Caucasian cloak and silver-ornamented belt, with his fur hat cocked over his ear, had gone up to Stalin and, half-joking, half-serious, had started to curse him in the extravagant soldier fashion of the time. He ended by gesturing as though to draw his great curved saber, and told Stalin that one day he would lop his ears off.[21]

Stalin said nothing, listening white and tight-lipped. The incident was taken as a bad joke, or at most an insult beneath political notice. Shmidt, after all, had accepted the Party decision which he objected to so strongly, and for nearly a decade he continued to serve. In fact, the Trotskyites were allegedly to find him suitable conspiratorial material precisely because he was "under no suspicion in the Party."[22] As to his rudeness, after all, Stalin had defended "rudeness" among comrades. And, indeed, that sort of thing from a rough soldier would not have been much regarded earlier on, or by any of the leaders but Stalin.

From the start, it was clear that Shmidt's arrest was not an isolated act. The "cases" of Shmidt and Kuzmichev are among those named in the indictment of the Zinoviev Case as "set aside for separate trial in view of the fact that the investigation is still proceeding." In court, Mrachkovsky spoke of a "terroristic group of people including Shmidt, Kuzmichev and some others whom I do not remember," which already implied a larger military organization. Reingold, too, mentioned them as forming only a part of a "Trotskyite group of military men," which had a number of other members whose names he did not know.

Kuzmichev, like Shmidt, was an old comrade of Yakir's. Another friend of his, Ivan Golubenko, Chairman of the Dnepropetrovsk Soviet, was also arrested in August 1936[23] as a Trotskyite, though later transmuted to a spy. Already a member of "a counter-revolutionary Trotskyite–Zinovievite nationalist bloc"[24] in the summer of 1936, he was mentioned in January 1937 as a member of a terrorist group formed to assassinate both Stalin[25] and "the leaders of the Communist Party and the Soviet Government of the Ukraine."[26] He is said to have really been associated with Ordzhonikidze's attempts to halt the Terror.

These arrests, and particularly Shmidt's, caused considerable worry in military circles in the Ukraine. No one believed he was guilty. Although he had once voted for Trotsky, he had long since "repented" of this. And throughout August, there were further arrests. On 25 September came that of Divisional Commander

Yu. Sablin. A woman NKVD officer, Nastya Ruban, who knew Yakir, went to him secretly and told him that she had seen the materials against Sablin, and it was quite clear that he was not guilty. Three days later, her death by heart attack was announced. It was soon learned that it had really been suicide.[27]

Meanwhile, in the Lubyanka, Shmidt was being interrogated "in all degrees" by top-ranking NKVD operatives, including the Head of the Special Department, M. I. Gay, and the notorious Z. M. Ushakov, on the charge of planning to kill Voroshilov. Documentary evidence was produced: a route card of Voroshilov's movements at the maneuvers, as issued to all commanders. For some time, Shmidt denied all the accusations.[28]

While Shmidt and Kuzmichev had been implicated in the preliminary interrogations of the Zinoviev Trial prisoners and publicly named in the indictment, it was only in the course of the trial itself that, on 21 August 1936, a more senior figure, and one of the Tukhachevsky group proper, was unexpectedly brought in. Dreitzer, who had finished his evidence on 19 August, was recalled. And as the last evidence given at the whole trial, he implicated Putna. This officer was now alleged to have been in direct contact with Trotsky and Ivan Smirnov. Smirnov denied that Putna had anything to do with it. But Pikel, Reingold, and Bakayev corroborated Dreitzer.[29] Putna, recalled from London, had been arrested on 20 August.[30] His wife learned of the arrest in Warsaw on her way to join him.[31] By 31 August, he had already admitted the existence of various Trotskyite groups.[32]

Corps Commander Primakov, though not so implicated at the Zinoviev Trial, had been arrested on 14 August.[33] He had already been in NKVD hands in, apparently, 1934,[34] so was particularly vulnerable. However, he denied all the charges, even at a confrontation before Stalin and the Politburo, for nine months.[35]

On the face of it, it was no more extraordinary for Trotskyite plots to involve Communists in the Red Army than in any other field. It could not easily be complained of as an attack on the Army as such. On the other hand, according to Dreitzer, Trotsky's instructions had included as a particular duty "to unfold work for organizing nuclei in the Army"[36]—a direct threat. During the autumn, there were rumors that a show trial of "Trotskyist" commanders in the Army was to be held, with Putna in the leading role. Tukhachevsky himself appeared to be under a cloud, if the lack of prominence given to him in the Army maneuvers was any guide. Voroshilov made sinister comments on lack of vigilance to the Kiev commanders during his visit to their autumn exercises.[37]

The fall of Yagoda was interpreted as, in part, a victory for the Army. German diplomatic reports of the time say that no more was to be heard of any Army trial, and that Tukhachevsky himself was fully "reinstated." And Stalin is now, in fact, reported at the December 1936 plenum mentioning material against Tukhachevsky which had proved unfounded.[38]

As ever, this relaxation proved to be simply another maneuver of Stalin's. Shmidt, Primakov, and Putna were not released, and Yezhov was soon planning a more effective blow at the military. There is an unconfirmed report that Putna was worked on from the start for evidence incriminating Tukhachevsky as a *British* spy.[39] This would, indeed, be natural from Putna's London post. And in the trials, the accused were often charged with working for several foreign powers. But, anyhow, the charge was not developed in later propaganda, and may have been overtaken by the Nazi connection.

As we have seen, at the Pyatakov Trial, Putna was once again incriminated—though still for terrorism only, not treason. On 24 January 1937, Radek remarked, as if in passing, that Putna had come to him "with some request from Tukhachevsky." An extraordinary exchange between Vyshinsky and Radek on the following day ran like this:

*Vyshinsky:* Accused Radek, in your testimony you say: 'In 1935 . . . we resolved to call a conference, but before this, in January, when I arrived, Vitaly Putna came to me with a request from Tukhachevsky. . . .' I want to know in what connection you mention Tukhachevsky's name?

*Radek:* Tukhachevsky had been commissioned by the Government with some task for which he could not find the necessary material. I alone was in possession of this material. He rang me up and asked if I had this material. I had it, and he accordingly sent Putna, with whom he had to discharge this commission, to get the material from me. Of course, Tukhachevsky had no idea either of Putna's role or of my criminal role. . . .

*Vyshinsky:* And Putna?

*Radek:* He was a member of the organization, and he did not come to talk about the organization, but I took advantage of his visit to have this talk.

*Vyshinsky:* So Putna came to you, having been sent by Tukhachevsky on official business having no bearing whatever on your affairs since he, Tukhachevsky, had no relations with them whatever?

*Radek:* Tukhachevsky never had any relations whatever with them.

*Vyshinsky:* He sent Putna on official business?

*Radek:* Yes.

*Vyshinsky:* And you took advantage of this in order to engage in your own particular affairs?

*Radek:* Yes.

*Vyshinsky:* Do I understand you correctly, that Putna had dealings with the members of your Trotskyite underground organization, and that your reference to Tukhachevsky was made in connection with the fact that Putna came on official business on Tukhachevsky's orders?

*Radek:* I confirm that, and I say that I never had and could not have had any dealings with Tukhachevsky connected with counter-revolutionary activities, because I knew Tukhachevsky's attitude to the Party and the Government to be that of an absolutely devoted man.[40]

An experienced NKVD officer who read this at once remarked that Tukhachevsky was lost. Why, his wife asked, since Radek's evidence so emphatically exculpated him? Since when, was the reply, had Tukhachevsky needed a character reference from Radek?[41]

The whole clumsy interchange must have been a set piece, doubtless dictated by Stalin himself, perhaps at Tukhachevsky's own insistence after the earlier mention of his name. Typically, it gave the Marshal full satisfaction in a superficial sense. He could hardly ask for a plainer assertion of his loyalty and innocence. But at the same time, the idea had been launched. And when Vyshinsky in his final speech complained of the accused having confessed much, but not enough, of their criminal connections, the foundations were laid for further development in his direction as in others.

When Shmidt finally broke down under severe interrogation, his confession was apparently circulated in the upper levels of the Party. Yakir determined to check the charges. He insisted on seeing Shmidt in jail. Shmidt had become very gray and thin, seemed apathetic, and spoke listlessly. Yakir described him as looking "like a Martian," a being from another planet. But when Yakir asked him if his confessions were true, Shmidt repudiated them. Yakir was not allowed to question him on the details, but had Shmidt write a note to Voroshilov denying all the accusations. Yakir took this to Voroshilov and told him that the charges were clearly false.

Yakir went back to Kiev well pleased with this result, but his pleasure did not last long. For soon after, Voroshilov rang him up and said that on the very next day Shmidt had reaffirmed his confessions, and wished to inform Voroshilov and Yakir that his early evidence was true.[42] (Shmidt had given, or was shortly to give, evidence which was not to be circulated to Yakir and the other commanders, for it implicated Yakir himself. The Divisional Commander was required to confess that at Yakir's instigation he had planned to raise his tank unit in revolt.)*

After all this, Yakir could not have believed in the accusations. And he is also reported as having said that those shot after the Pyatakov Trial were innocent.[43] It must have been clear to Stalin that Yakir was against the new purge. And his boldness in insisting on the interview with Shmidt shows him not lacking in undesirable courage.

On 3 March 1937, at the plenum itself, after the arrest of Rykov and Bukharin, Stalin spoke briefly about what harm "a few spies in the Red Army" could do. And Molotov "directly incited to the murder of the military cadres, accusing its participants of lack of desire to develop the struggle against 'enemies of the people.' "[44]

The crucial political victory of the Purge had been won at the plenum. The organizational basis for extending it was also now becoming adequate. It was in April that the NKVD, purged by Yezhov, became ready for further operations. It was "soon after the plenum" that "careerists and provocateurs in the organs of the NKVD fabricated a story 'on the counter-revolutionary military fascist organization' in the armed forces."[45]

Hitherto, Stalin's victims had almost all been former members of the oppositions. This was, of course, true even of Bukharin and Rykov. Now, for the first time, Stalin was to begin a massive offensive against his own supporters everywhere.

With the oppositionists, even Bukharin and Rykov, the Party elite may to some degree have felt that this was a sort of very rough justice after all—and justice had been rough in the Soviet Union for a long time. Or they may have been influenced to some extent by the notion that at least a potential alternative leadership was being dealt with. But if undoubtedly loyal followers of Stalin, men

---

*Shmidt was being interrogated "nine months before" the June Trial with a view to incriminating Yakir (I. V. Dubinskiy, *Naperekor vetram* [Moscow, 1964], pp. 243ff).

who had taken no part in opposition movements, were now to be destroyed, then no one was safe. And no principle was involved. In such circumstances, it was quite reasonable for Stalin to have thought that the Army leadership, whose representatives may have opposed even the Bukharin purge, or at any rate had only assented with obvious reluctance, might finally be driven into resistance. Stalin himself, in destroying the principle of political loyalty, would be undermining the restraints which had so held them. Thus it is natural enough that he should have planned his blow at the Army leadership to coincide exactly with the period when he was turning on his own insufficiently subservient followers.

Meanwhile, Stalin proceeded gradually. On Yagoda's arrest on 3 April 1937, his post as Commissar of Communications was taken by Army Commander Khalepsky, Tukhachevsky's tank expert—an absurd as well as a sinister transfer.

Corps Commander Gekker, Head of Red Army Foreign Liaison and thus a particularly sensitive figure in espionage charges, disappeared in April. During the same month, Corps Commander Garkavi, commanding the Urals Military District, was taken in. He was one of Yakir's closest associates; in fact, they were married to sisters. Again, Yakir showed undesirable boldness, by going to see Voroshilov and eventually Stalin. Stalin soothed him, saying that serious charges against Garkavi had been made by those already under arrest, but that if he was innocent he would be released.[46]

On 28 April 1937 *Pravda* published a pointed call to the Red Army to master politics and to fight the internal, as well as the external, foe. This powerful, if oblique, blow was understood by the already shaken High Command.

At the May Day Parade, Tukhachevsky was the first to arrive on the tribune reserved for the Army leaders. He walked alone, with his thumbs in his belt, to the reviewing stand. Yegorov then took his position, but did not look at or salute his colleague. Gamarnik also joined the silent rank. A gloomy and icy atmosphere surrounded the soldiers. At the end of the Army parade, Tukhachevsky did not wait for the civilian march-past, but walked out of the Red Square.[47]

He had been nominated to attend the coronation of King George VI. On 21 April, Yezhov reported that the NKVD had learned of a plot by German and Polish agencies to commit a terrorist act against Tukhachevsky if he went to the coronation in London, and next day the Politburo decided to avoid this "serious danger" by not sending him.[48] On 4 May, the British were told that for reasons of health Tukhachevsky would not now be able to go. Admiral Orlov took his place.

An officer who saw Tukhachevsky several times in May describes him as looking unusually gloomy after an interview with Voroshilov. A few days later, he went to see Voroshilov again. Voroshilov was cold and formal, and simply announced to him his removal from his post as Deputy Commissar of Defense and transfer to the Volga Military District, a backwoods command with three infantry divisions and assorted troops.

Tukhachevsky commented to a friend, "It is not so much a matter of Voroshilov as of Stalin."[49]

This posting, and others, were made official on 10 and 11 May, in a series of shifts among the higher officers which gave the clearest evidence yet of Stalin's animus. Gamarnik, as well as Tukhachevsky, was relieved of the position of Deputy Commissar of Defense. More deviously, Yakir was transferred from Kiev to

Leningrad; unlike Tukhachevsky's posting, this was not an obvious demotion. Nor were either of the two ignominiously rushed to their posts, remaining in Moscow and Kiev, respectively, until almost the end of the month.

At the same time, a decree (dated 8 May)[50] restored the old system of "dual command," with the powers of the political commissars being greatly increased relative to those of the fighting officers. The original powers of political commissars had been given them because the military specialists of the Civil War were mainly ex-Tsarist officers who were not regarded as trustworthy. The reimposition of the system on a Communist officer corps was an extraordinary demonstration of lack of trust in the new cadres. On 9 May, an "instruction" was put out calling for greater vigilance.[51]

Meanwhile, behind the scenes, the net was closing. On 22 to 25 April 1937, Yagoda's former Deputy, G. E. Prokofiev, and his former Head of the NKVD Special Department, M. I. Gay, who had interrogated Shmidt, were forced to give testimony about the criminal connections of Tukhachevsky and other officers with Yagoda. (Yagoda himself, at this stage, refused to confirm this.) On 27 April, A. I. Volovich, arrested Deputy Head (under Pauker) of the Operative Department, also implicated Tukhachevsky in a plot to seize power.[52] Also in April, the interrogators were ordered to get evidence from Putna and Primakov against Tukhachevsky, Yakir, Feldman, and others.[53]

Frinovsky, Yezhov's Deputy People's Commissar in charge of State Security matters, now called in the Deputy Head of the Moscow Province NKVD, Radzivilovsky, and asked him if he had any important military men among his prisoners. Radzivilovsky said that he had a General Staff officer, Brigade Commander M. E. Medvedev, lately expelled from the Party and the Army for "Trotskyism." Frinovsky said that a huge plot in the Red Army needed uncovering. Radzivilovsky obtained the necessary confession from Medvedev by "physical" means. On 8 May, he confessed that he had long been privy to a conspiracy in the central apparatus of the Red Army. Medvedev was brought before Frinovsky and Yezhov, and told them that his testimony was invented. Yezhov sent him back for further interrogation, after which he confirmed his earlier confession to Yezhov, who then forwarded it to the Central Committee.

Army Commander Kork of the Frunze Military Academy was arrested on 16 May. At first he denied the charges, but on 18 May he signed a confession that Yenukidze had recruited him to the Rightist conspiracy, to which the "Trotskyite" group of Putna and Primakov was also connected. Tukhachevsky, he said, had also joined the Rightists, and the intention was a military coup d'état.[54] On 8 May, after beatings and being kept without sleep, Primakov had finally admitted to plotting with Dreitzer, Shmidt, Putna, and Mrachkovsky. On 14 May, he implicated Yakir, and by 21 May, Tukhachevsky and others. On 14 May, Putna too had, under torture, implicated Tukhachevsky.[55]

On the basis of Medvedev's evidence, Feldman was arrested on 15 May.[56] Interrogated by Ushakov, Feldman at first denied all the charges. But after intensive interrogation, he signed a full confession of the plot, implicating "Tukhachevsky, Yakir, Eideman and others."[57] On 20 May, Yezhov sent Stalin, Molotov, Voroshilov, and Kaganovich the protocols of Feldman's interrogation, and asked for a decision on arresting the others now implicated.[58]

Thus by mid-May, three of the destined victims of the Tukhachevsky opera-tion were already under arrest, and the pressure was being increased on Tukhach-evsky and Yakir. At this time, Stalin, who read all the interrogation protocols, was seeing Yezhov almost every day (accompanied on 21 and 28 May by Frinov-sky) and taking "a direct part in the falsification of charges."[59]

And now, in addition to the charges of conspiracy, the themes of treason and espionage began to develop. The former head of the NKVD Foreign Department, A. Kh. Artuzov, who had been arrested on 13 May, was soon testifying to a pseudonymous plotter with the Germans, identifiable as Tukhachevsky (a report long known to the NKVD and hitherto rejected, an act now blamed on a cover-up by Yagoda).[60]

But a far more impressive "dossier" of evidence that Tukhachevsky was a German spy came into Stalin's possession at about this time.[61] It had been forged in the Ostabteilung of the German Sicherheitsdienst (SD). But the story is not as simple as that.

## STALIN AND FASCISM

> *I know how much the German people loves its Führer.*
> *I should therefore like to drink his health.*
> Stalin, 24 August 1939

Stalin's view of Fascism has some very peculiar features. It had, of course, long since been denounced as the worst form of bourgeois rule and "analyzed" as a form of control of the State by monopoly capitalists. But though *fascism* thus became a very evil word, the effects of this were considerably diluted by the method of calling the Social Democrats "Fascists" too—"Social Fascists." In the resulting confusion, the German Communist Party had been ordered, against its will,[62] to direct its main force against not the Nazis, but the Socialist–bour-geois coalition Governments, to the degree of the Prussian referendum of 1931 and the transport strike of 1932, in which Nazis and Communists actively coop-erated against the moderates.

When such tactics resulted in the victory of Hitler,* the crushing of the Ger-man Communist party was represented, according to the new Stalin style, as a victory. A new concept of Hitler as the "icebreaker of revolution"—the last des-perate stand of the bourgeoisie, whose failure would lead to the collapse of capi-talism—came into vogue.

When it became apparent that Hitlerism was *not* going to collapse—a conclu-sion Stalin seems to have reached at the time of the Nazi Roehm Purge in June 1934—Stalin was not to be inhibited by doctrinal reasons from coming to an arrangement with the new dictator. The difficulty was rather that Hitler appeared to be quite intransigently anti-Communist. As Hitler built up Germany's military and economic power, Stalin began a complex approach. Hitler's evident military threat could be blocked in two ways: by force or by agreement. If force was to be

---

*Who himself remarked that he could always turn a Communist into a Nazi, but could not do the same with a Social Democrat (Hermann Rauschning, *Hitler Speaks* [New York, 1940], p. 134).

necessary, then a powerful antifascist alliance needed to be built. If agreement were possible, it could best be achieved from strength. So from the mid-1930s, Soviet foreign policy, and Comintern tactics, were directed to creating a system of Party and State alliances against German power.

In 1936, following this shift in foreign policy orientation, Foreign Commissar Litvinov, long an advocate of alliance with the West, received every sign of support. Leaving a discussion, Stalin put his arm around Litvinov's shoulder and said that now it appeared they could agree. Litvinov (or so he later told Ehrenburg) answered, "Not for long. . . ."[63]

It has often been suggested that one of Stalin's motives for the Purge, and especially for the Army purge, was to give him the freedom of maneuver which finally produced the Nazi-Soviet Pact of 1939. The old pre-Nazi pro-German orientation had not been an ideological one, and alliance even with a very reactionary Germany against the "have" powers was in principle long since accepted by the Army and most of the Party. Only when Nazism was seen as an overt threat to the Soviet Union did a change come, with the Popular Front campaigns of the Comintern, the Franco-Soviet Pact, and so forth. But when it came, it was warmly accepted. The Rightist mood in country and Party saw in these State and Party alliances the possibility of an "opening to the Right," a reconciliation with democracy. Meanwhile, Tukhachevsky and the soldiery worked enthusiastically at a true modernization of the Army, to make it capable of facing not merely the Poles or Turks, but also the high military potential of a mobilized Germany.

But for Stalin, the fronts and pacts were matters not of conviction but of calculation.

As long as any qualms were able to make themselves felt in the Communist International, Stalin's freedom of action to come to an arrangement with the Germans was limited. The ideological conceptions, the socialist sentiments, were directed firmly on antifascist lines. As far as the international field was concerned, the crushing of all independent, undisciplined motivations was necessary if Stalin was to make the best bargain. Prisoners were predicting the Nazi-Soviet Pact in 1938 on the basis of the categories being arrested—in particular, the foreign Communists.[64]

When the Pact came in August 1939, the effects of years of hard organizational and propaganda work in the Comintern became visible. All over the world, with negligible and temporary exceptions, the Communist Parties accepted the switch and began to explain its necessity—sometimes in the later editions of papers which the same day had been urging a fight to the last against Nazism. Only individuals among the leaderships dropped out.

Even at the XVIIth Party Congress in 1934, Stalin had hinted of the alternative policy of agreement with Germany: "Of course we are far from enthusiastic about the Fascist regime in Germany. But Fascism is beside the point, if only because Fascism in Italy, for example, has not kept the U.S.S.R. from establishing the best of relations with that country."[65]

A pessimistic estimate was presented to Stalin by the NKVD Foreign Department in August 1935 about the strength of elements in Germany favoring settlement with Russia. But the officer making the report noted that it made no impact on Stalin's feeling that accord could be achieved.[66]

For Litvinov was right. From 1936, and on the basis of the threat of his alternative anti-German policy, Stalin began to put out feelers to the Nazis, through his personal emissaries.

The representative of Stalin's personal secretariat, his old henchman David Kandelaki, was sent as "Commercial Attaché" to the Soviet Embassy in Berlin to make these delicate approaches. In December 1936 Kandelaki approached Dr. Schacht at his own request to inquire about the possibility of enlarging Soviet–German trade. Schacht answered that a condition of this must be the ending of Soviet-sponsored Communist activity in Germany. Kandelaki went back to Moscow to consult Stalin and at about the turn of the year was given a written draft proposing the opening of negotiations either through ambassadors or, if the Germans so desired, in secret. The draft reminded the Germans that agreement had previously been suggested by the Russians.

On 29 January 1937 Kandelaki, with his deputy Fridrikhson, again visited Schacht with a verbal proposal from Stalin and Molotov for the opening of direct negotiations. Schacht said that these suggestions should be passed to the German Foreign Ministry, and added once more that he felt that Communist agitation would have to be damped down. On 10 February, Neurath saw Hitler about the proposals and wrote to Schacht the next day, sensibly saying that there was no practical point in getting an agreement from the Russians to cease Communist propaganda. On the main issue, he said that as things were at the moment the Russian proposals were not worth proceeding with. If, however, Russia was "to develop further along the lines of an absolute despotism supported by the Army," contact should certainly be made.

Meanwhile, the Pyatakov Trial had gone ahead, with its anti-Nazi implications. Even here, Stalin was able to have it both ways. General Köstring, the German Military Attaché who had been in effect implicated in the trial, was not declared *persona non grata*. This decision seems to have been taken after considerable pressure from the Germans and is, to say the least, curious.

For the time being, Stalin's approaches did not bear fruit. But the point had been made. The German leaders had had the advantages of an arrangement put before them.

Meanwhile, as Stalin's real approaches to Hitler went ahead, the nonexistent contact between the Soviet High Command and the Nazis was made the subject of the decisive accusations of treason.

In the murky world of the secret organizations, some measure of contact had already been established between the NKVD and Reinhardt Heydrich's SD.

After the suppression of the German Communist Party, operations against its underground remnant became simply a Secret Police matter. As with all sophisticated operations of this type, the Nazi secret agencies left some underground Communists untouched, with a view to retaining political contact.*

Among the organizations penetrated by both the NKVD and German espio-

---

*Indeed, in the occupied countries during the war, too, the Gestapo was in contact with the local Communist Parties, at least in the period before the German–Soviet war. In France, negotiations with the French Communist Party had reached the stage of discussing permission to let *L'Humanité* appear. In occupied Norway, Communist periodicals were briefly allowed. The position was similar in Belgium.

nage was the Union of Tsarist Veterans, with its main body in Paris. On 22 September 1937 the NKVD was to carry out, as a special operation, the kidnapping and murder of General Miller, its leader. This seems to have been in an attempt to put General Skoblin, Miller's deputy, in command of the organization. Skoblin had long worked as a double agent with both the Soviet and the German secret agencies, and there seems no doubt that he was one of the links by which information was passed between the SD and the NKVD. According to one version, the first move in the whole dark business, which "originated with Stalin,"[67] appears to have been an NKVD story sent through Skoblin to Berlin to the effect that the Soviet High Command and Tukhachevsky in particular were engaged in a conspiracy with the German General Staff. Although this was understood in SD circles as an NKVD plant, Heydrich determined to use it, in the first place, against the German High Command, with whom his organization was in intense rivalry.[68] For in Heydrich's motives, in this whole business, the compromising of the German Army ranked high. This side of it rather dropped into the background as the operation proceeded, and it does not anyhow particularly concern us.

The evidence that Stalin, or the NKVD, planted the idea with the Germans is far from conclusive. But whatever its origins, it is certainly true that it was only the atmosphere of extreme suspicion now engulfing the Soviet Union which made the idea seem worth pursuing from the German point of view. Meanwhile, the rumors trickled into Moscow. In January 1937, the *Pravda* correspondent in Berlin, A. Klimov, sent information that German Army circles were talking of their connections in the Red Army, especially Tukhachevsky.[69] And S. P. Uritsky, head of Red Army Intelligence, reported directly to Stalin and Voroshilov that there were rumors in Berlin of opposition among the Soviet generals, though he himself did not credit this.[70] The Soviet embassy in Paris sent a telegram to Moscow on 16 March that it had learned of plans "by German circles to promote a coup d'état in the Soviet Union" using "persons from the command staff of the Red Army."[71]

The most probable account[72] (to which Gomulka, when leader of the Polish Communist Party, gave his authority in a formal speech)[73] makes it out that towards the end of 1936, in a conversation with Hitler and Himmler, the pros and cons of "betraying" Tukhachevsky and crippling the Red Army were discussed, and a decision was taken. Several Soviet and other accounts[74] make it clear that the story of the German contacts with Tukhachevsky was originally "leaked" by the Nazis through President Beneš of Czechoslovakia. Beneš had the information as early as the end of January 1937 (and confidentially passed it on to the French, whose confidence in the Franco-Soviet Pact was considerably weakened by it).[75] He also, as several recent Soviet accounts agree, passed the reports to Stalin, in all good faith. Gomulka tells us that this false information had been planted some time before the documentary "evidence" arrived, so that preliminary reports of the "treason" were in Stalin's hands "at the time of the February–March plenum."[76]

The creation of the actual documentary evidence was an artistic job and took time. In March and April 1937, Heydrich and Behrens (who later became Chief of the SS in Belgrade and was executed by the Tito Government in 1946) directed the forgery of a "dossier" containing an exchange of letters over a period of a year between members of the German High Command and Tukhachevsky. Largely the work of the German engraver Franz Putzig, who had long been employed by the German secret agencies on false passports and so on, it consisted of thirty-two pages and had attached to it a photograph of Trotsky with German officials.[77] One later Soviet book quotes a number of Western and German accounts of the forgery of the dossier, and appears to accept that given by Colonel Naujocks, formerly one of Heydrich's men.[78] This says that the German security service got a genuine signature of Tukhachevsky from the 1926 secret agreement between the two High Commands by which technical assistance to the Soviet Air Force was arranged. A letter was forged using this signature, and Tukhachevsky's style was imitated. The letter carried genuine German stamps, and the whole dossier consisted of it and fifteen other German documents. The German generals' signatures were obtained from bank checks. Hitler and Himmler were shown the dossier in early May, and approved the operation.

A photocopy was in Prague within days. Beneš confirmed the existence of the plot to the Soviet Ambassador on 7 May, and on 8 May sent a personal secret message about it to Stalin. Heydrich's secret agent was put in touch with an officer of the Soviet embassy, and showed him two pages, asking payment for the rest. The officer immediately flew to Moscow and returned with full power to buy the whole dossier. Half a million marks were paid over (though these later turned out to be forged). And by mid-May, the documents were in Stalin's hands.[79]

Possession of this definite "proof" of treason may have contributed to a final decision on the conduct of the blow against the generals. On 20 May, Dmitri Shmidt was shot in secret without further ado.[80] On the same day, the emergency stories about the just-discovered plot began to be put about inside the NKVD. An official who left Russia on 22 May says that real panic was now gripping the officer corps.[81]

The same day saw the arrest of yet another of the leading figures in the alleged plot—Eideman. He was called out of a Moscow Party conference in the House of the Moscow Soviet, where he had been sitting on the presidium, and taken away by the NKVD.[82] The original pretext was that he had signed a Party recommendation for Kork. Like Yakir, Eideman is represented as having become disillusioned with the Purges. After a Party meeting in the spring of 1937, he had remarked quietly to a friend, "Last night they arrested another comrade here. It seems to me that he was an honest man. I don't understand. . . ."[83]

One officer describes a last conversation with Tukhachevsky. He was looking gloomy. When this was mentioned, he said that he had indeed had bad news. He had just learned of Feldman's arrest. "What a monstrous provocation!" he commented.[84] Tukhachevsky knew, in fact, that he was cornered. Driving to the station on his way to Kuibyshev, his chauffeur suggested that he should write to Stalin to clear up the obvious misunderstandings. The Marshal replied that he had already written.[85]

On about 24 May, Stalin, after consultation with Molotov, Voroshilov, and Yezhov, gave the order for Tukhachevsky's expulsion from the Central Committee and arrest.[86] On his arrival in Kuibyshev on 26 May, Tukhachevsky gave a short address in the evening to the District Military Conference. One who had known him well noted that in the two months since he had last seen him, his hair had begun to turn gray.[87]

He did not turn up at the next session.[88]

For he had been asked to call in at the offices of the Provincial Committee of the Party on the way to his headquarters. After a while, Dybenko, who he was relieving, came out pale-faced and told his wife that Tukhachevsky had been arrested.[89]

On the evening of 28 May, news of the transfer of Tukhachevsky's case to the "investigative organs" had reached the other generals, through some official though confidential channel.[90] So it is plain that the arrests after Tukhachevsky's were by no means bolts from the blue.

Tukhachevsky was interrogated by Yezhov personally, aided by the new Head of the NKVD Special Department, I. M. Leplevsky, and the ubiquitous Ushakov, now Deputy Head of that Department. By 29 May, the Marshal was confessing to espionage, links with the Germans, and recruitment by Yenukidze into Bukharin's conspiracy. Pages 165 and 166 of his testimony, when examined twenty years later, had on them forensically verifiable bloodstains.[91]

Army Commander Uborevich was the next to go. He was at a meeting in Minsk on 29 May when his A.D.C. passed him a note calling him urgently to Moscow. He excused himself and went to the station, where he was arrested as he entered his train. He told his wife and daughter, who were present, not to worry.[92] In the Lefortovo, Uborevich denied the charges, even after a "confrontation" with Kork. But after "physical methods" had been applied, he too confessed.[93]

Yakir was normally a cheerful man. A general who was present reports him as looking gloomy and *distrait* at a conference of the Kiev Military District, immediately after Tukhachevsky's arrest had become known to those present.[94] On 30 May, Voroshilov telephoned Yakir and ordered him to come urgently to a meeting of the Military Revolutionary Soviet. Yakir offered to fly, but Voroshilov told him to take the train—a clear indication that the Defense Commissar knew the plans of the NKVD in detail.[95]

Yakir took the 1:15 P.M. train from Kiev on the same day. At dawn on 31 May, the train stopped at Bryansk, where NKVD men boarded it and arrested him. His A.D.C., Zakharchenko, was not taken, and Yakir was able to send a message to his wife and son that he was innocent.

Yakir asked to see the warrant for his arrest, and when it was shown to him he asked to see in addition "the decision of the Central Committee." He was told that he could wait for that until he got to Moscow. He was bundled into a Black Maria; they drove to Moscow "at a hundred kilometers an hour"; and he was lodged in a solitary cell in the Lubyanka, where his chevrons and medals were ripped off.[96]

On 31 May, the last of the "conspirators" was dealt with. It was announced the next day that "former member of the Central Committee, Ya. B. Gamarnik, having entangled himself in connections with anti-Soviet elements and evidently fearing that he would be arrested, has committed suicide."[97]

There are several slightly different accounts of Gamarnik's end. The latest Soviet one, derived from his daughter, says that on 30 May, Blyukher visited Gamarnik, who was sick. Gamarnik was told that he would be a member of the court which was to try the Tukhachevsky plotters. Blyukher implied that if Gamarnik refused, he would himself be arrested. Gamarnik told his wife that he knew Tukhachevsky was innocent. On 31 May, Blyukher (or, in another account, Bulin) came in and said that Gamarnik had been fired. NKVD men sealed up his safe. When they had gone, he shot himself.[98] He was publicly attacked as a Trotskyite, fascist, and spy on 6 June.[99]

Meanwhile, from his cell in the Lubyanka, Yakir had written at once to the Politburo demanding immediate release or a meeting with Stalin. He assured Stalin of his complete innocence.

> He wrote: ". . . My entire conscious life has been spent working selflessly and honestly in full view of the Party and its leaders . . .—Every word I say is honest, and I shall die with words of love for you, the Party, and the country, with boundless faith in the victory of Communism."
> Stalin wrote on this letter: "Scoundrel and prostitute." Voroshilov added: "A perfectly accurate description." Molotov put his name to this and Kaganovich appended: "For the traitor, scum and [next comes a scurrilous, obscene word] one punishment—the death sentence."[100]

He was, instead, subjected to nine days' harsh interrogation, at which he was told that the "whole Yakir nest" had been arrested.[101] The charges presented to him were "so serious that in comparison the previous evidence for which Yezhov's interrogators had been working on Shmidt appeared to be amateurish concoctions."[102] That is, the Nazi connection was now being put forward, rather than mere Trotskyite terrorism, though the official title of the conspiracy remained "The Anti-Soviet Trotskyite Military Organization." A final day of beatings by Ushakov produced a confession from Yakir.[103]

From 1 to 4 June, the Military Revolutionary Soviet at the Commissariat of Defense, together with members of the Government, held an extraordinary session—the one to which Yakir had been invited, not knowing that the agenda consisted of a single item: the exposure of the counter-revolutionary military–fascist organization,[104] reported on by Stalin personally.

And now, after all the trouble and ingenuity which had been invested in it, he did not after all produce the "dossier." Instead, "in his statement, and also in many interjections, he based himself on faked evidence from repressed military men," though he also abused the accused at length as "agents of the Reichswehr."[105] He called for their execution, and denounced a number of other officers, including Army Commander A. I. Sedyakin, Head of Anti-Aircraft Command, and Divisional Commander D. A. Kuchinsky, Head of the General Staff Academy.[106]

Army Commissars Bulin and Slavin are said to have given offense to Stalin by not putting their names down to speak against the accused. However, other officers, like the Central Committee members three months earlier, joined in the denunciations; Dybenko is reported vilifying Gamarnik.[107]

The "dossier" seems to have had its use in giving the limited Stalin–Yezhov circle a proper sense of outrage and urgency. And since we are told that Stalin used it "to instruct the judges to pass a death sentence on Tukhachevsky,"[108] it is possible that they, or some of them, were shown or told about the document. But it received no official use. Stalin seems to have decided that he could after all manage without it, and that the well-tried system of confession could provide all the evidence needed. It would have been awkward even in a secret court if one of the officers could perhaps have exposed the fraud through some point which had escaped Yezhov's notice. And good fakes though they doubtless were, they had not been planned with a full feeling for the nuances of Stalin's technique.*

It seems clear, in any case, that "that quickfire court" found the accused guilty "on the basis of the verbal statements of Stalin at the Military Soviet" without the "dossier" being raised,[109] even to substantiate the charges of recruitment by Nazi intelligence which were laid. (In the indictment in the Bukharin Trial, it is asserted that that case was based on

> the materials not only of the present investigation, but also on the materials of the trials which have taken place in various parts of the U.S.S.R., and in particular the trial of the group of military conspirators, Tukhachevsky and others, who were convicted by a special session of the Supreme Court of the U.S.S.R. on 11 June 1937.[110]

Various allegations against the military were made in the Bukharin Trial, but they were all in the course of the evidence of various accused, and no "materials" from the military trial itself were produced.)

All the accused had eventually confessed under torture.

The interrogations continued right up to the morning of the trial, when Tukhachevsky was required to implicate Corps Commander Apanesenko and others. When Vyshinsky saw the accused, to complete the formalities (a process that took two to two and a half hours for the whole group), they admitted their guilt and made no complaints.[111]

Stalin, who was keeping direct personal control, saw Vyshinsky twice on 9 June, and, with Molotov, Kaganovich, and Yezhov, received Ulrikh on 11 June, doubtless to give final instructions.[112] The membership of the court which tried the generals consisted, in addition to Ulrikh as Chairman, of Marshals Blyukher and Budenny, Army Commanders Shaposhnikov, Alksnis, Belov, Dybenko, and Kashirin,† and Corps Commander Goryachev. Only the second and third survived the Purges.

When the court opened, Ulrikh stated the proceedings by asking, "Do you confess to the testimony which you gave at the NKVD interrogation?"

Although the defendants mostly confessed in general terms, only Primakov, who had been in prison for almost a year, admitted everything, and said that he had personally told the investigation of the names of more than seventy conspirators. Uborevich denied the charges, upon which the court had an hour's break and then went on to the other accused. The rest admitted that they (and Gamarnik) had had conversations about replacing Voroshilov, though denying that these had any criminal intent. Putna admitted that he had had personal relations with I. I. Smirnov, and Feldman that he had had them with Pyatakov; but they seem to have denied that these connections were criminal.[113]

They were also charged with various military errors. Budenny, from the bench,

---

*A minor point is that of the military men, they implicated Tukhachevsky only, and that they are said to have included Stalin's Ambassador first in Berlin and then in Paris, Surits, who was (by a curious quirk) one of the very few Ambassadors to survive the Purge.

† Shot on 14 June 1938 (*Sovetskaya istoricheskaya entsyklopediya*).

attacked them for overemphasizing the role of the tanks at the expense of the cavalry.[114]

As to complicity with the Nazis, the court relied on the fact that several of the officers had had connections with Germany: Kork had been Military Attaché in Berlin; Yakir had lectured at the German General Staff Academy; and Tukhachevsky had negotiated on the Soviet assistance in rearming Germany—but, as he said, this was before Hitler's coming to power.[115] Yakir confessed in a general sense, but when asked to confirm certain points said he could not add to his written evidence. Harangued by Ulrikh to the effect that the German officer attached to him on his last visit to Berlin had recruited him for Hitler, Yakir denied direct implication in espionage. Tukhachevsky denied connections with Polish espionage agencies, and more generally said merely that perhaps some contacts "might be considered espionage." Kork remained silent when the espionage charge was put to him. Uborevich said that he had not committed espionage.[116]

Another Soviet report says: "The court-martial was held behind closed doors. . . . Some witnesses' statements, which coincide, say that Tukhachevsky, speaking to one of the accused, who was talking about his connections with Trotsky, said, 'Have you been dreaming about all this?' "[117]

As usual, promises had been made to the accused that confession in court would save their lives.[118] All were condemned to death.

The military "judges" clearly had no real say, and it is plausible that (as one account, based on a conversation with the Assistant Head of the NKVD Foreign Department, has it) their signatures were attached to the verdict after the executions at a conference with Yezhov.[119] In any case, Stalin asked Yezhov how the members of the court had conducted themselves. Yezhov replied that apart from Ulrikh, only Budenny had cooperated enthusiastically, with the others almost silent. This angered Stalin.[120]

Rumors of the manner of the generals' end were many and various: it is reported that they were shot, not in the cellars, but in the courtyard of the NKVD building at 11 Dzerzhinsky Street, during the daytime, with NKVD trucks being revved up to cover the sound of the shots.

Khrushchev tells us that "when Yakir was shot he exclaimed: 'Long live the Party, long live Stalin!' . . . When Stalin was told how Yakir had behaved before his death, he cursed Yakir."[121]

Khrushchev reports this "long live Stalin!" as if it were a simple case of political devotion. But the generals were not really naive enough to believe that Stalin had no responsibility for their fate. Yakir was an old Communist, perfectly able to carry out political activity at the moment of death. And the program of support for Stalin, combined with condemnation of the NKVD, was already in existence. It was the line on which the maximum support for a program opposed to the Purge could be mobilized. It seems plausible to think that Yakir may have been trying, in fact, to establish an anti-Yezhov "platform."

But, at least equally compelling, we know he had thought of his family, and it was clearly not in their interests for him to utter words of defiance or abuse. He had made a last appeal for them. Two days before he was shot, he sent Voroshilov this letter:

To K. Ye. Voroshilov. I ask you, in memory of my many years of honest service in the Red Army in the past, to give instructions that my family, helpless and quite innocent, shall be looked after and given assistance. I have addressed the same plea to N. I. Yezhov.
Yakir, 9 June 1937.

On his copy, Voroshilov minuted, "In general I doubt the honesty of a dishonest person. K. Voroshilov. 10 June 1937."[122]

Yakir's attempt to save his family was unsuccessful. His wife, his "close companion for twenty years," was at once exiled to Astrakhan with her son Peter, and their passports were confiscated. In the Volga town, they met the families of Tukhachevsky, Uborevich, Gamarnik, and others. The boy's grandfather had hidden the paper containing the charge against Yakir from the mother, and she only saw it when Uborevich's wife showed it to her.

The papers published a faked letter from Mrs. Yakir repudiating her husband. She protested to the NKVD, which rebuffed her, but later told her in a threatening manner that it was willing to receive a withdrawal, though not necessarily to publish it.[123]

At the beginning of September, she was arrested. She was later liquidated, together with Yakir's brother, the wife of another brother and her son, and other relatives.[124] A woman cousin is reported as being sentenced to ten years' imprisonment in 1938.[125] Little Peti, now fourteen years old, was sent to a children's home. Two weeks later, at night, the NKVD took him, and he spent "many years" in camps and prisons. He chanced to meet his father's A.D.C. in one of the Arctic camps and learned from him the full story of the arrest.[126] (In 1961, when Khrushchev was visiting Kazakhstan, Peter Yakir approached him. "He asked me about his father. What could I tell him?"[127] At the time of Yakir's arrest and execution, Khrushchev had spoken of him as "riff-raff who wanted to let in the German Fascists.")[128]

Uborevich's wife (sent to Astrakhan on 10 June) had kept the charges against her husband from their little daughter, not yet in her teens; the girl learned of them from young Peter Yakir. On 5 September, Mrs. Uborevich was arrested by the NKVD. She was able to give her daughter a few photographs, and they never met again. Nineteen years later, in 1956, the daughter learned that her mother had died in 1941.

The daughter was taken to a children's home, where she found other young girls: Veti Gamarnik, Svetlana Tukhachevsky, and Slava Feldman. They were rounded up on 22 September and sent off, evidently to NKVD children's settlements.[129]

Tukhachevsky had a large family. "On Stalin's direct instructions, the wife of the Marshal, his sister Sofia Nikolayevna, and his brothers Alexander and Nikolai, were physically annihilated. Three of his sisters were sent to concentration camps, as well as the young daughter of the Marshal whom they interned when she reached the appropriate age."[130] This was Svetlana, eleven years old at her father's death; given a five-year sentence when she was seventeen, as "socially dangerous," she is later reported as having been in the Kotlas camp, south of Vorkuta, together with Uborevich's daughter.[131] The Marshal's mother, Mavra, also perished;[132] she had refused to repudiate him. His wife, Nina, is said to have first gone insane and to have been taken to the Urals in a straitjacket.[133] Two former wives of Tukhachevsky's, together with Feldman's wife, are reported to have been in a special "Wives and Mistresses" section of Potmalag—a camp area strict as to discipline, but comparatively mild as to living conditions—in 1937, and to have later been transferred to the Segeta camp.[134] Another of the Marshal's sisters announced that she was seeking permission to change her name. (The daughter and three sisters survived to attend a memorial meeting in his honor at the Frunze Military Academy in Moscow in January 1963.)

Gamarnik's and Kork's wives were also shot.[135]

## 1937–1938

As the Red Army's best generals were dragged off to execution amid a vast campaign of public abuse, Stalin and Yezhov launched the NKVD on the officer corps as a whole.

Four days after the Tukhachevsky executions, Brigade Commander Medvedev was tried and shot, on the charge only of Trotskyite ideas, though he told Ulrikh and the Military Collegium that he denied all accusations of counterrevolutionary crimes.[136] Within nine days after the trial, 980 officers had been arrested, including 21 Corps Commanders and 37 Divisional Commanders.[137] On 19 June, Yakir's subordinate, Divisional Commander Sablin, was shot. On 1 July, Corps Commanders Garkavi, Gekker, Turovsky, and Vasilenko and Divisional Commander Savitsky perished. (Garkavi's wife, Yakir's sister-in-law, was sent to camp, where she died in 1945; his two young sons, after some years in NKVD homes, were both killed in the Second World War.)[138] Twenty younger generals from the Moscow headquarters alone were also executed.[139] Almost the whole command of the Kremlin Military School was arrested.[140] The Frunze Military Academy, which Kork had headed, was swept by arrests. The Head of its Political Department, Neronov, was arrested as a spy. For a time, Shchadenko took over. Not a day passed without the arrest of a member of the staff. Almost all the instructors went to the jails.[141] Army Commander Vatsetis was giving a lecture. After an hour there was a short break, which ended with the announcement, "Comrades! The lecture will not continue. Lecturer Vatsetis has been arrested as an enemy of the people."[142] The students, too, were rounded up in droves. All who had references from Gamarnik, for example, were taken. So were those, and there were many of them, who had been sent to the academy from units whose commanders had been arrested.[143]

In the provinces, it was the same: in the Kiev Military District, 600 to 700 officers of the "Yakir nest" are said to have been arrested at this time.[144] A Soviet account of the Khrushchev period tells us that

> a new leadership arrived in the Kiev Military District, Shchadenko, a member of the Military Council, from the very first started to take an attitude of suspicion toward the members of the staff. He kept watch, without bothering to conceal it, on the commanders and political officers of the units and was thereafter acting hand in hand with the Special Department. He was also extremely active in the campaign to compromise the commanding officer personnel, which was accompanied by the massive

arrests of command cadres and political cadres. The more people were arrested the more difficult it was to believe in the charges of treachery, sabotage and treason.[145]

A Soviet engineer officer was one of a number who had been working under Yakir (and Berzin) to prepare secret partisan bases, and to train partisans, in the Ukraine. In 1937, they were arrested and accused of "lack of faith in the Socialist state" and "preparation for enemy activity in the rear of the Soviet armies"—or "training bandits and storing arms for them," as Voroshilov put it.[146] The bases were destroyed—to be much missed in 1941, when abortive attempts were made hastily to reconstruct them. The destruction of all but 22 of the 3,500 partisan detachments sent to the Ukraine in 1941 and 1942 is now largely blamed on this fact.[147]

The future Marshal Biriuzov tells in his memoirs of being appointed to be Chief of Staff of the Thirtieth Rifle Division, stationed in Dnepropetrovsk. When he arrived, he found that the entire command had been arrested, apart from a couple of junior staff officers—with a major in charge of the division. Biriuzov asked on what authority this officer had command, and got the answer, "We act according to regulations: when one chief leaves the division, he's replaced by the next in command. Just like in wartime."[148]

The Commander of the Seventh Cavalry Corps, Grigoriev, was called to the Kiev Military District Committee and accused of connections with the enemy. He was allowed to go back to his post, where he was arrested the next day,[149] and shot on 20 November, together with another Kiev District officer, Divisional Commander Dyumichev. Here we have a picture of the NKVD not feeling any necessity to put a general officer under arrest immediately he must have realized his case was hopeless. It cannot, in fact, have had much real fear of desperate military action, as is sometimes suggested.

Even retired veterans became involved. General Bougetsky, the Civil War hero whose wife had been crippled and son blinded while in the hands of the Whites, and who himself had lost his right arm in battle, was interrogated in the inner prison at Kiev. On the heart of this dignified sexagenarian they pinned the Nazi swastika and emptied a spittoon over his head. He was charged with an attempt to assassinate Voroshilov.[150] Juniors were treated even more brutally. A recent Soviet account tells us that in the Chita prison, a number of Air Force pilots were interrogated. One had his collar bone broken. They all had their teeth knocked out.[151]

In Minsk, Uborevich's "judge" and successor as Commander of the Byelorussian Military District, Army Commander Belov, was almost immediately in trouble. A member of Uborevich's "nest," Corps Commander Serdich (an officer of Yugoslav origin) was arrested on 15 July.[152] Imprudently enough, Belov intervened in his favor.[153] For the moment, Belov was not proceeded against, and presided impotently over the further massacre of his subordinates.

## PURGE OF THE POLITICAL COMMISSARS

At the beginning of August 1937, a conference of political workers in the Army was addressed by Stalin. He once more violently attacked enemies of the people.[154] Gamarnik's Political Administration suffered even more than the rest of the forces. At the top levels, there was a clean sweep. Gamarnik's deputy, A. S. Bulin, had been dismissed by 28 May,[155] and later arrested.[156] The other deputy, G. A. Osepyan, was already under arrest by the end of May and, refusing to answer questions, was shot on 24 (or 26) June. He was followed by almost all the heads of the political administrations and most of the members of the soviets of the military districts.[157] Ippo, Head of the Military–Political Academy in Leningrad, who had been criticized in April, was dismissed on 1 June for political blunders[158] and later arrested. By rank, all seventeen of the Army Commissars went, with twenty-five of the twenty-eight Corps Commissars.[159]

This purge of politicals swept the units as well. In the two months following the June 1937 meeting of the Military Soviet, arrests in the Fifth Mechanized Brigade of the Byelorussian Military District included the Brigade Commissar, the head of its political section, plus five out of the six Battalion Commissars, while the sixth was severely reprimanded.[160] A Soviet textbook speaks of "thousands" of leading Party workers in the Army and Fleet being repressed.[161]

Mekhlis, one of the most sinister and unpleasant of all Stalin's agents, was confirmed as Head of the Political Administration of the Army in December 1937. He had lately worked as editor of *Pravda,* but in the Civil War had served as a Political Commissar at Army level. He had a special quirk—to cashier and arrest many political workers on the grounds of their connection with the "anti-Party Army Byelorussian–Tolmachevite Group."[162] In fact, he was condemning the Political Commissars for this long-extinct deviation, which had consisted of enthusiasm for *greater* political control in the Army! In any case, the grouping of senior Political Commissars who had criticized the Party leadership in the late 1920s was, whatever its particular program, far too independent-minded for the new regime. Mekhlis had insisted that any who attempted to defend them, such as the Head of the Political Administration of the Byelorussian Military District, I. I. Sychev, deserved the same fate as this "band of spies."[163]

At the beginning of 1938, the number of political workers in the armed forces was only one-third of its official establishment. As the numbers still in position were 10,500, the implication is that at least 20,000 political workers had gone under.* By 1938, more than one-third of all the Party political workers had had no political education at all.[164]

The number of Party members in the Army shrank by about a half.[165] At the XVIIth Congress, Voroshilov had given 25.6 percent of the Army as Party workers, the Army numbering in February 1935 approximately 1 million: the net deficit here was therefore some 125,000.

## THE OFFICERS FADE AWAY

Everywhere—except as yet the Far East—the Purge began to strike at the whole command structure. The generals who had just been promoted to fill the vacant places now started to disappear.

At a meeting of the Military Soviet of the Caucasus Military District in

---

* "At least," because that is not to allow for replacements who must have come in: the proportion who had gone through military political schools, compared with that in 1934, had gone down by half. So of the 10,500, the assumption is that some 5,000 were fresh and raw.

November 1937, the new District Commander, N. V. Kuibyshev (brother of the dead Politburo member), criticized the purge of the Army as affecting its battle-preparedness. He was shortly afterward arrested.[166] And the same fate overtook the Military District Commanders all over the Soviet Union. By the summer of 1938, all who had held these posts in June 1937 had disappeared. At the center, a similar sweep took all eleven Deputy Commissars of Defense.

A Soviet account says that the Air Force and the tank and mechanized forces suffered most heavily.[167] Khalepsky of the Armored Forces, Alksnis of the Air Force, and Khripin, Alksnis's deputy, had made an excellent impression on foreign Military Attachés in the autumn 1936 maneuvers. Khalepsky, who had been relegated to the Communications Commissariat, was arrested in 1937 and shot in 1938.[168] Army Commander Alksnis was the youngest of the Tukhachevsky group, being barely forty. Backed by Corps Commander Todorsky, Head of the Air Force Academy, he had worked hard to save his juniors from persecution by NKVD. Alksnis is given on the electoral lists as late as 13 November, but by the last days of 1937 he was under arrest, together with Khripin (as was also Todorsky). Todorsky, arrested in the spring of 1938, was sentenced to fifteen years in May 1939. He survived (the only "repressed" Corps Commander to do so) and was released in 1953.[169]

The extraordinary deviousness of the NKVD is shown in Gorbatov's experiences. He learned he was in disfavor (for the second time) when, temporarily commanding the Sixth Cavalry Corps, he went to the stores officer to draw his winter uniform, and found that orders had been received from the corps political officer, Fominykh, then in Moscow, not to give him one. He went to Moscow and was arrested. His wife could not find out what had happened to him. No one would even tell her he had been arrested, until a girl whispered it to her in the corridor of the Red Army Officers' Hostel.[170]

Gorbatov has given a brief account of his interrogation. At the Lubyanka, he was at first treated fairly mildly, but bullying set in on the fifth day. He was in a cell with seven others, all of whom had confessed. He was then transferred to the Lefortovo prison, where he shared a single one-man isolator with two others. There he was tortured on the fourth interrogation, and five more torture sessions followed at two- to three-day intervals, from each of which he had to be carried back bleeding to the cell. There were then twenty days' rest, then five more bouts of torture. No confession could be wrested from Gorbatov, and on 8 May 1939 he was sentenced at a trial lasting four or five minutes to fifteen years' imprisonment plus five years' disfranchisement. The NKVD told his wife that as she was "young and interesting," she could easily get married again.[171]

Another officer, a former revolutionary sailor in the Baltic Fleet, is reported as also having refused to confess and actually being acquitted, getting a civilian job on his release. He was, however, rearrested six months later.[172]

But "many splendid comrades and political officers" confessed.

They were "persuaded"—persuaded by quite definite techniques—that they were either German or British or some other kind of spies. . . . Even in cases when such people were told that the accusation of espionage had been withdrawn, they themselves insisted on their previous testimony, because they believed it was better to stand on their false testimony in order to put an end as quickly as possible to the torment and to die as quickly as possible.[173]

One Divisional Commander is reported as confessing that he had "recruited" every officer in his division down to Company Commanders.[174] And there are many similar stories. Mekhlis even discovered and denounced a group of twelve terrorist-spies in the Red Army Chorus.[175]

Rivalries between the NKVD and the Army were of course natural in various fields. (The possession by the Police of a large armed force was itself an irritant.) But in addition, the military-intelligence network abroad operated to a certain extent independently of the Foreign Department of the NKVD, and there was a struggle to win it. When Tukhachevsky was arrested, the NKVD gained control. Almost all the military-intelligence agents were recalled from abroad and shot.[176] S. P. Uritsky, Chief of Soviet Military Intelligence—the "Fourth Bureau"—from 1935, was arrested on the night of 1 November 1937 and shot "soon afterward."[177]

His predecessor as Head of the Fourth Bureau, from 1920 to 1935, J. K. Berzin, who had held a post in the short-lived Soviet Latvian Government of 1919, had been sent to the Far Eastern Army on handing over. From there, he had gone to Spain, as virtual Commander-in-Chief of the Republican Armies under the name "Grishin." He had clashed with the NKVD, and was arrested on his return.[178]

The Commander of the International Brigade, "General Kleber," a Soviet officer whose real name was M. Z. Shtern, but was represented as a Canadian to suit international decorum, was accused of being a member of Berzin's "spy organization" and beaten on the legs with iron bars.[179] However, he was only sentenced to twenty-five years and sent to a labor camp, where he died.[180]

Brigade Commander "Gorev" (Skoblevsky), who had fought and won the Battle of Madrid for the Spanish Republic, was much feted on his return to the USSR. But soon afterward, about the end of 1937, "the hero of Madrid was slandered" and shot.[181] He is said to have been arrested only two days after receiving the Order of Lenin.[182]

Other military victims among Soviet veterans of the Spanish Civil War were to include the senior military adviser "Grigorevich" (G. M. Shtern), later promoted to Army Commander in the Far East, and the leading Soviet air ace in Spain, "Douglas," later, as Lieutenant General Smushkevich, Head of the Soviet Air Force; both were shot in 1941.[183] Marshal Malinovsky, until his death Minister of Defense, who was also in Spain, describes failing to obey two orders to return and finally getting a third threatening to list him as a "non-returner," upon which he went back, at a time when, fortunately for him, the worst period of the Purge was over.[184] Soviet civilians in Spain also fared evilly. Antonov-Ovseenko, who had operated in the delicate position of Soviet Consul-General in Barcelona, perished, as did Rosenberg, the Soviet Ambassador to the Republican Government. Rosenberg's crime seems to have been an attempt to arrange the exchange of prisoners with the Franco authorities. Stalin always regarded this sort of thing as suspicious, and was later to show resentment when the Yugoslav partisans entered into similar conversations with the German Command in the Balkans.[185]

## PURGE IN THE NAVY

In the Navy, the Purge was as sweeping as in the land forces. Of the nine Fleet Admirals and Admirals First Grade, only one (Galler) survived the Purge, to die in prison after the war.[186] First to be arrested was the brains of the Navy (though no longer holding naval position), R. A. Muklevich. Muklevich, a comfortable, strong-looking man, was an Old Bolshevik with an extraordinary career behind him. Born in 1890, he had become a Party member at the age of sixteen, and in the difficult years 1907 to 1909, still in his teens, had been secretary of the Party organization at Bialystok. He had been called up for the Imperial Navy in 1912 and been active in the Party's military work from then through the Revolution. During the Civil War, he had served on the staff of various armies and fronts, become Deputy Director of the Army Academy in 1921, then served with military aviation from 1925, and finally taken over effective control of the fleet from 1926 to 1927. As Director of Naval Construction, he had played a leading role in the modernization of the Soviet Navy. His clear view of the problems and unambitious efficiency made him a natural and welcome associate of Tukhachevsky's group.

He was arrested in May 1937.[187] He was not brought to public trial—indeed, there was no announcement made about the trial of any of the naval leaders. He and the Navy Commander-in-Chief, Admiral Orlov, were, however, denounced as accomplices of Tukhachevsky at the XVIIIth Party Congress in 1939. The attack on them, unlike those made on the Army men, contained a specific criticism of their military policies. People's Commissar for Shipbuilding Tevosyan announced that they had opposed the idea of a powerful surface fleet and that their removal had made it possible to build "a most mighty attacking force"[188]—a chimera which diverted a large amount of Soviet effort into a hopeless and pointless attempt to match the major naval powers with a battle fleet.

This is doubtless the factual basis to be found, as so often, for one of the incidents in Arthur Koestler's *Darkness at Noon:* the execution of the Fleet Commander "Bogrov" on account of a dispute about the nature of the future Soviet Navy. The precise issue, however, is rather different. Koestler has "Bogrov" advocating large, long-range submarines as against Stalin's view that small, short-range craft were required, the political distinction being that the former implies a policy of aggression and world revolution, and the latter one of coastal defense and a general defensive policy. In reality, the Stalinist view was the more, rather than the less, aggressive ("Stalin had threatened to mete out heavy punishment to anyone objecting to heavy cruisers").[189] Muklevich's attitude, doubtless dictated by a realistic appraisal of the possibilities, given actual Soviet resources, was a short-range, defensive one. When war came, the Soviet Navy lost effective control of the vital seas, and Muklevich was proved right posthumously—the Soviet Admiralty reverting to his views, though not acknowledging them.

In any event, this argument cannot have been the main motive behind the Navy purge, whose origins were clearly the same as those of the purge in the Army and in the country as a whole. It was less a matter of settling technical disputes by executions than of using technical disputes as one excuse for executions. Muklevich confessed after a week's severe torture in the Lefortovo prison.[190]

Next to fall was the Commander of the Naval Forces, Admiral Orlov, together with Admiral Sivkov, Commander of the Baltic Fleet, and Admiral Kozhanov, Commander of the Black Sea Fleet. Orlov was arrested in November 1937, but he seems to have been dismissed as early as June, when Admiral Viktorov, Commander of the Pacific Fleet and himself shortly to fall, was acting as Head of the Navy.[191]

With the leaders, their subordinates fell in scores.

The Navy by its very nature gave contact, or the possibility of contact, with foreigners. Soviet warships paid courtesy visits. They cruised in international waters. During the Second World War, these suspicious circumstances were to be much exacerbated, owing to collaboration with the Royal Navy at the Murmansk end of the Northern Convoy route. One of the chief figures in *One Day in the Life of Ivan Denisovich* is Buynovsky, "The Captain," who has actually spent a whole month on a British cruiser as liaison officer. "Then after the war some British admiral who should've had more sense sent me a little souvenir with an inscription that said: 'In gratitude.' I was really shocked and I cursed like hell, so now I'm inside with all the others."

The atmosphere had been established much earlier. Rear-Admiral Isakov, in his memoirs published in 1961,[192] tells a story of a flag officer of his acquaintance, Ozarovsky, who was wrecked in his small sailboat off the coast near Kronstadt. A Norwegian steamer came in sight and lowered a boat. Ozarovsky refused the offer of rescue, though his situation was desperate. Isakov describes Ozarovsky's feelings. He was bound to be saved. Although he himself could not have been seen from the shore, "the foreign steamer entering a prohibited zone would be seen at once. A cutter would be sent to the scene." And this in fact happened. Isakov visited him in hospital and asked why he had not let himself be brought to Leningrad by the Norwegians. Ozarovsky replied, "I should have had to give an explanation: when and how this meeting with foreign agents had been arranged and for how much I had sold our operational plans while the ship was passing through the channel." Isakov felt compelled to agree, and adds that even so Ozarovsky did not escape. He was arrested, interrogated, and tortured for the very reasons he had advanced.

In fact, the occupational hazards of the cadres in the Navy were even higher than those of the cadres in the Army. They had one very minor advantage. Except in the case of the Pacific Fleet, naval officers were usually British "spies," and, until 1939 at least, this carried slightly higher social status than attached to treason in favor of Germany, Japan, and Poland.

## A SECOND MILITARY MASSACRE

Orlov's case became associated with a new wave of military arrests launched in the early part of 1938, whose theme was made clear in a letter issued on Stalin's instructions calling for further purging of the armed forces, not only of enemies of the people, but also of "the silent ones" who had failed to take an active part in the Purge.[193]

The replacements of the slaughtered commanders of 1937 now went themselves to the Lubyanka. In the first days of January, Belov was recalled to Moscow. The train journey, we are told, was gloomy, full of recollections of similar ones of the previous year. On arrival, he was arrested; his intervention in favor of Serdich was now turned into a criminal matter.[194]

And now a second Marshal of the Soviet Union fell. Yegorov, a former Tsarist officer, was an older man than the members of the Tukhachevsky group, being fifty-five, a year younger than his former colleague in the Imperial Army, Shaposhnikov. He was one of Stalin's boon companions. Stalin is said to have offered Tukhachevsky's country villa to Yegorov after the execution, and Yegorov to have refused to take it.[195]

Yegorov had commanded the South-Western Front in the Polish Campaign, with Stalin as his political chief. He was one of the few figures from Stalin's old military entourage to suffer.

The first blow in the military purge had taken out all the military members of the Central Committee except Voroshilov, Budenny, Blyukher, and Yegorov. Yegorov is said to have complained that the extent of the purge was gravely affecting military efficiency. He was removed from his post as Deputy People's Commissar of Defense at the end of February 1938, and Stalin circulated to the Central Committee a note urging his expulsion from the Committee because he had been compromised in "confrontation" with the arrested conspirators Belov, Gryaznov, Grinko, and Sedyakin, and also because his wife was a Polish spy.[196] He was soon under arrest.

The same month saw the dismissal, and April the arrest on a civilian mission in the Urals, of Army Commander Dybenko,[197] who now commanded the Leningrad District. During the Civil War, Dybenko had served with Voroshilov and Stalin, but that was no longer sure protection. The huge sailor had led the mutiny of the *Imperator Pavel I* in 1916, and had commanded the Baltic Fleet sailors in the Revolution. He had once been married to the fiery aristo-deviationist Alexandra Kollontai. He had led the soldiers who suppressed the Constituent Assembly in 1918. But idealism had persisted for a time: he actually tried to resign from the Party when the death penalty was not, after all, abolished by the Soviet Government.[198] His closest friends at the Military Academy had been Uritsky, shot in 1937, and Fedko, who was brought on 2 February 1938 from Yakir's old post in the Ukraine to be Deputy Commissar for Defense for a short and insecure tenure.[199] They had all been sent from the Academy to take part in the assault on Kronstadt.[200] And now Dybenko was a German agent, though also (then a rarity) a spy for the United States, a group of Americans having visited Samarkand when he was commanding there.[201]

Not only old associates of Stalin's like Dybenko were now to perish (together with his wife).[202] There were still grudges to be paid against former enemies. Among those in jail was, as we have seen, Army Commander Vatsetis, first Commander-in-Chief of the Red Army, whom Stalin and others had attempted to remove as a traitor in 1919, but whom Trotsky had successfully defended. He had meanwhile held important posts in the Army Inspectorate and in the Military Academy.[203]

At the end of July came a second and even larger slaughter of the High Command, though no announcement was ever made. This went together with a major killing of political and other figures (see p. 420). As far as I know, this massive operation was referred to for the first time in an article of mine in *En-*

*counter* in October 1968. I then noted eleven death dates, military and civilian, to be found in various publications of the Khrushchev period. As I write, twenty years later, forty-six names (civilian and military) have become available with death dates 27 July to 1 August 1938, though so far few new names have been given in the *glasnost* literature of 1986 to 1990.

The military component of this mass operation included no fewer than nine Army Commanders—Alksnis of the Air Force, Belov of Byelorussia, Dubovoy, Dybenko (lately of the Leningrad Command), Levandovsky (until recently in the Far East), Khalepsky (former armored forces commander), Sedyakin (anti-aircraft), Vatsetis (former Civil War Commander-in-Chief), and Velikanov (unlike the others, newly promoted to this rank); Corps Commanders Gailit, Gribov, Gryaznov, Kuibyshev, and Kovtiukh (the legendary Civil War hero who appears under the name Kozhukh in A. S. Serafimovich's *Iron Flood,* which curiously enough continued to be sold without alteration after the purge of its hero, who was "brutally tortured");[204] Divisional Commanders Kuchinsky (Head of the General Staff Academy), Serdich, and Stigga; Fleet Admirals Orlov (Commander-in-Chief of the Navy) and Viktorov (his successor); Admiral Kireev; Army Commissars Berzin (lately in effect Commander-in-Chief of the Spanish Republican Army) and Okunev; Corps Commissar Ozolin; and the military theoretician (at one time briefly Chief of Staff of the Red Army) A. A. Svechin.

No doubt others not yet named perished; clearly the higher the rank, the more likely is its holder to be found in the reference books, so that nine Army Commanders to five Corps Commanders to four Divisional Commanders may not represent the real proportion. But even as it is, this is clearly a major blow to the Army and Navy: one not perhaps so striking, yet more massively devastating even than that of June 1937.

It may be worth stating that the military and political victims do not seem to have been taken in separate categories. One Army man was shot on 27 July; six soldiers and five civilians on 28 July; thirteen soldiers and thirteen civilians on 29 July; and six soldiers and two civilians on 1 August. This may not be entirely representative, but at least it appears to show that there was a blending of the two elements into a single alleged plot. Berzin was accused of belonging to the "anti-Soviet nationalist band Rudzutak–Berzin," which had served "British, French, and German intelligence."[205] Both were Latvian, to which the "nationalist" charge must refer (indeed, nine of the accused were Latvian). We are also told that the new Army plot was a matter of Right Socialist Revolutionaries and German, Polish, Finnish, and Latvian nationalists.[206] Then we learn that the accusations against Dubovoy included his having killed his superior, the legendary Shchors, during the Civil War, in order to take his place.[207] But a variety of charges of this nature had been melded together in previous trials. More generally, as far as the evidence goes, the political victims were accused of Rightist conspiracy, and we can perhaps assume that a military–Rightist plot was the main allegation.

One last major blow, against the Far Eastern Army, remained to be struck, and Marshal Yegorov and others were still to be dealt with. We shall go into that in a later chapter, and afterwards consider the whole effect of this unprecedented destruction of the officer corps. But it will already be obvious that if Stalin had destroyed a potential threat to his power, he had also inflicted enormous damage on Soviet defense.

# THE PARTY CRUSHED

*You have made of liberty a weapon for the executioner.*
Lermontov

## IN THE PROVINCES

April 1937 saw the beginning of intra-Party elections, the occasion for a great campaign in the press against those elements interfering, like Postyshev, with Party democracy, who were found everywhere. Some failures in this respect were dealt with harshly in the set-piece article which launched the campaign, "Internal Party Democracy and Bolshevik Discipline."[1] The author was Boris Ponomarev, still a member of the Central Committee of the Communist Party in 1988.

Among the first Central Committee members to be arrested were those from Leningrad. Outside Moscow, it was only in the northern capital, where Zhdanov ruled, and in Transcaucasia, under Beria, that local First Secretaries ready to purge without limit were already in control.

As a result of the Kirov murder,

> the Leningrad Party organization suffered particularly large losses. . . . For a period of four years there was an uninterrupted wave of repressions in Leningrad against honest and completely innocent people. Promotion to a responsible post often amounted to a step toward the brink of a precipice. Many people were annihilated without a trial and investigation on the basis of false, hastily fabricated charges. Not only officials themselves, but also their families were subjected to repressions, even absolutely innocent children, whose lives were thus broken from the very beginning. . . . The repressions . . . were carried out either on Stalin's direct instructions or with his knowledge and approval.[2]

But in fact the first waves of terror had struck at non-Party people and the mass of minor functionaries. Zhdanov had pursued the Stalin method. He had weakened the old Kirov cadre from below, replacing many of its junior veterans at the District Committee level. But he had not yet driven all Kirov's leading supporters, a number of them members or candidate members of the Central Committee itself, from the higher posts they held in the city and the province. In 1936, he had, indeed, removed and demoted Mikhail Chudov, Kirov's Second Secretary. A printer by trade, a Bolshevik since 1913, Chudov had been imported into Leningrad to reinforce Kirov in 1928. A full member of the Central Committee, he had been on the Presidium of the XVIIth Congress. In 1934, he had made Leningrad's funeral speech on Kirov and been on the Kirov Burial Commission. More than anyone, he represented the Kirov tradition in the city. Kirov's other closest associate, Kodatsky, was still in position.

The old Party leaders at this level were to prove unacceptable to Stalin throughout the country. But the Leningrad men were particularly unsatisfactory. First, they had been closely associated with Kirov and his platform, both of which had been the special objects of Stalin's hostility. And second, they were the very men who, on that December afternoon over two years before, had rushed into the corridor when they heard the shot that killed Kirov, and must have noticed—indeed, we are now told, *did* notice—the absence of guards and other suspicious signs.

The Leningrad purge had already been violent even by Soviet standards. In the ensuing period, as it affected the entire political and industrial leadership, it was worse than those almost anywhere else in the country—though this meant a matter of a nearly 100 percent destruction, compared with 80 or 90 percent elsewhere.* We happen to have fuller information about it than about the lesser provincial massacres which succeeded it, and it shows the sort of operation that now involved Party and population alike.

Zhdanov reported back from the plenum on 20 March 1937, at a Party meeting notable for attacks on various District Committees in the city. Zakovsky, Commissar of State Security, First Rank, spoke of "enemies still active" in the organization.[3]

Zakovsky was Zhdanov's right hand in the ensuing assault. His left—indeed, his only trusted aide at an executive level—was the infamous A. S. Shcherbakov, who had served with him from 1924 to 1930 in the Nizhni-Novgorod (Gorky) province, becoming local chief of agitation and propaganda. Shcherbakov, a figure more personally disliked even than Zhdanov, was a plump man with glasses and Western-style hair, combed back. He had gone on from Gorky province to the Central Committee apparatus, and had then been appointed, in 1934, Secretary of the Union of Soviet Writers! After a year (1936–1937) in Leningrad, he went on as a mobile purger to various reluctant provinces, apart from being briefly Head of the Political Department of Transbaikal Military District. During 1938 alone, he was to serve in fewer than four of these posts. Leaving Irkutsk completely crushed, he held two First Secretaryships in the Ukrainian provinces left empty by Khrushchev's purges, and then arrived in Moscow in the winter as the city's First Secretary. During the Second World War, he was to take over political control of the Army and to become Secretary of the Central Committee and candidate member of the Politburo. He died in 1945, allegedly at the hands of doctor-poisoners. A typical Zhdanovite career.

This group soon set to work. In May 1937, Zhdanov assembled the executive

---

*We are told by a Soviet historian that 90 percent of the members of Provincial and City Committees and Republican Central Committees were liquidated in 1937 and 1938 (Roy Medvedev, *Faut-il réhabiliter Staline?* [Paris, 1969], p. 42).

workers of the Provincial Committee and announced: "Two enemies—Chudov and Kodatsky—have been exposed in our ranks, in the Leningrad organization. They have been arrested in Moscow." No one spoke: "it was as if our tongues were frozen." A woman Old Bolshevik, later to spend seventeen years in a labor camp, went up to Zhdanov and said to him:

> Comrade Zhdanov, I don't know Chudov. He hasn't been in our Leningrad organization long. But I vouch for Kodatsky. He has been a Party member since 1913. I have known him for many years. He is an honest member of the Party. He fought all the oppositionists. This is incredible! It must be verified.

Zhdanov looked at her "with his cruel eyes" and said, "Lazurkina, stop this talk, otherwise it will end badly for you."[4]

This conference of the Party organization "uncovered and expelled from its ranks the Anti-Soviet Rightist-Trotskyite-double-dealers—the Japanese–German diversionists and spies."[5] (Expulsion was the extreme measure of Party discipline proper. In these circumstances it almost invariably meant "relaxation to the secular arm" of the NKVD, followed by arrest.) And this was only the first step: of the sixty-five members of the new City Committee elected on 29 May, only two were reelected on 4 June 1938 (while five others were transferred to posts outside the city).[6]

The long days of summer had set in in the northern capital, presenting a minor technical difficulty to Zakovsky's men. As the wave of arrests reached the top of the local Party, then swept downward again, involving those promoted to Party positions in the past year or two, and then out beyond them to the already stricken masses of the population, operations could no longer be conducted under the decent cover of night. For Leningrad is easily the most northerly of the great cities of the world, on the same latitude as the Shetland Islands and northern Labrador. In winter, daytime is extremely short, but in summer, as Pushkin says, one can read all night in one's room by the "Transparent dusk and moonless glitter." The rumbling and halting of police cars in the bright but deserted streets of the subarctic summer nights is said to have been particularly disturbing.

A man named Rozenblum, a Party member since 1906, had been arrested in connection with another case—that of the prominent Old Bolshevik Nikolai Komarov.

With the defeat of the Zinovievites in 1926, Komarov had taken over Zinoviev's own post as Head of the Leningrad Soviet. In 1929, he became unsatisfactory to Stalin: without actually supporting Bukharin, he had shown no enthusiasm in the struggle against him. Bukharin had told Kamenev in July 1928 that the higher functionaries in Leningrad "are mentally with us, but they are terrified when we speak of removing Stalin," so that they vacillated without being able to make up their minds. "Stalin," we are told elsewhere, "had met with a set-back in attempting to win the Leningrad people over to his cause, Komarov and the others, the successors of Zinoviev."[7] Komarov was removed and transferred to a post on the Council of National Economy in Moscow. In 1934, he was no longer a full member of the Central Committee, but remained a candidate member.

This and other transfers left Leningrad in the hands of men wholly loyal to the Party line. Yet most are perhaps best thought of as Stalinists with a slight Rightist tinge, a position to which Kirov himself to some extent evolved.[8]

Komarov remained a link to them. He was to be named later as an important figure in "the Leningrad group" of terrorists.[9] And through Rozenblum, the Komarov Case was somehow linked with Chudov's. But the latter was designed as a far more important affair, a public trial with all the trimmings. Rozenblum, who had already been subjected to "terrible torture,"[10] was brought before Zakovsky,

> who offered him freedom on condition that he make before the court a false confession fabricated in 1937 by the NKVD concerning "sabotage, espionage and diversion in a terroristic center in Leningrad." With unbelievable cynicism Zakovsky told about the vile "mechanism" for the crafty creation of fabricated "anti-Soviet plots."
>
> "In order to illustrate it to me," stated Rozenblum, "Zakovsky gave me several possible variants of the organization of this center and of its branches. After he detailed the organization to me, Zakovsky told me that the NKVD would prepare the case of this center, remarking that the trial would be public."
>
> ". . . You yourself," said Zakovsky, "will not need to invent anything. The NKVD will prepare for you a ready outline for every branch of the center; you will have to study it carefully and to remember well all the questions and answers which the court might ask. This case will be ready in four or five months or perhaps half a year. During all this time you will be preparing yourself so that you will not compromise the investigation and yourself. Your future will depend on how the trial goes and on its results. If you begin to lie and to testify falsely, blame yourself. If you manage to endure it, you will save your head and we will feed and clothe you at the Government's cost until your death."[11]

The trial, Zakovsky told Rozenblum, would involve Chudov, Chudov's wife, Lyudmila Shaposhnikova,* and three other Secretaries of the City and Provincial Committees: Boris Pozern, Party member since 1903; A. I. Ugarov; and Pyotr Smorodin—all candidate members of the Party's Central Committee.

As so often, we may note that the ground had been well prepared. Already, in August 1936, it had been alleged that several members of the group associated with Nikolayev had "enjoyed the confidence of a number of leading Party workers and officials of Soviet organizations in Leningrad"; it was this which had "ensured them every possibility of pursuing their preparations for a terroristic act against Kirov without the least fear of being discovered."[12]

As to political complexion, it seems clear that the Leningraders were to be treated as "Rightists." There was some truth in this, and their end represented the final crushing of the Kirov line.

The Leningrad Center Trial planned by Zakovsky never took place (in fact, announced trials of importance were held only in Moscow and Georgia). We do not know why.

The fate of Zakovsky's list of victims presents some peculiar features. Chudov and Kodatsky were executed on 30 October 1937. But Pozern, Smorodin, and A. I. Ugarov were still at large in mid-1938—Ugarov promoted to be First Secretary in Moscow—all three being shot only on 26 February 1939 (see p. 435).

---

*Also a member of the Provincial Committee and Secretary of the Leningrad Trade Unions.

This certainly shows that, as Zakovsky said, variants must have existed, some of them implicating men with whom he was sitting daily in the Provincial Bureau.

The Leningrad purge is the provincial one of which we are best informed, and it is illuminating to look at its scope. Those arrested included all the seven Leningrad members and candidate members of the Central Committee (Chudov, Kodatsky, Alexeyev, Smorodin, Pozern, Ugarov, and P. I. Struppe, Chairman of the Provincial Executive Committee). Other victims were A. N. Petrovsky, who had headed the Executive Committee and was later a Secretary of the Provincial Committee, and I. S. Vayshlya, Secretary of the Leningrad Komsomol. In addition, most of the other members of the Bureau, and "hundreds of the most active Party workers," including many Secretaries of District Committees in the city, perished. The purge also struck at the fighting service commands with Dybenko (G.O.C. Leningrad District and ex officio member of the Provincial Bureau) and the Commander of the Baltic Fleet, A. K. Sivkov. At the same time, the leading industrialists fell: the heads of all the great enterprises—"Lenenergo," the Kirov Works, the "Metallic" Factory—and many others.[13]

Of the 154 Leningrad delegates to the XVIIth Congress, only 2 were re-elected to the XVIIIth Congress: Andreyev and Shkiryatov, whose Leningrad affiliations were purely honorary. Of the sixty-five members even of the Leningrad Provincial Committee elected on 17 June 1937, only nine reappear a year later (four others had been transferred to positions outside the city).[14] As a survivor from among the lower officials in the Committee's apparatus was later to comment, "In 1937 I was to share the lot of many. I had an executive post in the Leningrad Province Party Committee and, of course, was also arrested."[15]

As the old cadres were annihilated, Zhdanov promoted his own men. Some of them (like Voznesensky, who became chairman of the local Planning Commission and then deputy chairman of the town Soviet before transfer to the central Government and eventual membership of the Politburo; A. A. Kuznetsov, promoted through District Secretaryships to Second and later First Secretary of the Provincial Committee, and later to become Secretary of the Central Committee; and Popkov, later also First Secretary of the Leningrad Committee) were shot in 1950 in a later "Leningrad Case."

These Leningrad events were repeated in the Provincial Committees throughout the country, with the amendment that (except in Beria's Caucasian fief and under Khrushchev in Moscow) the local First Secretaries could not be trusted, as Zhdanov was, to conduct their own purges.

So Kaganovich was sent to Ivanovo, Smolensk, and elsewhere; Malenkov to Byelorussia, Armenia, and so on; Zhdanov to Orenburg, Bashkiria, and other provinces; Shkiryatov to the North Caucasus. Everywhere they destroyed the old leaderships. As long as the Provincial Secretaries had to countersign orders for the arrest of prominent "Trotskyites" (which Eikhe mentions as one of his prerogatives as First Secretary in West Siberia),[16] they were, at the earlier stages, able and willing to block action—or, anyhow, to block the type of action now required by Stalin and Yezhov. In most cases, Moscow itself had to destroy the local leaderships. (The other method used by the Secretariat was to intrude, under the reluctant First Secretaries, Second Secretaries from the purging faction, as N. G. Ignatov was to be sent to undermine Postyshev.)

And so, we are told,

> The investigative materials of that time show that in almost all territories, provinces and republics there supposedly existed "Rightist–Trotskyite, espionage-terror and diversionary-sabotage organizations and centers" and that the head of such organizations as a rule—for no known reason—were First Secretaries of Provincial Party Committees or Republic Central Committees.[17]

When Kaganovich went to Ivanovo on 3 August, immediately on arrival he telegraphed Stalin: "First acquaintance with the material shows that Provincial Secretary Yepanechnikov must be arrested at once. It is also necessary to arrest Mikhailov, head of the Provincial Committee's Propaganda Department." Soon he was sending another telegram: "Acquaintance with the situation shows that Right–Trotskyist sabotage has assumed wide scope here—in industry, agriculture, supply, trade, public health services, education and Party political work. The apparatus of provincial institutions and the Provincial Party Committee are deeply infected."[18] His three-day visit to the city became known as "the black tornado":

> He accused the entire Party organization, which had great revolutionary traditions, of supposedly standing aloof, of being off to the side of the high road. At a plenary session of the Provincial Committee he pinned the label "enemy of the people" on the majority of executive officials without any grounds.[19]

When one of the city Secretaries, A. A. Vasilev, began to express doubt about enemy activity, Kaganovich had him expelled from the Party and arrested on the spot.[20] The local First Secretary, I. P. Nosov, followed, together with a whole list of other officials. Kaganovich was in frequent telephone contact with Stalin, who told him "not to be too liberal" and to make the operation larger and more ruthless—instructions he repeated to the local NKVD chief, Radzivilovsky, who was already "beating and torturing" officials to give testimony against more and more of their colleagues. (He was soon instructed to shoot 1,500 of them.)[21]

A Soviet account, in fictional form but evidently based on personal experience, describes the sort of scene which often occurred at the Provincial Committees.[22] On 23 July 1937 a member arrives at a meeting of one of these. It has been called at a few hours' notice and no agenda announced. When he arrives, the atmosphere is tense and silent. Everyone, as far as possible, sits in the back rows.

The first man to appear

> was then very powerful, both a People's Commissar and a Secretary of the Central Committee, virtually one man with seven faces. The hall was quiet. The People's Commissar frowned and was evidently displeased at how he had been greeted, being used to a triumphal reception. Some bright lad came to his senses and started clapping. Other people joined in and things took their proper course.
>
> After that the Bureau members of our Provincial Committee, headed by the First Secretary, appeared. They too were given a round of clapping, though a more feeble one. . . .

The report on agitation and propaganda work in the countryside ought to have been delivered by the Propaganda Secretary, but it was Kostyukov, the head of the provincial agricultural land administration, who got up to speak. He was a great one for making speeches, especially when it came to plans, hectares and fertilizers, but this time you could see his lips moving but nothing was audible. Some bolder spirit in the hall shouted: "Louder!"

Kostyukov raised his eyes from his notes and I felt ill—his eyes had the glassy look of a corpse. . . .

We heard him say:

"Two days ago Comrade Kazakov, Chairman of the Provincial Executive Committee, and I paid a visit to the Budenny Collective Farm. . . ."

The People's Commissar put his hands on his hips and in a curious way, whether expressing astonishment or derision, asked the speaker: "With whom? Who did you visit the collective farm with?"

"With Comrade Kazakov . . . "

It was only then that I noticed the absence of Kazakov from the Presidium. "How's that?" I thought to myself. "After all he is on the Bureau!"

The People's Commissar continued in the same incomprehensible tone: "So that therefore, if I understand you correctly, you consider Kazakov a Comrade? Answer me!"

Kostyukov went white and started stuttering . . . "Of course . . . if that is the case . . . Why shouldn't he be regarded . . . ?"

The People's Commissar looked at his wrist-watch, then glanced at the wings and some person there, not one of ours, immediately rushed over to him. The People's Commissar heard out this person's brief, momentary report and then declared . . . "I don't understand how you can conduct yourself in this way. I simply refuse to understand. . . . " He looked again at his wrist-watch and added, "The enemy of the people, Kazakov, was arrested twenty minutes ago. . . ."

. . . One of those sitting in the Presidium started applauding. The others backed him up, at first timidly, and then more energetically. A deep bass voice cried out: "Hurrah for our glorious NKVD!"

And I, too, cried "Hurrah!"

Kostyukov completely collapsed and, mumbling a few more words, left the rostrum to the sound of his own heels clicking on the floorboards. He was seen no more—he disappeared into the wings for good.

The People's Commissar again looked at his watch and in the same incomprehensible tone of voice addressed the Secretary for Propaganda: "Perhaps you can do duty for the last inadequate speaker?"

The Secretary walked across to the rostrum, as white as a sheet, gave a little cough, and started off relatively confidently:

". . . As the previous speaker already stated, we must complete the harvesting in a shorter period. . . . At the same time, Comrade Kostyukov failed to point out that . . ."

At these last words the People's Commissar again put his hands to his hips and inquired sneeringly: "Is Kostyukov your Comrade? Curious, very curious. . . ." Again a glance at his watch and the pole-axing words:

"The accomplice of the enemy of the people Kazakov, his henchman Kostyukov, was arrested fifteen minutes ago. . . ."

> Within forty minutes the entire bureau of the Provincial Committee and the entire
> Presidium of the Provincial Executive Committee had been swept into oblivion.

At the end of June, Kaganovich appeared before a specially summoned meeting
of the Smolensk Provincial Committee and announced that First Secretary Rumyantsev, who had held the area for Stalin since 1929, Second Secretary Shulman,
and a large group of the old leadership were "traitors, spies of German and Japanese fascism and members of the Rightist–Trotskyite gang."[23] They disappeared
without trace.

In Smolensk, we chance to be able to trace the impact of the Purge at the
local Party level. Belyi was a moderate-sized town and administrative area in the
Smolensk province. The Provincial Committee, itself already in trouble following
the February–March plenum, began to take it out on its subordinate bodies in
March 1937. The Belyi First Secretary, Kovalev, was put up in a four-day cere-
mony, to be abused and denounced by his local subordinates. Various speakers
attacked him for having lived with a Trotskyite in 1921, having behaved like a
local dictator, having been a deserter from the Red Army, and so forth. There
were more than 200 Communists present, accounting for a large section of the
local Party membership, and it is clear that a number of them had not yet grasped
the tone of the new-style Party. Questions from the floor pointed out that everyone
approved of Kovalev at the time and asked why they had not said anything earlier.
But one of Kovalev's more sophisticated accusers claimed that he had been silent
because Kovalev had, for four years, forbidden him to speak!

The representative of the Provincial Committee, while arranging the removal
of Kovalev, spoke more moderately than some of the rank-and-file delators, saying, "I do not have sufficient basis to call Kovalev a Trotskyite," but that the
matter would be investigated.

When, in June, the Provincial Committee was itself unmasked, a hysteria of
arrest and accusation seized Belyi. On 26 and 27 June, a further meeting there
saw violent denunciation of Kovalev and all the other members of the local leadership of his time. The whole of the Kovalev leadership fell, and on 18 and 19
September a plenum of the District Committee was held to destroy those who had
succeeded them. The new local Secretary, Karpovsky, was accused of having
been an agent of Rumyantsev's, of having once belonged to a bandit gang, of
having relatives abroad, of maintaining connections with a sister who had married
a former merchant. Karpovsky defended himself, saying that he not only had not
been a bandit, but had killed several bandits. He had received a letter from an
aunt in Romania, but had not seen her since she left Russia in 1908. Both his
sister and her former merchant husband were now employed in useful work. A
friend who had fought with Karpovsky testified that the two of them had fought
against bandits. But speaker after speaker attacked the Secretary in the most violent terms, and even this friend finally said weakly that he had just not been aware
of Karpovsky's membership in a bandit gang. All Karpovsky's associates fell with
him or shortly afterward. By the end of the year, a completely new team, all
strangers to Belyi, was in charge. The Party membership, which had been 367 on
1 September 1934, had gone down to less than 200.[24]

Almost as striking as the calls for terror from above was this hysterical lynching mood of what now became a dominant section of the lowest Party organizations. For while the upper and middle levels of the Party were being wiped out, Moscow's envoys everywhere found denouncers, like Nikolayenko in Kiev, to give them "evidence" against those they wished to destroy.

A Soviet article of the Khrushchev period entitled "The Dossier of a Provocateur"[25] describes how a Party member in Azerbaijan made his career during the purges by denouncing prominent Party colleagues to the NKVD. Among those he denounced were three Secretaries of the Azerbaijan Central Committee and the former Chairman of the local Council of People's Commissars. The "provocateur," I. Ya. Myachin, was until these revelations a well-known and well-liked local Communist whom "Communists for forty years had known simply as 'Vanya.'" At one time, he had held the post of Deputy People's Commissar for the Azerbaijan textile industry.

His belated undoing was the fact that he typed two copies of all his denunciations, sending one "to the NKVD, addressed to Bagirov's underlings," and the other, which he signed, to the archives, where it was added to a file which lay on a shelf "for a quarter of a century" until an archivist discovered it. It covered Myachin's activities for the period February to November 1937, and contained material "compromising" fourteen Party, Soviet, and economic leaders. A typical victim was accused of attempting "to give instructions to counterrevolutionaries to keep their mouths shut" because once on a bus he advised against talking about sabotage. In justification of his activities, Myachin said, "We thought this was what we had to do. . . . Everybody was writing. . . ." He was, of course, by his standards, quite right.

And, by such means, the Purge struck everywhere. In the Urals, in the newest industrial area, a "Ural Uprising Staff" was discovered, headed as was customary by the First Secretary, Kabakov, of the Sverdlovsk Provincial Committee, full member of the Central Committee. It was a "bloc of Rights and Trotskyites" and also included Social Revolutionaries and Church leaders.[26]

All the many industrial trusts in the area suffered as well; the Heads of Uralmash, Uralmed'rud, Levikhostroi, Sevkabel', and others, and their leading engineers, were of course arrested. Other institutions purged included the Bacteriological Institute, which lost "almost all" its staff, including its director, Professor Kuteyshchikhov, who committed suicide in jail. The Institute was closed down, its building being taken over by the NKVD, which certainly needed the space. One cell alone in the local prison now held twenty-seven wives of arrested officials.[27]

Malenkov went to Kazan in August 1937 to a plenum of the Tatar ASSR Provincial Committee, at or after which the First Secretary, Lepa, and most other high officials were arrested. At the same time, railway officials of the area were arrested on Kaganovich's orders.[28]

Zhdanov oversaw similar operations in various provinces and republics. In Karelia, he violently attacked the leadership—Irglis, Gylling, Rovio, and others, all of whom were arrested as Finnish spies. All the ten Finnish-language newspapers were closed down.[29] At a meeting of the Bashkir Provincial Committee on 4 to 6 October 1937, Zhdanov announced that the leading posts were held by "bourgeois nationalists, Trotskyites, fascist diversionists, spies and murderers."

Ya. B. Bykin, the local First Secretary, was "an old spy." He and almost all the local Party and Government leadership were arrested, including all the members of the Party Bureau and heads of departments. The local prison was not large enough for such an operation, and the victims were shot in "ravines and quarries," Bykin's pregnant wife among them.[30]

In Novosibirsk, the daughter of the head of the West Siberian medical department, Maxim Thallmann, tells us, in a recent Soviet article, how on 16 August 1937 her father was arrested with most of the local leadership. Her mother, sister of the former Central Committee member Vladimir Milyutin, followed on 3 September, and then all the leaders' wives and children over sixteen (only a few of the arrested survived). The daughter, aged seventeen, was one of 250 then held in a local NKVD children's home, and this was only one of several such homes.[31]

There were some special cases. Yosif Vareikis, who had been very much in Stalin's confidence, and had served as First Secretary in Voronezh and Stalingrad, was now First Secretary of the Far Eastern Territory. He telephoned Stalin in September 1937 with a query about the reasons for the arrest of certain Communists.[32] In the conversation he put some question about the arrest of Tukhachevsky. He had served with him in the Civil War, when the two had at one time been seized by Social Revolutionary mutineers, whom they had eventually suppressed.

Stalin shouted, "That is not your business. Don't interfere in what doesn't concern you. The NKVD knows what it's doing." He then went on to say, "Only an enemy would defend Tukhachevsky," and threw down the telephone. Vareikis was deeply shaken. He told his wife that he could hardly believe it was Stalin.

On 30 September, he got a telegram summoning him to the capital on official business. On 9 October, he was arrested a few stations out of Moscow. His wife was arrested four days later. He was mentioned as a plotter in the Bukharin Trial,[33] and was later shot. It seems very probable from the context that the conversation must have had something to do with the position of Marshal Blyukher, who commanded in the Far East, and that Stalin's lapse into open rage may have reflected a real anxiety about trouble from the Far Eastern Army.

## IN THE REPUBLICS

In the Republics, things went in the same way as in the provinces of Russia proper. In the Byelorussian Republic, the "verification" of Party cards ordered in 1935 and 1936 was used by Yezhov to expel, in connection with an alleged anti-Soviet underground, "more than half of the entire membership,"[34] The local officials opposed these actions, which amounted to the first phase in the destruction of the old Party and the rebuilding of another on its ruins. After the February–March plenum, on 17 March 1937, V. F. Sharangovich, as an emissary of the center, was sent to take over the Byelorussian First Secretaryship.

The resistance was widespread at the highest level in the Republic. M. M. Goloded, Chairman of its Council of People's Commissars, "cast doubt upon the results of the verification" at a meeting of the local Central Committee.[35] This was made the occasion for the dispatch of Malenkov, in June 1937, to destroy the leadership.

A plenum of the Byelorussian Central Committee was summoned. Violent accusations of espionage were made.[36]

Chervyakov, Chairman of the Byelorussian Supreme Soviet—that is, "Head of State" of the "sovereign republic"—committed suicide. Goloded was charged with "bourgeois nationalism,"[37] arrested on the way to Moscow, and shot.[38] Almost the entire leadership of the Republic, "including the Central Committee secretaries . . . the People's Commissars, and many leaders of local Party and Soviet bodies and representatives of the creative intelligentsia were expelled from the party and many of them were arrested."[39] Throughout the summer and autumn, the purge spread down to the local and mass level.

At a local Party Congress held in mid-June, Sharangovich warmly celebrated the purge then in progress. His own fall came at a Byelorussian Central Committee plenum in August, when Ya. A. Yakovlev, sent there from Moscow, denounced him in turn.[40] The resolutions referred to "the Polish spies, Goloded, Sharangovich, Benek, Chervyakov and other wreckers and diversionists." Sharangovich's fate is typical of a significant phenomenon. The new generation of Stalinist careerists, who had adapted themselves completely to the new system, still found themselves arrested. This is particularly the case among the first and most energetic batch who had worked up to high positions. They were succeeded by younger but similar characters, who again often fell quickly. The shortness of their tenure has been explained as follows:

> People of their type tended, in their unscrupulousness and zeal, to carry the Party line to absurd extremes, with the result that their actions had later to be explained away as deviations. People of this type were also inclined by nature to corruption and the exploitation of their positions for personal advantage. They thus roused the hatred and envy of their juniors. This further contributed to the shortness of their stay in office.[41]

Stalin's idea, announced at the February–March plenum, of having two stand-ins for every post, showed foresight, but did not go far enough. In many cases, it was only the fourth or fifth nominee who was to keep the post through the ensuing years.

Apart from politicians and engineers, the Byelorussian purge struck most heavily at the cultural leadership—and at the Linguistic Institute and the Commissariat of Education, in particular, where the principle of the separate Byelorussian nationality had been concentrated. Byelorussians, almost invariably, were ex officio Polish spies, owing to the geographical position of the Republic.[42] On 29 and 30 October 1937 there was a mass execution of Byelorussian cultural and political figures: M. M. Dzenishkevich, Byelorussian Second Secretary, and at least eleven others, including the poets Yu. A. Taubin and M. S. Kulbyak, together with such other writers as I. D. Kharik, A. Volny, and V. P. Kaval.[43]

The Byelorussian case is interesting in that it seems to show a rather more stubborn opposition than that offered in the Provincial Committees, perhaps owing to some reliance on local feeling. This was to be far more noticeable in the Ukraine, where a large concentration of high officials made final subjugation a more difficult matter.

In Georgia (where in 1919 the Mensheviks had won 105 out of the 130 seats in the National Assembly),* there was by now no need of a purge at the top. The thin-face, pince-nezed Beria, the old OGPU operative Stalin had infiltrated into the Transcaucasian First Secretaryship in 1931, was in full control, and had already been purging enthusiastically. As early as 11 August 1936 he had even shot, in his own office, the Armenian First Secretary, Khandzhyan.[44]

So Georgia's intra-Party purge was violent but routine. No emissary of the Central Committee was required to enforce it. But the Republic was the scene of several publicly announced trials, though these were not actually *held* in public.

The most important came on 10 to 12 July 1937. Men as prominent—on the narrower stage of Georgian Bolshevism—as the leading victims of the Moscow Trials were brought to trial. It was evidently intended, originally, to make this, too, a show trial. For all the men involved were old enemies of Stalin's. Chief among them was Budu Mdivani, former Premier of Soviet Georgia, whose defense against Stalin Lenin had undertaken just before his death—whose case, indeed, had been Lenin's final reason for wishing to remove Stalin from the General Secretaryship. With him were the Old Bolshevik Okudzhava and others.

Their trial is said to have been decided on at the February–March plenum.[45] But they had long since been incriminated. Mdivani had been denounced as long ago as 1929 for illegal Trotskyite activity,[46] but had become reconciled to the Party because, as he said, he felt too old to start another. At the Zinoviev Trial, though Mdivani's name was not mentioned, the "Georgian deviationists" were, as we saw, specially noted as having had an attitude which "as is well known was terroristic from 1928 onwards." At the time of the Zinoviev Trial, this was a record: no other group had then been charged with terrorist plans before the 1930s. At the Pyatakov Trial, Mdivani was accused of having planned a terrorist act against Yezhov, and another against Beria.[47] And after his death, at the Bukharin Trial of 1938, he was described as a British agent.[48]

He was arrested in early October 1936. To the first attempts to get him to confess, he is said to have answered, "You are telling me that Stalin has promised to spare the lives of Old Bolsheviks! I have known Stalin for thirty years. Stalin won't rest until he had butchered all of us, beginning with the unweaned baby and ending with the blind great-grandmother!"[49] He was then "cruelly beaten" and held in "hot" and "cold" cells: from the former, where he spent several days, he was taken out in half-dead condition, with his pulse barely detectable. He was also threatened with the death of his children, and was told that his wife had already been buried in the prison grounds. (The wife, their four sons, and their daughter all perished, though one daughter-in-law survived imprisonment.) On 15 January 1937, he finally confessed.[50] At the trial, however (where they were accused of terrorism, espionage, and links with émigré Georgian Mensheviks), he and Okudzhava are reported as having "fiercely denied their guilt."[51] The Georgian Supreme Court sentenced them to death, and they were shot.

Two parallel trials in the two Autonomous Republics within Georgia—Adzharia and Abkhazia—removed the equivalent veterans there on 29 September and 29 October, respectively. In the former, the Old Bolshevik Nestor Lakoba, who had died on 28 December 1936 as a result (it is now said) of some intrigue of

---

*The vote had been Menshevik, 640,000; Bolshevik, 24,000. The latter had won no seats at all.

Beria's,[52] was posthumously accused of a plot on Stalin's life.[53] Lakoba's wife was tortured for evidence against her husband. The interrogators threatened to shoot her fourteen-year-old son if she did not testify, but she refused. She died as a result of the torture, and the son was shot.[54]

Meanwhile, a fresh assault on the new generation of second-line leaders was mounted. The dates of arrest of a number of Georgian and Transcaucasian Communists rehabilitated in 1964 and 1965 are given as 1 to 3 September 1937. A general terror operation without the publicity of the oppositionist trials was starting. Over 1937 and 1938, 4,238 promotions to senior Georgian Party, State, and economic posts were made—that is, to leadership posts.[55] The *total* Party membership had been 34,000 at the XVIIth Congress, and the implication is that virtually the whole leading cadre was destroyed.

The Armenian Party had been under general attack since May. "Suspicious people" were found to be in the Party apparatus.[56] During the summer, Ter-Gabrielian, who had been Chairman of the Council of People's Commissars in 1935, was interrogated for seven hours in the office of the head of the local NKVD about alleged embezzlement on the railways, and killed on the spot. Stalin then sent a letter to the Armenian Central Committee alleging that Ter-Gabrielian had been a plotter liquidated by his accomplices to cover their traces.[57]

On 15 September 1937 a plenum of the Armenian Central Committee was held in Yerevan, and the decisive blow was struck. The All-Union Central Committee was represented by Mikoyan, supported by Beria and Malenkov. Under the New Constitution, Armenia no longer formed part of the old "Transcaucasian Socialist Federal Soviet Republic" ruled by Beria. It still came under his aegis in a general way, but in this case it was not thought to be an intrusion when Malenkov was sent "on Stalin's direct instructions"[58] to carry out the operation. Malenkov stopped off at Tbilisi on his way to Yerevan to concoct a story about the death of Khandzhyan, whom Beria had shot, to their mutual satisfaction. The rest of the Armenian leadership was now to be blamed for the crime.[59]

The First Secretary, Amatouni, is said to have put up a stout resistance and to have shouted back, "You lie!" He was, however, arrested, together with the Second Secretary, the Chairman of the Council of People's Commissars, the President of the Republic, and the head of the NKVD, and was denounced as an enemy of the people on 23 September.[60] Almost the entire leadership of Armenia's Central Committee and Council of People's Commissars was illegally arrested. Malenkov personally interrogated the prisoners, "using proscribed methods" in the process.

In this third week of September 1937, there was a wave of mass arrests throughout the Republic. Of the Bureau of sixteen members and candidate members elected in June 1935, none were left at the end of September 1937. Of those who formed the new Bureau in 1937, only two remained in 1940. Of the Central Committee of fifty-five elected in June 1937, only fifteen were reelected just a year later in June 1938, and they included the nonlocal names of Stalin, Beria, and Mikoyan. About thirty of those removed can be traced as having been expelled from the Party and probably arrested.

As in Georgia, the whole second level of the Party went too. "Over 3,500 responsible Party, Soviet, economic, military, and Komsomol officials were arrested . . . in a few months of 1937 alone. Many of them were shot without a trial and the requisite investigation."[61] On the last day of the year, the execution of eight leading Armenian officials was announced, together with—ironically enough—the posthumous disgrace of Khandzhyan.[62]

The launching of mass arrests in both Georgia and Armenia in September was not a coincidence. A general decision to destroy the old Parties in the national Republics seems to have been taken. By midsummer, the entire Government of the Tatar Republic was under arrest.[63] September saw the sudden start of a press campaign conducted in more violent terms than ever, on a threat about which not much had been heard for some time: bourgeois nationalism. Such articles as "The Rotten Position of the Daghestan Provincial Committee" became common. From about 8 September, the Parties in the minority areas were subjected, under heavy headlines, to a continual stream of abuse. In Uzbekistan, Kirghizia, Kazakhstan, Bashkiria, Karelia, everywhere, large groups of traitors were found in the leaderships—in fact, constituting the leaderships. (The most prominent of these—the Uzbek—we will deal with in connection with the Bukharin Trial; see p. 356.)

The pattern that emerges in the Purge in the Republics and provinces is a striking one. It amounts to this: an operation planned in Moscow and carried into effect by missions from the center almost everywhere destroyed the old Party, raising up instead from the rank and file a special selection of enthusiasts for a new organization of terrorists and denouncers. What requires the most emphasis is the sheer extent of the changes, the completeness of the liquidation of the hierarchy. At the center, Stalin had already created his own cadres, and infiltrated them into high position. In the coming months, the ravages were to be very great in Moscow too, but there was a continuity provided by a handful of men at the top and a group of Stalin's junior nominees in the instruments of power. In the provinces, the "black tornado" really uprooted the old "Party-line" Stalinists, the veterans who represented a continuity, however tenuous, with the old Party of the underground, of 1917, and of the Civil War. This amounted to a revolution as complete as, though more disguised than, any previous changes in Russia.

We may incidentally note a lesser point: whereas previously the Party Secretary had been the most powerful man in any area, it was now the NKVD chief who counted. Over the next year or two, the new Party executives were to regain a good deal of their power. But for the moment, the police—themselves purged and purged again—were the direct agents of the center and executors of its main missions.

## DEVASTATED AREA: THE UKRAINE

*And Kiev groaned with sorrow.*

The Armament of Igor

Stalin's victory over the Party was assured when he crushed moderate hopes at the February–March plenum. All that was left to do was to set the machinery of the purges in motion. There was to be one last flicker of resistance—in the Ukraine.

In the Central Committee, the great cities, the provincial capitals, the smaller Republics, those who had opposed the Purge were isolated figures impotently awaiting their fate. In the Ukraine alone, most of the old leadership, based on its local Central Committee, remained in control. The demotion and removal of Postyshev had removed one hostile leader. But Petrovsky at least was one of the doubters. Postyshev's place was taken by his predecessor in the post, Khatayevich, a full member of the All-Union Central Committee, who had been on the Ukrainian Politburo since 1933. A considerable purge in the lower ranks took place under an order from the All-Union Central Committee in the weeks following the February–March plenum; nearly one-fifth of Ukrainian Party members were expelled,[64] and two-thirds of the provincial and one-third of the local leaderships were changed.[65] But in the main, the old leadership was reelected at the Ukrainian Party Congress in May–June.

This Congress passed resolutions condemning errors in all ideological fields— the press, the Marx-Lenin Institute, the Institute of Red Professors, and elsewhere—and made strong attacks on Postyshev and the old Kiev leadership. Kossior, who had been comparatively mild at the time of Postyshev's demotion, now spoke of lack of vigilance at the top which had allowed Trotskyites to penetrate the Kiev Provincial Committee.[66] A day or two later, he denounced Postyshev by name for "co-opting numerous enemies" into the provincial apparatus.[67] It was presumably the unfortunate Karpov who was meanwhile referred to by a Moscow Party periodical in a denunciation of "a former secretary of the Central Committee" of the Ukraine, who had refused to believe accusations that one of his staff was a Trotskyite and had left him in a post in which, until his arrest, he had access to secret documents.[68]

The Ukrainian Party had a special history. Lenin had underestimated Ukrainian national feeling. The 1917 vote in the Ukraine for the Constituent Assembly was 77 percent to the Social Revolutionary parties, 10 percent to the Bolsheviks. The local Soviets were usually under anti-Bolshevik control. From 1917 to 1920, Ukrainian nationalist regimes of various types were in existence, and Bolshevik rule was imposed and reimposed vary largely from outside.

Unlike the situation in Russia proper, an important section of the Ukrainian Communist Party itself had originally come from the Left Social Revolutionaries. Their main body in the Ukraine had turned nationalist, under the name Borotbist. This party was dissolved early in 1920, and several thousand of its members, including Lyubchenko and Grinko, entered the Communist Party.

Time and time again, Bolshevik leaders sent to the Ukraine with strong centralizing views modified them over the years. The attempt to rule solely as agents of a foreign power, through a handful of Quislings, was seen as in the long run nonviable. It was a problem of the type which repeated itself in Hungary and elsewhere after the Second World War.

Chubar, who was to be moderate on this issue, became Premier of the Ukraine in July 1923. But in 1925, Kaganovich was sent to Kiev as First Secretary. His centralizing policy was unpopular in the local Party, which otherwise had no quarrel with Stalin. Stalin himself writes of a demand from the Ukraine in 1926 that Kaganovich be replaced by Grinko and Chubar.[69] Stalin, involved in his great struggle at the center, did not wish for a quarrel with the more moderate faction in the Ukraine simply on this local issue. When, in July 1928, Kaganovich was removed from the Republic, Stalin, as Bukharin put it, "bought the Ukrainians by withdrawing Kaganovich from the Ukraine."[70] He was replaced by Stanislav Kossior, a short, bald, bullet-headed Pole who backed Stalin unreservedly right up to the Yezhov period.

In the years of dispute with the Left and Right oppositions, Stalin's calculations proved correct. The Ukrainian Party gave no trouble. There seems to have been very little Trotskyism in it. And in fact, the national minorities in general disliked Trotsky more than Stalin. Even after experience of Stalin's rule, an Ossetian Communist believed that while Trotsky's intended method of rule was in general identical with Stalin's, on the nationality question Trotsky was "even more reactionary."[71]

And the Ukrainian experience with the oppositionists had not been reassuring. Pyatakov, who had briefly ruled in Kiev during the Civil War, had put the view that the Ukraine must submit to Russia very bluntly: "Can we declare that the form of existence of proletarian-peasant Ukraine can be determined solely and absolutely by the working masses of the Ukraine? Of course not!"[72]

In the early 1930s, the collectivization campaign had turned the Ukraine, more than anywhere else, into a battlefield between the Party and the population, and Party solidarity was the decisive criterion. Non-Communist nationalism remained powerful. The trial of forty-five leading cultural figures as a "Union for the Liberation of the Ukraine" in March and April 1930, and the similar trials which followed it, were directed against a real resistance.

This extreme and rigorous purge erased the old Ukrainian intellectuals and left the Old Bolshevik Skrypnik, in the Commissariat of Education, as the protector of only a residue of Ukrainian culture. This, however, he determined to defend.

There is no doubt that Skrypnik and his genuine feeling of resistance to Moscow represented a powerful trend among the rank and file of the Party. But the rest of the leadership were in a different position. Stalin's war on the peasantry had truly placed them in a position in which, in Lenin's phrase, "who-whom?" was the only immediate question. Whatever their hidden reservations and whatever they may have thought of the plans which had led to the crisis, they could no more be expected to indulge them than a general fighting a desperate battle can spend time arguing about the strategic errors of the High Command.

But still, they seem to have become shaken and exhausted by the loyal fulfillment of Stalin's collectivization orders.

On 24 January 1933 a resolution of the All-Union Central Committee attacked the Ukrainian Party: "The Party organs in the Ukraine have not succeeded in carrying out the Party charges entrusted to them in the areas of organization of grain storage and completion of the plan for grain collection."

This heralded the climax of the fearful terror-famine which reached its peak in March and April 1933, leaving millions dead in the Ukraine.[73] Three of the seven Provincial Secretaries were censured and removed, together with three members of the local Politburo and Secretariat. And Postyshev, hitherto Secretary of the All-Union Central Committee, was sent to the Republic as Second Secretary, with plenary powers. Throughout 1933, non-Ukrainian Party workers of more unquestionable loyalty were transferred into the Republic from Russia. (It is estimated that there were some 5,000 of these.)[74]

From 8 to 11 June 1933 Skrypnik was strongly attacked. He refused to recant, and was violently rebuked by Postyshev for his attitude. Other attacks followed in the press, and on 7 July he committed suicide. His example may have been the Ukrainian writer Khvylovy, who had just done the same when accused of excessive Ukrainian feeling.

Skrypnik had been one of the three representatives of underground organizations who had gone to the conference of Bolshevik leaders in Paris in 1909. The day after Skrypnik's suicide, *Pravda* described it as "an act of cowardice": Skrypnik, "an unworthy member of the Central Committee," had fallen prey to bourgeois–nationalist mistakes. And, as Petrovsky said, "It was not easy for us to ward off these nationalist attacks, since the chief aggressor was an Old Bolshevik, Skrypnik."[75] However, Petrovsky added, Moscow had helped "by sending well-known Party members to aid us."

Skrypnik's supporters were disposed of by the unmasking of a "Ukrainian Military Organization" consisting mainly of the post-1930 generation of academic leaders in the Institute of Linguistics, the State Publishing House, the School of Marxist Philosophy, and the Shevchenko Institute of Literary Scholarship. Many further trials of intellectuals followed. But after Skrypnik's death, there were no major attacks on the Party cadres of the Ukraine until Postyshev's fall in early 1937. When Chubar was called to Moscow to be All-Union Vice Premier, he was replaced as Chairman of the Ukrainian Council of People's Commissars by Panas Lyubchenko, a former Borotbist, who shared his views—a slight and light-bearded figure with a sensitive, intellectual face, who had given satisfaction by his firmness in the collectivization struggle.

But there were long-standing feuds and factions in the Ukrainian Party. By the time the purges started, Postyshev and the Head of the Ukrainian NKVD, Balitsky, were working against Lyubchenko. They were later joined by M. M. Popov, Third Secretary of the Ukrainian Central Committee, who around the end of 1936 fabricated a "case" and went to Stalin and Kossior to demand Lyubchenko's dismissal and arrest as a "Borotbist" plotter.[76]

But Stalin, as we have seen, was now turning against Postyshev. And after the February–March plenum not only Postyshev, but also Balitsky and Popov were transferred from the Ukrainian Party, and a purge swept the Party officials at the provincial and local level. With the defeat of the Postyshev-Balitsky-Popov group, it looked as though Lyubchenko and the remainder of the leadership were in a strong position. But, in fact, both factions were destined to destruction.

A Politburo commission from Moscow, which included Molotov and Yezhov, is reported in Kiev about this time, seeking further changes but meeting with some resistance.[77] At any rate, a new offensive was soon prepared, and a new NKVD People's Commissar for the Ukraine was named: I. M. Leplevsky, fresh from his triumphs in the Tukhachevsky investigation. He brought with him a large force of new NKVD men.[78] And Kossior, who had earlier shown some signs of resistance to the purge, was now put under strong pressure, and saved himself temporarily by accepting and implementing Moscow's directives.

When Army Commander Yakir was arrested, his interrogators had "sought an admission that Balitsky was a member of the military conspiracy." On 7 June

1937, Yakir testified that Balitsky had done good work, but had falsified certain cases, including the one against Lyubchenko, and that Balitsky and Postyshev had falsely attacked Ukrainian nationalists, again meaning Lyubchenko and his circle.[79]

Lyubchenko's great detractor M. M. Popov, arrested on 17 June 1937, by 22 June was confessing to a "military fascist organization" aiming to kill Stalin and overthrow the Soviet regime. But now not only Balitsky, but also Lyubchenko (and Postyshev's replacement as Ukrainian Second Secretary, M. M. Khatayevich) were implicated. At the same time, Popov testified more vaguely to the Polish "connections" of Kossior, Postyshev, and Lyubchenko.[80]

Balitsky (who had just assumed his new post as Head of the Far Eastern NKVD) was arrested on 7 July. By 26 July, he had implicated many of his NKVD juniors in the Ukraine.

Signs began to accumulate of pressure being put on the Ukrainian leaders. When greetings were sent to Chkalov and his aircrew on 20 June 1937, those from Moscow were signed with the names of the leaders, but that from the Central Committee of the Communist Party of the Ukraine was anonymous, contrary to previous practice. On 15 July, "leading organs" in the Republic were attacked, in particular for the transfer of Postyshev's "Trotskyites" from Kiev to other posts throughout the Ukraine. On 21 July, the Ukrainian Radio came under heavy attack.[82] At the same time, the Ukrainian Komsomol was severely criticized, and one of its Secretaries, Klinkov, denounced as an enemy of the people;[83] and the Central Committee of the Ukrainian Party was criticized as such for "tolerating the subversive work of the enemy among the youth."[84]

In "glorious, royal Kiev city," commanding the great plain from the cliffs of the Dnieper, everything appeared normal to the uninformed observer. In the tranquil Ukrainian summer, the concerts went on regularly in the cypress-walled outdoor auditorium. But even the musicians were under pressure, with all the other cultural agencies, and the Director of the Ukrainian State Opera, Yanovsky, was soon to be among those denounced as fascists.

A plenum of the new Ukrainian Central Committee met on 29 August. Kossior, with the new NKVD Commissar, Leplevsky, ran it in the harshest Stalinist spirit. The agenda was "1. On the discovery of the nationalist anti-Soviet organization. 2. Other matters."

First it was proposed that a number of enemies of the people who had already been arrested should be expelled from the Committee: Khatayevich, Sarkisov (Donets Provincial Secretary), and at least twenty others named. Kossior then announced that he had received a document from Yezhov with the confession of A. A. Khvylia, Head of the Ukrainian Arts Administration, implicating Lyubchenko.

Khvylia, also a former Borotbist, had been the subject of an NKVD accusation in the autumn of 1936, accused of being a nationalist and counter-revolutionary. Lyubchenko and Kossior had vouched for him and others in a "confrontation" in Stalin's presence. However, he had been rearrested on 13 August 1937, with other former Borotbists, and he eventually confessed. By 23 August, evidence of a plot by former Borotbists was in Yezhov's hands. And with this document as his text, Kossior denounced the new "bourgeois nationalist" organization just uncovered, which had had close contacts with "the previously unmasked anti-Soviet organization" headed by Yakir, Balitsky, and Popov. Lyubchenko was the leader of this new conspiracy.[85]

At 11:00 A.M. on 30 August, Lyubchenko rose to defend himself, but was shouted down by Leplevsky and others. Zatonsky, a former physics teacher, now Ukrainian Commissar for Education, and one of the most prominent Ukrainian Old Bolsheviks, more vaguely implicated, tried to cover himself by allegations that not only Lyubchenko but also his wife were members of the nationalist organization. Many violently attacked Lyubchenko, though Petrovsky and a few others remained silent. Kossior then proposed the expulsion and arrest of Lyubchenko, and this was carried. The case of Zatonsky was referred to the Politburo.[86]

Lyubchenko, still not under arrest, went back to his house and shot himself and his wife. *Pravda* (omitting reference to his wife), announcing his suicide on 2 September, attributed it to his "being entangled in anti-Soviet connections." (But a recent Soviet analysis of the affair tends to the view that NKVD men came to arrest him, he resisted and was shot, and they then disposed of his wife as an inconvenient witness.)[87] Grinko, USSR People's Commissar of Finance, the other major ex-Borotbist, was arrested in Moscow on the same day.[88]

Over the next year, the whole of the local Politburo, Orgburo, and Secretariat were arrested, with the exception of Petrovsky. Of the 102 members and candidate members of the Ukrainian Central Committee, 3 survived. All 17 members of the Ukrainian Government were arrested. All the Provincial Secretaries in the Ukraine fell.

The Purge swept through every sort of establishment in the Republic. The State industrial enterprises, the municipal councils, the educational and scientific bodies—all lost their leaders by the hundred. The Ukrainian Union of Writers was practically annihilated.

Violent attacks on Ukrainian institutions started to appear. The Kiev and Kharkov radio stations were accused of having broadcast funeral marches after the announcement of the verdict in the first two trials, while the Kiev station had actually gone off the air while the verdict on the generals was being transmitted. This was the result of "an enemy organization" which the Ukrainian Central Committee had failed to understand.[89] The educational system was attacked as being riddled with nationalists.[90] The museums were also full of spies concerned only to stress anti-Russian Ukrainianism.[91] The Republic had even failed to celebrate Peter the Great's victory at Poltava.[92]

The oppositionists in the three Great Trials were traitors, Trotskyites, spies, and accomplices of the fascists. But they were not shown as actually describing themselves as fascists pure and simple. In the Ukraine, though, it was not a "Bloc of Rights and Trotskyites" that was revealed, but nothing less than a "National Fascist Organization" headed by Lyubchenko, leader of the Soviet Government of the Republic, and including Grinko, People's Commissar of Finance in Moscow, Balitsky, Zatonsky, Yakir, and a variety of leading figures in the Ukrainian Government and Central Committee, and such cultural lights as Yanovsky.

For the moment, however, Kossior was spared. At a meeting of the Kiev Party organization on 15 and 16 September 1937, he delivered another attack on "the band of bourgeois nationalists uncovered in the Ukraine." Zatonsky was "severely blamed" and in reply "could not say anything."[93] Zatonsky was refused entry to the October 1937 plenum of the Central Committee in Moscow; on 3 November, he was called out of a university meeting in Kiev and arrested.[94]

The turnover was equally rapid at the local level. Kudryavtsev, who had replaced Postyshev in his lesser post as Secretary of the Kiev Provincial Committee of the Party and made some of the most violent attacks on Lyubchenko in August, was removed at the end of 1937, to be denounced as an "enemy of the people,"[95] and his successor, D. M. Evtushenko, followed on 17 April 1938. They were later linked as the centers of a hostile leadership which had subverted most of the District Secretaries of the province.[96]

Lyubchenko was succeeded as Premier by a young Communist, M. I. Bondarenko. He, too, was arrested within two months,[97] and for a time there was no Premier at all. Instead, the names of unknown subordinates of Petrovsky appeared on decrees.

Then another Premier, N. M. Marchak, was appointed. He was demoted to Deputy Premier by February 1938,[98] and was soon afterward under arrest. He is said to have been drinking heavily with Leplevsky one night, and to have exchanged with him some remarks skeptical of Tukhachevsky's guilt, a point on which Leplevsky was particularly well informed. The next morning, Marchak remembered this and thought that Leplevsky might have been acting as a provocateur. He rang Yezhov and denounced Leplevsky, who was arrested. Leplevsky, in turn, implicated Marchak, and both confessed to conspiracy, terrorism, and espionage.[99] Leplevsky's replacement, the third Ukraine NKVD Commissar to be appointed within a year, was Uspensky, himself to fall within months.

The Purge was so complete and so quick that legal authority virtually disintegrated. There was no longer a genuine quorum of the Ukrainian Central Committee or a body capable of appointing a Government. People's Commissars, irregularly appointed, emerged for days or weeks and then themselves disappeared. The unprecedented sweep of the political leadership marked the effective destruction of the Ukrainian Party. The Republic became little more than an NKVD fief, where even the formalities of Party and Soviet activity were barely gone through.

Finally, in January 1938, a presumably spurious plenum of the Ukrainian Central Committee elected Khrushchev First Secretary.[100] Khrushchev brought with him from Moscow a new Second Secretary, Burmistenko, who had served in the Cheka for many years in the 1920s and later worked closely with Stalin's personal secretariat. As Chairman of the Council of People's Commissars, he brought Demyan Korotchenko (or Korotchenkov; in 1939, in the *Stenographic Report of the XVIIIth Congress,* his name is actually given with its Ukrainian spelling in the list of the new Central Committee, and with its Russian spelling in the list of delegates to the Congress).

In May and June 1938, the entire Ukrainian Government was again replaced. Between February and June, all twelve new Provincial Secretaries were again removed, together with most of their Second Secretaries.[101] At the XIVth Congress of the Ukrainian Party in June 1938, the new Central Committee had, among its eight-six members and candidates, only three survivors from the previous year— all nonpolitical or honorary figures. The continuity of rule had for the first time been completely destroyed. Not one member of the new Politburo, Orgburo, or Secretariat had previously served.

The Politburo was a farcical rump with only six members: Khrushchev, Burmistenko, and Korotchenko; the Commander of the Military District, Timoshenko; the latest NKVD chief of the Republic, Uspensky; and the ubiquitous Shcherbakov, who was in the Republic for a few months to purge a couple of Provincial Committees.

They reconstructed the Party from the ground up. In 1938, 1,600 Party members were raised to be Secretaries of District and City Committees in the Ukraine.[102] Among those who benefited was the young Leonid Brezhnev. He had been raised to Deputy Mayor of Dneprodzerzhinsk in May 1937. In 1938, under the Khrushchev regime, he was promoted to be head of a department of the Dneprodzerzhinsk Provincial Committee, and by the following year was a Secretary of that Committee. He never looked back. (Few were so lucky. Between 1938 and the next Republican Party Congress in 1940, attrition remained high, if not so high. Of the 119 elected in 1940, 73 were new members.)

Stalin and Khrushchev had succeeded in destroying the old Party cadres in the Ukraine, and replacing them with men distinguished only by disciplined acquiescence in, or enthusiasm for, the new method of rule. This did not solve the problem of the Ukrainian people. Stalin was to tell Roosevelt at Yalta that "his position in the Ukraine was difficult and insecure."[103] And he later regretted that it was impracticable to deport the entire nation, as he had done with the smaller Chechens and Kalmyks.[104]

## AT THE CENTER

While the punitive expeditions sent out by Stalin and Yezhov harried the provinces, Moscow remained the storm center. Of the seventy-one full members of the Central Committee, about two-thirds were normally stationed in the capital: all the full members of the Politburo except Kossior; the People's Commissars; the heads of Central Committee departments, of the Komsomol, of the trade unions; the Comintern's managers—all the concentration of power of a highly centralized machine.

Over this major sector of the Purge, Stalin and Yezhov themselves presided. They received valuable help from Molotov and Voroshilov when required, but on the whole Stalin kept an extremely tight personal grip on proceedings, working through Yezhov alone.

In 1937 and 1938, Yezhov sent in to Stalin 383 lists, containing thousands of names of figures important enough to require his personal approval for their execution.[105] As Yezhov was only in power for just over two years—and, in fact, his effective working period was rather less—this means that Stalin got such a list rather more often than every other day of "persons whose cases were under the jurisdiction of the Military Collegium." A samizdat historian of the 1970s indicated that the lists included 40,000 names.[106] However, a Soviet periodical now tells us that at a recent plenum of the Central Committee, the total number shot, whose names appeared on lists signed by "Stalin, Molotov, Kaganovich, and Malenkov," though perhaps over a longer period, was given as 230,000.[107] At any rate, we can envisage Stalin, on arrival at his office, as often as not finding in his in-tray a list of a few hundred names for death, looking through, and approving them, as part of the ordinary routine of a Kremlin day. We are told in recent Soviet articles that on 12 December 1937 alone, Stalin and Molotov sanctioned 3,167 death sentences, and then went to the cinema.[108]

The lists were in the following form:

Comrade Stalin,

I am sending for your approval four lists of people to be tried by the Military Collegium:

    List No. 1 (General)
    List No. 2 (Former military personnel)
    List No. 3 (Former personnel of the N.K.V.D.)
    List No. 4 (Wives of enemies of the people)*

I request sanction to convict all in the first degree.

                                              Yezhov

The post-Stalin speaker who quotes this adds that "first degree" conviction meant death by shooting. The lists were examined by Stalin and Molotov, and on each of them is the notation:

Approved—J. Stalin
         V. Molotov.[109]

We learn that in one such set of lists (on 20 August 1938) of 736 names, 200 were of military men and 15 were of wives. The 12 December 1937 list cited above included, with a smaller list of 239 shot on 3 December, 49 members of the Central Committee.[110]

As to the executions not requiring approval at quite so high a level, on 18 October 1937 alone, Yezhov and Vyshinsky, acting as a "troika," considered 551 names, sentencing every one of them to be shot. It will be seen that in a sixteen-hour working day, this would give them less than two minutes per case.[111] That their speed was not up to Stalin and Molotov's best effort is probably due to the fact that they had to initial each name, rather than just read them through and sign the list.

Decisions to make an arrest, and even warrants, were often signed months before the arrest was carried out. And, in the same way, leading figures were sometimes decorated with high Orders on the very day of their arrest.[112] The reason given by an NKVD officer is that the police informed only their immediate superior about the progress of their investigations, and Yezhov informed only Stalin.[113]

When Yezhov once sent a list of names to Stalin with a note "For eventual arrest: to be verified," Stalin wrote on it, "don't verify. Arrest."[114] Ulrikh and Vyshinsky reported regularly to Stalin (and sometimes to Molotov and Yezhov) about the trials and sentences. "Ulrikh presented every month a report on the general number of people sentenced for 'espionage, terrorist and diversionary ac-

---

* "List 4" executions included the wives of Kossior, Eikhe, Chubar, and Dybenko (*Pravda*, 3 April 1964).

tivity.' Stalin read all the reports: on the state of the crop, coal production and, dreadful to say, of the number of people deprived of life."[115]

Molotov is named as suggesting sentencing "by lists," rather than by consideration of individual cases. It is certainly true that orders went out to arrest categories rather than individual suspects. A former Chairman of the Byelorussian Council of People's Commissars tells of being present when the local NKVD chief, Boris Berman, complained to the local First Secretary, A. A. Volkov, "Yezhov has sent again an order to arrest old Communists. But where shall I find them? There are none left."[116]

As in the rest of the country, the new offensive had started in May 1937.

Fitzroy Maclean, watching Stalin on the Red Square reviewing stand on 1 May, was already struck by the rest of the Politburo, who "grinned nervously and moved uneasily from one foot to the other, forgetting the parade and the high office they held and everything else in their mingled joy and terror at being spoken to by him." Stalin's own expression varied between "benignity and bored inscrutability."[117]

They might well feel alarm, for one of their members was absent. His colleagues had perhaps already "discussed" his case, in the same way that Zhdanov's Leningrad Committee was to "discuss" Chudov's. Yan Rudzutak, member of the Party since 1905, who had spent ten years in Tsarist prisons and exile, a former full member of the Politburo and now a candidate member, was not among his old comrades. His arrest had apparently just taken place.[118] He was seized at a supper party after the theater. The NKVD arrested everyone present. Four women among them are reported in the Butyrka, still in bedraggled evening dress, three months later.[119] His dacha was taken over by Zhdanov.[120]

Rudzutak was arrested as allegedly a Rightist, leader of a "reserve center" ready to take over if Bukharin's was exposed, because "nobody had ever known of any difference between him and the Party."[121] This is, in fact, an admission that Stalinists of long standing were now, for the first time, being arrested—especially (but not only) if they showed any signs of opposing the Purge. Rudzutak, in particular, had one very black mark against him: his failure to recommend the death penalty for Ryutin when Head of the Control Commission in 1932.

Through May, another great heroic diversion, parallel to the exploits of the aviators of the previous year, was spread in the papers day after day. This was the landing, under the direction of O. Shmidt, of Papanin's group at the North Pole, a fine exploit. The officers of the airlift that took them in and set them up were welcomed by the Party leaders, decorated, and publicized round the usual celebrations. At the same time, the camp on the ice drifted through the months, from time to time sending loyal greetings from—and receiving thanks at—the farthest-flung outpost of the Party and State.

Through the spring and early summer, the other great nonpolitical news was a series of plays and ballets attended by the leaders of the Party and the announcement of long lists of awards to People's Artists in these fields.

Meanwhile, as a particularly fine summer lay on the great plain, the arrests went on. Former oppositionists continued to fall. Nikolai Krestinsky, former member of the Politburo and Secretary of the Central Committee, had been removed from the Foreign Commissariat to be Assistant People's Commissar of Justice of the RSFSR in March.[122] On his transfer, he spoke approvingly of his removal to the Party cell, saying that even ex-oppositionists should not, in present circumstances, work in the Foreign Commissariat, where leading figures should have the absolute confidence of the leadership and a spotless past.[123]

At the end of May, he was arrested. After a week-long interrogation,[124] he started to confess on about 5 June.[125] He had been severely tortured, and is described in a recent Soviet article as being in the Butyrka prison hospital for some days with his whole back like a single wound.[126] Bukharin, with whom he was to appear in court as a fellow conspirator nine months later, had just begun his evidence.[127]

The way in which any sort of connection with the arrested oppositionists was made a crime can be seen in the case of the veteran Lomov, Party member since 1903, who, representing the Moscow Bureau of the Bolshevik Party, had (after Trotsky) been Lenin's most enthusiastic supporter in the Central Committee in pressing for the seizure of power in November 1917.

> In June 1937, an official of the U.S.S.R. State Planning Commission sent a letter to Stalin alleging that G. I. Lomov (Oppokov) a member of the Bureau of the U.S.S.R. Council of People's Commissars' Soviet Control Commission, had been on friendly terms with Rykov and Bukharin. Stalin wrote on this letter the instructions: "To Comrade Molotov. What to do?" Molotov wrote: "I'm for arresting this scum Lomov immediately, V. Molotov." A few days later Lomov was arrested, charged with membership in a Right Opportunist organization, and shot.[128]

Lomov was to be mentioned at the Bukharin Trial as a fellow conspirator with Bukharin against Lenin.[129]

But even now, opposition was not entirely crushed. In the last week of June, another plenum of the Central Committee was held—ostensibly to discuss vegetable production. It was the scene of mutual denunciations and disappearances on the spot. Nazaretyan (not, indeed, a member of the Central Committee, but of the lesser Central Revision Commission), whom Ordzhonikidze had saved in the early 1930s, was arrested while actually on his way to the Kremlin to attend the plenum.[130] In a few months, Stalin had progressed far in his ability to loose the Secret Police, without attention to political protocol, on to his opponents. His speech is said to have been in ruthless style, demanding, for example, less "coddling" of prisoners.[131]

In the meeting hall, many faces were already missing—Bukharin's and Rykov's, Rudzutak's and Chudov's, Gamarnik's and Yakir's, Yagoda's and a dozen others. But the spirit of resistance had not yet been entirely quelled. "After the February plenum of the Central Committee a campaign was raised in the conspirators' circles against Yezhov . . . an attempt was made to discredit Yezhov and the work he was doing in the Party, to slander him."[132] Even as late as this June plenum, there was an attempt to block the terror. Pyatnitsky, Kaminsky, and others had met for what came to be called "the cup of tea" to discuss resistance. Filatov, Mayor of Moscow, was among those present and appears to have given them away (he himself was shot later).[133]

At the plenum, when it was proposed to grant extraordinary powers to Yezhov and the NKVD, Pyatnitsky spoke strongly against it, and said that, on the contrary, the NKVD was now out of hand and should be more tightly controlled. During the break, several members of the Central Committee advised him to withdraw his statement, and Molotov suggested that he should think of his wife and family. However, he stuck to his guns.

The next day, Yezhov announced that the NKVD had evidence of Pyatnitsky having been an agent of the Tsarist police. Krupskaya defended his character on the grounds that Lenin had regarded him as one of the best Bolsheviks. Yezhov proposed a vote of censure against Pyatnitsky. Kaminsky and Krupskaya voted against. Stalin asked why Pyatnitsky did not say what he thought about this. Pyatnitsky then said that if he was not needed he would go, and left. On 7 July, he was arrested.[134] (As Molotov had foreseen, Pyatnitsky's wife was arrested and not seen again. His son Igor spent many years in labor camp, and his younger son was placed first with foster parents and then in an NKVD children's home.)[135] Kaminsky also spoke against the purges. Among other things, he attacked Beria, denouncing him as a former agent of the Azerbaijan nationalist intelligence service.[136] Kaminsky, who had joined the Bolshevik Party as a medical student some years before the Revolution, was arrested that day and was later shot.[137] His wife was only jailed for two years, and survived.[138]

In the midst of the swing into total terror, yet another diversion was provided by Russian airmen. In June, Chkalov and his crew flew their ANT-25 over the North Pole to Falkland, Oregon, and in July Gromov flew another to San Jacinto, California, setting a world distance record. The two flights, both fine achievements, were the occasion for a further great press campaign: pages and pages of newspapers filled with greetings, meetings, lives of the airmen, photographs, and so on. When Chkalov finally crashed on 15 December 1938, Belyakin, Head of the Main Administration of the Aircraft Industry, Usachev, Director of the plant where the plane had been built, and Tomashevich, the designer, were shot for sabotage.[139]

The papers continued to carry general calls to vigilance and accounts of various methods used by the enemy. *Pravda* drew attention to misprints in the local press which amounted to sabotage—for example, a reference to the *bedy* (sorrows) rather than the *pobedy* (victories) of Socialism. And local trials were frequently reported. But the great blow was that now being delivered against the leading cadres of the regime, which was to ravage the old Central Committee and destroy the next level of the Party command in their thousands.

For it was now, starting in May 1937, that the flower of Stalin's long-nurtured administrative and political machine began to go. After Rudzutak, no member or candidate member of the Politburo was to be arrested during the year, and several officials only just junior to them hung on until a specially mounted top-level operation in November and December took them. But for the moment, there was a broad sweep of their subordinates, running as high as men like Antipov,[140] Vice Chairman of the Council of People's Commissars, Party member since 1902, several times arrested under Tsarism, and organizer of underground printing plants, who had been among the half-dozen appearing with the Politburo on the May Day platform.

In the Central Committee apparatus, Malenkov's Department of Leading Party

Organs was overseeing a thorough "renewal." Another figure who was to be named though not produced as one of the most important links in the Bukharin plot was Ya. A. Yakovlev, former People's Commissar for Agriculture, and now Head of the Agricultural Department of the Central Committee. He figured prominently in the press over June, and was the *rapporteur* to the June plenum on its sole published item of discussion, vegetables. In the autumn, he fades out until his extraordinary transmogrification into a Rightist in March 1938—an odd appellation for the man who had been a chief operator in the collectivization field.

Another head of a Central Committee department now to disappear had at one time almost reached the summits of power—K. Ya. Bauman, Head of the Central Committee's Scientific Department. He had been Secretary of the Central Committee and candidate member of the Politburo (as Uglanov's replacement) for a few months in 1929 and 1930. An enthusiastic Stalinist, he had been the scapegoat for the first excesses of collectivization, but he had remained on the Central Committee. Bauman's wife was also arrested, and his fourteen-year-old son, Volik, sent away to a home.[141] Bauman was shot on 14 October 1937. With him went most of the staff of his department. The Head of the parallel, but more important, Agitation and Propaganda Department, Stetsky, an old economist who had held the post since 1929, was also arrested about this time.

Cynicism prevailed as well as terror. A senior Army officer in prison mentioned that he was once cheerfully greeted at a reception by Molotov's wife, with the words "Ah, Sasha, whatever's this? Why haven't you been arrested yet?"[142] She had become Head of the Cosmetics Trust (a post she was to hold for some years) through the elimination of her boss, Chekalov, who was sent to the Vorkuta railway camps,[143] and she was to be a member of the 1939 Central Committee, which replaced the men now disappearing. Her own arrest came in 1948.

An atmosphere of fear hung over the Party and Government offices. People's Commissars were arrested on their way to their jobs in the morning. Every day, another Central Committee member or Vice Chairman of a People's Commissariat or one of their more important underlings was disappearing. In one sphere alone, for the moment, joy prevailed. Yezhov was awarded the Order of Lenin on 18 July, an occasion for photographs, leading articles, and general celebrations. Vyshinsky received the same award on 21 July, though with less panache.

Orders were now also handed out to many leading police officials. On the completion of the Mdivani Case, the Georgian NKVD men received their reward. One notes among them the names of men who a year later were to replace the current operators in Moscow and elsewhere, and who were only to perish at the end of the Beria epoch, in 1953 to 1955: Goglidze, Kobulov, Rapava, and their like.[144] Other awards went to a group of Yezhov's men, including the dreadful Ushakov, Frinovsky, and, as a junior, the long-surviving L. E. Vlodzimirsky, who was to serve Beria and be brought back by him in 1953 to be Head of the Section for Investigating Specially Important Cases, and be shot in December of that year.

Yezhov himself was now to get the highest accolade, a town named for him. On 22 July, Kaganovich's protégé, the ex-OGPU man Bulganin, was appointed Chairman of the Council of People's Commissars of the Russian Republic. The fall of his predecessor, Sulimov, involved a change in the name of the town of

Sulimov, capital of the Cherkess Autonomous Province, which was now suitably renamed Yezhovo-Cherkessk.

Bulganin's later colleague and rival Khrushchev was conducting his own purge in the local machine of the city and province to the satisfaction of the authorities. He had started in late March, as in Leningrad.[145] Now, at a meeting of the Moscow Provincial Committee on 23 August, he made a series of attacks on local leaders like Filatov, which presaged his disappearance, with many others. Ukhanov, Khrushchev's Chairman of the Moscow Soviet until recently, was now filling one of the ministerial vacancies as People's Commissar for Local Industry, and it was from there that he was seized. Like Antipov, Yakovlev, Stetsky, and Sulimov, he was a full member of the Central Committee.

August saw one of the biggest tourist influxes ever to reach Russia. The visitors noted no public gloom. Once again, a great Soviet flight was being celebrated—that of Levanevsky and his N-209 around the Union. The papers were full of celebrations, though they had time also, towards the end of the month, to announce the award of Orders of Lenin to the hard-worked Military Jurists, including Ulrikh, Matulevich, and Nikitchenko[146] (the last two described as Vice Presidents of the Military Collegium), and to Prosecutors like Roginsky.[147]

Meanwhile, the Commissars and Vice Commissars of the economic Commissariats went the way of Ukhanov. Some—like Chernov, Commissar for Agriculture, removed on 30 October; Grinko, Commissar for Finance; and Ivanov, Commissar of the Timber Industry—were to appear in the next great trial. Others, like M. Rukhimovich, Commissar for the Defense Industry, who had been appearing with the highest leadership for a few months and lost his post in October 1937[148] (being replaced by Kaganovich's brother, M. M. Kaganovich), were to be tried in secret. Rukhimovich had supported Stalin against all the oppositionists; earlier he had been one of Stalin's and Voroshilov's closest accomplices in the intrigues against Trotsky in Tsaritsyn in the Civil War. In the same category comes Lyubimov, People's Commissar for Light Industry, who was removed, with both his Assistant Commissars, on 7 September.[149]

By the end of the year, few Commissars apart from Voroshilov and Kaganovich remained. In addition to those already named, the Commissars for Communications (Khalepsky), for Internal Trade (Veitser), for Heavy Industry (Mezhlauk), for Education (Bubnov), for Justice (Krylenko), and for Sea and River Transport (Yanson) were arrested, together with successive heads of the National Bank and their subordinates.

For the moment, we may consider one last case in more detail—that of the naturally sensitive Commissariat of Foreign Trade. Its head, Rosengolts, was removed on 15 June for "other work." Both his assistants, Eliava and Loganovsky, disappeared—Eliava to be shot during the year.[150]

Rosengolts, broad-shouldered, strong-minded, and Jewish, was an excellent administrator. He had in the past few years accommodated himself to the new style of rule. He had been brought up in a revolutionary family. When only ten years old, "My hand, the hand of a child, was used to hide illegal literature during the night and to recover it in the morning from a place where the hand of a grown-up could not reach."[151] He joined the Bolshevik Party at fifteen or sixteen and was first arrested when sixteen years old. At the age of seventeen, he was nominated as a delegate to the Party Congress. During the Revolution, he fought in Moscow, and in the Civil War was prominent at various fronts. He had ruled the Donbas in a ruthless fashion. After a brief flirtation with the Trotsky opposition, he was appointed to the London Embassy. In 1928, he returned and had since worked in the Government, holding his present post since 1930.

Rosengolts was still referred to as "Comrade" in the June decree releasing him from his post, and for some time no further move was made against him. This was in accordance with a common practice of Stalin's. Arrest was decided on; the dismissal occurred; and then for months the victim was left in some minor post, never knowing when the blow would fall. An American resident in Moscow in August 1937 describes a high official seen, day after day, on a balcony opposite waiting to be arrested. "Waiting was killing him. He waited three more weeks while the G.P.U. watched and while his wife wasted away. Then the G.P.U. came." [152] Some survivors have described this as psychologically more wearing and destructive even than the eventual imprisonment and interrogation, and they add that the state to which a man was reduced made the process of interrogation a fairly easy one for the NKVD. In fact, some of its work had been done for it already without its officers having to move a finger, a useful saving of energy in a hard-worked organization.

Rosengolts was left to sweat it out for many weeks. He was still at large in August, when he made several desperate efforts to get an interview with Stalin— later to be interpreted as an assassination attempt. [153] On his wife, "a jolly, red-haired girl, very imperfectly educated and brought up in a religious household," [154] the weeks and months of anxiety must have been frightful. She did all she could think of.

When her husband was finally arrested, the routine NKVD search revealed, sewn into his hip pocket, a small piece of dry bread wrapped in a strip of cloth. Inside the bread was a piece of paper on which she had written, as a charm against evil fortune, eight verses from Psalms 68 and 91, ancient cries of the helpless against their oppressors:

L X V I I I

1. Let God arise, and let his enemies be scattered: let them also that hate him, flee before him.

2. Like as the smoke vanisheth, so shalt thou drive them away: and like as wax melteth at the fire, so let the ungodly perish at the presence of God. . . .

X C I

1. Whoso dwelleth under the defence of the most High: shall abide under the shadow of the Almighty.

2. I will say unto the Lord, Thou art my hope, and my stronghold: my God, in him will I trust.

3. For he shall deliver thee from the snare of the hunter: and from the noisome pestilence.

4. He shall defend thee under his wings and thou shalt be safe under his feathers: his faithfulness and truth shall be thy shield and buckler.

5. Thou shalt not be afraid for any terror by night: nor for the arrow that flieth by day;

6. For the pestilence that walketh in darkness: nor for the sickness that destroyeth in the noon-day. . . . [155]

## CLOSING IN ON THE POLITBURO

As the tempo of the public side of the Purge eased somewhat in the autumn of 1937, Stalin began to prepare the next phase. A number of figures, including Bukharin and Rykov themselves, were under interrogation with a view to public trial. A number of unsatisfactory Stalinists like Rudzutak and Antipov, though they were still perhaps resisting, lay ready as a possible reserve for the Bukharin Case, or alternatively as the central figures of a later trial. But much remained to be done.

The rank and file of the February–March waverers had been crushed. But the senior figures involved were still in positions in the highest leadership. Until they, and any others who had shown restiveness or independence, could be eradicated, there was a flaw, a weak spot, in the structure of autocracy. They were not, like Zinoviev and Bukharin, men long removed from the centers of power, or even, like Pyatakov, men long relegated to second-rank positions in the Government and Party. It is true that they constituted a minority and that—except for Kossior's and (previously) Postyshev's control of the Ukrainian machine—they had little grip on any true instruments of power. They nevertheless represented a higher potential of trouble than their predecessors. The one serious combination which, Stalin may have thought, remained was a combination of a group of "moderate" leaders with the Army. Nor was the striking down of the Army leaders in June 1937 entirely conclusive. Other commanders survived who could conceivably give trouble. In any case, Stalin proceeded with his usual combination of gradualness and ruthlessness.

But first, certain technical moves were called for. Since the decree of August 1936, people had been making a nuisance of themselves by complaining that their snap trials and executions were illegal. At any rate, on 14 September a decree was issued to introduce "simplified trial procedures," in cases under Articles 58 (vii), 58 (viii), and 58 (ix) of the Criminal Code. It forbade appeals and also petitions for clemency, the right to which had been restored in 1936 with the object of deceiving Zinoviev and Co. More interesting still, the new decree "eliminated publicity in court trials."[156] There are some obvious anomalies: in the first place, many trials must already have been held without any, or any effective, public attendance; second, the Bukharin Trial, with its vast publicity, was yet to come. Still, however we take the decree, it may perhaps reflect some sort of decision by Stalin to bring public trials to an end as soon as the one then in hand was over. It is sometimes argued that the partial failure of the Bukharin Trial itself led to the dropping of any further court proceedings. This decree shows that the decision may have been taken earlier. It is indeed true that the Bukharin Case seems to have been giving Yezhov a good deal of trouble. While Pyatakov and Radek were ready for open court in four months, nine months had already passed since Bukharin's and Rykov's arrest, and they were not to be adequately prepared for another three or four months yet. However, the plans for the Bukharin Trial were now, as we shall see, reaching the stage at which all possible ingredients had been established—assassination, medical murder, industrial and agricultural sabotage, espionage, bourgeois nationalism, and treason. Each trial so far had added crimes to the roster, but after this there would be no further lesson to rub in.

On 2 October came a law increasing the maximum term of imprisonment from ten to twenty-five years.[157] And a short plenum on 11–12 October celebrated the end of overt opposition by electing Yezhov a candidate member of the Politburo. At the same time, twenty-four members and candidates were expelled.[158] This plenum also saw the fall of a prominent figure in circumstances even more high-handed than had previously been noted.

The People's Commissar for Education, Andrei Bubnov, was one of the most prominent of all Old Bolsheviks. He had been a delegate to the 1907 Congress, a candidate member of the Central Committee in 1912, and a member of the original Political Bureau, which existed for a short time in November 1917. With Pyatakov, he had organized the Communist revolt in the Ukraine in August 1918. A Democratic Centralist in the early days, he had switched to Stalin's side as early as 1923, rigorously purging faction in the Army, and had served loyally ever since. At the October plenum, he went with his Ukrainian opposite number as Education Commissar, Zatonsky, to the Central Committee building, but, on showing their Central Committee membership cards, they were told by the NKVD officer on duty that they could not be admitted without further documents which had not been issued to them. Bubnov went back to his Ministry and worked late. At midnight, his secretary came in trembling and told him that the radio had just announced his removal for inability to cope with his duties. The next day, he handed over to the transient Tyurkin,[159] and was arrested in December.[160]

While announcements of local Party trials and death sentences continued, they were now for a time rarer, and they were not given front-page treatment. The great propaganda campaign receded. The press began to fill with the preparations for elections to the Supreme Soviet. Every type of electoral article appropriate to a democracy began to appear—"Women Voters, a Powerful Force," for example. And following them, the nominations of all the leaders in good odor, and page after page of enthusiastic meetings all around the Union, filled the papers day after day through October.

But Stalin was preparing for action against his unsatisfactory followers. A document (still in existence) was signed by Stalin, Molotov, and Kaganovich in November, to sanction "the arraignment . . . before a court of the Military Collegium of a large number of comrades from the ranks of prominent Party, State and military workers."[161] The 1961 speaker who gave this information went on to say, "Most of them were shot. Those innocently shot and posthumously rehabilitated include such prominent Party and State figures as Comrades Postyshev, Kossior, Eikhe, Rudzutak and Chubar; People's Commissar of Justice Krylenko; Unshlikht, Secretary of the U.S.S.R. Central Executive Committee; People's Commissar of Education Bubnov, and others."

This strongly implies (though it does not actually assert) that these men were on the list referred to. Some, indeed, were already under arrest, but under the old procedure were presumably still being interrogated with the intention of any formal "arraigning" being postponed until the confessions had been obtained. What is more extraordinary is that some of the arrests now authorized were not carried out for weeks or months—that the accused remained in high posts for longish periods.

The procedure with regard to ordinary Party members seems to have been that just before an arrest, the NKVD would inform the local Party committee or, in the case of important members, the Central Committee that a warrant had been issued. The member was then expelled from the Party in secret session and was not informed of the expulsion until arrested. Sometimes the period between these clandestine expulsions and the arrests was quite long. A case is reported of a District Party Secretary in the Ukraine who was secretly expelled by the Ukrainian Central Committee in March 1938 and not arrested until July, meanwhile carrying on as usual and even expelling other members.[162] (Again, a foreign Communist arrested on 19 June 1938 was shown the order for her arrest dated 15 October 1937.)[163] Needless to say, the procedure was contrary to Party statutes.

Who the "prominent . . . military workers" referred to were has not been made explicit, but they were now falling, or about to fall, in numbers, as we have seen. The "others" must include the important figure of V. I. Mezhlauk, who now held the Commissariat of Heavy Industry, and had since the spring been appearing on platforms with the Politburo itself.[164] Mezhlauk, plumply square, balding, with glasses, was arrested in December 1937.[165]

Unshlikht, a Pole in the Dzerzhinsky tradition, had been a pro-Bolshevik member of the Polish Social Democratic Party since 1900. A member of the Petrograd Revolutionary Committee, he had served in the Civil War with Tukhachevsky, in the Sixteenth Army, and had been wounded. He had later been Vice Chairman of the All-Russian Cheka. Trotsky had thought him "an ambitious but talentless intriguer." By the end of the year, he too had been arrested.[166]

Meanwhile, Postyshev still held his post in Kuibyshev and was still a candidate member of the Politburo. Kossior was still First Secretary of the Ukraine and a full member of the Politburo; Chubar, Vice Chairman of the Council of People's Commissars and a full member of the Politburo; and the others in their relevant posts.

Even Postyshev, in spite of demotion, was still not proceeded against. He is now said to have had a last conversation with Stalin, after he had been transferred to Kuibyshev, and to have frankly denounced the Purge, at least as it applied to loyal Party members.[167] However, in June, he had been given reasonable headlines for his speech to the Party conference in his new fief at Kuibyshev: it was a call, extreme even by the standards then prevailing, for the vigilant uprooting of Trotskyites.

Eikhe, a large, serious-looking man, smooth-moustached, with a reputation for ruthlessness, a Party member since 1905, was made People's Commissar for Agriculture in Chernov's place on 30 October.[168] In the West Siberian Territory, which had hitherto been his satrapy, Vyshinsky had alleged[169] an inadequate number of prosecutions for counter-revolutionary activity in 1937, a fact which may well have been due to Eikhe's attitude or at least have figured in the later charges against him.

On 3 November 1937 a poster for the Republican elections, consisting of portraits of the Politburo, was put out. It contained all the full members, including Kossior and Chubar, but of the candidate members only Zhdanov and Yezhov were shown. Eikhe, Postyshev, and Petrovsky were thus demonstratively snubbed. In fact, throughout this period, signs of degradation were visited on the candidate members of the Politburo who were later to fall. They were omitted from honorary Presidiums. Large numbers of lists of nominations for the December election of the Supreme Soviet starting in late October usually left them out (and often omitted Kossior too).* But they were included in the conventional letter of important figures refusing multiple nomination on instructions of the Central Committee.[170] And all (Kossior, Postyshev, Eikhe, Chubar, and Petrovsky) were returned in the elections which followed.

For the best part of two months, until the actual voting of 12 December and afterward, these elections were given intense prominence and publicity. Every day, articles, photographs, lists of places where Politburo members would speak, the addresses of meetings to their candidates, and a vast apparatus of joyful expectancy reigned on paper. Mass resolutions were printed under such headings as "With Joy We Vote for Nikolai Ivanovich Yezhov"; poems, such as one by Stalin's Kazakh hack bard Dzhambul, "People's Commissar Yezhov," gave a view of the police chief which would have been thought excessively rosy if applied to a ruler like Good King Wenceslas.

Throughout December, articles and statements on the elections continued to appear. There were many reports from abroad of, for example, "The Great Impression Made in England." And so the days drew on. As the election publicity gradually petered out, there were other themes for the public—for example, the centenary of the Georgian poet Rustaveli—eked out with much Stakhanovite conferencing.

But the year was not to end without a demonstrative killing. Only five months had separated the Zinoviev and Pyatakov Trials. Since then, eleven had passed, and the Bukharin Case was still not ready. As an interim measure, a group of men who were not prepared to confess was tried *in camera* under the 14 September law.

On 20 December 1937 the papers ran page after page to celebrate the twentieth anniversary of the VCHEKA–OGPU–NKVD, with pictures of Dzerzhinsky and Yezhov. That body's vigilance had been demonstrated the previous day by the announcement of a purge in the bread-distribution organizations. Workers' meetings sent applause, and poems about the splendid role of the Secret Police appeared in profusion. *Pravda* carried a long article by Frinovsky, and also a long list of awards, including the Order of Lenin to Boris Berman. Among this feast of laudatory generalization, a short announcement drew attention to the more practical side of the work of Yezhov's men. It said that on 16 December, Yenukidze, with Karakhan, Sheboldayev, Orakhelashvili, and others, had been tried before the Military Collegium of the Supreme Court as spies, bourgeois nationalists, and terrorists, had confessed, and had been executed.[171]

In the Bukharin Trial, Yenukidze was to be made the central villain of terrorist activity, held responsible for the organization of the murder of Kirov, and said to have instructed Yagoda to tell Zaporozhets not to hinder the act.[172] He was also to be responsible for plotting the murder of Gorky.[173] Orakhelashvili, who had been Secretary of the Georgian Central Committee, had for the past five years acted as Deputy Director of the Marx-Engels-Lenin Institute in Moscow. He is now said to have lost his life as a result of objecting to Beria's book on the

*Petrovsky and Eikhe, though not Postyshev, were included in one list (*Pravda,* 2 November 1937).

Bolshevik movement in the Caucasus, which was heavily faked to give Stalin a major role.

Although the charges and the supposed confessions did not impress, there seemed no reason to doubt that such a trial had indeed taken place as stated. It was only in the 1960s that death dates given for the accused made it clear that the whole thing was a complete lie. Karakhan had been shot on 20 September (with several others, including I. A. Teodorovich, Head of the Society of Former Political Prisoners); Yenukidze and Sheboldayev had perished on 30 October (with other leading figures, including thirteen other full members of the Central Committee, such as Chudov, Kodatsky, Rumyantsev, Khatayevich, and Lobov). Sheboldayev's wife, Lika, a niece of Rudzutak, was severely interrogated, with threats to her newborn baby, and is reported going mad.[174] Nazaretyan was also shot on 30 October. His wife, Klavdia, with her seven-year-old son and five-year-old daughter, were taken to a special prison for women and children, a former church. Later they were sent to camp, but the daughter was eventually retrieved by a "brave aunt." Klavdia was apparently sentenced to eight years, released in 1946, rearrested, but survived to be rehabilitated.[175]

Orakhelashvili, indeed, had been executed on 11 December, only five days before his supposed trial; he was not even tried by the Supreme Court, as stated, but by a troika of the Georgian NKVD (his wife had been shot on 17 September).[176]

At any rate, none of the supposed leading defendants at the "trial" of 16 December were in fact alive when it took place. Why Stalin played this elaborate farce is unknown.

Another massacre of the 30 October type had taken place on 26–27 November. N. S. Komarov was then shot, as was E. I. Kviring, former secretary of the Bolshevik faction in the Duma; Ya. S. Hanecki, who had secured Lenin's release from Austrian jail (his daughter was also arrested);[177] N. A. Kubyak, former Secretary of the Central Committee; D. E. Sulimov; Nosov; and at least fourteen other important figures, including M. M. Nemtsov, secretary of the Society of Old Bolsheviks.

On 21 December, there was a grand ceremonial meeting for the NKVD in the Bolshoi Theater in the presence of Kaganovich, Molotov, Voroshilov, Mikoyan, and Khrushchev. The whole of the full membership of the Politburo, including Kossior and Chubar (who were not present), were elected to the honorary Presidium, but only Zhdanov and Yezhov among the candidate members, the remaining places being taken by Khrushchev and Bulganin. Mikoyan was the main speaker, lavishing praise on Yezhov as "a talented faithful pupil of Stalin . . . beloved by the Soviet people," and as having "achieved the greatest victory in the history of the Party, a victory we will never forget." He concluded, "Learn the Stalinist style of work from Comrade Yezhov, as he learned it from Comrade Stalin!"[178]

In January came an important plenum of the Central Committee and the presentation of a new Government to the Supreme Soviet. The positions of Postyshev and Kossior were affected.

In Kuibyshev province, Postyshev had tried to make up for his earlier opposition to the purges by extremely harsh action. He was now accused of excesses in this line. Malenkov, reporting, accused him of "by cries of 'vigilance' hiding his brutality in connection with the Party." When Postyshev replied that almost all the Secretaries of District Committees and Executive Committees were in fact hostile elements, Molotov, Mikoyan, and Bulganin accused him of exaggerating, Kaganovich brought up his supposedly similar errors in Kiev the previous year,[179] and Malenkov summed up that his acts, and refusal to admit them, were an obvious "provocation." (Malenkov was not even a candidate member of the Committee. Only twenty-eight of the seventy-one full members elected four years earlier were now in fact available to constitute the "plenum.")[180]

Postyshev, still described as "Comrade," was replaced as candidate member of the Politburo by Khrushchev.[181] (This was the last occasion on which a removal from Politburo was officially announced. Henceforth, names simply disappeared from lists and photographs.) *Pravda*'s leader of the same day denounced the heads of certain Party organizations, giving that of Kuibyshev as an example, for having around them "sworn enemies of the people," while expelling honest elements. The Central Committee resolution menacingly noted that the NKVD had had to intervene to save slandered Party members expelled in the province.[182] Postyshev had also in fact received a confidential Party censure while in Kuibyshev for "protecting enemies of the people."[183] Stalin had now suggested that Postyshev might be removed from the Politburo, remaining a member of the Central Committee, and this was voted unanimously. However, his case was referred to the Control Commission, which reported that he had known of and worked with the Right–Trotskyite organization, and he was expelled from the Party.[184] But he was not arrested for a few days. He had a small flat in Moscow, where he was visited after this by his fighter-pilot son.[185] There he seems to have remained until his arrest on 21 February.

Kossior, in Kiev among the crumbled remnants of his power, had had a bad year. His brother I. V. Kossior, also a member of the Central Committee, had died in apparent good odor on 3 July, though it was later revealed that his death was, in reality, a suicide like Ordzhonikidze's.[186] Another brother, V. V. Kossior, an old oppositionist, had been given ten years in 1934 and been implicated again in the Pyatakov Trial;[187] during the summer, he had been one of a batch of oppositionists brought from Vorkuta to Moscow and shot. Kossior and Petrovsky went to Kiev on 26 January 1938 and were welcomed at the station by the supposititious Ukrainian Central Committee. On 27 January, its "plenum" released Kossior from his post.[188] The First Secretaryship of the Ukraine was transferred, as we have seen, to the coming man, Nikita Khrushchev.[189] But far from falling into immediate oblivion, Kossior was appointed instead Vice Chairman of the USSR Council of People's Commissars and President of the Soviet Control Commission.

In fact, the new Government presented by Molotov to the Supreme Soviet on 19 January 1938 had as its three Vice Premiers S. V. Kossior, Chubar, and Mikoyan, while Eikhe was People's Commissar for Agriculture.[190]

The Vice Chairmen of the Council of People's Commissars cannot indeed seriously have thought of themselves as holding powerful positions. Both Voroshilov and Kaganovich, in charge of important departments and invariably ranking senior to them in Party listings, were not at this time Vice Premiers—an adequate demonstration of the post's comparatively decorative significance.

Even so, we have the extraordinary spectacle of Molotov taking the chair at a meeting of the Council of People's Commissars, the official order for the trial and arrest of several of whose members he had already signed. At meetings of Molotov and the Vice Premiers, two out of the three supposedly contributing to policy discussions were actually no more than dead men talking, whose opinions were by now quite meaningless.

During the Khrushchev period, it was customary to speak of the January 1938 plenum as marking a return to legality, it being thought suitable for such a turn of events to mark Khrushchev's promotion to the highest levels. Indeed, the resolution of the plenum as ever speaks strongly against unjust expulsions from the Party, and this, with the attacks on Provincial Committees for the same error, which were to continue throughout the year, gave that impression to those who wished to receive it. But there was no sign of any real improvement. A Soviet account given in April 1964 managed to satisfy the demands both of Khrushchev and of truth by saying, "The January 1938 plenum of the Central Committee of the All-Union Communist Party somewhat improved the situation. However, repressions did not cease."[191]

It was Yezhov himself who made some of the most critical remarks about the wickedness of expelling members wrongly. Throughout the Terror, the leadership had constantly spoken against unfair expulsions—with the aim, however, of destroying its subordinates. For example, as we have seen, in the 1937 attack on Postyshev, the real motive of which was to remove an objection to the Terror, the official line was condemnation of inadequate Party democracy. In fact, this can be traced even in the Central Committee's key letter of the summer of 1936, which spoke strongly against unprincipled expulsions.[192]

The January 1938 resolution criticizes a large number of local Party organizations in addition to that of Kuibyshev for such practices, blaming officials such as "the former Secretary of the Kiev Provincial Committee of the Communist Party of the Ukraine, the enemy of the people Kudryavtsev," "the exposed enemy of the people" Shatsky (Head of the Leading Party Organs Administration of the Rostov Provincial Committee), and so on, and telling pathetic tales of honest Bolsheviks, and even their relatives by marriage, who had lost their jobs as a result of incorrect denunciation.

The persistence of this theme is remarkable. Clearly, it was a great advantage to blame Postyshev and others for inhumanity rather than for belated humanity. In this way, the central leadership could, or might think it could, avoid some of the unpopularity arising from its own actions. But we might perhaps go further and see in this a sign that Stalin, right from the start, had determined to put the odium on his instruments and to destroy them when their task was completed. If so, he was to some degree successful. The "Yezhovshchina" remained the popular name for the Reign of Terror, and with the disappearance of Yezhov himself, some of the curse was taken off the surviving leadership.

On 9 and 10 February 1938, as if to mark the continuity of the Purge, a fresh group of fourteen or fifteen significant figures perished. They included A. P. Smirnov, Kaminsky, and Muklevich. M. I. Erbanov, First Secretary of the Buryat-Mongol ASSR, was among them. Purged with him was his Second Secretary, A. Markizov. Markizov's daughter, Gelya, was in a famous photograph taken in 1936 in which she is held in Stalin's arms, which indicated his love of children; and it continued to appear after he had orphaned her. In fact, a sculpture modeled on the photograph was set up in the Stalinskaya Metro station.[193]

Meanwhile, arrests and denunciations continued. N. V. Krylenko, now serving as People's Commissar for Justice, was attacked in January at the first meeting of the Supreme Soviet, for neglecting his duties in favor of mountain climbing and chess, and was not reappointed. When he had handed over (to Ulrikh's subordinate, N. M. Rychkov), Stalin personally telephoned him to reassure him about future work. He was, of course, on the list of those to be arrested, and was in fact arrested the same night, 31 January 1938, with some of his family.[194]

Krylenko, whom Lenin had appointed Commander in Chief of the Army immediately after the Revolution, had impressed Bruce Lockhart in 1918 as an "epileptic degenerate" and is referred to in 1938 by a fellow prisoner as "notorious and universally despised."[195] He had conducted the prosecution in such faked trials as the Shakhty Case and the Menshevik Trial. As to his other interests, he had shown farcical dogmatism at a Congress of Chess Players in 1932:

> We must finish once and for all with the neutrality of chess. We must condemn once and for all the formula 'chess for the sake of chess,' like the formula 'art for art's sake.' We must organize shockbrigades of chess-players, and begin immediate realization of a Five-Year Plan for chess.[196]

On his arrest, he is reported being treated with special indignity in the Butyrka "to take the conceit out of him."[197] But he was soon taken to the Lefortovo for serious interrogation. The original charge was of connections with the Bukharin conspiracy, and the creation of a wrecking organization in the Commissariat of Justice, in which he had personally enlisted thirty people. On 3 March, he confessed that he had belonged to an anti-Soviet organization since 1930. But by 3 April, this was put further back, and he was confessing to having worked against Lenin before the Revolution and having plotted with Bukharin, Pyatakov, and Preobrazhensky after it.[198]

In general, secret executions of prominent committee members already arrested, and arrests of many of those still at large, continued.

The Party, as it had existed a year previously, had been broken. From District Secretaries to People's Commissars, the veterans of Stalin's first period of rule had fallen to Yezhov's assault. But further blows were being prepared for the terrified survivors.

# NATIONS
# IN TORMENT

*Of all the treasures a State can possess, the human lives of its citizens are for us the most precious.*

Stalin

It is very hard for the Western reader to envision the sufferings of the Soviet people as a whole during the 1930s. And in considering the Terror, it is precisely this moral and intellectual effort which must be made. To demonstrate the facts is to provide the bare framework of evidence. It is not the province of the investigator to do more. Yet it cannot but be that these facts are offered for moral judgment. And however coolly we consider them, we should think in terms of Pasternak, breaking off his *Sketch for an Autobiography* before the Terror with the words "To continue it would be immeasurably difficult. . . . One would have to talk in a manner which would grip the heart and make the hair stand on end."

Thus far we have dealt with the Purge as it struck the Party. Information about this side of it, especially from Soviet sources, is much richer than for the larger but less dramatic fate of the ordinary Soviet citizen. Yet for every Party member who suffered—and many of *them* were scarcely political in any real sense—six or seven others went to the cells.

The figures we have so far been covering were consciously involved to a greater or lesser degree in a political struggle whose rules they understood. They had themselves in many cases been responsible for the imprisonment or death of peasants and others by the million in the course of collectivization. Our pity for their own sufferings should doubtless not be withheld, but it can at least be qualified by a sense of their having a lesser claim to sympathy than the ordinary citizen of the country. If Krylenko was to go to the execution cellars, he had sent to their deaths, on false charges, hundreds of others. If Trotsky was to be assassinated in exile, he had ordered the shooting of thousands of the rank and file, and gloried in it. Pushkin once described an earlier generation of Russian revolutionaries as "positively heartless men who care little for their own skins, and still less for those of others." We may accept this about such people as Rosengolts. But it plainly does not apply to his wife. In her, we can already see the fate and the feelings of an ordinary non-Communist, caught up in the frightful tensions and agonies of the Great Purge.

The oppressive feeling that hung over everything is well illustrated by a comparison made by Dudorov, in *Doctor Zhivago:*

> It isn't only in comparison with your life as a convict, but compared to everything in the thirties, even to my favorable conditions at the university, in the midst of books and money and comfort; even to me there, the war came as a breath of fresh air, an omen of deliverance, a purifying storm. . . . And when the war broke out, its real horrors, its real dangers, its menace of real death, were a blessing compared to the inhuman power of the lie. . . .

It is difficult for those of us who have lived in fairly stable societies to make the imaginative effort of realizing that the heads of a great State can be men who in the ordinary course of events would be thought of as criminals. It is almost equally hard to get the feeling of life under the Great Terror. It is easy to speak of the constant fear of the 4:00 A.M. knock on the door, of the hunger, fatigue, and hopelessness of the great labor camps. But to feel how this was worse than a particularly frightful war is not so simple.

Russia had undergone Terror before. Lenin had spoken of it frankly as an instrument of policy. During the Civil War period, executions simply of "class enemies" were carried out on a large scale. But the circumstances were different in many ways. In those days, it was, as it were, a hot Terror. Injustices and brutalities were perpetrated throughout the country, but they were seldom part of a big planned operation from above. And they were openly described in their true colors. Those were indeed terrible days, when the Cheka squads were shooting class hostages in scores and hundreds. Those who went through them might have though that nothing could be worse.

But Lenin's Terror was the product of the years of war and violence, of the collapse of society and administration, of the desperate acts of rulers precariously riding the flood, and fighting for control and survival.

Stalin, on the contrary, attained complete control at a time when general conditions were calm. By the end of the 1920s, the country had, however reluctantly, accepted the existence and stability of the Soviet Government. And that Government had, in turn, made slight economic and other concessions which had led to comparative prosperity. It was in cold blood, quite deliberately and unprovokedly, that Stalin started a new cycle of suffering. First had come the Party's war on the peasantry. When this had done its worst and things were settling down again in the mid-1930s, the Great Terror was again launched cold-bloodedly at a helpless population. And the cold-bloodedness was compounded by the other distinguishing quality of the Stalin purge—the total falsehood of all the reasons given for it and accusations made during it.

There was another factor. In the First World War, as Robert Graves notes in *Goodbye to All That,* a soldier could stand the squalor and danger of the trenches only for a certain time. After that, the wear and tear became too great. After the first month, under the tensions of trench life, an officer began to deteriorate a little. "At six months, he was still more or less all right; but by nine or ten months . . . he became a drag on the other officers. After a year or fifteen months, he was often worse than useless." Graves notes that over the age of about thirty-three, and particularly over forty, men had less resistance. Officers who had done two years or more often became dipsomaniacs. Men went about their tasks "in an apathetic and doped condition, cheated into further endurance." It had taken Graves himself, he says, some ten years to recover. He adds that none of this was due simply to physical conditions; in a good battalion, physical illness was rare.

What is so hard to convey about the feeling of Soviet citizens in 1936–1938 is the similar long-drawn-out sweat of fear, night after night, that the moment of arrest might arrive before the next dawn. The comparison is reasonable even as to the casualty figures. The risk was a big enough one to be constantly present. And again, while under other dictatorships arrests have been selective, falling on genuinely suspected enemies of the regime, in the Yezhov era, just as in the mudholes of Verdun and Ypres, anyone at all could feel that he might be the next victim.

> The whole people were the victim, including those who were not directly affected by the repressions. Even those who had not had a family member, relative, or friend suffer (true, there were not all that many of them): even they experienced the fear and all sorts of burdens and, in general, to put it mildly, had by no means an easy time of things—the exceptions to this general rule were relatively insignificant in number.[1]

And the public trials, as another Soviet periodical points out, everywhere "created an atmosphere of total suspicion and fear."[2]

Fear by night, and a feverish effort by day to pretend enthusiasm for a system of lies, was the permanent condition of the Soviet citizen.

## DENUNCIATION

For Stalin required not only submission, but also complicity. The moral crisis arose in a form well described by Pasternak. In 1937 (he later told Dr. Nilsson),

> on one occasion they came to me . . . with something they wanted me to sign. It was to the effect that I approved of the Party's execution of the Generals. In a sense this was a proof of their confidence in me. They didn't go to those who were on the list for liquidation. My wife was pregnant. She cried and begged me to sign, but I couldn't. That day I examined the pros and cons of my own survival. I was convinced that I would be arrested—my turn had now come! I was prepared for it. I abhorred all this blood. I couldn't stand things any longer. But nothing happened. It was, I was told later, my colleagues who saved me indirectly. No one dared to report to the hierarchy that I hadn't signed.[3]

But few could match the moral grandeur of the great poet. Everyone was isolated. The individual, silently objecting, was faced with vast meetings calling for the death "like dogs" of the opposition leaders, or approving the slaughter of the generals. How could he know if they were not genuine, or largely so? There was no sign of opposition or even neutrality; enthusiasm was the only visible phenomenon. Even the children and relatives of the arrested got up to denounce their parents.

The disintegration of family loyalty was a conscious Stalinist aim. When, in November 1938, Stalin destroyed the leadership of the Komsomol, headed by

Kosarev, his complaint was that the organization was not devoting itself to vigilance activities, but sticking to its statutory obligation as a political training ground for young Communists. Stalin's idea of a good young Communist demanded not this sort of political training, but the qualities of an enthusiastic young nark.

Many denunciations were made out of fear. If someone heard an incautious word, and failed to report it, it might be he who would suffer. There are many accounts of Party members, unable to think of any enemies of the people among their acquaintances, being severely censured by their own branch secretaries as "lacking in revolutionary vigilance." There are many stories of conversations between old acquaintances which became too frank and ended with each of them denouncing the other. Any conversation that strayed even slightly from the orthodox could only be conducted between old and trusted friends, and with great circumspection. Ilya Ehrenburg's daughter had an old shaggy poodle which had learned the trick of closing the dining-room door as soon as the guests began to talk in a guarded way. As it was given a slice of sausage for its vigilance, it became expert at guessing the type of conversation.[4]

Not every responsible citizen did his duty as a delator. One director gave a lift to the mother of an enemy of the people, an old woman, and was told by his chauffeur:

> Comrade Director, I may be a son of a bitch who must report everything he sees and hears. Believe me or not, but I swear by my own mother that I will not report this time. My own mother is just a plain woman, not a fine lady like this one. But I love her and, anyhow, thank you, Victor Andreyevich, as one Russian to another.

And in fact this incident was never brought up against the director, though many less serious "crimes" were to be alleged against him.[5]

Nevertheless, just as Nazism provided an institutionalized outlet for the sadist, so Stalinist totalitarianism on the whole automatically encouraged the mean and malicious. The carriers of personal or office feuds, the poison-pen letter writers, who are a minor nuisance in any society, flourished and increased.

"I have seen," says Ehrenburg, "how in a progressive society people allegedly dedicated to moral ideas committed dishonorable acts for personal advantage, betrayed comrades and friends, how wives disavowed their husbands and resourceful sons heaped abuse upon hapless fathers."[6] A Soviet story of the Khrushchev period tells, as reasonably typical, of a geology student who denounced another because he heard him, at a dance, telling his girl friend that his father had been executed—a fact that he had failed to disclose at the Institute.[7] After the first student reported it, his colleague disappeared, to serve fifteen years in a labor camp.

Individual denouncers operated on an extraordinary scale. In one district in Kiev, 69 persons were denounced by one man;[8] in another, over 100.[9] In Odessa, a single Communist denounced 230 people.[10] In Poltava, a Party member denounced his entire organization.[11]

At the XVIIIth Party Congress, when the "excesses" of the Purge period were being belatedly and peripherally criticized, one was now made to confess his methods, which had involved removing fifteen local Party Secretaries. Another well-known slanderer, in Kiev, applied for a free pass to a resort on the grounds that he had worn out his strength in "the struggle with the enemy," a remark which caused loud laughter at the Congress.[12]

Extraordinary results came from purely lunatic denunciations. Many poison-pen letters were mere malignant fantasy. There were odder cases yet, such as the Red Army deserter Sylakov, who gave himself up in Kiev with a dramatic tale of an anti-Soviet plot in which he played the leading part. His original story was of planning an armed raid on a post office to provide funds for a terrorist organization, but of having decided instead to throw himself on the mercy of Soviet justice. This was not much use to the NKVD. After Sylakov had been badly kicked and beaten, a quite different version was worked out, involving not him and a few vague friends, but his military unit. The leader of the plot was now not Sylakov, but his commanding officer. They had planned terroristic attacks on Government leaders. Almost the whole unit, from the C.O. to the drivers, were arrested, with many of their wives. Sylakov's two sisters, both working girls, his old and crippled mother, and his father were all pulled in too. So was an uncle who had only met his nephew once and who, having served as a corporal in the old Army, was transmuted into a "Tsarist general."

This absurd case proliferated fantastically until "there was not a single cell in Kiev prison which did not contain someone involved in the Sylakov plot."[13] When Yezhov and his latest representative in Kiev, Uspensky, fell late in 1938, Sylakov and his fellow accused were reinterrogated with a view to getting them to withdraw their confessions. Some of them, fearing a trick, refused, and had to be given tough treatment once again—to force them to withdraw false confessions involving them in crimes carrying the death penalty! Sylakov himself was finally sentenced to three years' imprisonment for denunciation only.

But the NKVD did not, of course, leave denunciation on an amateur and voluntary basis. Everywhere it organized a special network—the *seksots,* recruited from among the general population.

*Seksots* were divided into two types: the voluntary, malicious degenerates out to injure their neighbors, together with "idealists" who were convinced that they were working for the cause; and the involuntary, who were drawn into it out of fear, or (very often) promises of the alleviation of the fate of an arrested member of the prospective *seksot's* family. These last hoped that if they kept strictly to the truth and reported nothing disadvantageous about their friends, no harm would be done. But once started, they were trapped; the pressure became greater and greater. The *seksot* who failed to produce information was himself automatically suspect. As the population became more and more careful in its talk, more and more harmless acts and words had to be reported, misinterpreted, and finally invented to slake the NKVD's insatiable appetite for plots.[14]

One Ukrainian *seksot* is described as having become a genuine convert to Communism, though unable to join the Party owing to former White Army connections, and therefore wishing to serve the cause in the one way which appeared to be open to him. At first, he abused no confidences and reported impartially. "He was only doing his duty, and doing one's duty is always pleasurable. When he had occasionally to overcome his own scruples or likes and dislikes in carrying it out, he felt a positive hero."[15] But naturally, simple hints of feelings hostile to the Government were not in themselves sufficient, for the NKVD of course knew that such could be found in a large section of the population. He put up a struggle, but was himself threatened as having concealed evidence. Gradually going to pieces, he started first to "interpret" remarks, until slowly the distinction between truth and falsehood faded out in his mind. Even so, he failed to give satisfaction because he retained a sense of the plausible, and his inventions were too limited for his superiors, so he was himself arrested.

The Soviet press had recently published material from the archives about informers—for example, a letter from one who was by now himself a prisoner, claiming clemency because of his earlier services in denouncing Vareikis and a number of others, including writers and actors, and after his own arrest, numerous fellow prisoners.[16]

In some areas, bounties were paid for denunciation. In one Byelorussian village depicted in a recent Soviet article, 15 rubles a head was paid, and a group of regular denouncers used to carouse on the proceeds, even singing a song they had composed to celebrate their deeds.[17]

Every account of life in a Soviet office or institution, even before the Great Purge, is replete with intrigues. Such, doubtless, would be true of most other countries. But the resources available to a keen intriguer in Soviet conditions made it a far greater menace, since the normal method of getting on was to "compromise" and have expelled from the Party, and as often as not arrested, either one's rival or, if his position was for the time being too strong, one of his subordinates—through whom he could eventually be undermined. One rough estimate was that every fifth person in the average office was in one way or another an NKVD stool pigeon.[18]

Weissberg speaks of the foundry industry, with which he had connections through experiments to improve blast furnaces. Following Gvakharia, Ordzhonikidze's nephew and one of the geniuses of the industrialization drive, all the directors of the big foundries in the Ukraine were arrested:

> A few months later their successors were arrested too. It was only the third or fourth batch who managed to keep their seats. In this way the direction of the foundry industry came into the hands of young and inexperienced men. They had not even the normal advantages of youth in their favour, for the choosing had been a very negative one. They were the men who had denounced others on innumerable occasions. They had bowed the knee whenever they had come up against higher authority. They were morally and intellectually crippled.[19]

And, of course, this applied not only to industry, but to the whole of the new ruling cadre. As a Soviet periodical complained in 1988, it was "the conscious result of negative selection, of the horrible social selection which went on in this country for decades."[20]

Right through the Purge, Stalin's blows were struck at every form of solidarity and comradeship outside of that provided by personal allegiance to himself. In general, the Terror destroyed personal confidence between private citizens everywhere. The heaviest impact of all was, of course, on the institutional and communal loyalties which still existed in the country after eighteen years of one-party rule. The most powerful and important organization drawing loyalty to itself and its ideas rather than to the General Secretary himself was the Party—or rather its pre-Stalinist membership. Then came the Army. Then the intellectual class, rightly seen as the potential bearer of heretical attitudes. These special allegiances attracted particularly violent attention. But in proceeding to attack the entire people on the same basis, Stalin was being perfectly logical. The atomization of society, the destruction of all trust and loyalty except to him and his agents, could only be carried out by such methods.

In fact, the stage was reached which the writer Isaak Babel summed up, "Today a man only talks freely with his wife—at night, with the blankets pulled over his head."[21] Only the very closest of friends could hint to one another of their disbelief of official views (and often not even then). The ordinary citizen had no means of discovering how far the official lies were accepted. He might be one of a scattered and helpless minority, and Stalin might have won his battle to destroy the idea of the truth in the Soviet mind. "Millions led double lives," as the grandson of the executed Army Commander Yakir was to write later.[22] Every man became in one sense what Donne says he is not—"an island."

Not that everyone blamed Stalin. His skill in remaining in the background deceived even minds like Pasternak and Meyerhold.[23] If men—albeit nonpolitical—of this caliber could feel so, it is clear that the idea must have been widespread. The fear and hatred of the population was concentrated on Yezhov, who was thus unconsciously making himself ready to be the scapegoat, the eponym of the "Yezhovshchina."

## MASS TERROR

As "the number of arrests based on charges of counter-revolutionary crimes grew tenfold between 1936 and 1937,"[24] the purge extended itself outward from the Party victims to include all their contacts, however slight. For example, in 1932 the Party Secretary of the Urals, Kabakov, had visited some workers' quarters and chanced to look in at an apartment where he found only the mother at home. She told him that her son had gone on a rest cure after being overworked, but had to do it at his own expense. Kabakov ordered the management of the trust employing the worker to pay the expenses. Five years later, when Kabakov was arrested (see p. 222) someone informed the NKVD that he had visited this worker and given him protection. The worker was himself at once pulled in, and accused of "bootlicking" Kabakov.[25]

Thirteen accomplices had been found for Nikolayev, who had really acted alone. This became a general principle. "Vigilance" was made the test of a good citizen or employee, as well as of a good Party member. The NKVD everywhere, and all public organizations and economic institutions, were under continual pressure to show their worth in uprooting the enemy. Every man arrested was pressed to denounce accomplices, and in any case all his acquaintances automatically became suspects.

In the show trials themselves, some of the confessions automatically implicated not just individual or groups of political associates, but also wide circles completely outside the Party struggle. For example, in his evidence in the Bukharin Trial,[26] Zelensky pleaded guilty to the fact that 15 percent of the staff of the Central Cooperative Union "consisted of former Mensheviks, Socialist-

Revolutionaries, anarchists, Trotskyites, etc. In certain regions the number of alien elements, former members of other parties, Kolchak officers and so on . . . was considerably higher.'' These elements were, he said, assembled to ''act as a center of attraction for all kinds of anti-Soviet elements.'' The way this would snowball almost automatically, and throughout the country, is obvious.

Yet it was not only this process of association that gave the Purge its increasingly mass character. In the 1930s, there were still hundreds of thousands who had been members of non-Bolshevik parties, the masses who had served in White armies, professional men who had been abroad, nationalist elements in the local intelligentsias, and so on. The increasingly virulent campaign for vigilance against the hidden enemy blanketed the whole country, not merely the Party, in a press and radio campaign. And while the destruction of hostile elements in the Party was going forward, it must have seemed natural to use the occasion to break all remaining elements suspected of not being reconciled to the regime.

For this sizable part of the population was already listed in the files of the NKVD and its local branches under various headings, such as

AS     anti-Soviet element

Ts     active member of the Church

S     member of a religious sect

P     rebel—anyone who in the past was in any way involved
     in anti-Soviet uprisings

SI     anyone with contacts abroad

Such categories were not in themselves legal grounds for prosecution, but they automatically made those listed natural suspects and almost automatic victims when an NKVD branch was called upon to show its merits by mass arrests.

We have a more detailed division of these suspect categories in the lists of dangerous elements issued on the annexation of Lithuania by the USSR in 1940.[27] Since even by January 1941, after half a year's occupation, there were admittedly only 2,500 Communists in the country,[28] few of the worst suspects—real Trotskyites—could be found. And no threat to Stalin's position as a whole could come from so small a territory. But in the selection of those whose elimination was required to turn the country into a more or less reliable fief, we can see some of the way of thinking which had been applied to Russia itself. The lists itemized all former officials of the State, Army, and judiciary; all former members of non-Communist parties; all active members of student corporations; members of the National Guard; anyone who fought against the Soviets (that is, in 1918 to 1920); refugees; representatives of foreign firms; employees and former employees of foreign legations, firms, and companies; people in contact with foreign countries, including philatelists and Esperantists; all clergy, former noblemen, landlords, merchants, bankers, businessmen, owners of hotels and restaurants, and shopkeepers; and former Red Cross officials. It is estimated that these people covered about 23 percent of the population.[29]

In the Soviet Union, many in these categories had already died or emigrated. But many were left. And around each was a widening circle of colleagues and acquaintances who automatically entered the field of suspicion by "association with alien elements." Anyone in a job worked under a State official who might turn out to be a Trotskyite. Anyone, anywhere, might find that he bought his groceries from a former kulak or was neighbor to an Armenian bourgeois nationalist.

Thus in Nikopol, when the Party Secretary fell, the NKVD arrested his

assistants, his friends, the men and women whom he had put into jobs anywhere in Nikopol. The Commandant of the Nikopol garrison went into the hunters' bag, then the local Prosecutor and all his legal staff, finally the Chairman of the Nikopol Soviet . . . the local bank, the newspaper, all commercial institutions were "cleansed" . . . the manager of the Communal Administration, the Chief of the Fire Brigades, the head of the Savings Institution. . . . Crowds of women and children swarmed around the NKVD building in Nikopol at all hours, in spite of the bitter cold.[30]

A recent Soviet comment on the purges is that as against the argument, sometimes met, that the purges were largely confined to party officials, "they hit everyone—doctors, intellectuals, peasants, atheists, priests, industrial managers, diplomats, former private businessmen."[31] In the Butyrka, Eugenia Ginzburg's cell mates were, as she puts it, "a much broader section of the population" than in the "special block" in Kazan: "There were many peasants, factory workers, shop girls, office clerks."[32] Roy Medvedev, again, mentions about 1,000 arrested in a single factory.[33] In fact, as the Soviet trade-union organ *Trud* recently put it, it is "a myth that the working class was not touched by the repressions," for statistics show that "millions of all sections of the population suffered."[34]

In Moldavia "an absolute majority of the repressed were workers and peasants often semiliterate or illiterate, with no interest in politics."[35] Figures given in the Soviet press for Kursk province imply that about 20 percent of the arrests were in the countryside—that is (for the USSR as a whole), about 1.5 million.[36] A recent Soviet article describes how in the writer's home village of 100 households, one day in April 1937, two policemen arrived, stopped the farm work, and arrested all the men between twenty and fifty years old, on charges of having started the sowing too late for sabotage reasons. Numbering sixty-five in all, they were taken off in lorries, the writer's father among them. (In 1956, the writer learned that his father had not survived.)[37]

Thus while officialdom, the intelligentsia, and the officer corps were prime victims, by mid-1937 practically the entire population was potential Purge fodder. Few can have failed to wonder if their turn had come. Pasternak, in the bitterly matter-of-fact passage with which he ends the main body of *Doctor Zhivago*, gives the expectations of the time:

One day Lara went out and did not come back. She must have been arrested on the street, as so often happened in those days, and she died or vanished somewhere, forgotten as a nameless number on a list which later was mislaid, in one of the innumerable mixed or women's concentration camps in the north.

Russians who had been abroad and came back toward the autumn of 1937, like Ilya Ehrenburg, were deeply shocked by the change. Even on his way through from Spain, when he rang his daughter from Paris, he could get nothing out of her except conversation about the weather. In Moscow itself, he found that writer after writer and journalist after journalist had disappeared. In the *Izvestiya* office, they had given up putting nameplates outside the doors of department heads; as the messenger girl explained, "Here today and gone tomorrow." In the ministries and the offices, it was everywhere the same—empty seats, haggard faces, and an extreme unwillingness to talk.[38] An American journalist living in a block of about 160 apartments in the summer of 1937 notes that the Secret Police had made arrests in more than half of them, "and our house was no exception."[39]

There were various methods of avoiding arrest. A well-known scholar avoided the first wave of the Purge by pretending to be a drunkard. Another, taking the same line a little further, got drunk and created a disturbance in a public park, thus getting six months for a minor criminal offense and avoiding political trouble.[40] By a curious irony, some genuine enemies of the regime—perhaps more prescient than most—escaped by simply fading into the background. For example, Nicholas Stasiuk, who had actually been Minister of Supply in the anti-Communist Rada Government in the Ukraine in 1918, survived in Mariupol working as a park attendant until the German occupation during the Second World War, when he became a leading figure in the nationalist movement in the area.[41]

There was sometimes a period between disgrace and arrest which a lucky individual might make use of by leaving the main centers. S. G. Poplawski (who was to be installed by Stalin as Deputy Commander-in-Chief of the Polish Army after the war) was at the Frunze Military Academy in 1937. Expelled from the Party and the Academy, he at once left Moscow to avoid the next step. "A year or a year and a half later"—that is, presumably after the fall of Yezhov—he reappeared and was then rehabilitated and readmitted to the course.[42]

Again,

> the editor of the Kazan newspaper, Kuznetsov, who was to figure in my charge sheet as belonging to the same "underground group," disappeared into the wilds of Kazakhstan and was never arrested because they lost track of him and eventually stopped looking. Later he even had his translations of Kazakh odes to "Stalin the Great" and "Father Yezhov" published in *Pravda*.[43]

In general, moving frequently was a certain protection, since it usually took "at least six months or a year" before the local NKVD paid much attention or accumulated enough evidence against a figure whom there was no exceptional reason to persecute. It also took a great deal of time before his personal documents from the NKVD of his previous place of residence were forwarded, "particularly as all such documents were dispatched by special NKVD express messenger and not through the ordinary post." Sometimes they never arrived at all.[44] Siberia, in particular, was a good place to go. Comparatively speaking, the local authorities were glad to have settlers, hardly distinguishing between people in forced exile and those freely arriving. The NKVD in a province in European Russia would have little interest in providing suspects for its Siberian opposite number, and though it could have a man under "suspicion" brought back, this was troublesome and hardly worth going through, except in important cases.

But moving was an option open to few, and was often no more than temporary protection. The arrests came, eventually, in millions.

Vyshinsky's assistant, Roginsky, who got a fifteen-year sentence, continued to argue in camp that the regime was justified in isolating from the community large numbers of people who might cause trouble and in continuing to exploit to the maximum, regardless of any guilt or innocence, the labor of those who were economically "old and useless."[45] More sophisticated NKVD and Party members would defend the Purges on subtler grounds. Even if mild jokes or criticism of the Government was all that had taken place, this was a potential for future active opposition, and the NKVD, by excising such people, was carrying out a justified preventive operation.

In the factories, public denunciation meetings of the established type spread to the workers as a whole. A Soviet novel of the Khrushchev period typically describes such a works scene in 1937:

> A short man in a lambskin cap angrily announced, "My foreman Sereda failed to issue me with cement. I thought at the time this was suspicious. Yesterday I learned that Sereda was concealing his relationship with one of Makhno's followers who married his cousin!"
>
> "The fitter Tsvirkun when taking up employment concealed the fact that his old man was an elder of the church!" announced a second speaker.
>
> A third speaker proceeded to expose his former comrade whose parents had been deprived of electoral rights for sabotage during the period of collectivization. . . .[46]

The extension of the Purge throughout the country was not, as sometimes suggested, just the result of too much eagerness on the part of local NKVD officials who let things get out of control. On the contrary, it was insisted on from the center. For example, on 29 November 1936 Vyshinsky was already ordering that within a month all "criminal cases of major conflagrations, accidents, and output of poor-quality products be reviewed and studied with the aim of exposing a counter-revolutionary and saboteur background in them." In certain areas, where few prosecutions on charges of counter-revolutionary activity had been brought, severe censure was issued from the Public Prosecutor's Office in Moscow. In 1937, only eight cases in this category were brought to court through a large part of Siberia, and Moscow blamed this on "a weak and inadequate struggle to stamp out the nests of saboteurs."[47]

Arrest quotas were imposed from above. An NKVD local officer who had been in charge of the small Ukrainian district of Chrystyneska is reported in jail as telling of an order sent to him to arrest 3,800 people; even arresting all former prisoners, all those reported by *seksots* and others would not have fulfilled the quota, so he had to ask village soviets to nominate lists, himself being arrested for this.[48] At a higher level, the 1938 Head of the Byelorussian NKVD was reproached for not matching the Ukrainian bag of Polish spies, and managed to pull in 12,000, many of them Jewish shopkeepers.[49]

In general, occasional highly organized mass trials and much more frequent mass arrests marked the period. In May 1937, the Far Eastern press announced fifty-five death sentences in such trials;[50] in June, another ninety-one; in July, another eighty-three; and so on through the year. In Byelorussia from June onward, hardly a week went by without wrecking and espionage being discovered in various industrial enterprises, the Academy of Sciences, the Polish theater, the physical culture groups, the banks, the cement industry, the veterinary services, the bread-supply organization, and the railways. (The local railway authorities were denounced on 8 October 1937 and charged with being not only Polish but also Japanese spies, in accordance with railway tradition.) In Central Asia, it was the same: 25 executions were announced in Kazakhstan[51] and 18 in Uzbekistan[52] in November. In January 1938 came 26 in Kirghizia[53] and another 134 in Uzbekistan.[54]

On 28 July 1937 E. G. Evdokimov assembled the Party leadership of the North Caucasus Territory and gave instructions for a long-planned superpurge in the area. On 31 July, the local phase of this "general operation" was launched in the Chechen-Ingush Republic in the North Caucasus: 5,000 prisoners were crammed into the NKVD prisons in Grozny, 5,000 in the main garage of the Grozny Oil Trust, and thousands of others in various requisitioned buildings. In the Republic as a whole, about 14,000 were arrested, amounting to about 3 percent of the population. Shkiryatov in person oversaw a further mass operation in October.[55]

The cold-blooded administrative organization of such mass arrest and deportation comes out very clearly in Serov's Order No. 001233 for the Baltic States:

> Operations shall be begun at daybreak. Upon entering the home of the person to be deported, the senior member of the operative group shall assemble the entire family of the deportee in one room. . . . In view of the fact that a large number of deportees must be arrested and distributed in special camps and that their families must proceed to special settlements in distant regions, it is essential that the operations of removal of both the members of the deportee's family and its head shall be carried out simultaneously, without notifying them of the separation confronting them.

## ARREST

Whether as part of such a special operation, or in the ordinary course of routine arrests, it was usual to take action in the small hours. Two or three NKVD men, sometimes brutal, sometimes formally correct, would knock and enter. A search was made which might be brief but could take hours, especially when books and documents had to be examined. The victim, and his wife if he had one, sat under guard meanwhile, until finally he was taken off. A quick-witted wife might in the long run save his life by getting him some warm clothes. By dawn, he would usually have been through the formalities and be in his cell.

A general describes his arrest:

> At two in the morning there was a knock on the door of my hotel room.
> "Who's there?" I called.
> A woman's voice answered: "A telegram for you."
> "Obviously from my wife," I thought as I opened the door.
> Three uniformed men came into my room and one of them told me point-blank that I was under arrest.[56]

A poet writes of his, also at night:

"Go with you"
>                    you ask, looking for your coat,
Your arm fumbles for the sleeve.
You feel overcome by a sudden weakness—
In such a moment you tire as in a lifetime. . . .

It seems a ravine has opened under your feet,
And the ceiling seems to fall on you.
There is suddenly not enough air in the room—
You breathe
>                    with an effort.[57]

The New Constitution, indeed, had guarantees against unjustified arrest. Under its Article 127, no one might be "arrested" except by order of a court or with the consent of the Prosecutor. This was anyhow not of much value in the absence of an independent judiciary; and the judicature of the USSR was officially defined as "a means of strengthening the Socialist regime, guarding the rights of citizens and repressing the enemies of the people and the Trotskyite–Bukharinist agents of foreign espionage organizations."[58] But in any case, a distinction was made between "arrest" and "detention." A man might be "detained" without the sanction of the court or Prosecutor in "all cases where public order and security is threatened." Moreover, Article 45 of the Corrective Labor Codex reads: "For reception into a place of deprivation of freedom it is obligatory to have a sentence or an order by organs legally empowered thereunto, *or an open warrant.*"

In fact, a prosecutor's warrant seems generally to have been provided, though sometimes formalities were dispensed with. For example, a case is reported from the Ukraine in which the police arrested two chance visitors for whom they had no warrant together with the man they were after; each of the two accidentally arrested spent five months in jail before managing to get out.[59] Cases of mistaken identity, particularly of persons with common names like Ivanov, are also occasionally noted. Such prisoners were usually released after a few weeks or months, but cases are mentioned of their having confessed to espionage or other crimes before the mistake was discovered. Even then, they were sometimes released.[60]

Releases were most exceptional in 1937 and 1938. One prisoner had incurred a five-year sentence for wondering why an old actress (Ekaterina Korchagina-Aleksandrovskaya) had been nominated for the Supreme Soviet in the autumn of 1937, when a number of harmless "cultural" figures were so used to improve the governmental image. He was condemned for "speaking against a candidate of the Communist and non-Party bloc." A friend, Lev Razgon, got him to tell his wife to approach the actress herself, who went to the NKVD and complained. They told her that the offender had been jailed as a spy for the British and Japanese, and showed her thick files supposedly containing the evidence and sentence. However, he was able to send his real sentence, still in his possession, to be shown to Korchagina. Three weeks later, he was released.[61]

There are many accounts of the NKVD insisting that anyone released (usually after 1938) should sign a guarantee not to reveal what had happened to him in jail. A Soviet newspaper recently quoted one such:

I, Sternin, N. V., pledge never and nowhere to speak of what became known to me between 11 June 1938 and 11 July 1939 about the work of the organs of the NKVD. It is known to me that on any breach of this I will be accountable under the strictest revolutionary laws, for divulging state secrets.[62]

Wives were not told where the arrested had been taken. The method of finding where they were was to go from prison to prison. In Moscow, wives would go to the "information center" opposite the Lubyanka, at 24 Kuznetsky Most; then to the Sokolnika; then to the Taganka; then to the office of the Butyrka, in its small courtyard; then to the Lefortovo military prison; and back again. When the head of the queue of hundreds of women was reached, an official was asked to accept the 50 rubles a month to which as-yet unconvicted prisoners were entitled. Sometimes a prison administration, perhaps through bureaucratic incompetence, would not admit that it held the man in question until the second or third time round. One Moscow wife found a girl aged about ten in front of her in the queue with a dirty little wad of ruble notes. She was paying it in her for father and mother, both arrested.[63]

Anna Akhmatova's son, the young Orientalist Lev Gumilev, was in jail in Leningrad. "During the frightful years of the Yezhov terror," the poet says in the foreword to *Requiem,*

I spent seventeen months in prison queues in Leningrad. One day someone "recognized" me. A woman with blue lips standing behind me, who had of course never heard my name, suddenly woke out of the benumbed condition in which we all found ourselves at that time and whispered into my ear (there everyone spoke in a whisper):
    —Could you describe even this?
And I said:
    —I can.
Then something resembling a smile flickered over what once had been her face.

Akhmatova speaks of her own mouth as one "through which a hundred million people cry," and asks that if a monument to her is ever put up, it should be at the prison gates in Leningrad where she stood for 300 hours. In 1940, she was allowed to see her son, and afterward wrote the poem which is number 9 in *Requiem,* feeling that she was going mad.

Young Gumilev was again, or still, in jail in 1956 when Fadeyev made an appeal to the Prosecutor's Office, saying that "although he was only a child of nine when his father was no more, he, as the son of N. Gumilev and of A. Akhmatova, was at all times a convenient target for career-seeking and hostile elements who sought to make accusations against him."[64] This makes it clear that he was, like so many others, the victim of his relationships.

Women who actively tried to get their husbands released almost never succeeded. One typically describes being called to a local NKVD headquarters at midnight and simply being told, "I order you to stop running about like a lunatic trying to get your husband released! I order you to stop bothering us! That's all! Get out!"[65]

After a husband had been sentenced, it was again difficult to trace him. One method was to write to the addresses of camps of whose existence a woman had heard from other wives. Sometimes, after a wife received a long series of printed forms saying that her husband was not at such-and-such a camp, he could be found[66] and, in certain types of sentence, parcels accepted.

For the wives, indeed, life was very bad. General Gorbatov remarks, "I often thought of my wife. She was worse off than me. I was, after all, in the company of other outcasts, whereas she was among free people among whom there might be many who would shun her as the wife of an 'enemy of the people.' "[67] And all reports agree that the women lost their jobs, their rooms, and their permits, had to sell possessions, and had to live on occasional work or on the few relatives who might help them. Ignorant of their husbands' fate, they faced a worsening future.[68]

## TO THE CELLS

The arrested man first was taken to a reception point in one of the prisons, signed in, and submitted to a strict physical search and an examination of his clothes seam by seam. Bootlaces and metal attachments, including buttons, were removed. These searches were made at intervals during imprisonment. At the same time, thorough cell searches were carried out about once a fortnight.

In the cells, while there were variations around the country, the prisoner would find much the same routine—intense overcrowding, inadequate food, boredom, and squalor, between bouts of interrogation. Life in the Tsarist prisons is universally described as very considerably preferable to those now developed. In particular, there had not been the overcrowding.

A prisoner who had been in Moscow's Butyrka Prison in 1933 says that while in that year there had already been 72 men in a 24-man cell, there were no fewer than 140 in November 1937.[69] In a woman's cell supposed to hold 25, 110 women were crowded. Planks covered the entire floor and the few beds, apart from a small part of the central gangway, a table and two large latrine buckets. It was impossible for the prisoners to lie on their backs, and when lying on their sides, if one wanted to turn over, it could only be done by negotiating with the prisoners on either side to do it all together.[70] The cell in which Pugachev had been held alone before his execution was now occupied by sixty-five people.[71]

Most of our descriptions of prisons are those in Moscow, Leningrad, or the Ukrainian capital. The impression given is scarcely a favorable one: in the Shpalerny, a four-man cell held up to forty.[72] But conditions seem to have been a good deal better there than in the provincial jails. Several accounts remark on prisoners from Chelyabinsk or Sverdlovsk, on arrival in the packed cells of the Butyrka, exclaiming that the place seemed a holiday camp compared with their previous experiences.[73] A civilian official describes being shown around Pervouralsk jail: "the stench struck me like a physical blow."[74] Where the overflow was too great, as in some of the Siberian towns, vast pits were sometimes dug and roofed over, and the prisoners simply herded in. By the autumn of 1937, a Kharkov prison built for about 800 held about 12,000.[75] In Novosibirsk, about 270 men were crammed into a forty-square-meter cell.[76]

In the most crowded cells, conditions were literally lethal. In a letter in a recent issue of a Soviet newspaper, a survivor describes an 8-man cell in Zhitomir prison into which 160 men had been crowded. They had to stand up, pressed tightly against one another. "Five or six died every day"; the bodies "continued to stand up because there was no room to fall down."[77]

Overcrowding was treated differently in Moscow than in the provinces. In Moscow, space was gained by having the prisoners sleep under the beds and on boards between the beds. By this means, it was possible to accommodate up to three men to the square yard. In provincial prisons, beds and boards were taken out to make room for more inmates. In some, as we have seen, people slept in rows, lying on their sides; but when cells were even more crowded, half the occupants had to stand while the other half slept, packed, on the floor.[78]

Each cell elected its *starosta,* or cell leader, who was responsible for keeping order, allocating sleeping places, and so forth. The new prisoner was put next to the reeking slop bucket, or *parasha,* getting better places as his seniority increased.

In the morning, a short time was given for ablution and excretion. For example, 110 women in one cell were allowed forty minutes with five lavatories and ten water taps.[79]

In prisons in the big cities, at least before they became too crowded, prisoners were taken to the baths every ten days. Sufficient soap was issued. Clothing was regularly disinfected. In most of the provincial prisons, however, conditions were already filthy.

During the "Yezhovshchina," the usual daily ration was 500 to 600 grams of black bread, 20 grams of sugar, and thin cabbage soup twice a day. In some prisons, there was also a tablespoonful of groats and hot water three times a day.

In the Butyrka, alternate days saw cabbage soup and fish soup, about a pound of black bread, and a meal of lentils, barley, or groats in the evening. This is described by a woman prisoner as being worse than what she was managing on in town after losing her husband and her son, but, even so, good in comparison with what she was to get in the camps.[80] These rations were usually delivered regularly and fully. Prison diet seems to have been calculated to be just enough to keep a more or less motionless prisoner alive.

It was unhealthy fare. But the general conditions were more unhealthy. Prisoners showed a peculiar grayish blue tinge from long confinement without light or air.[81] The main diseases resulting were dysentery, scurvy, scabies, pneumonia, and heart attack. Gingivitis was universal.[82]

But the prison administration was held strictly responsible for the actual life of every prisoner. This was taken to such paradoxical lengths that "in the same cell you would find prisoners suffering severely from the effects of interrogation about which nobody bothered, while every conceivable medicine for the prevention and cure of colds, coughs and headaches were regularly distributed."[83] And great precautions were taken against suicide.

Doctors reluctant to interfere with the course of the interrogation would sometimes treat prisoners whose ribs had been broken under a different diagnosis, but giving them the right treatment.[84] Medical conduct in a provincial prison is reported as being in a different spirit, the examination being conducted quite openly with a view to seeing how much the prisoner could stand. A certificate issued was quite frank about the beatings and was evidently entered in the official records without a qualm. This was in early 1938.[85]

The company, apart from a plague of stool pigeons, was usually good, especially in Moscow, and innumerable cases are given of kindness and self-sacrifice—as when (a Hungarian Communist reports) a prisoner, back from even worse conditions, was allowed a bed to himself for a whole day by the 275 men crammed into a 25-man cell, and was given extra sugar from their rations.[86] Lectures were given on a large variety of subjects, and much storytelling was also done. Herling mentions too that

> every cell contains at least one statistician, a scientific investigator of prison life, engrossed day and night in assembling a complicated jig-saw of stories, scraps of conversation overheard in corridors, old newspapers found in the latrine, administrative orders, movement of vehicles in the courtyards, and even the sound of advancing and receding footsteps in front of the gate.[87]

All prisoners report cases of Party officials who remained loyal, and held either that Stalin and the Politburo knew nothing of what was happening or, alternatively, that they themselves were not qualified to judge these decisions, and simply had the duty of obeying Party orders, including confession.

There were other types. In one of the cells of the Butyrka, there were the sons of five moderately important officials. Four of them were the typical brutalized product of the new privileged youth of Stalinism. They had freely denounced their parents and boasted of it, taking the view that there was no reason why they should harm their own prospects to look after relics of the past. Only the fifth, the son of General Gorbachev (the executed "daredevil"),[88] was a decent youth.[89]

Smoking was permitted. All games were forbidden. Chess was, however, played illegally, with men made out of bread or other objects. In one of the women's cells in the Butyrka, a fortune-telling game with matches was played. When a wardress saw people with matches, she would count them, and if there were exactly the number required for the game (forty-one) the owner was punished.[90]

Books are reported as available in two Moscow prisons, the Lubyanka and the Butyrka (though at the height of Yezhov's power, they seem to have been prohibited). These libraries were good, containing the classics, translations, histories, and scientific works—sounding much better than those of British prisons or, indeed, hospitals or cruise liners. The Butyrka's was particularly fine. The reason was that it had been used for political prisoners in Tsarist times, and the big liberal publishing houses had always given free copies of their books to these jails.[91] That of the Lubyanka was largely of books confiscated from prisoners.

After Yezhov's appointment, new and harsher regulations came into force. All windows were blocked with shutters—still called "Yezhov muzzles"—which left only a small piece of sky visible. (They had, indeed, been in use in the Lubyanka, and the equivalent Shpalnery prison in Leningrad, for some years.)[92] After the Bukharin Trial, as a "reprisal," these panes were shut except for ten minutes a day. Bread became moldy, clothes damp, and walls green; joints ached "as though some creature were gnawing them."[93] The penalty for the slightest offense, such as the possession of a needle, was the punishment cells with only from one-half to two-thirds of the already small prison ration, deprivation of outer clothing, and permission to lie down only at night, and then on the stone floor.[94] Punishment cells had, logically enough, to be even worse than ordinary ones. A

Soviet writer mentions three grades of them in Yaroslavl in 1937. In one there was light, and the prisoner kept his or her clothes. The next was a moldy hole in the wall, totally dark and cold, with only a vest permitted and bread and water once a day. She was in it for five days for the offense (in any case not committed by her) of writing her name in the washroom. From the remaining "first" category, which she escaped, "people came out only to die."[95]

The trees and flowers which had grown in some prison yards were meanwhile cut down and the ground asphalted over. Zabolotsky, in his poem "The Ivanovs," had spoken of trees "standing . . . behind railings, under lock and key." He was himself to be deprived of the sight of even these.

At the same time, as far as possible, the more liberal warders were liquidated, and only the least popular guards were retained, after reindoctrination courses.[96]

Some prisoners, particularly those under interrogation in especially important cases, were kept in "inner prisons." So were certain men already serving sentences. The regime in these "inner prisons" was quite different from the bullying squalor of the main buildings. Unlike the mass cells, with fetid air and prisoners pressed close together on bare boards, which nevertheless had a certain social life, of discussion and even occasional scientific and literary lectures from specialists, the inner prisons were "living graves."[97] The cells were clean, without overcrowding; each prisoner had his own bed and even linen; and clothes were actually washed once a month. But no noise, not even loud speech, was permitted. The spyhole in the cell door opened every few minutes. The prisoner had to be in bed from 11:00 P.M. to 6:00 A.M. During the day, he could sit down but not lean on anything. There was nothing whatever to do—on inadequate diet. Isolation was complete; Weissberg, in isolator cells in the Ukraine and then in Moscow, only learned about the outbreak of war at the end of October 1939. There were only a few hundred prisoners in an "inner prison" at a time when thousands and tens of thousands might be in the outer one.

Such a prisoner had to undress in such a way that his hands could be seen and, when sleeping, to keep his arms outside the covers. Weissberg says that this was because a prisoner had once plaited a length of string under the cover and hanged himself with it; in any case, it would have been the only opportunity for making any illegal object.[98] If a warder saw a prisoner's hands hidden, he would enter the cell and wake the prisoner each time he detected him.

In the "inner prisons" proper, communication by tapping was almost impossible, and was seldom replied to as being probably the work of a provocateur.[99] Elsewhere there was a certain amount of it.[100] The method is that described by Arthur Koestler in *Darkness at Noon*—the so-called Dekabrist alphabet, dating from the prisoners of the 1820s.*

In the isolation cells, the psychological problem was intense. A former actor from the Bolshoi Theater who had served five years gave the following "lesson":

> First, you must detach yourself from reality—stop thinking of yourself as a prisoner. Make believe that you are a tourist who temporarily finds himself in an unfamiliar environment. Don't admit to yourself that conditions here are very bad, because they

*The alphabet is arranged, in imagination, in a square of horizontal and vertical lines. To show a letter, you tap its coordinates in the horizontal and then the vertical.

may get even worse, and you should be prepared for that. Don't become too involved in the everyday life of the isolator. Try not to hear its sounds, especially at night, or to smell its smells. Try not to be aware of the guards, don't look at them, ignore the expression on their faces. Stop making-believe about the possibility of your being released soon from the isolator. Do not attempt to regain your freedom by means of a hunger strike, or by admitting your guilt, or by appealing for mercy to the authorities. Stop pining for the friends you have left behind in the free world.[101]

A special category of prison consisted of the half-dozen "political isolators," notably those at Suzdal, Verkhne-Uralsk, Yaroslavl, and Aleksandrovsk. These dated from earlier days of the regime, when they had been thought of as a comparatively humane method of removing factious Communists and other left-wing "politicals" from public life. Even in the early 1930s, treatment in these prisons was comparatively humane. During the purge, they sank to the normal level. A Soviet commentator says of the food in the Yaroslavl isolator in 1937 that it "contained no vitamins whatever. For breakfast we got bread, hot water, and two lumps of sugar, for dinner—soup and gruel cooked without any fat, and for supper—a kind of broth reeking of fish oil."[102] But the isolators still preserved some special characteristics. They mostly held no more than 400 to 500 prisoners. Typically at Verkhne-Uralsk, there were cells holding either 10 to 25 or 3 to 8 prisoners, with in addition a number of solitary cells. It was usual for important prisoners serving sentences, but not expendable—in that further trials were planned for them—to be held in these.

## THE GREAT PRISONS

Of the five main prisons in Moscow, three—the Lubyanka, the Lefortovo, and the Butyrka—were for "politicals" only, though they were also held in the other places of detention with nonpoliticals. The Lefortovo was the great torture center, though torture was also practiced on a lesser scale in the Lubyanka and in the "special section" of the Butyrka.

The *Lubyanka* was free of bugs, and the same is reported of some of the Kiev prisons, though bugs usually abounded. (In spite of the far cleaner and more sanitary conditions in the German concentration camps compared with the Soviet labor camps, the same does not seem to have been true of the prisons. The Berlin Central Prison on the Alexanderplatz is described as being more lice-ridden than prisons in Moscow.)[103]

The corridors of the Lubyanka were clean, smelling of carbolic and disinfectant. It is the best known of the NKVD prisons, since it lies within the headquarters of the Police Ministry, and has been the scene of the most famous imprisonments, interrogations, and executions. But though its great wedge looming over Dzerzhinsky Square is only a few minutes' walk from the Kremlin and the general tourist area, it is seldom pointed out to visitors even now.

It was originally the headquarters of an insurance company. The Cheka took over the old building, and over the years built over the entire block. The original building is pre-Revolutionary Gothic; the rest of the block was rebuilt in two bursts: one in 1930-functional, and the other in postwar wedding-cake style. The People's Commissariat consisted of the whole outer section. Inside is a courtyard, and within the courtyard is the nine-story prison section. This was originally a hotel or boarding house run by the insurance company, and though considerably adapted has not been rebuilt. As a result, the rooms used as cells are less unpleasant than the cells in the other prisons. The windows—though largely blocked by shutters—are of good size.

The Lubyanka had about 110 cells, which were fairly small. It seems improbable that more than a few hundred prisoners were held there at a time.

Prisoners who were unsatisfactory in the preliminary interrogations at the Lubyanka were often transferred to the 160-cell *Lefortovo*—in particular, the military. No clear account of the atrocities practiced in the Lefortovo is available. We are told that prisoners who had been there and were transferred to the Butyrka regarded the beating up in the latter prison as child's play compared with their previous sufferings.[104] The Lefortovo was built just before the First World War in a more or less star shape, with blocks radiating from the center. It had the advantage that there were water closets actually in the cells.

The *Butyrka,* started in the eighteenth century to house the captured rebels of the Pugachev insurrection, is by far the largest prison. It consists of a number of vast barrack-like blocks, centered on the old section, "the Pugachev Tower," in which the great rebel had been held before his execution. In the Purge, it held about 30,000 prisoners.[105]

Gorbatov, who was tortured in the Lefortovo, says that the Butyrka was an immense improvement. Prisoners got half an hour's exercise a day instead of ten minutes every other day. It had large exercise yards, unlike the cramped squares of the Lefortovo.[106] Exercise was taken, walking in pairs, with hands behind backs and eyes to the ground. Any swinging of arms or raising of heads was immediately stopped.[107]

Women with newborn babies are reported in the Butyrka.[108] On the other hand, others were brought in who had had to leave children, and nursing babies, unattended at home. They had their breasts bandaged to stop the milk.[109]

The *Taganka,* and other prisons holding politicals and others, were like the Butyrka, but dirtier and less efficient.[110]

A special small prison some ten or twenty miles out of Moscow, the *Sukhanovka,* deserves mention. It had a particularly fearful reputation among prisoners, who knew it as "the dacha."[111] It was a single-story building, consisting of a set of isolators; and torture was the normal method of procedure. It is said to have been built specially for the Rudzutak–Postyshev intake. It was the one place were the regulations were observed so strictly that the warders literally never spoke at all to the prisoners.

In Leningrad, there was a similar system. The *Shpalerny* prison, described as comparatively clean and orderly, fulfilled the role of the Lubyanka in Moscow with about 300 cells. The larger *Nizhnegorodsky,* too, had a number of one-man cells for important prisoners. The *Kresti,* equivalent to the Butyrka, with about 30,000 prisoners,[112] was more squalid altogether, with sixteen men sharing what had been a one-man cell in Tsarist times.[113] A special *Transfer Prison* held those already sentenced to camps. (And outside, tourists were being shown as a horror of the past the cells of the old Peter Paul Fortress, where a handful of politicals had been held in considerably better circumstances before the Revolution.)

Whether in one of these or in prisons of various degrees of rigor, malnutrition, and overcrowding, the arrested citizen awaited the authorities' next move. As a general thing, physical conditions were usually far worse in the provincial jails in Minsk, Gomel, Vyatka, or Vologda, but regulations were less tightly enforced; there was more offhand brutality, but also more chance of a comparatively sympathetic warder, who might even warn against informers.[114] As an experienced prisoner puts it, "The dirtier the prison, the worse the food, the rougher and more undisciplined the guard, the less danger there was to life."[115]

## CRIMINAL TYPES

In his cell in this new community, the arrested man might be interrogated at once, or he might wait for some time. Meanwhile, he would discover in discussion with his cell mates what his crime was likely to be. At the beginnings of the purge, those arrested often thought that the other people in the prisons were actually guilty of something, and that only their own case was a mistake. By 1937, the outside public had come to realize that the accused were innocent, and people brought in took it for granted that their cell mates were in the same boat as themselves. The chances of anyone there being actually guilty of anything whatever were very small. One sometimes hears the view still expressed in the West that the Great Purge, though unforgivably striking at many innocent men, at least destroyed, in passing, the genuine spy networks of hostile powers. Such was not the view of Gomulka, who remarks that the Terror "only facilitated the work of the intelligence services of the imperialist states."[116]

In fact, from the purely intelligence point of view, the Japanese, Polish, and Latvian services at least seem to have gained all the information they required. And apart from direct operations, the mere fact of (for example) the defection, owing to fear for his life, of the Far East NKVD chief, Lyushkov, to the Japanese in 1938 must have put them in possession of a veritable treasure house of information—and this defection was a direct result of the Terror!

There is one important earlier case generally recognized as that of a genuine spy—Konar, who became Assistant People's Commissar of Agriculture until accidentally exposed. He was a Polish agent who had been given the papers of a dead Red Army soldier in 1920, and in ten years had thus risen high in the hierarchy, until exposed by someone who chanced to have seen the real Konar. As to minor agents, a number of books mention, as an extreme rarity, "real" spies or men who at least might possibly have been guilty.[117] There is one such, the "Moldavian," in Solzhenitsyn's camp in *One Day in the Life of Ivan Denisovich.* In a Kiev prison in 1939, there was much pride and astonishment on all sides that one of the prisoners was a genuine Polish spy. Once he had admitted his own guilt, he was badly beaten to get him to implicate Party officials in Kiev.[118]

Prisoners recognized, in most cases of arrest, that there was an "objective characteristic" basic to their cases. This might be social origins, past or present posts, relationships or friendships with someone, nationality or connection with a foreign country, or activity in specific Soviet organizations. This probable "real" cause of arrest was at once plain to cell mates, though it was never mentioned by the interrogators.[119]

For although there were many categories, membership in which was liable to bring arrest—such as foreign connections, high military rank, and so forth—these were not the crimes officially charged. Nor did they *automatically* lead to arrest. "We can even quote cases of German Communists who were not arrested, although they were political refugees."[120] Arrest depended on a variety of secondary factors.

One peasant in Kharkov jail accounted for his arrest by the fact that he had been arrested on a false charge four years previously, and released with apologies. This, he thought, must make the NKVD think that he had reason to dislike it. This was apparently not an unusual case. "Hundreds of thousands of people were arrested during the Purge for no other reason than at some time in the past the Soviet authorities had done them an injustice."[121]

To have had anything to do with foreigners was one almost certain road to arrest. People who had actually been abroad—for example, footballers like the three Starostin brothers, stars of the prewar period—were almost all in camps by the 1940s.[122] In general, sport was thoroughly purged: "loathsome counter-revolutionary work" at the Institute of Physical Culture led to the denunciation and arrest of the "human degenerates" concerned, who included I. I. Kharchenko, Head of the All-Union Committee on Physical Culture and Sports Affairs.[123] Philatelists were arrested en bloc, as were Esperantists, for their international connections.[124] Professor Kalmanson, Assistant Director of the Moscow Zoo, had been educated abroad, so was assumed to be a "spy" by his cell mates. After his first interrogation, he triumphantly told them that he was only a "wrecker"—16 percent of his monkeys having died of tuberculosis (a lower figure, he pointed out, than the London Zoo's). But they were vindicated by his second interrogation, which reached "the main question"—espionage for Germany.[125] Everyone connected with the organizations for contact with "Friends of the Soviet Union" abroad was automatically suspect. These organizations sponsored pen-pal exchanges. One young science student is mentioned as being sentenced as a German spy because he had, on this basis, been writing to a Communist in Manchester, though his letters had consisted almost entirely of Soviet propaganda.[126]

All direct contact with foreign consulates was likely to prove fatal. Doctors who had treated German Consuls; a veterinarian who had dealt with consular dogs; even more indirect connections, such as the veterinarian's son, were arrested in the Ukraine; and another man, an old caretaker, always explained in prison that he was there as "the brother of the woman who supplied the German Consul's milk."[127] Another had copied and given to the Polish Consul the weather forecast pinned up in the public park.[128]

An opera singer who had danced longer than permitted with the Japanese Ambassador at an official ball is reported in camp. A cook had applied for a job advertised in *Vechernaya Moskva,* the evening paper. It turned out to be at the Japanese Embassy. She got the job but was arrested for espionage before she had time to start it.[129] Another typical case is of two engineers and their families, arrested in the winter of 1937/1938 because of a gift parcel one of them had received from an uncle in Poland, consisting of two pairs of shoes, some crayons, and a couple of dolls. The engineer who had not received the parcel, but was a friend of the one who had, got ten years.[130]

A Greek doctor was charged with espionage on the grounds that he had written to relatives in Salonika describing the characteristics of some fish being bred with a view to the extermination of malarial mosquitoes.[131] In December 1937, Greeks were arrested everywhere. Later, the Greek-inhabited area of Mariupol, on the Black Sea, was thoroughly purged in connection with a special Greek nationalist plot which was to create a Greater Greek Republic over a large part of the Ukraine. Its "Minister of Education" was in fact a Russian, but he had been Professor of Ancient Greek at Kharkov University and had spent a year in Athens. The "Prime Minister" had been an adviser on minority questions to the Ukrainian Central Committee.[132]

Chinese were also arrested en bloc. One is reported as having been charged with taking a job as a tram driver in Kharkov, with the aim of crashing it into any car on the tracks in front of him which contained members of the Soviet Government.[133] The national minorities in Russian towns were virtually eliminated. In September 1937, the Armenians in the Ukraine were rounded up. There were 600 of them in Kharkov.[134] The Latvians were arrested the same month. An alleged Latvian secret organization had worked for a Greater Latvia stretching over a large part of Russia, including Moscow.[135]

Members of the smaller national minorities were in as "bourgeois–nationalist" plotters. So were, in most cases, members of larger groups like the Ukrainians. One commented:

> I was bound in any event to be regarded as a Ukrainian bourgeois nationalist. True, I had never had anything to do with Ukrainian nationalism, and had never had any sympathy with it, but I had a typically Ukrainian surname, and I had several sympathizers with Ukrainian nationalism among my acquaintances.[136]

It is an interesting fact that there were almost no accusations through the Great Purge of allegiance to any genuinely reactionary idea. Those accused were almost always linked with the Mensheviks, the Armenian progressive nationalist "Dashnaks," the Socialist Revolutionaries, or Communist deviationist groups—practically never with Monarchists, Kadets, and the like.

The Jewish Social-Democratic Bund was a particularly fatal association, and many Jews qualified for accusation as either Bundists or Zionists. A case is quoted of an elderly Jew who had worked as a defense lawyer in earlier trials in the Donets Basin and had conducted himself in a way that antagonized the NKVD—by asking it for documents which might be helpful to the defense and so forth. He had learned enough not to defend himself, and on his arrest signed everything that was put before him without reading it. He later found that he had installed himself as a leader of a Bund group, in touch with other counter-revolutionary organizations, including one headed by the Provincial Party Secretary, Sarkissov (a candidate member of the Central Committee). On one occasion, he was told that he was going to be "confronted" by an important accomplice called Abramsohn, of whom he had never heard. When this man was brought in, the investigator said, "Stop looking at each other as if you'd never met before," so he immediately remarked, "Hello, Abramsohn." "Hello, er . . . er . . . ," the other started, having to be prompted with his chief's name. Then they both signed the records of their confessions about each other without looking at them.[137]

Genuine Bundists, on the contrary, are always reported as being the most refractory in interrogation, being better educated in Marxism than their interrogators, and toughened by a harder underground life in Tsarist times than that of the Bolsheviks.

All former Socialist Revolutionaries were arrested. Weissberg tells[138] of a man in Kharkov jail who had joined the Bolsheviks in 1917, but who in 1905 had distributed among the Tsar's soldiers leaflets provided by the Socialist Revolutionaries. He had then been a young student and, far from being a member of the Party of Socialist Revolutionaries, did not even realize that there was any difference between it and the Bolsheviks.

Almost all ex-Mensheviks were also arrested. We are told that "in 1937–1941 ninety-seven to ninety-eight percent of Russian socialists were physically annihilated."[139]

But everybody with unorthodox ideas of any sort was liable to end up in the camps. Jehovah's Witnesses were automatic victims. But there were also too-enthusiastic members of legal religions, such as the Baptist mentioned by Solzhenitsyn. Tolstoyans are widely reported, including an aged Tolstoyan woman whose twelve-year-old granddaughter had fought the NKVD officers to try to prevent her arrest.[140]

Priests had always had a difficult time under the Soviet regime. Now they became almost automatically suspect of capital crimes. Trials of priests were announced throughout the Union. One in Orel in the summer of 1937, involving a bishop, twelve priests, and others, had as one of the accusations "publishing prayers in Old Slavonic."[141] Other accusations were less credible. Three bishops sentenced in February 1938 had "agitated for the opening of previously closed churches," but their further crimes included sabotage.[142] The main Soviet authority of the time mentions that Buddhists were commonly agents of Japan, engaged in sabotaging bridges and farms.[143] It was also true that "the activity of the counter-revolutionary Muslim priesthood in the U.S.S.R. is directed by the Japanese Secret Service."[144] Many were accused of railway sabotage.[145] One Tatar Imam who had been allowed to visit Mecca was naturally suspect and was soon arrested as a German spy. A "meeting" of about forty leading mullahs, in fact all under arrest, but acting as if it were a normal assembly, accepted the charges against him, and he was shot.[146] The authorities also "destroyed not a few nests of spies directed by 'holy' Catholic priests" who had been responsible for the sabotage of factories, bridges, and railways as well as espionage.[147]

If it was neither nationality nor past nor ideas that brought a prisoner in, it might be relationship: the purge within the Party, the Government, and the Army automatically spread in that way. Each of the accused had relatives, and acquaintances who also had relatives. We have already noted (p. 235) the four categories sent by Yezhov to Stalin of people to be shot, of which List 4 is the simple "Wives of enemies of the people."[148] We have seen the liquidation or imprisonment of the generals' relatives. The military men had, it is true, been shot in comparative haste without public trial. Confessions in the longer-drawn-out affairs were in part obtained by promises not to kill the surviving dependents. Stalin's promises were sometimes kept. A woman prisoner met in labor camps twelve wives, two daughters, two sisters, and a daughter-in-law of prominent purgees.[149] Eight years was the usual sentence.

Typical of purgees of the second rank was Zalpeter, a commander of Stalin's bodyguard, a Lett, who was arrested, together with his wife. She refused to confess, but was finally confronted with her husband in a very bad state, who mumbled that she had said she would get rid of a picture of Stalin that hung in their new flat (formerly Yagoda's). For this, she got eight years.[150]

The wives of the Soviet elite adjusted most slowly of all to their situation in the cells. Their position was an especially difficult one. They had nothing to confess and were unable even to deny the charge, since it was simply of being "wives of enemies of the people."[151] In many cases they had not, as their husbands had, understood the dangerous possibilities before them. On arriving in the cells, some of them were priggish and intolerant of women who had been under arrest for a long time—believing that these earlier cases must have been guilty of some genuine offense.[152]

Even when not arrested, families suffered terribly. An attempted mass suicide is reported by a group of four thirteen- and fourteen-year-old children of executed NKVD officers, found badly wounded in the Prozorovsky Forest near Moscow.[153] The daughter of an Assistant Chief of Red Army Intelligence, Aleksandr Karin (who was arrested and shot, with his wife), was thirteen in the spring of 1937. The Karin apartment was taken by one of Yezhov's men, who turned her out into the street. She went to her father's best friend, Shpigelglas, Assistant Head of the Foreign Department of the NKVD, who put her up for the night, but was virtually ordered the next day, by Yezhov's secretary, to throw her out. Shpigelglas remembered she had relatives at Saratov and sent her there. Two months later she came back: "She was pale, thin, her eyes filled with bitterness. Nothing childish remained in her." She had meanwhile been made to speak at a meeting of the Pioneers, approving the execution of her father and mother and saying that they had been spies.[154]

When Weissberg was in the sick bay of the Kharkov prison, there were a number of children there, including a boy who was nine years old.[155] When, early in 1939, the Soviet press started to report the arrest of various NKVD officers for extorting false confessions, one case at Leninsk-Kuznetsk in the Kemerovo province concerned children as young as ten years old.[156] Four officers in the NKVD and the Prosecutor's Office received five- to ten-year sentences. In all, 160 children, mainly between twelve and fourteen, had been arrested and subjected to severe interrogation, and had confessed to espionage, terror, treason, and links with the Gestapo. These confessions were obtained with comparative ease. A ten-year-old broke down after a single night-long interrogation, and admitted to membership in a fascist organization from the age of seven. Similar mass trials of children took place in various other cities.[157] (There is, indeed, one report of a genuine children's organization which planned to avenge arrested parents by killing the NKVD officers they held responsible.)[158] But, in general, as a Soviet speaker has pointed out, "not only the workers themselves were victims of repression, but also their families, down to the absolutely innocent children, whose lives were thus broken from the beginning." [159]

Another "category" was composed of automatic suspects—anyone connected with production, and in particular engineers. In their case, no guesses were needed. They were saboteurs to a man. It did not matter if their record was generally good. Stalin himself had said:

> No wrecker will go on wrecking all the time, if he does not wish to be exposed very rapidly. On the contrary, the real wrecker will show success in his work from time to time, for this is the only means of staying on the job, of worming himself into confidence, and continuing his wrecking activity. [160]

In the economy, the security mania of the NKVD seems to have been genuine. For quite apart from the persecution of actual people, it imposed by about the end of 1935 a system through which guards and watchmen multiplied enormously in the factories, research institutes, and so forth throughout the country. This was in part supposed to be for the prevention of theft, but also against the penetration of "secrets," many of which were not secret even by Soviet standards and almost none of which would have been regarded as secret in any ordinary community. Moreover, there already existed in every Soviet institution a "secret department," covering both the political reliability of personnel and the technical secrets; and into its safes anything remotely confidential had to be put each night. It is now stated that in 1939 there were, in a labor force of 78,811,000, no fewer than 2,126,000 guards and watchmen—*not* counting NKVD militia—and only 589,000 miners and 939,000 railwaymen. [161]

In this atmosphere, any failure, or any accident, in the economic sphere automatically became sabotage. In the absence of genuine opposition acts, any breakdown had to be made to serve, just as Molotov's accident at Prokopyevsk had had to be inflated into an assassination attempt in the absence of any genuine one. And already at the Pyatakov Trial, railway accidents had been put to the account of the accused, with Vyshinsky graphically recounting the sufferings of the murdered passengers. In the Bukharin Trial, livestock deaths were attributed to the conscious activities of the plotters. Sharangovich said in evidence, "In 1932 we took measures to spread plague among pigs"; and later, speaking of horses, "In 1936 we caused a wide outbreak of anemia." Sharangovich also mentions a number of particular plants—a cement works, a flax mill, a pipe foundry, a power station—in Byelorussia (where he was First Secretary) as having been sabotaged under his instructions. Failures in the grossly overextended first Five-Year Plan were very widespread indeed. But even if the local First Secretary was usually responsible, in every case subordinates were involved.

On the economic side, Soviet statistical and planning methods led to an endless strain on skilled management. The planning figures were always unrealistic. To admit failure meant instant arrest, so the directors concealed it as best they could. This led to a vicious circle with doubly erroneous figures in the ensuing period. When the gap grew so large that it could not be concealed, a scapegoat had to be found, and "then there is a crisis and the Chief Director and a number of officials are sent to camps, but those who take their place have to employ the same methods all over again; the system as it stands leaves them no option." [162]

The directors who organized the new works faced appalling tasks. Lyk-hachev, of the Stalin Automobile Works in Moscow, had to try to direct 25,000 men, with crises about administration, raw material, or simple negligence arising almost hourly. At the Gorky Works in Gorky, an even larger factory wore out the director, Diakonov, even before his arrest. The head of the automobile industry, Dybets, and his assistant were arrested in 1938. In the same year, in the metallur-gical factury in Sverdlovsk, the Old Bolshevik director, Semion Magrilov, shot himself in his office, leaving a long letter attacking the Terror. All those suspected of having read it were arrested and disappeared.[163] By the beginning of 1940, this factory had 2 engineers and 31 technicians with the right qualifications, and 270 without. Magnitogorsk had 8 engineers and 16 technicians with diplomas, and 364 without. In general, as a Soviet legal journal tells us, "hundreds of thousands with no qualifications" now took over the engineering and technical work, with disastrous results.[164] Production, stagnant in 1937 and 1938, actually went down in 1939.[165]

The railways were subjected to particularly Draconian laws. The Criminal Codex of the RSFSR, in its Article 59, covered "crimes against the system of government," including various offenses on the railways which "lead, or might lead, to the breakdown of State transport plans" and of which some examples given are the accumulation of empty trucks and the dispatch of trains off schedule. The prescribed punishment was up to ten years or, if done with malicious intent, the death sentence.

Kaganovich also devised the so-called theory of counter-revolutionary limit-setting on output, with the help of which he organized the mass destruction of engineering and technical cadres. "In a short period of time most of the directors of railroads and of the railroads' political departments and many executive offi-cials of the central apparatus and lines were dismissed from their jobs and later arrested."[166]

As to "sabotage" itself, on the Soviet railways at this time there was an accident of some sort every five minutes. As we have seen in dealing with the Pyatakov Trial, this led to the slaughter of the railway cadres. Kaganovich had made a tour of the railways of the Far East early in 1936. Following this, the Military Collegium went on tour and handed down five death sentences and ten long jail terms in Krasnoyarsk and Tomsk in March, for wrecking for "foreign intelligence services." This was only a beginning:

> In his speech at a meeting of railway activists on 10 March 1937, Kaganovich said:
> "I cannot name a single road or a single system where there has not been Trotys-kyite–Japanese sabotage. Not only that, there is not a single branch of railway trans-port in which these saboteurs have not turned up. . . ." Under Kaganovich arrests of railway officials were made by lists. His deputies, nearly all road chiefs and polit-ical section chiefs, and other executive officials in transport were arrested without any grounds whatever.[167]

On 10 August 1937 Kaganovich wrote to the NKVD demanding the arrest of ten responsible officials in the People's Commissariat of Transport. The only grounds were that he thought their behavior suspicious. They were arrested as spies and saboteurs and were shot. He wrote, in all, thirty-two personal letters to Yezhov, demanding the arrest of eighty-three transport executives.[168]

The North Donets railway was the only line not involved in these sweeping arrests of early 1937. In August, the heads of the line were called to Moscow and instructed to find saboteurs. An estimate by the Director of Locomotive Service of the line is that about 1,700 of the 45,000 employees were arrested within months. In mid-November, he himself was called to the NKVD and asked how he proposed to end sabotage. As he was unable to think of any cases of sabotage—the line being an exceptionally efficient one—he was bitterly harangued and during the next wave of arrests was pulled in, on 2 December 1937, without a warrant or charge. His wife and six-year-old son were thrown out of his house two days after his arrest, and he was subjected to severe interrogation, with beatings, together with a number of other prisoners, including several station masters and the deputy head of the line.[169]

Special railwaymen's prisons were set up, in small towns like Poltava. Arrested railwaymen were kept in coaches in unused sidings. Special military courts traveled around the country dealing with them.[170] They were almost invariably Japanese spies. The reason for this was that the Soviet Union had in 1935 handed over the Chinese Eastern Railway to the Japanese. The Russian railwaymen who had operated it and who now returned to the Soviet Union were almost the only nondiplomatic Soviet personnel who had been living abroad, and on their return they were automatically high-grade suspects. (With their families, they are said to have numbered about 40,000.) And they had meanwhile worked on all the railway systems and recruited their colleagues.

## INTERROGATION

Whether soldier or intellectual, Ukrainian or engineer, the arrested man might thus deduce or learn from his acquaintances what the exact charge would be. And this was important. For when he went to interrogation, it was NKVD practice not to tell him what he was in for, but to let him frame his own confession—unless he proved "obstinate" after a few interrogations, when he might be enlightened.

Article 128 of the Code of Criminal Procedure of the RSFSR laid down that the charge against a person under investigation must be presented not later than forty-eight hours after his arrest. This procedure was not observed. In fact, it contradicted the basic NKVD method. In many cases, charges were not presented until months or years afterward; and in some cases, not at all.

Sometimes there were special preliminaries. The Hungarian Communist writer Jozsef Lengyel describes being taken from the ordinary cell in which 275 men lived "on, between and under twenty-five iron bedsteads" to a much worse one for a fortnight's softening up prior to interrogation. In this "hermetically closed space" in the moist heat from human beings and radiators, bread fresh in the morning was white with mold by midday. Some of his cell mates had strokes, and some went insane. Although Lengyel only got jaundice and open sores on arms and legs, his former cell mates did not recognize him when he was returned to the ordinary prison.[171]

A woman teacher held in solitary confinement in darkness for forty days to confess her espionage motive in approaching the British Consulate for a visa also returned to her cell quite unrecognizable.[172] Worse was the "kennel" at the Lubyanka, described by the critic Ivanov-Razumnik—a true Black Hole with sixty men packed into a heated basement cell about fifteen feet square, with no ventilation but the slit under the door, for a week or even more. Eczema, nausea, and palpitations were universal.[173] This was a variation on the old "steam room" technique used by the OGPU in the 1920s. A Soviet writer describes also the "standing cell," where, in darkness, a prisoner had room only to stand with his hands at his side, virtually immured. A Secretary of the Tatar Provincial Committee was held thus for two days and taken out unconscious.[174]

Interrogation took place mainly at night. A warder would enter a mass cell and murmur the initial letter of a man's name, upon which those this fitted would give their names until the right man answered. He would then be taken out.[175]

All accounts of experiences in the great prisons mention that when escorting prisoners along corridors to interrogation or for other purposes, the warders continually made a clicking sound with their tongues or with their belt buckles, so that others on similar errands would know in advance. The purpose of this, evidently a definite regulation, was to stop anyone from recognizing prisoners from other cells. If two prisoners were about to meet in a corridor, one had his face to the wall while the other went by. In the Butyrka yard, which sometimes had to be crossed, were little sentry-box-style sheds, into which one or the other of two passing prisoners could be shunted.

Eventually, down the stairs ringed with antisuicide nets, the prisoner would arrive at the office of the interrogator, where he might, for the moment, be fairly politely received. The routine questions started: "Do you know where you are? . . . You are in the heart of Soviet Intelligence. . . . Why do you think you are here? . . ." A confession was now required. In the case of the ordinary prisoner, preparation for public trial did not arise, and the confession was merely a horrible formality required under NKVD custom to justify a sentence which was usually ready for issue. That is, as far as the accused himself was concerned. For interrogation had one further purpose—the implication of hitherto unnamed accomplices.

The interrogation technique almost invariably started, not with an accusation, but with the question "Will you tell me what hypothesis you have formed of the reason for your arrest?" This is said to have been based on a questionnaire used by the Holy Inquisition.[176]

The "Yezhov method," as NKVD officers called it, threw the task of building the case against him on the arrested man. If the accused simply gave an innocent account of everything he had done, tougher methods were used, but it still remained up to the victim to find the right line of confession. Prisoners, with the more or less obvious connivance of the authorities, became expert in helping the newly arrested to devise suitable and satisfactory confessions, thus saving everybody trouble, on both sides.[177]

There were various tricks of interrogation. The interrogator might be polite and speak rather in sorrow, and then change to abuse. The obscene cursing of the interrogated was routine. In some cases, it had its effect. In others, not: Weissberg recounts that he found it quite interesting.[178]

Many NKVD interrogators were often aware of the complete falsehood of the charges, and some of them would even admit it. Most, however, even though not crediting the full details, "professed to believe that they contained a grain of truth, and this sufficed to justify their actions in their own eyes." [179] This applied particularly to the earlier generation of NKVD men. After they themselves were liquidated, the newer intake were much simpler Stalinists, who often seem to have believed to a great extent in the accused's guilt.

For the police machine, too, was ruthlessly purged. We are told that "the staff of the Lefortovo Prison was wiped out entirely four times." [180] In all, as we have seen, 20,000 NKVD men perished. [181]

The turnover of interrogators, as the NKVD itself was purged, was good for the morale of resisting prisoners. Two mention that "each of the present writers outlasted more than ten of his examining magistrates; one of them outlasted more than a dozen. In both instances this included the magistrate who ordered the arrest." [182] In Chelyabinsk, one prisoner was saved from execution when the Head of the Provincial NKVD angrily exclaimed, "The investigation was conducted by enemies of the people. Now we've got to start all over again." [183] NKVD officers under arrest were usually interrogated more severely than others. They were more pessimistic about the outcome, and "were extremely stubborn and reluctant to confess for they knew what lay ahead of them." [184] They are reported as highly nervous, expecting to be taken out and executed at any moment.

We have already dealt with the basic techniques of interrogation. In run-of-the-mill cases, the "conveyor" remained at first the main system, punctuated by physical assault. A typical case is that of the young secretary of a factory director arrested as one of a Trotskyite sabotage ring. She was kept standing for two days with short interruptions and then half-throttled by the examiner until she signed a confession which enabled the NKVD to arrest her chief and the thirty-odd other members of the factory's sabotage group. [185]

The conveyor would break down almost anyone in four to six days, and most people in two. Its single disadvantage was that it consumed time and energy. There came a point when the arrests outpaced the interrogative capacity of the NKVD, and the simpler method of beating became routine, under the rubric "simplified interrogation procedures." [186] We can date this change precisely. It was on 17–18 August 1937. In Moscow, Kharkov, and elsewhere, it suddenly came into force. At the Kholodnaya Gora Prison interrogation section, a prisoner describes having to stuff his ears with bread to get any sleep that night on account of the shrieking of women being beaten. [187] In Kazan jail, the first victim was the wife of the Premier of the Tatar ASSR. [188] In the Butyrka that summer, one floor of a whole wing of one of the prison buildings was set aside for night interrogation. From 11:00 P.M. until 3:00 A.M., the inmates of nearby women's cells were kept awake: "over the screams of the tortured we could hear the shouts and curses of the torturers." A woman would go half-mad thinking that she recognized her husband's screams. [189]

The appearance of mere local initiative was preserved. The weapons were almost always boots, fists, and table legs. But Stalin and Yezhov no longer needed to heed any complaints from within the Party, and the rather half-hearted cover to a widely known reality seems more a matter of preserving conventions than anything else. Stalin seems, in fact, to have issued official instructions on torture proper as early as the beginning of 1937, though they remained confidential even from Provincial Party Secretaries until he confirmed the orders, both retrospectively and prospectively, in the secret telegram to them on 20 January 1939 when, after the fall of Yezhov, one or two objectors had begun to make themselves heard[190] (see p. 122).

Several victims note that the NKVD respected certain formalities. Of course, their methods of interrogation were a clear breach of the law. But declarations signed by prisoners were very rarely suppressed. They had to be copied and filed in the dossier.[191] So when Beria took over, he found that some prosecutors were still attaching the complaints made by the accused about "illegal methods of investigation" to the examination record. He took this up with Vyshinsky, who gave instructions that it was not to occur again, though in some cases the prisoners' statements could be preserved on file, not attached to the records of the case.[192]

Whichever interrogation method was applied to a given victim, the required confession followed the same routines. As early as 1931, the foundations had been fully established. A surgeon had confessed his intention to poison the Dnieper River. A lawyer had confessed first to blowing up a bridge, then to planning terrorism, and finally to being a Japanese spy. An electrical engineer was to have commanded a battery of artillery to bombard the workingmen's quarter of Dniepropetrovsk. Another accused confessed to having met former President Poincaré.[193]

There is a report of a former senior official in the Ukrainian timber industry who at the beginning of the 1930s had made a confession in connection with the Industrial Party Trial, that he had had too little timber felled in order to spare the woods for their former owners, whose rights he aimed to restore. He had been sentenced to ten years but released after a year and—like many members of this particular conspiracy—restored to high position. On his re-arrest, he was required to confess that he had had too much timber felled in order to ruin the forests. Another forester had had to confess that he had special tracks cut in the forests to open the way for Polish or German tanks.[194]

One typical style of charge was that against Mrs. Weissberg, arrested in April 1936. She was a ceramicist, and it was alleged that she had surreptitiously inserted swastikas into the patterns of teacups she had designed, and had hidden two pistols under her bed with a view to killing Stalin.[195] A Jewish engineer was accused of having designed a large scientific institute in the form of half a swastika, for reasons of Nazi ideology.[196] A woman potter had designed an ashtray which resembled, or could be made to resemble, a Zionist Star of David. She was arrested, and the stock destroyed.[197] Koestler mentions a German Communist doctor who was charged with injecting patients with a venereal disease, spreading rumors that venereal disease was incurable, and being a German spy.[198] Professor Byelin, of Kiev University, was charged with espionage for mentioning in a textbook the depth of the Dnieper at various points. Another professor—a Jewish refugee from Germany—had given German agents details about the navigability of the Siberian River Ob. A third had forwarded to the Japanese reports about the political attitude of Jewish children.[199] One Kiev workman confessed to having tried to blow up a kilometer-long bridge over the Dnieper with a few kilograms of arsenic, but having had to abandon the attempt owing to rainy weather.[200] Speaking of a middle-aged washerwoman type, accused of consorting with foreigners in expensive restaurants and seducing Soviet diplomats to worm secrets out of them, a Soviet writer bitterly comments, "This was July 1937, when no one cared any longer whether charges bore the slightest semblance of probability or not."[201]

There is a Soviet account published in Khrushchev's time of an Old Bolshevik serving a fifteen-year sentence for "terrorism," in that he had murdered himself. The NKVD maintained that he had stolen the dead man's papers and passed himself off in his place. When he had NKVD officers call a witness who had known him since childhood, and identified him at once, they threw her out and sentenced him notwithstanding.[202]

When a big case was afoot, local interrogators sometimes tried to gain credit by finding accomplices for it, on their own initiative, among their prisoners. After the Tukhachevsky Case, a junior interrogator attempted to involve Weissberg in a connection with the Reichswehr, to build up a new military conspiracy. His superior, on the other hand, meant to produce Weissberg as a witness in the Bukharin Trial, a role to which he was better suited, since he had at least met Bukharin.[203]

There is an account of a case in the Ukraine in which fifty students were charged with forming an organization to assassinate Kossior, who had been named as one of the senior intended victims in the great Moscow Trials. A year's work on this case, which was a structure of great intricacy, had been performed by the interrogators. In 1938, however, it became known that Kossior himself had been arrested as a Trotskyite. Everyone thought that the students would be released. But a new interrogation immediately started, and they were beaten up for having lied to the NKVD. After a few days, the stool pigeons in the cells let them know what they were supposed to confess this time. It was to change their deposition, putting in the name of Kaganovich for that of Kossior. The NKVD could not face the trouble of constructing a completely new fabrication. Finally everything was in order, and the students were sent off to labor camps.[204]

The demand for denunciation was a difficult matter of conscience with many. One Armenian priest with a good memory confessed to recruiting all his countrymen he had buried in the past three years. A newly arrested prisoner would sometimes find a list of unused dead men made available by his cell mates.[205] The denunciation of people already arrested and sentenced was not regarded as discreditable.

But, of course, such tactics only seldom satisfied the examiners, and most people gave way enough to implicate outside contacts whose names were presented to them as already suspect by the very fact of acquaintance.

On the whole, the NKVD officers showed a niggling, self-righteous, and bureaucratic brutality, treating the prisoners like cattle about whom any question of sympathy simply did not arise. But there are many reports of odd exceptions, showing that even in these circumstances the Russian style of humanism sporadically persisted. Two ex-prisoners note,

> There were many officials of all grades, from simple warder to prison governor, who again and again defied regulations and risked their own freedom by finding opportunities of making prisoners' lives easier by secretly giving them food or cigarettes, or even merely speaking a cheering and comforting word to them.[206]

Jozsef Lengyel, however, recounts that though he remembers "humane guards" and "decent commandants," the investigators were without exception despicable.[207] (This minor divergence certainly reflects the increasing brutalization of the NKVD: Koestler's "Gletkin," even, is a figure of the Yagoda rather than the Yezhov period.)

An NKVD sentry was returning a prisoner to his cell, after an interrogation in the Butyrka. They stopped at a tap for the prisoner to wash the blood off himself. As he did this, he was shaken with sobs. The sentry said:

> Don't take it too hard, Comrade! Life's hard on us all, one just has to bear it. Maybe he did beat you for no good reason, but think nothing of it. Probably his black heart aches more than your white body. You can wash the blood off just like that, but what about him? Where's the water that can clean his black heart . . . ?

The prisoner, an Army officer named Vasilev, returned to his cell much cheered, and spoke of the special humanity of the Russian people.[208]

A woman prisoner, a German Communist, reports a guard on the deportation train as saying to her, when she was in tears, "Don't cry. It won't be as bad as all that. You'll live through it and get home again." (She was later, when handed over to the Nazis, to note in the same way the occasional kind and thoughtful Gestapo man.)[209] Eugenia Ginzburg tells a similar story.

In 1937 (though this is a somewhat different point), some of the old NKVD officers continued to show sympathy for obviously innocent and nonoppositionist Old Bolsheviks. A Soviet account by Antonina Levkovich, who was arrested as "the wife of an enemy of the people" in 1937 following an appeal for her already arrested husband, quotes several instances of kindness. They often turned out badly for all concerned. After a month spent in bad conditions on the way from Moscow to Kirghizia, she and her companions found an NKVD officer who tried to save them from starvation. He was charged with "intolerable pity for wives of enemies of the people" and had to shoot himself to avoid arrest.[210]

Such things are worth recording. But at the best of times, they were most exceptional. The norm was callous brutality, or at best cloddish indifference to death and suffering. A Soviet writer remarks of the interrogators, "They were all sadists of course. And only a handful found the courage to commit suicide. Pace by pace, as they followed one routine directive after another, they climbed down the steps from the human condition to that of beasts. . . . But this happened only gradually."[211] The few humane officers and guards did not anyhow survive Yezhov's purge of the NKVD. His new intake of NKVD troopers were well-trained, well-fed, heartless young thugs. Any display of human sympathy, they had firmly implanted in them, was a concession to bourgeois feeling and a form of treachery in the class struggle. As the Purge broadened, it also got worse.

## "TRIAL"

With interrogation completed, the cases were transferred to the judicial and quasi-judicial bodies for sentence. Since 1934, the competent court in political cases was the Military Collegium of the Supreme Court. It had a large staff and was able to mount many cases simultaneously. It took mere minutes even for leading officials (see p. 421) or generals (see p. 92). A lesser figure, Eugenia Ginzburg, describes her seven-minute trial before the Collegium in 1937. The Court returned in two minutes with a "verdict" which she estimates must have taken twenty minutes to type.[212] Thus the Collegium got through tens of thousands of cases over the years of the Terror. From 1 October 1936 to 30 September 1938, it passed 36,157 sentences—30,514 of death and 5,643 of imprisonment.[213] But these constituted a very small proportion of those condemned.

Those who came before a court were judged according to the Criminal Code, whose long Article 58 covered all forms of remotely political crime. This article was broad enough, or so it might have been thought, to encompass anyone the NKVD wished to "repress." And it had long been Draconically interpreted. A Supreme Court ruling of 2 January 1928 had laid down that counter-revolutionary offenses were committed "when the person who committed them, although not directly pursuing a counter-revolutionary aim, wittingly entertained the possibility of this arising or should have foreseen the socially dangerous character of the consequences of his actions."[214] The definition of terrorism was gradually extended to violent acts against a wide range of people. Not only all Party officials, but also members of grain-procurement commissions (in 1930), shock workers (in 1931), and "pioneers" (in 1934) were covered.[215]

A law of 7 August 1932 introduced the death penalty for a wide range of offenses against State property, and the courts seem to have been invited to extend it still further in practical action.[216] Again, to take an example from the field of sabotage,[217] a law of August 1935 established as such the gleaning of wheat by peasant women, who had hitherto been able to save a certain amount in this way. Peasant women were commonly given ten years for this offense.[218]

Vyshinsky strengthened such tendencies by a simple interpretive method:

> He proposed that the deliberate burning of State or public property be adjudicated, regardless of motive and intent, under Article 58, paragraph 9, of the Russian Republic Criminal Codex (Sabotage). Consequently, acts committed without counter-revolutionary intent (for instance, arson for reasons of personal enmity, revenge, etc.) had to be adjudicated under the articles on State crimes. Vyshinsky declared that there are no ordinary criminal offenses, that these offenses now became crimes of a political order. He recommended that ordinary criminal cases be reviewed for the purpose of imparting a political character to them.[219]

To take a specific crime:

> Vyshinsky demanded that counter-revolutionary intent must mandatorily be sought in all criminal cases linked with shortcomings connected with the harvesting campaign. In his view shortcomings in the harvesting campaign were in many cases caused by the activity of saboteurs, who had to be "rendered harmless." For example, during the harvesting campaign of 1937 it was revealed that a number of crops had become infested with ticks. This infection was ascribed to the activity of hostile counter-revolutionary elements, and in connection with this a great number of criminal cases were instituted. Many of the indictments linked with tick infection in grain crops were completely unfounded. Yet Vyshinsky demanded that the prosecutors insist on severe punishment in all criminal cases instituted in connection with crops infested with ticks.[220]

When it came to the actual trial, "he repeatedly maintained that in a criminal trial probability of guilt was perfectly adequate. Instructing prosecutors in the 'art of identifying saboteurs,' Vyshinsky maintained that this is achieved not by comprehensive, full and objective evaluation of the evidence gathered in a criminal case, but by so-called 'political flair.' "[221]

And the legal processes were eased by his ruling that "it is pointless to repeat without particular need what has already been established in the preliminary investigation."[222]

As a result, we get such extraordinary results as a woman who got ten years under Article 58, Section 10, for saying, after his arrest, that Tukhachevsky was handsome,[223] or an artist getting five years for adding to the slogan "Life has become better, life has become more joyful: Stalin" the letter $u$, changing the meaning of "Life has become better . . . for Stalin."[224] Failure to inform, treated as complicity, was severely dealt with. In a minor case, only producing a six-year sentence even for the principal, the noninformer got three years under Article 58 (xii).[225] Under the same Article, a man was sentenced to three years for "smiling in sympathy" while some drunken dockers at another table in Odessa were telling one another anti-Soviet anecdotes.[226] A Tatar woman, originally listed as a Trotskyite, was reallocated as a bourgeois nationalist by the NKVD official concerned, on the grounds that "they'd exceeded the quota for Trotskyites, but were short on nationalists, even though they'd taken all the Tatar writers they could think of."[227] A twenty-year-old mathematician, with no political interests, was sentenced simply because his mother, an old Socialist Revolutionary, was rounded up in 1937. He had actually been born in a Tsarist jail.[228]

Court procedures were at best formalities. Still, the Supreme Court and its Military Collegium at least required the presence of the accused, though as a leading Bulgarian Communist victim notes of a session of the Collegium which sentenced him, "No prosecutor. No witnesses. No co-accused. No defender."[229]

But comparatively few cases were dealt with by a court. Article 8 of the Corrective Labor Codex states, "Persons are directed to corrective labor who have been sentenced thereto by *(a)* sentence in a court of law; *(b)* decree of an administrative organ." This latter was usually the NKVD "Special Board," as set up by laws of 10 July and 5 November 1934 (replacing the Judicial Collegium of the OGPU).

The Special Board consisted of the Deputy Head of the NKVD, the Plenipotentiary of the NKVD of the RSFSR, the Head of the Main Administration of Militia, and the Head of the Union Republic NKVD where the case had arisen. The Prosecutor-General of the USSR or his deputy was also to participate.[230]

The Special Board's sentences were originally limited to five years, but this was either abolished or ignored fairly soon; terms of eight and ten years are soon mentioned. But in any case, while a man who served out a term imposed by a court was often released, one sentenced by the Board was simply resentenced to a further period when his sentence expired. The formalities were completed in Moscow, and the new sentence was announced to the accused in camp by a local representative of the NKVD.

The Special Board was usually given "cases for which the evidence was not sufficient for turning the defendant over to a court."[232] The defendant had no right to defense, and cases were tried in absentia, which—as a Soviet law journal has remarked—"created the preconditions for deliberately passing unjustified, harsh sentences."[233]

And if the Criminal Code was interpreted with great elasticity by the courts, even that was found too restrictive for most cases before the Special Board. Article 58 was generally cited as a basis, but the accused were liable under the following heads:

| | |
|---|---|
| K.R.T.D. | Counter-revolutionary Trotskyite Activity<br>Usual sentence five to ten years |
| K.R.D. | Counter-revolutionary Activity<br>Usual sentence five years or more |
| K.R.A. | Counter-revolutionary Agitation<br>Usual sentence five years or more |
| Ch.S.I.R. | Member of the Family of a Traitor to the Fatherland<br>Usual sentence five to eight years |
| P.Sh. | Suspicion of Espionage<br>Usual sentence eight years |

The last an offense perhaps unique in the world's legal history.

In addition, those in the following categories could be simply labeled by the Prosecutor and sent to camp without even the Special Board routine:

| | |
|---|---|
| S.O.E. | Socially Dangerous Element<br>Usual sentence five years |
| S.V.E. | Socially Harmful Element (that is, common criminals)<br>Usual sentence five years[234] |

This power to inflict punishment when there was admittedly no crime was provided for in Article 22 of the "Principles of Criminal Jurisdiction," given in the Basic Criminal Code, which reads as follows:

> Punishment in the form of exile can be applied by a sentence of the State Prosecutor against persons recognized as being socially dangerous, without any criminal proceedings being taken against these persons on charges of committing a specific crime or of a specific offense and, also, even in those cases where these persons are acquitted by a court of the accusation of committing a specific crime.

In early 1937, sentences were still on the light side. A typical K.R.T.D. case is of an electrician arrested at that time, who had formerly known some Trotskyites and in whose room there was found, on his arrest, a copy of the first edition of *The History of the Civil War* (which, of course, gave many of the facts of Trotsky's role in the period covered). For this, he got three years.[235] Another man, a former Trotskyite, was sentenced to a longer term because he had traveled from Moscow to Leningrad on 1 December 1934.[236] Another got three years for possession of a K.R.A. rhyme about Feuchtwanger and Gide.[237] For copying Lenin's Testament, the usual sentence was ten years, under Article 58, Section 10, for anti-Soviet agitation, though sometimes death was imposed.[238] A professor of astronomy got five years (K.R.A.) for having objected to his daughter marrying an NKVD man.[239] A typical P.Sh. case was of a professor who had been a prisoner of war in Austria in 1915—his *sole* offense.[240] The decree of 14 September 1937[241] established what amounted to completely extrajudicial procedures for counter-revolutionary crimes, and sentences grew greater. Moreover, those arrested in 1933 or 1935 were now retried, and the comparatively mild sentences of three or five years of those earlier days were "translated . . . into the language of 1937."[242]

After a Special Board "trial" (in his absence), the accused eventually received the sentence, on some convenient occasion. One prisoner mentions simply being handed a grubby typewritten sheet in his cell by a woman trusty, an ex-prostitute, to the effect that the Special Board of the NKVD had condemned him to five years in camp.[243]

In spite of the vast amount of paperwork, loose ends proliferated. It is said that in the Butyrka a whole block was occupied by prisoners who could not be sent to camps because not only were there no warrants against them, but no papers of any sort existed in connection with them. They had been condemned as groups, and the judges had not been able to compile dossiers, while the labor camps would only accept prisoners with papers.[244]

The Special Board continued to have this legal position throughout the Stalin period. But while the Board in its official form went on handing out prison sentences (though longer ones than in the previous period), a new and illegal body emerged from it. As early as 27 March 1935, a mere order of the NKVD gave the powers of the Special Board to committees of three NKVD officers, though a representative of the Prosecutor's Office was to be present at their proceedings, and they were only empowered to inflict the same sentences as the Special Board proper. On 30 July 1937, though this was never announced, new and deadly "Troikas" were set up on Stalin's instructions (though "on Kaganovich's initiative" and formally established by a "special instruction" from Vyshinsky), with the power to impose the death penalty.[245] Recalling, no doubt consciously and with a view to suggesting revolutionary urgency, the so-named emergency tribunals of the Civil War, they now in fact often—as "Dvoikas"—consisted merely of two members. At the center, as we have seen, Yezhov and Vyshinsky fulfilled this role.

Troikas were established in all the provinces and Republics; their composition varied a little, but seems usually to have consisted of the NKVD chief as Chairman, the Provincial or Republican First Secretary, and the Chairman of the local Executive Committee (or a representative of the Prosecutor's Office). A recent Soviet article tells us that in practice, the NKVD chief initialed the sentence and it was then carried out, the other two adding their initials ex post facto. As with the Special Board, the defendant was not present at the proceedings of the Troikas. They inflicted the death penalty in absentia on a vast scale. In Uzbekistan, the Soviet press lately noted, the Republic's Troika ordered 40,000 executions in 1937 to 1938, which would mean over 1 million for the USSR as a whole. (And this, of course, over and above the sentences by the Supreme Courts of the Union and Autonomous Republics, the Military Tribunals, and similar bodies. Moreover, executions could be carried out without even the pretense of a trial, by "special order," as with G. E. Prokofiev and his subordinates in 1937 and M. S. Kedrov and others in 1941.)[246]

Orders for further executions came from Moscow. Yezhov telegraphed the NKVD chief in Frunze, capital of Kirgizia: "You are charged with the task of exterminating 10,000 enemies of the people. Report results by signal." The form of reply was, "In reply to yours of . . . the following enemies of the people have been shot," followed by a numbered list. An order to the Sverdlovsk NKVD called for 15,000 executions. Another, to a small town near Novosibirsk, ordered 500, far above normal capacity, so that the NKVD had to shoot priests and their relatives, all those who had spoken critically of conditions, amnestied former members of White Armies, and so on, who would ordinarily have got five years or less.[247] In February 1938, a recent Soviet account tells us, Yezhov himself went down to Kiev to call a special NKVD conference to order 30,000 more executions in the Ukraine.[248]

For all the various forms of trial, official death sentences are estimated at not over 10 percent.[249] However, this is based only on the information given to relatives, and there was falsification on a large scale, with the sentence of "ten years without the right of correspondence" in fact meaning execution; all the identified bodies in the mass graves at Vinnitsa and Kuropaty were of people who had had such sentences.

A Soviet authority of the Khrushchev period remarked that "many were exterminated without trial or investigation."[250] Vyshinsky himself favored the extralegal method. He several times said, "When it is a question of annihilating the enemy, we can do it just as well without a trial."[251] There seem, in fact, to have been few executions without "trial," apart from the liquidation of oppositionists already in camps, until 1937. The first blow seems to have been against foreigners resident in Russia, including naturalized Soviet citizens. With no important defenders in the Party and susceptible to the charge of contact with foreign espionage, they began to go to the execution cellars in large numbers late in 1936.

It was usually obvious when an execution was to take place in a central prison. Several warders and an NKVD officer would appear at the cell door, which otherwise seldom happened. There was sometimes time to say goodbye and hand over any remaining property, such as clothes, to one's cell mates.

The cellars of the Lubyanka were really a sort of basement divided into a number of rooms off corridors. Later on, in ordinary routine, the condemned handed in their clothes in one of these rooms and changed into white underclothes only. They were then taken to the death cell and shot in the back of the neck with a TT eight-shot automatic. A doctor then signed the death certificate, the last document to be put in their files, and the tarpaulin on the floor was taken away to be cleaned by a woman specially employed for that purpose.[252] (Execution with a small-bore pistol is not, as might seem, very humane. Of the 9,432 corpses exhumed at Vinnitsa, 6,360 had needed a second shot; 78, a third shot; and 2, a fourth shot, while many others had been struck over the head with some blunt object to finish them off. Again, we are told in a recent Soviet article that in the mass graves at Kuropaty the sand thrown above a new batch of those executed could still be seen moving some time later.)[253]

At the Lefortovo, the corpses were cremated, and other crematoria seem also to have been used: a tombstone to "ashes of unknown persons" recently noted at the Danilovskii Monastery is believed to cover some who were executed and never identified.[254] Elsewhere in Moscow, at the Kalivnikovskoye Cemetery in the heart of the city, there was what has now been described in the Soviet press as "Moscow's Babi Yar," where "naked bodies were brought in carts in the middle of the night during the thirties, with rags stopping the two bullet holes in their heads."[255]

The final documents in a case were a note to the sanitary-burial services of the NKVD: "please take six, twelve, or some such a number of corpses, date, signature," and on the other side, "six, twelve, or some such a number of corpses cremated, date and signature of the director of the crematorium." This refers to important cases, not to those merely shot and buried in mass graves.[256]

And so it was elsewhere. In Gorky, for example, during the height of the Purge, one estimate is that from fifty to seventy executed corpses were taken out daily from the NKVD headquarters on Vorobievka Street. One prisoner was employed to whitewash the walls of the cells of executed prisoners immediately after they were taken to the NKVD headquarters for execution. This was to cover the names that they had scratched on the walls.[257]

As I write, mass execution sites are known in several places: the one in Vinnitsa, discovered by the Germans in 1943, where over 9,000 corpses were exhumed, even though part of the area remained uninvestigated; one between Khabarovsk and Vladivostok, where some 50,000 seem to have been executed in 1937 and 1938; one at Gorno-Altaisk; one at Bykovnya, near Kiev; one, with over 46,000 bodies, near Leningrad; one near Tomsk; one close to the well-known Polish grave site at Katyn; near Chelyabinsk; near Poltava; in Donetsk; near Voronezh; and, above all, the mass grave at Kuropaty, near Minsk, of which much was written in the Soviet press in 1988 and 1989, which became the eponym of the later discoveries and where no fewer than 50,000 victims lie buried, while considerably higher estimates have been given in the Soviet press.[258] These included many from newly annexed western Byelorussia in 1939 to 1941 (five of the eight mass graves actually dug up were of western Byelorussians, and three were from 1937 and 1938, though this may not be representative). The total in any case is unexpectedly large, especially when five more sites are reported waiting investigation in or near Minsk alone, with others in the Byelorussian provincial capitals. And Byelorussia had in 1937–1938 about one-thirtieth, or 3.4 percent, of the Soviet population, and even in 1939–1941 only about one-eighteenth, or 5.6 percent. The great majority of the dead were peasants and workers.[259]

So the Purge had gone on, striking further and further into every layer of the population until finally it reached the mass of the peasantry and the ordinary workers (often accessories in sabotage cases). Although many at this level were shot, most escaped

> with a simple confession that, for purposes of counter-revolutionary agitation, they had alleged that there was a shortage of certain foods or of petrol or that shoes man-

ufactured in Soviet factories were of inferior quality, or something of the kind. This was sufficient for a sentence of from three to seven years' forced labor under Article 58.[260]

Many accounts by former prisoners contain stories like the following: in September 1937, several hundred peasants were suddenly brought in to Kharkov prison. None of the officials in the prison knew what they had been arrested for, so they were beaten up to produce some sort of confession. But the peasants did not know either. Finally, a case was put together:

> The charges against them were relatively light. Most of them were merely asked to confess that they had carried on counter-revolutionary agitation and sabotage. They had planned to poison wells and burn down barns, and they had put a spell on Stalin and agitated against grain collections. All mere bagatelles. But about twenty of them were in more serious trouble. They were accused of a plot to steal horses, ride into the nearest town and proclaim an insurrection. The church bells were to ring out and at that sign the countryside was to rise. Nothing of all this had actually happened: the wells had not been poisoned, the cattle had not been harmed, the barns had not been burned down, the horses had not been stolen, the bells had not rung out, and the countryside had not risen. The whole thing was a complete invention.[261]

For the remainder of the Yezhov period, they dominated the prison. They came in groups almost identically composed. First the chairman of the collective farm was arrested. He would give the names of his committee as accomplices, and they would name their foremen, who would involve the ordinary peasants. Peasants usually confessed as soon as they found out what was required of them. The NKVD at this stage let them know what was needed informally through its own stool pigeons. They went off to the camps in the far north in batches twice a week.[262]

Even out on the far Soviet periphery, a British observer, then in Lenkoran, Azerbaijan, saw lorry following lorry at intervals throughout the day, filled with Turkic peasants under NKVD escort. Ships, including passenger boats taken off their ordinary routes for the purpose, were waiting to take them across the Caspian.[263]

Already in the summer of 1937, a later Soviet writer notes "the tremendous scale of the operation": "All the agencies were inhumanly overworked. People were run off their feet; transport was insufficient; cells were crowded to bursting; courts sat twenty-four hours a day!"[264]

An NKVD officer arrested in November 1938 said that for six months it had become clear to the NKVD that the Purge could not go on in its present form.[265] The NKVD by now had files proving that almost every leading official everywhere was a spy. Many of them were never arrested. An example is Professor Bogomolets, at the time of his death President of the Ukrainian Academy of Sciences; at least ten statements from arrested scientists were on the record involving him as a fascist spy.[266]

The snowball system had reached a stage where half the urban population were down on the NKVD lists. They could not all be arrested, and there was no particular reason to take one rather than another. All the old "categories" had been largely liquidated: former partisans, Old Bolsheviks, oppositionists, and so on. The new arrests in the NKVD itself were a sign that this was understood. The feeling also got around that a vast number of people had been arrested quite indiscriminately, and now "they don't even know what to do with them."[267]

Not less than 5 percent of the population had been arrested by the time of Yezhov's fall—that is, already at least one in twenty. One can virtually say that every other family in the country on average must have had one of its members in jail. The proportions were far higher among the educated classes.

In 1938, even from Stalin's point of view, the whole thing had become impossible. The first substantial question an interrogator asked was, "Who are your accomplices?" So from each arrest, several other arrests more or less automatically followed. But if this had gone on for a few more months, and each new victim named only two or three accomplices, the next wave would have struck at 10 to 15 percent of the population, and soon after that at 30 to 45 percent. There are many theories of Stalin's motives throughout the whole horrible business, and the question of why he stopped the mass Terror at this stage has puzzled many commentators. But we can see that the extreme limits had been reached. To have gone on would have been impossible economically, politically, and even physically, in that interrogators, prisons, and camps, already grotesquely overloaded, could not have managed it. And meanwhile, the work of the mass Purge had been done. The country was crushed.

# ON THE CULTURAL FRONT

*Mandelshtam always said that they always knew what they were doing: the aim was to destroy not only people, but the intellect itself.*

Nadezhda Mandelshtam

The Russian intelligentsia had for over a century been the traditional repository of the ideas of resistance to despotism and, above all, to thought control. It was natural that the Purge struck at it with particular force. The Communists not only took seriously the whole principle of right and wrong ideas, and the necessity of crushing the latter, but also increasingly developed theories of form and method within the arts and sciences, so that someone otherwise an orthodox Party man in every way could yet hold opinions in biology or dramatic production which would lead directly to his fall.

In Soviet conditions, the academic world overlapped that of government to a larger degree than was then common elsewhere. The economists had been involved in the State Planning Commission, and had mostly been purged in the early 1930s. But in other spheres, too, such as foreign affairs and culture, there was a considerable overlap. We hear of a "professor" in the Foreign Affairs Commissariat appealing to Molotov to intercede for his father, arrested through what he took to be a misunderstanding. Molotov minuted, "To Yezhov: Can it be that this professor is still in the People's Commissariat of Foreign Affairs and not in the NKVD?" Whereupon the writer of the letter was unlawfully arrested.[1]

During March, April, and May 1937, articles appeared attacking deviation in history and economics, and among the "cadres" of literature. A special article by Molotov sharpened the tone of the campaign.[2]

Historians were particularly vulnerable. The whole school of Party historians which had followed Pokrovsky were arrested. They were often labeled terrorists. In fact, it is extraordinary how many of the leading terrorist bands were headed by historians. Sokolnikov mentioned in the most natural way at his trial that "arrests had begun among the historians."[3] Prigozhin, one of the leading terrorist executives of the group then before the court, was a historian. So were Karev, Zeidel, Anishev, Vanag, Zaks-Gladnev, Piontkovsky, and Friedland, named at the 1936 and 1937 Trials as active terrorists. Friedland is mentioned by Radek as leading a terror group actually "consisting of historians": this "we, among ourselves, called the 'historical or hysterical' group."[4] Professors were a convenient class of suspect because they were in a position to recruit plausible terrorists in the persons of students—also a much-arrested class. It was said in evidence at the 1937 Trial, as a normal thing, that the terrorist organization in Siberia sought its cadres "chiefly among the young people in the universities."[5]

Friedland and the others were Party historians and automatically involved in controversy. But the non-Party academic world was also in a difficult position. While the man in the street could cease to talk a great deal, the professors were bound to continue giving lectures before public audiences which inevitably contained informers on the alert for anything which could possibly be interpreted as "hostile." (Colleagues, too, might be serving the police. A successful and erudite professor in Dniepropetrovsk, who had matters in his past which the NKVD used against him, is described as a most efficient agent provocateur.)[6]

A professor of ancient history, Konstantin Shteppa, first lost favor as a result of describing Joan of Arc as high-strung. Joan had been treated in a hostile fashion or ignored until the mid-1930s, but with the coming of the Popular Front in France she had been referred to as a heroine of a national resistance movement, so that the professor's remarks deviated from the Party line. After considerable trouble about this, he was again censured for a reference to the legend of Midas in an unfortunate context. Then, speaking of ancient and Christian demonology, he happened to remark that country people are always backward. Unfortunately, Trotsky, like many others, had expressed the same thought. Finally, in dealing with the Donatist movement in North Africa, at the time of the Roman Empire, he had shown that it was in part a national as well as a peasant rebellion, thus becoming a bourgeois nationalist. At this time, in 1937, his friends and colleagues were being arrested on a large scale.

> I was naturally sorry for my friends, but I was not only sorry for them. I was also afraid of them. After all, they could say things about conversations we had had, in which we had not always expressed the orthodox view. There had been nothing criminal in these conversations; they had contained no attacks on the Soviet power. But the trivial criticisms and grumbles and expressions of resentment and disappointment which occurred in every conversation forced every Soviet citizen to feel guilty.[7]

Then came the suicide of Lyubchenko and his wife, N. Krupenik. Unfortunately, the wife had been a university lecturer, and the whole staff of Kiev University naturally became high-grade suspects. A vast network of bourgeois nationalists in the universities and cultural agencies came to light. Nevertheless, the professor was not arrested until March 1938. After a severe interrogation for fifty days, by a series of thirteen "magistrates," he was charged with complicity in an attempt to assassinate Kossior. The fall of Kossior led to the withdrawal of this charge in his and many other cases, and for it was substituted espionage for Japan. This was based on the following facts: the professor had for some time been head of the "Byzantological" Committee of the Ukrainian Academy of Sciences. The term then came to be regarded as reactionary and was replaced by "Near East." This connection with the "East" was regarded as adequate for at least some suspicion of sympathy with, and espionage for, a country a good deal farther east. It was shown that the professor had lectured on Alexander the Great and Hannibal to senior Red Army officers. This had given him contact with the Army and therefore the opportunity to carry out espionage. It was then proved that he had actually met foreigners in the person of Professor Hrozny, the great specialist in Hittite history, who had "recruited" him through another Byzantologist who had lectured in the Soviet Far East, thus getting very near Japan. Finally, an indirect contact was found with a professor in Odessa who had actually met the Japanese Consul there. The reports passed through this espionage link to Tokyo consisted of remarks about the "political morale" of the Army, and here a genuine fact was established in that the accused had once told a colleague that some senior officers had confused Napoleon III with Napoleon I, and Alexander the Great with Caesar.[8]

When things became easier, after Yezhov's fall, some of the surviving academics withdrew their confessions, the charges began to be toned down, and eventually, in the early autumn of 1939, the professor was released. He was lucky. Others were still going, from V. G. Sorin, of the Institute of Red Professors, repressed as an enemy of the people in 1939, who died in prison or camp in 1944,[9] down to non-Party lecturers. (Sorin is said to have been willing to supply Stalin with suitable texts, but "he drew the line at *inventing* texts and *falsifying* quotations.")[10] At the February–March 1937 plenum, Zhdanov had complained that of the 183 members of the Institute of Red Professors, 32 had been arrested between 1933 and 1936, and 53 more had more recently been found to be enemies of the people.[11]

At a Party meeting in a university, where a member was denounced with the approval of the chair, it sometimes happened that a supporter would rise and ask for proof of the charges against his colleague. The makers of such demands were invariably denounced for counter-revolutionary attitudes, always silenced, and often arrested. At a meeting of the Kiev Academy of Sciences, for example, someone denounced Professor Kopershinsky. Another Communist scientist, Kaminsky (not the Minister of Health), remarked, "Where class instinct speaks, proof is unnecessary." He, too, was later arrested. The Secretary of the Academy was publicly accused in the local press of having demanded proof about a similar denunciation.[12] He was one of the thirteen successive Secretaries of the Academy between 1921 and 1938, all of whom were arrested. (Of the seven Principals of Kiev University in the same period, six were arrested and one died a natural death.)[13]

In the Byelorussian Academy of Sciences, too, a "center for the espionage work of enemies of the people" was discovered, including most of those in leading positions—thirty-seven names are listed for eight institutes.[14]

The Academy of Sciences covers a wide range of disciplines. But we should note that the purge was violent not only among Byzantologists and so on, whom a technologically minded State can perhaps do without at a pinch, but also among scientists proper. The physicist Weissberg describes the situation at the Kharkov Physics Institute:

'Listen,' I said. 'Our Institute is one of the most important of its kind in Europe. In fact there is probably no other institute with so many different and well-equipped laboratories. The Soviet Government has spared no expense. Our leading scientists were partly trained abroad. They were constantly being sent to leading physicists all over the world at Government expense to supplement their knowledge and experience. Our Institute had eight departments each headed by a capable man. And what's the situation now? The head of the laboratory for crystallography, Obremov, is under arrest, and so is the head of the low-temperature laboratory, Shubnikov. The head of the second low-temperature laboratory, Ruhemann, has been deported. The head of the laboratory for atom-splitting, Leipunsky, is under arrest, and so are the head of the Röntgen department, Gorsky, the head of the department for theoretical physics, Landau, and the head of the experimental low-temperature station, myself. As far as I know, Slutski, the head of the ultra-short-wave department, is the only one still at work.

'Amongst those arrested is the founder of the Institute, Professor Obremov—its first director; Professor Leipunsky, member of the Academy of Sciences and later again director of the Institute; Professor Lev Davidovich Landau, the leading theoretical physicist in the Soviet Union.* Landau had already been forced out of the Institute by the G.P.U., and he went to Moscow to work with Professor Kapitza. I supervised the building of our low-temperature experimental station, but before it could be put into operation I was arrested. My successor was Komarov. He has also been arrested. Who is to carry on?

'. . . You need five years to train an engineer, and even then the Government had a very great deal of trouble before it could get suitable engineers for its new factories. But a capable physicist needs from ten to fifteen years' training.'[15]

Matvei Bronshtein, a brilliant young physicist, was married to the writer Lydia Chukovskaya. He was arrested, and shot on 18 February 1938. She then wrote the story "Sofia Petrovna" (which only appeared in Russia in 1988, in the Leningrad magazine *Neva*). She had actually read it to Anna Akhmatova and eight others, who agreed that it could not be kept in the flat of the "wife of an enemy of the people." And the NKVD, in fact, soon heard rumors and searched her place. A friend took it, but died in the siege of Leningrad. Before dying, however, he dragged himself to his sister's to give her the manuscript to keep. After the war, the sister kept it, by arrangement with Chukovskaya, until she died in 1956. Then, after the dead woman's belongings were dispersed, Chukovskaya finally found it in the bottom of a dust-covered wastepaper basket. Few such documents (for the story is factual) survive. It might have been published in Khrushchev's time, but she refused to change a word.[16]

The purge also extended into the more technical sciences. For example, Academician Berg writes:

Thereafter there came difficult times: 1937, the loss of one's close friends. Soon I too was arrested on a basis of a ridiculous and stupid denunciation. I spent precisely 900 days in prison. I was let out shortly before the war. During these years radiotechnology suffered an enormous loss. Institutes and laboratories were closed down and people disappeared.[17]

Sergei Korolev, the unique genius behind the Soviet early space program, was sent to Kolyma, but eventually brought to the NKVD prison aviation group KOSOS near the Yauza River. He had been told that "our country doesn't need your fireworks. Or maybe you're making rockets for an attempt on the life of our leader?" He was contemptuous of the regime, and fully expected to be shot.[18]

---

*Landau, long one of Russia's foremost scientists, has described how he nearly died in prison as a "German spy." His colleague Peter Kapitsa, with extraordinary bravery, finally persuaded Stalin of his value (*Komsomolskaya pravda*, 8 July 1965).

The aircraft designer A. N. Tupolev was arrested on 21 October 1937. He was kept standing "for many hours on end. Since I am a heavy man it was rather tough." [19] But on the advice of Muklevich, who was one of his cell mates, he confessed before worse befell him. [20] (His wife was also arrested.) [21]

The charge was of having sold plans to the Germans for use on the Messerschmidt 109. [22] (The aviator Levanevsky had a couple of years earlier denounced him to Stalin as a wrecker.) In November 1938, Tupolev withdrew some of his testimony, and in the following years asserted his innocence in several appeals. He finally only got a ten-year sentence. He was later (foreign policy having changed) accused of being a French spy, but was in fact released in 1941. He had meanwhile worked, with other scientists, in one of the NKVD's prisoner research units, of the type described in *The First Circle*. [23]

Another aircraft designer, Chaikovsky, was also arrested. His wife, arrested too, was one day given her clothes, taken to a manicurist and hairdresser, and told she was to meet her husband, but must not let him know that she, too, was in jail. He was reassured, and told her that he could now do the technical work they were giving him in the Lubyanka with an easy mind. However, he seems to have been shot later, [24] as were most of the leading figures in the aircraft industry. [25]

Generally speaking, the sciences in some way connected with policy or ideology fared worst. Sciences impinging on agriculture fared badly on both counts. The Meteorological Office was violently purged as early as 1933, for failing to predict weather harmful to the crops. [26] In part on similar grounds, astronomers connected with sunspot research fared badly. The Solar Service had in fact been set up in 1931 to help predict long-range weather patterns, with the usual imperfect results, though there were also charges of un-Marxist theories of sunspot development. [27] But astronomy in general suffered a devastating purge, conducted by the Stalinist pseudo-astronomer Ter-Oganezov. This started in early 1936, and soon the press was attacking the great Pul'kovo Observatory, which had in its earlier days been known as "the astronomical capital of the world." The distinguished astronomer B. V. Numerov, arrested in November, admitted after severe beatings that he had organized a counter-revolutionary astronomers' group for espionage, terror, and wrecking. It had "drawn a significant number of scientific workers into its orbit."

In all, about twenty-seven astronomers, mostly leading figures, disappeared between 1936 and 1938. Work at Pul'kovo almost ceased, and the observatories at Tashkent and elsewhere also suffered severely. Russian astronomy, which had led the world, was devastated. [28] It is curious to recall that Stalin's own first job was at an observatory.

Biology was, of course, a particularly sensitive field. With the rise of Lysenko in the early 1930s, a fierce "ideological" struggle commenced. Already in 1932, G. A. Levitsky and N. P. Avdoulov, cytologists, were arrested, but were later released. Other biologists were arrested about the same time.

In December 1936, the more prominent Professor I. J. Agol was arrested on charges of Trotskyism and was executed. Professor S. G. Levit, Head of the Medico-Genetic Institute, was expelled from the Party on the grounds that his biological views were pro-Nazi. (The People's Commissar for Health, G. M. Kaminsky, was also criticized for defending him.)[29] Levit was arrested in about May 1937 and died in prison. A number of other prominent biologists, such as Levitsky, Karpechenko, and Govorov, also perished, as did the celebrated N. M. Tulaikov, Director of the Cereals Institute, who was arrested in 1937 and died in 1938 in one of the White Sea labor camps. The botanist A. Yanata was shot, on 8 June 1938, for having proposed chemicals to destroy weeds, contrary to the urging of Lysenkoites.[30] Max Levin, former head of the 1919 Bavarian Soviet Republic, seems also to have perished in his biological rather than his political capacity.[31]

In this field, as in the political, the lesser figures were arrested first, and the net thus closed round their superiors. The biggest game was Academician N. I. Vavilov, the great geneticist, Lenin's favorite. He had given up his position as head of the Lenin All-Union Academy of Agricultural Sciences in 1935 to A. I. Muralov, until then Deputy Commissar for Agriculture. Muralov was arrested on 4 July 1937 and succeeded by Professor G. K. Meister. Meister was, in turn, arrested at the beginning of 1938, and Lysenko took the job after a squalid and deadly intrigue.

Vavilov himself was in trouble early in 1940 for some argument about the right agricultural policy to pursue in the parts annexed from Finland. An open quarrel with Lysenko followed. In August, he was touring the Ukraine. While in Cernauti, he was suddenly recalled to Moscow, and arrested on 6 August. The files on his case (to which leading biologists were given access after the fall of Lysenko in 1964) contain a letter from Beria to Molotov as Politburo member in charge of science, requesting permission for this arrest. Vavilov was under interrogation for eleven months and was questioned over a hundred times. He was tried on 9 July 1941 by the Military Collegium on charges of Rightist conspiracy, espionage for England, and other matters. He was sentenced to death.

The veteran biologist D. N. Pryanishnikov, together with Vavilov's physicist brother, had interviews with Beria and Molotov to try to have him released, but without success. Pryanishnikov also seems to have intervened through Beria's wife to try to get better prison conditions for his old colleague, and he even had the extraordinary temerity to nominate Vavilov for a Stalin Prize in 1941.

Vavilov was now held in Saratov prison. He introduced himself to his cell mates: "You see before you, talking of the past, Academician Vavilov, but now, according to the opinion of the investigators, nothing but dung." Held in the condemned cell, a windowless underground block, without any exercise, for nearly a year, he was almost saved by his election in 1942 as a Fellow of the Royal Society in London, and his sentence was commuted to twenty years. But it was too late. Dystrophy had gone too far; he was a "goner" and died on 26 January 1943. His wife and son had been evacuated from Leningrad to Saratov in 1942 and lived all this time within a few miles of the prison where he was dying. But they were informed that he was in Moscow and did not learn of his presence.[32]

The triumph of Lysenkoism was the most extraordinary of all the indications of the intellectual degeneracy of the Party mind which had followed on Stalin's replacement of the intellectual section of the apparatus by his own creatures, such as Mitin and Mekhlis, in the early 1930s. The villain of the piece from this point of view was the charlatan I. I. Prezent, who established the orthodoxy of the Lysenko line by a complex and superficially sophisticated manipulation of the Marxist phraseology. To do justice to Zhdanov, he at least was never wholly taken in by Lysenko, and the final destruction of Soviet biology was only accomplished in 1948, as part and parcel of his own political defeat and death. But meanwhile, impressive verbalization, backed by vicious intrigue, secured Lysenko's position of supremacy even if not yet of monopoly.

Another field in which a wholly erroneous doctrine was declared orthodox was linguistics. By the late 1920s, the teachings of N. Marr, who held that all language derives from the four sounds *rosh, sal, ber,* and *yon,* became accepted as the Marxist line. It is a view otherwise universally dismissed. As a result, old professors first were exiled, later had their books withdrawn, and in 1937 and 1938 were usually arrested. A major case was that of Professor E. D. Polivanov, a friend of Mayakovsky, arrested in 1937 and shot on 25 January 1938.[33] (Stalin abandoned Marrism in 1950, censuring its adherents for having bullied the anti-Marrites.)

This was followed by the "Dictionary Affair," about which little is known except that the French writer Romain Rolland managed to get the sentences commuted to imprisonment.[34]

But the heaviest toll of all seems to have been among the writers. They were threatened from two directions. A theory of correct aesthetic *method* was imposed on them, and at the same time the *content* of their works was subject to intense scrutiny. It emerged in the 1950s that of the 700 writers who met at the First Congress of the Union of Soviet Writers in 1934, only 50 survived to see the second in 1954.[35] A recent estimate is that 90 percent of the membership was repressed.[36] After the XXth Party Congress in 1956, it was confidentially admitted that "there were more than 600 writers who were guilty of no crime, and whom the Union [of Writers] obediently left to their fate in the prisons and camps." Aleksandr Solzhenitsyn, telling of this, adds that in reality "the list is still longer. . . ."[37] And the Soviet researcher Eduard Beltov has lately revealed that he has long collected a list of a number of writers verified as dead in the repressions— though this also includes the post-1938 purges. He has the names of "nearly 1,300." But he adds that this is incomplete, that Vasil Bykov, in his capacity as a deputy in the Byelorussian Supreme Soviet, recently applied to that body's Presidium for information on several dozen Byelorussian writers who disappeared at this time, and that the local "law enforcement authorities" had "no information" about eighteen of those names.[38] In the country as a whole, about 150 littérateurs, including some 75 members of the Union of Soviet Writers, could not be traced at all. In all, the organ of the Union now tells us, some 2,000 literary figures were repressed, of whom about 1,500 met their deaths in prison or camp.[39]

In connection with the Zinoviev Trial in August 1936, a series of hysterical articles in *Literaturnaya gazeta* attacked Trotskyite writers. They had infiltrated the Writers' Union apparatus. Numbers of well-known authors were denounced, including I. I. Kataev (who had allegedly received Trotskyite "directives" in 1928, sent money to Trotskyites then in internal exile, and "retained his ties with Trotsky"), Tarasov-Rodionov (who also "for years had ties with class enemies"), and Galina Serebryakova, married in turn to Sokolnikov and Serebryakov; she survived years in camp, but the others did not. At the same time, the periodical attacked scores of other "enemy" writers throughout the Soviet Union.[40]

The spring of 1937, in part in connection with Yagoda's fall, saw the end of the former Russian Association of Proletarian Writers (RAPP), which had bullied the writing community from an extreme Marxist position in the early 1930s before being repudiated by Stalin in 1932 in favor of Socialist Realism. L. L. Averbakh, its leading figure, was a relative of Yagoda by marriage and was denounced as a Trotskyite and arrested in mid-April,[41] together with the playwright V. Kirshon[42] (a delegate to the XVIIth Party Congress), who was eventually shot in the political–military massacre at the end of July 1938. Dmitry Mirsky, a prince who had fought in the White Army, had been converted to Communism while in exile in England, and had returned to the USSR, was now referred to by *Literaturnaya gazeta* as "that filthy Wrangelist and White Guard officer."[43] The leading Polish Communist poet, Bruno Jasienski, was also denounced in connection with the RAPPists. At his first interrogation in the Lefortovo, the examiners seized him by his shoulders and stamped on his feet.[44] He was, of course, accused as a Polish spy—in connection with the case of T. F. Dombal (shot on 4 December 1938). He was given a fifteen-year sentence as such, but also as a French spy. A friend met him in the Vtoraya Rechka camp near Vladivostok, now barely recognizable from sickness, hunger, and exhaustion, but denied entry to the hospital, though he was apparently admitted before he died in 1939.[45]

There were certain definite grudges to be paid off. Isaak Babel, Russia's finest short-story writer, had served in Budenny's Cavalry Army in the Civil War and the Polish Campaign, and in 1924 published his extraordinary collection of Civil War stories, *Konarmiia*. Budenny had protested vigorously as each vignette forming the book came out. He regarded the ruthlessly clear-eyed stories as a slander, preferring the hack heroics of the ordinary correspondents. Gorky, recognizing Babel's very different talent, had protected him.

Babel wrote of the Revolution, "It's eaten with gunpowder and the very best blood is poured over it." It was Babel who at the Writers' Congress of 1934 had spoken of the "heroism of silence," a phrase and an activity to be condemned bitterly as a sign of alienation from the regime. Babel knew Yezhov's wife. Although he knew it was unwise, he sometimes went to see her to "find a key to the puzzle." He gathered that whatever Yezhov's role, it was not at the bottom of it.[46] He ceased to be published in 1937 and at the end of May 1939 was arrested in his dacha at the writers' settlement at Peredelkino. He is said to have resisted arrest and was shot on 27 January 1940, a week before Meyerhold, whose case was connected with his.[47]

Babel, in addition to offending a minor figure like Budenny and bringing into disrepute the First Cavalry Army, from which Stalin was now drawing an inadequate substitute for a High Command, is said to have made a rash joke about the General Secretary. But his offense was small compared with that of Boris Pilnyak, another talent to have arisen from the Revolution. His *Naked Year,* about a provincial town in 1919, is a most extraordinary representation, in which the struggle for bare existence brings out the excess, the eccentricity, of the range of Russian character.

As early as the 1920s, Pilnyak had become involved in one of the most obscure and doubtful crimes attributed to Stalin. In the spring of 1924, Frunze was appointed Deputy Commissar for War—and in practice took over control of the Army, with little resistance from Trotsky, before Trotsky's actual removal in 1925. He seems to have sympathized mainly with the Zinoviev–Kamenev group. In the late summer of 1925, he fell ill, and died on 31 October of that year. The rumor in Moscow was that he had been ordered by the Central Committee—that is, in effect, by Stalin—to undergo an operation which in fact killed him. If Frunze had died in 1936 or 1937, the existence of such a rumor would have been perfectly natural. The significant thing is that it circulated at so early a date—at a time, that is, when Stalin had not given any precedents.

Later Soviet books on Frunze have been notably touchy on the point. One biography[48] elaborates at some length about doctors who said that an operation was really necessary, and who tended him through his last illness. This is a book by one of those military historians who have elsewhere been so frankly hostile to Stalin's acts against the generals. Unless (as is, of course, quite possible) other interventions took place on its publication, one tends to think that exculpation from such a source shows that Stalin is really believed not guilty by some of those who would be anxious to know.

The most extraordinary thing is that the rumor was given public circulation. On its basis, Pilnyak, hitherto an almost entirely nonpolitical writer (who had said that he knew nothing of politics and not being a Communist could not write like one), produced his *Tale of the Unextinguished Moon,* subtitled *Murder of the Army Commander.* The hero, Gavrilov, is described as a well-known Red Army leader who returns to Moscow on orders and reads in the papers that he has come back for an operation. He has had stomach ulcers, but is now fully recovered. He goes to see a man described as the most important of the "three who lead" the Party, who orders him to have the operation. The doctors examine him, and report that an operation is necessary, but afterwards in private conversation say that it is not. The operation is performed, and he dies of an overdose of chloroform. The story has a very sinister and gloomy tone. It was about to be printed in *Novyy mir,* but the issue was confiscated and the editors admitted in the following number that accepting it had been a mistake, and printed letters describing it as "a malicious slander of our Party." In the circumstances then prevailing, there were many copies circulating, and the story was printed in 1927 in Sofia.

It is clear, indeed, that no one with any political sense would have written a story like *The Tale of the Unextinguished Moon,* and it seems likely that Pilnyak was put up to it by some friend more deeply involved in the struggles of the time. But no more was said about the matter for the moment.

In 1929, Pilnyak was President of the All-Russian Union of Writers, a genuine association then resisting the maneuvers of RAPP to enforce ideological and bureaucratic control of the writers. (Mayakovsky's suicide in 1930 is now attributed, in part, to persecution by officials of RAPP.)[49] In the face of opposition from all the best writers, and to a large degree from Maxim Gorky too, the RAPPists failed in their task, and, as we saw, later lost favor and were themselves purged. But this did not save the non-RAPP writers.

Pilnyak's last effective work, *Mahogany,* served as a pretext for action against him. It was published in Germany as a preliminary to its coming out in Russia, then a common practice for copyright reasons. But it was then denounced as anti-Soviet and its publication abroad alleged to be a White Guard provocation. Pilnyak was now in great trouble and ready to submit to any ruling. Zamyatin, chairman of the Leningrad branch of the Writers' Union, was also under attack; his *We* (on which Orwell was to draw for *1984*) had been published abroad in much the same circumstances as Pilnyak's *Mahogany*. He boldly demanded to be allowed to leave the country, refused to retract, and exposed the whole mechanism which literary persecution was already setting in motion, mild though its actions were compared with later developments. He said that the Moscow branch had passed its resolution "without hearing any defense: first there was a condemnation and only then an investigation. I imagine that no court in the world has ever heard of such a procedure." He added that he could not belong to an organization that behaved like this and resigned his membership in the Union. Finally, Maxim Gorky interceded for both Pilnyak and Zamyatin in *Izvestiya:*

> . . . We have got into the stupid habit of raising people up into high positions only to cast them down into the mud and the dust. I need not quote examples of this absurd and cruel treatment of people, because such examples are known to everybody. I am reminded of the way in which petty thieves were lynched in 1917–18. These dramas were generally the work of *obyvateli* [obtuse philistines] and one is reminded of them every time one sees with what delight people throw themselves on to a man who has made a mistake, in order to take his place.[50]

Pilnyak was "allowed" to settle down to write pro-Soviet literature, while Zamyatin's boldness was rewarded by permission to leave the country. Zamyatin was one of the few trained Marxists among Soviet writers, and on this account he had rejected Bolshevism, which was welcomed in a vague and romantic fashion by Futurists like Mayakovsky—at a time, indeed, when the Futurists of Italy were showing a similar romanticism toward the other new and dynamic movement, Fascism.

Pilnyak worked at a conformist novel, *The Volga Flows into the Caspian Sea.* Yezhov personally oversaw the production, listing fifty-odd passages for amendment. Pilnyak became deeply depressed, and told Victor Serge, "There isn't a single thinking adult in this country who hasn't thought that he might get shot."[51] (But he had the courage to intervene when Serge was arrested in 1933.) In May 1937, he was attacked flatly for "counter-revolutionary writing,"[52] and was arrested on 28 October 1937.[53] It has now been stated in Moscow that he was shot in April 1938 (and not at the later date given in reference books for the past twenty years).[54] The charge, or one of the charges, was of being a Japanese spy—he had actually visited Japan.[55] His wife, the actress Kira Andronikova, mother of his three-year-old son, Boris, was sentenced to eight years.[56]

Other prose writers of mark who perished include Pantaleimon Romanov, author of *Three Pairs of Silk Stockings;* Artyom Vesyoly; and S. Tretyakov, author of *Roar China.* Mikhail Koltsov, of *Pravda,* under suspicion as an agent of Lord Beaverbrook,[57] was arrested on 12 December 1938. Sentenced by Ulrikh on 1 February 1940 to ten years without the right of correspondence,[58] he was shot at once. Others who were arrested but survived include Yuri Olesha and Ostap

Vyshnia. Vyshnia, accused of planning to assassinate Postyshev and others, was released in 1943, and had to write deriding those abroad who had protested at his supposed liquidation.

Poetry in the USSR was already a dangerous trade. Nikolai Gumilev, Anna Akhmatova's former husband, had been shot as a counter-revolutionary, on Agranov's orders, in August 1921, the month which also saw the death of Alexander Blok, long past his brief enthusiasm for the Red Guard, from anemia due to malnutrition. Yesenin had committed suicide in 1925, and Mayakovsky in 1930.

And now many of the best surviving poets in Russia were destroyed.

The poet Vladimir Smirenski (Andrei Skorbny) had been given ten years as early as 1931, for participation in a group which had discussed politics almost entirely in relation to art.[59] We do not know the charges against most of the poets who now went to their deaths. It seems that they were seldom accused of poetic crimes as such, though a case is reported of a young poetess arrested for writing a "hymn to freedom" which was construed as "preparation for terrorism," and sentenced to eight years in the Karaganda camps.[60] There is no information about the eventual charges against such men as Nikolai Klyuev, Yesenin's disciple, whose best poem, his "Lament" for his friend and teacher, sighs, "If I could only touch peace." He had already in the 1920s spent three days in the Leningrad OGPU's steam room,[61] and been released. He was again arrested in 1933 for "kulak agitation" and counter-revolutionary verses and was exiled to Arctic Narym. Gorky managed to have him moved to the far more tolerable Tomsk, but he was eventually rearrested and is reported dying in a prison train and being buried at some Siberian halt.[62]

The poet Pavel Vasiliev is said to have defended Bukharin as "a man of the highest nobility and the conscience of peasant Russia" at the time of his denunciation at the Pyatakov Trial, and to have damned the writers then signing the routine attacks on him as "pornographic scrawls on the margins of Russian literature."[63] On 7 February 1937 he left his wife, Elena, to go to a barbershop for a shave, accompanied by his host's son.

> Some minutes later the boy returned.
> "Lena, they've arrested Pavel. . . ."
> . . . In all the prisons they answered alike, to the question: "Is there a Vasiliev amongst those arrested?"
> "No, Vasiliev, Pavel Nikolaevich, is not listed."
> Months went by. Some woman instructed her:
> "Prepare a parcel. He'll be in the place where they accept it."
> It was true—the parcel was accepted in one of the prisons. Moreover they said that she could come again on 16 July.
> On 16 July the person on duty said: "He's been transferred to another place."
> And twenty years later, petitioning for her husband's posthumous rehabilitation, Elena Aleksandrovna discovered that it was precisely on 16 July that Pavel Vasiliev ceased to be.[64]

The leading Georgian poet, Yashvili, killed himself with a shotgun on 22 July 1937[65] as the result of the arrest of other Georgian literary figures, in particular his friend and equal the poet Titsian Tabidze.[66] In Boris Pasternak's *Letters to Georgian Friends,* we read of the Russian poet's brave and devoted attempts to help and console Tabidze's family after his disappearance, until his wife was finally informed of his execution (on 16 December 1937) when he was rehabilitated seventeen years later.

Many Armenian writers were shot. The poet Gurgen Maari, who survived, tells how "I was arrested at night on 9 August 1936. I was not surprised. A month previously the First Secretary of the C.C. of the Armenian Communist Party, Agasi Khandzhyan, had tragically perished. The atmosphere in the House of Writers was very oppressive."[67]

He was in solitary confinement for many months without even being allowed out for exercise. It was not until two years after his arrest that he was "tried":

> The Military Collegium of the Supreme Court of the Soviet Union is in session. I confess to terrorist acts, to the wish to separate Armenia from the Soviet Union and unite her to the imperialist camp. I intended to kill Beria. . . .
>
> The court was a closed one, the trial lasted three minutes. . . . I was condemned to ten years' deprivation of liberty. Once again Sianos [a jailer, formerly in the same orphange as Maari] accompanies me. This time to the cell for sentenced prisoners.
>
> "How many did you get?" he asked in a whisper.
>
> "Ten years."
>
> "Thank God. You've got off lightly."
>
> "Ten years," I repeat.
>
> "For the third night running, when they've taken people out, they've shot them," he whispers. . . .

The forty people in his cell included two architects, three writers, four engineers, and one People's Commissar; all the rest were Government employees and Party workers. The opinion of the pessimists was that their prison sentences were just for the sake of form and that they would be shot in any case. However, "in the autumn of 1938 we were crammed into lorries one night and—covered with tarpaulin like forbidden goods—were taken to the station. It was empty at the station, there was not a living soul—only troops."

For six months, the prisoners lived in the Vologda city jail. Then they were taken to Krasnoyarsk, where "a large army of prisoners composed of representatives of many of the peoples of the Soviet Union swarmed. Inhabitants of Central Asia stood out particularly in their bright national costumes."

A medical examination determined who was to be sent on to Norilsk in the Arctic. It was then, for the second time in three years, that Maari managed to see himself in a mirror. He could hardly recognize himself. At the Siblag ("Siberian" Prison Camp) in Norilsk, he made friends with Egert, once a famous film actor. He was marched with 200 others to another camp; most of the 200 died later. Maari himself was there until 1947. He briefly describes two camp commandants: one hated "intelligent swine" and sent them to do the heaviest work; the other, who liked books, eased his lot a good deal.

Released in 1947, Maari was not permitted to publish anything under his own name as his civic rights had not been restored, and in 1948 he was rearrested. This time, the cell was full of troops returning from German captivity. In 1948 and 1949, he was incarcerated in nine prisons in nine towns. He and his fellows were then classed as "exiles for life."

The Ukrainian creative intelligentsia, as we have seen, had been struck down on a vast scale every year since 1930.[68] The Ukrainian poets perished in their majority for "nationalist" reasons: sixteen, starting with Vlyzko in 1934, are named as executed or dying in camps between then and 1942—almost all at Solovetsk, though a few were in Kolyma. A group of neo-classicist poets, Mykola Zerov, Pavlo Fylypovych, and others, was tried in Kiev in January 1936 for nationalism, terrorism, and espionage. One temporary survivor, the poet Mykhalo Dray-Khamara, got a five-year Special Board sentence on 28 March 1936, but seems to have died in camp in 1938 or 1939.[69]

There seems to have beeen another Ukrainian writers' case in October 1937. At any rate, A. S. Mikhailyuk is given as dying on 23 October and M. V. Semenko on 24 October 1937—a case perhaps associated with that of Ukrainian Politburo member V. I. Porayko, later to be denounced as a prominent fascist, shot on 25 October. Two more Ukrainian writers of note, M. G. Yoganson and G. O. Kovalenko, perished on 27 and 28 October 1937, respectively; and two more, Slisarenko and P. P. Fylypovich, on 3 November. Yet another concentration of Ukrainians is to be found on 12 to 14 January 1938, with the writer N. Filyansky and the old revolutionaries S. D. Visochenko and A. K. Serbichenko.

And so it was in all the non-Russian Republics. Their men of literature were almost automatically regarded as bourgeois nationalists, since, of course, they had been working in the national traditions of their own languages. In Byelorussia (see p. 224) most of the leading writers were shot. In Kazakhstan, the death dates of almost all the main figures are given as 1937 to 1939.[70]

The mean viciousness of such campaigns can be seen in speech after speech and periodical after periodical. It is at random that we quote from an attack in *Revolyutsiya i natsional' nosti*[71] on a Russian–Upper Mari dictionary by the alleged "bourgeois nationalist SR" Epin, who had omitted words like *dekulakization, opportunism, kolkhoznik,* and the like, though "in order to mask his wrecking policies" included a few revolutionary words in a section at the end on "new terms." He had also omitted the names of Marx, Lenin, Stalin, Molotov, and Voroshilov from his dictionary. This was all called "counter-revolutionary."

The Leningrad poet Nikolai Zabolotsky, who exalted a starling's song against "the tambourines and kettledrums of history," was arrested on 19 March 1938 "on a faked political accusation."[72] A "counter-revolutionary writers' organization" had been "uncovered" in Leningrad (though its alleged leading members, Nikolai Tikhonov and Konstantine Fedin in Moscow, were never arrested). Those implicated in what was also called the *"Pereval* Case," after the magazine in which they had collaborated, included the poets Benedikt Livshits and Boris Kornilov, who were shot in the autumn of 1938; Elena Tager, a short-story writer, who spent ten years in labor camp; and at least five others (all of whom were shot or died in camp). Connections were also made with poets elsewheree in the USSR, like the Georgian Tabidze and D. I. Kharms.

Zabolotsky was interrogated for four days without a break, and tortured. (One of the charges was that a poem of his was a satire on collectivization.) On his return to his cell, he tried to barricade himself in and fought the warders who came for him. He was then beaten even more severely and taken in a state of collapse to the prison psychiatric hospital, where he was held for two weeks, first in a violent, then in a quiet ward. On recovery, he was literally pushed into a common cell designed for twelve or fifteen, which now held seventy or eighty, and sometimes a hundred prisoners. "People could lie down only on their side, jammed tight against each other, and even then not all at once, but in two shifts." (Such arrangements had been "worked out by generations of prisoners . . . who had gradually passed on their acquired skills to newcomers.") At night, the cell was pervaded by "dumb terror" at the screams as "the hundreds of sergeants, lieutenants, and captains of State Security, together with their assistants got down to their routine tasks" in the main Liteyni prison. Meanwhile, several Soviet writers are reported as coming to Zabolotsky's defense, and, together with his failure to confess, this seems to have led to the removal of his name from the list of major plotters. He was later transferred to a two-man cell in the Kresty, now inhabited by ten. In September or early October, he was sentenced by the Special Board to eight years. On 8 November, he was sent to Sverdlovsk, and on 5 December started a sixty-day train journey in a forty-man railway wagon, suffering the usual horrors, and ended up at Komsomolsk-on-the-Amur, at hard labor in the notorious Bamlag. For part of the time, he is reported employed in the camp draftsman's office, which may have saved his life. He was released in 1944 and returned from exile in 1946; his sentence was annulled in 1951. However, his health had been undermined, and he was an invalid until his death seven years later.[73]

The beautiful poet Marina Tsvetaeva had gone abroad soon after the Revolution to join her husband, the literary critic Sergei Efron, who had fought in the White Army. She had written of the "deadly days of October." In the 1930s, her husband was recruited by Soviet agents and joined a Soviet-supported movement for the return of émigrés to Russia. He was one of the first to be allowed back by the Soviet authorities, and he disappeared without trace soon after his arrival. Their daughter went from Paris to seek him and also disappeared. (He had been executed, while the girl was to spend sixteen years in prison camps.)[74] In 1939, Marina Tsvetaeva followed them. On 31 August 1941, worn out by long suffering, she committed suicide in the provincial town of Yelabug.[75]

Her scintillating poetry became widely known and circulated in manuscript. But in spite of its influence and popularity in literary circles, it was not to be published until 1957. Much of it had to wait longer, in particular a cycle of romantic lyrics connected with the tragedy of the White Army:

> Where are the swans?
> The swans have left.
> Where are the ravens?
> The ravens have stayed.

Even in 1957, the publication of a short selection of her most harmless verses was soon called "a gross political error."[76]

Another talent of the first rank, Osip Mandelshtam, was a sick man, with a nervous complaint. In 1934, he was called in to the NKVD on an order signed by Yagoda himself, interrogated the whole night, and then sent to prison. He had written an epigram on Stalin. Pasternak is reported to have pleaded for him with Bukharin, a sign of Pasternak's naïveté. (It seems to have been now that Stalin rang up Pasternak and asked if Mandelshtam was a good poet.) Other writers went to Yenukidze, still influential. At this time, when the Terror had not got into its stride, such interventions may have been helpful. In any case, the poet was sentenced merely to three years' exile at Cherdyn, a small town near Solikamsk, for "conspiracy." He attempted suicide, and his wife appealed to the Central Committee.

Mandelshtam was transferred to Voronezh, a tolerable provincial town. He was able to return to Moscow in May 1937, but could not get permission to remain. On 2 May 1938 he was again arrested, taken to the Butyrka, and sentenced by the Special Board to five years' forced labor in the Far East on 2 August 1938. Sent off by train on 9 September, he arrived on 13 October at the Vtoraya Rechka Transit Camp, from which prisoners were sent on to Kolyma. But he seems to have become half-demented, and was rejected from the transports. In his calmer moments, he sometimes recited poetry to his fellow prisoners, and once he was told that a line of his had been scratched on the wall of a death cell at the Lefortovo: "Am I real and will death really come?" When he heard this, he cheered up and for some days was much calmer. He suffered from the cold in his tattered leather coat, and seems to have got little food, dying, apparently of hunger, on 26 December 1938.[77] He had written of his times:

> But your spine has been smashed,
> My beautiful, pitiful era,
> And with an inane smile
> You look back, cruel and weak,
> Like a beast that has once been supple,
> At the tracks of your own paws.

As with other citizens in all these arrests, the blind chance of "objective characteristics" prevailed. In December 1937, so Ehrenburg tells us, his son-in-law Boris Lapin tried to account for various arrests of intellectuals: "Pilnyak has been to Japan; Tretyakov often met foreign writers; Pavel Vasilyev drank and talked too much; Bruno Jasienski was a Pole. . . . Artyom Vesyoly had at one time been a member of the Pereval literary group; the wife of the painter Shukhayev was acquainted with the nephew of Gogoberidze. . . ."[78]

Writers sometimes intervened for their colleagues, occasionally with partial or eventual success. Tikhonov, Kaverin, Zoshchenko, Lozinsky, Tyanova, Shklovsky, and Chukovsky are named as doing so for Zabolotsky, Vygodsky, and others.

But there were denouncers as well as victims, cowards and bullies as well as brave men in the literary world, as elsewhere. When Pasternak was refusing to sign the authors' circular applauding the killing of the generals—only to escape because the organizers added his name anyway—Yakov Elsberg, the author of several books about Herzen, Shchedrin, and others, who had formerly been Kamenev's secretary, now embarked on a course of deletion to remove the taint of this association, denouncing his former RAPP associates and others. Another, N. V. Lesyuchevsky, denounced Zabolotsky, Livshits, Kornilov, and the other Leningraders. He was still alive and was feebly defending himself in 1988.[79]

During the "Thaw" of 1962, the Moscow writers' organization managed to secure the expulsion of Elsberg on a charge of having informed in the 1930s. The equally notorious case of Lesyuchevsky was raised, then shelved. But when the organization fell briefly into the hands of a liberal leadership at the end of that year, the members voted once more to reopen the case, again abortively.[80] Such men lasted, indeed, while an honest Stalinist like Fadeyev, who had tried to save some of his political enemies, committed suicide in 1956 on the exposure of his patron.

Besides mere police spies, there were men who had simply sold out to Stalin, like Alexei Tolstoy, who wrote that "Dostoevsky's Stavrogin was a typical potential Trotskyite" and made a career as a regime hack. There were others who just accepted the killing of their colleagues. Surkov remarked long after the rehabilitations, "I have seen my friends, writers, disappear before my eyes, but at the time I believed it necessary, demanded by the Revolution."[81]

In fact, the whole cultural world was under attack. Plots were discovered everywhere—for example, among the staff of the Hermitage Museum.[82] The public arts suffered almost equally. The composer N. S. Zhelayev had been a friend of Tukhachevsky, and when he was arrested even the NKVD men were astonished to find that he had not yet taken down a picture of the late Marshal.[83] The conductor E. Mikoladze was shot in 1937.[84] Many actors are reported in the camps—such as Shirin, sent to labor camp for saying, "Don't feed us Soviet straw; let's play the classics."[85] Well-known actresses like O. Shcherbinskaya (an ex-wife of Pilnyak) and Z. Smirnova followed them.[86] Actresses and ballerinas are frequently mentioned in the camp literature: a typical arrest was under Article 58, Section 6, of a ballerina who attended a dinner arranged by foreign admirers.[87]

The celebrated Natalia Sats, creator of the Moscow Children's Theater, had been Tukhachevsky's wife, and was arrested in 1937 and sent to Rybinsk camp. She is reported there at several dates in the 1940s, but survived and was eventually released.

But the greatest victim in the theater was Vsevolod Meyerhold. At the beginning of 1938, a short decree announced the "liquidation" of the Meyerhold Theater as "alien to Soviet art." It added that the question of Meyerhold's further work in the theater was being "studied."[88]

On 15 June 1939 Meyerhold was invited to make a public self-criticism at a meeting of producers presided over by Vyshinsky—himself, as the artist Yuri Annenkov remarks, a well-known producer of dramas of a certain type.[89] Meyerhold retracted, but also (in one account) counterattacked:

> The pitiful and wretched thing that pretends to the title of the theater of socialist realism has nothing in common with art. . . . People in the arts searched, erred, and frequently stumbled and turned aside, but they really created—sometimes badly and sometimes splendidly. Where once there were the best theaters in the world, now— by your leave—everything is gloomily well regulated, averagely arithmetical, stupefying, and murderous in its lack of talent. Is that your aim? If it is—oh!—you have done something monstrous! In hunting down formalism, you have eliminated art![90]

Meyerhold was arrested a few days later. He was severely tortured, and wrote in an appeal to Vyshinsky that fortunately the interrogator Rodos had only broken his left arm so that he could still use a pen. Rodos, he added, had also urinated in his mouth.[91] He was shot on 2 February 1940.[92] His wife, the actress Zinaida Raikh, who had formerly been married to Yesenin, was found dead in their flat after his arrest, with, reportedly, her eyes cut out and seventeen knife wounds. Only documents were missing, and there was no police investigation.[93] Her death was thought of by prisoners to be intended as a general threat to wives.[94]

Meyerhold's theater had predeceased him. The disappearance of anyone led also to the disappearance, or reassignment, of his artifacts. On the arrest of the sculptor Kratko, all his works disappeared from the galleries. When A. N. Tupolev was arrested, the "ANT" types of plane were rechristened. One prisoner reports a physicist who had with four collaborators completed a paper and lectured on it at the Academy of Sciences. The paper appeared in the scientific journals under the name of the two collaborators who had not been arrested.[95] Unorthodox works simply vanished into the files of the NKVD, where any that have not been destroyed still lie, with Gorky's last notebooks and Marina Tsvetaeva's last poems.

Nor have we dealt with the more general effect of actions such as those described in reducing what had been a lively culture to a terrified level of almost unrelieved conformism. We have only been able to give a few illustrations of the way in which the Purge hit the creative minds of Russia—half a dozen stories and a handful of names, including the greatest in the country. A Georgian paper in the Khrushchev era asked rhetorically, "How many eminent writers, poets, artists, scholars and engineers perished in Georgia, repressed illegally, subjected to torture, exiled or shot?"[96] The same might be said of the USSR as a whole, where, as a more recent Soviet article puts it, "There came about a tragic, unthinkable annihilation of culture, science, the best part of the intelligentsia. . . ."[97] The few cases we have spoken of, and briefly, must stand for a holocaust of the things of the spirit.

# IN THE LABOR CAMPS

*No one who has not sat in prison knows what the State is like.*
Tolstoy

The fate of the prisoner who had the good fortune to escape being taken to the execution cellars was to be dispatched to a Corrective Labor Camp.

The Corrective Labor Codex defines three types of camp:

1. Factory and agricultural colonies where "people deprived of freedom" are "trained and disciplined." (Article 33)
2. Camps for mass work which includes those in "distant regions" for "class-dangerous elements" requiring "a more severe regime." (Article 34)
3. Punitive camps for the "strict isolation" of those "previously detained in other colonies and showing persistent insubordination." (Article 35)

The first category was mainly for very minor offenses against factory discipline, and for petty thieves. All sentenced under Article 58 or by the Special Board went initially to category two.

The labor camp was one of the pillars of Stalin's whole system. Concealment of its nature from the West was one of his most extraordinary triumphs.

For the evidence on the camps was, by the late 1940s, overwhelming and detailed. Thousands of former inmates had reached the West, and their wholly consistent stories were supported by a good deal of documentation, such as the many labor-camp forms and letters reproduced in David J. Dallin and Boris I. Nicolaevsky's *Forced Labour in Soviet Russia* and, indeed, by the Corrective Labor Codex of the RSFSR, produced with much effect by the British delegation to the United Nations in 1949. Yet it was possible for Western intellectuals to disbelieve this material, and to join in Soviet-sponsored campaigns condemning all who revealed it as slanderers.

And, indeed, there had long been an alternative Soviet story. There were, it is true, corrective labor establishments of a highly beneficent type. Their operations could be seen in such works as Pogodin's play *The Aristocrats,* which showed how prisoners were reclaimed at labor on the White Sea Canal and elsewhere. Pogodin represents bandits, thieves, and even "wrecker" engineers being reformed by labor. A regenerated engineer, now working enthusiastically at a project, has his old mother visit him. The kindly camp chief puts his car at her disposal, and she is delighted at her son's healthy physical appearance. "How beautifully you have reeducated me," a thief remarks, while another sings, "I am reborn, I want to live and sing."

And much of the hostile evidence came from people who had been unjustly imprisoned in camps, and who had come to oppose the Stalin regime. They were, therefore, "anti-Soviet," and purveyors of "anti-Soviet propaganda." By this system, no evidence whatever of any facts unpalatable to Stalin could ever be admissible. As Bertrand Russell wrote of a labor-camp book:

> The book ends with letters from eminent Communists saying that no such camps exist. Those who write these letters and those fellow-travellers who allow themselves to believe them share responsibility for the almost unbelievable horrors which are being inflicted upon millions of wretched men and women, slowly done to death by hard labour and starvation in the Arctic cold. Fellow-travellers who refuse to believe the evidence of books such as Mr Herling's are necessarily people devoid of humanity, for if they had any humanity they would not merely dismiss the evidence, but would take some trouble to look into it.[1]

As Russell truly remarks, it was "millions" who suffered. And here we have a point on which admissions only began to appear in the Soviet media in 1987 to 1989. While the publications in Khrushchev's time of such books as *One Day in the Life of Ivan Denisovich* and of various memoirs by former camp inmates amounted to an acknowledgment that the long-disputed evidence produced in the West was accurate through and through, this applied to the nature of the camp system, not—or not explicitly—to its extent.

What many people of good will found hard to believe was less the existence of the system, in all its unpleasantness, than the numbers of prisoners alleged to be detained in them. When figures like 10 million were mentioned, it was an almost instinctive feeling that this did not accord with common sense, with normal experience. Nor, of course, did it. But, then, the reality of Stalin's activities was often disbelieved because they seemed to be unbelievable. His whole style consisted of doing what had previously been thought morally or physically inconceivable.

Even so, it is difficult not to reject the larger figures out of hand as "obviously" exaggerated, and a very definite effort has to be made when we consider the evidence. This is multifarious, but inexact, and estimates have ranged from about 5 million upward. I am inclined to accept a figure of about 7 million purgees in the camps in 1938. This cannot, in any case, be very far wrong.

A detailed list of camp groups covering 35 clusters was given as early as 1937[2] (a cluster usually included about 200 camps of around 1,200 inmates each). In 1945, on the basis of reports from Poles allowed to leave under the Soviet–Polish treaty, a far more comprehensive account was given, together with a map, showing 38 administration clusters and groups (including 8 under Dalstroy—the "Far Eastern Construction Trust").[3] In 1948, Dallin and Nicolaevsky, on the basis of careful research, were able to list and describe the operations of 125 camps or camp clusters, mentioning that a number of others had been reported but not wholly confirmed.[4]

Like the other mechanisms from which Stalin constructed the Purge, the labor camps were no new invention.

With a few exceptions, our major accounts of labor-camp life come from intellectuals who were sent to them from 1935–1936 on. For the victims of the Yezhov terror included a higher proportion of urban, and of foreign, intellectuals than had the repressions of earlier years. As a result, we are inclined to think of the system as arising, or passing through an enormous quantitative or qualitative change, at the beginning of the Great Purge proper. There are, indeed, a few accounts by "intellectuals" from the earlier period—for example, Professor Tchernyavin—and these differ little from later ones. But on the whole, those who suffered in the first half of the 1930s were mainly peasants, who were less inclined to write books about their experiences—even though an equivalent proportion of them ended up in Western Europe as a result of the captures and migrations of the war.

There is one important exception. When Victor Kravchenko sued *Les Lettres françaises* in 1949 for having declared his book *I Chose Freedom* a fake, many otherwise unforthcoming refugees in the West sent in affidavits of experiences of theirs which confirmed his story, and a number of these were peasants who had been in camps from as early as 1930.

Their accounts[5] (and earlier ones) make it clear that the system already existed in much the same form, if with fewer inmates, at this earlier stage. Brutalities are described, indeed, which for a time became less common in the mid-1930s. This probably signifies the automatic hostility of the NKVD cadres to those whom they were able to think of as a genuinely hostile class element—kulaks. At the same time, the tradition of the Russian *vlast,* of straightforward beating for the clods of peasants, compared with a certain restraint toward the intelligentsia who might have influential friends and relations, still prevailed. Later on, of course, the latter class became, if anything, the target of yet greater extremes of brutality. But up to 1936, preferential treatment of political prisoners could still be claimed even by imprisoned Trotskyites, a category later to be marked out for specially vicious treatment.

Camps seem to have been in existence as early as mid-1918, but the decrees legalizing them were passed in September 1918[6] and April 1919.[7] The first true death camp seems to have been at Kholmogori, near Archangel, in 1921. A list of sixty-five concentration camps administered in 1922 by the Main Administration of Forced Labor is given in the directory and address book *All Russia* of 1923.[8] This Administration was merged in October 1922 with the Corrective Labor Section of the Commissariat of Justice, and the whole brought under the NKVD as the Main Administration of Places of Detention.

The first great camps were in the Solovetsky Monasteries in the far north. Here, in Tsarist times, the monks of the oldest tradition of isolation from the world had withstood a siege from 1668 to 1676, defending their faith in the Old Belief against the reformism of the time. When the camps were set up, some of the old monks were retained for a time to teach the convicts how to operate the fisheries. They were later liquidated for sabotage.[9] At the Solovetsky camps, health conditions were very bad. Epidemics reduced the population from 14,000 to 8,000 in 1929 and 1930.[10] In general, these were bad times in all the camps springing up around the White Sea. The average life span in them between 1929 and 1934 "did not exceed one or two years."[11] This was almost always due to corruption and inefficiency among the jailers. The remedy was a conventional one. "The G.P.U. commission would come down from Moscow and shoot half the administration, after which convict life returned to its normal horror."[12] The original Solovetsky "Camp of Special Designation" was changed in 1936 into a "Prison of Special Designation," and in 1939 the surviving prisoners were transferred by sea to Norilsk and Dudinin.[13]

The statute on Corrective Labor Camps which governed the later period was adopted on 7 April 1930. The camps took their modern form at a time of vast expansion of the network.

The most careful estimates of the camp population over the pre-Yezhov period run as follows:

In 1928, 30,000.

In 1930, over 600,000.

In 1931 and 1932, a total of nearly 2 million in "places of detention" can be estimated from figures given for the allotment per prisoner of newspapers, and a Moscow scholar recently estimates that of "over" 15 million dekulakized in the collectivization of 1930 to 1932, 1 million of the males of working age were sent directly to labor camps.[14]

In 1933 to 1935, Western estimates run mainly at the 5 million level (70 percent of them peasants),[15] and in 1935 to 1937, a little higher.[16] But recent Soviet analysis suggests that (omitting deportees held in NKVD "Special Settlements") the true figure may be lower, in the 2 to 4 million range. A Soviet textbook of the 1930s gives the maximum numbers at forced labor *(katorga)* in Tsarist times as 32,000, in 1912, and the maximum total of all prisoners as 183,949.[17]

## TO THE CAMPS

This established system awaited the new intake. After sentence, the prisoners were crammed into Black Marias, of a type originally produced before the Revolution; they had then been designed for seven persons, but by narrowing the cellular partitions to a minimum, now took twenty-eight.[18] Then, usually at night, they were loaded into the railway wagons taking them to their destination, either cattle wagons which had carried twelve horses or forty-eight men in the Tsarist wars and now held up to a hundred prisoners,[19] or the specially made "Stolypin trucks," named after the Tsarist Minister—though, as a Soviet writer says, "Why were these appalling narrow penal wagons called Stolypin trucks? They were of quite recent origin"—which often held twenty to thirty people in six-man compartments.[20] These journeys to the camps might last months. For example, one prisoner describes a forty-seven-day railway journey from Leningrad to Vladivostok.[21] Such trips are sometimes described as worse than the camps themselves. The crowded goods wagons were practically unheated in the winter and unbearably hot in the summer. Inadequate food and drinking water and sanitary arrangements caused great suffering and a high death rate. A foreign Communist complains of spending six weeks in a ship's hold, on "one of the widest rivers in the world," with only seven fluid ounces of drinking water a day.[22]

The train guards, from the so-called convoy troops of the NKVD, were particularly brutal and negligent. During transport to the camps, the NKVD's regulation mania was not even formally observed when it came, for example, to rations. Sometimes there was nothing to drink the "tea" ration from. Often rations gradually got smaller and smaller, and the guards started failing to distribute them at all. Even the water to be provided was often forgotten for a day or two.[23] A Soviet woman writer complains of the suffering caused by the provision of only one mug of water a day for all purposes on the long run from Moscow to Vladivostok.[24]

A Pole who collated the accounts of his countrymen deported in 1939 and 1940 remarks:

> It seems almost impossible for any human being, when not experiencing any particular sensations of anger or vindictiveness and when not in danger of thereby being deprived of it himself, persistently to refuse to hand in a bucket of water to fifty or sixty human beings shut in under such conditions. It is a fact that these men did refuse to do so, and could keep up this attitude throughout journeys lasting four, five and six weeks. There were whole days of twenty-four hours when not a drop of anything to drink passed into the cars. There were periods even of thirty-six hours.[25]

The writer adds that in examining "many hundreds"[26] of accounts, he has noted one case of a guard passing in an extra bucket, and five others of the doors being opened for ten minutes or so to relieve the fetor of the cars. Of the doctors or medical orderlies attached to each train, he found a few cases of "a little more than blank indifference" to particular children, and two records of decided kindness.[27] The brutalization Bukharin had noted in the Party had reached down and everywhere reinforced a more archiac brutality. These train journeys were highly debilitating. A Soviet writer, later rehabilitated, describes a party of men being marched from Vladivostok Transit Camp to the embarkation point for Magadan immediately after coming off the train, without food. After several had collapsed and died, the remainder refused to go on, whereupon the guards panicked, started kicking the corpses, and shot a number of others.[28]

There is an interesting postwar account in the *British Medical Journal** of a medical examination of twenty-four women, former inhabitants of East Prussia, who had just excaped to western Germany after returning to the Eastern Zone from Soviet labor camps. On their way to the latter, they had been packed about eighty to a truck, and they lived on bread and a spoonful of sugar a day. But the worst deprivation was the lack of water. It was estimated that about 40 to 50 in one transport of 2,000 women died en route. In one of the camps described, it was estimated that about half the women died in the first eight or nine months, mostly from intestinal diseases.

It was usual for political prisoners to be robbed almost at once of their most valued possessions, such as warm clothing and good footwear, either on the journey or immediately on arrival at camp. This was done quite openly under the eyes

---

*23 April 1949. This was at a later time, but the conditions described are exactly parallel.

of the guards. The old criminal underworld of Tsarist Russia, which since the Time of Troubles had developed as an extraordinary milieu with its own dialect and its own law, had been greatly reinforced, and its character much modified, by the tumults of the Civil War and the famine of the early 1920s. Already then, the *bezprizorniye,* the homeless orphan children assembling in gangs and living by their wits, had become a problem. Collectivization and other social experiments disrupted millions more families and provided large reinforcements to these now maturing criminals.

The percentage of "criminals" was around 10 to 15 percent, but the majority of these were of the petty embezzler type, rather than *urkas* proper, who were seldom more than around 5 percent of a camp total. In some camps, indeed, there were none or almost none—particularly the more severe camps like the one described in Solzhenitsyn's *One Day in the Life of Ivan Denisovich,* where almost all prisoners were in under Article 58, as interpreted by the Special Board. In other camps, their rule, which led to the slow murder of many politicals at night in the barracks when guards did not dare to interfere, was the norm. By 1940, the NKVD was often more fully in control, permitting only, in mixed camps such as Kargopol, regular rape hunts. Even these were largely suppressed in 1941. But later, a considerable relapse seems to have taken place. And in no case was there any serious interference with ordinary robbery and beating up.

Soviet sources as long ago as the 1960s confirmed all this. General Gorbatov relates:

> While we were in the Sea of Okhotsk misfortune befell me. Early in the morning, when I was lying half-awake as many of us did, two "trusties" came up to me and dragged away my boots which I was using as a pillow. One of them hit me hard on the chest and then on the head and said with a leer: "Look at him—sells me his boots days ago, pockets the cash, and then refuses to hand them over!"
>
> Off they went with their loot, laughing for all they were worth and only stopping to beat me up again when, out of sheer despair, I followed them and asked for the boots back. The other "trusties" watched, roaring with laughter. "Let him have it!" "Quit yelling—they're not your boots now."
>
> Only one of the political prisoners spoke up: "Look, what are you up to? How can he manage in bare feet?" One of the thieves took off his pumps and threw them at me.[29]

Similar things happened to Gorbatov on several other occasions. Once, buying a tin of fish from a "trusty," he had his money stolen, together with letters and photographs of his wife, by criminals who refused to return even the latter. (When he opened the tin, it was full of sand.)[30]

He was surprised to see that the guards did nothing to discourage this sort of thing. At the Maldyak gold-field camp in the Magadan area, where he served his sentence, there were 400 politicals and 50 common criminals. The latter had all the privileges and in one way or another did the politicals out of much of their meager food ration:

> Work at the goldfield was pretty killing, particularly so considering the bad food we were given. The "enemies of the people," as a rule, were detailed for the heaviest jobs, the lighter work being given to the "trusties" or common criminals. . . . [I]t

was they who were appointed foremen, cooks, orderlies, and tent seniors. Naturally enough the small amounts of fat released for the pot chiefly found their way into the bellies of the "trusties." There were three types of rations: one for those who had not fulfilled their quota, another for those who had, and a third for those who had exceeded their quota. The latter automatically included the "trusties." They did little enough work, but the tally clerks were of their persuasion and so they swindled, putting to their own and their mates' credit the work that we had done. As a result the criminals fed well and the politicals went hungry.[31]

Outside the camps proper—that is, in the transit camps and stations—the criminals continued to be almost completely out of control. One of their customs was to gamble with one another for the clothes of some strange political; the loser then had to pull them off the victim and hand them over to the winner. This game was also played for prisoners' lives. A Hungarian who was in Vorkuta in 1950 to 1951 reports it played by fifteen-year-old juvenile criminals, the loser then knifing the chosen victim. These young delinquents, usually aged from fourteen to sixteen, were seldom seen in the usual camps, being held in special centers. They were far more terrifying than any other element in Soviet society: their egos were completely unsocialized. Killing meant nothing at all to them. They formed the hard core of the "hooligan" youth element which still persists in the Soviet Union and, politically speaking, may be thought to form the potential storm troops, on one side or another, in any future upsets in the country.

Gorbatov mentions a criminal with fingers missing who explained to him that he had "lost" a political's clothes to another criminal, and before he could steal them to hand them over, the political had been transferred. So he was at once tried for negligence by his mates and sentenced to the loss of his fingers. The criminal "prosecutor" demanded all five, but the "court" settled for three. "We also have our laws," the victim commented.[32] In another case, one who, in a mass rape aboard the convict ship *Magadan,* had taken a woman the leader of his band had marked down, had his eyes put out with a needle.[33] Another leader, also on a convict ship, had gambled his brigade's bread ration away at cards. He was tried and cut to pieces.[34]

In fact, the criminals (who had such names as "The Louse," "Hitler," and "The Knout"), known at the time of the Purges as *urkas* and later as *blatniye,* in the 1950s had come to call themselves "Those with the Law"—that is, their own code.

One of its provisions (though the *urkas* later split into two factions on the issue) was refusal to work. Since the *urka* groups had sanctions just as effective as any disposed of by the camp administration, nothing could usually be done about this. One commandant is reported given the *urkas* jobs in the camp which existed only on paper. As Gorbatov describes above, the criminals in effect had arrangements with the authorities to ensure that the politicals worked on their behalf as well as on their own.

## WOMEN IN CAMPS

Women criminals, who formed a high percentage of all women in the camps, were in the main tough and shameless—though one prisoner mentions a woman of the criminal class who never took her knickers off even in the washroom: it was said that the tattooing on her belly was so indecent that "even she was a little embarrassed by it."[35] The criminal women referred to themselves as "little violets" and sneered at the politicals as "little roses." But they were somewhat restrained in their attitude towards nuns.[36]

Women on the whole seem to have survived much better than men. For this reason, we have perhaps a disproportionate number of accounts of the camps from their hands. In fact, they seem to have numbered "less than ten per cent" of the total, and many of these were in the criminal group.[37] This was enough, all the same, to account for "the innumerable mixed or women's concentration camps in the north," to which Pasternak refers in *Doctor Zhivago*.

In the mixed camps, noncriminal women were frequently mass-raped by *urkas*, or had to sell themselves for bread, or to get protection from camp officials. Those who did not were given the heaviest possible tasks until they gave in. A typical story from the Baltic–White Sea Canal camps is of a young woman who refused to give in to an official, who thereupon assigned her to a team of ordinary criminals who the same night blindfolded her, raped her, and pulled out several gold teeth from her mouth. There was no one to whom she could complain, for the camp chief himself was known to have raped several prisoners.[38]

The guards were often brutal to them. A woman prisoner describes an attempt by a girl to evade work by hiding under the floorboards. She was attacked by the guard dogs and dragged out so violently by the guards that she was literally scalped. Serving five years for stealing potatoes, she was one of the sixteen- or seventeen-year-old girls frequently reported in the camps.[39]

Decent prisoners did what they could do for them. But the demoralization of their physical deterioration was intense. A man wrote of them, "I suppose there is no more horrifying sight for the normal man than a few hundred filthy, diseased-looking, shabby women. The deep-rooted romanticism of the male is outraged."[40] And they felt this keenly. All accounts agree that even the debilitating work and diet did not damp down their sexual feelings, as it did in the case of men. Hysteria was common from this cause.

A French peasant woman, divorced from a Russian and unable to leave the country, got an eight-year sentence as the wife of a traitor in November 1937. She describes being marched twenty-five miles and then left standing in the freezing rain outside the barbed wire for two hours while the camp officers were being shown a film.[41]

In the labor camps, there were seldom tractors or horses, and sleds of wood were pulled by the prisoners. If the team was made up of men, five were harnessed; if of women, seven.[42] A Polish journalist who served in the Pechora camps reports seeing several hundred women carrying heavy logs, and later rails for the railway.[43]

In 1937, a special camp, in the Potmalag complex, was set up which contained about 7,000 wives and sisters of enemies of the people. Some, transferred to Segeta on the Kirovsk railway, are said to have been amnestied in 1945.[44] But most were sent to a new camp, "ALZHIR," in the Karaganda complex. Prisoners there included wives of many enemies of the people—like those of Ryutin, Svanidze, Pyatnitsky, and Krestinsky—and sisters of Gamarnik, Tukhachevsky, and others.

Women who had been arrested included the pregnant. The wife of a Comintern official, an invalid with curvature of the spine, was arrested in the seventh month of pregnancy, and gave birth in the Butyrka. On the transit train, having no milk at all, she filtered the fish "soup" through her stockings to feed the baby. Their further fate is not stated.[45]

Children were also conceived and born in the camps. The mothers were allowed to feed them, but the babies were kept separately. "After a year they were removed to unknown destinations. It was explained to the mothers, 'You have broken the regulations. Connections with men are not permitted. Therefore the children are ours, not yours. They belong to the Security Organs, and we will bring them up.' " One estimate in a Soviet paper is that the "children of the NKVD" numbered 500,000 to 1 million.[46] There was a children's "special camp" near Akmolinsk, which later became an ordinary camp. About 400 children lived in barracks, in two or three levels of bunks. Later they were allowed to work, tending a herd of 250 cattle, and sewing.[47] A sad account of those in Bamlag's "children's *kombinat*" is given in a recent Soviet article, while in special children's prisons in Ashkhabad, the fate of seven- or eight-year-olds was "hunger and cold, beatings, humiliations."[48] In another such article, Lydia Chukovskaya tells of children born in the camps who at the age of five could not yet speak.[49]

### SETTING UP CAMP

In general, the great expansion of the Yezhov period was marked by the setting up of new camps. For example, in the Archangel area, the Kargopol "camp," consisting of a number of smaller camps in a radius of about thirty-five miles, containing in 1940 about 30,000 prisoners, was founded in 1936 by 600 prisoners who were simply put out of the train in the middle of the forest and who built their own barracks and fences. The death rate had been very heavy. The Polish and German Communist prisoners had died first, followed by the national minorities from Asia.[50]

Pasternak, certainly drawing on the experiences of friends who had suffered, described in *Doctor Zhivago* the setting up of a new camp:

> We got off the train.—A snow desert. Forest in the distance. Guards with rifle muzzles pointing at us, wolf-dogs. At about the same time other groups were brought up. We were spread out and formed into a big polygon all over the field, facing outward so that we shouldn't see each other. Then we were ordered down on our knees, and told to keep looking straight ahead in front on pain of death. Then the roll-call, an endless, humiliating business going on for hours and hours, and all the time we were on our knees. Then we got up and the other groups were marched off in different directions, all except ours. We were told: "Here you are. This is your camp."—An empty snow-field with a post in the middle and a notice on it saying: "Gulag 92 Y.N.90"—that's all there was. . . .
>
> First we broke saplings with our bare hands in the frost to get wood to build our huts with. And in the end, believe it or not, we built our own camp. We put up our prison and our stockade and our punishment cells and our watch towers, all with our own hands. And then we began our jobs as lumberjacks.[51]

In exactly the same way, a Pole describes being marched, in rags, to a spot on the frozen tundra where there was no more than a sign: "Camp Point No.

228." The prisoners dug pits to live in and covered them with branches and earth. The food was simply raw rye flour, kneaded with water.[52]

Another prisoner describes being marched to a temporary camp which would not hold, however squeezed, more than one-fifth of the prisoners. The others were left out in the mud for several days. They began to light fires made of bits of parts of the barracks, and were charged and beaten up by the guards. Twice a day, they had one-third of a liter of soup, and once a day about half a kilo of bread.[53]

On entry into an established camp, prisoners were allotted their categories for work. This might be done by a quick examination of the prisoners' legs.[54] A certificate of "first-class" health was required for the heaviest tasks. (A Soviet writer describes one being issued to a political four hours before her death from scurvy.)[55] Then they were marched to the barracks, where, typically, "two hundred men slept in fifty bug-ridden bunks," on boards or mattresses "full of heavy and hard-packed sawdust."[56]

Crowding was intense. The former director of a Kemerovo works describes negotiating with the NKVD for 2,000 slave laborers.[57] The trouble was not the number, but how to accommodate them in the existing camps in the area. The officials concerned were shown around a camp which appeared to be packed solid, but the commandant agreed with his superior that yet another layer of bunks could be put in.

There would be a stove, though not adequate to warm one of the Arctic huts "because the orderlies only brought in ten pounds of coal dust for each stove, and you didn't get much warmth from that."[58] In a corner would be the twenty-gallon latrine tank which prisoner orderlies carried off to empty daily—"light work for people on the sick list!"[59]

The company, apart from the complement of *urkas* who in a nonpenal camp would be lording it in the corridors, were of a varied lot of "politicals." There would be saboteurs—specialists and engineers. At first they mostly had technical jobs, but, as the mass purges grew in scope, so many engineers and specialists flooded the camps that the chance of appointment to a technical position which had previously saved so many of them became proportionately rare.

There were certain special categories. In Kotlas, there was a whole group of men of eighty years and older who had been sentenced in Daghestan as part of the "liquidation of feudal remnants."[60] And about 3,000 Moscow homosexuals were in camp at the "Third Watershed," on the Baltic–White Sea Canal.[61] But usually the intake was mixed.

An account of the Dzhezkazgan camp in a Moscow article of the Khrushchev period mentions a former Ambassador to China, a soloist from the Bolshoi Opera, an illiterate peasant, an Air Force general.[62] Common were soldiers, intellectuals, and especially Ukrainian and other nationalists, on the one hand, and members of religious sects, on the other. Solzhenitsyn points out that the Baptists were in the camps simply for praying. For this (at the time he writes of), "they all got twenty-five years, because that was how it was now—twenty-five years for everybody."[63] There are many reports of sectarians being beaten or sent to the isolator cells for refusal to work on Sundays.[64] A priest, beaten blind, was noted in 1937.[65]

As in all times of trouble and oppression, the millenarian sects flourished. In the great slave empires of the past, similar voices had always spoken for the oppressed and hopeless. Now they sometimes preached that the horrors of the present were a special trial, and that from the Russian people, degraded and demoralized, a "race of saints" would arise.[66] Even twenty years later, in Vorkuta, we are told that there was more religious organization (and sharper national feeling) among the minority groups still settled there after their camp experiences than in other districts.[67]

Prisoners' rights were virtually limited to making written protests and complaints. The result: "Either there was nothing or it was rejected."[68] Such applicants made a prisoner unpopular with the authorities.

In the penal camps proper, however, there was considerable freedom of speech:

> Somebody in the room was yelling: "You think that old bastard in Moscow with the moustache is going to have mercy on *you?* He wouldn't give a damn about his own brother, never mind slobs like you!"
>
> The great thing about a penal camp was you had a hell of a lot of freedom. Back in Ust-Izhma if you said they couldn't get matches "outside" they put you in the can and slapped on another ten years. But here you could yell your head off about anything you liked and the squealers didn't even bother to tell on you. The security fellows couldn't care less.
>
> The only trouble was you didn't have much time to talk about anything.[69]

Almost every account quotes cases of people who remained devoted to "the Party and the Government" and attributed their arrest to error.[70] These bored and annoyed the other prisoners considerably. In some cases, though not in all, they turned informer. There were, in any case, a number of these by common NKVD practice. Informers who were recognized as such were always killed sooner or later. If the NKVD had been unable to extricate them in time, it made no complaint about their deaths. Herling gives an account of a revenge taken on a notorious former NKVD interrogator who was recognized in the camp, and when badly beaten up, but not killed, complained to the guards, who did nothing to save him so that he was finally killed a month later after endless persecution and attempts to appeal.

## BEHIND THE WIRE

Reveille is usually reported as at 5:00 A.M.—a hammer pounding on a rail outside camp headquarters. Anyone caught a few minutes late getting up could be sentenced on the spot to a few days in the isolator. In the winter, it would still be dark. Searchlights would be "crisscrossing over the compound from the watchtowers at the far corners."[71] Apart from the guards and the barbed wire, most camps also relied on dogs, their long chains fastened by a ring to a wire running from watchtower to watchtower. The noise of the ring screeching along the wire was a continual background.[72]

The prisoners' first thought, all day, was of food, and it is now that the breakfast, the best meal of the day, was served. (We will consider food, the center of the entire norm system and the key to Stalin's plans for efficient slave labor, later.)

Then they were assembled and marched off to work, in gangs of twenty or thirty. The order (known to prisoners as "the prayer")[73] would be given:

> Your attention, prisoners! You will keep strict column order on the line of march! You will not straggle or bunch up. You will not change places from one rank of five to another. You will not talk or look around to either side, and you will keep your arms behind you! A step to right or left will be considered an attempt to escape, and the escort will open fire *without* warning! First rank, forward march![74]

Apart from sleeping, the prisoners' time was their own only for ten minutes at breakfast, five minutes at the noon break, and another five minutes at supper.[75] They lost so much sleep that they fell asleep instantly if they found a warm spot, and on the Sundays they got off, which was not every Sunday, they slept as much as they could.[76]

The shoe situation varied. "There'd been times when they'd gone around all winter without any felt boots at all, times when they hadn't even seen ordinary boots, but only shoes made of birch bark or shoes of the 'Chelyabinsk Tractor Factory model' " (that is, made of strips of tires that left marks of the treads behind them).[77]

Clothes were usually carefully patched and repaired: "rags tied around them with all their bits of string and their faces wrapped in rags from chin to eyes to protect them from the cold. . . ."[78]

Ulcers are reported as common, through filthy clothes. Clothing was cleaned and disinfected occasionally, and baths were also provided. Solzhenitsyn implies that in the penal camp he describes, a bath was available about every two weeks.[79] But often there was "no soap for either bathing or laundry."[80]

To go sick for the odd day was possible with a minor complaint. But to be recognized as sick and put on a sick diet was usually fatal. In any case, even a man feeling ill might not be allowed to go sick, as there was a quota: "He was allowed to excuse only two men in the morning, and he'd already excused them."[81] As a rule, the infirmary took in only those who were plainly dying—"and not all of them," a Soviet woman writer recalls.[82]

In one camp, still under construction, a sick inspection is described:

> The *naryadchik* and the *lekpom* [medical assistant], armed with clubs, enter the pit. The chief asks the first man he sees why he does not come out. 'I am sick,' is the answer. The *lekpom* feels his pulse and pronounces him all right. Then blows shower upon the man and he is kicked out into the open. 'Why don't you go to work?' the chief asks the next man. 'I am sick,' is the stubborn answer. The day before, this prisoner went to the *lekpom* and gave him his last dirty louse-infected shirt. The *lekpom* feels his pulse and finds high fever. He is released from work. A third man replies that he has neither clothes nor shoes. 'Take the clothes and shoes from the sick one,' the chief rules sententiously. The sick one refuses, whereupon his things are taken off him by force.[83]

The veteran convicts in *One Day in the Life of Ivan Denisovich* have learned that it is necessary to march as slowly as possible to the morning job, otherwise they get hot too early, and "won't last long."[84] And in fact, those who survived the first months became fantastically skilled in the arts of survival. At the same time, customs useful to them became thoroughly established and traditional. For example, Solzhenitsyn describes the prisoners' habit of picking up odd scraps of wood on the building site and marching back with them.[85] This was illegal, but the guards did nothing about it until they reached camp again. They then ordered them to throw down the wood, as they, too, needed extra fuel and were unable to carry any in addition to their submachine guns. But only a certain amount of the wood was dropped. At the next checkpoint, the warders repeated the order. Again, only a certain amount of wood was dropped, and the prisoners reached the quarters with a portion of their original gleanings. It was necessary, and in the interests of both guards and warders, that the prisoners be able to get away with some wood; otherwise they would have no incentive to bother to carry it in, and guards and warders would not have got their share. But no overt arrangement had ever been made. The agreement was wholly unspoken. We see, in such things, the development of the rules and traditions of a whole new social order, in microcosm.

A genuine caste feeling seems to have been arising, with the prisoner beginning to be regarded as actually an inferior being, just as in ancient times. The sentiment gradually spread that "mere contact" with the prisoners was "an insult to a free man." "It is considered inadmissible for a non-prisoner to eat the same food as a prisoner, to sleep under the same roof, or have any friendly relations with him." Things reached the stage where the head of a camp admonished the man in charge of the disinfestation chamber for allowing a shirt belonging to a free mechanic employed in the power plant to be put in with the prisoners' clothes for delousing.[86] As a recent Soviet article puts it, a camp commandant did not regard the prisoners as human.[87]

Free citizens in Kolyma sometimes tried to help prisoners they came in contact with. In particular, we are told, "doctors, engineers, geologists" would try to get their professional colleagues employed according to their capacities. A geologist now described as "a hero of the north" lost his own life owing to an attempt to defend some of the Kolyma inmates. One of his interventions is described:

> "These people might die!"
> "What people?" the representative of the camp administration smiled, "These are enemies of the people."[88]

As a camp official told a foreign prisoner, "We are not trying to bring down the mortality rate."[89]

A recent Soviet account tells of a commandant refusing the camp doctor's insistence that convalescents not be sent to work in the forest on 400 grams of bread a day. The commandant answered, "I spit on your ethics!" and sent out the 246 men convalescing, who were all dead in a week.[90]

There are many accounts of camp officials, and even doctors, who came to regard the prisoners as their personal serfs. This selection of slaves was sometimes similar even in detail to the illustrations of books about Negro slavery, as when the chief of a Yertsevo camp section, Samsonov, honored the medical examination with his presence, and with a smile of satisfaction felt the biceps, shoulders, and backs of the new arrivals.[91] It has been maintained that the Soviet forced-labor system might be considered as "a stage on the way to a new social stratification which might have involved slavery"—that is, in the old-fashioned overt sense—though the trend was changed by later events.[92]

A Soviet critic has remarked that

the whole system in the camps Ivan Denisovich passed through was calculated to choke and kill without mercy every feeling for justice and legality in man, demonstrating in general and in detail such impunity of despotism that any sort of noble or rebellious impulse was powerless before it. The camp administration did not allow the prisoners to forget for a single moment that they had no rights at all. . . .[93]

In the 1940s, "a prisoner had to take his cap off at a distance of five paces when he saw a warder, and keep it off till he was two paces past him."[94] Solzhenitsyn tells of a muddled count, leading to recount after recount, and another time an extra count when a missing prisoner has been found:

"What's all this about?" the chief escort screamed. "D'you want to sit on your asses in the snow? That's where I'll put you if you like and that's where I'll keep you till morning!" And he sure would. He wouldn't think twice about it if he wanted. It'd happened plenty of times before and sometimes they had to go down on their knees with the guards pointing their guns at the ready.[95]

Reports of physical violence are common.[96] Refusal to work seems to have been punished variously: in the Far Eastern area, by immediate shooting; elsewhere, by stripping the offender and standing him in the snow until he submitted or by solitary confinement on 200 grams of bread. For a second offense, death was usual. And in camp, not only "sabotage" but also "anti-Soviet propaganda" might be treated as a capital crime.[97]

Occasional tightening of lax discipline in the camps led to the sudden infliction of penalties on a large scale. Appeals to the regulations were treated as repeated and willful refusal to work. In 1937, 400 prisoners were executed in a batch in Karaganda on such charges.[98] A "mutiny" is reported in a camp near Kemerovo near the end of 1938. It was, in fact, a strike against rotten food. Fourteen of the ringleaders, twelve men and two women, were shot in front of all the rest of the prisoners, and then details from each hut helped to dig the graves.[99]

Apart from these executions for "disciplinary" reasons, often announced openly in the camps with the purpose of intimidating the occupants further, there were many killings of a different kind. Orders would come from Moscow for the liquidation of a given number of ex-oppositionists, and the quota would then be fulfilled by a cursory reinterrogation—not on activity in the camps, but on newly discovered circumstances in connection with the original offense, transforming it into a capital crime. For mass operations of this kind, special commissions were on occasion sent down, and given special powers and premises where the doomed men were transferred for investigation and death. For example, one such center was established in an abandoned brick factory in the Vorkuta area, where some 1,300 politicals are reported executed in the winter of 1937.[100]

In most of the main camp areas, there seem also to have been established special and highly secret "Central Isolation Prisons" covering a given group of camps. To one such, in Bamlag, we are told that some 50,000 prisoners were "transferred" for execution in the two years 1937 and 1938. The victims were tied up with wire like logs, stacked in trucks, driven out to a selected area, and shot.[101]

The Hungarian Communist writer Lengyel, himself a camp veteran, describes one of these special extermination camps in the Norilsk area, as what is evidently intended as authentic background, in his story "The Yellow Poppies": the camp is wound up first by the execution of the remaining prisoners, and then by special NKVD squads who move in and execute all the staff and guards. Owing to the permafrost, it is impossible to bury the bodies, and they are piled into veritable hills and covered with truckloads of earth, the whole matter remaining unknown even in neighboring camps, and even when the camp site itself is later reoccupied as a prison hospital.

Prisoners are also reported shot to check epidemics, as in December 1941 at Kozhva, where the victims are said to have included the Bulgarian Communist leader Danko Sapunov.[102] There have also long been unofficial reports of barge-loads of prisoners no longer able to work, or otherwise superfluous, being sunk in the Arctic seas. One of the missing groups of Polish officers is believed to have been killed in this way, and we are also told that this is how the poet Narbut perished.[103] The Soviet press has lately confirmed the use of this method of liquidation—reporting, for example, that such was the fate of two leading Ukrainian intellectuals: the writer Hrihory Epik and the director Les Kurbas.[104]

The routine punishment was the punitive "isolators" built in each camp, and quite deadly. At Solzhenitsyn's,

> the fellows from 104 had built the place themselves and they knew how it looked— stone walls, a concrete floor, and no window. There was a stove, but that was only enough to melt the ice off the walls and make puddles on the floor. You slept on bare boards and your teeth chattered all night. You got six ounces of bread a day and they only gave you hot gruel every third day.
>
> Ten days! If you had ten days in the cells here and sat them out to the end, it meant you'd be a wreck for the rest of your life. You got T.B. and you'd never be out of hospitals as long as you lived.
>
> And the fellows who did fifteen days were dead and buried.[105]

Even among those who avoided the cells, all the deficiency diseases were rife. Solzhenitsyn's hero, who had lost teeth from scurvy in the Ust-Izhma camp in Pechora "at a time when he thought he was on his last legs,"[106] was lucky enough to recover. With scurvy, wounds opened and abscesses suppurated. Pellagra was equally common. Pneumonia, usually fatal, was a normal hazard. And the direct effects of undernourishment, "swelling of the feet and face, and, in its final and lethal stage, swelling of the abdomen," were constantly to be seen.[107] In the farming camps, epidemics of brucellosis are reported.[108] In the northern camps, gangrene, resulting in amputation, was frequent.[109] Tuberculosis was often the immediate cause of death. After about two years, women prisoners tended to develop a continuous hemorrhage of the womb.[110]

It later became routine, when a corpse was taken to the morgue, "to crack his skull with a big wooden mallet to make sure."[111]

Escapes were occasionally made, but very seldom with any success. They were acts of desperation; but, of course, there was enough desperation to produce them. In the Pechora area, the NKVD offered a reward of eleven pounds of wheat to anyone turning in an escaped prisoner. In the early 1930s, escaped prisoners in other regions were sometimes sheltered by the peasantry, but this was very seldom true among the terrorized kolkhozniks of the Purge period. There were, nevertheless, rare successes. Gypsies, in particular, sometimes reached encampments of their own race where its solidarity saved them from discovery. And odd individuals, like the Spanish Communist general El Campesino, made completely successful escapes.

Recaptured prisoners were always brutally manhandled, and almost invariably shot.

For any escape on the march to the camps from the railheads, the guards were charged with complicity and sentenced to two or three years, which they continued to serve as guards but without pay. This made them extremely vigilant. In the camps, too, "if anybody got out it was hell on the guards and they kept on the go without food or sleep. It made 'em so mad they often didn't bring the fellow back alive."[112]

One consequence of this vigilance was continual counting of prisoners:

> The lieutenant stood still and watched. He'd come outside to double-check the count. That was the routine when they left the camp.
> 
> The men meant more to a guard than gold. If there was one man missing on the other side of the wire, he'd soon be taking his place. . . .[113]

> They counted you twice on the way out—once with the gates still shut, so they knew if they could open them, and then a second time, when you were going through the gates. And if they thought there was something wrong, they did a recount outside.[114]

This is one of several interesting parallels with Dostoevsky's account of forced labor in the 1840s, in *The House of the Dead:*

> The prisoners are lined up, counted and called over at dawn, midday and nightfall, and sometimes more often during the day, depending on the suspicions of the guards and their ability to count. The guards often made mistakes, counted wrongly, went away and then came back again. Eventually the wretched guards would succeed in arriving at the right figure and lock up the hut.

In a general comparison between this century and the last, we note that in Dostoevsky's time prisoners had considerably more freedom of action inside the camp, and were not under such strict guard outside either, though Dostoevsky mentions that his convicts are serving "incomparably" the worst of the three types of hard labor. With the exception that in Dostoevsky's camp the main sanction is frightful floggings, which sometimes result in death, rather than the "isolators," the life of the convict was on the whole preferable in his descriptions to those of Solzhenitsyn and the others. Each convict has his own box with a lock and key. Prisoners keep domestic animals. They do not work on Sundays or feast days, or even on their own name days. Jews and Moslems have parallel privileges. The food is greatly superior, and prisoners on the sick list go into town to buy "tobacco, tea, beef; on Christmas Day, suckling-pig, even goose." They even have enough bread to spare for the horse of the water carrier.

The convicts in *The House of the Dead* are all, indeed, really guilty of one or another offense—often murder, like the hero Goryanchikov—though there are about a dozen political prisoners out of thirty.

Dostoevsky's type of camp was abolished in the 1850s. (He makes the point that he is "describing the past.") But even nonliterary prisoners in Stalin's camps were able to make other comparisons—for example, one prisoner was a Polish Communist who had served two years in Wronki jail in Poland for political offenses. In the Polish jail, the prisoners had been locked in only at night, by day they were allowed in the garden; they were allowed any books from outside, unlimited correspondence, and weekly baths; there were five of them in a large room.[115]

## THE PENAL EMPIRE

In the vast empty spaces in the north and the Far East, areas as big as fair-sized countries came under complete NKVD control. There were many camps scattered through the Urals, in the Archangel area, and more especially in and around Karaganda and on the new railway being built from Turkestan to Siberia. But in these, the NKVD administered only comparatively small enclaves. Even in the huge Karlag complex around Karaganda, where there were about 100,000 prisoners, they were in camps scattered over an area the size of France among other settlements, mostly of deported "free" labor. (These so-called free exiles were men and women whose innocence was absolutely clear even to the examining judges. In some areas, they were often little more than vagabonds, sleeping under bridges, begging their bread, and seeking work or even arrest to save themselves from starvation.)[116]

The two biggest true colonies of the NKVD empire were the great stretch of northwestern Russia beyond Kotlas, comprising roughly what is shown on the map as the Komi Autonomous Soviet Socialist Republic, and the even vaster area of the Far East centered on the gold fields of Kolyma. These regions had, before the NKVD took over, populations of a handful of Russians and a few thousand Arctic tribesmen. A decade later, they held between them something between 1.25 and 2 million prisoners. For these great areas we have accounts from both Soviet and émigré publications. *One Day in the Life of Ivan Denisovich* is set in the northeastern camps. General Gorbatov's *Years Off My Life* covers his experiences in Kolyma. These and other Moscow-published works confirmed and complemented the large amount of material long available in the West.

The Soviet Arctic is a world of its own. The feeling of having been thrown out from normal life was accentuated by the physical phenomena. In winter, there is the extreme, extravagant cold; the short days in which a swollen, livid sun raises itself for a few hours above the horizon—or, in the Arctic proper, simply lightens the sky somewhat without appearing; the soundlessly flickering ion-stream of the aurora borealis. In summer, the long days; the mosquitoes; the slushy swamp of the melted surface, with its alien vegetation—bog cotton and dwarf willow a few inches high; and below it, hard as rock, the permafrost. South of this true tundra is the even wilder forest belt, the taiga, where the great complex of timber camps lay.

Most of the northern camps were separated from the country as a whole by vast stretches of empty land, sparsely inhabited by tribal hunters, the Chukchi, Yakut, Nentsi—the last being the Samoyeds, cannibals, from whom Ivan the Terrible had recruited his fiercest guards. Most of these were happy to turn in prisoners for a bounty, having in any case a general hostility to Russians.

## KOLYMA

The largest camp area was that which came under Dalstroy, the Far Eastern Construction Trust. The exact boundaries of Dalstroy's control have never been exactly determined, but it seems to have included all the territory beyond the Lena and north of the Aldan, at least as far east as the Gydan Range—a territory four times the size of France.

Its prison population was never as large as the Pechora region's, being usually around 500,000. But the death rate was so high that more individual prisoners inhabited its camps at one time or another than any other region. Since it was supported by sea, and the number of ships, their capacity, and their average number of trips are known with reasonable accuracy, we can compute a probable minimum of 2 million dead.[117]

The main concentration of camps was in the Kolyma gold fields, based on Magadan, with its port of Nagayevo.[118] Gold mining started on a big scale in the early 1930s. In 1935, a series of awards was announced in the gold-mining industry, with great publicity to all concerned. Most of those named were mentioned as working at Kolyma, under E. P. Berzin, the "Director." High among the awards of Orders, a different decree was inserted—commuting the sentences and restoring the civil rights of five engineers in the gold industry for their services.

Berzin is described as comparatively reasonable about prisoners' complaints.[119] He, his wife, and his chief assistant, Filipov (who is said to have committed suicide in Magadan prison), were arrested, together with scores of others, in 1937, in Yezhov's purge of the NKVD. There seems to have been some apprehension of resistance, and Berzin was promised awards and promotion, feted by the NKVD "delegation," and only arrested on the airfield.[120]

He was succeeded by K. A. Pavlov, who, through his deputy, Garanin, launched on a campaign of, even by NKVD standards, maniac terror, torture, and execution, with the shooting in 1938 of an estimated 26,000 men in a special camp, Serpantinka, set up for the purpose. Garanin was soon shot, and his successor, Vyshnevetsky, also lasted a very short time, receiving fifteen years for a disastrous expedition intended to open up new areas.

Pavlov himself was promoted to head Gulag, and was succeeded in Kolyma by Ivan Nikishov, described as "icily, mercilessly cruel." He married an NKVD woman, Gridassova, who was put in charge of the women's camp at Magadan. They lived in a comfortable country house forty-five miles northwest of Magadan, in their own hunting preserve.[121]

The slave route to Kolyma had its own Middle Passage, the trip to Magadan from Vladivostok by boat, with thousands of prisoners battened down under hatches.

The trip took a week or more, and was much feared. An alternative route was tried to Ambarchik on the Arctic Ocean, at the mouth of the Kolyma—a 4,000-mile voyage through difficult seas, taking some two months. The first ship sent that way, the *Dzhurma,* was caught in the autumn ice, and when it arrived in Ambarchik the following year (1934), none of its 12,000 prisoners remained. This was at a time when the exploring ship *Chelyushkin* was caught in the ice and sank, and there was worldwide interest in the safety of its crew camped on the ice. American and other offers to try to rescue them by air were refused, and it has been suggested that the reason was that their camp was only a couple of hundred miles from the wintering place of the *Dzhurma,* which might have been stumbled upon by foreign fliers.[122]

More usually, the shorter passage to Magadan, on the *Dzhurma,* the *Indigirka,* the *Dalstroy,* and other freighters, was the prisoners' route. The ships, referred to by Andrei Sakharov as "death-ships of the Okhotsk Sea,"[123] were the scene of the worst of the *urkas'* acts. It was on the *Dzhurma* that General Gorbatov lost his boots (see p. 313). By 1939, the guards were not entering the prisoners' hold, only waiting outside with raised guns when the prisoners were let out on deck in small groups to go to the latrine. As a result, the *urkas* had a freer hand than at any other time. There were always numbers of murders and rapes. In 1939, on the *Dzhurma,* the criminals managed to break through a wall and get at the provisions, after which they set the storeroom on fire. The fire was held in check, though it was still burning when the *Dzhurma* entered port. But there was no attempt to release the prisoners locked in the hold, and a great panic ensued when they realized that if it came to the point, they would be abandoned.[124] A similar tale—perhaps a version of the same event—is told by a Soviet writer. The ship took fire. Male prisoners tried to break out and were battened down in the hold. "When they went on rioting the crew hosed them down to keep them quiet. They then forgot about them. As the fire was still burning the water boiled and the wretched men died in it. For a long time afterwards the *Dzhurma* stank intolerably."[125]

On another occasion, several hundred young girls, sentenced for unauthorized absence from arms factories and so on, were in a compartment of the hold on their own. Again the *urkas* managed to break through and raped many of them, killing a few male prisoners who tried to protect them. This time, the combination of the rapes, the breakage, and the murders resulted in the arrest of the commander of the ship's guard.[126]

On arrival at Nagayevo, first "the sick were carried ashore on stretchers and left on the beach in tidy rows. The dead were also neatly stacked so that they could be counted and the number of death certificates would tally."[127]

The survivors found themselves in a strange land.

The Kolyma Basin alone is almost as big as the Ukraine. It is intensely cold: the temperature may go down to $-70°C$.[128] Outside work for prisoners was compulsory until it reached $-50°C$.[129] In spite of this, in 1938, fur was banned in the Dalstroy camps, and only wadding permitted; felt shoes were replaced by canvas. The rivers of the region are ice-bound for eight to nine months of the year. A camp rhyme ran:

> Kolyma, wonderful planet,
> Twelve months winter, the rest summer.

For about two months in winter, there is no sunrise at all. One calmly written account of the Kolyma camps has as a natural chapter heading: "Sickness, Self-mutilation, Suicide."[130]

Not, of course, that these were limited to Kolyma. But in Kolyma the death rate was particularly high, and the despair rate, too. Gorbatov, a strong man with great will power who had even resisted interrogation successfully, tells us that he barely survived less than a year in the gold camps. The death rate among the miners is estimated in fact at about 30 percent per annum,[131] though it varied to some extent with location, type of work, and personality of commandant. A Kolyma prisoner comments that it is rarely possible to live on the camp ration for more than two years. By the fourth, at the very latest, the prisoner is incapable of work, and by the fifth year he can no longer be alive.[132] In one of the Kolyma penal camps which had started a year with 3,000 inmates, 1,700 were dead by the end, and another 800 in hospital with dysentery.[133] In another—a regular camp—it is estimated that 2,000 out of 10,000 died in a year.[134] Of some 3,000 Poles, over a period of about fifteen months, about 60 percent were counted dead.[135] A Soviet article of 1988 says that "of every one hundred inmates of Kolyma, only two or three survived."[136]

In a camp there described in the Khrushchev-period press,[137] inmates did a twelve-hour day. The food ration for 100 percent norm was 800 grams of bread per day. Nonfulfillment of norms, through whatever cause, automatically entailed a reduction of the bread ration to 500 grams. This was just above starvation level; any further reduction to 300 grams (as a punitive measure) meant certain death. Work at the surface gold sites was performed in accordance with a strict division of labor. Two men had to start a bonfire, and this had to be done without matches, by the ancient method of striking sparks with flints. Another man had to fetch water from the frozen river and melt it. Next, the deeply frozen ground had to be softened, then excavated, and the sand passed through sieves in search of gold.

Three youths of about seventeen appeared in this camp. They looked younger than their age, perhaps because they were so thin as to be almost emaciated. After the death of the father of one of them, the son had found a collection of Lenin's works, and in the last volume an envelope containing a copy of Lenin's Testament. Not keeping it a secret, he and his closest associates were arrested on a charge of terrorism and counter-revolution, and sentenced to fifteen years' hard labor. So there they all were—three boys and two girls in Kolyma and others of the youthful group dispersed in other prison camps.

There were several women's camps in the Kolyma area. Eugenia Ginzburg (the mother of the writer Aksyonov), who became a nurse just in time to save her life, and survived to be rehabilitated, gives an account of the Elgen camp which makes it clear that it was a killer. She describes the impossibility of the tree-felling norm, the trade in sex, the using up of the "quota" of medical exemptions on the common criminals, and the sole methods of survival—"threats, intrigue and graft." Women prisoners who had become illegally pregnant in illicit camp intercourse were among those sent to Elgen. They were allowed to try to feed their babies, but milk hardly came, owing to the rations and work, and after a few weeks usually ceased altogether, whereupon "the baby would have to fight for its life" on patent foods. As a result, "the turnover of 'mothers,' was very rapid."[138] Even worse was the women's disciplinary camp at Mylga where they worked in the gypsum quarries.[139]

Gorbatov and others note NKVD officers saving old mates in the services or the Party by giving them easy jobs. This old-boys' network was all very well for those with good connections. A Soviet source gives the other side of the picture. A commandant discovered his former general among the doomed *dokhodyagi*—"goners"—and gave him a post in the store. A Jew called Dodya Shmuller, who had been a trouble to the authorities through constantly demanding his rights under the regulations, was then in the punitive isolator on 300 grams of bread a day, and unlikely to survive. When he heard of the general being saved, he put in one last formal complaint, about his ration, but merely received a further spell in the isolator.[140]

Another disciplinary case is of a team accused of concealing gold which they had dug up. Their quarters were thoroughly searched, but nothing was found. However, in order to "teach the men a lesson," the whole team was sentenced to solitary confinement in a punitive section known as "Stalin's Villa." Only a few survived.[141]

For administration was even harsher than elsewhere, and more capricious too. One prisoner in Kolyma finished his sentence at the end of 1937 and was given a paper to sign stating that he had been notified of his liberation. However, he was not given any document to identify him as a free citizen, and could not leave the camp without one. He continued to work as a convict with the ambiguous status of "free prisoner." He did not protest, as even so he was doing better than most people, who simply got a fresh sentence. At the end of 1939, he was finally given his certificate of liberation and allowed to choose a place of residence in European Russia apart from his home area.[142]

By a circumstance unique in the history of the labor-camp zones, Magadan was visited in 1944 by the Vice President of the United States, Henry Wallace. With him, representing the Office of War Information, was Professor Owen Lattimore. They both wrote accounts of what they saw, which differ in various respects from the information we have from ex-prisoners.

Wallace found Magadan idyllic.[143] The horrible Nikishov, he noted approvingly, "gambolled about, enjoying the wonderful air." He noted Gridassova's maternal solicitude, and much admired the needlework which she showed him. The true story of the needlework[144] is that women prisoners capable of producing this were able to sell it for extra rations to the NKVD aristocracy's wives to decorate their apartments. It was normally produced, that is, after a ten- or twelve-hour working day in conditions comparable with those adversely commented on by Thomas Hood in *The Song of a Shirt*. (In a similar way, Solzhenitsyn mentions three "artists"[145] in his camp, who gained certain privileges "as a reward for doing pictures free for the higher ups.")

Lattimore condemned the hardness of the Tsarist system in Siberia.[146] But this had now, fortunately, passed. The Soviet opening up of the north was "orderly,'' being controlled by ''a remarkable concern, the Dalstroy . . . which can be roughly compared to a combination of the Hudson Bay Company and the T.V.A.''

He was equally impressed with ''Mr.'' Nikishov and his wife. ''Mr. Nikishov, the head of Dalstroy, had just been decorated with the Order of Hero of the Soviet Union for his extraordinary achievement. Both he and his wife have a trained and sensitive interest in art and music and a deep sense of civic responsibility.''

Lattimore approvingly quotes another member of his party on a local ballet troupe which provided ''high-grade entertainment,'' which, he adds, ''just naturally seems to go with gold and so does high-powered executive ability.'' Lattimore notes, too, that unlike the old gold rushes, with their ''sin, gin and brawling,'' Dalstroy concentrated on greenhouses where tomatoes, cucumbers, and even melons were grown to make sure that the hardy miners got enough vitamins. The tomatoes that Lattimore was so lyrical about were indeed grown in the area. A prisoner describes some under the charge of a bullying but efficient woman doctor at a prisoners' hospital in the northern region of Kolyma. Most of the tomatoes went to officials and staff, but at least some reached the patients, which is remarked on as an extraordinary thing.[147]

Nikishov had indeed shown some of the executive ability Lattimore attributes to him. For the reception had been very well organized. All prisoners in the area were kept in their huts. Watchtowers were demolished. Various other deceptions were undertaken. For example, Wallace was shown a farm, the best in the area; fake girl swineherds, who were in fact NKVD office staff, replaced the prisoners for the occasion. All the goods that could be scraped up in the neighborhood were put in the shop windows, and so on.[148]

The party was actually taken to a gold mine in the Kolyma Valley. Lattimore prints a photograph of a group of husky men bearing little resemblance to accounts of the prisoners from current Soviet or other sources. It is captioned ''They have to be strong to withstand winter's rigors.''[149] The comment is a sound one, but when it came to real prisoners it worked out the other way: since they were not expected to withstand the winter's rigors, it was unnecessary to keep them strong.

## PECHORA

No other camp area had quite the reputation of Kolyma for isolation, cold, and death. But there were others which ran it close—in particular, the vast prison region at the northeastern corner of European Russia in the basin of the Pechora River. Even its name, though there is no river of Europe outside Russia larger than it, except only the Danube, is practically unknown in the West. Its basin is larger than the British Isles, or than New England, New York, and New Jersey. Here, between Kotlas, the gateway to the area, and the Vorkuta coal-mining district, lay the largest single concentration of forced labor in Russia, holding more than 1 million prisoners.

In Vorkuta, the temperature is below zero Celsius for two-thirds of the year, and for more than 100 days the *khanovey,* or ''wind of winds,'' blows across the tundra. The climate killed those from the southern parts of Russia very quickly;

few would be alive after a year or two.[150] As has been seen, much of our evidence comes from this region.

The head of the Pechora camps in 1936 was NKVD Major Moroz, who is variously described as particularly cruel and as sensible enough to give good rations and good conditions in exchange for good work. He himself had briefly been a convict between high NKVD appointments. And he later disappeared. His assistant, Bogarov, a man of the most brutal and ferocious appearance, seems in fact to have been as humane as his post permitted, and to have been behind these improved conditions.

Moroz was succeeded by "a confirmed sadist," Kashketin, of whom it was said that the only safety from him lay in his being ignorant of one's existence. After a few months of his rule, there were 2,000 convicts in the isolators of a single camp group, of whom only 76 survived. Kashketin's brutality availed him no more than Moroz's humanity: he, too, disappeared with all his subordinates at the end of the Yezhov period.

Norilsk, on the Arctic Ocean, was developed as a metallurgical project. A recent article in *Izvestiya* tells us that though there was death on a large scale from "unbearable toil, dystrophy, scurvy, and catarrhal diseases," there are about 2 million *survivors* of the "nightmare barracks" from the intake of the postwar years still alive today, a striking testimony to the number in the camps.[151]

And so it was, on a smaller but still vast scale, throughout the NKVD's realm, from the White Sea to Sakhalin, from the great complexes of Karaganda to the virtually unrecorded "death camps" of the Taymyr and Novaya Zemlya, from (as Solzhenitsyn puts it) the Pole of Cold at Oy-Myakoi to the copper mines of Dzhezkazgan.

## SLAVE ECONOMICS

The millions of slave laborers at the disposal of Gulag played an important economic role, and indeed became accepted as a normal component of the Soviet economy.

An ad hoc Committee of the United Nations appointed under resolutions by UNESCO and the ILO, and consisting of a prominent Indian lawyer, a former President of the Norwegian Supreme Court, and a former Peruvian Minister of Foreign Affairs, reported in 1953 in a sober document leaving no doubt of the "considerable significance" of forced labor in the Soviet Union.

State-owned slaves were common in the ancient world. For example, the Laurion silver mines were operated by Athens on that basis. The Romans, too, had their *servi publici*. The Head of the Department of War Engineering Armaments, RSFSR, wanting some hundreds of prisoners for urgent work during the war, was told by the NKVD official responsible that there was a shortage. "Malenkov and Voznesensky need workers, Voroshilov is calling for road builders. . . . What are we to do? The fact is we haven't yet fulfilled our plans for imprisonment. Demand is greater than supply."[152]

We think of the lumber camps as typical. But the best estimate seems to be that (of the comparatively low camp population of early 1941) only about 400,000 were held at lumbering. The other main categories were

| | |
|---|---|
| Mining | 1,000,000 |
| Agriculture | 200,000 |
| Hired out to various State enterprises | 1,000,000 |
| Construction and maintenance of camps and manufacture of camp necessities | 600,000 |
| General construction | 3,500,000 [153] |

Even in the great lumbering area of the northwest, a high proportion of prisoners were building the Kotlas–Vorkuta railway. Many others were erecting (like Solzhenitsyn's hero) various industrial and mining buildings.

It has often been pointed out that slave labor is economically inefficient. Karl Marx had the same view:

The lowest possible wage which the slave earns appears to be a constant, independent of his work in contrast to the free workers. The slave obtains the means necessary to his subsistence in natural form, which is fixed both in kind and in quantity, whereas the remuneration of the free worker is not independent of his own work. [154]

Slavery thus owed part of its inefficiency to lack of incentives.

The same point is put by the Webbs, in a passage worth quoting at length as representing a certain way of looking at Soviet affairs common in the 1930s. They are criticizing Professor Tchernyavin's first-hand account of the camps he served in:

It is to be regretted that this testimony—very naturally strongly biased—mixes up personal observation and experience of conditions that are, in all conscience, bad enough, with hearsay gossip unsupported by evidence, and with manifestly exaggerated statistical guesses incapable of verification. The account would have carried greater weight if it had been confined to the very serious conditions of which the author had personal knowledge. His naive belief that this and other penal settlements are now maintained and continuously supplied with thousands of deported manual workers and technicians, deliberately for the purpose of making, out of this forced labour, a net pecuniary profit to add to the State revenue, will be incredible by anyone acquainted with the economic results of the chain-gang, or of prison labour, in any country in the world. [155]

It is quite true that the mass arrests remain basically a political phenomenon. The slave-labor motive can only have been secondary. The engineers and scientists, the doctors and lawyers, were not arrested simply to provide a corps of incompetent lumberjacks. As Weissberg says:

After twenty years of endless trouble and enormous expense the Soviet Government finally developed a working body of really capable physicists. And now what's happened? Shubnikov, one of the leading low-temperature physicists in the country, is to help dig a canal in the Arctic. So is our first director, Professor Obremov, also a leading Soviet physicist and an expert on crystallography. Can't you imagine what expensive navvies men like Shubnikov and Obremov are. [156]

But once people were arrested, the extraction of their physical labor ensured at least some contribution to the economy, and (granted the initial irrationality of the whole Purge) there is nothing contrary to reason and common sense in Stalin's typical decision to integrate them into his economic machine. To this extent, the Webbs are simply wrong as to Stalin's motives.

Moreover, Stalin was well aware of Marx's economic objection to slavery. And with his usual refusal to accept precedent, he sought to overcome it by the simple but untried method of *not* giving the slave a flat subsistence, but linking his rations to his output. In this way, it was thought, the lack of incentive Marx had pointed to was overcome.

It is quite true that the forced-labor projects were, anyhow, like much else in Stalin's economy, often totally misconceived even on their own terms. During the great wave of arrests in 1947, a Soviet account tells us, Stalin remarked at a meeting of the Council of Ministers that the "Russian people had long dreamed of having a safe outlet to the Arctic Ocean from the Ob River." Simply on the basis of this remark, decisions were taken to build a railway to Igarka. For more than four years, amid feet of snow, in temperatures down to −55°C in winter, and with swamps and mosquitoes in the summer, forced laborers toiled at this vast project, at more than eighty camp sites at intervals of 15 kilometers along the 1,300-kilometer stretch. The estimated cost, if it had ever been completed, was from 4 to 6 million rubles per kilometer. In the end, 850 kilometers of rail, and 450 of telegraph poles only, had been completed. After Stalin's death, the line, the signals, the railway stations, the locomotives, and all that had been erected were abandoned to rust in the snow.[157]

But this was an irrationality of the Soviet political and planning system itself. When it came to an ordinary operation, such as logging, it might seem that a method of providing very cheap labor had indeed been found.

Some prisoners made efforts on the spot to estimate the economic value of the camps. A friend of mine who was in a logging camp in the Vorkuta area worked for a time on the administrative side there (from 1950 to 1952) and says that the results were to a large degree faked or inflated, as in ordinary Soviet factories at that time. A great deal of the work which counted against norms was of a valueless nature, and although the prisoners themselves received the barest minimum of all necessities, the total cost of the camp, with guards, administration, and so forth, was much in excess of the value of its output. Antoni Ekart reports much the same of the Vorkuta mines[158]—which, however, would probably have been uneconomic even if run by free labor because of the distances involved and the total production effected. And a careful study[159] makes the supposed savings due to forced labor over the whole economy at best marginal.

A Soviet account reinforces this view. The writer recalls a conversation in which one of the technicians on the job, himself a former prisoner, commented on the suggestion that the use of convict labor for construction projects was relatively cheap:

> It merely seems so. After all the prisoners have somehow to be fed, shod, clothed, and guarded; special areas have to be constructed, provided with watchtowers for the guards—yes and for that matter the maintenance of the guards is a costly matter. Then also there is the physical training section and all the other "sections" which in fact only exist on paper . . . in fact a sizable establishment. Then there are those again who have to fetch the water for them, heat the baths and wash the floors. After

all there are a lot of things that human beings need. There are also many duty officers and personnel, the hewers of wood and drawers of water, the countless carpenters, clerks and other "scabs" as they are called in the camp! So that if one averages it out you must reckon one and a half ancillary persons for every one who actually works. The other main thing is that the guards cannot deploy the labor force as it ought to be: either one is not allowed to use the proper machinery, or else the foremen, not to mention the convicts themselves, simply have no time to stop and think about how to organize the labor force because of the consequent parades, inspections, and the rest of the to-ing and fro-ing.[160]

The maintenance of the guards, it may be remarked, was also a *military* debit. Throughout the war period, the camps continued to be guarded by picked NKVD soldiers, in a proportion of about one guard to twenty inmates. The Soviet Government thus forfeited the use of certainly no fewer than 250,000 trained and healthy troops.

Even so, in certain circumstances, forced labor does seem to have paid: coal from Karaganda was sometimes noticeably cheaper than that from the Donets Basin.[161] Moreover, there are certain fields where free labor would be inordinately expensive, and where slave labor is probably economically preferable—for instance, in the mines and strategic roads of northeastern Siberia. In 1951, in the United States Congress, the immense labor cost of setting up an American air base in Greenland was disclosed. We can be sure that the equivalents in northern Siberia were completed far more cheaply with slave labor than they could have been with even Soviet free labor. That is to say, while it is true that the forced-labor system was not limitlessly expandable, it may have paid in certain fields.

In any case, to start examining the economics of the operation in an abstract way is clearly a mistake. A man killed by squeezing a year or two's effort out of him is of more use than a man kept in prison. The camps were *politically* efficient. They effectively isolated masses of potential troublemakers, and were a great disincentive to any sort of anti-Stalinist activity, or even talk. Assuming that the political purging was necessary, the camps were a useful end product.

Like everything else in Stalin's epoch, the system operated by pressure from the top down. Every camp had its "plan," and every camp chief worked under a system of penalties and rewards. There were some odd results. Camp chiefs are reported as having kept recaptured prisoners whom they should have returned to their original camps. Again, in the prison at Kotlas, there was a group of prisoners consisting entirely of invalids and old people, whom none of the camps would accept, for obvious economic reasons. They remained there for over a year as the problem solved itself by their dying.[162]

## FOOD AND DEATH

In the camps, the commandants operated the norm system vis-à-vis the prisoners. As a general principle there were various "cauldrons," or food allotments. The principle is simple enough. Precise figures varied considerably, but the following shows a typical proportion. In the Kolyma camps, for men doing twelve to sixteen hours' heavy physical labor a day, eight months of it in very low temperatures, the daily ration, of very poor bread, is given as follows by a former prisoner writing in the West:

| | |
|---:|:---|
| for more than 100% of the norm | up to 930 grams (32 oz.) |
| for 100% | 815 grams (28½ oz.) |
| for 70–99% | 715 grams (25 oz.) |
| for 50–69% | 500 grams (17½ oz.) |
| disciplinary ration | 300 grams (10½ oz.) |

plus "soup," 3½ oz. of salt fish, and just over 2 oz. of groats[163]

A Soviet account of the same area gives

| | |
|---:|:---|
| for 100% fulfillment | 800 grams |
| nonfulfillment for whatever reason | 500 grams |
| punitive | 300 grams[164] |

The first is given in ounces in the original, so the slight discrepancy has no significance. What seems to be the abolition of the intermediate stage may be due to the fact that the Russian was serving there later—from 1942 until at least 1950—as against the other's circa 1938 to 1946. A Polish account, of 1940 to 1941, gives 500 grams for 50 percent norm and 300 for less.[165]

Another reported ration scheme, in one of the northern camps in the winter of 1941/1942:

| | |
|---:|:---|
| for the full norm | 700 grams of bread, plus soup and buckwheat |
| for those not attaining the norm | 400 grams of bread, plus soup[166] |

Most Arctic arrangements were probably close to these two. The ration outside the Arctic proper was rather lower, typically

| | |
|---:|:---|
| over 100% | 750–1,000 grams |
| 100% | 600–650 grams |
| 50–100% | 400–475 grams |
| penal (under 50%) | 300–400 grams[167] |

These rations may be compared with those of a camp system more familiar to Western readers—that of one of the Japanese P.O.W. camps on the River Kwai (Tha Makham). There, prisoners got a daily ration norm of 700 grams of rice, 600 of vegetables, 100 of meat, 20 of sugar, 20 of salt, and 5 of oil—for a total of 3,400 calories, but, as in Russia, very deficient in vitamins.[168] (Even in the 1980s in the USSR, the camp norm was of 2,400 calories only, mainly based on 700 grams of black bread.)

We can make certain other comparisons. In the Ukrainian cities in the famine period of the 1930s, the bread ration was 800 grams for industrial workers, 600 for manual workers, 400 for office employees. In the siege of Leningrad, in 1941 to 1942, about one-third to one-half of the population remaining in the city died of hunger, mostly during the first winter. The rations in the worst period were

| | |
|---|---|
| October 1941 | the basic ration was down to 400 grams of bread a day for workers and 200 grams for dependents |
| Late November 1941 | 250 grams for workers and 125 for dependents |
| Late December 1941 | up to 350 grams for workers and 200 for dependents[169] |

At Leningrad, there were small additional rations of meat and sugar; lumber workers got a supplementary ration above the norm; and a truly major difference is that in camps the prisoners never got their full ration, and if there was a bad or inedible portion of the original bulk ration, that was the part that went to them. Solzhenitsyn describes what happens to the groat issue:

Shukhov had had thousands of these rations in prisons and camps, and though he'd never had a chance to weigh a single one of them on a scale . . . he and every other prisoner had known a long time that the people who cut up and issued your bread wouldn't last long if they gave you honest rations. Every ration was short. The only question was—by how much?[170]

The reason was obvious:

When they left in the morning, the cook got an issue of groats from the big kitchen in the camp. It worked out to about two ounces a head—about two pounds for each gang. That is, a little over twenty pounds for everybody working on the site. The cook didn't carry that stuff himself on the two-mile march from the camp. He had a trusty who carried it for him. He thought it was better to slip an extra portion of the stuff to a trusty at the expense of the prisoners' bellies rather than to break his own back. Then there was water and firewood to carry and the stove to light. The cook didn't do that either. He had other prisoners and "goners" to do it. And they got their cut too. It's easy to give away things that don't belong to you.

All the cook did was put groats and salt in the cauldron, and if there was any fat he split it between the cauldron and himself. (The good fat never got as far as the prisoners. Only the bad stuff went in the cauldron. . . .) Then his only job was to stir the mush when it was nearly ready. The sanitary inspector didn't even do that much. He just sat and watched. When the mush was ready, the cook gave him some right away and he could eat all he wanted. And so could the cook. Then one of the gang bosses—they took turns, a different one every day—came to taste it and see if it was good enough for the men to eat. He got a double portion too.

After this, the whistle went off. Now the other gang bosses came and the cook handed them their bowls through a kind of hatch in the wall. The bowls had this watery mush in them. And you didn't ask how much of the ration they'd really put in it. You'd get hell if you opened your mouth.[171]

And so it was with everything: "They stole all the way down the line—out here on the site, in the camp, and in the stores too."[172]

The system was made more effective yet, in the lumber camps in particular, by turning it into a "brigade," a gang, matter, with collective responsibility for inadequate work:

You might ask why a prisoner worked so hard for ten years in a camp. Why didn't they say to hell with it and drag their feet all day long till the night, which was theirs?

But it wasn't so simple. . . . It was like this—either you all got something extra or you all starved. ("You're not pulling your weight, you swine, and I've got to go hungry because of you. So work, you bastard!")

So when a really tough job came along, like now, you couldn't sit on your hands. Like it or not, you had to get a move on. Either they made the place warm within two hours or they'd all be fucking well dead.[173]

The brigade leader, himself a prisoner, worked out with a foreman, "the team surveyor," the amount of work done by his brigade. Other camp officials then estimated the production compared with the "daily norm." Their decisions were then sent to the food department for rationing according to the output.[174]

More depended on the work rates than the work itself. A clever boss who knows his business really sweats over these work rates. That's where the ration comes from. If a job hasn't been done, make it look like it had. If the rates were low on a job, try to hike 'em up. You had to have brains for this and a lot of pull with the fellows who kept the work sheets. And they didn't do it for nothing.

But come to think of it, who were these rates for? For the people who ran the camps. They made thousands on the deal and got bonuses on top for the officers. Like old Volkovoy, with that whip of his. And all you got out of it was six ounces of bread in the evening. Your life depended on them.[175]

On one occasion, the gang boss gets "better rates." This means that "they'd have good bread rations for five days. Well, maybe four. The higher-ups always cheat on one day out of five."[176]

As to the quality of the food, the convicts in Solzhenitsyn's book discuss the film *Battleship Potemkin*. The maggots on the meat which cause the mutiny are thought to be unrealistically large, and this is explained as necessary from the film point of view. Then comes the comment: "If they brought that kind of meat to the camp, I can tell you, and put it in the cauldron instead of the rotten fish we get, I bet we'd . . ."[177]

He describes a meal:

The gruel didn't change from one day to the next. It depended on what vegetables they'd stored for the winter. The year before they'd only stocked up with salted carrots, so there was nothing but carrots in the gruel from September to June. And now it was cabbage. The camp was best fed in June, when they ran out of vegetables and started using groats instead. The worst time was July, when they put shredded nettles in the cauldron.

The fish was mostly bones. The flesh was boiled off except for bits on the tails and the heads. Not leaving a single scale or speck of flesh on the skeleton, Shukhov crunched and sucked the bones and spat them out on the table. He didn't leave anything—not even the gills or tail. He ate the eyes too when they were still in place, but when they'd come off and were floating around in the bowl on their own he didn't eat them. The others laughed at him for this.

. . . The second course was a mush made from *magara*. It was one solid lump, and Shukhov broke it off in pieces. When it was hot—never mind when it was cold—it had no taste and didn't fill you. It was nothing but grass that looked like millet. They'd gotten the bright idea of serving it instead of groats. It came from the Chinese, they said. They got ten ounces of it and that was that. It wasn't the real thing, but it passed for mush.[178]

The ration, and the whole estimate of norms, depended on all sorts of factors. First, the ideas of the officials in determining the piecework. For some types of work, it was on occasion set far above the possible—for example, in building the Kotlas–Vorkuta railway. It was impossible to do more than about 30 percent of the quota, so the ration, for this extremely hard work, was down to 400 grams.[179] On the extension down to Khalmer-Yu, average expectation of life was about three months.[180]

Again, the goodness or badness of the year's harvest immediately affected rations. The bad harvest of 1936 produced an appalling level of mortality from starvation in the camps in 1937.

Trouble was caused by the desire to eat anything at all. Rubbish boxes from the kitchens might be attacked by gangs. When these, in one camp, were thrown into the cesspool by the latrines, "even there the gangs waded after them."[181] When grass came up, every blade might be put in a tin and boiled and eaten. Grass eating was most common among intellectuals. Its long-term effects were deadly. Others tried to satisfy their appetites with boiling salt water, also ineffective.[182]

Even in Solzhenitsyn's penal camp, there are convicts who have served in worse places—a lumber camp where work went on until midnight if necessary to fill the quotas, and the basic ration was six ounces less.[183] In the area of the far north, to the east of the Urals, there seem to have been a number of camps of particularly rigorous regime, which are described as of "complete isolation." Only a few rumors about them have emerged, as no one seems in any circumstances to have been released. The death rate is said to have been very high. Novaya Zemlya had an extremely bad reputation—with few, if any, returning.

Special punitive camps are often reported. After the introduction of a new and harsher regime of *katorga* in the early 1940s, those so sentenced were deprived of blankets and mattresses for the first three years and otherwise subjected to harder labor, longer hours, and worse conditions.[184] Sometimes, as in the Dzhido camp, offending prisoners were put in chains for the remainder of their sentences.[185] For women, the Stalinogorsk camp was particularly severe: inmates worked in iron and coal mines. The second Alekseyevka camp, in the Kargopol group, a particularly bad one listed as a disciplinary camp but in fact full of foreign prisoners who had had no time to commit offenses in other camps, had a large number of Polish Jews who had escaped from the Nazi persecution and died like flies. They hated the Soviet regime more bitterly and passionately than anyone in the camps.[186]

In one respect, Solzhenitsyn was lucky. He was not in a lumber camp. Here rations were notoriously low, and work was extremely hard. Professor Swianiewicz, who was himself in a lumber camp at one time, says that the former inmates are inclined to overestimate the proportion of prisoners sent to such work, probably because they were "under the constant fear of being sent to the forest. It was the equivalent of a death sentence for a person not accustomed to heavy physical work to be assigned for a long period to a felling brigade."[187] One former assistant to a doctor in a northern camp says that in two successive winters about 50 percent of the workers in some forestry brigades died. Overall, about 30 percent of the labor force was lost by death or total exhaustion per annum.[188] A Pole who was briefly in Alekseyevka describes the visible death as extraordinary. He saw two drop dead as they left the gates with other brigades. In his own brigade, three died at the work site on the first day.[189] A very active man would sometimes remain healthy by producing 120 or 150 percent of his quota for a year or eighteen months, and then one night would be found dead of heart failure in his bunk.[190]

Even comparatively mild lumber camps were great killers. Finnish prisoners who were experts in the matter held that the norms prevailing were impossible even for the best-fed workers. They could only be brought down even to the barely tolerable level by various forms of cheating (tufta) and bribery—using the same logs over again by sawing off the stamped end, and so forth. Herling never came across a prisoner who had worked in the forest for more than two years. After a year, prisoners were usually incurable and, following transfer as "goners" to lighter work, retired to the mortuary.[191]

This was the last stage in the camps. When worn down, debilitated to the degree that no serious work could any longer be got out of them, prisoners were put on substarvation rations and allowed to hang around the camp doing odd jobs until they died. This category is recognized in Soviet as well as foreign books. Gorbatov, who describes the usual symptoms, confirms that to go sick was ordinarily fatal. For if you did, you had your ration cut and from that point there was no way out.[192] This corps commander was at one time able to sweep the camp office floors, and there found an occasional crust to keep him going. He was himself saved from death by a friendly doctor who got him transferred to an easier post. In general, throughout the period, all our sources emphasize that survival for any length of time was rare in most camps except among those qualifying for "functions"—office jobs or other work enabling them to escape the main labor of the camp in question.

During bad periods "the camps of the disabled and unfit . . . became the most populous, and the largest labor brigades were those of the woodcutters and the gravediggers."[193] The dead were buried in pits, with small wooden tags attached with string to their legs.[194]

One estimate is that a batch of prisoners in the camps would, on the average, lose half its number in two or three years.[195] An NKVD functionary who worked on the Baltic–White Sea Canal group of camps gave evidence[196] that there were 250,000 prisoners in these camps at the beginning of the Purges, and the death rate was 700 a day, a figure also given elsewhere.[197] However, 1,500 new prisoners came in daily, so the population continued to rise.

The mortality rate of the camps in 1933 is estimated at about 10 percent per annum, and in 1938 to be running at about 20 percent.[198] The 1936 prisoners were almost all extinct by 1940. A woman who worked in a camp hospital notes that patients sentenced in 1937 and 1938 filled it in 1939 and 1940, but by 1941 there were few of them to be seen.[199]

In any case, of those who went into the camps, only a small proportion ever came out again. For long, some of the best evidence we had came from German Communists withdrawn from the camps and handed over to the Nazis in 1939 and

1940, from Poles released under the 1941 treaty, and from others who, benefiting from exceptional circumstances, were in for equally short periods. In general, releases were very rare, and survival until the post-Stalin amnesties rarer still.

The length of sentence anyhow made little difference. (Those who were released were in any case all rearrested around 1947–1948.) Upon the expiration of a sentence, it was usual for prisoners to be called before a Special Section officer and given a few more years, though in some cases they were sent back to prison in Moscow or elsewhere, reinterrogated, and sentenced for fresh crimes.

> Shukhov sort of liked the way they pointed at him—the lucky guy nearly through with his sentence. But he didn't really believe it. Take the fellows who should've been let out in the war. They were all kept in till forty-six—"till further notice." And then those with three years who'd gotten five more slapped on. They twisted the law any way they wanted. You finished a ten-year stretch and they gave you another one. Or if not, they still wouldn't let you go home.[200]

We do know of people who lasted up to seventeen years and were then rehabilitated—Snegov, referred to in Khrushchev's Secret Speech, for instance, or Lieutenant-General Todorsky. They seem to have served in the less severe camps. But much of the published Soviet evidence until 1987 was from figures such as Gorbatov, who was among the rehabilitated officers of 1940 and would not otherwise have survived. (The routine of rehabilitation, in those few cases in which it applied, was slow. Gorbatov had, he later found out, been defended by Budenny, and on 20 March 1940 his sentence was rescinded and a review ordered. He did not get back from Magadan to the Butyrka until 25 December 1940. By 1 March 1941 he was in the Lubyanka, and on 5 March he was released.)

The other sort of Soviet witness was of the type of Solzhenitsyn, who says that though a man might possibly last ten years, any much longer period was out of the question—and this at a comparatively good period in camp history. Solzhenitsyn was in fact released after ten years, in the post-Stalin rehabilitations. He had fortunately been sentenced late in Stalin's life. A man sentenced in 1938 would have had to wait seventeen or eighteen years. Of those arrested in the period 1936 to 1938, we can hardly allow 10 percent to have survived; in fact, a Soviet historian tells us that 90 percent of those who went to camp before the war perished, while Academician Sakharov notes that only 50,000 of the more than 600,000 party members sent to camp, rather than executed, survived.[201] A million would be an outside figure. Of the other 7 million-odd, the number who died either by execution or in camps during the actual two-year Yezhov period may be taken as about 3 million.[202] The rest followed over a period of years, during which time their number was continually added to by the victims of later arrest.

A recent Soviet article puts it that "their death was caused by unbearable toil, by cold and starvation, by unheard-of degradation and humiliation, by a life which could not have been endured by any other mammal."[203]

In another we read,

> I often hear the word "lucky" from those I am recording. I was lucky—the firing squad was replaced by twenty-five years of hard labor; lucky—I waited for hours on the tundra to be shot but wasn't; lucky—I was transferred from general work to the meteorological station; lucky—I had enough time to take my daughter to my parents

before the arrest; lucky. . . . One day we shall learn how many people died in the prisons and camps and how many returned.[204]

A Soviet poet wrote as long ago as 1963, in *Izvestiya,*

> There—row on row, according to years,
> Kolyma, Magadan,
> Vorkuta and Narym
> Marched in invisible columns.
>
> The region of eternal frost
> Wrote men off into eternity,
> Moved them from the category of "living"
> To that of "dead" (little difference between them)—
>
> Behind that barbed wire
> White and grizzled—
> With that Special Article of the law code
> Clipped to their case files.
>
> Who and what for and by whose will—
> Figure it out, History.[205]

# THE GREAT TRIAL

*Le dernier acte est sanglant, quelque belle que soit la comédie en tout le reste.*

Pascal

Preparations for the greatest trial of all were in less expert hands than those which had produced the Zinoviev and Pyatakov shows. The NKVD veterans had gone. Agranov had by now followed Yagoda and his staff, being "in 1937 expelled from the Party for systematic breaches of socialist legality,"[1] or so a later Soviet footnote has it, as if asking us to believe that such practices were frowned on by the Party leadership of that year. He died, presumed shot, in 1938.[2] His wife was also shot.[3]

Instead of Molchanov and Mironov, Agranov and Gay, Yezhov's team for the 1938 Trial consisted basically of the experienced Zakovsky, promoted from Leningrad; Mikhail Frinovsky, who under Yagoda had been Commander of the NKVD's Frontier Troops; I. I. Shapiro, Head of Yezhov's Secretariat and of the new Section for Investigating Specially Important Cases; and to some extent Slutsky of the Foreign Department.[4] They were all themselves to perish, but meanwhile they had after all contrived a show not grossly inferior to its two predecessors. The plot was more complicated, and more horrifying, and there were faults of detail which attracted the censure of the stricter critics. But on the whole, it was a fair success.

It might be thought (as we have said) that no public trial was now necessary. The opposition and the semi-independent voices among Stalin's own supporters had been crushed. The third trial was in this sense little more than a victory parade. It brought together publicly every type of opposition, terror, sabotage, treachery, and espionage, and turned them into branches of one single great conspiracy. For the 1936 Trial, Molchanov had prepared for Stalin "a special diagram . . . a system of many colored lines on the diagram indicated when and through whom Trotsky had communicated with the leaders of the conspiracy in the U.S.S.R."[5] Such a diagram showing all the links in the Bukharin Case would be one of great complexity. The trial, which opened in the October Hall on 2 March 1938, had, indeed, taken over a year to prepare, but it was a production of far greater scope than the others.

For all the threads were now pulled together. The Rightists, Bukharin and

Rykov, were linked to Trotsky; to the earlier Zinovievite and Trotskyite plotters; to Trotskyites, hitherto considered ex-Trotskyites, who had not yet been tried; to the usual dozens of terrorist action groups; to the espionage organizations of several powers. They had set up at least two "reserve" centers; they had been involved in Yenukidze's plots; and they were closely concerned with that of Tukhachevsky. They had formed organizational connections with underground nationalist conspirators in half a dozen of the non-Russian Soviet Republics. Their own "Rightist" grouping had involved dozens of men thought to be loyal Stalinists, in high positions in the State. And, as a final touch, they had throughout had as a major accomplice Yagoda, with all his leading subordinates.

As Vladimir Voinovich comments of the shorthand report of the Trial in *The Ivankiad*:

> Don't regard it as a document, for it is not a document; don't think about methods of investigation, about why Krestinsky first offered one story, then another. Regard it as a work of art. And you will agree that you've never read anything like it in all of world literature. What well-defined characters! What a grandiose plot, and how cohesive and integrated everything was. It's just too bad that the characters were living people, otherwise you might be able to stand reading it.[6]

"In the dingy winter daylight and under the stale glare of the electric lamps,"[7] a wide variety of prisoners sat in the dock. In the first trial, Zinoviev and Kamenev, and to a lesser extent Smirnov and Evdokimov, were the only well-known figures. The second, with Pyatakov, Radek, and Sokolnikov, was less impressive still. And in each case, the supporting cast consisted mainly of third-rate alleged terrorists and only slightly more interesting engineers.

This time, three members of Lenin's Politburo stood in the dock—Bukharin, Rykov, and Krestinsky. With them were the legendary Rakovsky, leader of the Balkan and Ukrainian revolutionary movements, and the sinister figure of Yagoda, the Secret Police personified, looking right and left with a certain rat-like vitality. A group of the most senior officials of the Stalinist state who had for many years served it uncritically formed the bulk of the accused: Rosengolts, Ivanov, Chernov, and Grinko—all People's Commissars until the previous year; Zelensky, Head of the Cooperatives; and Sharangovich, First Secretary in Byelorussia. For the first time, two Asians, the Uzbek leaders Khodzhayev and Ikramov, denounced the previous year for bourgeois nationalism, took their places beside the European accused. These main political accused were supplemented by five minor figures: Bessonov, who had worked in the Soviet Trade Delegation in Berlin; Zubarev, an official of the Agriculture Commissariat; and the former secretaries of Yagoda, of Kuibyshev, and of Maxim Gorky. Last, by a fearful innovation, there were three men far from public life, the doctors Pletnev, Levin, and Kazakov—the first two highly distinguished in their field and the oldest men in dock (sixty-six and sixty-eight, respectively).

The indictment was a comprehensive one—of espionage, wrecking, undermining Soviet military power, provoking a military attack on the USSR, plotting the dismemberment of the USSR, and overthrowing the social system in favor of a return to capitalism. For these purposes, the accused had assembled this vast conspiracy of Trotskyites, Zinovievites, Rightists, Mensheviks, Socialist Revolutionaries, and "bourgeois nationalists" from the whole Soviet periphery. They had been in close cooperation with the military plotters. A number of them had been spies of Germany, Britain, Japan, and Poland since the early 1920s. Several of them had been Tsarist agents in the revolutionary movement. Wrecking had been committed in industry, agriculture, trade, and finance.

On the terror side, they had been responsible for the assassination of Kirov, which Yagoda had facilitated through Zaporozhets. But in addition, they had caused the deaths of Kuibyshev and of Maxim Gorky, hitherto regarded as natural (and of the former OGPU chief, Menzhinsky, and of Gorky's son Peshkov into the bargain). This had been done by medical murder. Yagoda was also charged with an attempt to poison Yezhov. And a variety of the more usual fruitless plans to assassinate Stalin and other leaders were also alleged.

A brand-new charge, against Bukharin alone of those in dock, was of having plotted to seize power in 1918 and to murder Lenin and Stalin at the same time.

We are now told that when, "thirteen months later," Frinovsky was himself interrogated, he recounted how he had "prepared" witnesses in this trial, and then brought them before Yezhov, who warned them not to change their stories in the public trial; if at any point before then they retracted, they were returned to interrogation. (But this 1939 confession by Frinovsky was not thought to necessitate any revising of the 1938 verdict.)[8] We also learn that rehearsals were held, and a recent Soviet document tells us how "Yezhov more than once talked with Rykov, Bukharin, Bulanov, and assured each of them that they would not be shot." To Bukharin, he said, "Conduct yourself well in the trial—I will promise you they will not shoot you."[9]

Once again Ulrikh presided, assisted by Matulevich and a new junior figure, Yevlev. And once again, Vyshinsky conducted the prosecution. Only the three doctors had defense counsel, and they were represented by two of the same lawyers who had done their bit for the prosecution in the same roles in the Pyatakov Trial.

## A CONFESSION WITHDRAWN

The first sensation of the trial came almost at once, when the accused were asked their pleas. These were all the usual "guilty," until Krestinsky was reached.

Krestinsky, "a pale, seedy, dim little figure, his steel-rimmed spectacles perched on his beaky nose,"[10] replied firmly to Ulrikh:

> I plead not guilty. I am not a Trotskyite. I was never a member of the bloc of Rights and Trotskyites, of whose existence I was not aware. Nor have I committed any of the crimes with which I personally am charged, in particular I plead not guilty to the charge of having had connections with the German intelligence service.
>
> *The President:* Do you corroborate the confession you made at the preliminary investigation?
>
> *Krestinsky:* Yes, at the preliminary investigation I confessed, but I have never been a Trotskyite.
>
> *The President:* I repeat the question, do you plead guilty?

> *Krestinsky:* Before my arrest I was a member of the Communist Party of the Soviet Union (bolsheviks) and I remain one now.

> *The President:* Do you plead guilty to the charge of participating in espionage activities and of participating in terrorist activities?

> *Krestinsky:* I have never been a Trotskyite. I have never belonged to the bloc of Rights and Trotskyites and have not committed a single crime.[11]

After the pleas, the court recessed for twenty minutes. It has been suggested that this was to give time to put a little pressure on Krestinsky. Probably; but the recess was only five minutes longer than that at the previous trials.

The court proceeded with the examination of Bessonov, who from his post as Counselor in the Soviet Embassy in Berlin was the alleged contact man with Trotsky and Sedov. Bessonov, a grim, gray-faced man with the air of an automaton,[12] had been arrested on 28 February 1937, the day after Bukharin and Rykov. He had denied the main charges until 30 December 1937, when a combination of torture and the conveyor finally broke him.[13] But meanwhile, he had been tried on 13 August before the Military Collegium of the Supreme Court ("composed of almost the same people as in the present Trial"),[14] which neither acquitted nor condemned him, but sent the case for further examination.

This can hardly mean other than that it had been decided to save him for a major trial: as a minor diplomat, and ex-Socialist Revolutionary, he was bound to be purged in any case. He must have appeared a suitable courier. The case is comparable with that of the Komsomols of 1935, saved for the Zinoviev Trial.

When Bessonov now confessed that he had indeed been involved in Trotskyite plots with Krestinsky, Vyshinsky referred to Krestinsky's refusal to admit this. Bessonov smiled. Vyshinsky asked, "Why are you smiling?" Bessonov replied, "The reason why I am standing here is that Nikolai Nikolayevich Krestinsky named me as the liaison man with Trotsky. Besides him and Pyatakov nobody knew about this."[15] Something of the mechanics of confessions implicating others, and of the whole tangled net of moral responsibility, comes through. In his final plea, Bessonov was to remark that it was not until Krestinsky implicated him in October 1937 that his resistance to interrogation started to become hopeless.[16]

In general, after Bessonov had made a few points about connections with Sedov and Pyatakov, his examination was largely turned into an excuse for baiting Krestinsky. The latter admitted he had met Bessonov in the West, but denied any Trotskyite links:

> *Vyshinsky:* And about Trotskyite affairs?

> *Krestinsky:* We did not talk about them. I was not a Trotskyite.

> *Vyshinsky:* You never talked about them.

> *Krestinsky:* Never.

> *Vyshinsky:* That means that Bessonov is not telling the truth, and that you are telling the truth. Do you always tell the truth.

> *Krestinsky:* No.

> *Vyshinsky:* Not always. Accused Krestinsky, you and I will have to examine serious matters and there is no need to get excited. Consequently, Bessonov is not telling the truth?

*Krestinsky:* No.

*Vyshinsky:* But you too do not always tell the truth. Is that not so?

*Krestinsky:* I did not always tell the truth during the investigation.

*Vyshinsky:* But at other times you always tell the truth?

*Krestinsky:* The truth.

*Vyshinsky:* Why this lack of respect for the investigation, why during the investigation did you tell untruths? Explain.

*Krestinsky:* (No reply.)[17]

A few minutes later, Bessonov spoke of Krestinsky's formulations. Vyshinsky interrupted in an unpleasant tone, "Briefly, because I think that Krestinsky will himself talk about these purposes later." And, after Bessonov had made his point, Vyshinsky turned to Krestinsky and asked, "Accused Krestinsky, do you recall such diplomatic conversations with Bessonov?" Krestinsky answered firmly, "No, we never had such conversations."[18]

Two minutes later, it was:

*Vyshinsky:* You do not remember the details, but Bessonov does.

*Krestinsky:* There was not a word said about the Trotskyite stand.[19]

Finally, the question of Krestinsky's confession was faced directly:

*Vyshinsky:* But what about your admission?

*Krestinsky:* During the investigation I gave false testimony several times.

*Vyshinsky:* You said, 'I did not formally belong to the Trotskyite centre.' Is that true or not?

*Krestinsky:* I did not belong to it at all.

*Vyshinsky:* You say that formally you did not belong. What is true and what is not true here? Perhaps it is all true, or it is all untrue, or only half of it is true? What percentage, how many grams of it are true?

*Krestinsky:* I did not belong to the Trotskyite centre because I was not a Trotskyite.

*Vyshinsky:* You were not a Trotskyite?

*Krestinsky:* No.[20]

Krestinsky went on to point out that he had abandoned Trotsky in 1927:

*Krestinsky:* I date my rupture with Trotsky and Trotskyism from 27 November 1927, when, through Serebryakov, who had returned from America and was in Moscow, I sent Trotsky a sharp letter containing sharp criticism. . . .

*Vyshinsky:* That letter is not in the records. We have another letter—your letter to Trotsky.

> *Krestinsky:* The letter I am referring to is in the possession of the Court investigator, because it was taken from me during the search, and I request this letter to be attached to the records.
>
> *Vyshinsky:* The records contain a letter dated 11 July 1927, taken from you during the search.
>
> *Krestinsky:* But there is another letter of 27 November. . . .
>
> *Vyshinsky:* There is no such letter.
>
> *Krestinsky:* That cannot be. . . .[21]

This was to be significant.

Pressed continually in a long exchange, Krestinsky gave his motives for earlier confessions:

> *Krestinsky:* At the preliminary investigation, before I was questioned by you, I had given false testimony.
>
> *Vyshinsky:* . . . And then you stuck to it.
>
> *Krestinsky:* . . . And then I stuck to it, because from personal experience I had arrived at the conviction that before the trial, if there was to be one, I would not succeed in refuting my testimony.[22]

Vyshinsky now called on Rosengolts, who confirmed Krestinsky's Trotskyism. Krestinsky, who had not been feeling well, slumped. Vyshinsky told him to listen. He replied that when he had taken a pill, he would be all right, but asked not to be questioned for a few minutes.

Rosengolts, then Grinko, gave evidence of Krestinsky's guilt. Krestinsky, recovering, continued to deny it:

> *Vyshinsky:* Here are three men on good terms with you who say what is not true?
>
> *Krestinsky:* Yes.

After several more denials, Vyshinsky again asked him directly, "When we interrogated you at the preliminary investigation, what did you say on this score?"

> *Krestinsky:* In giving testimony I did not refute any of my previous testimony, which I deliberately confirmed.
>
> *Vyshinsky:* You deliberately confirmed it. You were misleading the Prosecutor. Is that so, or not?
>
> *Krestinsky:* No.
>
> *Vyshinsky:* Why did you have to mislead me?
>
> *Krestinsky:* I simply considered that if I were to say what I am saying today—that it was not in accordance with the facts—my declaration would not reach the leaders of the Party and the Government.[23]

This clear statement of the position was greeted with a "shocked hush" from the audience.[24]

Questioning further about the preliminary examination, Vyshinsky asked, "If you were asked whether you had complaints, you should have answered that you had.'' And Krestinsky replied, ''I had in the sense that I did not speak voluntarily.''[25]

Vyshinsky then abandoned this line of questioning and turned to his official prey, Bessonov, who developed his connections with Trotsky at length, adding that Trotsky had hinted at the physical extermination of Maxim Gorky. The session ended with a further exchange with, and denial from, Krestinsky.

After a two-hour adjournment, the evening started off with the evidence of Grinko, former People's Commissar for Finance. He had been a Borotbist, and in the early 1920s had been dismissed from his post as Ukrainian Commissar for Education for excessive haste in carrying out Ukrainianization. In this capacity, he now implicated Lyubchenko and other lesser Ukrainians, such as Porayko, Deputy Chairman of the Ukrainian Council of People's Commissars, as members of the ''national-fascist'' organization. In his Moscow role, he brought in a number of other leading figures, such as Antipov, Rudzutak, Yakovlev, and Vareikis, as Rightist plotters. He described how Yakir and Gamarnik had instructed the Head of the Department of Savings Banks to ''prepare a terrorist act'' against Yezhov, and how other conspirators had arranged for an official of the Northern Sea Route to do the same against Stalin. His own main activity had been financial sabotage, which he had defined at the preliminary examination:

> The main object of undermining work in the People's Commissariat of Finance was the following: to weaken the Soviet rouble, to weaken the financial power of the U.S.S.R., to dislocate the economy and thus rouse among the population discontent with the financial policy of the Soviet power, discontent over taxes, discontent with bad savings bank service, delays in paying wages, etc., which were to result in wide, organized discontent with the Soviet power and were to help the conspirators to recruit adherents and to develop insurrectionary activities.[26]

This sort of theme—the blaming of all the errors and malpractices of the Soviet economy on sabotage by the accused—was to run through the trial. For all spheres of life, there was someone in the dock to answer for popular discontents. And the evidence tells us a huge amount about Soviet conditions.

Grinko, similarly, had been involved with Zelensky and others in trade hold-ups:

> *Grinko:* . . . Bolotin in the People's Commissariat of Internal Trade, carried on undermining activities, created a shortage of goods, goods difficulties in the country. . . . Zelensky, on the instructions of the bloc of Rights and Trotskyites, sent huge quantities of goods to the districts where there was a poor harvest and small quantities of goods to the districts where there were good harvests, and this caused goods to remain on the shelves in some districts and a shortage of goods in others.[27]

But once again, Vyshinsky diverged to attack Krestinsky. Again he was rebuffed by a firm, ''I deny that I talked with Fascists for Trotskyite purposes.''

At this, Rykov was called on. He, too, confirmed Krestinsky's guilt. Krestinsky once more asserted flatly that he knew nothing of any illegal activities, and the intervention of Ulrikh could get no more out of him.

But Rykov, too, proved unsatisfactory, though in a different way. In the period before his arrest, he had taken to heavy drinking, and reduced himself to a bad condition which the long strain of his imprisonment had, in its different way, done nothing to help. During cross-examination, he sometimes seemed to have gone to pieces, punctuating his answers with inane giggles.[28] But he rallied. At first he was vague:

> *Grinko:* From Rykov I learnt that Yagoda belonged to this organization, but I had no direct connections with Yagoda.
>
> *Vyshinsky:* (to the court): Permit me to question Rykov. Accused Rykov, did you tell Grinko about this?
>
> *Rykov:* I do not remember exactly, but I cannot exclude such a fact.
>
> *Vyshinsky:* Hence, you told him about Yagoda's membership?
>
> *Rykov:* Yes.

Now, wrecking was raised:

> *Vyshinsky:* Accused Rykov, do you corroborate this conversation with Grinko about wrecking?
>
> *Rykov:* I don't accept that. I deny it, not because I want to minimize my guilt. I have done much worse things than this.[30]

But then he got into his stride on the line which both he and (much more forcefully and consistently) Bukharin were to take throughout. That is, they admitted forming an illegal organization, confessed to giving it a terrorist "orientation," accepted full responsibility in the abstract for all the acts allegedly committed, but denied personal knowledge of or connection with any particular crime. They were thus able to point out that they were freely confessing to capital crimes, so that their denials of the particular acts could not be interpreted as attempts to evade the penalty.

The last to be examined on 2 March was Chernov. Ex-Menshevik and ex-theological student (like Bessonov—and Mikoyan and Stalin), he had been in charge of grain collection in the Ukraine in 1929 and 1930, and had more recently been serving as All-Union People's Commissar for Agriculture. He had been a ruthless executer of Stalin's will in the collectivization campaign, but apparently not a convinced one. He is reported as having said, during the 1930 slaughter of their livestock by the peasantry, that at least "for the first time in their sordid history, the Russian peasants have eaten their fill of meat."[31] He had started to confess on the day of his arrest.[32]

He now confessed to qualms about collectivization, and admitted sharing them, at the time, with a wide range of Ukrainian officials, including Zatonsky. But his main role in the dock was to take the blame for agricultural failures. He had only been removed from his post on 30 October 1937,[33] and could reasonably be blamed for much.

For example, there had been a good deal of livestock mortality. Back in September 1937, a spread of infective anemia among Soviet horses had been countered by the arrest of the Head of the Veterinary Administration of the People's Commissariat of Agriculture, Nedachin, the Head of the Veterinary Services of the Red Army,* Nikolsky, and a leading veterinary official in the Agricultural Commissariat, Chernyak, whose forthcoming trial was announced.[34] They had never again been heard of, but Chernov was now able to accept the blame for similar epidemics, spread through the agency of a different set of veterinarians:

> *Chernov:* . . . I performed the following acts of diversion. In order to cause heavy cattle mortality in Eastern Siberia, I instructed Ginsburg, Chief of the Veterinary Department, who belonged to the organization of the Rights, and through him the Chief of the Veterinary Supply Department, who also belonged to the organization of the Rights, not to supply anti-anthrax serum to Eastern Siberia, knowing that Eastern Siberia was particularly liable to anthrax. The serum was not supplied to Eastern Siberia. The preparations for this were made in 1935, and when there was an outbreak of anthrax there in 1936 it turned out that no serum was available, with the result that I cannot say how many exactly, but at any rate over 25,000 horses perished.
>
> Secondly, I instructed Ginsburg and Boyarshinov, Chief of the Bacteriological Department, to artificially infect pigs with erysipelas in the Leningrad Region and with plague in the Voronezh Region and the Azov-Black Sea Territory. . . .
>
> It is difficult to estimate the results, but at any rate it may be taken for granted that several tens of thousands of pigs perished owing to this diversive act.[35]

And a variety of other agricultural sabotage schemes, such as wrong types of crop rotation, the provision of bad seed, and so on, contributed to "lowering the harvest yield."

In Chernov's Ukrainian period, he had also undertaken to incense the middle peasants and Ukrainian national feeling generally by attributing the policies he had pursued to orders from Moscow. He had contacted Mensheviks abroad, and become a German spy. Rykov was his main connection in the Rightist center. Recalled, the ex-Premier again admitted the plot, but denied approving the actions. "All that he says is essentially and fundamentally true, but as to the part in which he said that I was in favour of distortions [of the agricultural policy], it seems to me he is wrong."[36] On the overthrow of the Soviet power, Rykov added, "I do not remember having such a conversation with Chernov, but of course the possibility of such a conversation is not precluded."[37] Finally, he denied various meetings with Chernov for wrecking purposes, and when Chernov said that to have neglected to give such instructions would have marked him as a very poor Rightist leader, he answered sardonically, "Perhaps I should have done as he says. It was a mistake on my part."[38] At which Ulrikh abruptly closed the day's session.

The next day, 3 March, started with the ex-medical student Ivanov, former

---

*The Senior Veterinary Surgeon of the Moscow Military District is reported in the Butyrka about this time. He was charged with destroying 25,000 horses of the cavalry reserve by issuing poisoned vaccine and was sentenced to death (R. V. Ivanov-Razumnik, *Memoirs* [London, 1965], p. 310).

People's Commissar for the Timber Industry. He had, of course, sabotaged that industry, on instructions from Rosengolts. Referring to the timber dumping which was a notorious aspect of Soviet trade policy in the early 1930s, he said:

> The most valuable timber was sold at reduced prices. This involved a loss to the Soviet State of several million roubles in foreign currency. Bukharin explained this measure as being an advance to the British bourgeoisie in return for the support it had promised. Otherwise, he said, we would not be taken seriously, and we would forfeit confidence.[39]

In the internal administration of lumbering, his main aim, curiously enough, had been the disruption of culture:

> Attention was chiefly devoted to hindering the technical re-equipment of lumbering, preventing the fulfillment of the plans of capital construction, especially in the cellulose and paper industry, in this way placing the country on a short paper ration and aiming a blow at the cultural revolution, interrupting the supply of exercise books and thus rousing discontent among the masses.[40]

He confessed also to having been involved in the "Left Communist" movement against Lenin, and to various attempts to organize insurrectionary bands (partly on British orders) and terrorist groups. In this connection, Bukharin was now questioned. He said he had ordered the formation of illegal organizations, but not insurrectionary bands. He had (though at a later date than that given by Ivanov) propounded an "insurrectionary orientation"—the Ryutin Platform. He had given no actual instructions for insurrectionary preparations, but he accepted the responsibility, in that a "practical worker" like Ivanov would doubtless go on to action on such a basis.[41]

When Vyshinsky said to him, "Hence, Ivanov's statements about connections with the British Intelligence Service . . . ," he interrupted, "I was totally uninformed about the Intelligence Service."[42]

The next questioning should, according to schedule, have been that of Krestinsky. But instead, a minor agricultural specialist from Chernov's Commissariat, Zubarev, appeared. He gave a good deal of evidence about disrupting the food supply.

*Vyshinsky:* Tell us the nature of your wrecking activities.

 *Zubarev:* . . . Causing confusion in seed cultivation, lowering the quality of the seeds, employing bad quality materials, bad sifting, careless storing, and the result of all this was not only a reduction in yield, but also a hostile mood of the peasantry, dissatisfaction with these so-called selected seeds. . . . My criminal activities consisted first of all in wrongly planning the sowing of vegetables. . . . Exactly the same kind of work was carried on in respect to retarding the development of fruit-tree nurseries.

  In respect to State farms, the main wrecking activities were that up to the last moment no proper rotation of crops was established, and in a number of State farms there was no rotation of crops at all. All this naturally reduced the yields. A large number of State farms which possessed large herds of cattle were left without fodder owing to the wrong crop rotation, and as a result we had the dying-off of cattle and slow development of the livestock farming. . . .[43]

And so on and so on. As well as with the Rights, he established connections with Muralov from the 1937 Trial. He had also organized a terrorist group in the Agriculture Commissariat, choosing Molotov as the prospective victim. He had carried out agricultural spying for Germany.

Zubarev's main contribution, however, was his recruitment as a Tsarist agent in 1908 and later. For Vyshinsky now produced a surprise witness. This was a police inspector of pre-Revolutionary days, Vasilyev, who had allegedly recruited Zubarev. The production of this aged Tsarist gendarme was treated by the court and "public" as a sort of comic turn. Even Vyshinsky was comparatively amiable to him, baiting him only with that puny malice which was the closest he could evidently get to good humor.[44]

With that, the morning session dragged to a close.

When the court reassembled at 6:00 P.M., Ulrikh announced to a tense court that the examination of Krestinsky would now take place. Vyshinsky interposed to say that he first wanted to put a few questions to Rakovsky.

He asked the old Bulgarian about the letter to Trotsky abandoning Trotskyism, which Krestinsky had referred to in the previous day's session. Rakovsky recalled it, and said it had been intended as a deception, and that Krestinsky had never broken with Trotskyism.

Vyshinsky then produced the letter, whose existence he would not acknowledge the previous day, and went on to argue that the letter itself, which spoke of the defeat of the opposition and the need to work in the Party, should be interpreted as a call to underhand subversion—a possible argument, indeed, but one scarcely compatible with an out-and-out deceptive surrender.

Finally he turned to Krestinsky. Did he accept this formulation?

Krestinsky, who was "looking more than ever like a small bedraggled sparrow,"[45] accepted it.

Vyshinsky asked if this meant that Krestinsky would now cease to deceive the court. The answer was a full confirmation of the evidence given at the preliminary inquiry. He admitted his guilt. On the first day, Krestinsky had occasionally been roused by Vyshinsky's taunts, but on the whole his tone is said to have been natural; it had now become flat and desperate.[46]

Vyshinsky pressed the point:

I have one question to ask Krestinsky: What, then, is the meaning of the statement you made yesterday, which cannot be regarded otherwise than as a piece of Trotskyite provocation in court?

Krestinsky: Yesterday, under the influence of momentary keen feeling of false shame, evoked by the atmosphere of the dock and the painful impression created by the public reading of the indictment, which was aggravated by my poor health, I could not bring myself to tell the truth, I could not bring myself to say that I was guilty. And instead of saying 'Yes, I am guilty,' I almost mechanically answered 'No, I am not guilty.'

Vyshinsky: Mechanically?

> *Krestinsky:* In the face of world public opinion, I had not the strength to admit the truth that I had been conducting a Trotskyite struggle all along. I request the court to register my statement that I fully and completely admit that I am guilty of all the gravest charges brought against me personally, and that I admit my complete responsibility for the treason and treachery I have committed.[47]

And now, despite Ulrikh's earlier announcement that the examination of Krestinsky was due, Vyshinsky at once dropped him and turned to the examination of Rykov. All this has very much the air of the prosecution playing safe, and not willing to risk a further retraction at this stage.

Stalin received regular reports on the case and gave advice. The latest Soviet account says that after he was informed of Krestinsky's retraction, he said, "You worked badly with that filth," and ordered a stop to be put to Krestinsky's talk. On the night of 2 March, "special measures" were taken. The interrogators dislocated his left shoulder, so that outwardly there was nothing to be seen. Bessonov is named has having told this version to the German engineer Hans Metzger in a prisoners' transfer train in 1939.[48] According to another variant, Krestinsky was also faced for hours with a battery of particularly bright lights, which damaged his already injured eyes, but only consented to confess on condition that the letter he had written to Trotsky should be put in the records.[49]

And if Krestinsky had hoped to rouse the other defendants to defy the court, he had had to recognize defeat. Indeed, he may never have hoped or intended his retraction to go beyond the first day, making what demonstration he felt to be in his power.

An alternative account leaked through NKVD circles was that Krestinsky's retraction and reaffirmation were a put-up job. Stalin was wishing to show that the defendants did not all confess like automata and thought that this single and temporary lapse would add a touch of verisimilitude.[50]

The arguments against this notion are very powerful. Krestinsky's phrasing during the first day sounds, on the face of it, genuine, and some of the points he makes seem to be both valid and extremely embarrassing to the prosecution. Vyshinsky's attitude is sinister in a way which appears more compatible with a genuine threat to Krestinsky than the appeal to his reason and conscience, which would be supposed to have produced the change in his evidence on the second day.

There is another and most suggestive piece of evidence from the trial itself. At the beginning, Vyshinsky announced the order in which he proposed to question the twenty-one prisoners. This was evidently a predetermined list, since it is repeated in the order in which they made their final pleas, except for one transposition among the minor characters. But the actual order of questioning was different. The first day went according to schedule—Bessonov, Grinko, Chernov. But on the second, Krestinsky should have had his examination-in-chief immediately after Ivanov. Instead, as we saw, the agricultural official Zubarev took the stand on the morning of 3 March, and in the afternoon Krestinsky was called upon not for a full examination, but only for a brief recantation. This, too, was preceded by the short and unscheduled interrogation of Rakovsky, undermining Krestinsky's point about the letter disavowing Trotskyism.

On the evening of 3 March, this was all that Krestinsky's examination amounted to. His full examination was postponed until the following afternoon, when the examinations of Rosengolts and Rakovsky were rescheduled, the former to precede and the latter to follow Krestinsky's. Rosengolts, as Krestinsky's alleged closest Trotskyite collaborator, established both Krestinsky's connections with Trotsky and the joint plotting activity of himself, Krestinsky, and the Tukhachevsky group in the days after the Pyatakov Trial and Bukharin's arrest. Krestinsky confirmed and elaborated all this, and Rakovsky rubbed it in afterward. All this seems to show an emergency procedure.

Nor is it difficult to see that the circumstances of his original interrogation were such as to make retraction possible. Krestinsky had been arrested at the end of May 1937. He confessed "after the lapse of a week . . . at the end of the first interrogation."[51] This was by torture in its most intensive form, and he was not, therefore, broken in the long-drawn-out fashion described on pages 124–127. It was just at that time that Bukharin was making his first confession, and it may be that it was momentarily intended to produce the next big trial at very short notice—and about as soon after the Pyatakov Trial as that had been after Zinoviev's.

If so, this perhaps came to nothing when Bukharin started to retract some of his confession (see p. 365), and the whole business of interrogating him had to begin over again. Meanwhile, with the spread of the Purge right through the Party, other useful additions to the case kept emerging, and it was nine months later that the trial took place.

However that may be, it is certainly the case that the NKVD seems to have had in its hands a leading prisoner who had not been brought into the right state for a trial by the most tried and successful procedure. Torture and the conveyor could produce confessions, but, as we have seen, the victim, once rested, recovered to the degree that he could retract them. He was not reduced to the degree of submission obtained by the longer method. Yet Krestinsky had confessed, and was being cooperative. There was no overt resistance to break.

Krestinsky's withdrawal of his confession was not unprecedented. During the Shakhty Trial, one of the accused (Skorutto) had refused to confess, been kept out of the court for a day on the grounds of illness, and then come back and confessed, only to withdraw the confession again, and the following day to reaffirm it. Again, in the Metro-Vic Trial, MacDonald withdrew, then reaffirmed, his original confession. It has never been thought that these withdrawals added anything to the credibility of the confession when finally produced.

Thus the argument that Stalin had planned the whole Krestinsky episode is a weak one. What seems more probable is that some such story was put round *within* the outer circles of the NKVD to account for the lapse. Another theory is that Krestinsky was replaced in the dock by a double or an actor. Observers present felt that it was someone different who appeared in the later phase of the trial. That Krestinsky did not appear to be "the same Krestinsky" after hours of NKVD attention seems natural enough. And recent long accounts in the Soviet press do not make the suggestion, speaking, in fact, of his reaffirming his confession after being "suitably worked over."[52]

In any case, Krestinsky's withdrawal, so dramatic and so cogent in its comments, barely affected the reception given to the trial by the foreign public. Stalin had won again.

## AN EX-PREMIER

Rykov's examination-in-chief came almost as an anticlimax. It started off mildly, soon coming to the alleged complicity of Yagoda in Rightist activity back in 1929. And now Yagoda, in turn, was questioned and gave one of those half-hearted affirmatives which any objective observer might have interpreted as a negative: "The fact is true, but not as Rykov puts it."

Rykov, who is said to have been "tortured quite brutally,"[53] still managed to inject a tone of irony into some of his remarks.[54] He went on to describe the supposed Rightist underground which arose after 1930. He then came to the Ryutin Platform—which, he said, he, Tomsky, Bukharin, Vasily Shmidt, and Uglanov had been responsible for. Ryutin had merely fronted for them, and Yagoda's protection had saved the main culprits. The Platform

> recognized (as far as I remember, and I do remember, for I had a share in editing it) methods of violence in changing the leadership of the Party and of the country— terrorism and uprisings. It was formulated so broadly as to constitute an instruction that measures of violence should be applied in whatever forms might prove to be at our disposal.[55]

The Rightists were, he added, a large organization: "it was not a question of a hundred or so people, but of numerous cadres," so that it was understandable that "the name Ivanov has no place in my memory."[56] A palpable irony about a People's Commissar and full member of the Central Committee.

When it came to kulak insurrections, Bukharin too was called on, and both Rykov and Bukharin admitted vaguely a connection with one in Siberia. Its location was put to Bukharin, who could not remember if the one given was right. He, too, mentioned the Ryutin Platform: "I have been questioned so many times about the Ryutin Platform. . . ."

Rykov now admitted to forming a terrorist organization headed by his former secretary, Ekaterina Artemenko, which he had instructed "to watch for passing Government automobiles," without result. He and Bukharin (again questioned) admitted forming another terrorist group, headed by a former Socialist Revolutionary, to assassinate Stalin and Kaganovich, but again without result. But both men were unsatisfactory as to details. Rykov said, "The Centre did not adopt a decision in such-and-such a year to kill such-and-such a member of the Political Bureau or the Government. The Centre took means that would enable such a decision to be put into effect if one were adopted . . ." at which point he was understandably interrupted by Vyshinsky. Bukharin, asked on whose initiative Semyonov, the Socialist Revolutionary, had acted, said, "I do not remember. Perhaps it was mine. At all events, I do not deny it."

Rykov involved the Rightists with the supposed plan of 1935 to seize power, with Yenukidze, Yagoda, Peterson, and others, which had also (he said) implicated Tukhachevsky and other generals. "We did not," he added, "succeed in making a real attempt. . . ." He went on to the connections with fascism, Menshevism, bourgeois nationalism, and other groupings. But as to detail, he again said he could only suspect, not know, what Grinko represented; and when Grinko was now called on, Rykov said, "I do not remember," when asked if his evidence was correct.

There followed a further three-way exchange between Vyshinsky, Rykov, and Bukharin on the dismemberment of the USSR and defeatism. Bukharin said that he did not take a defeatist line, "but am responsible for this affair." Rykov broke down and admitted the whole defeatist position on his own behalf and that of all the Rightists, but withdrew a suggestion he had made at the preliminary inquiry, that Bukharin was the man mainly responsible. At this, Vyshinsky openly expressed his annoyance.

After further confession to treasonable actions in Byelorussia, Rykov again rejected the charge of organizing livestock wrecking. He again denied knowledge of Ivanov's connections with the British. But he also, backed by Krestinsky and Rosengolts, confirmed the participation of Tukhachevsky in the bloc.

Rykov's testimony was not coherent, and took no perfectly clear line, but he had still contrived to make a number of substantial denials.

Next day, Sharangovich, the Byelorussian First Secretary, was first to be called. After the shifts and evasions of the previous evening, he made an excellent impression on observers sympathetic to the regime, with his frank and total admission of all charges. He had been a Polish spy since 1921, and had become a prominent member of the Byelorussian "national-fascist" organization, whose other members included Goloded, Chervyakov, and most of the Party leaders in the Republic. Rykov and Bukharin were directly involved in their crimes, which had included the formation of three terrorist groups: two of them had been intended to attack Voroshilov during the 1936 maneuvers.[57]

Sabotage, on a large scale, had been designed to cause discontent as well as disruption. He, too, had spread disease among animals:

> I must also say that in 1932 we took measures to spread plague among pigs, which resulted in a high pig mortality; this was done by inoculating pigs against plague in a wrecking fashion.[58]

> . . . Further, as regards rural economy, I should like to say something about our diversionist activities in horse-breeding. In 1936 we caused a wide outbreak of anaemia in Byelorussia. This was done intentionally, because in Byelorussia horses are extremely important for defence purposes. We endeavoured to undermine this powerful base in case it should be needed in connection with war. . . .
> As far as I can now recall, about 30,000 horses perished owing to this measure.[59]

More essentially, he took the blame for the early excesses of collectivization. These had been put through for anti-Party reasons:

> At that period there were still about 100,000 individual peasants in Byelorussia. We gave it out that an individual peasant who failed to join the collective farm was an enemy of the Soviet power. This was done for provocative purposes; in accordance with our provocative stand, we applied to the individual peasants who resisted collectivization such taxation measures which caused discontent and an insurrectionary spirit among the individual peasants.[60]

But fortunately Moscow had known better:

> . . . Later the Central Committee of the C.P.S.U. took measures to correct what we had done, and the situation changed. The spirit among the individual peasants, among those whom we had provoked, took a distinct turn for the better.

This interpretation of the events of 1929 and 1930 is a striking one, and shows a continual preoccupation with the peasantry on Stalin's part.

In industry, too, the "national fascists" had operated on a large scale:

> As to power development, here attention was mainly concentrated on the Byelorussian Regional Power Station, which feeds the industries of Vitebsk, Orsha and Moghilev. Fuel was supplied irregularly. Construction work was interfered with. Specifically, I can mention the Krichevsk Cement Works, the Orsha Flax Mills, the Moghilev Pipe Foundry. . . .[61]

## ASIAN NATIONALISTS

The Uzbek leader Khodzhayev followed Sharangovich. It will be convenient to take his case together with that of his colleague Ikramov, though the latter gave evidence the following day.

Hitherto "bourgeois nationalism" had been represented by Sharangovich and, to a lesser extent, Grinko. In the persons of the two Uzbeks, it was put forward in a more forthright form. They were not mobile *apparatchiks* like the two just named. Their entire careers had been spent in Central Asia, where they had successfully fronted for the imposition of Moscow rule on long recalcitrant populations.

They represented, as others represented in their different spheres, a much larger set of Party and State officials—implicating the First Secretary and Chairman of the Council of People's Commissars in neighboring Tadzhikistan, for example, as well as their own Republic's deviationists.

Khodzhayev seems to have really resented in some degree the centralizing and denationalizing tendencies of Stalinism, but Ikramov had not. In fact, they had led two opposed factions in the Uzbek Party, and they now attributed their alleged unity in struggling against the regime to pressure from the Rightist central group. Ikramov testified, "Under the pressure of Bukharin and the direct guidance of Antipov, the two nationalist organizations co-ordinated their work."[62]

Khodzhayev was by far the most prominent and effective Uzbek to have taken the Communist side right from the time of the Revolution, in the struggle against the old Emir of Bokhara. He had been a member of the Uzbek Central Committee Bureau since the first Congress of the Uzbek Party in 1925, and had long served as Chairman of the local Council of People's Commissars.

But he had not even been elected a delegate to the VIIth Congress of the Uzbek Communist Party, ending on 17 June 1937. On 27 June, his removal from the Chairmanship of the Uzbek Council of People's Commissars and expulsion from the Uzbek Central Executive Committee were announced, together with an attack on his counter-revolutionary nationalist positions.[63] He was clearly under arrest by this time. His brother, also prominent in the local Party, committed suicide.[64]

On 8 September, Khodzhayev and seven others, including four members of the Bureau of the local Central Committee, were denounced as enemies of the people, and Ikramov, the First Secretary of the Republic, and the current local Bureau, censured for insufficient vigilance.[65] Two days later, *Pravda* violently attacked Ikramov for defending a "Trotskyite" Secretary of the Uzbekistan Central Committee.[66] Ikramov was at this time in Moscow and, still not under arrest, had been "confronted" with Bukharin, Khodzhayev, Antipov, and others. He denied their testimony against him, in spite of four "conversations" with Yezhov.

A letter to the Uzbek Central Committee signed by Stalin and Molotov now drew its attention to the evidence against "Comrade Ikramov," as apparently proving "not merely political blunders, but also connections with the Trotskyite–Rightist group." The letter also "proposes that the Uzbek Central Committee consider the question of Comrade Ikramov and inform the Central Committee of the All-Union Communist Party of its opinion."[67] On 12 September, it was announced that Ikramov had been "unmasked" and expelled from the Party, and his case handed over to the investigating authorities.[68] He had been arrested "on Stalin's personal instructions."[69]

The Uzbek press now attacked him for weakness towards bourgeois nationalism, and specifically for supporting Khodzhayev.[70] It was presumably in support of Khodzhayev that Ikramov had protested in 1937 against the Purge, and thus incurred Stalin's displeasure.[71] (As an otherwise loyal Stalinist, Ikramov was the first defendant in the public trials to be rehabilitated.)

When his arrest was announced to the Party membership in Tashkent, the news was greeted "with warm applause."[72] He was confronted in jail with Bukharin,[73] who again implicated him, but he only confessed on the "sixth or seventh day" of the interrogation.[74]

Similar events, with similar timing, were sweeping Soviet Asia, as we saw in Chapter 8. In Kirghizia, the Chairman of the Council of People's Commissars was purged on 12 September,[75] and a call put out for ruthless measures against the local Central Committee.[76] In Tadzhikistan, the Chairman of the Council of People's Commissars, Rakhimbayev (arrested on 9 September 1937 at a Youth Day meeting at the Park of Rest and Culture); the President, Shotemor; Ashurov and Frolov, Secretaries of the Central Committee; and a number of others were denounced as nationalists or spies on 10 to 12 September. Rakhimbayev was accused in addition of keeping a harem of three wives.[77] (After the trial, *Pravda* again denounced these local leaders and "other swine.")[78]

Under the cold lights of the October Hall, Khodzhayev now confessed that he had been anti-Soviet since 1920. He and Ikramov had been in contact with the Rights, through Antipov, and had been instructed to work with the British for the secession of Uzbekistan as "a British protectorate." They had done a good deal of industrial sabotage on much the same lines as Sharangovich's. "Errors" of planning had been intentional:

> The ramp for the delivery of coal was planned for a capacity of 75,000 kW., whereas the power house was built for 48,000 kW., and the planned capacity of the station is 70,000 kW. You see, therefore, that the elements of wrecking were present in the very planning of the station.[79]

Their agricultural policy had been disastrous, and this was also intentional, as it caused hostility to Moscow:

> *Khodzhayev:* . . . This would have meant causing enormous discontent among the people, because we put it to them in this way: 'This is the Moscow plan, we are merely the servants of Moscow, we are carrying out Moscow's instructions. Don't you like it? Then complain to Moscow.' This is the task we set ourselves.
>
> *Vyshinsky:* A provocative task?
>
> *Khodzhayev:* A provocative task, set deliberately, and pursued for a number of years.
>> What did it lead to? It actually led to the destruction of the rotation of crops system, it led to diminution in the number of cattle, it led to a diminution in silk cultivation, because even here we pursued our wrecking activities, and in the long run it led to a diminution even of the cotton yield. And that is why for years Uzbekistan failed to fulfill its cotton plans. . . . If a peasant had ten hectares of land he had to sow eight or nine hectares with cotton. You will understand that if only one hectare is left for all the rest, the farm goes to ruin.[80]

But there was a more important economic aim—to develop an independent economy in Uzbekistan. This (in contradiction to the admissions made above) led to their planning the economy

> in such a way as to have less cotton, because it was an industrial crop which most of all bound Uzbekistan with the Union; secondly, we planned to develop agriculture in Uzbekistan so as to have more grain farming not only on the non-irrigated lands, but also on the irrigated lands, in order to be independent of Russian grain, and lastly, we planned the development of industry, road building, etc., in such a way as to be more economically independent than ever of Soviet Russia, of the Soviet Union, at the end of the First Five-Year Plan.

The economic side of "bourgeois nationalism" was thus well shown, and Khodzhayev made it explicit:

> I do not know whether the court is aware that the bourgeois nationalists, particularly in Central Asia, had a theory of organizing a self-contained economy, that is to say, of making the economy of the republic develop independently of the other parts of the Soviet Union, of making it possible for the republic to live without need for the rest of the Soviet Union in the event of possibilities arising for active, direct struggle.[81]

Ikramov gave similar evidence. He had had contacts with Zelensky, Antipov, and A. P. Smirnov, and Bukharin had stayed with him for a few days in 1933. Bukharin, called on, admitted discussing with him the Ryutin Platform, and "a vague allusion to terrorism," but denied any talk of wrecking.[82] At a further meeting, in 1935, the sinister point was raised that both Bukharin's and Ikramov's wives had been present, though the seditious conversation had taken place in their absence. Bukharin denied that on this occasion politics had been discussed at all. Here came a sharp exchange with Vyshinsky:

> *Vyshinsky:* And you, the leader of an underground organization, met a member of your organization, one whom you enlisted, met him two years later, and did not try to verify whether he still adhered to your counter-revolutionary organization, you showed no interest in this, but began to discuss the weather in Uzbekistan. Is this how it was, or not?
>
> *Bukharin:* No, this is not how it was. You are putting a question which contains in itself an ironical reply. As it happens, I figured I would meet Ikramov again, but by chance this meeting did not take place because he did not find me in.
>
> *Vyshinsky:* You have an extraordinarily good memory for exactly those meetings which did not take place.
>
> *Bukharin:* I do not remember the meetings which did not take place, because they are a phantom, but I do remember those which did materialize.[83]

Ikramov gave a long account of Antipov's vital role in organizing Central Asian subversion. Antipov had insisted on terrorism, and personally boasted that "whoever the Rights had decided to kill would never reach Central Asia."[84] And Ikramov, too, implicated the polygamist Rakhimbayev and his Tadzhik group.

## TO RUIN THE ECONOMY

The examinations of Rosengolts and Krestinsky on the evening of 4 March were satisfactory to the prosecution. Rosengolts and Krestinsky testified that they, with Rudzutak and Gamarnik, had constituted the main center of the conspiracy after the arrest of Rykov and Bukharin in February 1937. They had then relied almost entirely on the projected Army coup.

Their connections with German espionage, arranged through Trotsky, had dated back to 1922–1923. Krestinsky admitted to the meeting with Trotsky in person which he had denied on 2 March. Trotsky had given full instructions for all types of treason, espionage, sabotage, and terror.

The only slightly awkward moments were when Krestinsky said that he, Rosengolts, and Gamarnik had "discussed the necessity for a terrorist act" against Molotov, but had made no actual preparations for it (Vyshinsky commented sharply that this amounted to the same thing), and when Rykov, again called on briefly to confirm conversations with and about Tukhachevsky, denied them.[85]

Rykov and Bukharin, too, were incidentally all but exculpated of all the recent activity attributed to them by Krestinsky's remark that "Trotsky said that we should not confine ourselves to Rykov, Bukharin and Tomsky, because although they were the recognized leaders of the Rights, they had already been compromised to a great extent and were under surveillance," so that Rudzutak, whom no one suspected, should be the connection. But this "surveillance," and the admission that it made Rykov and Bukharin unsuitable conspiratorial colleagues, in effect disposes of the possibility of their guilt—and this from 1933 on, covering the whole period of the Kirov and other alleged murders.

Rosengolts confessed to various embezzlements, including sabotage in the export of iron. This seems to refer to pig-iron exports, which in fact had been under a directive bearing Stalin's signature, with the deliveries superintended by Yezhov.[86]

Rakovsky was now questioned. He was the son of a landowner in the Southern Dobrudja, at first part of Bulgaria, but transferred to Romania a few years after his birth. He was prominent as a Bulgarian Socialist at the age of twenty, when he represented the party at the Congress of the Second International. He took a doctorate of medicine at Montpellier, and went back to the Balkans, where he was arrested a number of times for involvement in the Romanian revolutionary movement. In 1916, he was again arrested in Romania, and imprisoned at Jassy, where the Russians freed him in May 1917. He went to Petrograd and in 1919 became a member of the Central Committee of the Russian Communist Party and Chairman of the Council of People's Commissars of the Ukraine. Becoming attached to Trotsky's views, he lost his high posts and from 1924 to 1927 was Soviet Chargé d'Affaires in London and then Ambassador in Paris. He was recalled to Moscow in November 1927 and was expelled from the Central Committee in the same month, for supporting the Left opposition. He defended the opposition viewpoint at the XVth Party Congress. In January 1928, he was expelled from the Party and deported to Astrakhan, and later to Barnaul. It had not been until February 1934, one of the very last, that he had recanted and been readmitted to the Party. He had been implicated in the Pyatakov Trial and was arrested on 27 January 1937.[87] Apart from the doctors, he was easily the oldest of those in dock. And even among his veteran fellow accused, his record stood out as long and legendary.

The sixty-five-year-old revolutionary had refused to testify to the NKVD for eight months,[88] one of the best records in the trials. He now confessed that he had been a British spy since 1924. His disavowal of Trotskyism in February 1934 had been designed to deceive the Party.[89]

On his rehabilitation, he had been sent to Japan at the head of a Red Cross delegation, and this was made the occasion for him to incriminate the then Soviet ambassadors in the Far East, Yurenev and Bogomolov. He himself became a Japanese as well as a British spy.

Vyshinsky got in one particular unfair smear. Rakovsky's father had been a landlord.

> *Vyshinsky:* Hence I am not mistaken when I say that you were a landlord?
>
> *Rakovsky:* You are not mistaken.
>
> *Vyshinsky:* Well, now. It was important for me to establish whence you received your income.
>
> *Rakovsky:* But it is important for me to say what this income was spent for.
>
> *Vyshinsky:* This is a different matter.[90]

Everyone among the Old Bolsheviks knew that Rakovsky had spent everything he had on the revolutionary movement—financing the Romanian Socialist Party, which he had founded, and its paper, which he edited, and also subsidizing Russian and other revolutionaries. Now provoked enough to try to draw attention to these facts, he was instantly silenced.

When Rakovsky began to refer to the "opposition," Vyshinsky interrupted briskly:

> In your explanations today you are generally permitting yourself to use quite a number of such expressions, as if you were forgetting that you are being tried here as a member of a counter-revolutionary bandit, espionage, diversionist organization of traitors. I consider it my duty to remind you of this in my interrogation of you and ask you to keep closer to the substance of the treasonable crimes which you have committed, to speak without philosophy and other such things which are entirely out of place here.[91]

Rakovsky finished by explaining that his surrender after eight months had been due to getting information, during the summer of 1937, about the Japanese attack on China and the extent of Nazi and Italian intervention in Spain.[92] This "had a stunning effect on me. Rancour and ambition fell from me." He decided that his "duty was to help in this struggle with the aggressor, that I would go and expose myself fully and entirely, and I told the investigator that on the following day I would begin to give complete, exhaustive testimony."

This sounds, in the context of interrogation and exhaustion, a credible exposition of the "Rubashov" motive—more so, indeed, than the reluctant and partial confession of Bukharin, on whom "Rubashov" was founded.

Rakovsky's evidence, adjourned over the night, had lasted until the morning of 5 March. The court then took Zelensky, a much less interesting figure. He had, however, a past in the highest Party ranks, as a former (1923–1925) Secretary of the Central Committee and Secretary of the Moscow Party organization, who had been removed for inadequate hostility to Zinoviev and Kamenev. He had merely been transferred to be Secretary of the Party's Central Asian Bureau from 1924 to 1931, and had never lost his place on the Central Committee. In his Asian capacity, he had already been implicated as an agent of Trotsky by Ikramov and Khodzhayev. But his main role now was to explain how he had given rise to popular discontent; in the position he had held from 1931 to 1937, as Chairman of the Consumer Cooperatives—that is, virtually the entire official distribution network—he had had unexampled opportunities for doing this.

Starting with an account of his work as a Tsarist police agent in the Party from 1911, he admitted complicity in Kamenev's actions in 1924, and recruitment by A. P. Smirnov into the Rightist "organization" in 1928–1929. After Smirnov's exposure (that is, in 1933), his contact became Antipov, under whose instructions the whole shop system was badly disrupted:

> *Zelensky:* . . . The Rights engineered interruptions in the supply of commodities of everyday use to the trading organizations. Thus, for instance, interruptions of this kind were engineered in the Kursk Region in the first quarter of 1936, in the sugar supply. Many shops were out of sugar for two or three weeks. Similar interruptions were engineered in the Leningrad Region in the *makhorka* supply; there were similar interruptions in the summer of 1936 in the bread trade in a number of rural districts of the Byelorussian S.S.R. situated near the frontier.
>
> To give you some idea of the character of these interruptions, I will point out the following: out of 30,000 shops inspected by the coopera-

tive trade sections of the Soviets and by trade inspectors, there was no salt in 3,700 shops in the first quarter of 1936. Out of 42,000 shops, 2,000 shops had no sugar on sale. In the third quarter of 1936, 1,600 shops out of 36,000 had no *makhorka,* so that these were not isolated cases, but rather widespread.[93]

And again:

*Vyshinsky:* Was there a case in 1936 when Moscow was left without eggs through your fault, through the fault not of you personally, but of one of the active participators in this conspiratorial bloc?

*Zelensky:* There was.

*Vyshinsky:* Do you remember when this made itself most acutely felt?

*Zelensky:* I cannot recall the month just now, but I can mention the following fact. In 1936 fifty carloads of eggs were allowed to spoil, from wrecking motives.[94]

He had also dislocated the accounts system:

*Zelensky:* It seems to me that the question of overcharging, short measure and short weight should be clear to everybody; it is very obvious. It consists in the following: when a man comes into a shop to make a purchase, he is overcharged, given short measure and short weight, that is, he is named a price higher than the one at which goods should be sold, or is given shorter weight than he is entitled to, or is sold goods not of the proper quality.

*Vyshinsky:* Why is this done?

*Zelensky:* To arouse discontent among the population. . . . Prices are fixed by the trading organizations or by the salesmen in the shops very often at their own discretion, that is, without control. And so it is almost impossible to detect a man who overcharges the consumer. This matter assumed a serious and widespread character. To give some idea of the extent of this wrecking work, I may mention that of 135,000 shops that were inspected by the co-operative inspectorate, cases of overcharging and defrauding purchasers were established in 13,000 shops. The actual number was considerably larger.

Another important form of wrecking, also designed to arouse the discontent of the population, was the freezing of trade by dispatching goods to the wrong districts or at the wrong times. For example, there were cases when summer goods were sent in winter and vice versa, when winter goods arrived in the shops in summer.

*Vyshinsky:* That is, the public was offered felt boots in summer and summer shoes in winter?

*Zelensky:* Yes.

All this was partly due to his staff:

*Zelensky:* . . . I had instructions, and I pursued the aim of contaminating the apparatus with alien, hostile, anti-Soviet and insurrectionary elements. How contaminated the apparatus of the Centrosoyuz was may be judged from the fact that when I was in charge of it about 15 percent of the staff of the Centrosoyuz consisted of former Mensheviks, Socialist-Revolutionaries, anarchists, Trotskyites, etc. In certain regions the number of alien elements, former members of other parties, Kolchak officers, and so on, as, for example, in the Krasnoyarsk Territory, Irkutsk and West Siberia, was considerably higher.[96]

He then got into a curious altercation with Vyshinsky:

*Vyshinsky:* . . . But how did matters stand with butter?

*Zelensky:* We don't sell butter in the rural districts.

*Vyshinsky:* I am not asking you what you sell. You were above all selling the main thing—your country. I am speaking about what measures were taken by your organization to disrupt trade and deprive the population of prime necessities. Apart from sugar and salt, do you know anything concerning butter?

*Zelensky:* I told you that the co-operatives do not sell butter in the rural districts. . . .

*Vyshinsky:* I am asking you: have you any knowledge of criminal operations with regard to supplying the population with butter, particularly cheap grades of butter, or not? Operations which were effected on the orders of your 'bloc of Rights and Trotskyites'; are they known to you or not?

*Zelensky:* Yes, they are.

*Vyshinsky:* In what did they consist?

*Zelensky:* They consisted in the following: in making butter, all the produce purchasing organizations used the international standards fixing quality of butter.

*Vyshinsky:* That is not the point.

*Zelensky:* That is the point.

*Vyshinsky:* No.

*Zelensky:* What do you mean? This was done. . . .

*The President:* Accused Zelensky, no cross-talk, and keep to the point. . . .

*Vyshinsky:* And was the butter which was issued for sale always of good quality, or did you try to spoil its quality too?

*Zelensky:* Yes.

*Vyshinsky:* Were there cases when members of your organization connected with the butter business threw glass into the butter?

*Zelensky:* There were cases when glass was thrown into the butter.

*Vyshinsky:* Were there cases when your accomplices, fellow participants in the criminal plot against the Soviet power and the Soviet people, threw nails into the butter?

*Zelensky:* There were.

*Vyshinsky:* For what purpose? to make it 'tastier'?

*Zelensky:* That is clear.

*Vyshinsky:* Well, that is organized wrecking and diversive activities. Do you admit that you are guilty of this?

*Zelensky:* I do. . . .

In addition to his vaguely unsatisfactory and undignified style of reply, Zelensky balked at a major question:

*Vyshinsky:* Did you take part in the wrecking, diversive, terrorist and espionage work of this bloc?

*Zelensky:* I did take part in wrecking and diversive work.

*Vyshinsky:* About espionage work you so far say nothing?

*Zelensky:* (No reply.)

*Vyshinsky:* Do you answer for all the criminal activities of the bloc?

*Zelensky:* I do.

—this last a weak ploy by Vyshinsky.

Zelensky did, however, admit contact with A. V. Alexander, the British Labour and Cooperative leader, with whom he had discussed the possibilities of a Rightist Government in Russia.

Ikramov's examination, which we have already covered, came next. When he had finished, first Bessonov was again questioned. He gave evidence of connections with Socialist Revolutionary émigrés, with Trotsky, and with the Nazis.

## BUKHARIN IN DOCK

And now, at last, the main subject of the trial was brought to questioning. Vyshinsky started his duel with Bukharin.

After his arrest, Bukharin had been confronted with Radek, who, however, had qualified his evidence against him, saying that Bukharin had objected to the degree of Trotsky's commitment to the Germans,[98] and refusing to confirm some of the more vicious charges.[99] In *The Great Terror,* I wrote that Bukharin had not been tortured. This was based on general report, though also on a definite statement by Mikoyan after Stalin's death.[100] From recent Soviet articles, it does not appear to be true. Perhaps Frinovsky's order "beating permitted," with which the investigation of the case "started,"[101] was not applied in its full vigor. But we are now told that, though Bukharin held out for three months, threats to his wife and infant son, combined with "methods of physical influence," wore him down, and he now wrote to Stalin, "Dear friend, if it is necessary for the Party, I will go to trial as you wish."[102] At interrogations on 1 and 28 June 1937, he confessed that the Ryutin Platform expressed his own views and that many others shared them, including Rykov and Tomsky, but also Uglanov, Rudzutak, Antipov, Lomov, Unshklikht, and others.[103] It is reported that he now agreed, in a long talk with Yezhov and Voroshilov—as "representatives of the Politburo"—to confess to all the charges, including that of having planned to assassinate Lenin.

But when, two days later, his confession, amended and corrected by Stalin personally, had been given to him to sign, he was so shocked that he withdrew his whole confession. The examination started all over again, with a double team of interrogators. He finally agreed once more to testify, but refused to say that he had planned Lenin's death.[104] One of the charges brought against him in court, that of espionage, was not raised at all during his interrogation. It was doubtless felt that he was unlikely to agree to it, so it now was sprung on him for the first time at the trial.[105]

He had evidently decided on his tactics after considering the earlier cases. His confession, like Rykov's, avoided admitting direct complicity in any of the worst overt acts, but accepted general responsibility. Anything less would have doubtless led to his omission from the trial and the execution of his wife. As it was, Vyshinsky threatened to stop his evidence.

Before Vyshinsky could speak, Bukharin asked the court to allow him to present his case "freely" and to dwell on the ideological stand of the "bloc." Vyshinsky at once asked for the request to be denied, as limiting the legal rights of the prosecution. Bukharin then said that he confirmed his evidence at the preliminary inquiry. He then made his carefully phrased acceptance of guilt:

> I plead guilty to being one of the outstanding leaders of this 'bloc of Rights and Trotskyites'. Consequently, I plead guilty to what directly follows from this, the sum total of crimes committed by this counter-revolutionary organization, irrespective of whether or not I knew of, whether or not I took a direct part in, any particular act.[106]

He had, he admitted, planned the forcible overthrow of the Soviet power, and "with the help of a war which prognostically was in prospect," relied on the help of foreign States to which territorial concessions would be made.

*Vyshinsky:* And also by means of weakening the defensive power?

*Bukharin:* You see, this question was not discussed, at least not in my presence.

As to wrecking, "the orientation on wrecking was adopted." But again, when a concrete question was put:

*Vyshinsky:* As you see from the trial, the circumstances were concrete enough. Did you and Khodzhayev discuss the fact that too little wrecking was being done, and being done badly?

*Bukharin:* About accelerating wrecking there was no talk.[107]

Bukharin then admitted that the bloc stood for the assassination of the leadership. Vyshinsky immediately asked whether the Kirov murder had been committed on the instructions of the bloc.

*Bukharin:* I do not know.

*Vyshinsky:* I ask you, was this assassination committed with the knowledge and on the instructions of the 'bloc of Rights and Trotskyites'?

*Bukharin:* And I repeat that I do not know, Citizen Prosecutor.

*Vyshinsky:* You did not know about this specifically in relation to the assassination of S. M. Kirov?

*Bukharin:* Not specifically, but . . .

*Vyshinsky:* Permit me to question the accused Rykov.

*The President:* You may.

*Vyshinsky:* Accused Rykov, what do you know about the assassination of Sergei Mironovich Kirov?

*Rykov:* I know nothing about the participation of the Rights or the Right part of the bloc in the assassination of Kirov.

*Vyshinsky:* In general, were you aware of the preparations for terrorist acts, for the assassination of members of the Party and the Government?

*Rykov:* As one of the leaders of the Right part of this bloc, I took part in the organization of a number of terrorist groups and in preparations for ter- rorist acts. As I have said in my testimony, I do not know of a single decision of the Right centre, through which I was related with the 'bloc of Rights and Trotskyites', about the actual commission of assassinations. . . .

*Vyshinsky:* About the actual commission. So. Do you know that one of the aims of the 'bloc of Rights and Trotskyites' was to organize and commit terrorist acts against leaders of the Party and Government?

*Rykov:* I said more than that, I said that I personally organized terrorist groups. But you are asking me whether I knew of such aims through some third person.

*Vyshinsky:* I am asking whether the 'bloc of Rights and Trotskyites' had any rela- tion to the assassination of Comrade Kirov.

*Rykov:* I have no information regarding the relation of the Rights or the Right part of the bloc to this assassination, and therefore I am convinced to this day that the assassination of Kirov was carried out by the Trot- skyites without the knowledge of the Rights. Of course, I might not have known about it.[108]

Vyshinsky, baffled, then called on Yagoda, who said that both Rykov and Bukharin were lying: Rykov had been present, with Yenukidze, at the meeting which had discussed the question. However, Yagoda now started to drop peculiar hints on his own:

*Vyshinsky:* After this, did you personally take any measures to effect the assassina- tion of Sergei Mironovich Kirov?

*Yagoda:* I personally?

*Vyshinsky:* Yes, as a member of the bloc.

*Yagoda:* I gave instructions. . . .

*Vyshinsky:* To whom?

*Yagoda:* To Zaporozhets in Leningrad. That is not quite how it was. . . .

*Vyshinsky:* And then you gave instructions not to place obstacles in the way of the murder of Sergei Mironovich Kirov?

> *Yagoda:* Yes, I did. . . . It was not like that.
>
> *Vyshinsky:* In a somewhat different form?
>
> *Yagoda:* It was not like that, but it is not important.[109]

Vyshinsky hastily dropped the matter and started to question Bukharin about the allegation that he had intended to kill Lenin. Bukharin admitted that there had been a plan in 1918 to arrest Lenin, but when Vyshinsky asserted that this must mean to kill him, he pointed out that Dzerzhinsky had actually been arrested by Socialist Revolutionaries at the time, and not killed. Conceding that Stalin and Sverdlov, too, were to have been arrested, he added that "under no circumstances" were the three to have been killed. Vyshinsky postponed the question until witnesses were called.

Bukharin was then allowed to start to speak at length. Ulrikh told him to stick to his "criminal anti-Soviet activities," but after ten or fifteen minutes he was still expounding a theory of the way Rightism inevitably led to the restoration of capitalism. Ulrikh interrupted to say he must not make his defense plea now.

Bukharin countered: "This is not my defense, it is my self-accusation. I have not said a single word in my defense. . . ."[110] Nor, strictly speaking, had he. And he now went on to admit that his program would have meant "a lapse into bourgeois-democratic freedom," which (Vyshinsky pointed out, and he accepted) meant in effect "outright rabid fascism"!

Vyshinsky turned to espionage:

> *Vyshinsky:* Then why was it so easy for you to join a bloc which was engaged in espionage work?
>
> *Bukharin:* Concerning espionage work I know absolutely nothing.
>
> *Vyshinsky:* What do you mean, you don't know?
>
> *Bukharin:* Just that.
>
> *Vyshinsky:* And what was the bloc engaged in?
>
> *Bukharin:* Two people testified here about espionage, Sharangovich and Ivanov, that is to say two *agents provocateurs*.[111]

Here Bukharin was cleverly turning the trial's tactics against its originators. Ivanov had, on his own evidence, been a Tsarist agent provocateur in the revolutionary movement—for a Bolshevik audience, no lower form of life, no more untrustworthy character, could exist. His evidence was automatically worthless. But at the same time, Bukharin was surely suggesting that he was still following the same trade, under different orders.

Vyshinsky now scored a point by turning to Rykov, who again admitted knowing that espionage was being conducted by the Byelorussian "national fascists," and that "in my opinion, Bukharin also knew." Bukharin simply retorted that he had not known. His connections with the Austrian police, which Vyshinsky raised, "consisted of my imprisonment in an Austrian fortress."

> *Vyshinsky:* Accused Sharangovich, you were a Polish spy, although you have been in prison?
>
> *Sharangovich:* Yes, although I have been in prison.
>
> *Bukharin:* I have been in a Swedish prison, twice in a Russian prison, and in a German prison.[112]

Bukharin went on to elaborate the negotiations for and the structure of the alleged "bloc," from his conversation with Kamenev in 1928 on, with special attention to the Ryutin Platform. Again Ulrikh intervened, "So far you are still beating about the bush, you are saying nothing about your crimes."

Bukharin spoke of the planned coup of 1935 by Yenukidze and Peterson—of which nothing had ever come. And, continuing his evidence at the next session, on the morning of 7 March, he developed this theme to include the Tukhachevsky group. (Vyshinsky here objected to his use of the term "palace coup.") He admitted also sending insurrectionary organizers to the provinces, but denied all knowledge of their connection with White Guard and German fascist circles. Again there was a long tussle as Vyshinsky tried to get him to admit and Rykov to confirm that he knew of this. But this time, Rykov rallied and supported Bukharin's point.

Rykov went on to deny knowing that Karakhan was a spy. And on the whole issue of negotiation with Germany, Bukharin admitted that Trotsky had spoken of ceding the Ukraine, but that he himself "did not consider Trotsky's instructions as binding on me." On Karakhan's alleged negotiations:

> *Vyshinsky:* Did you endorse these negotiations?
>
> *Bukharin:* Or disavow? I did not disavow them; consequently I endorsed them.
>
> *Vyshinsky:* I ask you, did you endorse them, or not?
>
> *Bukharin:* I repeat, Citizen Prosecutor: since I did not disavow them, I consequently endorsed them.
>
> *Vyshinsky:* Consequently you endorsed them?
>
> *Bukharin:* If I did not disavow them, consequently I endorsed them.
>
> *Vyshinsky:* That's what I am asking you: that is to say, you endorsed them?
>
> *Bukharin:* So then 'consequently' is the same as 'that is to say'.
>
> *Vyshinsky:* What do you mean, 'that is to say'?
>
> *Bukharin:* That is to say, I endorsed them.
>
> *Vyshinsky:* But you say that you learnt of this *post factum*.
>
> *Bukharin:* Yes, the one does not contradict the other in the slightest.[113]

Vyshinsky again started to hammer at the espionage theme, raising with Rykov the matter of the Byelorussians. And now, for half an hour, came one of the most striking exchanges in the whole of the public trials:

> *Vyshinsky:* Isn't this an espionage connection?
>
> *Rykov:* No.
>
> *Vyshinsky:* What kind of connection is it?

*Rykov:* There was an espionage connection there, too.

*Vyshinsky:* But was there an espionage connection maintained by a part of your organization with the Poles on your instructions?

*Rykov:* Of course.

*Vyshinsky:* Espionage?

*Rykov:* Of course.

*Vyshinsky:* Bukharin included?

*Rykov:* Of course.

*Vyshinsky:* Were you and Bukharin connected.

*Rykov:* Absolutely.

*Vyshinsky:* So you were spies?

*Rykov:* (No reply.)

*Vyshinsky:* And the organizers of espionage?

*Rykov:* I am in no way better than a spy.

*Vyshinsky:* You organized espionage, so you were spies.

*Rykov:* It may be said, yes.

*Vyshinsky:* It may be said, spies. I am asking, did you organize connections with the Polish intelligence service and the respective spy circles? Do you plead guilty to espionage?

*Rykov:* If it is a question of organization, then in this case, of course, I plead guilty.

*Vyshinsky:* Accused Bukharin, do you plead guilty to espionage?

*Bukharin:* I do not.

*Vyshinsky:* After what Rykov says, after what Sharangovich says?

*Bukharin:* I do not plead guilty.

*Vyshinsky:* When the organization of the Rights was set up in Byelorussia, you were at the head of it; do you admit that?

*Bukharin:* I have told you.

*Vyshinsky:* I am asking you, do you admit it or not?

*Bukharin:* I took no interest in Byelorussian affairs.

*Vyshinsky:* Did you take an interest in espionage affairs?

*Bukharin:* No.

*Vyshinsky:* And who did take an interest?

*Bukharin:* I received no information with regard to activities of this kind.

*Vyshinsky:* Accused Rykov, was Bukharin receiving any information with regard to activities of this kind?

*Rykov:* I never spoke to him about it.[114]

After going over the ground again, Vyshinsky only got Rykov back to his old line:

*Rykov:* I mean to say that we did not personally direct this development; however, it is not a question of direct leadership but of general leadership. We absolutely and definitely bear responsibility for this.

*Vyshinsky:* There is no point in making a pious face, accused Bukharin. Better admit what exists. And what exists is the following: you had a group of accomplices, fellow-conspirators in Byelorussia, headed by Goloded, Chervyakov and Sharangovich. Is that right, Sharangovich?

*Sharangovich:* It is.

*Vyshinsky:* And on Bukharin's and Rykov's instructions, and under their leadership, you established connections with the Polish intelligence service and with the Polish General Staff? Is that right, Sharangovich?

*Sharangovich:* Absolutely right.

*Vyshinsky:* Under your leadership also with regard to the espionage connections. Is that right, Sharangovich?

*Sharangovich:* Absolutely right.

*Vyshinsky:* Consequently, who was the organizer of the espionage in which you engaged?

*Sharangovich:* Rykov, Bukharin.

*Vyshinsky:* Hence, they were spies.

*Sharangovich:* Quite right.

*Vyshinsky:* Just as. . . .

*Sharangovich:* As I myself.

*Vyshinsky:* Be seated.
(To Rykov): Accused Rykov, did Goloded tell you in 1932 that all more or less important appointments of people to responsible posts in Byelorussia were first co-ordinated with the Polish intelligence service?

*Rykov:* Yes.

*Vyshinsky:* Did Bukharin know of this?

*Rykov:* I cannot say.

*Vyshinsky:* You do not know. You do not want to betray your pal?

*Rykov:* What I mean to say is that in those cases when I know that he is not telling the truth, I am exposing him, but in those cases when I do not know, I cannot and shall not do it.

*Vyshinsky:* I am asking you with regard to the fact that the Poles were giving their consent to the various appointments to official posts in Byelorussia. Was this known to your leading centre?

*Rykov:* I knew of it. As for Bukharin, I never spoke to him about it. I also knew that Chervyakov and Goloded maintained connections, not only with me, but with Bukharin and Tomsky as well. Whether they spoke of this to Bukharin I cannot say, because I was not present at those conversations.

> *Vyshinsky:* Do you think that it would have been natural for Goloded to speak to Bukharin about this question? Or did they have to keep it a secret from Bukharin?
>
> *Rykov:* I think that, naturally, he spoke to Bukharin, but what they talked about I do not know.
>
> *Vyshinsky:* I shall ask you now by way of making a supposition: do you suppose that Bukharin knew of this?
>
> *Rykov:* This circumstance. . . . I prefer to speak only of what I knew; and as to what I do not know—my position in the court room is not such as to allow me to advance suppositions.[115]

On his conversations with Bukharin, Rykov went on to say: "I do not recall any conversations dealing especially with this espionage work. I do not exclude the possibility that there were such conversations, but I do not remember."[116]

After a long exchange with Rykov about the meaning of some of his preliminary evidence, which Rykov pointed out was meant not as fact but as supposition, Vyshinsky turned to Bukharin, who immediately remarked, "I was not asked a single word about this during the preliminary investigation, and you, Citizen Prosecutor, did not question me for three months, not a single word."[117]

At this Vyshinsky lost his temper and shouted that Bukharin was not going to instruct him about how to conduct an investigation. He then turned on Rykov again, but got no further.

He concluded weakly: "Permit me to consider it established that Rykov and Bukharin knew the substance of the treasonable connection which included espionage. Is that correct, Rykov?"

> *Rykov:* That is, espionage followed.
>
> *Bukharin:* So it appears that I knew something from which something followed.[118]

Ulrikh turned the accused back to the theme of the proposed coup d'état. Following that, Bukharin denied having told Khodzhayev about an agreement with Germany, and after further argument about this Vyshinsky again lost his composure, and Bukharin was able to remark, "There is nothing for you to gesticulate about." Ulrikh called him to order, and Vyshinsky launched on a harangue: "I will be compelled to cut the interrogation short because you are apparently following definite tactics and do not want to tell the truth, hiding behind a flood of words, pettifogging, making digressions into the sphere of politics, of philosophy, theory and so forth. . . ."

Bukharin replied calmly, "I am answering your questions," and went on to deny having told Khodzhayev about connections with British spies. Vyshinsky had remarked, during his burst of rage, that "according to all the material of the investigation you are obviously a spy of an intelligence service." Bukharin now took him up on this point:

> *Bukharin:* During the year I spent in prison I was not once asked about it.
>
> *Vyshinsky:* We are asking you here in an open proletarian court, we are asking you here in this court before the whole world.

*Bukharin:* But you did not ask me this before.

*Vyshinsky:* I am asking you again, on the basis of the testimony which was here given against you: do you choose to admit before the Soviet Court by what intelligence service you were enlisted—the British, German or Japanese?

*Bukharin:* None.

*Vyshinsky:* I have no more questions to put to Bukharin.[119]


The court adjourned on that note. The Prosecutor had been defeated.

When the session resumed, Bukharin listed his contacts with émigré Mensheviks and Socialist Revolutionaries, and the concessions to be made to Germany. He again went out of his way to deny espionage, and say that the military conspirators had spoken to Tomsky of "opening the front" in case of war, but he had disapproved:


*Vyshinsky:* And did you talk to Karakhan about opening the front?

*Bukharin:* Karakhan said that the Germans were demanding a military alliance with Germany.

*Vyshinsky:* And are the gates closed to an ally?

*Bukharin:* Karakhan gave me an answer to this question.

*Vyshinsky:* That the gates are closed to an ally?

*Bukharin:* No.

*Vyshinsky:* That means to open the gates?

*Bukharin:* Pardon me, there was no alliance yet.

*Vyshinsky:* But there were expectations, plans?

*Bukharin:* Well, just now the Soviet Union has an alliance with France, but that does not mean that it opens the Soviet frontiers.[120]


Vyshinsky now went on to the crime with which Bukharin alone of those on trial was charged—the plan to assassinate Lenin in 1918. The prosecution produced three prominent Left Communists of that period, Yakovleva, Mantsev, and Ossinsky—the last (originally Prince Obolensky) still a candidate member of the Central Committee elected in 1934.

At the time, Varvara Yakovleva, a candidate member of the small 1917 Central Committee, had been the more prominent, and with Bukharin, Pyatakov, and V. M. Smirnov had resigned when the decision to accept the Peace of Brest-Litovsk had been taken.

She now fully confirmed Vyshinsky's story. Bukharin had no difficulty in showing that the alleged illegal activities of early 1918 were not illegal at all, and that in fact the Leftists, with the Trotskyites then roughly aligned with them, held a majority and hoped to enforce their views through ordinary Party channels. *After* this majority had been lost, he admitted, conversations had taken place with a view to arresting Lenin and forming a new government. (Bukharin had indeed thought of arresting Lenin for twenty-four hours with a view to making it easier to change the Government, and had given the whole story as long ago as 1924.)[121]

There had also been conversations with the Left Socialist Revolutionaries, who had dropped out of the Soviet Government on the peace issue. What Bukharin denied was that there had been any sort of plan to kill Lenin or complicity with the Socialist Revolutionaries. He went on to point out that many who had been Left Communists at the time—including Kuibyshev and Menzhinsky—were not for that reason now regarded as enemies. He was ruled out of order. A series of points—including the fact that he had been wounded by a bomb thrown by the Left Socialist Revolutionaries at a time when he was now charged with conspiring with them—were similarly ruled on.

Mantsev's evidence followed the same lines, and Ossinsky gave a rather more restricted account, omitting certain points against Bukharin. Bukharin denied the evidence about the assassination plan, and twice hinted strongly at the reason for the witnesses' attitude:

> *Vyshinsky:* Consequently, you assert that Mantsev's testimony in this part and the testimony of witness Yakovleva are false?
>
> *Bukharin:* Yes, I do.
>
> *Vyshinsky:* How do you explain the fact that they are not telling the truth?
>
> *Bukharin:* You had better ask them about it.[122]

And later on:

> *Vyshinsky:* You must somehow explain the fact that three of your former accomplices are speaking against you.
>
> *Bukharin:* You see, I have neither sufficient material nor the psychological requisites to clear up this question.
>
> *Vyshinsky:* You cannot explain.
>
> *Bukharin:* Not that I cannot, I simply refuse to explain.[123]

Getting no further with this, Vyshinsky called two new witnesses—the old Socialist Revolutionaries Boris Kamkov and Vladimir Karelin. They were in "neat blue suits," their faces "grey and corpse-like."[124] They had been in prison for years. An even more important Socialist Revolutionary, Maria Spiridonova, was implicated with her comrades.[125] She had been arrested on 8 February 1937, with twelve other former Left Socialist Revolutionaries, in Ufa, where they were living in exile. They were first accused of terrorist plots against the Bashkir Communist leadership. But then the whole of that leadership was itself arrested, and charges of plotting against Stalin and Voroshilov were substituted. On 25 December 1937 they were sentenced on these and other charges by the Military Collegium to various terms of imprisonment—in Spiridonova's case, twenty-five years—the charges now including setting up a "center" to unite all opposition parties, preparing peasant uprisings, and so on. After a hunger strike, she was held in isolation, finally in Orel.[126] But she seems to have refused to cooperate in the present trial.

Kamkov had apparently been released during the 1920s, but was back in prison no later than 1933.[127] Kamkov now said that he understood from others that Bukharin had been informed of Socialist Revolutionary intentions, but he could not himself testify to this directly. He denied that there was any "joint decision" by the Left Socialist Revolutionaries and Left Communists. Vyshinsky again became flustered at the firm attitude of the old revolutionist, and when Bukharin tried to ask a question, he burst out with "I request the accused Bukharin not to interfere in my interrogation. I am restraining myself enough, and I request my opponent to restrain himself. . . ."[128] Kamkov again denied the point. Vyshinsky abandoned the witness without putting the point about Lenin's assassination.

Karelin was more amenable, and confirmed the plan to kill Lenin. He also brought in an entirely separate action—the genuine attempted assassination of Lenin on 30 August 1918 by the freelance *Right* Socialist Revolutionary Fanny Kaplan. This, he said, had been insisted on by Bukharin, and his insistence transmitted through the Left Socialist Revolutionaries. Ossinsky, called on to confirm this, said he had heard some vague gossip about Kaplan's shot being inspired by the anti-Government stand of the Lefts, but "I can say nothing of Bukharin personally" in such a connection.

Bukharin denied the whole thing:

*Vyshinsky:* Ossinsky spoke on the subject.
*Bukharin:* Ossinsky said that he could say nothing about me.[129]

Vyshinsky then tackled Bukharin directly, in an attempt to make him concede that the atmosphere in the Party had been so heated in 1918 that assassination would have been rational. Bukharin denied this, and again denied the evidence:

*Vyshinsky:* But why do both former 'Left' Communists and 'Left' Socialist-Revolutionaries say so—everybody?
*Bukharin:* No, not everybody: of two 'Left' Socialist-Revolutionaries, only one said it.[130]

With a final "categorical denial," Bukharin's examination was over.

In the indictment, the cases of Yakovleva, Mantsev, Ossinsky, Kamkov, and Karelin are among those mentioned as being the subject of separate proceedings. The death dates of both Kamkov[131] and Karelin[132] are now given as 1938. We can presume that they were in fact executed for their alleged part in the plan to assassinate Lenin, and similarly with Ossinsky, sentenced in secret by the Military Collegium and shot on 1 September 1938.[133] Yakovleva, whose evidence had been the most satisfactory, survived until 1941.[134]

## THE DOCTOR-POISONERS

On the morning of 8 March, the most horrible and obscure of all the crimes alleged against the bloc were reached. Over the next two days, the system of alleged "medical murders" carried out directly under Yagoda's orders was the main subject of examination.

The plan to charge the opposition with these medical murders seems to have been adopted soon after Yezhov took over the NKVD. Of the doctors concerned, as we shall see, Pletnev was already embroiled in the NKVD's plans by December 1936. Pletnev's hope "as late as 5 March" (1937)[135] that the medical world would protect him presumably refers to the date of his arrest. Kryuchkov, Gorky's secretary, also involved, was denounced (with other writers associated with Yagoda) on 17 May, but his date of arrest is now given as 5 October, with the arrest dates of others directly involved in the poison plots as Dr. Levin, 2 December; Maximov-Dikovsky (Kuibyshev's secretary), 11 December; and Dr. Kazakov, 16 December—which may indicate that a final decision to go ahead with these charges was not made until a fairly late stage.[136]

There were four of these alleged murders. First, in May 1934, Menzhinsky, Yagoda's predecessor as Head of the OGPU, had been killed by his favorite doctor, Kazakov, under instructions from Levin. Then, in the same month, Gorky's son Maxim Peshkov had been killed by Levin and Pletnev. Next came Kuibyshev, killed by Levin and Pletnev; and finally Gorky himself, killed by Levin and Pletnev.

The sixty-eight-year-old Dr. Levin gave the first evidence. "He, together with Yagoda, was the organiser"[137] of the medical killings. He had served in the Kremlin since 1920 "on the staff of the medical services of the NKVD."[138] Levin had worked for Dzerzhinsky, Menzhinsky, and Yagoda, which can certainly be taken as showing him not merely in the *medical* confidence of the OGPU–NKVD; as he said himself, he enjoyed "a definite recognition and confidence in me on the part of the head of" the OGPU.[139] He also "had a feeling that I would perish with Yagoda."[140] In fact, he may be regarded as to some degree another of Yagoda's NKVD circle, all of whom were to go to the execution cellars.*

Levin remarks, too, that he has "told the truth from the first day I entered prison."[141] If that is taken at its face value, it is so different from the attitudes of other non-Party accused that it indicates a high state of discipline vis-à-vis the NKVD.

Bukharin, in a brief cross-questioning of Dr. Levin, asked if he had not been a counter-revolutionary saboteur in 1918 after the Bolshevik seizure of power, as if this were a generally known fact.[142] This question seems quite irrelevant—and indeed, if anything, damaging to the accused in general—but if we seek a special

---

*Apart from the other two doctors actually on trial, it may be noted that two more were implicated: Dr. A. I. Vinogradov, of the medical service of the OGPU (*Bukharin Trial*, p. 518), proceedings against whom had been "terminated owing to his death" (ibid., p. 35); and the political Khodorovsky, Head of the Kremlin Medical Administration until 1938, who had presumably not yet ripened (and whose death date was later given as 1940) (*XI s''ezd RKP(b) mart–aprel' 1922 g. Stenograficheskiy otchet* [Moscow, 1961]).

implication, it must be that Levin had been especially susceptible to NKVD black-mail and threats about his past.

Levin gave model evidence on the layout of the alleged crimes. As developed in his and the other testimony, it amounted (1) to getting Kazakov, Menzhinsky's pet quack, to kill him by an overdose of his patent method, so that Yagoda could inherit the leadership of the OGPU; (2) to killing Peshkov by having Gorky's secretary, Kryuchkov, get him drunk and leave him passed out on a garden bench in the cold (though it was May), and loosing Levin, Vinogradov, and Pletnev on him when he caught a chill; and (3) to arranging bonfires to affect Gorky's weak lungs,* and then taking him to see his granddaughters when they had colds, which he caught, thus also falling into the hands of Levin and Pletnev. Kuibyshev (4) had simply been given bad treatment for his heart, but had finally died for lack of medical attention, which, in the circumstances, it might have been thought, he was lucky to avoid.

Levin explained how Yagoda had recruited him in a highly plausible way, which brought a sigh even from the trained audience:

> *Levin:* He said: 'Have in mind that you cannot help obeying me, you cannot get
> away from me. Once I place confidence in you with regard to this thing,
> once confidence is placed in you with regard to this matter, you must appre-
> ciate it and you must carry this out. You cannot tell anybody about it. No-
> body will believe you. They will believe not you, but me. Have no doubts
> about this but go ahead and do it. You think it over, how you could do it,
> whose services you could enlist for this. I will call you in a few days.' He
> reiterated that my refusal to carry this out would spell ruin for me and my
> family. I figured that I had no other way out, that I had to submit to him.
> Again, if you look at it retrospectively, if you look back at 1932 from today,
> when you consider how all-powerful Yagoda appeared to me, a non-Party
> person, then, of course, it was very difficult to evade his threats, his or-
> ders.[143]

Kazakov was called to corroborate Levin's story about Menzhinsky. Unlike Levin and Pletnev, Kazakov was not a doctor of reputation, though evidently honest in his eccentricities. He employed (as Bulanov was to remark) "very intricate drugs that were not only unknown to medicine, but not very well known to Kazakov himself."

Menzhinsky had sworn by Kazakov's "lysates" method. In Dr. Levin's evidence, there is a sardonic description of "much talk of a miraculous medicine" produced by a Professor Schwartzman, who had earlier made a good impression on Menzhinsky, ending in disappointment: "Then there was another sensation, there was a lot of publicity about Ignaty Nikolaievich Kazakov and he (Menzhinsky) turned to Kazakov. . . . He was one of the small group of important people

---

*Levin*: . . . Gorky loved fire, flames, and we made use of this. A bonfire would be lit up for him. Just when Gorky would feel the fatigue after his work all the chopped branches were gathered together, and a flame kindled. Gorky would stand near this bonfire, it was hot there, and all this had a harmful effect on his health (*Bukharin Trial*, p. 537).

at that time who were under the impression that they were being helped by him a great deal.''[144] There had even been a special meeting of the Council of People's Commissars to discuss Kazakov's method—one of several examples of the leadership's tendency to swallow ideas rejected by specialists of the science in question.

Kazakov confirmed Levin's evidence, and said he had been taken to see Yagoda personally, submitting out of fear on hearing the remark "If you make any attempt to disobey me, I shall find quick means of exterminating you."[145]

Yagoda was now called. He looked very different from his old self. His hair seemed whiter, and his former jauntiness had gone.[146] But he still showed a certain bitter energy. His evidence was extraordinary, and must be significant—even though he was to withdraw it later in the day.

*Vyshinsky:* Accused Yagoda, did you instruct Levin to tell Kazakov that he would be asked to come and have a talk with you?

*Yagoda:* The first time I saw this man was here.

*Vyshinsky:* So you gave no such instructions to Levin?

*Yagoda:* I gave instructions to Levin to talk it over . . .

*Vyshinsky:* With whom?

*Yagoda:* With Kazakov, but I did not receive him personally.

*Vyshinsky:* I am not asking you whether you received him or not; I am asking you whether you instructed Levin to talk it over with Kazakov.

*Yagoda:* I gave no instructions to talk to Kazakov.

*Vyshinsky:* You just said here that you gave Levin such instructions.

*Yagoda:* I gave Levin instructions to bring about the death of Alexei Maximovich Gorky and Kuibyshev, and that's all.

*Vyshinsky:* And how about Menzhinsky?

*Yagoda:* I did not bring about the death of either Menzhinsky or Max Peshkov.[147]

Vyshinsky called Kryuchkov, who confirmed his role in killing Peshkov on Yagoda's orders. He then turned on Yagoda again and read from his evidence at the preliminary examination confessing to the Menzhinsky and Peshkov murders:

*Vyshinsky:* . . . Did you depose this, accused Yagoda?

*Yagoda:* I said that I did, but it is not true.

*Vyshinsky:* Why did you make this deposition if it is not true?

*Yagoda:* I don't know why.

*Vyshinsky:* Be seated.
'I summoned Kazakov and confirmed my orders. . . . . He did his work. Menzhinsky died.'
Did you despose this, accused Yagoda?

*Yagoda:* I did.

*Vyshinsky:* Hence, you met Kazakov?

*Yagoda:* No.

*Vyshinsky:* Why did you make a false deposition?

*Yagoda:* Permit me not to answer this question.

*Vyshinsky:* So you deny that you organized the murder of Menzhinsky?

*Yagoda:* I do.

*Vyshinsky:* Did you admit it in this deposition?

*Yagoda:* Yes.

*Vyshinsky:* When the Prosecutor of the Union interrogated you, what did you answer to this question about your part in the murder of Menzhinsky?

*Yagoda:* I confirmed it also then.

*Vyshinsky:* You confirmed it. Why did you confirm it?

*Yagoda:* Permit me not to answer this question.

*Vyshinsky:* Then answer my last question: Did you file any protest or complain with regard to the preliminary investigation?

*Yagoda:* None.

*Vyshinsky:* Are you filing any now?

*Yagoda:* No.[148]

Taking up the Peshkov murder, Vyshinsky went on:

*Vyshinsky:* So everything that Kryuchkov says . . .

*Yagoda:* It is all lies.

*Vyshinsky:* You gave him no such instructions regarding Maxim Peshkov?

*Yagoda:* I have stated, Citizen Prosecutor, that with regard to Maxim Peshkov I gave no instructions. I see no sense in his murder.

*Vyshinsky:* So Levin is lying?

*Yagoda:* He is lying.

*Vyshinsky:* Kazakov is lying?

*Yagoda:* Yes, lying.

*Vyshinsky:* Kryuchkov?

*Yagoda:* Is lying.

*Vyshinsky:* You gave Kryuchkov no instructions regarding the death of Maxim Peshkov? At the preliminary investigation you . . .

*Yagoda:* I lied.

*Vyshinsky:* And now?

*Yagoda:* I am telling the truth.

*Vyshinsky:* Why did you lie at the preliminary investigation?

*Yagoda:* I told you. Permit me not to reply to this question.[149]

This last was spoken "with such concentrated venom and fury," an American observer notes, that the whole audience gasped with "dismay and terror."

When Ulrikh intervened, Yagoda turned on him and said (in a phrase not included in the official report): "You can drive me, but not too far. I'll say what I want to say . . . but . . . do not drive me too far."[150] Again everyone was shaken. If Stalin was present in the hidden room above the Tribunal, where during this trial a trick of the light at one point made him clearly visible,[151] even he might for a moment have wondered whether his whole plan was not about to be wrecked.

Yagoda, more than any of the others, had reason to resent the trial. He, more than anyone, had performed irreplaceable services for Stalin. His arrest had so affected him that he could not sleep or eat, and Yezhov had feared for his sanity. Slutsky, the insinuating Head of the NKVD Foreign Department, had been sent to talk to him. Yagoda complained about the ruin of the police organization he had built up over fifteen years, and one day remarked that God must after all exist: from Stalin he deserved only gratitude, but from God the fate which had actually overtaken him.[152]

But his present demonic outburst was left in the air. Vyshinsky turned back to Levin. Levin now developed the Kuibyshev and Gorky murders, and Yagoda confirmed them. Towards the end of the morning, when Levin was going into the detail of Gorky's death, Yagoda suddenly said, "May I put a question to Levin?" Though such cross-examination by defendants had been usual practice in the previous days of the trial, Ulrikh hastily replied, "After Levin finished his testimony." Yagoda, making it clear that his question was immediately relevant, insisted. "This concerns Maxim Gorky's death!"

Ulrikh, evidently fearing the worst, cut him off, "When the accused Levin finishes, then by all means." He shortly ordered a thirty-minute adjournment. After this Vyshinsky said, ". . . I think the accused Yagoda wanted to put questions to the accused Levin."

*The President:* Accused Yagoda, you may put questions.

> *Yagoda:* I ask Levin to answer in what year the Kremlin Medical Commission attached him, Levin, to me as my doctor, and to whom else he was attached.[153]

When this question had been answered, with no reference whatever to Gorky's death or to any of the other crimes, Yagoda said he had no more questions. It will be seen that what he wanted to say before the adjournment cannot have been the same as what he actually asked after.

Levin was then questioned by his "defending lawyer," Braude. Two points were made. First, Levin said of the "directing organization" behind the murders, "I knew nothing about it. I learnt about it only at the trial itself." He then reiterated what was evidently, in one way or another, a powerful motive for obeying those capable of carrying out such measures: "What frightened me most was his threat to destroy my family. And my family is a good, working, Soviet family."[154]

The court had earlier announced an Expert Commission of five doctors. The morning session of 8 March concluded with the following exchange:

> *The President:* Have the expert witnesses any questions to ask the accused
> Levin?
>
> *Shereshevsky and* The expert witnesses have no questions to ask; everything is
> *Vinogradov:*\* quite clear.[155]

The evening session of 8 March saw the evidence-in-chief of Bulanov (Ya-goda's personal assistant) and of Yagoda himself. Bulanov, a veteran NKVD officer—he had been in charge of the expulsion of Trotsky from the country in January 1929—testified to the special version of the planned coup involving Yenu-kidze, Yagoda, and the seizure of the Kremlin, and developed its links with the Tukhachevsky group and with Karakhan's German negotiations. He went on to say that Yagoda had protected Uglanov and Ivan Smirnov in their interrogations and had ordered no search to be made when Zinoviev and Kamenev were arrested. He implicated all the old NKVD chiefs in the plot, and described how Yagoda had ordered Zaporozhets to "facilitate" Kirov's assassination, and how Zaporozh-ets had released Nikolayev on his first attempt and later killed Borisov. It must have seemed curious that Yagoda, arranging through Zaporozhets to let Nikolayev in to kill Kirov, had not thought to do something similar in Moscow by the agency of Pauker and Volovich, in charge of Stalin's personal security, and both now implicated as plotters.

A new crime was now developed—Yagoda's attempt to kill Yezhov after the latter had taken over the NKVD in September 1936. Bulanov and another officer, Savolainen (whose case was sent for separate trial), had sprayed a mercury solution six or seven times in Yezhov's office, and on the rugs and curtains, together with some other, unidentified poison.

Bulanov went on to describe a special poison laboratory that Yagoda had had fixed up under his personal supervision. Yagoda was, Bulanov said, "exceptionally" interested in poisons. This laboratory is believed to have really existed (Yagoda had been a pharmacist by profession before the Revolution). Given the characters and the motivations, this is one crime which appeared to be possibly genuine: Yezhov's health, it was alleged, was "considerably impaired."[156] But a recent Soviet account quotes Yezhov at his own interrogation a year later as saying with a smile that obviously people could not get into his office so easily, and that he had made the whole thing up "to look better in Stalin's eyes."[157]

On the medical poisonings, Bulanov remarked, plausibly enough, "As far as I know, Yagoda drew Levin into, enlisted him in the affair, and in cases of poi-

---

\*Professors Shereshevsky and (V. N.) Vinogradov were to survive Levin by many years. In 1952–1953, they themselves were to go through the same process. Vinogradov, who was seventy on 3 November 1952, was arrested a few days later, and proved to have been "an old agent of British Intelligence." He had, it was announced on 13 January 1953, been one of the murderers of Zhdanov (whose death certificate on 31 August 1948 he had signed). On Stalin's personal order, he was put in chains. Shereshevsky's name was not announced as one of those arrested, but in the larger list of those released when the Doctor's Plot was repudiated by Beria on 4 April 1953, it turned out that he, too, had been implicated and arrested. This later batch of doctor-poisoners, who survived by the happy chance of Stalin dying in the meanwhile, had been treated with particular brutality. It was to them that Stalin's order "Beat, beat and beat again" was applied by General of State Security M. D. Ryumin, Head of the Section for Investigating Specially Important Cases and Assistant Minister of State Security (himself shot in July 1954) (Khrushchev, *Secret Speech*).

soning generally, by taking advantage of some compromising material he had against him.''[158]

Bulanov asserted that Kazakov had indeed visited Yagoda, in spite of the latter's denials. Kazakov again confirmed this. Vyshinsky then put it once more to Yagoda:

> *Vyshinsky:* After this testimony, which establishes your part in the poisoning, do you continue to deny it?
>
> *Yagoda:* No, I confirm my part in it.

And then:

> *Vyshinsky:* Accused Bulanov, and was the killing of Maxim Peshkov also Yagoda's work?
>
> *Bulanov:* Of course.
>
> *Vyshinsky:* Accused Yagoda, what do you say to that?
>
> *Yagoda:* I admit my part in the illness of Peshkov. I request the court to hear this whole question *in camera.*[159]

Yagoda is described as having looked cornered and desperate during the earlier session, but he now appeared crushed, and gave his evidence in a toneless voice.

Vyshinsky next tried to implicate Rykov in Gorky's murder, on the grounds that Yenukidze had once allegedly said to him that an end should be put to Gorky's political activity. Rykov answered that doubtless Yenukidze meant murder by this, but that he himself had not so understood it at the time. He then put a question to Bulanov, who had spoken about "Rykov's archives" being looked after by Yagoda: What were the contents? Bulanov said that he did not know, but Rykov had clearly established that there was an alleged mass of documentary evidence which no one had produced in court.

Yagoda's own evidence-in-chief followed. A recent Soviet account has it that Yezhov promised Yagoda his life if he incriminated Bukharin,[160] but if so Yagoda's confidence in Yezhov's word cannot have been high. His voice was now utterly weary and so faint that it could barely be heard. He stumbled through a written statement, "reading it as though for the first time."[161] He confirmed his long connection with the Rightist plotters from 1928 on. In the early days, he had supplied Rykov and Bukharin with tendentious material from the NKVD secret files, for use in their anti-Party struggle. It was due to his activities in the NKVD that the Rights, and the "bloc of Rights and Trotskyites," had not been uncovered and liquidated until 1937–1938. He had appointed conspirators to all the leading posts in the Secret Police—Molchanov (on Tomsky's express instructions), Prokofiev, Mironov, Shanin, Pauker, Gay, and others. He had joined in Yenukidze's plot to seize the Kremlin, and it was on Yenukidze's orders that he had arranged for Zaporozhets's collaboration in the Kirov assassination.

But when cross-examination started, he still showed a remnant of resistance. Bulanov's evidence about trying to kill Yezhov, he said, had been wrong in detail, and correct only in "essence."

Vyshinsky then taxed him with espionage. Yagoda replied, "No, I do not admit being guilty of this activity." He admitted shielding spies in the NKVD:

> *Vyshinsky:* I consider that since you shielded this espionage activity, you helped them, assisted them.
>
> *Yagoda:* No, I do not admit being guilty of that. Had I been a spy, I assure you that dozens of states would have been compelled to disband their intelligence services.[162]

This sensible remark did not deter the Soviet leaders from the practice of nominating the heads of their Secret Police as imperialist employees.

Rykov again raised the question of his "archives." Yagoda said, "I had no archives of Rykov's." Bulanov then reaffirmed his evidence about these, and when Yagoda challenged him to mention any of their contents, he said he could not. Yagoda finally commented contemptuously, but tellingly, "In any case, had the archives really existed, in comparison with the other crimes, the Rykov archives are a trifle."

Later he refused to admit that he had protected Mensheviks:

> *Vyshinsky:* But in any case you shielded this, even very insignificant role of the Mensheviks?
>
> *Yagoda:* I shall not be able to give you an answer to this question.
>
> *Vyshinsky:* Allow me to quote to Yagoda his testimony in Vol. II, p. 135: 'Question: You are shown a document from the materials of the People's Commissariat of Internal Affairs, containing a report on the Menshevik center abroad and on its active work in the U.S.S.R.' Do you recall this fact?
>
> *Yagoda:* Yes, I know, only I shall not be able to give you an answer to this here.[163]

When it came to the medical numbers, he was still not entirely satisfactory. First he admitted his "part in causing Max's [Peshkov's] sickness," but when Vyshinsky pressed him to plead "guilty to causing, as you express it, Peshkov's sickness," he simply answered that he would give all his explanations *in camera*. Vyshinsky asked twice more, with the same result. Finally:

> *Vyshinsky:* Do you plead guilty or do you not?
>
> *Yagoda:* Permit me not to answer this question.[164]

The only distinction between what Yagoda had admitted and Vyshinsky's formulation was that the former spoke simply of "his part in causing" and the latter of "guilt for" Peshkov's death. Yagoda seems to have been implying either that he had caused the fatal illness in an unintentional way or, more likely, that he did not accept the major guilt. Whether either version is true is another matter.

Yagoda went on to admit to killing Menzhinsky and to reluctantly becoming involved in the murder of Gorky, at Yenukidze's insistence. When Vyshinsky went through his crimes at the end of the day, asking in turn whether Yagoda was guilty in the cases of Kirov, Kuibyshev, Menzhinsky, and Gorky, he did not refer to Peshkov—a minor victory for the accused.

Levin's defense counsel, Braude, then cross-examined:

> *Braude:* Allow me to ask you, what methods did you employ to secure Levin's consent to commit these terrorist acts?
>
> *Yagoda:* In any case not such as he described here.
>
> *Braude:* You yourself went into detail about this at the preliminary investigation. Do you confirm this part of your testimony?
>
> *Yagoda:* It is exaggerated, but that doesn't matter.[165]

Vyshinsky now attempted to involve Bukharin in the Gorky murder. Bukharin defended himself effectively. The "evidence," even at its face value, was simply that Tomsky had once said to him in conversation that the Trotskyites were opposed to Gorky and had some idea of a "hostile act" against him. A hostile act could be anything from a newspaper article up, and in any case such a conversation, as he pointed out, could not possibly prove that he, Bukharin, had murdered the writer.

Kryuchkov, Gorky's secretary, followed. He had left Peshkov lying in the snow in March or April, without result, and finally managed to leave him out to catch a chill in May; Levin and A. I. Vinogradov had managed to persuade other doctors and nurses to give the patient a fatal dose of laxative. When Gorky, in turn, had been given a cold, Pletnev and Levin had insisted on overdoses of digitalis.

The most tragic of all the figures in the great trials was examined on the morning of 9 March. Professor Dmitry Pletnev, a sixty-six-year-old heart specialist, had long enjoyed a reputation as Russia's leading doctor, the pride of the profession. Now, for the first time (if we except the petty crook Arnold) a figure from outside the whole machinery of state, the whole political controversy, stood for trial—and confessed. He, above all, represented the silent non-Party masses whose sufferings in the Purge were otherwise hidden from sight.

When Yezhov had decided that a confession from Levin alone would clearly not be impressive enough, he had turned his attention to Gorky's other main physician. But Pletnev had been before the Revolution a member of the liberal Constitutional Democratic (Kadet) Party. There was no question of appealing to him on the basis of Communist morality. But equally, he had avoided politics since the Revolution, and no political blackmail against him was possible.

Yezhov's solution was nasty even by Yezhov standards. A preliminary decision on the story of medical murders must have been taken soon after he succeeded to Yagoda's post. An NKVD provocateur, a young woman usually employed to compromise foreigners, was sent as a patient to Pletnev. After a couple of consultations, she accused him of having assaulted her two years previously.[166] By December 1936, she was coming to his house, annoying his daughter and housekeeper, and he complained to the police.[167]

They affected to take up his complaint, but instead went into hers, and claimed to believe it. Pletnev appealed to his medical and personal connections to help him. (He was treating Ordzhonikidze and others.)[168] As late as 5 March, the official account tells us, he was still expecting that such help would be forthcoming.[169]

But the contrary was true. On 8 June, *Pravda,* by a very rare exception to its policy of not dealing with individual crimes, published under the sensational headline "Professor—Rapist, Sadist" an account in three half-columns. Pletnev had (it told) thrown himself upon the woman patient "B" on 17 July 1934, and bitten her severely on the breast. This had done her a permanent injury which Pletnev, though no expert in breast disorders, had tried to cure. Not succeeding, and being pestered by the woman, he complained to the police, who took the matter up. On 17 January, she had written him a letter, described by *Pravda* as "a striking human document":

> Be accursed, criminal violator of my body! Be accursed, sadist, practicing your foul perversions on my body! Let shame and disgrace fall on you, let terror and sorrow, weeping and anguish be yours as they have been mine, ever since, criminal professor, you made me the victim of your sexual corruption and criminal perversions. I curse you.
>
> "B"

A short statement was added, signed by Vyshinsky, to the effect that the Section for Investigating Specially Important Cases had the matter in hand—that is, I. I. Shapiro, who was in fact to be Pletnev's interrogator throughout.[170]

On the day after the publication of this article, the papers were full of accounts of meetings of a whole series of medical organizations vilifying him—the Moscow Association of Doctor-Therapeutists, the Medical Union, and others. The following day, the equivalent organizations from other parts of the country sent in their protests, from Kiev, Tula, Sverdlovsk, and elsewhere, denouncing the villainous doctor, the disgrace to Soviet medicine. Among the doctors speaking to, and signing, violent resolutions attacking Pletnev, one finds the names of M. Vovsi, B. Kogan, and V. Zelenin, who were (like Drs. Shereshevsky and V. N. Vinogradov) to be tortured by the MGB in 1952–1953 in the later Doctors' Plot.

Pletnev was sentenced, in a trial which took place on 17 to 18 July 1937, to two years' imprisonment. The press said that he had confessed. And thus, crushed and dishonored, denounced by his colleagues, found guilty of a disgraceful offense, he found himself in the cells of the Lubyanka, "where a still greater misfortune awaited him."[171]

Just before the present trial, Pletnev had the formal confrontation with Vyshinsky, as Prosecutor, in the Lefortovo. When it was finished, Vyshinsky said to him, "I would like you to explain to me how you took to terror . . . it interests me psychologically." Pletnev replied that he would confirm all the lies in court, and not spoil the show, but that for now he asked to be returned to his cell, since it disgusted him to talk to Vyshinsky.[172]

Now, under Vyshinsky's questioning, he confessed his role in the murders of Kuibyshev and Gorky. He spoke of the "violent threats [made by Yagoda] against me and against my family."[173]

He mentioned a connection with Dr. Nikitin, Tolstoy's favorite physician, who had been one of a number of doctors exiled some years earlier. But he said that he did not believe Nikitin to be politically minded[174]—an honorable rebuttal of what was presumably a false charge against a distinguished colleague.

Pletnev's defense lawyer, Kommodov, elicited his splendid medical record. Then Vyshinsky reexamined on that, raising the assault case. Pletnev made an attempt to reject the charge, but he was borne down by Vyshinsky, now in one of his most arrogant and bullying moods:

*Vyshinsky:* How many years did you say was your standing as a physician?

*Pletnev:* Forty.

*Vyshinsky:* You consider your standing as irreproachable?

*Pletnev:* Yes, I do.

*Vyshinsky:* Irreproachable?

*Pletnev:* Yes, I think so.

*Vyshinsky:* During these forty years you have never committed any crime in connection with your profession?

*Pletnev:* You are aware of one.

*Vyshinsky:* I am asking you because you state that your work for forty years was irreproachable.

*Pletnev:* Yes, but since I denied that time . . .

*Vyshinsky:* Do you think that the sentence in the case which is well known to you, the case of an outrage which you committed against a woman patient, is a blot on your reputation?

*Pletnev:* The sentence, yes. . . .

*Vyshinsky:* Is that sentence a blot on your reputation or not?

*Pletnev:* It is.

*Vyshinsky:* So there were moments of disgrace during these forty years?

*Pletnev:* Yes.

*Vyshinsky:* Did you not plead guilty to anything?

*Pletnev:* I cannot say that I did not plead guilty to anything.

*Vyshinsky:* So you did plead guilty to something?

*Pletnev:* Yes.

*Vyshinsky:* Is this a blot on your reputation?

*Pletnev:* Yes.[175]

Kazakov, the remaining doctor, confirmed his part in Menzhinsky's death. But at the end of his evidence, he defended his method and asserted that "lysates" could after all not have harmed Menzhinsky:

*Vyshinsky:* For what purpose did you introduce these lysates? To kill Menzhinsky?

*Kazakov:* (No reply.)

*Vyshinsky:* Did you introduce the lysates for this end? Were you certain that they would assist your crimes?

*Kazakov:* You see, lysates have a dual effect.

*Vyshinsky:* You dare to assert that these lysates were harmless for Menzhinsky?

*Kazakov:* Yes. These three lysates were harmless.

*Vyshinsky:* And could you have fooled Yagoda?

*Kazakov:* (No reply.)

*Vyshinsky:* In view of the impossibility of getting a direct answer to this clear question, I request the court to adjourn the session and to make it possible
for the Commission of Experts to answer the questions I have put
to Kazakov.[176]

After a half-hour adjournment, the Commission of Experts supported Vyshinsky's view of the matter:

Such a combination of methods of treatment could not but lead to the exhaustion of
the heart muscles of the patient V. R. Menzhinsky, and thereby to the acceleration of
his death.

| Moscow, | Expert Witnesses: |
| --- | --- |
| 9 March 1938 | Professor D. A. Burmin, Scientist of Merit |
| | Professor N. A. Shereshevsky, Scientist of Merit |
| | Professor V. N. Vinogradov |
| | Professor D. M. Rossisky |
| | V. D. Zipalov, Doctor of Medicine |

Vyshinsky then read out admissions made by Kazakov at the preliminary investigation. Under these pressures, Kazakov finally confirmed his guilt in the matter.
Vyshinsky was then finally able to say:

Inasmuch as we have a definite finding from the Commission of Experts, and Kazakov
has repudiated his statement about the neutrality of these lysates, I think that the
question can be considered closed.[177]

The last accused, Maximov-Dikovsky, was then examined. He admitted having been placed in Kuibyshev's secretariat by Yenukidze, and explained how he
had helped the medical killers to dispose of Kuibyshev.

Vyshinsky then produced a medical "witness," Dr. Belostotsky, who had
been present during Gorky's last illness and now testified against Pletnev and
Levin. The final report of the Expert Commission, confirming all the medical
accusations and the attempt on Yezhov's health, was then presented.

It will be seen that the evidence in the case of these medical murders is
confused and incomplete. We can be sure that those on trial were innocent of all
the charges of treason, conspiracy, espionage, and sabotage. We can be virtually
certain, on the other hand, that Yagoda's responsibility for the murder of Kirov
was correctly established—with the minor amendment that his instructions were
received not from Yenukidze but from Stalin. But with the murky tale of the
deaths of Menzhinsky, Peshkov, Kuibyshev, and Gorky, we are on different ground.

There are two problems: Were they murdered? And, if so, were they murdered by the doctors, or by one or any of them?

The first point to establish is that reliance on the binding force of the Hip-

pocratic Oath will not take us far. Either the five doctors (Levin, Pletnev, Kazakov, A. I. Vinogradov, and Khodorovsky) were guilty as charged or the five
doctors on the Expert Commission, and the witness Dr. Belostotsky, were, in their
capacity as doctors, accomplices in judicial murder.

A similar pattern was to be repeated in 1952–1953. In the later Doctors'
Plot, either the doctors, or some of them, procured the murder of Zhdanov (and
in this atmosphere the fact of their rehabilitation by a political group not wishing
the matter to go further by no means disproves this possibility) or Dr. Timashuk—
their denouncer—was actively willing to have her colleagues submitted to torture
and death, and the new Commission of Medical Experts who certified that the
doctors were guilty—and were afterward censured for having doing so—were accomplices in an action which would ordinarily have led to the liquidation of their
colleagues. In neither case can the doctors be blamed, as can the true instigators.
On the contrary, the degradation of a humane profession under political terror
makes the story even more revolting.

Drs. A. I. Vinogradov and Khodorovsky, dead in unknown circumstances in
the hands of the Secret Police; Drs. Levin and Kazakov, shot to death in the
cellars of the Lubyanka; and Professor Pletnev, killed later, did not commit all or
any of the crimes they were charged with. They may all seem to us to have been,
in a way, martyrs—the unknown, confused, and pathetic martyrdom suffered by
ordinary people caught up more or less accidentally in maneuvers of power by
leaders to whom human life and standards of truth counted for nothing.

A number of other doctors were implicated in one way or another, though
not publicly, in the Gorky affair (and were known in imprisonment as "Gorky-
ists"). For example, Professor G. M. Danishevsky, chairman of the Scientific
Council of the People's Commissariat of Health,[178] and a Dr. Loevenstein[179] were
reported in the Pechora and Yertsevo camps, respectively.

The argument that no post-Kirov murders in fact took place is a simple one.
Stalin needed a few more assassinations to lay at the door of the oppositionists,
and could only produce them by representing natural deaths as murders. This is a
perfectly sound point as far as it goes. But it is an entirely negative one, and does
not enable us to pronounce one way or the other, meaning no more than "*if* the
deaths were natural, Stalin might have produced an identical story."

The (equally general) argument on the other side is equally strong: that Kuibyshev and Gorky were obstacles to Stalin, and we all know what Stalin did to
obstacles. Nor is it in the least out of character to suppose that he and Yagoda
would have been prepared to use the method of murder, if available.

We must turn, rather, to the details. In the first place, there is Yagoda's
evidence of the morning of 8 March, when he pleaded guilty to the murders of
Kuibyshev and Gorky, and not guilty to those of Peshkov and Menzhinsky.

On the whole, Yagoda's initial evidence seems to have been true, or as true
as was possible in the circumstances, on most other matters. His account of the
Kirov murder seems quite authentic, except on the point of who instructed him to
carry it out, and even that is hinted at in his remarks that "it was not quite like
that," when describing the relevant meetings; for this can best be taken as implying that someone's name has been left out or wrongly reported. Again, he pleaded

not guilty to the charge of espionage, and there is no doubt that this was the truth. So when we come to his anomalous pleas on the four medical murders, there is at least some ground for paying attention to what he is saying.

On the Menzhinsky case, we have the added detail of Kazakov's last-minute retraction of the whole essence of his evidence. This seems decisive. Menzhinsky was almost certainly not murdered by his doctors. (He may, of course, have been killed in some other fashion.)

On Peshkov, on the face of it the whole idea of his murder seems almost pointless. Yagoda justly remarked, ''I see no sense in his murder.'' That Peshkova was Yagoda's mistress really adds little to his motive. He did not propose to marry her; he was married already and made no attempt to murder or divorce his wife over the following three years. Moreover, the murder method (reflected in the death of the loyal old sheep in *Animal Farm*) is a trifle unconvincing.

With Kuibyshev and Gorky, though—that is, precisely the two killings Yagoda freely admitted to—we have cases in which Stalin had definite and pressing political motives for murder.

This does not prove that he killed them. In Kuibyshev's case, all we can say is that he is now named as one of Stalin's three main opponents of the purge in the Politburo, and that Stalin procured the death of both the others (Kirov and Ordzhonikidze) by devious, though differing, means—the latter by a faked heart attack. So Kuibyshev's ''heart attack'' is not by any means to be accepted simply at face value. Moreover, his survival through 1935 might have constituted a severe obstacle to Stalin's plans, and he died at precisely the time Stalin was turning against the other main opponents of the killing of Zinoviev and Kamenev.

But as against that, we have no positive evidence of murder. We can, indeed, exculpate the doctors. If Kuibyshev was murdered, it was not done by them. On Kuibyshev's death, documents now published in the Soviet Union show that he did indeed suffer from heart trouble and that, ''feeling very poorly,'' he asked to be excused from a session of Gosplan, on which the writer comments, ''It is probable that this was a regular heart attack.''[180] (But it has recently been speculated in a Soviet periodical that Stalin may indeed have killed Kuibyshev.)[181]

Gorky's death is the most interesting and important. For here we have a case where the survival of a sick man for a few months might have gravely hampered Stalin's plans for the August 1936 Trial, whose postponement until after the holidays could perhaps have led to resistance in the Politburo and Central Committee. But how could Gorky be silenced, apart from the international scandal of arrest? As Vyshinsky put it, though with different intent, in his concluding speech: ''How in our country, in the conditions that exist in the Soviet State, could it be made impossible for Gorky to display political activity except by taking his life?''[182]

But again, it is clear that the doctors, or at any rate those tried, were innocent. Even such credulous observers as Walter Duranty strongly doubted their guilt.

A possible alternative is perhaps that Gorky was indeed murdered, but not by Pletnev and Levin, now long since rehabilitated.

As I write, in 1989, opinion is still current in Moscow that Stalin procured Gorky's death. Such talk goes back a long way; for example, a ''Gorkyist'' doctor in one of the Vorkuta camps, wrongly identified as Pletnev, told a confidante in the early 1950s that Gorky had been given poisoned sweetmeats, which also killed one of his attendants.[183] As evidence, this does not amount to much. However, there is one piece of more cogent testimony. In the summer of 1963, an old American acquaintance of Gorky visited his eighty-six-year-old widow, Ekaterina Peshkova, in Moscow. Of her son's death, she said quite calmly that she had no doubt that it was natural. When the visitor remarked that people now said that Gorky's, too, had been natural, she became very agitated and exclaimed: "It's not quite so, but don't ask me to tell you about it! I won't be able to sleep a wink for three days and nights if I tell you."[184]

Mme. Peshkova's evident conviction that Peshkov's death was natural and Gorky's not fits in with Yagoda's testimony in court. As with his evidence on the Kirov Case, we seem to be driven to the ironic conclusion that, alone among the accused, the story told by the ex-Police Chief was essentially true! And if this is so, his confession to the Kuibyshev murder, alone among the other three, is best explicable as indicating that Kuibyshev, too, was really murdered. But this is a matter of deduction rather than evidence: we cannot at present at all exclude the possibility that the timely death of these men Stalin wanted out of the way was, after all, natural. Nor does it seem very probable that more will be forthcoming even when the Soviet archives are opened up. For it is rather unlikely that plans for this style of killing are committed to paper.

And there we must leave this murky and horrible episode.

When the doctors and their organizers and accomplices had been dealt with, the Expert Commission, as we have said, made its report, confirming their guilt, and for full measure establishing the damage to Yezhov's health, evidenced in his urine. Apart from a short session *in camera* at which Yagoda (it was announced) "fully admitted organizing the murder of Comrade M. A. Peshkov," the hearing was concluded. But before adjournment, Vyshinsky recalled Rosengolts for one petty smear.

He described the good-luck token found in Rosengolts's pocket (see p. 241), and asked the court's permission to read it. In a sneering tone, amid titters from the audience, he read out eight verses of the Psalms—"Let God arise, and let his enemies be scattered . . ."—and then asked Rosengolts, "How did this get into your pocket?"

> *Rosengolts:* My wife put it in my pocket one day before I went to work. She said it was for good luck.

Vyshinsky continued on a humorous note, "And you carried this 'good luck' in your hip pocket for several months?"

> *Rosengolts:* I did not even pay attention . . .
>
> *Vyshinsky:* Nevertheless, you saw what your wife was doing?
>
> *Rosengolts:* I was in a hurry.
>
> *Vyshinsky:* But you were told that this was a family talisman for good luck?[185]

At this, he winked at the crowd, which roared with laughter,[186] and the hearings were at an end.


## THE LAST ACT

The court reassembled on 11 March for the final speeches and pleas. Vyshinsky's speech for the prosecution lasted all morning. He started with a violent harangue:

> It is not for the first time that the Supreme Court of our country is examining a case involving the gravest crimes directed against the well-being of our country, against our Socialist fatherland, the fatherland of the working people of the whole world. But I will hardly be mistaken if I say that this is the first time that our court has had to examine a case like this, to examine a case of such crimes and such foul deeds as those that have passed at this trial before your eyes, before the eyes of the whole world, a case of such criminals as those you now see in the prisoners' dock.
>
> With every day and hour that passed, as the court investigation on the present case proceeded, it brought to light even more of the horror of the chain of shameful, unparalleled, monstrous crimes committed by the accused, the entire abominable chain of heinous deeds before which the base deeds of the most inveterate, vile, unbridled and despicable criminals fade and grow dim.[187]

He then came to the whole crux, from the point of view of Stalinist logic:

> . . . The historical significance of this trial consists before all in the fact that at this trial it has been shown, proved and established with exceptional scrupulousness and exactitude that the Rights, Trotskyites, Mensheviks, Socialist-Revolutionaries, bourgeois nationalists, and so on and so forth, are nothing other than a gang of murderers, spies, diversionists and wreckers, without any principles or ideals. . . .
>
> The Trotskyites and Bukharinites, that is to say, the 'bloc of Rights and Trotskyites', the leading lights of which are now in the prisoners' dock, is not a political party, a political tendency, but a band of felonious criminals, and not simply felonious criminals, but of criminals who have sold themselves to enemy intelligence services, criminals whom even ordinary felons treat as the basest, the lowest, the most contemptible, the most depraved of the depraved.[188]

Interrupting his argument with remarks about "a foul-smelling heap of human garbage,"[189] he traced the continuity of counter-revolution back to the Shakhty and "Industrial Party" Trials.

Attacking the entire past careers of Bukharin and the others, he rehearsed their current crimes. Of Zelensky, for example, he said:

> I shall refer here to the most abominable practice of mixing glass and nails with foodstuffs, butter in particular, which hit at the most vital interests, the health and lives of our population. Glass and nails in butter! This is so monstrous a crime that, in my opinion, all other crimes of the kind pale before it.

He went on to explain:

> In our country, rich in resources of all kinds, there could not have been and cannot be a situation in which a shortage of any product should exist. . . .
>
> It is now clear why there are interruptions of supplies here and there, why, with

our riches and abundance of products, there is a shortage first of one thing, then of another. It is these traitors who are responsible for it.[190]

A method of explaining economic failure which any Government might envy.

He attacked the line taken by Bukharin—"the damnable cross of a fox and a swine"—and Rykov:

> The former wanted to prove here that, actually speaking, he did not favour the defeat of the U.S.S.R., that he did not favour espionage, nor wrecking, nor diversive activities, because in general he was not supposed to have any connection with these practical matters, for he was the 'theoretician', a man who occupied himself with the problematics of universal questions.[191]

He was particularly incensed with the refusal of Bukharin and Rykov to accept responsibility for the Kirov murder:

> Why did people who had organized espionage, who had organized insurrectionary movements and terrorist acts, and who, on their own admission, had received instructions from Trotsky on terrorism, suddenly, in 1934, stand aloof from the assassination of one of the greatest comrades-in-arms of Stalin, one of the most prominent leaders of the Party and the Government? . . .
>
> Bukharin and Rykov have admitted that the assassination of leaders of the Party and the Government, of members of the Political Bureau, was part of their plans. . . . Why should we assume that, having entered into negotiations with Semyonov for the organization of the assassination of members of the Political Bureau, Bukharin deletes from this list of persons who are to be slain one of the most influential members of the Political Bureau who had distinguished himself by his irreconcilable fight against the Trotskyites, Zinovievites and Bukharinites? Where is the logic in such behaviour? There is no logic in it. . . .
>
> Finally Rykov admitted that in 1934 he instructed Artemenko to keep a watch on the automobiles of members of the Government. For what purpose? For terrorist purposes. Rykov was organizing the assassination of members of our Government, of members of the Political Bureau. Why should Rykov make an exception in the case of Sergei Mironovich Kirov, who nevertheless was assassinated on the decision of this accursed bloc? He made no such exception![192]

In the medical murders, too, Vyshinsky pointed out that Bukharin admitted everything but actual knowledge or responsibility. Dismissing "an opinion current among criminologists that in order to establish complicity it is necessary to establish common agreement and an intent on the part of each of the criminals, of the accomplices, for each of the crimes,"[193] he demanded the death penalty for all except Rakovsky and Bessonov.

He concluded that the others

> must be shot like dirty dogs! Our people are demanding one thing: crush the accursed reptile! Time will pass. The graves of the hateful traitors will grow over with weeds and thistles. . . . Over the road cleared of the last scum and filth of the past, we, our people, with our beloved leader and teacher, the great Stalin, at our head will march as before onwards and onwards, towards Communism![194]

In the evening, the doctors' defense lawyers made their pleas, putting the blame on Yagoda.

Then came the last pleas of the accused. Bessonov remarked that he had loyally returned to Moscow from abroad even when under suspicion. Most of the others simply accused themselves, Bukharin, and Rykov. Ivanov put in the remark, a sinister foreshadowing of future cases:

> The reason, I think, why Bukharin has not told the whole truth here is because throughout the whole period of the revolution he has fought the revolution and to this day has remained its enemy, and because he wants to preserve those remnants of the hostile forces which are still lurking in their dens.[195]

Krestinsky went into his splendid record in the Party, starting as an eighteen-year-old boy in 1901, his leadership in Bolshevik underground organizations, his many arrests, his work as Lenin's "organizational assistant." He made the telling point, "I consider it necessary to stress the fact that I had absolutely no knowledge of the terrorist acts enumerated in the second section of the indictment, and that I learnt about them only when I was handed a copy of the indictment,"[196] and went on to explain his retraction as due in part to the fact that "it seemed to me easier to die than to give the world the idea that I was even a remote accessory to the murder of Gorky, about which I actually knew nothing."[197]

Rykov, trembling and livid, made a sound defense. He admitted his general guilt, and then added:

> . . . But the State Prosecutor has charged me with something in which I had no direct part, and which I cannot admit. He has charged me with adopting a decision, or with giving directions for the murder of Kirov, Kuibyshev, Menzhinsky, Gorky and Peshkov. . . .
>
> The evidence brought against me in this connection has been set forth here in detail; it is based upon the statements of Yagoda, who refers to Yenukidze. Nothing more incriminating was brought against me at the trial. . . .
>
> The assassination of Kirov has formed the subject of two trials. Both the direct perpetrators and the organizers and leaders of this assassination have appeared in court. I do not recall that my name was mentioned then.[198]

He went on to rub in one extremely telling point. When it came to the alleged attempt on Lenin of twenty years previously, the prosecution had produced eye-witnesses, there were confrontations, and in fact direct evidence.

> Why then, on the question of my participation in the assassination of five most important political figures, should a decision be taken on the basis of indirect evidence?
>
> This, it seems to me, would be incorrect. At any rate, I deny any charge of my participation in these five assassinations.[199]

Until his arrest, he had believed that Gorky had died a natural death. It was only at the trial itself that he had "first learnt of such members of our counter-revolutionary organization as Ivanov."[200]

He concluded with a formal plea of guilty—"This responsibility of mine of course transcends all the discrepancies which still remain regarding certain facts and certain details"—and called on any surviving Rightists to "disarm."[201]

Rakovsky said:

> I confess to all my crimes. What would it matter for the substance of the case if I should attempt to establish here before you the fact that I learned of many of the

crimes, and of the most appalling crimes of the 'bloc of Rights and Trotskyites' here in court, and that it was here that I first met some of the participants?[202]

He went on to denounce Trotsky and Trotskyism, and to point out that his evidence had been entirely satisfactory to the prosecution.

Rosengolts* rehearsed his revolutionary past, starting when, as a child of ten, he had hidden illegal literature. He made a reference to his children, and then ended by unexpectedly beginning to sing a well-known song about the USSR: ". . . I don't know any other country where we can breathe so freely." The NKVD men in the audience are reported jumping to their feet in case their intervention was needed. But Rosengolts then broke down and resumed his seat.[203]

Yagoda, too, "in low fear-ridden tones,"[204] dwelt on his underground work for the Party, from the age of fourteen, and of such later services as "vast construction jobs—the canals" (that is, the forced-labor projects). He continued to oppose Vyshinsky on one point:

> I am not a spy and have not been one. I think that in the definition of a spy or espionage we will not differ. But a fact is a fact. I had no direct connections with abroad, there are no instances of my directly handing over any information. I am not jesting when I say that if I had been a spy dozens of countries could have closed down their intelligence services—there would have been no need for them to maintain such a mass of spies as have now been caught in the Soviet Union.[205]

The doctors and secretaries pleaded Yagoda's threats to them. Levin lapsed by referring to his great esteem for Gorky, and had to be called to order for "blasphemy." Pletnev mentioned his medical work, adding that the NKVD had given him facilities to write a monograph; he had known nothing of the "bloc." Bulanov criticized his fellow accused:

> I think, perhaps I am mistaken, that some of them showed signs of wanting to deceive the Party even now, although each of them invariably began by saying that he fully and entirely shares responsibility, pleads guilty and is answerable. But this was a matter of form, general declarations. In a number of cases they tried to deny their guilt by pleading ignorance of some point.[206]

Bukharin's speech, even more than Rykov's, was a brilliant development of the line he had taken throughout. He admitted leadership of the "bloc of Rights and Trotskyites," and accepted political responsibility for all the crimes. For instance:

> I admit that I am responsible both politically and legally for the defeatist orientation, for it did dominate in the 'bloc of Rights and Trotskyites', although I affirm that personally I did not hold this position. . . .
> I further consider myself responsible both politically and legally for wrecking

---

*It is a curious fact that Stalin was later (in his Report to the 1939 XVIIIth Congress) twice to name Rosengolts first among the 1938 conspirators—once in a general list of spies and so on, running "Trotsky, Zinoviev, Kamenev, Yakir, Tukhachevsky, Rosengolts, Bukharin," and then on the 1938 Trial alone, "Rosengolts, Rykov, Bukharin and others." This seems to reflect some special animus on the part of the dictator, and fits in with the special jab at Rosengolts on the "talisman," doubtless ordered from above.

activities, although I personally do not remember having given directions about wrecking activities. I did not talk about this. I once spoke positively on this subject to Grinko. Even in my testimony I mentioned that I had once told Radek that I considered this method of struggle as not very expedient. Yet Citizen the State Prosecutor makes me out to be a leader of the wrecking activities.[207]

As Bukharin destroyed the prosecution case against him, "Vyshinsky, powerless to intervene, sat uneasily in his place, looking embarrassed and yawning ostentatiously."[208]

While accepting group responsibility, Bukharin went on to deny that the group, as apart from the central "bloc" of politicians, existed:

Citizen the Prosecutor explained in the speech for the prosecution that the members of a gang of brigands might commit robberies in different places, but that they would nevertheless be responsible for each other. That is true, but in order to be a gang the members of the gang of brigands must know each other and be in more or less close contact with each other. Yet I first learnt the name of Sharangovich from the indictment, and I first saw him here in court. It was here that I first learnt about the existence of Maximov, I have never been acquainted with Pletnev, I have never been acquainted with Kazakov, I have never spoken about counter-revolutionary matters with Rosengolts, I have never spoken about it to Zelensky, I have never in my life spoken to Bulanov, and so on. Incidentally, even the Prosecutor did not ask me a single question about these people. . . . Consequently, the accused in this dock are not a group.[209]

The bloc had supposedly been formed in 1928, long before Hitler came to power: "How then can it be asserted that the bloc was organized on the instructions of fascist intelligence services?"

On espionage he took the same line: "Citizen the Prosecutor asserts that I was one of the major organizers of espionage, on a par with Rykov. What are the proofs? The testimony of Sharangovich, of whose existence I had not even heard until I read the indictment."[210] The prosecution had proved that he had met Khodzhayev and discussed politics, and taken this as proof of espionage contact. There was no logic here.

He went on similarly to "categorically deny my complicity in the assassination of Kirov, Menzhinsky, Kuibyshev, Gorky and Maxim Peshkov,"[211] and in the 1918 case with Lenin:

As to the plan of physical extermination, I categorically deny it, and here the logic to which Citizen the State Prosecutor referred, namely, that forcible arrest implied physical extermination, will not help in the least. The Constituent Assembly was arrested, but nobody suffered physically. We arrested the faction of the 'Left' Socialist-Revolutionaries, yet not a single man of them suffered physically. The 'Left' Socialist-Revolutionaries arrested Dzerzhinsky, yet he did not suffer physically.[212]

He then remarked tellingly, "The confession of the accused is a medieval principle of jurisprudence."[213]

Vyshinsky flushed at the words.

Thus Bukharin refuted the charges in detail. But he admitted them in general. He had been a counter-revolutionary conspirator in "this stinking underground life." He had "degenerated" into an enemy of Socialism. He attacked Western commentators who had suggested that the confessions were not voluntary, and rejected the sympathy to be expected from Western Socialists. He was guilty of treason, the organization of kulak uprisings, the preparation of (unspecified) terrorist acts. He hoped that his execution would be "the last severe lesson" to those who had wavered in their support of the USSR and its leadership.[214]

At 9:25 P.M. on 12 March the court retired. It returned and pronounced verdict at 4:00 A.M. on 13 March. All the accused were found guilty on all charges. All were sentenced to death except for Pletnev, who got twenty-five years; Rakovsky, twenty years; and Bessonov, fifteen years. Pletnev was resentenced, this time to death, on 8 September 1941, and was shot on 11 September 1941, as were Rakovsky and Bessonov. Bessonov's liquidation is reported to have occurred in Orel prison, where Spiridonova was also executed at this time; and perhaps it was there that this final winding up of the Bukharin Trial took place.[215]

An Old Bolshevik remarked that apart from the use of relatives as hostages, he saw the 1938 confessions as based on total lack of political hope. In addition, in spite of everything, Stalin had continued his promise not to execute the Bukharinites. They knew he had gone back on his word in most other cases, but "a little hope goes a long way in such circumstances."

Bukharin, nevertheless, must have known that his own attitude in court, fulfilling the minimum requirements only, would cost him his life. He had said in court that he was "almost certain" he would be dead after the trial. He and Rykov, unlike Zinoviev and Kamenev, were ready for death. They are said to have died firmly defying their captors.[216]

In 1965, Bukharin's "last letter" was published in the West.[217] This was at a time when there was talk of an official rehabilitation of Bukharin and Rykov. And, in fact, they had at least been exculpated of spying and terrorism, though only at a fairly obscure conference of historians.[218] And Ikramov, Krestinsky, Zelensky, Khodzhayev, and Grinko had actually been rehabilitated, making nonsense of the charges against the rest. However, full rehabilitation of the two principals did not come for another twenty-three years.

The "last letter" appeals to future leaders of the Party and denounces the NKVD and its use of the "pathological suspiciousness" of Stalin. This "hellish machine" can transform any Party member into a "terrorist" or "spy." He was not guilty, would cheerfully have died for Lenin, loved Kirov, and had done nothing against Stalin. He had had no connection with Ryutin's or Uglanov's illegal struggle.

Bukharin's wife, Anna Larina, was arrested soon after the trial. She is reported spending six months in a small cell permanently ankle-deep in cold water, but survived to serve eighteen years in labor camp and exile. Their small son was brought up by Anna's sister and for twenty years knew nothing of his parenthood.[219] It was Anna Larina who, in the final days before Bukharin's arrest, had learned his "letter" by heart; it was finally published in Moscow in 1988.

Bukharin's crippled first wife, Nadezhda, had written to Stalin several times asserting his innocence, and turned in her Party card after his arrest. She was arrested in April 1938, and her surgical corset taken from her so that she was in continual pain. However, she refused to confess. She was interrogated at intervals until March 1940, when she was shot. Her brothers, brother-in-law, and other relatives were also arrested and were shot, died in prison, or disappeared in camps.[220]

Bukharin's daughter by his second marriage, Svetlana, had been left at liberty when he was arrested. At the end of the year, she was encouraged to write, and sketch, for an article in *Pionerskaya pravda,* which appeared on 28 December 1937. She later interpreted this as being a method of showing her father that the family was not being persecuted, but that if he gave further trouble, this unspoken bargain might be changed. She and her mother in fact were not arrested until later. She herself was convicted without an indictment: "is adequately convicted in being Bukharin's daughter."[221]

Ikramov's wife and his four brothers were shot, and his elder son was arrested (Ikramov himself was informed of all this while in jail). His younger son, Kamil, ten years old at the time of the trial, was only arrested in 1943.[222]

Yagoda's wife is reported in camp, though she was eventually shot, while two sisters and his mother seem to have died in camps as well.[223] Ivanov's wife is reported in camp,[224] and the wives of Rakovsky and Ossinsky in the Butyrka.[225] Rykov's wife was also in the Butyrka, in 1937, anxious and ignorant of her husband's fate.[226] She did not survive, and their daughter was sentenced to eight years in camp "to be used only for general labor,"[227] and in the event served twenty years. During 1938 at least, Bukharin's father and Rosengolts's wife are said not even to have been arrested.[228] As for the family of Tomsky, who had sensibly predeceased the other "conspirators": his two elder sons were arrested and shot; his wife and youngest son were imprisoned.[229]

During the whole period of the trial, from the announcement on 28 February 1938 that it would take place until the actual executions, the papers had, of course, been full of the demands of workers' meetings that no pity be shown to the "foul band of murderers and spies." Leaders and articles rubbed it in. A Conference on Physiological Problems at the Academy of Sciences passed a resolution of thanks to the NKVD. The folk "poet" Dzhambul produced his usual verse contribution to *Pravda,* "Annihilate." The verdict of the court was received with many expressions of public joy.

Life, which had cast the Bukharin reactionaries aside, was represented mainly by the heroes of the Soviet Arctic expedition who had been landed at the pole some months earlier and were now in the news. There was celebration first of their rescue from the ice floe and then, on 16 March, of their arrival back in Leningrad on the icebreakers *Yermak* and *Murmanets.* Papanin and his gallant comrades were, as before, given the full treatment day after day, with receptions, decorations, public meetings, and a vast press spread.

A further sign of the rejection by the forward-looking Soviet people of all the dark forces of the past was shown in the elections to Union Republic Supreme Soviets. As Stalin was to remark so tellingly in his Report to the XVIIIth Congress in 1939,[230] the executions of Tukhachevsky and Yakir were followed by the elections to the Supreme Soviet of the USSR, giving the Soviet power 98.6 percent of all taking part in the voting. At the beginning of 1938, "Rosengolts, Rykov, Bukharin and others" had been sentenced, and after this, elections to the

Supreme Soviets of the Union Republics gave the Soviet power 99.4 percent of all taking part in the voting.

As for the effects of the trial, once again neither the ineptitudes of the plot nor the partial denials of the accused made any difference. The extravagances included those long since established. Once more, a vast network of assassins was discovered. At least eight groups were working on the destruction of Stalin, Molotov, Kaganovich, Voroshilov, and Yezhov. And, this time, they were shown not simply to be under the protection of high officials in the Party and the Army, but actually to have been nourished and sponsored by the NKVD itself. Seldom can terrorists have had such advantages as those supposedly enjoyed by the plotters. Apart from half a dozen members of the Government, including the Head of the Secret Police itself, they actually had on their side the NKVD officers Pauker and Volovich, responsible for guarding their prospective victims. But the results had been negligible. Assassinations had indeed been carried out, but only by doctors. By adding these in, the total successes of all the groups of assassins exposed at the three trials consisted of Kirov killed; Molotov perhaps slightly shaken in a car accident; Kuibyshev, Gorky, and Menzhinsky "poisoned" by their doctors; and Gorky's son given a chill and then doctored to death. It is an unimpressive result, and the conclusion—that the best way to assassinate anyone was to wait until he got ill—was not very encouraging to anyone desiring speedy action. A minor curiosity, again unnoticed by enthusiasts, is that the indictment cites against the accused diversionary acts in the Far Eastern Territory, and in particular certain specified train wrecks, on the instructions of Japanese intelligence, and the verdict finds them guilty of this, but no attempt at all is made to prove it in the evidence! The reason for this anomaly is not clear, though it might conceivably be that the relevant witness balked at the last moment.

Another oddity of the trial was again the implication of a whole series of important figures who were, however, not produced. As Grinko had remarked, the "bloc" included "a number of other people who are not now in the dock."[231] Major roles in the conspiracy, as important as those played by any of those appearing in court, were alleged to have been played by Yenukidze, Rudzutak,[232] and Antipov,[233] while A. P. Smirnov, Karakhan, Uglanov, V. Shmidt, and Yakovlev[234] had roles notably more important than the second level of those appearing in the dock.* Yenukidze and Karakhan had indeed been shot without public trial. But why? And as to the others, why did they not appear? Such questions were scarcely asked.

On an even more essential point, Bukharin's calculation that his tactics would adequately expose the falsity of the charges against him seems to have been too subtle. It was, of course, plain that he denied all overt acts of terrorism and espionage. But who was affected by this? Serious independent observers in any case did not credit the charges, and would not have done so even if he *had* confessed to all of them—any more than they did in the case of Zinoviev. But to the greater political audience for whom the trials were enacted, the impression re-

---

*Other members of the Central Committee implicated include Vareikis, Lyubimov, Lobov, Sulimov, Kabakov, Razumov, Rumyantsev, and Komarov.

ceived was simply that "Bukharin had confessed." For those who even noted that the confession had only been partial, the fact that he had admitted to organizing a terrorist conspiracy outweighed his rejection of actual terrorist acts. Indeed, this last even gave a certain color to Vyshinsky's thesis that Bukharin, though driven to admit the essentials, was trying to wriggle out of particular crimes.

Stalin had once again won the battle of wits. For he understood, as the intellectual Bukharin did not, that political effects did not depend on simple logic, just as, in the 1920s, his opponents had "won" the arguments at Congresses in the debating-point sense, without affecting his practical victory.

All the accused except Yagoda were rehabilitated in 1988.

# THE FOREIGN ELEMENT

> *The N.K.V.D. organs . . . could extend the category of "enemy of the people" to everyone who dared to utter a word of criticism.*
>
> Wladislaw Gomulka

## IN THE COMINTERN

The Purge also operated abroad and against foreigners in the USSR. The most obviously purgeable of the latter were the foreign Communists in the apparatus of the Comintern. It was more particularly the Communist Parties which were illegal in their own countries that bore the brunt. First of all, their leaderships were mainly ready to hand in Moscow. Then again, there was no democratic opinion back in Germany or Yugoslavia or Italy which could raise objections. There were almost no victims, even in Moscow, among British or American Communists, who were thus not called upon to run the risks, either at home or in Russia, which the rest of the Comintern Parties had to face. Their protection derived from the nature of the regimes they were working to overthrow.

Lenin, in creating the Comintern, skimmed off a lively section of the European revolutionary Left, which might have otherwise fertilized a broad and unified movement and barred the way to Fascism. It became instead a set of parties founded strictly on the Bolshevik model, and constitutionally subordinated to the Comintern—which always remained under effective Soviet control. After a while, these parties' leaderships were selected and their tactics dictated by Moscow—almost invariably with disastrous results.

The last flicker of independence in the Comintern took place in May 1927. In the presence of Stalin, Rykov, Bukharin, and Manuilsky, the Executive Committee of the Comintern was asked by Thälmann to condemn a document of Trotsky's on the Chinese question. All present were prepared to do so, when the Italian delegates—Togliatti and Silone—said that they had not seen the document. It turned out that no one else had either. The Italians objected that though Trotsky was doubtless wrong, they could hardly be expected to subscribe to a formal condemnation of something they had not seen. It was explained to them that the Soviet Politburo thought it inexpedient to circulate it. The session was adjourned so that the old Bulgarian Communist Kolarov could go over the question with the recalcitrant Italians in private. He told them quite frankly that it was not a question of getting at the truth, but of the struggle for power. The Comintern must go along with the Soviet Politburo majority, and that was all there was to it. The Italians still persisted in their attitude, and Stalin typically withdrew the motion.[1] This appeal to independent judgment was, however, the last.

Silone left the Party. Togliatti must have decided that his choice was of submitting to Stalin and hoping to exert some influence, or going under; he chose the former course, and persisted in it, as an accomplice in many a far grosser breach of confidence, in later years.

Henceforward, the Comintern—after the removal, at that time peaceable, of various supporters of Trotsky and Bukharin—became merely another element in Stalin's political machine. As early as 1930, a member of the Yugoslav Politburo observed that apart from men of "limited intelligence" like Pyatnitsky and Remmele, the Comintern leaders appeared to him to be "men at one time remarkable, but now demoralized or exhausted."[2]

The Comintern and its organs were by the nature of their work particularly liable to the charge of contact with foreign countries. The Communist Party of the Western Ukraine, which had been kept organizationally separate from the Communist Party of Poland, was already being purged as a nest of spies in the late 1920s.[3] In 1936, a purge took place in the Communist Party of Latvia in which numbers of the Party's leadership then in Moscow were repressed "for treachery and treason." This amounted to "in effect the dissolution" of the Party.[4] The Latvian Party had been little more than a branch of the Soviet Party—in earlier times, even officially so—though many Latvians, like Rudzutak, were prominent in Russia, and their origin was used against them. The Estonian Communist Party, too, was denounced as "compromised." So few Estonian Communists survived that on the Soviet annexation of their country in 1940, one of the highest posts went to a man of Estonian origin who had hitherto been an assistant station master in the North Caucasus.[5] The entire Lithuanian Central Committee was also arrested, and charged with working for the Lithuanian government.[6] In any case, all this was a mere preliminary. In 1937, the storm broke over the main body of foreign Communists.

In the dingy corridors of the Hotel Lux, the Comintern officials led a rather bohemian existence. Full of foreigners with nowhere else to go, the hotel became something like a frontier village raided nightly by bandits. Occasionally there was trouble. One Polish Communist shot down several NKVD men before he was overcome.[7]

On 28 April 1937 Heinz Neumann, former member of the German CP's Politburo, was arrested. After being one of the leading foreigners in the Canton Commune, with his friend Lominadze, he had been removed from the leadership of the German Communist Party early in the 1930s, but had been working for the Party in Moscow since 1935.

Neumann's "dark, petite, vivacious and gay"[8] wife describes his arrest. At one o'clock in the morning, three uniformed police officials and the manager of the Lux, Gurevich—himself certainly an agent—came in and roused Neumann. Forbidding the couple to speak in German, they made a long search, lasting until dawn, of his documents, taking a trunkful and sixty books of allegedly oppositionist content. When Neumann was finally taken out, he said to his wife, "Don't cry."

> 'That's enough. Get a move on, now,' ordered the leader. At the door, Heinz turned and strode back, took me in his arms again and kissed me. 'Cry then,' he said. 'There's enough to cry about.'[9]

In December 1937, Neumann was removed from the Lubyanka, and he was evidently sentenced about then, since the order confiscating his goods was handed to his wife in January 1938.[10] He seems to have been transferred to the Butyrka in the summer of 1938 and still not to have signed any confession.[11] His wife had by then been sentenced to five years as a socially dangerous element.

Three other members of the German Politburo disappeared at about the same time: Hermann Remmele, Fritz Schulte, and Hermann Schubert—the last arrested in July.[12] Schubert was denounced by an Austrian woman Communist for having mentioned Lenin's 1917 deal with the Germans in connection with Trotsky's alleged relations with the Nazis. Togliatti then managed the attack on him.[13] Other prominent German victims included Hans Kippenberger, head of the Party's military apparatus; Leo Flieg, the organizational secretary of its Central Committee; and Heinrich Susskind and Werner Hirsch, editors-in-chief of *Rote Fahne,* together with four of their assistant editors. (Hirsch seems to have been saved from a Nazi prison and allowed to go to the USSR by the intervention of Goering's wife, who knew his family.)[14] Remmele is reported as going mad in camp, and always coming to blows with both guards and fellow prisoners.[15]

The veteran Hugo Eberlein had been the only genuine delegate at the conference at which the Comintern was founded. The "delegates" allegedly representing foreign countries were mostly just foreigners in the Soviet service; for example, Unshlikht represented Poland. Eberlein had instructions from Rosa Luxemburg to oppose the formation of the new International and did so firmly (though abstaining in the final vote).

His arrest was now reported in a Swiss paper, and he gave a press conference denying it, only to be arrested the next day. He is reported as being brutally interrogated while he was suffering from asthmatic attacks in the Lefortovo prison, and to have been sentenced to twenty-five years.[16] When with a group of prisoners being moved from Kotlas to Archangel, he was too ill to travel and was shot.[17]

For lesser figures any excuse served, as with Soviet citizens. One German Communist was arrested for saying that the only Nazi with principles was Goebbels. This was construed as "counter-revolutionary agitation."[18] Another was accused of "counter-revolutionary agitation against the Soviet State" on the grounds (in any case false) of having belonged to the opposition within the *German* Communist Party from 1931 to 1932.[19] A Soviet writer reports a German Communist in the Butyrka in 1937 with body scars from the Gestapo and crushed fingernails from the NKVD.[20]

Several of the arrested were Jews. This did not save them from charges of fascist espionage, any more than it had Yakir. An interrogator is quoted as saying, "The Jewish refugees are Hitler's agents abroad."[21] The German occupation of Czechoslovakia resulted in Czechs, too, being regarded as German agents. One

Czech is reported as having had to confess that he became a German agent early in the First World War, at a time when neither Czechoslovakia nor the Soviet Union existed.[22]

Willi Münzenberg, the German Communist Party's propaganda genius, was summoned to Moscow to share the fate of Flieg, who had been arrested as he stepped off the train on arrival from Paris (as is also reported of Eberlein; one or the other was evidently the leading German Communist who was brought in, in precisely these circumstances, to Ivanov-Razumnik's cell in the Butyrka, in his neat Western suit—horrified to learn from those present that he was, of course, a Nazi spy).[23] Münzenberg refused to go and was expelled from the Party in 1938. He was in France and was interned at the outbreak of war in the following year. When the refugee camps were opened by the French in view of the Nazi advance in 1940, Münzenberg struck for the Swiss border with another inmate. A few days later, his body was found in a forest near Grenoble, hanging from a tree. His face was battered, and reports make it clear that suicide is unlikely.[24]

After the Nazi-Soviet Pact, in 1939, about 570 German Communists were assembled in the Moscow prisons.[25] A number of them were sentenced by the Russians, but the majority were told that they had been judged by a Special Commission of the NKVD and expelled as undesirable aliens. These German Communists, who included Jews and men especially wanted by the Nazis for armed resistance to them during the street fights of the early 1930s, were hustled over the bridge to German-occupied Poland at Brest-Litovsk, while NKVD men checked the lists with Gestapo men. They included the widow of Erik Mühsam, the poet, and the composer Hans David, a Jew eventually gassed by the Gestapo in the Maidanek concentration camp.* The actress Carola Neher, who was originally on the list, disappeared in Russia instead.[26] She was sentenced to ten years but is believed, according to a recent Soviet article, to have been shot in Orel in 1941. Her son had been taken from her, and only found out his parents' names in the late 1960s.[27]

The son of Ernst Torgler, the main German defendant at the Leipzig Trial, who had been Communist leader in the Reichstag, was then about thirteen. He appeared at protest meetings in the West and eventually went to Russia. There he got a long sentence as a German spy. He was reported at a camp in the Komi area in the far north, where he had the job of disposing of bodies. He had by this time become completely assimilated into the young criminal element. After the Nazi-Soviet Pact, he too was handed over to the Gestapo with the other German Communists.[28]

The Hungarian losses were also heavy. They included Béla Kun, leader of the 1919 Communist Revolution in Hungary, himself. His conduct of the Terror

---

*There were cases, the other way round, of people who had been in Nazi camps and went to Russia on release. A woman who had done three years in a Nazi concentration camp got eight years as a Trotskyite on arrival in Russia owing to her acquaintance with a German Communist who had fallen under suspicion. Her husband had "repudiated" her, but still contrived to send her occasional parcels (Eleanor Lipper, *Eleven Years in Soviet Prison Camps* [London, 1951], p. 7). Another case is quoted of a Viennese Jew who had withstood nearly a year in Dachau, but committed suicide in a Soviet camp (D. J. Dallin and B. I. Nicolaevsky, *Forced Labour in the Soviet Union* [London, 1948], p. 38).

in Budapest preceded even worse actions when, on fleeing to Moscow, he was put in charge of the newly conquered Crimea, and was censured and withdrawn by Lenin for his excessive cruelties. He then operated in the Comintern, and had been partly responsible for the Communist fiasco in Germany in 1921. He has been described as "the incarnation of intellectual inadequacy, uncertainty of will, and authoritarian corruption." [29]

A meeting of the Executive Committee of the Comintern in May 1937 saw his fall. Manuilsky made a speech violently denouncing him for insulting behavior to Stalin and contacts with Romanian Secret Police since 1919. The other members of the ECCI looked on in silence.* Kun, who was quite unprepared for the attack, went white. He "roared like a mortally wounded lion: 'This is a terrible provocation, a conspiracy to get me murdered. But I swear that I have not wanted to insult Comrade Stalin. I want to explain everything to Comrade Stalin himself.' " But everything had been set up in advance. As Kun, pale and shocked, left the room in a dead silence, two NKVD men escorted him out. [30] But he was not arrested immediately. A few days later, Stalin telephoned and "gaily asked Kun to receive a French reporter and refute a rumour of Kun's arrest." This he did; the denial was published; and he was arrested soon afterwards. [31] He had had several members of his own Politburo arrested earlier. [32]

Béla Kun was taken to the Lefortovo, where he was tortured. He is reported as having been kept standing on one foot for periods of from ten to twenty hours. When he returned to his cell after interrogation, his legs were swollen and his face was so black as to be unrecognizable. [33] He was in the same cell as Muklevich. [34] He was then held in the Butyrka until his execution for espionage—as an agent of Germany since 1916, and of Britain since 1926. [35] This took place on 29 August 1938. [36] It seems clear that the formalities were complied with, for he is described as having been "sentenced on the basis of a faked indictment." [37] Kun's frail wife, Irina, was arrested on 23 February 1938, [38] and got eight years, going first to Kolyma, [39] but survived and was eventually released. His son-in-law, the Hungarian poet Hidas, was also sent to a labor camp. [40]

Of the other leaders of the Hungarian Revolution of 1919, twelve more People's Commissars of the then Communist Government in Budapest were arrested. These included the Grand Old Man of Hungarian Communism, Dezso Bokanyi, and Jozsef Pogány, known under the name of John Pepper as the Comintern's representative to the American Communist Party. Of the twelve, two survived imprisonment. Theorists like Lajos Magyar also perished.

Many Italian Communists died—such as Edmondo Peluso, who had been with Neumann in the Canton Commune. He got a letter out of prison begging friends for help and saying that his strength was failing through torture, but that they should believe his innocence. Because this was suspected to be a police trap, there was no response. The few who were later released found that their stories of prison were not believed. Togliatti's brother-in-law Paoli Robotti was arrested in 1937. The torturers broke his teeth and incurably injured his spine, [41] but he was eventually released and was later, in 1961, to say that he had kept silent

---

*Among them were Wilhelm Pieck (later to precede Ulbricht in the leadership of East Germany), Kuusinen, Togliatti, Gottwald, and Wang Ming.

about all this because it was not the business of Italian, but of Soviet, Communists to speak.[42]

Few had Robotti's luck. Most of the actual leadership was protected by Togliatti's docility in the face of Stalin's line. But about 200 Italian Communists perished. Eugenia Ginzburg mentions an Italian woman Communist screaming in the punishment cells of Yaroslavl on being beaten and hosed down with icy water.[43]

Gorkić, the General Secretary of the Yugoslav Communist Party, was arrested in Moscow in the summer of 1937. His Polish wife had already been seized as a British agent. Almost the whole of the Yugoslav Central Committee followed him, together with a large number of the remaining Yugoslav Communists; of these, more than 100 "found their death in Stalin's prisons and camps."[44] They included such men as Vlada Copić, the Party's Organizational Secretary, newly back from command in the International Brigade in Spain. Tito came to Moscow at this time and lived on the fourth floor of the Lux. He later said that he never knew whether he would get out alive or awake in the night "to hear the fatal knocking at my door."[45] He noticed that there was a tendency in the Comintern to dissolve the entire Yugoslav Party—as was being done with the Polish and Korean Parties. Finally, he was allowed to form a new Central Committee. As soon as he could, he transferred it to Yugoslavia and Western Europe, where it had some chance of survival.

The then First Secretary of the Finnish Communist Party, Arvo Tuominen, gives a long list of Finnish leaders shot, and says that "nearly all Finns then living in the Soviet Union were labelled 'enemies of the people.' " These Finnish Communists were involved through a confession obtained from Otto Vilen, "gained by Stalinist beating methods."[46] They were spies in the service of France, Germany, Norway, and so on. Of those not shot but sent to camp, most died, though one woman member of the Finnish Politburo drowned herself in a stream in the Solovki prison area.[47]

The tiny Romanian Party lost many of its most prominent members, including Marcel Pauker (not to be confused with the NKVD officer)* and Alexandru Dobrogeanu, shot on 4 December 1937. Pauker himself is said to have been accused of collusion with Zinoviev and shot without trial.[48] But in general, it was the early connection of the Romanians with Rakovsky which proved fatal. Little reference seems to have been made to this micro-purge until, at the trial in Bucharest in 1952 of the Politburo member Vasile Luca, an attack was made on "the treasonable clique of Marcel Pauker."† Bulgarian Communists were also much persecuted. Dimitrov's fellow defendants at the Leipzig Trial, Tanev and Popov, were jailed.[49] Popov survived and was rehabilitated in 1955. Chervenkov, later to be the Stalinist ruler of Bulgaria, hid in Dimitrov's flat until interceded for. There were many other victims. One Bulgarian is mentioned in a Vologda camp being thrown into a hole in the ground without food for thirteen days, and dying.[50]

---

*Pauker is said to have been denounced by his wife, Anna Pauker (D. J. Dallin, *Soviet Espionage* [New Haven, Conn., 1956], p. 100).

†The Luca Trial gives a curious example of nature imitating art—in this case, the career of Snowball in *Animal Farm*. Luca, who had hitherto featured as having played a heroic role in the Hungarian Revolution of 1919, was now exposed as having actually commanded a machine-gun unit on the other side.

A recent Bulgarian article tells us that "more than a thousand of the 1,200 to 1,400 Bulgarian political émigrés in the U.S.S.R. found themselves in forced labor camps, and only about one hundred of them came back to Bulgaria."[51] The main leadership, such men as Iskrov, Lambrev, and Vasilev, were Nazi or Bulgarian spies. Exiles settled in the Ukraine were charged with a plot to annex that country to Bulgaria.[52]

And so it was with all the émigré groups. For example, Tanaka, a leader of the Japanese Communist Party, was put through the conveyor and torture and is reported liquidated.[53]

But the heaviest casualties fell on the Poles. The Polish Communist Party was very much a special case in its relations with Moscow. It derived in the main from the Social Democratic Party of the Kingdom of Poland and Lithuania*— admitted on a basis of autonomy, together with the Jewish Bund and the Lettish Social Democrats, into the IVth Congress of the Russian Social Democrats in 1906, when the Mensheviks and Bolsheviks were still technically united. A. S. Warski and Dzerzhinsky were then elected members of the joint Central Committee as its representatives.

The Poles on the whole backed the Bolsheviks, though with reservations. Their leader Rosa Luxemburg had written privately that the Bolsheviks' support would be valuable in spite of their "Tartar-Mongolian savagery." Although Lenin was soon involved in organizing factions in the Polish Party, and in a series of polemics with Rosa Luxemburg and others, the quarrels were domestic in a sense which was not true of the relations with other foreign organizations. There was much coming and going between the Parties, then and later. When Poland became an independent state, Poles who had worked with the Bolsheviks and remained on Soviet soil became members of the Russian Communist Party pure and simple. We have only to think of names like Dzerzhinsky, Radek, Menzhinsky, and Unshlikht (as with the parallel Lettish cases of Eikhe, Rudzutak, and others). A Pole could be transferred between the new Communist Party of Poland and the Russian Communist Party at will. Marchlewski, named head of the Polish "Government" established behind the Red Army lines during the 1920 invasion of Poland, became, after the debacle, a Soviet diplomat. As a natural corollary, the Polish Party, insofar as its organizations within Soviet territory were concerned, was involved in the Purge in much the same way as the Soviet Party proper—Warski was, after all, practically an Old Bolshevik in almost the same sense as Rykov or Kamenev.

The Poles in Russia were to some degree comparable with the Irish in England; there were many of them, and they often played important roles in the life of the larger country. The Purge affected not only the Polish Party members, but the Polish population as a whole. The total Polish population is shown as 792,000 in the USSR census of 1926. The 1939 census (not indeed reliable) shows 626,000. Figures of their actual losses in the Purge are hard to come by. According to a Polish Communist, about 10,000 Poles from Moscow alone were shot at the time of the Bukharin Trial, with a total of 50,000 in the country as a whole.

---

*This is not the place to go into the complex origins of Polish Communism, in the two factions of the old Polish Social Democratic Party and the left wing of the Polish Socialist Party.

Arrests of Polish Communists had taken place sporadically all through the 1930s. Now the Party as a whole was caught up in an unprecedented campaign of almost literal annihilation, both organizationally and physically. The survivors in the whole of the Polish Communist movement and its following are said to have been about seventy or eighty in number. A Polish leader remarks, "Almost all the leaders and active members of the K.P.P. then in the Soviet Union were arrested and sent to camps."[54] It is certainly true that when a Polish Communist Government had to be formed in 1944, the leaders were scraped up from all over the place. The few who had the luck to remain in Polish jails, like Gomulka, had superimposed on them men like President Bierut, formerly (under the name Rutkowski) an NKVD interrogator, and as economic chief, Minc, who had been a lecturer in an institute in Central Asia.

On 20 and 21 August 1937 Warski, Budzynski, and others were shot.[55] Warski is said to have gone mad under interrogation and to have imagined that he was in the hands of the Gestapo. A number of Polish Communist leaders then in Poland were invited to Moscow for "consultation." They included Ring and Henrykowski, both members of the Polish Politburo. The latter saw what was going on, and for weeks never ventured out of his room at the Lux except on nocturnal shopping for supplies. All eventually disappeared.[56] From 1937 to 1939, all twelve members of the Central Committee present in Russia, and several hundred others, were executed. Among those who perished were all the Party's representatives on the Executive Committee and the Control Commission of the Comintern, including the veteran Walecki.

Before his arrest, Walecki provided an example of the way old revolutionaries had become humiliated and degraded. Walecki, who had always given friendly greetings to Neumann's wife, met her in the Lux soon after Neumann's arrest. "I smiled and nodded," she remembers, "but he looked away deliberately and there was an embarrassed, rather guilty expression on his face."[57] Walecki was to confess that he was a spy.[58] By 11 September 1937, the whole Polish Politburo had been arrested. Stalin signed a proposal on "cleaning up" the Polish Party on 28 November 1937.[59]

Usually Stalin, after purging a Party, could make use of the struggles over power and policy invariably prevalent to select a new leadership. But in this case, "both factions" in the Polish Communist Party in 1937 were accused of "following the instructions of the Polish counter-revolutionary intelligence."[60] It seems to have issued its last official statement on 8 June 1938 and to have been finally dissolved by a vote of the Presidium of the ECCI on 16 August 1938. "Agents of Polish fascism" had "managed to gain positions of leadership" in it, according to the report of the Comintern delegate to the Soviet XVIIIth Party Congress, Manuilsky. (Manuilsky, making this report, referred also to police agents in the Hungarian and Yugoslav Parties.) When the accusations were announced to the Polish members of the International Brigade in Spain, they were received with silence and tears.[61]

The final batch of leaders, like Kostrzewa, were shot in 1939, when accounts were being settled with the whole Comintern apparatus. The left-wing poets Stande and Wandurski and other literary men perished; the most important was Bruno Jasienski, of whom we have written in Chapter 10.

The total dissolution of the Polish Communist Party was an extraordinary measure. It reflected simply the physical destruction of its cadres. It probably suffered little more than the Ukrainian Party. But Stalin could not, of course, simply dissolve the Ukrainian Party, since he needed someone to rule in Kiev. He did not, at the moment, have any immediate need of a group for ruling Poland and doubtless reflected that—as it turned out in practice—he could scrape one up from somewhere when and if required. The Polish Party, moreover, was one in which hostility to the forthcoming Nazi-Soviet Pact, with its partition of Poland, was likely to be strong.

The wives of the arrested foreigners suffered like those of the Russian victims. But they had no relations to turn to. They remained entirely at the mercy of official caprice. First, they were involved in a continual struggle with the manager of the Lux, who soon contrived to transfer them from their rooms to a separate, older building on the other side of the courtyard, crowded in with other wives. From here, too, they were eventually evicted.

Their papers were not in order, and they had to queue up regularly every five days to renew them. It was impossible to get jobs. They could live only by selling their possessions and books.

It was common to try to keep the children from knowing what had happened to their fathers. Margarete Neumann quotes a conversation:

"Is your daddy arrested too?"
"No, my daddy's on holiday in the Caucasus."

And then the eleven-year-old daughter of one of the arrested comrades destroyed the child's illusion: "Oh, he's in the Caucasus, is he? Why does your mother pay money into the prison, then? A fine Caucasus that is!"[62]

But sooner or later, the wives were themselves arrested. On a single night in September 1937, all the Polish wives were taken. One that can be traced got eight years' forced labor,[63] and this seems to have been the usual sentence.

The Soviet representatives in the Comintern machinery were also destroyed, being blamed for collusion in the penetration of the enemy into the constituent Parties. The exception was Manuilsky himself, who acted as Stalin's agent throughout. Described as a third-rate mind, he was willing to be the Comintern equivalent of a Mekhlis or a Shkiryatov and thus survived.

In his report on Comintern matters to the XVIIIth Congress, after dealing with the Polish case, he significantly added, "It was the failure of Comintern workers that they allowed themselves to be deceived . . . and were late in taking measures against the contamination of the Communist Parties by enemy elements."

This referred primarily to two other members of the Central Committee of the CPSU: Pyatnitsky and Knorin. Pyatnitsky was, apart from Manuilsky, the chief Soviet operator in the Comintern. He had served on its Executive Committee since 1923, and ran the key Organization Department.[64]

V. G. Knorin, another Soviet representative on the Comintern Executive Committee, controlled the German and other Parties. A Latvian, he is described as an honest man, but a dogmatist.[65] He seems to have been denounced for permitting nationalist deviations as early as 1936. He was arrested in June 1937[66] as a Gestapo agent and is said to have been tortured particularly badly.

Their subordinates fell with them, including their immediate aides, Grollman and Idelson. One of the "lists" Stalin signed for execution consisted of 300 Comintern operatives.[67] Between 23 May and 1 June 1937, a wave of arrests swept the organization.[68] The Head of the Foreign Communications Department, Mirov-Abramov, was taken with all his staff. It is said that he was accused of espionage for no fewer than fifteen countries.[69] He was named as a link between Yagoda and Trotsky in the Bukharin Trial. Alikhanov, Head of the Cadre Department, was also arrested in the summer of 1937,[70] as were the Heads of the Propaganda Department, the Organization Department, and the Press Section. We can trace none of them further, presumably because they were shot en masse, under the list system.

In general, a clean sweep was made of the organization, apart from such pliant figures as Kuusinen. Dimitrov alone tried to save some of the victims.

## KILLERS ABROAD

It was comparatively easy to deal with the foreigners in Moscow. The operation of the Purge in foreign countries called for more secret techniques.

In December 1936, Yezhov organized in the NKVD an "Administration of Special Tasks." Under it were the so-called mobile groups, charged with special assassinations outside Russia.[71]

There was one problem in particular which he faced. He could not so easily dispose of the old NKVD cadres operating abroad under the Foreign Department as he could those in the internal departments. They could refuse to come and be arrested. He coped with this by two methods. First of all, when he arrested the other heads of departments in the Lubyanka, he left Slutsky to carry on in the best of odors. The Foreign Department, it became known, was not to be submitted to the purge needed for its more corrupt confreres.

Numbers of operatives, impressed by this idea, returned to Russia, where they were mostly "transferred" and executed. The fate of some of them became known. For example, in the summer of 1937, the NKVD Resident in France, Nikolai Smirnov, was recalled to Moscow and executed. At first, Yezhov pretended that he had simply been transferred to an underground job in China. But the true story leaked out to the NKVD station in France because the wife of another officer had chanced to see the arrest of Smirnov, when she was about to call on him at the Hotel Moskva. Yezhov then put out the story that Smirnov had been a spy for France and Poland. The NKVD officers in France deduced that this was untrue from the simple fact that their cipher for communication with Moscow was not changed. If Smirnov had indeed been a French spy, it must then be assumed that he had betrayed the cipher. Similarly, the old network of informers he had built up continued to operate, contrary to the laws of espionage.[72]

This sort of thing encouraged defection. Yezhov therefore strengthened his appeal for loyalty by another method. The mobile groups had as one of their first priorities the making of an example of any colleague who broke with Stalin.

Ignace Reiss, an NKVD Resident in Switzerland, broke with the regime in

July 1937. His body, riddled with bullets, was found on a road near Lausanne. The Swiss police also found in the abandoned baggage of the friend of Reiss's who had betrayed him a box of poisoned chocolates, apparently intended for his children.[73]

Agabekov, former OGPU Resident in Turkey, had broken with the regime as early as 1929. He was murdered in Belgium in 1938.[74] Walter Krivitsky, whose book is a useful source for this period, had been NKVD Resident in Holland. On 10 February 1941 he was found shot in a hotel room in Washington.

When the situation among the spies abroad had been largely cleared up, it became possible finally to dispense with Slutsky. But in order to avoid troubling the agents still in the field, this was done tactfully. His death on 17 February 1938 was announced in a short friendly obituary the next day.

In fact, he appears to have been poisoned by Frinovsky, by then Deputy Head of the NKVD, in his office (though a recent Soviet account makes it suicide). Slutsky's deputy, Shpiegelglas, was suddenly called in and told that Slutsky had had a heart attack. Slutsky lay in state in the main hall of the NKVD club, with a guard of honor. But many NKVD officers had some smattering of forensic medicine and at once noticed on his cheeks the spots indicating cyanide poisoning.[75]

## IN SPAIN

Slutsky had recently given important service in Spain, which by now had become a major theater of operation for the Purge—not only at the level of Yezhov's mobile groups, which roamed the country arresting and killing deviationists on the international scale, like Camillo Bernini. For there were also larger political issues: the supression of Spanish "Trotskyism" and the gaining of effective control of the Spanish Government.

As early as December 1936, the Soviet press was speaking of the necessity for the elimination of POUM, the heretical Marxist Party of Catalonia,[76] equivalent of the British ILP—that is to say, revolutionary Socialists opposed to Communist methods. It was not in any real sense "Trotskyite" (and the few genuine Spanish Trotskyites did not belong to it). While its Twenty-ninth Division (in which George Orwell served) was fighting against Franco on the Aragon front, the Russians were able to secure its suppression.

Jesús Hernández, one of the two Communists in the Spanish Republican Government, tells us how he was summoned by the Soviet Ambassador, Rosenberg, and introduced to Slutsky, then going under the pseudonym Marcos. Slutsky said that the suppression of POUM was an urgent matter. Not only was it openly criticizing the Soviet Union, and in particular the Zinoviev and Pyatakov Trials, but it was attempting to bring Trotsky to Spain.

(There seems to be nothing in this latter allegation, but if the Russians believed it, Stalin might well have had qualms. In a civil war or revolution, it could have been argued, Trotsky's name was "worth 40,000 bayonets." In fact, such an idea was chimerical, and even to Spaniards not basically hostile to Trotsky the disadvantages of his presence must have outweighed the advantages.)

Rosenberg remarked that he had often told Spanish Prime Minister Largo

Caballero that the liquidation of POUM interested Stalin personally, but that Largo Caballero would not listen to this. Slutsky made it clear that an alternative method was to be found—a provocation mounted by the NKVD which would allow the seizure of power in Barcelona by the Communists, and give them the excuse to get rid of Largo Caballero if he attempted to undo the *fait accompli*.

The operation was prepared by Antonov-Ovseenko, then Soviet Consul General in Barcelona, and Ernő Gerő, later to be overthrown in the leadership of the Hungarian Communist Party by the revolution of 1956, and at that time senior Comintern operative in Spain.

On 3 May 1937, the subservient Spanish Communist whom they had intruded into the leadership of the Catalan police, Rodríguez Sala, seized the Barcelona telephone exchange from the anarcho-syndicalist CNT trade unionists who had controlled it since the beginning of the war. The left-wing organizations, including POUM, resisted, and after four days of fighting, which is said to have caused about 1,000 deaths, they were put down by specially prepared police troops brought in from Valencia and elsewhere. On 15 May, the Communist Ministers in the Spanish Cabinet asked for the formal suppression of POUM. But even so, Largo Caballero again refused.

Stalin's orders to get rid of Largo Caballero and to put in Dr. Negrín as Premier were now transmitted to the Spanish Politburo at a meeting with the Comintern representatives, including Togliatti and Gerő.[77]

Immediately after the formation of the Negrín Government, the new Director-General of Security, the Communist Colonel Ortega, told Hernández that Orlov, the NKVD chief for Spain, had had him sign a number of warrants for the arrest of POUM leaders, without his superior, the Minister of the Interior, being informed. Orlov himself told Hernández that the leaders of POUM would be "exposed" as being in collusion with a group of Franco spies already under arrest.

Hernández recounts that the majority of the Spanish Communist leadership, though acting loyally in accordance with the Comintern directives, was disgusted with the whole affair. The Secretary-General, José Díaz (who was later to jump or be pushed from his window in Tbilisi), spoke of "this spiritual death" which had come over him. Togliatti and Dolores Ibarruri ("La Pasionaria"—a Communist who was never to be afflicted with qualms of conscience) had sent the Assault Guards' Commander in Catalonia an order to arrest the POUM leadership.

On 16 June, Andrés Nin, Political Secretary of POUM and former Secretary of the Red Trade Union International in Moscow, who had held the portfolio of Justice in the Catalan autonomous Government, was arrested. He was taken to Alcalá, to a prison in Communist hands. There he was seized by a group of men, including Orlov and Vittorio Vidali (an old Comintern agent later to be involved in the murder of Trotsky, and after the war to lead the anti-Titoite Communists in Trieste). He was removed to El Pardo and there submitted to a Soviet-style investigation. First he was interrogated for thirty hours in relays, without success, and then tortured. "At the end of a few days, his face was no more than a formless mass."[78] However, no confession could be obtained from him, and he seems either to have been killed or to have died under interrogation. El Campesino was told that he was buried on the spot.[79]

The formation in France of the Committee for the Defense of POUM and, even more, a strong but simple letter demanding merely a fair deal and treatment of the POUM accused, signed by Gide, Mauriac, Duhamel, Roger Martin du Gard, and others, seems to have had an effect in Spain and even on Negrín. In the case of the senior POUM *leaders* still surviving, the Government was able to insist on no further "disappearances," though the rank and file were shot freely. Julián Gorkin, representative of POUM on the Central Committee of the People's Militia, was one of those who survived.

Hernández takes the view that an important motive of Stalin's was to show that not only in Russia, but also in a "democratic" country governed by the Popular Front, Trotskyites had been proved traitors. Thus it was a question not simply of pursuing the feud and destroying all Trotskyite bases, but also of obtaining an ostensible non-Soviet confirmation of the existence of Trotskyite plots.

Meanwhile, the vulnerable units of the International Brigade were being combed for Trotskyites. For example, Walter Ulbricht was conducting among the German Brigaders the Spanish end of the purge which was sweeping the German Communists in Moscow. (The seconded Red Army commander "Kleber," commanding the International Brigade, was removed in February 1937 and soon afterward arrested.) The Soviet soldiers in Spain, who must have resented the NKVD actions, were often shot on return, as we have seen.

Ironically, as Stalin carried out his will as regards purges and control over the political machinery in Spain, he lost interest in the outcome of the actual war. Ehrenburg tells us that though the Soviet authorities expressed great indignation at Fascist and Nazi intervention in Spain, as soon as it became evident that the Republicans were fighting a losing battle, this interest became a mere formality. Ehrenburg's own dispatches, sometimes sent with considerable risk, were cut, altered, or simply thrown into the wastepaper basket.[80]

Many Spaniards who managed to escape the final debacle made their way to Moscow—150 in a single boat.[81] About 6,000, including 2,000 children, is the figure given.[82] They found themselves facing a different danger.

This wave of political refugees of the Left had been preceded by others. After the defeat of the Socialist rising in Vienna in 1934, several hundred members of the Socialist defense organization Schutzbund took refuge in Russia. They were welcomed as heroes, and marched past in a body in the Red Square to applause and congratulations. By mid-1937, they had been arrested and sent to camps "almost without exception."[83] Some of their dependents, with children to feed and no source of income (having been fired from their jobs), went in 1938 to the German Embassy, now controlled by the Nazis, in an attempt to get back to their homes. The Nazis put them up in the Embassy building and escorted them to the Soviet Registration Office for Foreigners to get permission to go back. Apparently, some succeeded.

The Austrians were, in the main, non-Communists. While, like them, the Spanish Republican rank and file was gradually deported to Central Asia and elsewhere, the leadership of the Spanish Communist Party became involved in the more political Purge that had long been sweeping the Comintern apparatus and the foreign Parties based in Moscow. Soon General González (El Campesino), after a long wrangle with a Comintern commission, was digging in the Moscow Metro, preparatory to being sent to a northern labor camp; and the General Secretary of the Spanish Communist Party, Díaz, had died in dubious circumstances. They were known casualties. In all, by 1948, only 1,500 of the 6,000 are reported to have survived.[84]

## THE TROTSKY MURDER

Abroad, one major piece of unfinished business remained. Rakovsky had remarked in his last plea that "even beyond the Mexican meridian Trotsky will not escape that complete, final, shameful ignominy which we all are undergoing here." But this prediction had not yet been fulfilled in a literal sense.

Since his expulsion from the Soviet Union in 1929, Trotsky—from Turkey, Norway, and finally Mexico—had loomed hugely in the Stalinist mythology as a diabolical figure, sunk in the morass of Nazi intelligence and finally responsible for the whole vast plot whose subordinate branches were continually being uprooted in Russia by a vigilant NKVD. In reality, he was trying to organize a political movement on a world scale. Odd sects of the Communist movement joined his Fourth International. But in the USSR itself, his influence was practically nil. He was a figure offstage in all the events we have recounted. His main participation in Soviet affairs was simply as a commentator and analyst from outside. In his *Bulletin of the Opposition,* he presented his ideas of the current situation in the country, and made recommendations for correct action by anti-Stalinist Communists.

For all his vigor and polemical skill, his ideas are notable mainly for two things. First, a total lack of solicitude for the non-Communist victims of the regime: no sympathy whatever was expended, for example, on the dead of the collectivization famine. Second, an unbelievable ineptitude in political judgment. It is natural that there should hang about Trotsky the glamor of a lost cause. This is a normal historical sentimentalism, reminding one of Scottish feelings about Bonnie Prince Charlie, entertained by many who would admit when it came to it that there is a vast difference between their hero fleeing persecuted through the Western Isles and the certainly unpleasant results of an actual Jacobite restoration.

To attribute too much political virtue, or political intelligence, to Trotsky, as Malcolm Muggeridge has done, on account of his "vivacious pen" or even of the combination of "an independent mind . . . courage, high spirits and unshakeable resolution," seems a similarly romantic view.[85] Muggeridge gives the impression of a "rebel" against all tyranny. But this needs to be very severely qualified. During the period when Trotsky held power, he was, whatever his personal magnetism, a ruthless imposer of the Party's will who firmly crushed the democratic opposition within the Party and fully supported the rules which in 1921 gave the ruling group total authority. And the crushing of the Kronstadt rebellion was as much his personal battle honor as the seizure of power had been. He was the leading figure among the doctrinaire Leftist Bolsheviks who were finding it hard to stomach Lenin's concessions to the peasantry, and preferred a far more rigorous regime, even before Stalin came round to the same view. Trotsky might have carried out such policies less crudely than Stalin. But he would have used, as ever, as much violence as he thought necessary—and that would not have been a small amount.

But more destructive still to the image of the "good old rebel" was his attitude to the Stalin regime. Even when in exile during the 1930s, Trotsky was not by any means a forthright revolutionary out to destroy a tyranny. His attitude was rather that of a "loyal opposition." In 1931, he published his key manifesto, "The Problems of the Development of the U.S.S.R." This accepted the main lines of Stalin's program, defined Stalinist Russia as "a proletarian State," and simply quarrelled with Stalin about which "phase" of evolution toward Socialism had been attained. Trotsky stood, in fact, not for the destruction of the Stalinist system but for its takeover and patching up by an alternative group of leaders.

In the autumn of 1932, Trotsky wrote in a letter to his son:

> At present Miliukov, the Mensheviks and Thermidorians of all sorts—will willingly echo the cry "Remove Stalin." Yet, it may still happen within a few months that Stalin may have to defend himself against Thermidorian pressure, and that we may have temporarily to support him. . . . This being so, the slogan "Down with Stalin" is ambiguous and should not be raised as a war cry at this moment.[86]

In his *Bulletin,* Trotsky wrote, "If the bureaucratic equilibrium in the U.S.S.R. were to be upset at present, this would almost certainly benefit the forces of counter-revolution."[87]

Trotsky was always arguing that a "Thermidor" was being prepared, with the support of "petit-bourgeois elements." Obsessed with comparisons with the French Revolution, he continually spoke of Thermidor and Brumaire. The parallels between Stalin and either the Directory or Napoleon are interesting, but the differences are so great that for purposes of practical politics they are not worth taking into account. Stalin's regime—indeed, Lenin's regime—had its own laws of development and potentialities. And when Stalin established his autocracy, it was comparable with other despotisms of the past, but hardly with those of eighteenth- and nineteenth-century France. Trotsky was attentive to the lessons of history, but they were not the lessons of Russian history. If instead of worrying about Barras and Bonaparte he had given some thought to Ivan the Terrible, it might have been more to the point.

Trotsky had objected to Lenin's machine right up to 1917, but having then accepted it, had never again denounced it in principle or seen that Stalinism, or something like it, was its natural product. The furthest he went was to say that it was "rather tempting" to suggest that the Stalin system was "already rooted in Bolshevik centralism, or, more sweepingly, in the underground hierarchy of professional revolutionaries."[88]

Since Stalinist historiography is so extravagantly unreliable, there has been a tendency for historians to accept Trotsky's account of certain events. In the intrigues following Lenin's death, he was by no means straightforward, but at once "devious and faint-hearted," and his own account is "pathetic in its half-truths and attempts to gloss over the facts."[89] This is natural enough, and the only problem is why Trotsky's virtually unsupported word should have been so widely accepted. Partly, no doubt, because his books, written under the comparatively critical eye of the West, were not so wildly and unashamedly falsified as their Stalinist competitors; partly because the Trotskyite tradition has trickled here and there into the mainstream of independent historical writing. But Trotsky had never failed in his duty to suppress or misrepresent facts in the interests of politics. And his general reliability on the period in question could have been considered in the light of his accusation that Stalin poisoned Lenin. There is no evidence whatever that this is true, and Trotsky himself only brought it up many years later—in 1939. The only serious point in favor of it is not evidential at all, but simply a consideration of *cui bono* insofar as Lenin's death saved Stalin from the loss of his main positions of power. But it is more reasonable to see in Trotsky's accusation a lesser, mirror image of Stalin's own habit of mind in making wild accusations of treachery against political opponents.

When people say that Trotsky had an attractive personality, they are speaking mainly of his public persona, his appearance before great meetings, his writings, his dignity. But even so, he repelled many who felt him to be full of vanity, on the one hand, and irresponsible, on the other, in the sense that he tended to make a bright or "brilliant" formulation and press it to the end regardless of danger.

Stalin's colorless, short-view remarks carried more conviction. Their very drabness gave them a realism. In a period of comparatively down-to-earth problems, the great revolutionary (like the great "theoretician" Bukharin) did not feel at home. Whatever his aberrations, Trotsky had a good deal in him of the European Marxist tradition. As Russia lapsed into isolation, the Asian element he had before the Revolution denounced in the Bolsheviks came to the fore. A Soviet diplomat told Ciliga that the country was, after all, Asiatic: "The way of Gengis Khan and Stalin suits it better than the European civilization of Lev Davidovich."[90]

Trotsky's vanity, unlike Stalin's, was, practically speaking, frivolous. There was something more histrionic about it. He had shown himself no less ruthless than Stalin. Indeed, at the time of the Civil War, he had ordered executions on a greater scale than Stalin or anyone else. Even in this, he showed some of the attributes of a poseur—the Great Revolutionary dramatically and inexorably carrying out the cruel will of history. If Trotsky had come to power, this concern for his image would no doubt have made him rule in a less ruthless, or, rather, a less crudely ruthless, fashion than Stalin. The Soviet peoples would perhaps have been able to say

> . . . What his hard heart denies,
> His charitable vanity supplies.

Stalin's pragmatic approach gave the impression of a sounder man, and in a sense this was a true impression. He was always capable of retreat—from the calling off of the disastrous collectivization wave in March 1930 to the ending of the Berlin Blockade in 1949. Stalin's skills in Soviet political methods make Trotsky look superficial, and the conclusion seems inevitable that he had far more to him than his rival. A mind may be intelligent, abilities may be brilliant; yet there are other qualities less apparent to the observer, without which such gifts have a certain slightness to them. Trotsky was a polished zircon; Stalin was a rough diamond.

Trotsky and his son Lev Sedov had been deprived of Soviet citizenship on

20 February 1932. They had not, as is sometimes said, been condemned to death by the courts, at least not openly. It had been announced as part of the verdicts in the Zinoviev and Pyatakov Cases that they would be liable to immediate arrest and trial "in the event of their being discovered on the territory of the U.S.S.R."

Trotsky boldly challenged the Soviet Government to seek his extradition from Norway, which would have meant the examination of his evidence in the Norwegian courts. Instead, it put pressure on the Norwegian Government to expel Trotsky. Through the painter Diego Rivera, he obtained asylum from President Cárdenas of Mexico, and on 9 January 1937 reached that country in a Norwegian tanker.

Like Lenin, who welcomed and protected Malinovsky and other Tsarist spies within the Bolshevik Party, even when they came under suspicion from the rest of his entourage, Trotsky proved gullible about his contacts. Lenin's defense had been the rather inadequate one that even while Malinovsky was betraying Bolsheviks, he was also having to work hard and well to make new ones. Trotsky took the view that if he refused to meet any but his oldest and closest disciples, he would lose important opportunities to preach his doctrines and gain new followers.

The plot against Trotsky was tied in with the murky world of Soviet espionage in the United States, and some of it was only unraveled after the arrest of Jack Soble in 1957.

Soble had spied on Trotsky as early as 1931 and 1932, with useful results. The next NKVD agent to penetrate Trotsky's political family was the extraordinary Mark Zborowski, of whom it has been said that he everywhere "left behind a trail of duplicity and blood worthy of a Shakespearean villain," and who, after establishing himself in the United States as a respectable anthropologist at Columbia and Harvard, was finally exposed and convicted on charges of perjury in December 1958, getting a five- to seven-year term.[91]

Zborowski had managed to become Sedov's right-hand man, and had access to all the secrets of the Trotskyites. He was responsible for the robbery of the Trotsky archives in Paris in November 1936. Although he never committed any murders himself, remaining a finger man, he seems to have played some role in the killing of Ignace Reiss.[92] He also nearly procured the death of Walter Krivitsky in 1937, and did succeed in having Trotsky's secretary, Erwin Wolf, murdered in Spain. The young German Rudolf Clement, secretary of Trotsky's Fourth International, seems also to have been conveyed into his murderer's hand by Zborowski, in 1938. A headless body found floating in the Seine in Paris was tentatively identified as Clement's; in any case, he has not been seen since. On 14 February 1938 Trotsky's son Lev Sedov died in suspicious circumstances in a Paris hospital.[93] Since Zborowski was the man who rushed him there, there is a very strong presumption that he informed the NKVD killer organization of the opportunity which now presented itself.

That Trotsky himself survived as late as 1940 is probably due to the breakdown of the NKVD Foreign Department as a result of Yezhov's and then Beria's purge of it and the difficulties produced by the defection of high officers like Lyushkov and Orlov.

Moreover, after some sort of attempt on Trotsky's life which seems to have been made in January 1938, very strict security measures were taken at the villa where he now settled at Coyoacán, outside Mexico City. Apart from Trotsky's own guards, considerable police protection was provided.

The planning of the attempts on Trotsky was now entrusted to a large staff, who made minute preparations. The Trotsky dossier in the NKVD registry at 2 Dzerzhinsky Street occupied three floors.[94]

We can certainly deduce a main motive of Stalin's as the simple physical destruction of all alternative leaderships. No further blackening of Trotsky's character was necessary or possible. In every sense except that of killing his great enemy, Stalin could only expect a political debit from the operation. It was the same concern as was to be shown in the execution of long lists of military and other men already serving in camps, at precisely the two defensive crises of the Second World War.

The organization of Trotsky's murder was assigned to Leonid Eitingon, a high NKVD officer, who was given virtually unlimited funds for the purpose. Eitingon had been sent to Spain to work under Orlov, taking the pseudonym Kotov, in 1936. He had already had considerable experience of terrorist activity abroad. He continued with this career for many years. The agent Nikolai Khokhlov, sent to Germany to assassinate anti-Soviet émigré leaders, who defected to the West in April 1954, had worked under him. (Eitingon seems to have been sentenced to twelve years' imprisonment after the fall of Beria in 1953, but to have been released in the late 1960s, getting a job in publishing.)

Eitingon set off for Mexico, taking with him Vittorio Codovilla (a founder of the Argentine Communist Party and a trusted Stalinist, who had been involved in the murder of Andrés Nin) and Vittorio Vidali, another of the most formidable of the killers from Spain.

The Mexican Communist Party, under its leader Herman Laborde, had been a genuine political trend, and was lukewarm about such action against Trotsky. As part of the move against Trotsky, Laborde and his followers were purged and an intransigent group, including the painter Siqueiros, placed at the head of the Party.

Taking the name of Leonov, Eitingon organized his first attempt on Trotsky on a lavish scale. The central figure was Siqueiros.

On 23 May 1940 Siqueiros and two accomplices collected a number of submachine guns, police and Army uniforms, and some ladders and incendiary bombs, together with a rotary power saw. He dressed himself as a major in the Mexican Army and put on a disguise. At about 2:00 A.M., he assembled the twenty men he had chosen, and they drove in four cars to Trotsky's fortified villa. Some of the police had already been lured away; the others were trussed up at gunpoint. The telephone lines were cut, and the sentry on duty, an American called Harte, was rushed and overwhelmed. The force broke into the patio and swept the bedrooms with tommy guns for several minutes. They then pulled out, leaving several incendiaries and a large dynamite bomb. The latter failed to explode. Trotsky was slightly wounded in the right leg; his ten-year-old grandson was also hit. His wife received some burns from the incendiaries. Otherwise, the attack was a failure.

The body of Harte was found, shot, buried in the grounds of a villa rented by Siqueiros.

The Mexican Communist Party disowned the attack and dissociated itself from Siqueiros and Vidali. By 17 June, the identity of the attackers had been established by the Mexican police.

Siqueiros was arrested in a hideout in the provinces in September 1940, but although the facts were established, great political pressures were now brought to bear. At the same time, "intellectuals and artists" urged the President to take into account the fact that "artists and men of science are considered as the bulwark of culture and progress."[95]

As a result, the court accepted Siqueiros's plea that the firing of 300 bullets into the bedrooms had been for "psychological purposes only," without any intention of killing or hurting anyone. Evidence that when Siqueiros heard of Trotsky's survival he had exclaimed, "All that work in vain!" was disregarded. The facts about Harte's death were found not to constitute a prima facie case of murder. The judge claimed that the accused did not form a "criminal conspiracy," since a conspiracy could not be made for a single temporary job but must have "stability and permanence." They were even acquitted of impersonating police officers, on the grounds that though they had dressed up in uniforms, they had not actually attempted to usurp any police functions.

While Siqueiros was still out on bail, a convenient invitation to paint some murals in Chile, at the instance of the Chilean Communist poet Pablo Neruda, led to his decamping thither. So even the light sentence he might have got for the crime still attributed to him—stealing the two automobiles outside the Trotsky house—was avoided.

On the failure of Siqueiros, Eitingon had put his second plan into operation. Four days after the first attempt, Ramón Mercader was introduced to Trotsky for the first time.

Mercader's mother, Caridad, a Spanish Communist, seems to have become sexually entangled with Eitingon during the Civil War in Spain, when she had worked in the liquidation squads. The NKVD made a practice of securing the passports of members of the International Brigade who had been killed. Mercader was given one which had originally belonged to a Yugoslav-Canadian volunteer killed in action early in the war. It had been reforged under the name of "Jacson"—a curious example of the absurd slips which crop up in these otherwise highly skilled operations, though in fact this attracted no attention.

The plot now reached into the world of outwardly respectable New York Leftism, which at the time was seething with intra-Communist intrigue, and provided a ready recruiting ground for Yezhov's men. In fact, general supervision of the murder seems to have come under the purview of the permanent Resident of the NKVD, the Soviet Consul-General in New York, Gaik Ovakimian, who was later exposed, in May 1941, and expelled from the country.

The details—some of which are even now a little obscure—do not concern us here. But it is at least interesting to note—in this, as in the great espionage cases of the 1940s and 1950s—how many people, of whom their non-Party acquaintances would have certainly denied any possibility of their joining in such activity, were, from factiousness, revolutionary romanticism, and even idealism, to become willing or half-willing accomplices in a vulgar murder.

These put Mercader in touch with Sylvia Ageloff, an American Trotskyite who was a social worker. He seduced her and entered into a relationship with her which passed for marriage. She was entirely innocent of the planned crime. Through her, he was admitted to the Trotsky household.

Over the next few months, Mercader made five or six visits and, as Sylvia Ageloff's husband, became reasonably established. On 20 August, he arrived at Trotsky's villa, ostensibly to have an article he had written criticized. He wore a raincoat. A long dagger was sewn into the lining. A revolver was in his pocket. But his actual weapon, a cut-down ice axe, was in his raincoat pocket. (An NKVD murder—of a Soviet Ambassador—by a strong assassin using an iron bar is reported by the Petrovs.) Mercader was an experienced mountain climber, and his choice of the ice axe as an assassination weapon was based on considerable experience of its use and power. Outside, his car was parked facing the right way for a quick move, and around the corner another car with his mother and an agent was waiting. Eitingon, in yet a third car, was a block or so away.

Trotsky had two revolvers on his desk, and the switch to an alarm system within reach. But as soon as he started to read Mercader's article, the assassin took out his ice axe and struck him a "tremendous blow" on the head.

Mercader had planned to leave quickly. But the blow was not immediately lethal. Trotsky screamed for "very long, infinitely long," as Mercader himself put it, "a cry prolonged and agonized, half-scream, half sob," according to one of the guards—who now rushed in and seized the assassin.

Trotsky was operated on, and survived for more than a day after that, dying on 21 August 1940. He was nearly sixty-two.

Mercader, coming to trial after Siqueiros, seems to have hoped that he, too, might get a light sentence. Perhaps the judge would hold that he had been teaching Trotsky how to climb the Alps. But he was sentenced to twenty years' imprisonment, which he served. Even after his identity had been established by fingerprints, he refused to admit who he was or why he had committed the murder. The official Stalinist version was that he was a disgruntled Trotskyite, and that the NKVD had nothing to do with it.

Mercader's imprisonment was passed under conditions superior to those prevailing in Soviet prisons and camps. The Mexican Revolution had effected genuine reform. A visitor notes, "His cell, spacious and sunny . . . with a little open-air patio in front, contained a neat bed and a table loaded with books and magazines." He was also, under Mexican law, allowed women in his cell. (On his release, he went to Czechoslovakia, moving from that country, when it became too liberal, to Moscow in 1968, though he is later reported in Havana.)

Eitingon and Señora Mercader left by the prepared escape route. She was received in Moscow by Beria, presented to Stalin, and decorated, for her son and herself.[96]

And, indeed, the destruction of Stalin's last great opponent must have caused great satisfaction in the Kremlin. For once, it might have been noted, a prediction of Trotsky's had been literally fulfilled. He had written of Stalin, in 1936: "He seeks to strike, not at the ideas of his opponent, but at his skull."

# CLIMAX

*Each day too slew its thousands six or seven.*
Byron

After the Bukharin Trial, Stalin and Yezhov turned their attention to the remnant of opposition at the top.

This final wave of the Purge in the inner Party, directed against his own supporters, was well defined by a circular put out under Stalin's instructions, in April 1938, calling for a "liquidation of the consequences of wrecking" in which the " 'silent' politically spineless people should also not be forgotten." [1]

Various loose ends were tied up; for example, the First Secretary in Kazakhstan, L. I. Mirzoyan, whom Stalin had attacked at the January plenum, was arrested "on Stalin's personal orders." [2]

There remained bigger game. Postyshev's arrest was not immediately followed up. Eikhe, Kossior, and Chubar, the doomed members of the Politburo, still featured, though not regularly, with the other members in formal listings, telegrams from the Soviet expedition at the North Pole, and so forth.

Eikhe and Kossior, appearing in good standing until the last week in April, went first. Eikhe was arrested on 29 April, and Kossior (mentioned in an electoral list as late as 28 April) at about the same time [3]—in accordance with the NKVD custom of arresting people just before holidays, during which no attempt could be made to trace them.

Stalin was now wholly ignoring the formalities. We are told that there was no "exchange of opinions or Political Bureau decisions" about the arrest of Kossior—or in any "other case of this type." [4]

No announcement was made, then or ever, though his arrest must have become known immediately to those interested, for Kiev Radio just ceased to announce itself as Radio Kossior, as it had done for some years. [5] The press had other matters to think of. For most of May and June, the new election campaign built up in newspapers, meetings, and any other feasible fashion, on the lines of the fanfares of the previous winter. (When the elections finally took place on 26 June, it was to the accompaniment of another exploit by "Stalinist falcons"—a nonstop flight to Khabarovsk in the Far East by Kokkinaki.)

The absence of both men from the 1 May demonstrations was noted. Chubar was still there. He can be traced as receiving official greetings as late as 9 June. By 1 July, he was no longer listed.

Chubar was later said to have been concerned with shortcomings in industry, and to have had qualms about the new agricultural system. He had been closely associated with Ordzhonikidze and was not pleased with the development of the cult of personality. In the period before his own removal, he is reported as "deeply indignant" about the facts he had learned about illegal repressions. He did not believe that people he had known and worked with for years were really spies. His views on this became known to those in charge of the Purge. On his removal from membership in the Politburo and Vice Chairmanship of the Council of People's Commissars, he was sent for the moment to work at Solikamsk in the Urals. But he remained there for only "a few months . . . soon he was arrested."[6]

Meanwhile Eikhe, in the new torture center for top officials at Sukhanovka, was being interrogated by the notorious Z. M. Ushakov. Soon his ribs were broken, and he was confessing to being leader of a "reserve net supposedly created by Bukharin in 1935."[7]

This was presumably what was mentioned at the Bukharin Trial as "another reserve centre," allegedly existing at the end of 1935 or the beginning of 1936, when Rykov was supposed to have urged Chernov to get in touch with it "through Lyubimov."[8] It was "another" reserve center because there was also reference to "the parallel group of Rights" allegedly led by Antipov.

There is at least some slight logic in this representation of the latest victims as "Rightists." They had had no connection whatever with the Trotsky or Zinoviev oppositions, and though they had equally opposed the Bukharinites in 1929–1930, they had been in favor of a lessening of the Terror and reconciliation with Bukharin.

The plan for the next trial was, in any case, changed. Eikhe was instructed to remove his name as reserve center leader and substitute Mezhlauk's.[9]

This left a number of ready victims for the first trial planned wholly against Stalinists, leaving the more recently arrested Politburo members and some others in reserve for future use.

On 28 July, Yezhov sent Stalin a list of 138 names, asking for permission to execute them. Stalin and Molotov signed, "Shoot all 138."[10] Thereupon, on 27 to 29 July, and after the weekend on 1 August, there took place in secret by far the largest massacre of the leadership in the whole period. We have already noted the twenty-four known military victims (see p. 212). In addition, at least twenty-two leading political, diplomatic, and cultural names can be identified. They included Rudzutak, formerly full member and more recently candidate member of the Politburo; V. I. Mezhlauk; Pyatnitsky; Rukhimovich; Knorin; Stetsky; M. I. Frumkin, who had been the leading Rightist spokesman in the late 1920s; Ya. A. Yakovlev; and Krylenko. V. M. Kirshon, a playwright with strong political connections, was among the other victims. In every case we can trace, they were "tried" by the Military Collegium. How the military and political elements in the supposed plot were melded is not clear, but (for example) the civilian Rudzutak was directly linked to the Army figure Berzin, as a Latvian spy, as was Army Commander Alksnis, who was "savagely beaten" by a special team.[11]

Rudzutak pleaded his innocence. He had made a confession, but now retracted it and asked that

> the Party Central Committee be informed that there is in the NKVD an as yet not liquidated center which is craftily manufacturing cases, which forces innocent persons to confess; there is no opportunity to prove one's non-participation in crimes to which the confessions of various persons testify. The investigative methods are such that they force people to lie and to slander entirely innocent persons in addition to those who already stand accused. He asks the court that he be allowed to inform the Party Central Committee of all this in writing. He assures the court that he personally never had any evil designs in regard to the policy of our Party because he had always agreed with the Party policy pertaining to all spheres of economic and cultural activity.[12]

However, "sentence was pronounced on him in twenty minutes and he was shot." The charges included espionage for Germany.[13]

Krylenko's trial also lasted twenty minutes, and the protocol ran to nineteen lines only.[14] Twenty minutes was also the time taken by the trial of M. E. Mikhailov, Provincial Secretary of Voronezh.[15] Pyatnitsky (who had been severely beaten by the NKVD officer Langfang, undergoing eighteen torture sessions and suffering broken ribs, internal injuries, and a lacerated face)[16] was accused of espionage for Japan and other countries in addition to having been a Tsarist police agent.[17]

We can trace a few relatives of the accused: Rudzutak's wife was sent to labor camp;[18] his brother is reported to have emigrated to America and taken the name Rogers, but to have returned in the early 1930s at the invitation of his then-powerful relation; he and his wife are reported shot, and their nineteen-year-old daughter, Senta, arrested and sentenced to death for espionage for the United States, but reprieved and sent to the Vorkuta camps.[19] Yakovlev's wife is reported sentenced to death.[20] Rukhimovich's young daughter Elena was jailed in 1939 (together with the daughters of Shlyapnikov's ally, Medvedev; of Lomov; of Smilga; and of Krestinsky) for having formed an "anti-Soviet group."[21] Unshlikht's sister, Stefanie Brun, got eight years;[22] Mezhlauk's first wife also got an eight-year sentence and died of dysentery in a transit camp in the Far East.[23]

This case marks a turning point in the Purge. There were to be no more public trials of Party figures. But it is also interesting because it comes at the moment when Stalin was beginning to show distrust of Yezhov.

Yezhov had been appointed People's Commissar for Water Transport (in addition to his NKVD Commissariat, Secretaryship of the Central Committee, and membership on the Executive Committee of the Comintern) on 8 April 1938. This is often thought of as the beginning of his decline. But in fact his new Commissariat's main component was the Soviet Merchant Marine, an important Secret Police area from both the security and the intelligence points of view. He seldom went to the Water Transport Commissariat, leaving the NKVD veteran E. G. Evdokimov in charge. Others from the NKVD now ran the Timber Industry and Communications Commissariats. And on the same day as Yezhov's new appointment, Kaganovich took over Railways in addition to Heavy Industry; but one of Yezhov's Deputy Commissars in the NKVD, L. N. Bel'ski, became First Deputy

People's Commissar of Railways, with the Head of the NKVD Transport Department, M. A. Volkov, as another Deputy Commissar, and other NKVD officers in posts there. In addition, several NKVD men now took over as Provincial Party Secretaries. All in all, Yezhov's power seemed strongly on the increase.

However, this now began to change.

One Party organization had remained not indeed exempt from purging, but only carrying out such purging as benefited its own leader—that of Georgia under Beria. It seems very out of character for Yezhov not to have attempted the destruction of the leading cadres in Tbilisi, and there are indeed reports that he was maneuvering to do this in 1938.[24] It is said that Beria was to be arrested,[25] but successfully appealed, being supported by Molotov and others.[26]

Beria's appointment on about 20 July 1938 to be Deputy Head of the NKVD can only be interpreted as the beginning of Yezhov's decline. It was a post that had previously been held by men like M. Berman and Agranov—that is, not one suitable for an important Party figure. In fact, Beria was clearly being prepared as a possible successor. He moved into the dacha just vacated by Chubar.[27]

There is a report that Yezhov and Kaganovich had clashed, not on any question of the desirability of the Great Purge, but on a more direct issue of power. Kaganovich himself supervised the purging of his Commissariats and other organs under his own control, but resented NKVD intrusion except for the technical purposes of arrest, shooting, and so on. According to one account, Yezhov began to implicate Kaganovich himself, and had already forced Bondarenko, Head of the Kharkov Tractor Works, to make statements compromising him.[28]

On one view, the immediate reason why Stalin listened to the voices being raised against Yezhov is that he had failed to set up further public trials, in particular that of the Rightist "reserve center," plus a second Military Trial.[29]

It is quite conceivable that Yezhov had been charged with setting up a fourth great trial, and had failed in the assignment. If this were so, the coincidence of Beria's appointment and the immediately following secret trial or trials would signify the winding up of an unsatisfactory project by the new management.

But Stalin had for some time been shooting prominent Central Committee members without such formality, and it is difficult to see what further benefits he could now gain from another public trial. Every possible lesson had been rubbed in in the Bukharin Trial. As far as a second Military Trial was concerned, the first had not taken place in public, and the second could have been announced in precisely the same way. Indeed, the mere fact that the new batch of military conspirators was dispatched without public announcement seems to show that Stalin no longer felt the need for such.

Whatever plans Stalin may have had for the future, it was, anyhow, at this point that he abandoned public trials of oppositionists. None of the figures still under arrest was brought before public courts, though almost all seem to have had confessions tortured out of them and to have been brought before these twenty-minute sessions of the Military Collegium.

It seems to have been difficult to extract reliable and durable confessions from the new Stalinist prisoners. Rudzutak (and Eikhe after him) would not repeat before the secret courts which eventually tried them the confessions they had made under torture. This had been true of a number of those who had fallen in the earlier phase of the Purge, but there had been an adequate residuum of confessors. None of the new victims, though, had anything whatever to reproach themselves for from the point of view of having collaborated in any of the oppositions, and could hardly be asked to "disarm." This had been true only of one or two second-rank prisoners in the Bukharin Trial.

Some of the difficulty may have resided in the fact that those in this middle generation were still rather more than personal nominees or members of Stalin's extremist entourage. They were still men following their political convictions, attached to Stalin as a leader, but not committed to the idea of his leadership as a matter of ideological dogma. Unlike the men Stalin had assembled from the earlier generation, and against many of whom he was able to exert something like black-mail, almost all the younger cadres were secure in the consciousness of their general and political innocence (if not from our point of view, at least from their own).

Through the autumn, the NKVD Commissar continued to appear with his old prominence; in fact, he was often named higher than his official standing in the Politburo—sometimes before Mikoyan, Andreyev, and Zhdanov.

And he continued his policies. The Purge had grown in size, until finally it had reached such monstrous proportions that even Stalin seems to have seen that the time had come to ease off. This was a matter of major policy: the midsummer changes were perhaps no more than the first moves towards an alternative, based more on particular failures than on the realization that a dead end was being reached in the entire Terror.

## DIPLOMATS

Meanwhile, another rumored trial failed to take place. After the Bukharin Trial, it had been rumored that a special trial of diplomats, centering on Antonov-Ovseenko, would be held. But in fact they were dealt with seriatim.

Soviet diplomats had already suffered severely. For example, Tairov, Ambassador to Mongolia, had been shot in June 1937. Both Krestinsky and Sokolnikov had served as Deputy People's Commissars for Foreign Affairs. Karakhan had been Ambassador in Berlin. Various lesser figures had been involved in the trials—for example, Chlenov,[30] of whom it was said in the Bukharin Trial indictment that his case would be subject to special proceedings. Others implicated in the Bukharin Trial were Yurenev, Ambassador to Berlin; Bogomolov, Ambassador to China; and Sabanin, Director of the Legal Department of the People's Commissariat of Foreign Affairs.[31] (Yurenev and Bekzadian, Ambassador to Hungary, were among the victims of the July 1938 massacre.)

At the Foreign Commissariat, an NKVD officer, Vasily Korzhenko, was appointed Chief of Personnel,[32] and he and his family moved into Krestinsky's Moscow house.[33] The treatment of the Commissariat's staff for comparatively minor offenses was interestingly described in a Soviet article of the Khrushchev period.

V. N. Barkov had long been Head of the Protocol Department:

On one occasion, on the instructions of Dekanozov, who was at that time a Deputy People's Commissar for Foreign Affairs and who, as it afterward appeared, was one of the most active members of the Beria gang, Barkov had to meet a foreign correspondent. Under the regulations in force, on the day of his talk with the correspondent, Barkov had to see Dekanozov without fail, but Dekanozov was nowhere to be found. Obeying the orders he had received, Barkov saw the correspondent.

On the following day Dekanozov summoned him.

"Who gave you direct permission for the interview?"

"I could not find you anywhere."

"You could not have tried very hard."

The dressing down went on for a long time. Barkov lost his temper and said:

"But on that day you could not be found!"

"Oh! It's like that is it?" said Dekanozov menacingly, and closed the interview.

On that day Barkov never returned home. His relations only saw him eighteen years later.[34]

The People's Commissar himself, Litvinov, beginning in 1937, and for the rest of his life, kept a revolver to hand, "so that if the bell rang in the night, he would not have to live through the consequences."[35] His Deputy People's Commissar, V. S. Stomonyakov, attempted suicide on arrest, to die in the prison hospital.[36]

Diplomats disappeared by the dozen. They had, indeed, had genuine contacts with foreigners, so that the presumption of their guilt was, by Yezhov's standards, overwhelming. They were recalled and shot; in his memoirs, Ehrenburg says that few survived.[37] He names nine that he knew personally whom Stalin liquidated.

But no trial took place. In particular, Antonov-Ovseenko simply went through a routine processing. He had been a Menshevik until 1917. He had led two local rebellions in 1905 and 1906 and had been sentenced to death in 1906. He had been arrested several times for underground activity afterward. (This record shows, incidentally, how mistaken is the notion that the Mensheviks were politically inactive because their views on party organization differed from Lenin's.) Joining the Bolsheviks in 1917, he had led the attack on the Winter Palace which overthrew the Provisional Government.

It was he who had burst into the Government room, announcing, "In the name of the Military Revolutionary Committee, I declare you arrested." He commanded on the Ukrainian front in the Civil War and later became Head of the Political Administration of the Army.[38] Here he had supported Trotsky and was removed in favor of Bubnov. He remained a Trotskyite until 1928, when he submitted, like other oppositionists. He had since been employed in State and diplomatic posts, latterly in Spain.

Antonov-Ovseenko was held in a cell on the third floor of the Butyrka prison. He was ill and (as is often reported of the undernourished and overinterrogated) had swollen legs. But he bore himself boldly and entertained his cell mates with stories of Lenin, the October Revolution, and the Spanish Civil War. One of them was Yuri Tomsky (youngest son of Mikhail Tomsky), who has given an account of Antonov's last days.[39] At the interrogation, Antonov refused to sign anything, though the protocols of the interrogation ran finally to 300 pages. One day when they were being gone through, there happened to be a radio on in the investigator's office. The NKVD man, I. I. Shneyderman, called Antonov an "enemy of the people." The prisoner retorted, *"You* are an enemy of the people. You are a regular Fascist.'' The radio started to broadcast a mass meeting. "Listen! Listen to how the people celebrate us. They trust us in everything, and you will be annihilated. There,'' the NKVD official added, "I have had a medal on your account'' (an Order of the Red Star, in the 19 December 1937 Honors List).[40]

Antonov-Ovseenko was sentenced to ten years with the group executed on 8 to 10 February 1938, but was in fact shot. When he was taken from his cell to execution, he took off his overcoat, shoes, and jacket and distributed them to the other prisoners, and then remarked (young Tomsky tells us), "I beg anyone who gets to freedom to tell the people that Antonov-Ovseenko was a Bolshevik and remained a Bolshevik till his last day.'' The chief warders then led him away.

Antonov had himself served as State Prosecutor in the early 1930s. He had to wait twenty-five years for his message to be published to the Russian people. All the same, he was lucky. The Mensheviks who died in camps after the 1931 Trial or the Social Revolutionaries like Spiridonova were not similarly vindicated.

Meanwhile, other diplomats were being recalled for execution. The Soviet Minister in Bucharest, Ostrovsky, hesitated to return to Moscow, but went back when Voroshilov, with whom he had served in the Civil War, gave him a personal assurance of his safety. He was arrested on reaching the frontier,[41] though only sent to labor camp.[42] Others who disappeared included the Soviet envoys to Warsaw, Kaunas, Helsinki, Kabul, Copenhagen, and Riga.[43]

The veteran of the Baltic Fleet Mikhail Raskolnikov was Soviet Ambassador to Bulgaria, where the NKVD officer sent to purge the legation implicated everyone from the chauffeur, Kazakov, to the Military Attaché, Colonel Sukhorukov.[44] Raskolnikov himself refused to return to Russia when recalled in April 1939. He was nevertheless rehabilitated in Khrushchev's time (later restored to the category of traitor, he was more definitively rehabilitated in 1987). This must partly have been due to his particularly fine record in the Revolution and the Civil War, his total lack of involvement in any opposition, and his death within a few months (September 1939). Even Ehrenburg in his published memoirs mentioned having met him at the time when he was deciding to stay abroad and having sympathized with his position. Raskolnikov wrote an offensive letter to Stalin, which was published in the émigré *Novaya Rossiya* on 1 October 1939 after his death, and also a more moderate statement which appeared in another émigré journal, *Poslednie Novosti*, on 26 June 1939. In the latter, he says firmly to Stalin, "You yourself know that Pyatakov did not fly to Oslo''—showing that a good deal was known, and discussed, in Party circles.

## KOMSOMOL

One major organization remained under its original Stalinist leadership—the Komsomol.

Kosarev had been sent by Stalin to purge the Leningrad Komsomol after the defeat of Zinoviev at the XIVth Party Congress in December 1925. In 1926, the opposition bloc had made a powerful attempt to secure the support of the young and of the students. Most of the "Trotskyist'' protest groups were composed of young intellectuals, who attacked Party control over the Komsomol. Half the members of the Leningrad Komsomol Committee were expelled.

Kosarev had been boldly denounced by Kotolynov, then a leading Zinoviev-ite in that body, for tactics of sheer bullying. He went on to practice these in Moscow, becoming a secretary of the Central Committee of the Komsomol in 1927 and its General Secretary in 1929.

Thenceforward, the organization had been a willing tool of the General Secretary, a sort of "Stalinjugend." Even this was not adequate, as Stalin held that "the very first task of all Komsomol education work was the necessity to seek out and recognize the enemy, who had then to be removed forcibly, by methods of economic pressure, organizational-political isolation, and methods of physical destruction."[45] In fact, he wanted the organization to become a youth auxiliary of the NKVD.

On 21 July 1937 Kosarev was summoned by Stalin and Yezhov and harangued for an hour and a half about the inadequate role played by the youth organization in vigilance and denunciation.[46] He did his best to satisfy their demands.

A trial now took place of some members of the Central Committee of the Komsomol: Lukyanov, Secretary of the Moscow Komsomol; Saltanov, editor of *Komsomolskaya pravda;* and others.[47] In the Ukraine, the youth leadership had already been purged in January, apparently in connection with Postyshev's offenses. On 22–25 July, the Ukrainian Komsomol Central Committee was simply dissolved: its counter-revolutionary organization had been headed by its First Secretary, S. Andreev,[48] who was shot in the mass execution of 27 November 1937.

At the provincial level, when the Smolensk Komsomol was cleaned up in October 1937, it was charged that "Fascists, penetrating even into the Central Committee of the Komsomol, had now been exposed." On 11 October 1937 the new local First Secretary, Manayev, reported that his predecessors, "the enemies of the people Kogan and Prikhodko," had undermined 700 kolkhoz Komsomol organizations. The Pedagogical Institutes, the Technicum, the intermediate schools had been "filled" with hostile people, as were the Pioneer organizations. Local secretary after local secretary was listed as a criminal. Already, from one-half to two-thirds of the members of committees and secretaries of organizations had been replaced.

However, Manayev himself was criticized for giving money for medical treatment to enemies of the people under arrest and for "criminal slowness" in uprooting enemies. The representative from Moscow said that the bad work of the provincial organization was possibly due to the fact that there were enemies in it yet to be unmasked.

The discussion consisted of a new torrent of denunciation. The Vyazma delegate, mentioning in passing that his district had lost five secretaries in the past few years, attacked the current holder of that office as "completely corrupt" and "a polygamist." Although a number of hostile people had been expelled, so far they had only scratched the surface. As to teachers, another delegate claimed that out of 402 in his district, 180 were alien elements.[49]

As the denouncers came to the fore, Kosarev found that there were some more enthusiastic than himself.

A young woman called Mishakova from the Komsomol *apparat,* put up to it (it was later said) by Malenkov, made an attempt to compromise and destroy the leadership of Kosarev's appointees in the Komsomol organizations in the Chuvash Republic. Kosarev intervened directly, prevented the proposed purge, and removed her. Mishakova wrote to Stalin on 7 October 1938. Two or three days later, she was invited to see Shkiryatov, whom Stalin had detailed to examine the case.

The whole incident, which had doubtless been arranged beforehand for that purpose, was used to complete the ruin of the last small power group which had gone through the Yezhov period unscathed. As late as 6 November, a speech of Kosarev's to a ceremonial Komsomol plenum was promptly reported in *Pravda*. But on 19 to 22 November, a plenum of the Young Communist Central Committee was held. Stalin, Molotov, and Malenkov attended. Stalin strongly defended Mishakova and turned the occasion into a violent attack on the Kosarev leadership. A few days later, the majority of that Central Committee were arrested. Beria in person came for Kosarev, the first time he had done such a thing.[50] This is almost certainly significant, as is the absence of Yezhov's name from the entire investigation. For the Police Commissar was about to fall. According to one NKVD source, Kosarev was accused of plotting with him.[51]

By 1939, Mishakova was a secretary of the Komsomol, in which capacity she was able to tell this story, accompanied by references to the "Kosarev gang," to the XVIIIth Congress, as a tribute to Stalin's sense of justice. By that time Kosarev, after torture at the hands of the NKVD interrogator Shvartsman, had been shot.

The purge of the Kosarev leadership, in its social aspect, has been interpreted as the removal of a genuine, if Stalinist, youth cadre in favor of a new conformity and anti-egalitarianism associated with the sons of the new bureaucracy.[52]

As with their seniors, the Komsomol Central Committee was devastated: of 93 full members elected in 1936, 72 were arrested; of 35 candidate members, 21 were arrested; 319 of the organization's 385 provincial secretaries were "repressed," as were 2,210 of the 2,750 district secretaries.[53]

The pre-Kosarev leaders of the Komsomol had naturally fared badly, too. The original First Secretary, E. V. Tsetlin, had been expelled from the Party as a Rightist in 1933 and arrested, but was released and returned to membership; rearrested on 16 April 1937, he was sentenced on 2 June 1937 to ten years by the Military Collegium, and to death by the local NKVD Troika at Ivanovo on 16 September 1937. His successor, O. L. Ryvkin, was sentenced to death by the Military Collegium on 7 August 1937. The third, L. A. Shatsky, was sentenced to five years by the Special Board in March 1935, and (as we have seen) to death by the Military Collegium on 10 January 1937. P. I. Smorodin, the next, whom we have already met in his later Leningrad career, was shot on 22 February 1939. The fifth, N. P. Chaplin, was "repressed" and died 25 September 1938. The next, A. I. Milchakov, only served sixteen years in labor camp and survived.[54]

## A LAST BLOW AT THE ARMY

The Far Eastern Army had not been treated quite as the rest of the forces had. For strategic reasons, it had been organized as something like an independent entity.

It was the only great body of troops commanded by a Marshal—the tough, competent, and practically experienced Blyukher.

Blyukher, though his name suggests a German origin, was in fact of pure Russian descent. His peasant grandfather had had the name given to him by some whim of his landlord during the days of serfdom.[55] Ironically enough, there was something of the German stance to him. Dark and grizzled, he had a square, bull-like face with a large close-clipped moustache in the *feldwebel* manner covering his large upper lip. He was now forty-eight.

He had been a worker in a wagon factory and had served a thirty-two-month sentence for leading a strike while still twenty years old. He first came to prominence when, with V. V. Kuibyshev, he had established an isolated Bolshevik enclave amid a sea of White Armies, in the Samara area. In the distinguished Civil War career which followed, he had been one of the first to be given the Order of the Red Banner. Later, under the pseudonym Galen, he had acted as chief military adviser to Chiang Kai-shek. He is said, back in the early 1930s, to have opposed collectivization in the Far East on military grounds and, with Voroshilov's support, to have obtained a certain exemption there; and there was also talk of some connection with Syrtsov.[56]

While Blyukher was still in Moscow in June 1937 in connection with the Tukhachevsky "Trial," the NKVD struck at his Army. His new Chief of Staff, Sangursky, is said to have become involved (with the Party Secretary of the Far Eastern Territory, Kutev) in what Stalin felt to be some sort of political intrigue against the leadership.[57] He was now arrested and tortured. Another account has him implicating literally hundreds of officers and in 1938 repudiating his confession and claiming that saboteurs in the NKVD were attempting to weaken the Army.[58] Sangursky is reported as still alive in Irkutsk jail in 1939,[59] full of remorse for having, under torture, given away so many officers as fellow conspirators. He was then facing a further charge—conspiracy with Yezhov to wreck the Army!

With Sangursky went the Deputy Chief of Staff, the Chief of Combat Training, and the Chief of Intelligence. In the autumn of 1937, Ingaunis, commanding the Far Eastern Air Force, was also in the Butyrka, having been severely tortured in the Lefortovo and confessing to espionage. The NKVD noncommissioned officer who tore off his insignia and Orders in the Lubyanka remarked, "Well, they certainly handed out medals to all sorts of counter-revolutionary swine!"[60] The Head of the Army's Political Administration was arrested, too. At the same time, most of the political leadership in the eastern provinces were seized.

Even so, as far as the Army is concerned, this phase only lasted about five weeks, and was not so intense or on such a mass scale as in the other military districts. It ended with Blyukher's return to his post.

For meanwhile, an even more important consideration had arisen: on 30 June, some patrol fighting had broken out between Soviet and Japanese troops on the Amur, and on 6 July the Japanese had seized Bolshoi Island in that stream. In spite of protests, the Russians made no attempt to dislodge them. There is no doubt that this was a probing action by Japanese military elements, who took the view that the local Soviet capacity to fight had been largely paralyzed by the Purge.

Blyukher at once started to repair as far as possible the disorganization that had already set in. Tukhachevsky's execution, followed by the arrests in the Far Eastern Army, had left him deeply depressed.[61] But in the face of the military threat, Stalin made no further move against him for the time being.

During the winter, various arrests were carried out. Corps Commander Rokossovsky had been beaten senseless and dragged off to prison, together with a number of other officers of his unit. When Rokossovsky came before a "court," its president said that it had the evidence of one of his fellow conspirators, Adolf Kazimirovich Yushkevich, who had confessed that he and Rokossovsky had belonged to a counter-revolutionary center and had had certain instructions and tasks.

> "Can the dead give evidence?" Rokossovsky asked, when he was allowed to comment.
> "What do you mean, the dead?"
> "Well, Adolf Kazimirovich Yushkevich was killed in 1920 at Perekop. I mentioned to the investigator that Yushkevich served in the Cavalry Group, but I accidentally forgot to mention his loss."[62]

Rokossovsky was merely imprisoned, and was one of those lucky enough to be released when the pressure had died down.

Meanwhile, things were to get worse.

Corps Commander Khakanian, Head of the Political Administration of the Far Eastern Army, was arrested on 1 February 1938. And at the end of June 1938, when every other part of the Army, and of the country, had been dealt with, Mekhlis arrived in Khabarovsk with a group of new political commissars. At the same time, the sinister Frinovsky steamed in, in a special train, with a large NKVD staff. The great purge of the Far Eastern Army, of which they had been cheated in 1937, was now at hand.[63]

Mekhlis and Frinovsky first destroyed their own representatives. Mekhlis replaced the officers of the political administration; the "Gamarnik–Bulin gang" was later said to have been particularly active in the Far East.[64] Frinovsky arrested and shot the sixteen leading NKVD officials of the area. He was balked of one major figure. The Far Eastern NKVD Chief was G. Lyushkov, who had been Deputy Head of the Secret Political Department under Molchanov in the days of the Zinoviev Trial. One of the few of such a rank still left over from the Yagoda regime, he had been so far spared because of his friendly relations with Yezhov. He had now decided it was time to push his luck no further, and on 13 June he had slipped across the Manchurian border with a vast amount of intelligence information for the Japanese.[65]

Having prepared the police and political striking forces, Stalin's emissaries turned on the Army proper. Blyukher's new staff and commanders were arrested wholesale. His Deputy Commander, his new Chief of Staff, his new Air Commander, Pumpur—who had served in Spain—and his leading Army Commander, Levandovsky, recently transferred from the Caucasus, all disappeared. (Pumpur was later released, but was rearrested and shot in 1942.) But now it was not only a matter of a few seniors. Forty percent of the commanders up to regimental level, 70 percent of divisional and corps staffs, and over 80 percent of the front staff were seized, as NKVD lorries raided the officers' quarters night after night. Blyukher was soon "standing amidst the shambles of what had been his command."[66]

Once again he was reprieved, and for the same reason as before. The Japanese had seen their chance. On 6 July 1938 they launched a probing attack with limited objectives on Lake Hassan.

Fortunately, there were still a few competent officers who had survived or been transferred to the area—in particular, Corps Commander Shtern, who had recently been Chief Military Adviser in Spain and was now given command of one of the armies into which Blyukher's front had been reorganized. He was to have time to fight his battle and report on it to the next Party Congress and even to be elected to the new Central Committee before he, too, disappeared.

After five weeks of intermittent fighting, the Far Eastern troops first contained the Japanese and then pressed them back. By 11 August, the battle was over. A week later, on 18 August, Blyukher was recalled to Moscow.[67]

The "Stalin air route," pioneered with such panache at the time of the Zinoviev Trial, was being put to typical use by the General Secretary. A special pilot, Alexander Golovanov, later to rise to be Chief Marshal of the Soviet Air Force until his removal after Stalin's death in 1953, had been allotted by the NKVD for urgent travel by members of the Central Committee and Government. In 1935 and 1936, he had served in the labor-camp administration in Siberia. Now he was provided with a special multi-engined aircraft, and in 1937 and 1938 this was used to transport arrested officials from the Far East and elsewhere.[68] He had lately carried most of Blyukher's subordinates and their NKVD escorts back to Moscow.

But the Marshal himself went by train. He was not yet, however, under arrest. At the end of August, he made a report to the Military Soviet of the People's Commissariat of Defense. "Criticism was sharp and one-sided." Voroshilov attacked him, while Stalin, who had always defended him previously, remained silent. Later Voroshilov told him that he was not to return to the Far East, but to remain at the disposal of the Military Revolutionary Soviet "until a post suitable for a Marshal" could be found. Meanwhile, he should go on leave to Sochi, the resort in the Caucasus.[69]

Blyukher telegraphed his wife to return, adding that his health was poor. He put some money aside for her, in case he was arrested. For the chances of this now seemed high. She and the family joined him soon afterwards, together with his brother, Pavel, commander of an Air Force unit in the Far East. By this time, he had learned of the arrest of Army Commander Fedko, Assistant Commissar of Defense, which seems in some way to have been associated with his own. Fedko put up armed resistance and ordered his guard to hold the NKVD men at gunpoint while he telephoned Voroshilov, who told him to yield "temporarily."[70]

On 22 October, on Stalin's personal orders,[71] four men in black civilian suits entered Blyukher's place and arrested all the family. Blyukher and his wife were taken to the Lefortovo, where Beria personally conducted the first examinations. He was then continuously interrogated by other NKVD officers working in shifts. The charge was of having been a Japanese spy since 1921, and of having planned to escape to Japan with the help of his Air Force brother, Pavel (this second charge at least was not totally implausible; after all, Lyushkov had just done precisely that). The Marshal was now told that in addition to the rest of the family, his first wife, Galina, had been arrested in Leningrad. (He had taken the pseudonym Galen from her name.)[72] Apart from using all these hostages, the NKVD also offered him an inducement: if he confessed, he would get off with a ten-year sentence. However, he refused to sign the protocol.[73]

On 28 October 1938, medals were awarded to the heroes of the recent fighting in the Far East, including Shtern. The true victor was now undergoing severe torture by his NKVD interrogators.

There is no evident reason for the NKVD to have practiced or feigned on this occasion the haste with which the May–June 1937 purge of the Tukhachevsky group had been carried out. And unlike the procedure not only in that case, but even in the July 1938 military executions, we learn from a Soviet publication of the Khrushchev period that Blyukher was killed "without court or sentence."[74] It was also stated that "uninterrupted interrogation broke down the health of this virile man."[75] And we are now told that by 6 November, he had been beaten until "unrecognizable" and died as the result of "inhuman beatings" though without signing any confession.[76] (Fedko and Khakanian, his presumed associates, were not to be executed until the following February.)

His wife, Glafira, spent seven months in solitary confinement in the Lubyanka,[77] then eight years in camps, but survived. Their five-year-old daughter was sent to an NKVD orphanage in Kemerovo, where her mother eventually found her, being the first mother ever to appear there.[78]

There have always been rumors that Blyukher, or some of the officers round him, had seriously entertained the idea of a revolt. There is no reliable evidence of this, though Lyushkov gave information to the Japanese about "opposition groupings" in Siberia. Much of this was seen, and transmitted back to Moscow, by the Soviet spy Richard Sorge. And whether it was factual or speculative, it seems from the timing that it may have been used against Blyukher.[79]

The true reasons for proceeding against the Marshal seems to have been that he was a comparatively independent-minded soldier, and (as a candidate member of the Central Committee) a politician, in a position of power and influence. His fall and death mark the end of the last tenuous hope of action against Stalin. By the beginning of November, official listings of the military leadership ran Voroshilov, Mekhlis, Shchadenko, Shaposhnikov, Budenny, Kulik, Timoshenko.[80] For the first time, the Purge operatives ranked before the surviving soldiery. A few days later, the same order of listing contained an even more insulting and symptomatic insertion: Frinovsky, briefly become People's Commissar for the Navy, immediately after Voroshilov.[81]

## THE FALL OF YEZHOV

It was around the end of October that the first overt moves against Yezhov took place. Kaganovich and others persuaded Stalin to appoint a secret Commission of the Central Committee to report on the NKVD. Its members were Molotov, Beria, Vyshinsky, and Malenkov. It reported in mid-November, in terms hostile to Yezhov: two secret resolutions of the Central Committee criticized irregularities in investigative methods, and called for "recruiting honest people" to the security agencies. Over the next few weeks, several of Yezhov's men were removed from their posts.[82] Finally, on 8 December 1938, it was announced that his rule, at once pettifogging and bloodthirsty, had come to an end. He was replaced as People's Commissar for Internal Affairs by Beria, retaining only his Commissariat of Water Transport.

For a time, Beria appeared together with Yezhov on the platforms and in the formal lists. Yezhov had by January dropped back to his former "correct" seniority in these lists, lowest of the candidate members of the Politburo (Khrushchev being absent in Kiev). He is last publicly mentioned on the presidium for the anniversary of Lenin's death, on 22 January.[83]

Although not a delegate to the XVIIIth Party Congress, in March, he was present as a member of the outgoing Central Committee. And when the Congress's "Senioren Konvent," or informal Council of Elders, met to consider names for the new Central Committee, Yezhov's went forward. There were no objections until Stalin said he thought him unsuitable, since he was involved in a plot with Frinovsky and others to use Stalin's own bodyguard to assassinate him. Yezhov answered that it had been he who had exposed this plot. But Stalin retorted that this was only to cover himself; moreover, he had arrested many innocent people while protecting the guilty. Stalin ended by telling those present that in his opinion Yezhov was unfit to serve on the Central Committee, though it was, of course, up to them to decide.[84]

But Yezhov was only arrested in early April, at the Water Transport Commissariat, where he had chaired the Collegium but not taken part in the discussions, keeping silent or making paper airplanes. He is reported as confessing freely, and implicating others as required. He was charged with framing innocent people, with plotting to kill Stalin and seize power,[85] and with being a British spy since the Civil War.[86] But he was not shot until the following year.[87] Frinovsky had remained Commissar for the Navy until removed and arrested in March. Otherwise, Yezhov's leadership group in the NKVD had almost all been purged by the end of 1938. About 150 of his followers were shot.[88]

By March 1939, Beria's men were everywhere in power; his own Georgian following held many of the major NKVD posts—in Moscow, Merkulov and Kobulov; in Leningrad, Goglidze; in the Maritime Province, Gvishiani; in Byelorussia, Tsanava.[89] These were what was later to be characterized as the "Beria gang," until they all fell together in 1953.

The appointment of Beria is usually taken as a convenient date to mark the end of the Great Purge. Of Beria!—that is, of a man whose name, even in official Soviet circles, is now the very embodiment of terror and torture. And yet there is some sense in the convention.

Yezhov's removal was a simple piece of Stalinist expediency. The fact that most of his subordinates were executed under Beria was a simple matter of political mechanics. For apart from Yezhov himself and his personal nominees, the leading purgers, Stalin's own agents, did not suffer. Shkiryatov, who had acted as Yezhov's assistant, simply returned to Party work, and died, fully honored as Head of the Party Control Committee, a year after Stalin's own death, in 1954. Mekhlis and Vyshinsky also survived into the 1950s. As for Malenkov, he flourished greatly in the years that followed, together with his rival Zhdanov.

In fact, throughout the Purge, Stalin had largely avoided public responsibility. And now, when the Terror had gone as far as it conceivably could, he could profitably sacrifice the man who had overtly carried out his secret orders, the man the Party and public then blamed most.

It would perhaps be going too far to compare the situation too closely with one common in despotisms—like the Byzantine favorite who "instead of being suffered to possess the reward of guilt was soon afterwards circumvented and destroyed by the more powerful villainy of the Minister himself, who retained sense and spirit enough to abhor the instrument of his own crimes." Stalin had perhaps no strong liking for Yezhov, who never figures as one of his boon companions. But it would doubtless be Yezhov's narrow political comprehension, rather than any moral deficiency, that his superior might despise. The comparison is, rather, with the old autocratic tradition of disposing of the executioner who has killed one's rivals and thereby attracted to himself the main hatred of the survivors—a matter, in fact, of a common historical action which the wretched Yezhov had not the wit to foresee.

As we have said, by mid-1938 the NKVD itself, at the lower, operational level, had already wished to stop the progress of the Purge for obvious reasons. At the rate arrests were going, practically all the urban population would have been implicated within a few months. But it was caught in its own system. It was impossible for it not to arrest a man who had been denounced as an agent of Hitler. And an interrogator who did not demand the names of accomplices from each of his victims would soon himself come under denunciation for lack of vigilance or enthusiasm. By this time, the idea had grown among prisoners that the more denunciations they made the better;

> Some even held the strange theory that the more people were jailed the sooner it would be realized that all this was nonsense and harmful to the Party. . . . My neighbor on the plank bed in the camp at Kolyma had once been head of the political department of a railway. He prided himself on having incriminated some 300 people. He said, as I had often heard in prison in Moscow, "The worse it is the better it is— like that, it will all be cleared up more quickly." [90]

And, in fact, this was of some effect in the railway context (though no doubt elsewhere as well). The Byelorussian leaders complained that the NKVD had arrested every second railway official and that the system was near paralysis. [91]

Weissberg recounts the arrest in the spring of 1938 of the secretary of the Kharkov medical council. [92] A man with an excellent memory, he knew the names of all the doctors in the city and denounced them all, pointing out that he was in an especially good position to have recruited them and that they were in any case largely from hostile social classes. He refused to name any of them as the leader of the plot, claiming that post for himself. The doctor told his cell mates that he had been inspired to take this course by reading about the case of a witch burning in Germany at the time of the Inquisition when a young theologian charged with intelligence with the devil had at once pleaded guilty and named the members of the Inquisition as his accomplices. The interrogators were unable to torture him, as he had confessed, and the case went up to the archbishop, who put an end to the business.

A climax of the mass Purge came in the first half of 1938, and the following months saw something of a diminution of pressure. Whether this was due solely to a simple loss of momentum at the lower, operational level, or to political pressures being put on Yezhov from above, is not clear. Stalin's discontent with Yezhov certainly began in the early summer, when the plans to bring Beria in must have been laid. But he left Yezhov in office, and veteran prisoners speak of a climax of brutality in September.[93] In October, the number of Military Collegium sentences actually increased.[94]

Even before Yezhov's fall was formalized, a significant case was reported from Omsk, where the Regional Prosecutor and his assistant were tried for abuse of authority, unjustified arrests, and detention of innocent people in prison, sometimes for as long as five months. They were sentenced to two years' imprisonment.[95]

This sentence seems only a partial triumph for justice. A few shootings of NKVD interrogators for extorting false confessions by violence are reported to symbolize the actual end of the Yezhov period. Captain Shiroky, of the Kiev NKVD, was sentenced after having been made Head of the Moldavian NKVD. One prison mentions him as a "not particularly harsh examining magistrate."[96] Five other Moldavian NKVD men were also shot.[97] There had, indeed, been occasional similar trials before, and speeches throughout the Purge period are full of condemnation of unjust persecutions. But this time, the demonstration was clearly intentional. When certain Party officials became too free with their criticisms of police methods, though, Stalin pulled them up sharply with the telegram of 20 January 1939, explaining that torture was authorized (see p. 122).

At the same time, certain cases which had become more of a nuisance than they were worth were dropped. For example, for the physicist Weissberg an agitation had been raised in the West to which even very left-wing scientists had subscribed. Moreover, papers in his investigation had been inadequate and muddled. It was now abandoned. (Weissberg explains how technical difficulties arose: when it was more or less accepted that the charges against him would be withdrawn, it was found that there were over twenty witnesses who had provided the evidence and it would be necessary to examine them all over again, and by this time they were, of course, scattered in camps throughout the country.)

The gross result of Beria's assumption of the NKVD was that a proportion of those in prison awaiting trial were released, making a good impression on the populace. Of those already in camp, apart from certain special rehabilitations, like those of some military men in 1940, almost none were freed. An NKVD officer, himself under arrest, predicted this:

'Some of us will be released just to make it clear there has been a change; the remainder will go off to the camps to serve their sentences just the same.'
'What will be their criterion?'
'Chance. People are always trying to explain things by fixed laws. When you've looked behind the scenes as I have you know that blind chance rules a man's life in this country of ours.'[98]

But in the towns and villages of the Soviet Union, the pressure of haphazard mass arrests greatly eased. The country had been broken, and henceforward a limited number of arrests of men who had given some sort of cause for suspicion of disloyalty was sufficient to maintain the habit of submission and silence.

In general, Beria consolidated and institutionalized the system. From the "Yezhovshchina," he developed, rather than an emergency operation against the people, a permanent method of rule.

## STALIN AND BERIA CONSOLIDATE

The imprisoned Politburo members were not among those fortunate enough to benefit by the fall of Yezhov. While Ushakov and Nikolayev were at work on Eikhe, their colleague Rodos was submitting Kossior and Chubar to "long tortures," receiving "detailed instructions from Beria."[99]

Rodos was to be described by Khrushchev as "a vile person with the brain of a bird and morally completely degenerate."[100] Summoned in 1956 before the Central Committee Presidium, he said, "I was told that Kossior and Chubar were enemies of the people and for this reason, I, as an investigative judge, had to make them confess that they were enemies. . . . I thought I was executing the orders of the Party."[101] Khrushchev expressed great indignation at this answer, but all the same it is the only justification he gives for the activities of himself and his surviving colleagues during the same period.

On 22 to 26 February 1939, Kossior, Chubar, and others came to trial with another group of figures from politics and the Army, who appear to have been called the "Military–Fascist Center." Corps Commander Khakanian was shot on 22 February, and Marshal Yegorov on 23 February (though we are recently told that Yegorov, reported by Ulrikh to Stalin as "tried" and shot, died under interrogation).[102] On 23 February also came the execution of Kosarev, after a trial which lasted for ten minutes; he had been severely tortured, but had not confessed. The charges included espionage for Poland.[103] Presumably, the remainder of the Komsomol leadership was tried on the same day.

On 25 February the three survivors of the abortive Leningrad Center that Zakovsky had mounted in 1937 were shot—B. P. Pozern, P. I. Smorodin, and A. I. Ugarov. So were others, including the chairman of the Uzbek Council of People's Commissars, S. Segizbayev.

On 26 February came the turn of Kossior, Chubar, and Postyshev. Kossior had been produced by Yezhov, before the latter's fall, at a "confrontation" with Petrovsky in the presence of Stalin. Kossior, completely broken, had admitted that he was a Polish spy and, on another account, to terrorism.[104] Postyshev had also confessed.[105] Others shot that day include Army Commander Fedko. He had confessed to being a German spy when Beria brought Voroshilov to see him in Lefortovo.[106] Mirzoyan, too, was now shot, having confessed to being an agent of Bukharin, and implicating all the other Kazakh leaders.[107]

Others shot at this time included several of the most prominent NKVD men, such as Boris Berman (sentenced on 22 February).[108] Among them was Zakovsky (who had been badly tortured). He is said to have been a British spy.[109] Thus by a certain irony, Zakovsky seems to have perished in the same case as the Leningraders who had been his intended victims.

We are told in a recent article in *Izvestiya* that those now sentenced were "taken directly to the cellars," and that "it was all done in such haste that a man had scarcely been shot when others sentenced to death were coming down the corridor."[110]

Kossior's two surviving brothers, Kazimir and Mikhail, perished too, as did his wife, Elizaveta, put on "List 4" and shot;[111] and the wife of one brother is reported attempting suicide on receiving a ten-year sentence.[112] Postyshev's oldest son, Valentin, was shot, and his other children were sent to labor camps.[113] His wife, Tamara, was viciously tortured night after night in the Lefortovo, often being returned to her cell bleeding all over her back and unable to walk.[114] She is reported shot. Chubar's wife was also executed.[115] Kosarev's wife and his seventeen-year-old daughter were sentenced to ten years, and his father-in-law, the Rector of the Trade Academy, was shot.[116]

There remained one Politburo figure who, though in bad odor, was not under arrest—Petrovsky. His position had now been extremely difficult for two years.

Among the Leningraders arrested in 1937 was his elder son, Peter, who had edited the local *Leningradskaya pravda*. Petrovsky, candidate member of the Politburo and Head of State of the Ukrainian Republic, was unable to get news of him. He met a "stone wall of silence." Friends, "high officials in the Party and State," made several attempts to find out the facts. Finally they had to give up. The strictest instructions had been given to prevent anyone from discovering what went on "behind the walls of the Lubyanka." Young Petrovsky never emerged alive.[117] Another son, Corps Commander L. G. Petrovsky, was expelled from the Party and Army, but though arrested was later released.[118]

Meanwhile, in July 1937, when various illegalities were being perpetrated in the Ukraine without the consent of the leadership, Petrovsky had written to Kalinin, his titular superior, complaining that the principles of Party democracy were being overborne.[119] This is consistent with his failure to join in the denunciations at the Ukrainian plenum that month.

He had, it is said, "become critical of the personality cult."[120] But on 4 February 1938 he was awarded the Order of Lenin for his sixtieth birthday. And he remained theoretically Chairman of the Ukrainian Supreme Soviet throughout the fall of all his colleagues. After a conversation with Stalin which he described as "short and painful," he was removed, in June 1938, from his Ukrainian posts.[121] This was, it was pointed out in Khrushchev's time, done "unconstitutionally."[122] At the 7 November Parade, he did not appear with the leadership, and was henceforth not to be named in the listings.

A political case was concocted against Petrovsky in the usual way. The caretaker of a villa near Kiev which had been used by the Ukrainian leaders made, after beatings, a confession incriminating him. Petrovsky's secretary is also reported under arrest in the same circumstances.[123] A brother of Petrovsky is reported in the Butyrka in 1938.[124]

In March 1939, during the XVIIIth Congress, charges were made as a result of which he was not elected to the new Central Committee: he was accused of friendship with K. V. Sukhomlin, Ukrainian Politburo member since exposed as a Japanese spy; of having failed to report his knowledge of S. V. Kossior's connections with foreign counter-revolutionary organizations; and of having (presumably in the 1920s) opposed Kaganovich's nomination as Ukrainian First Secretary.[125]

In fact, there is no doubt that a case against him, long prepared, was now to be launched. But Stalin held his hand. Petrovsky was relieved of his membership in the Presidium of the Supreme Soviet (his last and titular appointment) on 31 May 1939 in a public fashion and with the title "Comrade"—an indication that his name was not yet unsayable.

He had been unable to get any employment for some months, living on whatever his wife could earn. Finally, in June 1939, he was allowed to take up the post of Assistant Director of the Museum of the Revolution, offered him by another former Duma member, Fedor Samoilov, which he held until Stalin's death.[126] His name disappeared from reference books, and most foreigners imagined that he had been executed. But it continued to appear in one single list, that of former Bolshevik members of the Duma. Stalin shot none of them;[127] the others, all third-rate figures, survived to die natural deaths. Since I first noted this, an account has appeared from the Petrovsky family archives, in which Stalin shouts at Petrovsky that his former membership in the Duma would not save him.[128] But it did, or something did.

Petrovsky survived Stalin, only dying in 1958. In fact, he was the first figure to be restored to favor after Stalin's death. A decree of 28 April 1953[129] awarded him the Order of the Red Banner of Labor in connection with his seventy-fifth birthday and "his services to the Soviet State." His real birthday was on 4 February, at a time when Stalin was still alive, when nothing had been said of it. So the incident was quite plainly a conscious political demonstration, made during Beria's attack on the Stalin heritage.

During the Purge period, Petrovsky had certainly suffered, if less than many. Yet it would perhaps not be inappropriate to recall that, when Commissar of Internal Affairs in 1918, he had ordered the unconditional shooting of all engaged in any sort of "White Guard" activity.[130]

At the same time as the February 1939 executions came an event which caused little stir. One last ex-oppositionist remained. Krupskaya had been able to do little during these years, though Stalin had allowed her to save from death one or two figures like I. D. Chigurin, arrested in 1937—even though, his health ruined and not fully rehabilitated, he had to live in poverty thereafter. Although still a member of the Central Committee, Krupskaya had only the minor job of Assistant People's Commissar for Education, and even there was "deprived of the possibility of influencing decisions in education."[131]

She died on 28 February, and Stalin himself carried the urn with her ashes at her funeral.

> Nadezhda Krupskaya will no more protect
> The innocent, the dying, those executed like rats[132]

even to the slight extent that she had done so. The very next day, the head of the Commissariat of Education's publishing house ordered his subordinates, "Don't print another word about Krupskaya." A part of her works was sent off to the

"special store" sections of libraries; part was buried in oblivion and not repub-
lished.[133] One Soviet account has it that she was poisoned, but others deny it.[134]

## THE XVIIITH CONGRESS

The XVIIIth Party Congress on 10 to 21 March 1939, which saw Yezhov's fall,
was the scene of the complete consolidation of all Stalin had striven for since that
of 1934. The changes were extraordinary.

Of the 1,966 delegates to the previous Congress, 1,108 had been arrested for
counter-revolutionary crimes.[135] Even of the residue lucky enough to survive, only
59 now appeared as delegates. Of these, 24 were old Central Committee members, leaving *only 35 of the 1,827 rank-and-file delegates of five years previously—less than 2 percent!* This is an indication of how literally we may take the
thesis that Stalin created an entirely new Party in this period.

The list of the Central Committee membership now elected shows that 55 of
the 71 who had been full members in 1934 had gone, and 60 of the 68 candidate
members. Of the 115 names no longer appearing, which included some natural
and some possibly natural deaths, 98 had been shot, as Khrushchev later stated in
the 1956 Secret Speech. The most recent official account gives the total sooner or
later killed by an executioner, by a murderer (Kirov), or by their own hand as
107.[136] The discrepancy is due to the inclusion or otherwise of suicides, assassinations and so on, and of those shot at a later date, such as Lozovsky.

In the new Committee one can note the groupings—no longer political factions, as in the pre-Stalin period, but personal followings—which were to contend
for Stalin's favor over the next fourteen years, and for power thereafter.

Zhdanov and his group are well represented, with himself, Shcherbakov, Ko-
sygin, and A. A. Kuznetsov as full members, and Popkov and Rodionov as candidate members. The first two were to be the alleged victims of the later Doctors'
Plot, and three of the other four were to be shot in the "Leningrad Case" of
1949–1950.

Another group was associated with Malenkov: he and V. M. Andrianov in
the Central Committee; Pervukhin, Ponomarenko, Pegov, Tevosyan, and Malyshev as candidate members—together with Shatalin, Malenkov's closest associate, on the Revision Commission.

Beria was better represented still. With himself, Bagirov, and V. N. Merkulov on the Central Committee, and Gvishiani, Goglidze, Kobulov, Dekanozov,
Arutinov, Bakradze, and Charkviani as candidate members (plus Tsanava on the
Revision Commission), we see his control in the Secret Police and in the political
mechanism in the Caucasus. (There were four other NKVD representatives—Nikishov, Head of Dalstroy; V. P. Zhuravliev; Kruglov; and Maslennikov as candidate members—a total of ten secret police on the Central Committee, by far the
highest number yet.)

Khrushchev, too, had his band—four full members of the Committee from
his own selection in the Ukraine.

Stalin's own personal group was also, of course, fully represented, with
Mekhlis, Shkiryatov, Poskrebyshev, Shchadenko, and Vyshinsky.

In the Politburo, the losses had been less great than at the lower level. But they were still remarkable. Kirov had been assassinated, and Kuibyshev had died or been poisoned. Ordzhonikidze had been either murdered or forced into a suicide which was scarcely different from murder. Rudzutak had been shot eight months earlier; Kossior, Chubar, and Postyshev, just before the Congress. Petrovsky had been removed, and was in Moscow, uncertain of his fate and begging for a menial post. Of the four who had been brought in between the Congresses, Khrushchev and Zhdanov were balanced by Eikhe, in prison awaiting execution, and the doomed Yezhov. Of four of the fallen leaders, it has now been specifically said that they were tortured (Rudzutak, Eikhe, Kossior, and Chubar).

On 22 March 1939, four promotions were made in and to the Politburo, of those who had served Stalin most satisfactorily during the recent period. Zhdanov and Khrushchev were raised to full membership; Beria became a candidate member, as did Shvernik, who after Tomsky's removal in June 1929 had been appointed head of the unions. He had adequately transformed them into organizations for mobilizing and disciplining labor.

There is a notable difference in Stalin's treatment of the more senior generation of his supporters on the Politburo and those promoted later. If we take the members of that body who supported him against the oppositions: of the eleven promoted to it up to July 1926, six survived right through the Purges, two were physically destroyed by informal means (Kirov and Ordzhonikidze), one died in doubtful circumstances (Kuibyshev), one, though removed from his posts, survived until after Stalin's own death (Petrovsky), and only one was "tried" and shot (Rudzutak). But of the eight promoted from July 1926 until the end of 1937, only one (Zhdanov) survived. All the others were executed.

This distinction should perhaps be interpreted as follows: in the earlier period, it was not a question of Stalin simply nominating rapidly promoted figures from the second rank of the Party. He was bound to rely on men who had reached high position to some extent on their reputations, and who in any case were widely enough known to the leading circles of the Party and had good enough Party records for their presence not to appear absurd on a body still containing distinguished and widely known oppositionists.

They were men who, in however minor a way compared with the Trotskys and Bukharins, yet represented a continuity with Lenin's leading cadre. Some of them, like Kaganovich, were eager supporters of the Great Terror. Others, like Molotov, may have had qualms but became enthusiastic accomplices, whether through fear or from other motives. More reluctant figures, like Kalinin, remained useful figureheads. In disposing of them, Stalin inclined to roundabout and concealed methods. But the Eikhes and Postyshevs carried little more Party prestige than the other members of the Central Committee, and they were as readily expendable if they failed to satisfy.

The new leadership, Stalinist in every sense, made the Congress a triumphal celebration. At the same time, dissociating themselves from Yezhovism, the most notorious Purge operators deplored more strongly than ever the excesses of the Purge.

Shkiryatov quoted at length an incident of a man in Archangel wrongly removed from his job, arrested, and restored as a result of an appeal to the Central Committee. Zhdanov referred to a man who had written 142 denunciations, all false, and raised a number of cases in which individual Party members had been wrongly expelled, including such incidents as one in Tambov province, where the expulsion and wrongful arrest of one man led to the expulsion from the Party of his wife and seven other members, and from the Komsomol of twenty-eight Young Communists, while ten non-Party teachers lost their jobs.

Khrushchev's ally Serdyuk expressed horror at a denunciation of a large number of enemies of the people in the Party apparatus in Kiev which had turned out on investigation to be signed by someone using a false name, and to be in the handwriting of the Head of the Cultural Section of one of the District Committees. Another case, also in Kiev, was of a woman teacher who in 1936 and 1937 had denounced a large number of innocent people, and also obtained by blackmail and threats 5,000 rubles from various organizations and three free trips to a resort; Serdyuk explained to the disgusted delegates that her slanders had been written at the dictation of "enemies of the people since unmasked," and that she herself had been sentenced to five years.

Stalin himself summed up: the Purge had been accompanied by "grave mistakes," indeed "more mistakes than might have been expected." "Undoubtedly," he went on, "we shall have no further need of resorting to the method of mass purges. Nevertheless, the Purge of 1933–6 was unavoidable and its results, on the whole, were beneficial." [137]

The phrase "1933–6" might have struck the layman a little oddly. The fact is that the expulsions from the Party at that time had been constitutionally and publicly authorized, while the later Purge had not ever been formalized, and so could be taken as irrelevant.

Party executions, in fact, continued. Over the next years, Stalin and Beria wound up most of Yezhov's unfinished business.

In July 1939, the Prosecutor's sanction for Eikhe's arrest was at last obtained, to some extent legalizing the position. Eikhe was presented with the charges against him on 25 October 1939, and wrote to Stalin protesting his innocence— and blaming the frame-up in part on Trotskyites he now took credit for having persecuted in West Siberia. Ushakov and Nikolayev-Zhurid, he added, had "utilized the knowledge that my broken ribs have not properly mended and have caused me great pain," as the result of which he had incriminated himself and others. He asked for an end to "the vile provocation which wound itself like a snake round many persons, in large measure through my meanness and criminal slander." [138] There is a story that, temporarily insane by torture in 1938, he had cried out that he confessed his "guilt of belonging to a criminal organization which goes by the name of the Central Committee of the All-Union Communist Party (bolsheviks)." [139]

One of the charges against Eikhe is a trifle mysterious. He was accused of being responsible for certain "resolutions of the Central Committee of the All-Union Communist Party (bolsheviks) and of the Council of People's Commissars." He pleaded that the resolutions in question "were not made on my initiative and without my participation," and were "in any case correct." Those made without his "participation" can only have been resolutions of the Council of People's Commissars, to which he did not belong until October 1937. The natural explanation would seem to be that the charge was a general one, made against a number of accused, some of whom *had* participated.

Eikhe's letters to Stalin were ignored, though evidently kept on file. On 2 February 1940 he was finally brought before a court, where he withdrew his confessions and again attributed them to torture by the investigator, and was then shot. (His wife was also executed.)[140] It is interesting, in view of the previous association of political and military executions, that Admiral Dushenov, Commander of the Northern Fleet, former sailor on the *Aurora,* perished on 3 February (though on one in other ways inaccurate fictional account, he died in a labor camp).[141] But these executions are chiefly remarkable as being included in a final settlement with the Yezhovites. The operation seems to have taken place in two phases: one around 26 and 27 January, and the other around 2 to 4 February. Frinovsky was shot on 3 February, and NKVD veteran M. A. Trilisser, Soviet representative on the Executive Committee of the Comintern (under the pseudonym Moskvin), on 2 February, together with Mikhail Kol'stov and the producer Meyerhold. Meyerhold's alleged accomplice in the writers' conspiracy, Isaak Babel, had been shot on 27 January, charged in addition with links with Yezhov. We now learn that several veteran NKVD men—I. M. Kedrov, L. I. Reykhman, and V. P. Golubev—were shot on 25 to 27 January while others, like Ushakov and Nikolayev-Zhurid, are also given as shot "in January 1940"—so they preceded their victim Eikhe to the grave, if only by days and as part of the same alleged conspiracy. Some recent Soviet sources give 1 April 1940 as Yezhov's death date, but a more authoritative statement says "January 1940,"[142] so this set of killings seems to mark Stalin's final winding up of the Yezhovshchina.

None of those liquidated at this time could be considered as anything resembling an alternative political leadership to which the Party or the country might have turned in a crisis of the regime. In fact, few figures of any repute still survived. Bubnov had been shot, or died in prison, on 12 January 1940.* (His daughter Valya was sent to labor camp.)[143] And the last leading figure of the Stalinist cadres to go was Antipov, who (presumably having been the token non-death sentence in one of the earlier mass killings) was liquidated in Stalin's elimination during the first German advance of all former such cadres remaining. Stalin's victory on the political front had been complete. Now, in the disaster arising from his own miscalculation, no move to replace him was possible. Subjected to this very severe test, the Purge proved to have accomplished its object.

---

*This date for Bubnov has been given officially for the past quarter of a century; however, a very recent Soviet listing has him shot on 1 August 1938, with the others *(Izvestiya TsK KPPS,* no. 12 [1988]).

# BOOK III

# *AFTERMATH*

*. . . hope once crushed, less quick to spring again.*
Matthew Arnold

# HERITAGE
# OF TERROR

*None of the evils which totalitarianism . . . claims to remedy is worse than totalitarianism itself.*

Albert Camus

"Zachto—why?" The last words of Yakov Livshits, Old Bolshevik and Deputy People's Commissar, as he awaited execution on 30 January 1937, got no answer. During the few remaining months that old Party members were still at liberty and able, occasionally at least, to talk of such things, his question was much repeated. If experienced politicians felt baffled, the man in the street was even more uncomprehending. "I asked myself and others, why, what for? No one could give me an answer."[1] As for victims, the first words on entering a cell were almost always, we are told, a shaken "But why, why?"[2] The prison and camp literature tells of the same phrase, "Why?" often found written on cell walls, and carved into the sides of prison wagons and on the planks of the transit camps.[3] The old partisan Dubovoy* (whose long white beard, of which he was very proud, the examining magistrate had torn out) even developed in jail the theory that the Purge was the result of an increase in the number of sunspots.[4]

The simplest form of true answer would, of course, be "to destroy or disorganize all possible sources of opposition to Stalin's progress to absolute rule." But we can also see, in the system he created after his victory, the specific form of despotism for which he had sacrificed the nation and Party.

The victory was inevitably marked by a good deal of dislocation, and stability had not been achieved when the Soviet Union was faced with international emergencies, starting with the Finnish War of 1939 to 1940, which became a desperate struggle for mere existence in the four-year war with the Nazis from 1941 to 1945, and its aftermath of reconstruction. It was not until 1947–1948 that the Stalinist State became politically and institutionally stabilized.

But meanwhile, two main objects had already been accomplished. A vast number of past or potential "hostile" elements had been destroyed or sent to labor camps, and the rest of the population reduced to the most complete silence and obedience. And, on the other hand, the Communist Party itself had been turned into something entirely new.

---

*Father of the Army Commander of that name.

This political transformation is to some extent masked by the fact that the organizational forms remained the same. But, in fact, the discontinuity between the Party of 1934 and the Party of 1939 was radical. The people opposed to Stalin had already been almost entirely eliminated from the leading organs of the party. Over the Purge period, the Stalinists themselves, except for a small and peculiar personal following, were destroyed. The extent of the discontinuity is plain if we consider the delegates to the XVIIth and XVIIIth Congresses. As we have seen, and it is worth repeating, *less than 2 percent* of the rank-and-file delegates of 1934 held their positions in 1939. The Communist Party of 1939 was more different from that of 1934 than Buchanan's Democratic Party was from Andrew Jackson's. If the latter case is more evident to historians, it is partly because, in the Communist case, emphasis on the continuous tradition, and thus concealment of the change, were of much greater political importance to the rulers.

The earlier leaders had wished to reserve all political rights for the limited leading membership of the old Party. Stalin, in destroying that Party, in a sense threw the positions of power open. He instituted the *carrière ouverte aux talents* in place of the old system. It is true that the "talents" required were of a special type. But at least any man, whatever his origins and however recently he had joined the Party, could be sure of a good post if he exhibited adequate servility and ruthlessness. But at the same time, among the new cadres of Stalinism, Party theory in its old justificatory form was still to be a basis. As Hitler had remarked, "Any violence which does not spring from a firm spiritual base, will be wavering and uncertain. It lacks the stability which can only rest in a fanatical outlook."[5]

A close student of, and victim of, the Purge acutely analyzes the thoughts of the truly orthodox among Stalin's operatives. Taking the case of a former NKVD officer known for his brutality, but gentle and even sentimental when himself a prisoner, he concludes:

> What would a Prygov say if he were required to defend himself in a court of law? He would not, we believe, refer to superior orders, but to the teachings of Marxism and Leninism as he understood them. Prygov was as loyal and obedient as an S.S. man. But his faith was founded on a conviction that it fully accorded with the demands of reason and conscience. He was fully convinced that his was no blind faith, but was founded on science and logic. He was brutal because the general line required him to be brutal. The general line, so long as it accorded with the fundamental tenets of Marxism, was everything to him. Without the allegedly scientific foundation of the general line, which was the backbone of his faith, all the instructions of the Party authorities would have lost their significance for him. He was convinced of the logical and ethical correctness of his Marxist principles, and on this conviction his faith depended.[6]

For the Stalinist Party maintained, in theory, the old doctrine and the old loyalty. But the discipline which had hitherto been due, in theory at least, to a corporate collective leadership now became the service of one man and his personal decisions. The loyalties and solidarities which had bound the membership now worked in one direction only—upward; sideways, as regards the Party comrades among whom there had subsisted some degree of common trust, only mutual suspicion and "vigilance" remained.

A new political system had been established. Not merely had the new men everywhere taken the place of the veteran cadres, but they had been given a long, severe, and testing exercise in the methods and attitudes of the new style of rule. The experience of the Purge had hardened and tempered them, as the collectivization struggle and, before that, the Civil War had tempered their predecessors. The alloy, however, was a new one. Dostoyevsky remarks, in *The House of the Dead*, "Tyranny is a habit; it grows upon us, and in the long run, turns into a disease. . . . The human being, member of society, is drowned for ever in the tyrant, and it is practically impossible for him to regain human dignity, repentance and regeneration."

A Communist philosopher saw Stalin

> as the apex of a pyramid which widened gradually toward the base and was composed of many "little Stalins": they, seen from above, were the objects and, seen from below, the creators and guardians of the "cult of the personality." Without the regular and unchallenged functioning of this mechanism the "cult of the personality" would have remained a subjective dream, a pathological fact, and would not have attained the social effectiveness which it exercised for decades. . . .[7]

At the apex, this led to an extravagant adulation of Stalin. A Congress delegate of 1939 remarked: ". . . At that moment I saw our beloved father, Stalin, and I lost consciousness. The 'hurrahs' resounded for a long time, and it was probably this noise which brought me to myself. . . ."[8] And this was reasonably typical. A whole literature was devoted to the *Vozhd*.

In the country as a whole, a new public mood had been created. The experience had given the ruled as well as the rulers a new impress. The population had become habituated to silence and obedience, to fear and submission. In the years which remained of Stalin's rule after the Purges, the all-out mass terror was no longer necessary. The machine had been started up, and could now be kept rolling without extraordinary efforts. It is true, in a sense, that the comparative calm which may reign in an autocracy following the elimination of all opponents or potential opponents is no less a manifestation of terror than the original killings—is, in fact, merely a product and consolidation of them: "Ubi solitudinem faciunt, pacem appellant."

In any case, the security organs never ceased to strike and strike brutally at all suspects. As late as 1940, Saratov jail was still holding ten men in cells for one or two.[9] Right through the period, millions of prisoners, replacing the losses by death, were dispatched to the camps, and the threat remained ever present in all minds; yet the intensity of 1936 to 1938 was never reached again. In one vast operation, the country had been silenced and broken, and from then on more selective terror sufficed. This was partly because a good proportion of the new recruitment of forced laborers came from local and partial actions, starting with the Baltic and eastern Poland, where the work of 1917 to 1939 in the rest of the USSR was compressed into a couple of years, in 1939 to 1941.

Apart from the approximately 440,000 Polish civilians sent to camp, in September 1939 the Russians took about 200,000 Polish prisoners of war. Most of the officers and several thousand soldiers were sent to camps at Starobelsk, Kozielsk, and Ostachkov. In April 1940, there were about 15,000 of them there, including 8,700 officers. Only 48 were ever seen again; they had been removed from the camps and sent to Soviet prisons. The missing group included 800 doctors and a dozen university professors.

When, under the agreement between the Poles and the Russians following the Soviet entry into the war, the former Polish prisoners were allowed to leave Russia and form their own army in the Middle East, the Polish representatives gave the Russians lists of names of soldiers who were known to have fallen into Russian hands and had not been released.

The Polish Ambassador, Professor Kot, raised the subject ten times with Molotov and Vyshinsky between October 1941 and July 1942, and always received the reply that all the prisoners had been released. When Kot met Stalin in November 1941, Stalin made a call to the NKVD on the subject. Whatever the answer was, Stalin then went on to the next point and would not discuss the matter further.

When General Sikorski saw Stalin on 3 December 1941, he was told that perhaps the missing men had got over the border into Manchuria. But Stalin promised to look into the question, saying that if any Poles had not been released, through local obstruction by NKVD officers, the latter would be disciplined.

In April 1943, the Germans announced the discovery of mass graves containing executed Poles in the Katyn Forest, near Smolensk. Within two days, the Russians produced a clear-cut official story of Polish officers in camps in the Smolensk area who had been left behind and had fallen into German hands—a totally different account from those which had previously been given by Stalin and his subordinates.

Allied leaders, while not all actively accepting the Russian story, took the line that no trouble should now be caused in view of the overriding importance of unity against Hitler. The Western press, however, accepted the Russian version almost unanimously. The American military paper *Stars and Stripes* even published a caricature of a Polish officer, represented as pretending to have been killed by the Russians.[10]

The Germans allowed access to the Katyn Forest to a large number of expert or interested parties—a European medical commission, containing experts from universities all over Europe, including neutrals such as Dr. Naville, Professor of Forensic Medicine at Geneva;* representatives of the Polish underground; senior Allied prisoners of war, who correctly refused to pronounce any opinion, but who reported confidentially to their Governments that the German story was quite clearly true.

Basically, the proof consisted of digging up previously untouched mass graves; examining the corpses, compacted under earth; finding on them Soviet newspapers and similar material going up to April 1940, and nothing later; and noting that they were mostly in thick clothing, as against the Russian story that the executions had taken place in the warmth of September 1941.

The bodies found at Katyn, 4,143 in number, represented only those who had been in the Kozielsk camp; 2,914 were identified, and 80 percent of them were among the lists of missing the Polish authorities had assembled.

---

*The only member to withdraw his evidence was the Bulgarian Dr. Markov, who did so after some months in prison when arrested by the Russians on their entry into his country.

What happened to the Poles from the other two camps, numbering about 10,400 men, remains unknown. There are stories that a number of Polish prisoners were packed into old barges and scuttled in the White Sea. And there are also tales of a mass execution and burial resembling Katyn in the neighborhood of Kharkov.[11]

The Nuremberg judges examined the Katyn Affair from 1 to 3 July 1946 in a derisory fashion, and did not mention Nazi responsibility for it in their verdict. No evidence of any sort has ever been forthcoming from German prisoners or captured material of Nazi responsibility for this particular crime.

But it is now hardly necessary here to say more. It is nowhere believed any longer that the Germans were responsible.

The significance, from the point of view of our theme, the Purges, is that we have here a clear-cut example of a mass execution carried out, without trial and in complete secrecy, as a routine administrative measure—and in peacetime.

One further case, this time of two individuals, is equally illustrative. Henrik Ehrlich and Viktor Alter, the leaders of the Jewish Bund Socialists in Poland, fell into Russian hands in September 1939 at the time of the Soviet–German invasion of Poland. They were both veterans of the Social Democratic movement in the old Russian Empire, and Ehrlich had been a member of the Executive of the Petrograd Soviet in 1917. They were taken to the Butyrka, charged with acting for the Polish Government in various infiltrations of saboteurs from 1919 to 1939. Ehrlich, who was on one occasion interrogated by Beria personally, insisted on writing all his answers. Alter replied simply to each question, "It is absolutely false, and you know it well."

After eighteen months, in July 1941, they were transferred to Saratov and condemned to death. They both refused to appeal, but after ten days their sentences were commuted to ten years' imprisonment. The amnesty granted to all Polish prisoners shortly afterwards resulted in their release in September and October, respectively. They were asked to organize a Jewish antifascist committee, and it was clear that their connections with old members of the Bund in the American trade unions—such as David Dubinsky—were much valued. Ehrlich became president and Alter secretary of this new organization, and the Soviet actor-producer Mikhoels was named a member of its Presidium. Beria personally sponsored the organization, while telling them that on all international questions Stalin took the final decision.

On 4 December, they went out of their hotel in Kuibyshev, and were never seen again. At first, the pretense was kept up that what had happened to them was unknown. But after protests from Clement Attlee and from the leading trade unionists in America and England, and also from important world figures like Albert Einstein and Reinholdt Niebuhr, Litvinov finally, in February 1943, sent a letter to the Head of the American Federation of Labor, William Green, explaining that Ehrlich and Alter had been arrested and executed for trying to persuade Soviet troops to cease contesting the advance of the German armies and to conclude an immediate peace with Nazi Germany. He added that they had been executed in December 1942—but their colleague, Lucjan Blit, who was with them in Kuibyshev until the moment of their arrest, believes that this is probably a mistake for December 1941.

Katyn and the Ehrlich–Alter Case are representative of a host of similar actions, both having exceptionally come to the notice of the world public through special circumstances. Apart from continuous attrition in the old lands of Russia, particular operations provided a flow of victims. After the Poles and Balts in 1939 to 1941, various other minorities were deported. In 1941, the Soviet Germans; in 1943 and 1944, seven entire nations, mainly from the Causasus, were arrested and deported en bloc.[12] German and Japanese prisoners of war filled the camps. In 1945 and 1946, the Western territories were again ravaged, and with the end of the war those Russian soldiers who had fought for, or merely been captured by, the Germans were mostly sent to camps on their return.

## THE PURGE AND THE WAR

Meanwhile, in 1941 to 1945, the country had felt the effects of the measures taken by Stalin against his military leaders.

Figures given over the past years vary slightly, depending on (for example) whether they refer to those holding ranks at the time of the original appointments in 1935, or include promotions made later. As now given in the Soviet press, the Purge accounted for

3 of the 5 Marshals

13 of the 15 Army Commanders

8 of the 9 Fleet Admirals and Admirals Grade I

50 of the 57 Corps Commanders

154 of the 186 Divisional Commanders

16 of the 16 Army Commissars

25 of the 28 Corps Commissars

58 of the 64 Divisional Commissars[13]

All 11 of the Vice Commissars of Defense went, as did 98 out of 108 members of the Supreme Military Soviet. Nor was the effect confined to the upper echelons. Between May 1937 and September 1938, 36,761 Army officers and "over three thousand" Navy officers were dismissed (of whom 9,579 had been arrested even before dismissal). But from 1939 to 1941, we are told, some 13,000 of these dismissed were re-enrolled, so that the total permanently repressed may be as low as 27,000. (This omits, of course, those repressed after September 1938, for which Soviet figures almost as high as those for 1937 and 1938 have been given, for a total over the whole period of 43,000.)[14] As Khrushchev later said, the Purges started "at company and battalion commander level."[15] And the chances of the repressed seem to have been lower than those in any other field: of one group of 408 Army men tried by the Military Collegium, 401 were shot and 7 sent to labor camp.[16]

The Soviet novelist Konstantin Simonov gives an account of a conversation between two generals—Serpilin and Ivan Alexeyevich— in his *Soldiers Are Made, Not Born.*[17] Ivan Alexeyevich comments that the Purge was not merely a matter of individual generals:

"The whole thing goes deeper. In the autumn of 1940 when the Finnish war had already ended, the Inspector-General of the Infantry carried out an inspection of reg-imental commanders and in the course of my duties I saw the resulting data. The review was attended by 225 commanders of infantry regiments. How many of them do you think had at that time graduated from the Frunze Academy?"

"I cannot really guess," said Serpilin, "judging from the preceding events, pre-sumably not very many."

"What if I tell you that there was not a single one to have done so?"

"It just cannot be . . ."

"Don't believe it then, if you find that easier. Well, how many of the 225 do you think had gone through ordinary military college? 25 of them! and 200 of them had come from junior lieutenants' courses and regimental schools!"

As Ivan Alexeyevich himself points out, 225 regiments constitute 75 divi-sions, or half the strength of the peacetime Army, a reasonable sample. What Simonov is saying, in effect, is that the Army purge (plus the comparatively minor Finnish War of 1939 to 1940) accounted for virtually every single regimental commander throughout the entire Soviet Army apart from those promoted to fill gaps higher up. Although fictional in form, the figures Simonov gives also appear in factual Soviet literature.[18]

Similarly, in his labor camp, Gorbatov

wondered how the officers newly appointed to high rank, with no battle experience, would deal with operations in a real war. Honest, brave men, devoted to their country they might be, but yesterday's battalion commander would be head of a division, yesterday's regimental commander of a corps; in charge of an army, or a whole front, there would be at best a former divisional commander or his deputy. How many futile losses and failures would there be? What would our country suffer just because of this?[19]

As is confirmed by Russian military writers, the Purge had indeed led to "inexperienced commanders" being promoted. As early as 1937, 60 percent of the commanding cadres in rifle units, 45 percent in tank units, and 25 percent in air units were given as in this category.[20] Moreover, "the cadre of leaders who had gained military experience in Spain and in the Far East was almost completely liquidated."[21]

Nor could the atmosphere fail to affect the discipline of the Army:

The policy of large-scale repression against the military cadres led also to undermine military discipline, because for several years officers of all ranks and even soldiers in the Party and Komsomol cells were taught to "unmask" their superiors as hidden enemies. It is natural that this caused a negative influence on the state of military discipline in the first war period.[22]

Mekhlis, in his report to the 1939 XVIIIth Congress, expressed horror and sorrow at "incorrect expulsions" from the Party which had taken place in the Army in 1935, 1936, and 1937, on the basis of "slander," instead of the correct method of "documents and facts."[23]

And over the next few years, a handful of generals were released—Rokos-sovsky and Gorbatov, for example. But still, as with the civilian purge (and the similar crocodile tears of Zhdanov), the arrests did not actually cease and cases continued to be processed. Herling mentions a number of Soviet generals with whom he shared a cell in 1940. Most of them had been badly beaten, and showed the marks of ill-mended broken bones.

Even now, the Red Army had considerable striking power in the right hands. This was shown over the summer of 1939. After a very shaky start, a build-up of superior forces (itself a feat), luckily entrusted to the one superlative soldier of the old First Cavalry Army, Zhukov, threw back the Japanese invaders of Mongolia in model fashion at Khalkhin-Gol. But even as this was being done, the armored tactics he had used, sponsored under Tukhachevsky (who with his group had by 1937 been beginning to create an "elite army emerging from the mass"),[24] were being condemned and abandoned, and within two months the tactical doctrine of the Red Army was back to old-fashioned "mass," and the tanks were distributed in packets to lesser unit commands.

The post-Purge promotions placed men totally unsuited or untrained for high command in key positions. None of them showed any capacity for strategic thinking, and even the tactical dispositions on the frontier were proof of "a dull or listless mind."[25] The rigidity of the military–political machine meant that failure at the top produced certain dislocation. The "mass" on which post-Tukhachevsky doctrine relied became too large and sluggish to be manipulated in such circumstances.

In the Finnish War of 1939 to 1940, the "initial incompetence of the Voroshilov–Mekhlis clique literally plunged the Red Army into disaster," says John Erickson.[26] He adds that apart from this high-level failure there was a fatal lack of the "nerve" that Tukhachevsky had insisted on in junior commanders: independence of spirit had been destroyed by the Purges.

The German General Staff's secret rating of the Red Army at the end of 1939 spoke of it as a "gigantic military instrument." Although finding the "principles of leadership good," it added "the leadership itself is, however, too young and inexperienced."[27] In 1940, German intelligence, warning against an underestimation of the Red Army, felt that nevertheless it would take four years before that Army was back to its 1937 level of efficiency.[28]

There were two positive ingredients in the gloomy post-Purge scene. First, Army Commander Shaposhnikov, the Tsarist colonel, had never lost Stalin's trust. Through the debacle, he contrived to seek out and promote talent. As Chief of Staff his powers were limited, but he brought into the senior command posts a number of efficient officers, even though not enough to make up for those rising through the whims of Stalin, Mekhlis, and Voroshilov.

Second, by great good luck, two of the old First Cavalry Army officers were fair, or good, soldiers. After Voroshilov's Finnish effort, Timoshenko, who had picked up the pieces and was now (7 May 1940) a Marshal, was made Defense Commissar. At the same time, Zhukov took the newly revived rank of full General, and then various key commands, culminating in his appointment as Chief of Staff in January 1941.

The reforms which took place between 1940 and the German attack on Russia in 1941 were inadequate, but without them the Red Army would probably have been completely ruined in the first weeks of Hitler's assault. Timoshenko, in effect, attempted to restore the position as it had existed under Tukhachevsky. But three years of degeneration could not be recouped in a few months.

Moreover, with Timoshenko, the grotesque Kulik, also from Stalin's Tsaritsyn entourage of the Civil War, and commonly described in the Soviet literature as a bullying incompetent,[29] was made Marshal and put in charge of the artillery arm; and another ineffective First Cavalry veteran, Tyulenev, became full General, together with Zhukov and Meretskov (the latter arrested early in the war and confessing under torture to being a terrorist plotter, but released in September 1941).

In fact, as a result of the 1940 promotions, four out of the five Marshals, two out of the three full Generals, and two of the new Colonel-Generals were from Stalin's Civil War group. Of the eight, two were to prove useful appointments. The others ranged from mediocre to disastrous. Stalin's concessions to military reality were not yet whole-hearted. We can be reasonably certain that but for the sharp jolt of the Finnish War, Timoshenko would not have been allowed to carry out his partial program of revitalization.

The task was tremendous—indeed, given the circumstances, impossible. But some improvement could be effected. The dual-command system was, after all, abandoned on 12 August 1940. In September, Mekhlis was removed from the Political Administration of the Army. A partial reversion to Tukhachevsky's training methods set in. To create a new leadership and a new spirit could nevertheless not be done in the time remaining. Timoshenko was a vast improvement on Voroshilov, but the latter, and a large number of Stalinist arrivistes, remained in positions of power. And Stalin himself, with his long refusal to face the possibility of a German attack, was in final control.

When the German invasion was on the point of being launched, a leading commentator was doubtful "whether any consistent plan for the defense of the Soviet Union existed, even at this late hour. . . ."[30]

Stalin's attitude towards the Nazi-Soviet Pact of 1939 is one of the most peculiar things about his entire career. The man who had never attached the slightest value to verbal assurances or paper promises does really seem to have thought, or hoped, that Hitler would not attack Russia. Even when overwhelming evidence was sent to him, by Soviet intelligence, by the British, by German deserters, that the Nazis were massing for attack, he gave strict orders that such reports should be treated as provocations. As far as can be seen, it was in the genuine hope of persuasion that he remarked to Schulenberg, "We must remain friends," and told Colonel Krebs, "We will remain friends with you in any event."[31]

During the 1939 to 1941 period, attacks on the British were encouraged, but no mention even of the word *fascism* was allowed. The Counselor of the Soviet Embassy in Paris, Nikolai Ivanov, was actually sentenced to five years for "anti-German views," and the sentence was confirmed—doubtless through bureaucratic inefficiency—in September 1941![32]

As an old Soviet diplomat remarked, the two years gained by the Nazi-Soviet Pact were almost completely wasted. He commented sourly, "He suspected his own closest comrades, but he trusted Hitler."[33]

It has been said that so much genuine enmity had been focused on Trotsky that Hitler, in comparison, seemed a shadowy figure, a bogeyman for use in frightening the Party rather than a real threat. There may be an element of truth in this, psychologically speaking. But Stalin's lack of contact with reality on the one point of the Nazi invasion had not been reflected in his attitude to Soviet–German relations during the earlier part of the Pact's duration. In 1939 and 1940, the Soviet Union had bargained hard, had refused to make definite commitments, and, though providing the Germans with various services appropriate to an ally such as the U-boat "Base North" near Murmansk, had conducted even the lowest-level negotiations with all the self-centered closeness and suspiciousness later shown in relations with the Anglo-American allies of a subsequent phase of the war period. The complete withdrawal from reality in the face of unpleasant facts is very much the aberration of 1941.

It seems likely that Stalin, realizing the incapacity of his Army and his re-gime in the face of the Germans, hoped against hope at least for a further year or two's grace. Everything had gone his way for years. He could scarcely, it seems, conceive of his luck failing. Be that as it may, the result of his attitude was the despairing and absurd messages which poured in from the frontier on 22 June—"We are being fired on. What shall we do?"

And yet the Soviet Army was larger in numbers, stronger in matériel, and at least as well equipped technically as the Germany invaders. There was only one element in which the armies were not comparable: the German Command, staff, and officer corps in general were of immensely superior quality. Although Hitler had removed a number of the higher officers, he had at least the sense to see that he could not fight a major war without a trained military cadre.

As the armies facing the Germans broke up under a task for which they had not been properly prepared or supported, Stalin reacted promptly. The Com-mander of the Western Front, Pavlov; his Chief of Staff, Klimovskikh; and his Signals and Artillery Commanders were shot. General Korobkov, commanding the battered Fourth Army, followed them. This did not save the three armies and four mechanized corps trapped between Minsk and Bialystok.

The Air Force, with 10,000 to 11,000 machines to the Luftwaffe's 5,000,[34] was almost annihilated in the first days of the war. A large proportion of Soviet aircraft were not of modern type. And the other faults of Stalin's rule in the Air Force reinforced the errors of industrial and design policy. First, training had been inadequate, and tactical methods were poor. Kesselring applied the term *infanti-cide* to the Luftwaffe's destruction of Soviet bomber formations.

And all these long-established errors were compounded by Stalin's last and most fateful blunder, the failure to believe in the imminence of attack. Large parts of the Air Force were caught on the ground and destroyed in the first hours. General Kopets, of the air arm, committed suicide, having lost 600 aircraft while imposing negligible damage on the Luftwaffe, and others were arrested and shot—for example, General Chernykh, commander of an aviation division in the West-ern Front, who had lost seven-eighths of his command, and General Ptukhin, commander of the Kiev District Air Force.[35] In all, between June and August 1941, about 8,500 Soviet planes were lost.[36]

The Russians also had a great superiority in the number of tanks, 11,000 or 12,000 to 4,300,[37] and here design had not fallen behind. The original Soviet tank defeats can be attributed almost entirely to bad tactical methods and worse staff work.[38]

In his biography of Stalin, Isaac Deutscher mentions that imprisoned officers (like survivors of the purged opposition) were "brought out of concentration camps and assigned to important work."[39] This needs to be qualified.

Three hundred experienced officers were being held in the Lubyanka in October 1941 while at the front battalions were being commanded by lieutenants.[40] A Soviet account refers to two lists of "men inside" who were liquidated in October 1941 and July 1942, respectively, at times when Stalin "considered the situation to be desperate." The October executions included, on the twenty-eighth of that month, and after severe torture, Colonel-General Shtern; three successive Heads of the Soviet Air Force—Loktionov, Smushkevich, and Rychagov—and a number of other senior officers, mainly artillery or Air Force (with three of their wives). They were shot without trial, on an administrative order from Beria.[41]

Moreover, a Soviet Marshal makes it clear that while some of the officers brought out of camps and rehabilitated gave good service, in many cases the men concerned had been ruined: "the moral, and often also the physical sufferings undergone in the prisons and camps had killed in them all the will, initiative and decisiveness necessary for a military man." He gives the example of a general (a Civil War hero who had been wounded eleven times) who was arrested and sentenced in 1939 to twenty years' imprisonment without any charges being presented apart from the simple formula "enemy of the people." In a camp of "severe regime," he became a bath attendant and was given five years more for stealing a few underclothes. He was released in 1943 and made Chief of Staff of an Army, but his sufferings had broken his character.[42]

The "Horse Marshals" commanded in 1941—all three from the old First Cavalry Army. Timoshenko, in the center, proved reasonably competent, though he, too, suffered heavy losses. On the southern and northern flanks, Budenny and Voroshilov were merely catastrophic, especially the former. Stalin's other protégé, Marshal Kulik, came to grief in a clumsy operation before Leningrad. General Tyulenev became involved in the disasters in the Ukraine. All four were removed, but none was shot (except, apparently, Kulik, but only after the war). As late as 1957, Tyulenev was defending Stalin's Lwów operations of 1920, the old wound in the side of the Soviet Army which had festered so long and so desperately.

With superior Soviet resources and vastly lengthened German communications, it was still only possible to avoid total defeat for three reasons. First was the continued existence of further reserves. Second was Allied aid. Third, and most important, was the selection of better commanders. This could only be done in the course of the endless battles of the great retreat. The incompetents who had been put in to replace an adequate command in 1937 and 1938 were weeded out by disaster. A new and efficient command was created by natural selection in the struggle itself. It was purchased, in fact, with the lives of hundreds of thousands of Russian soldiers, with hundreds of miles of Russian territory, and with a great prolongation of the war.

Tukhachevsky's military doctrines were reinstated in the directives of the *Stavka* for the counter-offensive at Moscow in 1941. The turn had come. But, as a Soviet Army officer once remarked to the author, it was owing to the purges that the road to Berlin involved the long and painful detour via Stalingrad.

Far from the Great Purge eliminating a Soviet fifth column, it laid the foundation for one throughout the country in 1941 to 1945. This was the first war fought by Russia in which a large force of its citizens joined the other side.

Among the more brilliant younger officers who had survived the Purge was General Vlasov. In the maneuvers of 1940, his Ninety-ninth Division had proved the best. A tall, powerful man with a stentorian voice and a fine flow of invective, he was, Ilya Ehrenburg tells us, popular with the troops and in favor with Stalin, who could not recognize a genuine potential "traitor."[43]

Vlasov, when captured, organized the Russian troops on the German side, in spite of great difficulties with the Nazi authorities. His program shows that he was entirely out of sympathy with Nazism, and only concerned with a democratic Russia—he was comparable, in fact, to the Irish revolutionaries of 1916 who sought German support against Britain, or the Burmese and Indonesians of the Second World War who came to agreements (or tried to) with the Japanese against the West. As a Polish prisoner in Russia remarks more generally, of the expectations in the labor camps:

> I think with horror and shame of a Europe divided into two parts by the line of the Bug, on one side of which millions of Soviet slaves prayed for liberation by the armies of Hitler, and on the other millions of victims of German concentration camps awaited deliverance by the Red Army as their last hope.[44]

Ehrenburg's implication that Stalin was effective at dealing with *imaginary* traitors is sound. In 1941, he destroyed the last remnants of alternative political leadership. Antipov was apparently shot on 24 August. In September, the survivors of the 1938 Trial still in prison—Rakovsky, Pletnev, Bessonov—were retried and shot, as was Maria Spiridonova, the Social Revolutionary leader. In October, two more political figures, former members of the Central Committee Goloshchekin and Bulatov, were shot with the Shtern–Loktionov group of officers.

It seems that such acts were widespread. A Pole mentions, in the Yertsevo camp, two generals, four lawyers, two journalists, four students, a high-ranking NKVD officer, two former camp administrators, and five other assorted nobodies being selected and shot in June 1941.[45]

In fact, the outbreak of war was made the occasion for a general increase in police activity and power. Individual grudges were paid off, and potential malcontents dealt with—as with the case of the widow of the Deputy People's Commissar of the NKVD in the Ukraine, Brunivoy, who had died under interrogation. She was arrested in 1937 and severely interrogated, with permanent injury to the kidneys and several broken ribs. She was released in 1939 and rehabilitated. She believed throughout that everything that had happened was the result of hostile elements in the NKVD, and wrote to Stalin and Vyshinsky to this effect. At the beginning of 1941, the NKVD officials in her case were tried and sentenced to short terms of imprisonment for the use of torture. She felt herself completely justified. Two days after the German invasion, on 24 June 1941, she disappeared once more.[46]

When the Russians withdrew before the German advance, attempts were made to evacuate NKVD prisoners. Not only was their labor needed, but they were, of course, expected to sympathize with liberators, even German ones. The retreat was so disorganized, especially in the Ukraine, that evacuation was often impossible. Killings on a mass scale took place. These are reported from Minsk, Smolensk, Kiev, Kharkov, Dniepropetrovsk, Zaporozhe, and throughout the Baltic States. Near Nalchik, in the Caucasus, there was a molybdenum *kombinat* operated by the NKVD with convict labor. The prisoners were machine-gunned on the orders of the Kabardino-Balkar Republic's NKVD Commissar.[47] There is another report of a group of 29,000 prisoners accumulated in the Soviet retreat. When threatened with a further German advance and the abandonment of the camp at Olginskaya, the NKVD released all those serving less than five years and on 31 October 1941 shot the remainder.[48]

More generally, we are told that mass shootings took place in the camps in November 1941, when the Germans were at the gates of Moscow; in early June 1942; and in September 1942, when Stalingrad seemed about to fall.[49]

And yet the war was also an occasion for the relaxation of certain pressures. Religion, for example, was no longer persecuted. The public reversion to the old patriotism heartened at least the Russians. Above all, there was everywhere hope that once the war finished, things would become easier: the collective-farm system would be abolished; the Terror would end.

Even apart from the sanguine mood of the people, the war brought a feeling of release, as Pasternak's characters remark:

> You could volunteer for front-line service in a punitive battalion, and if you came out alive you were free. After that, attack after attack, mile after mile of electrified barbed wire, mines, mortars, month after month of artillery barrage. They called our company the death squad. It was practically wiped out. How and why I survived, I don't know. And yet—imagine—all that utter hell was nothing, it was bliss compared to the horrors of the concentration camp, and not because of the material conditions but for some other reason. . . .
>
> . . . It was not only felt by men in your position, in concentration camps, but by everyone without exception, at home and at the front, and they all took a deep breath and flung themselves into the furnace of this deadly, liberating struggle with real joy, with rapture.[50]

## THE CONSOLIDATION OF STALINISM

But in proposing the toast at the victory banquet in the Kremlin in June 1945, Stalin spoke significantly of the "ordinary" people as "cogs in the wheels of the great State apparatus."[51] His intention, completely fulfilled, was the restoration of the old machine.

In the same month, it was made clear that the confession–trial system had been abandoned after 1938 because it was, in the then circumstances, no longer necessary, rather than because Stalin thought it unconvincing or useless. Sixteen leaders of the Polish underground Government and Army were placed on trial. The accused were headed by General Okulicki (who had taken over command of the Home Army following the surrender of General Bor Komorowski after the heroic Warsaw Rising) and Jankowski, the chief delegate in Poland of the Polish

Government. (Okulicki, then underground, had been asked to contact the Soviet Command, with a guarantee of safe conduct, but was arrested when he presented himself.) They and thirteen of their fourteen co-defendants pleaded guilty to charges of anti-Soviet activity. This was the last of the great public trials to be held in Moscow. Its aim was to discredit the Polish Resistance and to bring pressure on the Polish Government-in-exile to enter into a coalition with the Communist-sponsored Lublin Committee, then ruling Soviet-occupied Poland, on terms adequate to secure Communist predominance.

Although no more such trials were seen in Moscow, all over Eastern Europe the old method was employed, under direct Russian control, first (as in Russia) against non-Party elements, such as the Agrarian leader Nikola Petkov in Bulgaria and Cardinal Mindszenty in Hungary, and later with Communist leaders like Laszlo Rajk in Hungary and Traicho Kostov in Bulgaria.

The system of public confession to entirely false charges came to an abrupt halt in December 1949* when Kostov, Secretary of the Central Committee of the Bulgarian Communist Party, retracted his confession in open court and maintained this stand throughout the trial.

Kostov refused to change his mind in spite of the moral indignation of the court and the tearful appeals of his co-accused. Kostov was perhaps in a stronger position than most accused in earlier trials; he must long ago have become accustomed to the idea of death and torture in pursuit of his political aims. His conduct under "fascist" interrogation had been held up as an example to the Bulgarian Communist Party. He was still close to the period of his illegal life and had not— as perhaps Bukharin and others had—gone to seed after years of comfort. Moreover, he knew that the bulk of his party was silently behind him, and thus, perhaps, did not feel quite the isolation of the Russian oppositionists. In addition, he seems to have been particularly tough; in him, typical Bulgarian mulishness and resilience were developed to a high degree.

In Russia itself, there were almost no death sentences for three or four years after the war, apart from those on a few leading Vlasovites. Genuine collaborators with the Germans had been rounded up by the tens of thousands, and merely sentenced to labor camps, where they were joined by the Soviet soldiers returned from internment in Germany. In 1946 and 1947, a great wave of arrests struck at Jews, Army officers, and others, and soon afterwards all those who had been released in the meanwhile were again arrested. This reversal of an act of "rotten liberalism" was given official authorization by a decree of 1950, said to have been adopted "on the initiative of Beria and Abakumov."[52]

The camps were at first more deadly than ever. Of those sentenced in 1945 and 1946, few survived by 1953. The famine of 1947[53] was, of course, reflected in the camp rations, with the usual results. By the beginning of the 1950s, however, a reform and rationalization of the forced-labor system led to a drop in the

---

*The last show "trial" of the Stalin period, that of Slansky and others in Prague in November 1952, was announced as public. But this time, no Westerners were admitted. (The Slansky Trial was conducted under Soviet supervision. At the political level, Mikoyan was sent by Stalin in November 1951 to arrange for the next batch of arrests. At the Secret Police level, the scenario was supervised by M. T. Likhachev, Deputy Head of the Section for Investigating Specially Important Cases—himself to be shot with Abakumov in 1954—and other MGB officials.) (*Nova mysl*, no. 7 [10 July 1968])

death rate. Since almost no releases took place (one Kotlas commandant is quoted as saying that he had been in his post for eight years and had released one prisoner),[54] the camp population mounted, by Stalin's death, to its probable maximum of approximately 12 million.

This general consolidation of the labor-camp system reflected a consolidation of the whole State and economy into the form Stalin had evidently been aiming at since his achievement of full power. In the new society, forced labor was evidently intended as permanent economic form.

What Stalin had established was essentially a command economy and a command society. This applied at every level. The collective farms, with their tractors, were producing less food than the ill-equipped *muzhik* of 1914. But they were now economically and politically under control. They could no longer hold the market to ransom.

And so it was the whole way up the scale. Everywhere, orders from the center were not merely binding in principle, but enforceable in practice. There was no significant area in which the important decisions could not be taken in the Kremlin.

The resemblances between this and "Socialism," as Marx and others had envisaged it, were, formally speaking, not negligible. The capitalist no longer existed. The "petit-bourgeois" individual peasant had gone. The State controlled the economy. For those who held that in a modern industrial society the absence of capitalists could only mean Socialism, this was enough. Defined more positively, Socialism had indeed always had one further characteristic—in effect, its very keystone. The control of the State by the proletariat had been regarded as the essential. In Stalin's Russia, there was no sign at all of any such thing. This point was got over by verbal means. All the phraseology of the Workers' State was employed, in every conceivable context.

One may wonder how far Stalin thought that he had produced the Socialism the securing of which he had, as a young man, been converted to. There was indeed no longer any "ruling class." Although Stalin created (and admitted he was creating) a large privileged stratum, it had no rights of ownership over the means of production. Every privilege was held, in the last analysis, at the whim of the ruler.

In this unitary system, politics as such had disappeared, except in the form of intrigue at the highest level for Stalin's favor. In a sense, this may sound paradoxical; there was more "political" agitation and propaganda in the press and on the radio, in factory speeches and official literature, than anywhere in the world. But it was totally passive. It consisted solely of the handing down of, and working up of enthusiasms for, the decisions of the General Secretary. A new generation of industrial managers had risen, competent in the techniques of administration, in which the threat of the forced-labor camp spurred on the directors, just as a piecework system drove the worker to his limits by the threat of hunger. The new industrialists—even those at the highest level, like Tevosyan, Malyshev, and Saburov—were little more than the unquestioning technicians of the new scheme of things.

The planning system, which had been quite chaotic in the 1930s, now settled into a new rationality; increases in productivity—at least in the heavy industrial production which was Stalin's main interest—at last became regular. The system had huge wastages and inefficiencies. Its planning was, in many fields, largely mythical. And the general unworkability of its distribution network was made up for by a large extralegal market. But, all in all, the economy Stalin had created was at least an operating reality. Its built-in wastages were not great enough to prevent achievement of its main aim—the continuing investment in industry of a high proportion of the national income. They were, however, great enough to hold the expansion bought at such sacrifice down to a level lower than that of various capitalist countries.

Detailed comparisons were in any case impossible to make, owing to the secrecy and distortion of the Soviet statistical system of the time. But what provided confidence to the Party elite, and gained the admiration of certain intellectuals abroad, was the more general fact that industry had been "created" in a fairly backward country. It was hoped that the method might be applicable in the really backward lands of the East.

But the old Russia had not been all that backward. It had already been the fourth industrial power before the Revolution. In the reign of Nicholas II, the railway network had doubled in length in ten years, and there had been a great upsurge in the mining and metal industries. As Lenin said:

> . . . The progress in the mining industry is more rapid in Russia than in Western Europe and even in North America. . . . In the last few years (1886–1896) the production of cast metal has tripled. . . . The development of capitalism in the younger countries is accelerated by the example and aid of the older.[55]

And the trend continued right up to 1914.

Since 1930, Stalin had enlarged the industrial base. But he had done so by very wasteful methods—far more wasteful economically, and in human suffering, than those of the original Industrial Revolution. He had not made the best use of his resources, solving the problem of rural overpopulation by removing precisely the most productive section of the peasantry, and wasting much of the original skilled engineering force by decimating it on false charges of sabotage. (It is true, indeed, that a high proportion of Russia's skill had been killed or had emigrated during the Revolution itself.) Even in 1929 it was reasonably clear, economically speaking, that milder measures could have produced equally good results, as they had in Meiji Japan, for example.

As long ago as Khrushchev's time, *Kommunist,* the main theoretical and political organ of the Central Committee, summed up the charges against Stalin's planning system. He personally interfered with the work of planning organizations, enforced arbitrary goals, and radically changed plans in a way that made whole sections of them meaningless. He thus inflicted lasting harm on the Soviet planning work and on the Soviet economy. Indeed (*Kommunist* went on), it was Stalin who was responsible for lasting troubles in the Soviet economy which, to cover up his personal guilt, he used to ascribe to difficulties allegedly inherent in the rapid growth of the economy. In particular, "arbitrary planning caused immense damage to agriculture which still suffers from the results of the cult of Stalin's personality."[56]

Few would now maintain that Stalin's method was the only, or the best, way available—even to a one-party regime—to attain the degree of increased industrialization actually realized. But in any case, the basic economic benefits obtained, or supposedly obtained, by the Stalin regime were already in hand before the Purge proper started. Economically, in fact, there is no doubt that the Purge was disadvantageous: it removed a high proportion of the most skilled industrial leaders, from Pyatakov down; and at the same time, the camps were filled from an already overstretched labor pool. The rationale was that not of economics, but of despotism. With all the incentives to attain, or at least claim, the opposite, economic advance admittedly slowed down in 1938 to 1940.[57]

The lesson might seem to be that the use of terror in conditions when it may seem to some degree economically effective is nevertheless not a good idea even economically. For it cannot simply be switched off. It builds up its own interests and institutions, its own cadres and habits of mind. Any good it may be (in this sense) at a particular moment is likely to be offset at a later stage when it is no longer applicable, but still applied.

But even if one were to accept the Stalin method as a whole, writing off later losses as the inevitable payment for earlier successes, other issues arise. Stalinism might be one way of attaining industrialization, just as cannibalism is one way of attaining a high-protein diet. The desirability of the result hardly seems to balance the objections.

Meanwhile, Stalin pervaded every sphere. In philosophy, for example, he was celebrated as a profound critic of Hegel, as the first to elucidate certain pronouncements of Aristotle, as the only man to bring out the full significance of Kant's theories. On the tercentenary of Spinoza's birth, *Pravda* had put in several quotations from Stalin, having nothing to do with Spinoza or even philosophy.[58]

At a Moscow conference of experts held in 1963, a historian complained that in the postwar period "it was impossible frankly to share one's thoughts and doubts even with one's comrades, for fear of placing them in a difficult position."[59] Academician Evgeni M. Zhukov spoke of the "psychological trauma" suffered by historians who were "systematically imbued with the idea that theoretically sound works could only be written by a select *vozhd* and that profound thoughts and fresh deeds could proceed only from him." Thus "for almost twenty years—the period of the formation of the consciousness of a whole generation—independent creative thought by 'ordinary mortals' in the sphere of theory was placed in doubt."

A doctor, denouncing the effect on Soviet medicine, summed up:

> The main harm caused to science by the cult of the personality lay in the proclamation of a single opinion . . . "an inexhaustible fount of wisdom" as the supreme truth. . . . It is not accidental that in the course of discussions of concrete scientific problems, one concept or another was not verified by the experiments of its proposers but by references to scientific heritage, by mere quotation from the works of others.[60]

In the even more sensitive field of economics, independent thought was naturally treated with greater rigor. The Director of the Institute of Economics of the USSR Academy of Sciences remarked in 1962:

> Many Communists can still remember the havoc wreaked in the forties on the journal *Problems of Economics* for publishing an article by Professor Kubanin. In this article

he expressed the completely correct thought that we were lagging behind America in labor productivity in agriculture. The great scholar and major expert on the economics of agriculture paid for this correct thought with his life, while the journal was closed for its "heresy."[61]

The effect of the Stalinist attitude at the lower level is adumbrated by the First Secretary of the Georgian Communist Party, Mgeladze, who summoned workers from the Institute of Marxism-Leninism and the Institute of History of the Georgian Academy of Science and had them write a book on the history of the Party in Transcaucasia. When he was given the result, he announced, "I, as the author, like it. But be sure if there are any mistakes in it, you, dear friends, will all go to prison."[62]

Again, Stalin happened to say in an aside that the Azerbaijanis were obviously descended from the Medes. Although there is no basis for such a notion, it became established doctrine among the historians. Linguists spent fifteen years trying to find Median words in Azeri. "Eventually thirty-five dubious Median words were found, although the Median language itself is mythical."[63]

These few examples—which omit, for instance, the major scandal of Lysenkoism in Soviet biology—must serve as a general impression of the effect of Stalin's new regime on the intellect.

In the less stormy atmosphere of the post-Yezhov years, moreover, more careful attention could be paid to thought-crime and face-crime. An authoritative instruction, typical of many, ran:

> One must not content oneself with merely paying attention to *what* is being said, for that may well be in complete harmony with the Party program. One must pay attention also to the *manner*—to the sincerity, for example, with which a schoolmistress recites a poem the authorities regard as doubtful, or the pleasure revealed by a critic who goes into detail about a play he professes to condemn.[64]

The last years of Stalin's life saw a major, though unpublicized, series of purges. In 1949–1950 came a new "Leningrad Case." Voznesensky, member of the Politburo; A. A. Kuznetsov, Secretary of the Central Committee; and other leaders were shot. About 3,000 senior Party members in Leningrad were arrested, and treated with particular brutality, many of them being shot; and there were similar purges elsewhere. In 1952 and 1953, leading Jewish intellectuals perished by the hundred, and a wave of arrests culminated in the Doctors' Plot, with Stalin ordering the investigators, "Beat, beat and beat again," as Khrushchev tells us.

Stalin's execution of the main Yiddish writers in the "Crimean Affair" of 1952 is among the most extraordinary of all State acts. As Manès Sperber has said, these were Communists who had submitted to all the imperatives of the regime and of Stalin. "Like the others, they had betrayed their friends and their brothers every time that fidelity to the Party demanded it; but they were to die because they remained incapable of betraying their language and their literature."

Not long before Stalin died, *Pravda,* by an extraordinary exception, published an article by Herbert Morrison, the British Foreign Secretary.[65] It calmly but cogently set forth democratic objections to the Soviet system. An answer appeared at once, saying that Morrison was asking for freedom of speech for those it would be wrong to give it to—"the criminals who . . . killed . . . Kirov." It now turns out that it was precisely those people, and no others, who had freedom of speech.

The Stalinist version of the events of the Purge was, of course, the only one permitted in Russia itself. Many people there knew at first hand that this version was false, but anyone susceptible of indoctrination by terror or by sheer pressure of propaganda fell in with the official line.

Abroad, things were different. The West was not forced to accept the Stalinist version. Freedom of judgment and freedom of information prevailed, then as now. This did not prevent an extraordinary degree of success for the official Communist view.

## FOREIGN MISAPPREHENSIONS

> *If thou canst not realize the Ideal thou shalt at least*
> *idealize the Real.*
>
> Calverley

During the Purges, a young English Communist, John Cornford, published a poem:

SERGEI MIRONOVICH KIROV
(Assassinated in Leningrad, December 1934)

Nothing is ever certain, nothing is ever safe,
To-day is overturning yesterday's settled good.
Everything dying keeps a hungry grip on life.
Nothing is ever born without screaming and blood.

Understand the weapon, understand the wound:
What shapeless past was hammered to action by his deeds,
Only in constant action was his constant certainty found.
He will throw a longer shadow as time recedes.[66]

Cornford, with a first-class record at Cambridge University, went to Spain in 1936 and was killed near Córdoba, with the International Brigade, at the end of that year. There can hardly be a better illustration of the way in which the generous impulse in Western Communism could be befouled by Stalinism. The young man who gave his life in the cause of a supposed revolutionary humanism had been led by his allegiances to produce what is little more than a versification of Stalin's theory that the class struggle grows more bitter as the opponents of Communism become weaker, using as its text a crime allegedly committed by counter-revolutionaries, but actually by Stalin himself.

Time having, as Cornford suggests, receded, what has become plain is that not even high intelligence and a sensitive spirit are of any help once the facts of a situation are deduced from a political theory, rather than vice versa.

Although Cornford's case is instructive, and not only as regards his own time, he was not among those actively responsible for propagating and compounding the falsehood; he was, rather, at the receiving end. Between those in the West who accepted the Stalinist version of events and those who originally issued that version, there stood a number of journalists, ambassadors, lawyers, and students of Russia, whose direct and admitted duty it was to study the facts in detail and pronounce on them. Not every Western Communist, or every left-wing intellectual, could be expected to read with a critical eye the official reports of the Great Trials. Those who did, or who had actually attended them, and who from incompetence and blind (or cynical) partisanship transmitted a false analysis to the larger audience, may reasonably be thought somewhat blameworthy. A few examples of inadequate skepticism have already been noted.

Any recorder of these events must be tempted to compile a vast *sottisier* of misjudgments made by his compatriots and others in the West. It is scarcely a point that should be ignored, but it has been thought best to give no more than a few examples of the type of error which was made by many with high claims to clear judgment, moral enlightenment, and political knowledge. The contemporary effect on world opinion was an important aspect of the whole Purge operation. Stalin had himself considered it when he ordered the Zinoviev Trial: "He is not impressed by the argument that public opinion in Western Europe must be taken into consideration. To all such arguments he replies contemptuously: 'Never mind, they'll swallow it.' "[67]

The fact that so many did "swallow" it was thus certainly a factor in making the whole Purge possible. The trials, in particular, would have carried little weight unless validated by some foreign, and so "independent," commentators.

Foreign intervention had, as late as the mid-1930s, been able to secure certain results, particularly in view of Stalin's post-1935 policy of alliances. For example, in June 1935, the International Congress of Writers for the Defense of Culture was held in Paris. It was intended as a large-scale Popular Front occasion. Magdalene Paz insisted on raising the case of Victor Serge, arrested in 1932. After an uproar, in which she was supported by Salvemini and Gide, she was allowed to speak. The Soviet delegation consisted of Pasternak, Nikolai Tikhonov, Ilya Ehrenburg, Mikhail Koltsov, and the playwright Kirshon—the two last to perish shortly. Apart from Pasternak, these Soviet delegates resisted the debate strenuously and accused Serge of complicity in the Kirov murder, which had taken place two years after his arrest.[68] Afterward, Gide went and conveyed the writers' displeasure to the Soviet Ambassador.

Serge was released at the end of the year. This is an almost unique occasion on which foreign opinion was able to influence Stalin. It seems to show, however, that if articulate Western opinion had condemned the Zinoviev Trial with sufficient unanimity and force, it is conceivable that Stalin might, in this Popular Front period, have acted at least slightly less ruthlessly. In fact, those who "swallowed" the trials can hardly be acquitted of a certain degree of complicity in the continuation and exacerbation of the torture and execution of innocent men.

The facts that were concealed from (or by) progressive opinion in the West were twofold: the existence and extent of the mass slaughter and imprisonment; and the inconsistency and falsehood of the public trials.

From the start, there were three basic objections to the evidence in the trials. First, the alleged plots were totally out of character with the accused leaders, who had always opposed individual assassination, and were now, moreover, charged also with having been enemy agents throughout their careers. Second, the allegations were often inherently absurd—like the charge against Zelensky that he had put nails into the masses' butter with a view to undermining Soviet health. Third, some of the stories told in court were of events abroad, which could be checked; these contained demonstrable falsehoods—a meeting at a nonexistent hotel in Copenhagen, a landing at a Norwegian airfield during a month when no landings had taken place.

In the West, the facts were readily available. Hundreds of articles and books were published in which all these points were clearly and flatly demonstrated. Trotsky, the one accused at liberty, exposed the frame-up with incisive skill. The distinguished Commission headed by Professor Dewey examined the whole evidence in the most judicious and meticulous fashion, and published its findings. It was not a question of political argument, properly speaking, but of facts. Yet in spite of everything, these went unheard among large sections of well-informed people. There was no reasonable excuse for believing the Stalinist story. The excuses which can be advanced are irrational, though often couched in the formulas of intensive rationalization.

The Communist Parties everywhere simply transmitted the Soviet line. Communist intellectuals, some of them better informed about Soviet conditions and more inclined to frame their own answers, reacted variously. There were those who simply repressed the difficult material. Stephen Spender quotes an English Communist friend, when asked what he thought of the trials, as replying, "What trials? I have given up thinking about such things long ago." [69]

More representative was the attitude of Bertolt Brecht, who remarked to Sidney Hook at the time of the first trials, "The more innocent they are, the more they deserve to die." [70] Meanwhile, he had written a play about Nazi Germany: a father and mother are worried because friends of theirs are under investigation, and they fear the block warden. The husband, a teacher, does not know if they have anything against him at the school. "I am ready to teach whatever they want me to teach. But what do they want me to teach? If only I were sure of that." They worry about whether to put Hitler's picture in a more prominent position, or whether that will look like a confession of guilt.

> *Wife:* But there's nothing against you, is there?
>
> *Husband:* There's something against everybody. Everybody is suspected. It's enough if someone expresses any suspicion of you, to make you a suspected person.

And later one remarks, "Since when have they needed witnesses?" [71]

But the main theme of the play—taken as completely destroying the moral basis of Nazism—is the father's and mother's fear that their schoolboy son may have denounced them. This was at a time when, as Brecht evidently knew, the same sort of thing was going on in the Soviet Union. In fact, there was a widely praised and celebrated Soviet example of sons denouncing their parents. During collectivization, Pavlik Morozov, leader of his village group of young Communist "Pioneers" who were acting as auxiliaries in the attack on the peasantry, "unmasked" his father—who had previously been president of the village soviet but had "fallen under the influence of kulak relations." The father was shot, and on 3 September 1932 a group of peasants, including the boy's uncle, in turn killed the son, at the age of fourteen—thus, as it were, anticipating Stalin's age limit for executions. All the killers were themselves executed, and young Morozov became, until very recently, a great hero of the Komsomol. The Palace of Culture of the Red Pioneers in Moscow was named after him.[72] Even in the Khrushchev period, the Soviet press celebrated the "sacred and dear" Pavlik Morozov Museum in his own village: "In this timbered house was held the court at which Pavlik unmasked his father who had sheltered the kulaks. Here are reliquaries dear to the heart of every inhabitant of Gerasimovka."[73]

In Brecht's own case, it is noteworthy that a close connection, his former mistress the actress Carola Neher (who had played the lead in the *Dreigroschenoper*), was arrested in Russia and never seen again.

As Hubert Luthy has argued, Brecht himself was not attracted to Communism as part of the "Workers' Movement, which he had never known, but by a deep urge for a total authority, a total submission to a total power, the new Byzantine State Church—immutable, hierarchical, founded on the infallibility of the leader."[74] His political and semipolitical work invariably shows this pleasure at rolling in the muck for the sake of the idea. It seems to represent an extreme and degenerate version of Pyatakov's view of the Party.

It is perhaps natural that committed Communists should in principle have accepted and propagated untruths, in the old tradition of "pious fraud." But curiously enough, such a consideration seems partially to apply also to many elements of the non-Communist Left. Not in such a clear-cut manner, not so fraudulently or so piously, they yet tended to temper criticism, to put the best complexion on, or ignore, refractory events.

There was, indeed, much resistance among the tougher-minded Left. Edmund Wilson, reading the charges against Zinoviev and Kamenev while still in Russia, saw at once that they were faked. In the United States, the Dewey Commission had as its lawyer John F. Finerty, who had appeared for the defense in the Mooney and Sacco–Vanzetti trials. The Liberal *Manchester Guardian* was the strongest and most effective of British exposers of the trials. The orthodox Labour Party press did the same; that party also put out Frederick Adler's forthright and accurate pamphlet on the subject. And on the extreme Left, some of the most effective exposure was done by Emrys Hughes in the Scottish *Forward*. In fact, some Leftists (and not only Trotskyists and so on, who had a direct partisan interest) were perfectly clear-headed about the matter, while some people opposed to the principles of Communism accepted the official versions.

But on the whole, in the atmosphere of the late 1930s, fascism was the enemy, and a partial logic repressed or rejected any criticism of its supposed main enemy, the USSR. The Western capitals thronged with "the thousands of painters and writers and doctors and lawyers and debutantes chanting a diluted version of the Stalinist line."[75]

Appeals in favor of the trials were made by various Western writers, Feuchtwanger, Barbusse—even the sensitive Gandhi fan, Romain Rolland. In the United States, a manifesto attacking the Dewey Commission was signed by a number of authors, poets, professors, and artists—Theodore Dreiser, Granville Hicks,* Corliss Lamont, and others.

---

*Hicks later made the *amende honorable*.

Speaking of the attitude of many British intellectuals to the trials, Julian Symons remarks on the "monstrous incongruities that they willingly swallowed." He adds: "But they had not been deceived. In relation to the Soviet Union they had deceived themselves, and in the end one has to pay for such self-deceits."[76]

In the non-Communist, Popular Front–style Left, there were signs of unease. Britain's leading journal of the intellectual Left, the *New Statesman,* found the first trial "unconvincing," yet added, "We do not deny . . . that the confessions may have contained a substratum of truth." On the 1937 Trial, it said, "Few would now maintain that all or any of them were completely innocent." On the 1938 Trial, which it claimed was "undoubtedly very popular in the U.S.S.R.," it said that the confessions remained baffling, "whether we regard them as true or false," but that it could be concluded that "there had undoubtedly been much plotting in the U.S.S.R."—curiously combining a sense of the incredibility of the charges with a willingness to believe them.

One of the achievements of Stalinism was, in effect, that in spite of the fact that plenty of information was available contradicting the official picture, it was possible to impose the latter upon journalists, sociologists, and other visitors by methods which, on the face of it, seem crude and obvious, but which worked splendidly. Tourists visited Russia on a bigger scale in the Yezhov period than ever before. They saw nothing. The nighttime arrests, the torture chambers of the Lefortovo and the crowded cells of the Butyrka, the millions of prisoners cold and hungry in the great camps of the north were all hidden from them. The only dramatic scenes were the three great public trials. And these, too, were strictly controlled and did not depart much from a prepared script.

For if access to Russia was extensive, it was also imperfect. The Soviet Government at this time maintained its model prison at Bolshevo, which many foreign visitors were shown. The Webbs give it a laudatory account,[77] and it had also attracted favorable comment from D. N. Pritt, Harold Laski, and many others. One friendly visitor had the opportunity of gaining a rather broader view: Jerzy Gliksman, who, as a progressive member of the Warsaw City Council before the war, visited and reported enthusiastically on Bolshevo and the new humanitarian methods of criminology. A few years later, he found himself in camps more representative of Soviet penal practice.[78]

Other prisoners report occasionally passing through the model blocks—known to prisoners as "Intourist Prisons"—which were shown to foreign sociologists and journalists. Herling,[79] while in an ordinary cell in the Leningrad Transit Prison (which he describes as better than usual, with only seventy prisoners in a cell intended for twenty), was taken by chance through a model wing—evidently that described by Lenka von Koerber in her enthusiastic book about the Soviet prison system, *Soviet Russia Fights Crime.*

On the other end of the judicial process, the trials themselves, we have already quoted one or two Western reports. Of others, that of the eminent British pro-Communist lawyer Pritt, who attended the Zinoviev Trial, is especially interesting, since in his autobiography published in 1966, long after the Khrushchev revelations, he wrote that he *still* had "a Socialist belief that a Socialist state would not try people unless there was a strong case against them." He added, "What the Soviet views are now . . . I don't know."[80]

Every journalist Pritt spoke to thought the trial fair, and, he remarks, "certainly every foreign observer thought the same." This is not so, of course, but the fact that even considerable partisanship could suggest it is presumably a sign that far too many did think so. One can certainly detect in some of the journalists, in particular, a certain professional vanity—that *they* could be duped was inconceivable. Then, once committed, a sort of blindness came over them.

Walter Duranty of the *New York Times* spoke Russian, had been in Russia for years, and knew some of the accused. For years, he had built a disgraceful career on consciously misleading an important section of American opinion. He now described Ulrikh as "a hard judge but a just one"; said, "No-one who heard Pyatakof or Muralof could doubt for a moment that what they said was true"; and concluded, "The future historian will probably accept the Stalinist version."[81] He argued that Muralov and Pyatakov were so "impervious to pressure" that their confessions could not have been false, and found one of the strongest proofs of Pyatakov's guilt to be the fact that he was "the brains of heavy industry" and therefore Stalin would not have killed him unless his crimes were beyond pardon. As we have seen, this sort of common sense did not, in fact, apply.

Duranty's argument about Gamarnik's suicide is another example of the muddled advocacy thought acceptable in the period: "His suicide . . . proves that he had been engaged in some deal with the Germans."[82] Of the other military conspirators, Duranty argued that "they confessed" without long preparation, and this was an indication of the truth of the charges, while it also showed that confession was not necessarily the product of long interrogation. But of course the evidence that the Generals had "confessed" was simply that Stalin's press said they had done so! The trial was not public.

Professor Owen Lattimore was another noted apologist for the Stalin and similar regimes. In his *Pacific Affairs,* he wrote of Yezhov: "As to the suggestion that the new head of the secret service is likely to abuse his power just as Yagoda did, it is obvious that the publicity given in the Soviet Union itself to Yagoda's turpitude is a safeguard against any such thing"; and he described the trials themselves as a triumph for democracy on the grounds that they could only "give the ordinary citizen more courage to protest, loudly, whenever he finds himself being victimized by 'someone in the Party' or 'someone in the Government.' That sounds to me like democracy."[83]

Not only Leftists and journalists wrote this sort of thing. The American Ambassador Joseph Davies reported to the Secretary of State that there was "proof . . . beyond reasonable doubt to justify the verdict of guilty of treason."[84]

During wartime lectures, Davies used to get a laugh, which he greatly appreciated, to his answer to questions about fifth columnists in Russia: "There aren't any, they shot them all." Both parts of this piece of gallows wit are untrue. The men shot were not fifth columnists. And fifth columnists rose by the thousand, even in spite of the repulsive policies of the Germans. Most of them were, moreover, people who would never, under a moderately popular regime, have thought of going over to the enemy. Stalin's policies created a vast pool of potential treason which, had the Nazis not been foolish as well as foul, might well have decided the war.

This sort of reporting is more or less ephemeral. We should perhaps take more serious and studious treatments as still more reprehensible. Scholars and

Russian experts were duped to the same degree as journalists and lawyers. When Beatrice and Sidney Webb examined Soviet matters, and put their conclusions into their vast tome *Soviet Communism: A New Civilization,* the Constitution much impressed them. So did the constitutions and the statutes of the Party, the trade unions, the consumer cooperatives, the collective farms. And, indeed, if these documents had ever been put into operation, they might have produced the society the Webbs thought they saw. It doubtless never occurred to the Webbs, brought up in Britain, that official documents do not necessarily bear much relation to fact. As it is, their book is to be regarded less as an account of a real country than as a successor to the works of Sir Thomas More, Campanella, Plato, Harrington, and William Morris. It was unfortunate—and this, of course, applied not only to the Webbs—that the perfectly natural human activity of constructing Utopias should, through various misunderstandings, have been projected on to a real community with so little claim to it.

The Webbs assert flatly that Kirov's assassin "was discovered to have secret connections with conspiratorial circles of ever-widening range." On the executions immediately following the assassination, they say that those shot did not seem to have been proven accomplices in the assassination "or the conspiracies associated therewith," but that they were "undoubtedly guilty of illegal entry and inexcusably bearing arms and bombs."[85] "Undoubtedly" seems a strong word, when the sole evidence was a brief announcement to that effect in the Soviet press.

They describe the Moscow trials as "a tragic hangover from the violence of the revolution and the civil war."[86] Of course, there is a sense in which all these events are connected, but the image does not seem appropriate as it stands. A hangover which suddenly reaches its climax sixteen years after the events supposed to have caused it requires some special explanation.

The Webbs comment, truly though not perhaps in the sense in which they meant it, that the trials produced some international revulsion against the Soviet Union and that therefore "the Soviet Government must have had strong grounds for the action which has involved such unwelcome consequences." Claiming to attempt "a detached and philosophic interpretation" of the trials, they say that the whole manner of the confessions was convincing, and that "careful perusal of the full reports of the proceedings" left them with the same impression, though they express a reservation about Trotsky.[87]

They explain the confessions as due to Russian prisoners

behaving naturally and sensibly, as Englishmen would were they not virtually compelled by their highly artificial legal system to go through a routine which is useful to the accused only when there is some doubt as to the facts or as to the guilt or innocence of the conduct in question.[88]

This curious view of the comparability of the Soviet and British legal systems was shared by Professor Harold Laski, who noted that "basically I did not observe much difference between the general character of a trial in Russia and in this country." In Vyshinsky, with whom he had a long discussion, he found "a man whose passion was law reform. . . . He was doing what an ideal Minister of Justice would do if we had such a person in Great Britain—forcing his colleagues to consider what is meant by actual experience of the law in action." [89] This was indeed published before Vyshinsky's great days. But trials had already taken place in Russia, and with Vyshinsky's active participation, which might have produced qualms.

Another serious student of Russia (and of agriculture in particular) was Sir John Maynard, from whom it had been possible to hide the Ukrainian famine. On the trials, he remarked, "However much falsity of detail there may be, the Trials of the leading personages in 1936–38 were substantially justified by facts: and were probably the means of saving the U.S.S.R. from an attempted revolution which would have given to the Nazi Government an earlier opportunity." [90]

Sir Bernard Pares, a serious historian and long-established expert on all things Russian, was equally duped. The later editions of Pares's *History of Russia* cover the period to the end of the Second World War. Dealing with the Purges, he permits himself to say, "Nearly all admitted having conspired against the life of Stalin and others, and on this point it is not necessary to doubt them. . . . Radek, who spoke with consummate lucidity, gave what is probably a true picture." [91] On the Tukhachevsky case—of which, it may be remembered, no evidence whatever was made public—he merely points out that the Russian and German General Staffs had earlier been in contact, and therefore "it is by no means unlikely that there was a plot." A generation earlier, the conscience of the civilized world could be aroused by the false condemnation to imprisonment of a single French captain for a crime which had actually been committed, though not by him. The Soviet equivalent of the Dreyfus Case involved the execution of thousands of officers, from Marshals and Admirals down, on charges which were totally imaginary. It called forth instead, and not from Pares alone, comments like the above!

Of the trials in general, Pares concludes, "The plea that Stalin acted first to disrupt a potential fifth column . . . is by no means unwarranted." Elsewhere he remarks that "the bulky verbatim reports were in any case impressive" [92]—perhaps the most fatuous of all comments, and the fine fruit, as Walter Laqueur has said, "of fifty years of study of Russian history, the Russian people, its country, its language."

As an old authority on Russia, Pares had been opposed to the Soviet Government and revised his attitude in view of the Nazi threat. "Towards the end of 1935," his son comments, "my father set foot in Russia once more and any remaining doubts vanished at once. He had not left the Moscow railway station before his mind was flooded with the realization that the Bolsheviks were, after all, Russia." [93] This reliance on personal revelation and intuition, inadequately related to the real situation, is surely inappropriate and egocentric—a point worth making when we read similar accounts from more recently totalitarianized lands.

What happened in Russia under Stalin could not be understood or estimated in any commonsensical fashion, if by common sense we mean notions that sound reasonable and natural to the democratic Westerner. Many of the misunderstandings which appeared in Britain and America during the Great Trials were due to prejudice—not necessarily to prejudice in favor of the Soviet regime or of Stalin, but at least prejudice in regard to certain events or interpretations of them as inherently unlikely. The Great Trials were, and it should have been plain at the time, nothing but large-scale frame-ups. But it was extraordinarily difficult for many in the West to credit this, to believe that a State could really perpetrate on a vast scale such a cheap and third-rate system of falsehood. Bernard Shaw typically remarked, "I find it just as hard to believe that [Stalin] is a vulgar gangster as that Trotsky is an assassin." [94] Presumably, he would not have been surprised at some such events in quite highly organized societies like Imperial Rome or Renaissance Florence. But the Soviet State appeared to have a certain impersonality, and not obviously to lend itself to actions determined not so much by political ideas as by the overt personal plotting which had afflicted those earlier regimes.

There was another powerful factor. Both opponents of and sympathizers with the Russian Revolution thought of the Communists as a group of "dedicated" (or "fanatical") men whose faults or virtues were at any rate incompatible with common crime—something like the Jesuits of the Counter-Reformation. England has had little recent experience of revolutionary movements, and this idea persists. It is the type of general notion which the uninformed are likely to assume simply out of ignorance, and it has not lost its obscuring power to this day.

Men like Stalin, Kaganovich, Voroshilov, Molotov, and Yagoda had been members of the underground Bolshevik Party in the time of its illegal struggle against Tsardom. Whatever their faults, they had thus established at least enough bona fides to exempt them from the suspicion that they did in fact behave as they are now known to have done. Even now, doubtless, there are those in the West who find it hard to swallow the notion of the top leaders of the Soviet Communist Party writing obscene and brutal comments on the appeals for mercy of the men they knew to be totally innocent. The mistake was, in fact, in the idea held in this country about revolutionary movements. In practice, they not only are joined by simon-pure idealists, but also consist of a hodgepodge of members in whom the idealist component is accompanied by all sorts of motivations—vanity, power seeking, and mere freakishness.

Perhaps the commonest reaction was to believe that the case against the accused in the trials was exaggerated, rather than false in every respect. This formula enabled those who subscribed to it to strike what they felt to be a decent commonsensical balance. In fact, it was simply a mediocre compromise between truth and falsehood, between right and wrong.

And the trials were at least directed against rivals of Stalin. The idea that Stalin had himself organized the murder of Kirov, on the face of it his closest ally and supporter—a murder in strictly criminal style—would have been rejected as absurd. When it was suggested by a few ex-oppositionists and defectors, who knew more about the circumstances than most people, it was hardly thought worth discussing.

Such attitudes showed a basic misunderstanding of the range of political possibility in a nondemocratic culture. More particularly, they showed a failure to grasp Soviet circumstances and, above all, a misjudgment about Stalin personally. For Stalin's political genius consisted precisely in this: he recognized no limitations, either moral or intellectual, in his methods of securing power.

His calculation about the effect abroad was on the whole sound. It is true that the frame-ups were clumsy fabrications. It is also true that Stalin did not in fact silence everyone who knew anything about them. But he did not have to. The notion that things would have been very different if the frame-ups had been seamlessly perfect and if everyone who had known the truth had instantly been shot is a superficial one. Stalin had a clearer idea of the state of the public mind both in Russia and in the West. It is only too plain that he was right. Those who were prepared to believe his story believed it regardless of its peripheral faults, and rejected accounts put out by people who had had access to the correct information.

Thus a State prepared flatly to deny its own malpractices, and to prevent open access to the facts, could successfully persuade many people abroad, even in spite of a large and growing body of first-hand evidence from those who had actually experienced the Terror. This is a lesson that has clearly been learned by similar regimes in other parts of the world, and is still the basic principle of much misinformation that appears in the West.

The trials were overt acts. The other acts of the Purge were never announced. In particular, the size and nature of the labor-camp system only became known in the West through defectors, some of them former inmates. After the Poles in Russia were released in 1941 and 1942, thousands of accounts were available for checking, and dozens of first-hand descriptions were readily available in print. By 1948, as we have said, a very full analysis of the system listing hundreds of camps, together with reproductions of camp documents, was published by David J. Dallin and Boris I. Nicolaevsky.[95] The United Kingdom delegation to the United Nations was able to circulate the Corrective Labor Codex of the RSFSR; free trade-union bodies produced their own analyses.

The evidence was as complete and as consistent as it could conceivably be. It was widely rejected. Jean-Paul Sartre even defended the proposition that the evidence about the Soviet forced-labor-camp system should be ignored, even if true, on the grounds that otherwise the French proletariat might be thrown into despair. Why the labor-camp population should be sacrificed to the (rather smaller) membership of the CGT was not clear; nor, indeed, was it ever made plain why the views of the French proletariat, one of the few that has ever come largely under Communist influence, should prevail in world affairs any more than those of the anti-Communist British and American and German proletariats. Nor is it obvious at first sight why falsehood should demand the allegiance even of the intelligentsia. This sort of intellectual and ethical attitude might be treated as a passing aberration, a curiosity of history, and one might have thought that anyone holding it would have forfeited any public standing as a moral arbiter, at least in this sort of sphere. But this does not seem to have been the case, and if only for that reason is worth referring to.

During the 1940s and 1950s, there were many attempts to silence or discredit the evidence of men who had been in the camps, or otherwise given information about the Purge. This was particularly the case in France. In 1950, the writer David Rousset, of the Commission Internationale Contre la Régime Concentrationnaire, sued the Communist weekly *Les Lettres françaises* for libel. It had alleged that he had falsified a quotation from the Soviet penal code. As often in French political cases, themes much broader than the point supposedly at issue were developed. And, against a venomous defense by Communist lawyers, the facts of the forced-labor system were publicly established. One of the witnesses was Alexander Weissberg. An Austrian, a Jew, and (up to the time of his period in a Soviet prison) a Communist, he was continually subjected to abuse by the defense counsel in the style, "It turns my stomach to see a German testifying before a French court." The campaign to smear the witness did not work well in this instance, as he was able to produce an appeal which had been sent at the time of his imprisonment to the Soviet authorities testifying to his character and to his loyal service to the Soviet Union, and had been signed by a number of leading physicists, including the Communist Joliot-Curie.

The most useful and interesting *I Chose Freedom* by Victor Kravchenko was similarly smeared in one of the most thorough and vicious campaigns of the time. Older readers will probably recall the title with a vague feeling of unease, or hostility, induced by these methods.* Kravchenko, too, became involved in a court case in France, and in this instance the Russians sent witnesses to oppose him, while the French Communist Party mobilized a powerful legal and extralegal team.

The French Communist *Les Lettres françaises* had published an article supposedly by an American journalist called Sim Thomas, who had allegedly claimed that a friend of his in the OSS had admitted that Kravchenko's book was faked by that organization. Thomas was never produced, and it was later revealed by the editor concerned that he never existed. The trial proved a disaster to the Communists, though the French literary men concerned invariably countered facts supported by an impressive array of eyewitnesses by emotional appeals about the Battle of Stalingrad. They also put forward, to refute men who had actually been in labor camps and had otherwise suffered, witnesses such as the Dean of Canterbury and Konni Zilliacus, who found themselves able to assert that full, or at least admirable, liberty prevailed in the Soviet Union. The Soviet Government also sent a number of witnesses, but they proved unused to hostile cross-questioning, and were on the whole disastrous.

For example, the Soviet witness Vassilenko, who had been an official in the Ukraine during the Purges, answered questions about the period:

> *Izard:* What became of the following members of the Politburo who were in office before the purges in the Ukraine: Kossior?
>
> *Vassilenko:* I don't know him.
>
> *Izard:* Zatonsky?
>
> *Vassilenko:* I don't recall that name.
>
> *Izard:* They were the members of the Government of the Ukraine when you were working there. Balitsky?
>
> *Vassilenko:* I don't recall that name.
>
> *Izard:* Petrovsky?
>
> *Vassilenko:* He's working in Moscow.
>
> *Izard:* He wasn't purged?

*The obituary of Victor Kravchenko in *The Times* of 26 January 1966 was an extraordinary example of the carrying forward of sentiments common in the 1940s. Ignoring the question of the truth of his book (long since established) and the falsehood of the libels against him (established even at the time by the court), it represented it all as a reprehensible "Cold War" action.

*Vassilenko:* No.

    *Izard:* Khatayevich?

*Vassilenko:* I don't know where he is.

    *Izard:* Naturally! Lyubchenko?

*Vassilenko:* I don't recall that name.

    *Izard:* Disappeared! Sukhomlin?

*Vassilenko:* I don't recall that name.

    *Izard:* Yakir?

*Vassilenko:* I don't know.[96]

It will be seen that Vassilenko, under pressure, seems to have forgotten that the deaths in disgrace of both Yakir and Lyubchenko had been publicly announced. He was then asked what had happened to the four Secretaries of his own local provincial Party, and "did not know." Although himself a leading industrialist in the area, when asked about fifteen of the main managers and engineers, he denied knowing anything about what had happened to ten of them (two had died natural deaths). Unfortunately, when pressed about the missing ten, he snarled back, "Why do you make yourself the defender of people like them?"[97] a remark not compatible with ignorance of their fate. This public illustration of the official Soviet mind at work is of interest far beyond the particular context of the trial.

Kravchenko won his case, and won it flatly and clearly, as the non-Communist press of the West agreed. Much credit went to his lawyer, the Resistance hero and former Socialist deputy Maître Izard, who had himself been a prisoner of the Gestapo. But in the main, the result depended on the chance that Kravchenko was of quick intelligence, capable of coping with skilled French lawyers. And even with his victory, as the details began to be forgotten, the mud was again picked up, was flung, and stuck. As for Paris intellectuals without any knowledge of Russia, they had a sound safety mechanism: "All they had to know was that Kravchenko was opposed to the Soviet system. This proved he was wrong."[98]

Thirty years later, the *Les Lettres françaises* editor responsible, Claude Morgan, admitted in his autobiography, *Don Quichotte et les autres* that "Kravchenko was right." He said that after Kravchenko's death, he had wished "to pay him homage, but it was as yet too early. . . ."

Even when the existence of camps was admitted, they were described as of a most humane and reformatory nature. Pat Sloan, the British Communist chiefly concerned with cultural liaison with the USSR, wrote:

> Compared with the significance of that term in Britain, Soviet imprisonment stands out as an almost enjoyable experience. For the essence of Soviet imprisonment is isolation from the rest of the community, together with other persons similarly isolated, with the possibility to do useful work at the place of isolation, to earn a wage for this work, and to participate in running the isolation settlement or 'prison' in the same way as the children participate in running their school, or the workers their factory.[99]

And again: "The Soviet labour camp provides a freedom for its inmates not usual in our own prisons in this country."[100]

In 1966, he was prepared to comment on the above: "Among most writers on the U.S.S.R. in the 1930s, I have least to be ashamed of, or to wish to withdraw." [101]

The editor-in-chief of *Les Lettres françaises,* Pierre Daix, wrote:

> The camps of re-education of the Soviet Union are the achievement of the complete suppression of the exploitation of men by men; the decisive sign of the effort by victorious Socialism to achieve the liberation of men from this exploitation in liberating also the oppressors, slaves of their own oppression.

By a considerable irony, when *One Day in the Life of Ivan Denisovich* came out in a French edition, sponsored by the Friends of the Soviet Union, they selected Daix to write the preface; but Daix had, in fact, changed his views.

Active falsification by partisans and—worse—theoretical justification of falsehood by philosophers were not the only causes of delusion. In addition, a general vague good will towards the Soviet Union, even in the 1930s, led to a tendency to palliate or ignore the facts.

Dr. Margolin remarks that "an entire generation of Zionists has died in Soviet prisons, camps and exile"; and he comments that the Zionists of the outside world were never able to help them, not only because of the difficulties, but also because "we did not care. I do not remember seeing a single article about them in the prewar papers. Not the least effort was made to mobilize public opinion and alleviate their fate." [102]

If this is true of the intelligent, inquisitive, and internationally minded Zionist movement, with a special interest in a special group of prisoners, it applies much more to those in the West whose interest in the matter was, or might have been, the common bonds of humanity.

Whatever the Zionists felt, we should note that one great Jewish tradition remained clear and forthright in its attitude. The old Bund, the Jewish Social Democratic organization which had played a most important part in the old Left, though crushed in Russia, had continued to work in the Baltic States and Poland. And in the United States, some of the most effective militants in the New York Jewish Left had sprung from Bund circles. A great example is David Dubinsky, who throughout the period combined a firm radicalism with regard for the employers and an equally firm resistance to the Terror in Russia, and even during the war rebuffed pressures from "liberals" and from the State Department, which tried to dissuade him from protest against the executions of Ehrlich and Alter.

The effects of the Stalin era took a long time to sink in in the West. Indeed, they were rejected by many until admitted by the dictator's *diadochi.* A curious resistance prevailed in which evidence which would have been thought adequate about any other regime was rejected—a phenomenon ludicrously illustrated by (again) Jean-Paul Sartre in his introduction to Henri Alleg's book about torture in Algeria. Sartre said that we now know of the existence of torture in Communist countries as well, because of Khrushchev's admission and the evidence given at the trial of the Hungarian Police Minister Farkas. That is to say, evidence of the Alleg type, mere first-hand accounts, was to be admitted in the French, but excluded in the Russian, case.

Khrushchev's revelations in February 1956 did not affect some Soviet sympathizers in the West except to the degree that they feared that the disclosures might prove disturbing to those whose faith was less firmly founded.

After the publication of Khrushchev's Secret Speech, Professor Joliot-Curie asked Ehrenburg to be cautious when speaking about it, especially to his children; Khrushchev's revelations were disturbing to many Communists; he personally knew of many errors and mistakes, even of crimes committed,* but he understood also that drastic changes of the whole structure of the State would cause troubles and personal hardships. These troubles could happen in any country, and they would not perturb him personally. They might, however, have a quite different effect on those who knew less. So he wished that Ehrenburg, when speaking about the Soviet Union, would choose positive rather than negative events.[103]

Such is the perhaps rational attitude of a Communist. It is charitable to imagine that the great physicist had not really faced the facts of what he still thought of as unavoidable hardships. In any event, his case and the various others we have dipped into constitute a mere sketch and selection of an extraordinary potpourri of inhumanity and self-deception which a later generation might well take to heart.

## THE KHRUSHCHEV PERIOD

When Stalin died on 5 March 1953, his successors appealed against "panic and disarray."[104] But their qualms were unnecessary. Although the single will of the creator of the new State had now gone, the machinery he had created remained in existence. And aspirations among the citizenry toward a different order of things had no possible means of expression and organization.

We need not rehearse the history of the USSR over the post-Stalin period. It will be enough to note that its politics have been dominated by the problem of Stalin. Within three years came the major breakthrough of Khrushchev's Secret speech to the XXth Party Congress, which denounced the late dictator's arbitrary rule and exposed the falsification, based on torture, of the cases against certain non-oppositionist victims such as Kossior and Eikhe. The Secret Speech was a tremendous step forward. And it was followed, over the next eight or nine years, by the publication of a great deal of other material on the truths of the Stalin epoch. But passive and active opposition within the old apparatus was strong, and de-Stalinization remained incomplete and sporadic. The Speech itself had been opposed by Molotov and other members of the Party Presidium—equivalent of the old Politburo—and it was not published in the USSR until 1989. The official line tacked and veered between dramatic though partial denunciations of the former dictator (in, for example, 1956 to 1961) and considerably more positive estimates (in, for example, 1957 and 1963).

"The cult of personality," a curiously inadequate description, was the invariable category in which the Stalinist past was now criticized. This was, in effect, basically an allegation of vanity and flattery—not quite the essential which had made the rule of Stalin so deplorable. It mattered much less to his victims

---

*As Arthur Koestler points out, Professor Joliot-Curie intervened in the case of certain physicists imprisoned in the Soviet Union, implying realization that charges were not always sound (*The God That Failed,* ed. Richard H. Crossman [London, 1950], p. 79).

that towns were named after him than that he was ruling by terror and falsehood. It is true that the expression implies autocracy, but it remained slightly off target.

It proved compatible with allegations of extravagant tyranny, and equally with mere suggestions of the rather excessive application of necessary force— depending on the vagaries of politics. Above all, it made it possible to claim that the Soviet State and the Party were essentially healthy throughout the period:

> The successes that the working people of the Soviet Union were achieving under the leadership of the Communist Party . . . created an atmosphere in which individual errors and shortcomings seemed less significant against the background of tremendous success. . . . No personality cult could change the nature of the Socialist State, which is based on public ownership of the means of production, the alliance of the working class and the peasantry, and the friendship of peoples.[105]

But as the Italian Communist leader, Palmiro Togliatti, commented in 1956:

> First, all that was good was attributed to the superhuman, positive qualities of one man: now all that is evil is attributed to his equally exceptional and even astonishing faults. In the one case, as well as in the other, we are outside the criterion of judgment intrinsic in Marxism. The true problems are evaded, which are why and how Soviet society could reach and did reach certain forms alien to the democratic way and to the legality that it had set for itself, even to the point of degeneration.[106]

Time and again, the authorities made it clear that, in the words of a 1963 Central Committee resolution, they opposed "resolutely and implacably any attempt to undermine the foundations of Marxist-Leninist theory under the guise of the struggle against the personality cult, and all attempts to rehabilitate the anti-Marxist opinions and trends which were routed by the Party."[107]

One of Stalin's principles—the theory that the intensity of the class conflict, and hence the necessity of terror, increases as the power of the defeated classes diminishes—was denounced, though in its official form in the Party Program adopted at the XXIInd Congress in 1961, this denunciation was hedged with reservations:

> The general trend of class struggle within the socialist countries in conditions of successful socialist construction leads to the consolidation of the position of the socialist forces and weakens the resistance of the remnants of the hostile classes. But this development does not follow a straight line. Changes in the domestic or external situation may cause the class struggle to intensify in specific periods. This calls for constant vigilance. . . .[108]

The period also saw an evolution in the forms of the enforcement of State power. The Special Board of the MVD was abolished in September 1953.[109] The "Terror" Decree of 1 December 1934 was annulled on 19 April 1956.

In December 1958, the new Decree on State Crimes replaced the relevant articles of the Criminal Code dating from Stalin's time. Certain notorious excesses, such as Article 58 (i.c.), which openly inflicted penalties on the families of "traitors" fleeing abroad, even if they were totally unimplicated, were dropped. But the Decree remained Draconian and provided severe punishment for all forms of action, organization, or discussion hostile to the Government. Legal practice, too, received some degree of reform: Vyshinsky was denounced, together with his theory that confessions are the main element in a good case. But confessions were still used, and treated as valid—as in the Powers and the Penkovsky cases, in 1960 and 1963, respectively.

The labor-camp system remained in being, and no information about it was officially available. The general impression is that measures had already been taken to cut the death rate and to make forced labor economically more rational in 1950–1951. After the death of Stalin, camp regulations seem to have been more equitably enforced, partly as the result of mass strikes in the northern camps. The release of a large number of prisoners took place under amnesties and through rehabilitations. We are told, though this was given no publicity, that eventually about 100 commissions—1 for each main camp group—were sent out. Consisting of 3 members, they examined all the files and rehabilitated millions, mostly post-humously; present-day estimates are that about 8 million of the 12 million in the camps in 1952 were released.

The general picture is of some camps being virtually dissolved, some losing many of their inmates, and others remaining about the same. In many areas, prisoners were released into free exile. After rebellions in the camps in 1953 (Norilsk and Vorkuta) and 1954 (Kingur), prisoners seem to have been transferred farther east. Reports at the end of 1956, when the operations to reduce the number of prisoners were virtually at an end, showed little change in the Kolyma–Magadan complex. Repatriated prisoners of war estimated that over 1 million then still remained in the far eastern camps. Avram Tertz (Andrei Sinyavsky) remarked ironically of one camp, in *The Trial Begins,* that earlier "the amnesty had virtually emptied the camp of its inmates. Only some ten thousand of us, dangerous criminals, were left."

Discipline remained rigorous. Indeed, a decree of the Supreme Soviet of 5 May 1961 for the first time imposed the death penalty for certain "acts of aggression against the administration," short of murder, in the camps.

However one looks at it, the penal and police systems were reformed in the Khrushchev period. Equally, however one looks at it, they did not undergo essential change, did not become truly liberal.

The regime owed its legitimacy to its descent from Stalin and was committed to the correctness of Stalin's line as against both the Left and the Right oppositions of the 1920s and 1930s, and hence to his correctness on basic policy matters. At the XXIInd Party Congress in 1961, Khrushchev was indeed able to say publicly what had been "secret" in 1956, and Stalin's body was removed from Lenin's tomb; though even in 1989 it still lay in a fairly honorable position under the Kremlin wall, among the bodies of important "positive" figures of the second rank—and, perhaps significantly, next to that of Felix Dzerzhinsky, founder of the Secret Police.

Many of Stalin's personal group died in good odor after their patron's own death—Shkiryatov in 1954, Vyshinsky in 1955. Men like Kaganovich and Malenkov, though publicly accused by the Prosecutor-General of the USSR of "criminal violations of Socialist legality,"[110] also remained at liberty. The fall of Beria entailed the trials of a series of police officials of the old regime. In all, thirty-eight Security generals were deprived of their military ranks.[111] But others survived, such as Serov, who was Head of Army Intelligence until 1964. General Gorbatov, writing in the early 1960s, speaks quite naturally of his torturer, Stolbunsky—"I don't know where he is now"—and mentions meeting the despicable Commissar Fominykh, who had organized his removal, in a group of senior officers in 1962.

More basically, there was no serious attempt to deal with the Terror as a whole. The great plot ostensibly headed by Trotsky, backed by the Nazis, involving politicians, generals, engineers, doctors, and ordinary citizens by the thousand, was not explicitly denounced as a fabrication. Statements were made that demolished the authenticity of some of the main public accusations. Several of those named as conspirators in the 1938 Trial were rehabilitated. One major crime of the 1937 accused—the "attempt" on the life of Molotov—was openly described at the XXIInd Party Congress in 1961 as a frame-up. On the centerpiece of the whole Purge story (and the main crime of the 1936 accused in particular), the Kirov murder, we have seen that the official line was already rejected as unsatisfactory by Khrushchev in his Secret Speech of February 1956, and again, publicly, in his report to the 1961 Congress—each time with strong hints that Stalin had been the real organizer of the assassination. So, although the full truth was being extracted with painful slowness, enough had already been said to concede the total falsehood of the original Stalinist version.

We now know that the Tukhachevsky group were legally rehabilitated by the Supreme Court on 31 January 1957, and posthumously restored to Party membership on 27 February 1957. This and similar decisions were not published. It simply became plain from their reappearance in a favorable light in books and articles that they were now cleared of the charges. In this and the other cases, the published formalities were merely a note at the end of the encyclopedia entries: "Illegally repressed. Posthumously rehabilitated." Similarly, the executed Stalinists—Rudzutak, Chubar, Postyshev, Eikhe, Kossior, and the others—were seen to be in good odor, as were such men as Yenukidze and Karakhan.

One distractive ploy by the forces of obstruction was to give to the rehabilitated death dates differing from the true ones. This was done in part, Nadezhda Mandelshtam tells us, to transfer purge victims to the war period, and thus distance them from the Purges. Marshal Yegorov, Army Commander Fedko, and Vlas Chubar were among those given wartime deaths. And others were spaced out, if not so far; for example, Postyshev's was for twenty years dated to 1940.

No one was cleared from the Zinoviev or Pyatakov Trials. And in the Bukharin Trial, a fantastic situation persisted for years in which some of the accused were fully rehabilitated, and others not. Ikramov, Khodzhayev, Krestinsky, Zelensky, and Grinko were now in favor. But to rehabilitate, for example, Krestinsky without rehabilitating Rosengolts was to rehabilitate Burke while leaving Hare accused.

Yugoslav sources said, in the autumn of 1962, that Bukharin would shortly be rehabilitated.[112] This did not take place, though at a meeting of an All-Union Conference on Measures to Improve the Training of Scientific-Pedagogical Cadres in the Historical Sciences,[113] Pospelov said: "Students ask whether Bukharin and others were spies of foreign States. . . . I may state that it is sufficient to study the documents of the XXIInd Congress of the C.P.S.U. in order to say that neither Bukharin nor Rykov, of course, were spies or terrorists." This little-publicized partial exculpation is important in principle. But Bukharin's and Rykov's names were not restored to Party favor. Zinoviev, Kamenev, Pyatakov, I. N. Smirnov, Sokolnikov, and Rosengolts—to name some of the other leading figures at the public trials—remained totally unrehabilitated. So did a good many men who had not even come to public trial—for example, Preobrazhensky, Smilga, Uglanov, and Shlyapnikov.

Rehabilitation, as well as being done in this illogical and partial fashion, took a variety of forms. The maximum was the full-scale article with at least a remark at the end that the man named had fallen victim to slander as a result of the personality cult. The minimum was simply the mention of the former purgee's name in a neutral or favorable context. There was, indeed, something even more minimal, if one can so express it, than the above. It was now conventional in the "biographical notes" on people who had played a part in the earlier history of the Party and who were listed at the end of works dealing with that time to give, in addition to those of birth and death, the date of entering the Party. In the case of all those in good odor, this was phrased "Member of the Party from 1910," or whatever the date might be. In the case of those still unrehabilitated, this was invariably "Got into the Party [*Sostoyal v partii*] 1910." From this minor convention, it can be seen that, for example, Syrtsov was now, to this degree at least, restored to favor, while Preobrazhensky was not.

This curious, and typical, indirectness marked a failure to come to grips with the past. It is easily explicable. After Stalin's death, the machine he created continued to rule the country. The principle of one-party rule, the overriding competence of that party in all spheres of life, the preservation of its "monolithic" nature—and rule over it by a small central body—all continued.

All the leaders had arisen in the old machine during Stalin's time. The channels through which they rose remained as then established. And the principles of rule were, in general, those then brought to fruition.

The efforts of Khrushchev personally and of a number of intellectual and other figures had nevertheless made important, if partial, progress in uncovering the truth. The resistance from the whole traditionalist cadre at every level was natural. And it beat him.

## THE BREZHNEV REACTION

After the fall of Khrushchev in October 1964, an end was gradually put to speculative and risky initiatives in every field. This applied also to the matter of "Stalinism." The rehabilitation process virtually ceased, as did written discussions of the more sensitive areas of the Stalinist past. Stalin himself began to be treated at first with a rather cold respect and later with considerable favor, in spite of the protests of intellectuals. The system of government he created, as amended and improved under Khrushchev, was consolidated.

The extent of the reaction since Khrushchev's time could be seen in the treatment of Raskolnikov. In his military *Memoirs* (published in 1964), the introduction states flatly, "The C.C. of the C.P.S.U. has completely rehabilitated him, and restored him posthumously to party membership and to Soviet citizenship." Even as late as 1968, his Civil War record was favorably referred to;[114] but soon his photograph was removed from books, and various editors who had permitted favorable reference to him were reprimanded or dismissed. Finally, an article in the authoritative party organ *Kommunist* spoke of him as "a deserter to the side of the enemy and a slanderer of the party and the Soviet State."[115]

This was, indeed, a special case. More generally, those rehabilitated remained so, though the expression "Illegally repressed. Posthumously rehabilitated" disappeared from the reference books. And accounts of events of the Purges simply ceased to appear. For the moment, at least, the promise of better things after forty years in the wilderness showed little sign of fulfillment. The reason, basically, seems to be that the caravan was led by men skilled in the ways of the wilderness, and enjoying the powers they had gained and would certainly forfeit in a lusher land.

For Pyatakov's "miracle"—the idea that by sheer political organization the Party could create industry and the proletariat, which should in Marx's view have preceded the coming to power of Socialism, and having done that, go back to the main line forseen by Marx—had not worked out. The reason is plain. It had been a mistake to think that the Party would, after this Marxist detour, simply revert to a humanist democratic representation of the new proletariat. It was not the case that Stalinist methods could be used and then simply cast aside when specific economic and social aims had been achieved. Terror institutionalizes its own cadres, its own psychology. And the Party machine, whose loyalties for so long had been in practice simply to itself, whose interests for so long had been equally circumscribed, had become Djilas's "New Class," no more capable of easily changing its ways than the old classes and bureaucracies of the past had been.

The Stalin era was a past so atrocious that its repudiation brought obvious dividends to any succeeding regime, but its successors also inherited a set of institutions and a ruling caste indoctrinated in certain habits and beliefs. And in an important sense, the essence of Stalinism is less the particular periods of terrorism or special views on industrial organization than the establishment of the political set-up. And that still remained substantially unchanged.

Even the Khrushchevite "de-Stalinization" had consisted of little more than the abandonment (or even the denunciation) of a specific set of excesses associated with the late dictator. It did not amount to any change of substance in the *system* of political rule in the USSR or in the basic principles behind that system. Russia was still ridden by the Party machine, and the principle of *Partiinost*—the doctrine of the Party's right to rule and to decide on all questions of speed and direction—remained untouched. What took place, in effect, was simply the renunciation of excessive use of whip and spur.

There was now, in fact, a considerable effort to rehabilitate the NKVD: criticism was leveled at those who, basing themselves on the organization's role in the Purges, "are not averse to putting practically all the officers of the Cheka under a cloud."[116] A whole series of novels and plays appeared featuring Secret Police heroes.*

Those police officers condemned to imprisonment rather than death in the post-Beria purge were released—Eitingon, the organizer of Trotsky's assassina-

---

*For example, Yuri German, *I Am Responsible* and *The New Year's Eve Party;* Kozhevnikov, *The Shield and the Sword;* Bylinov, *The Streets of Wrath;* and Zalynsky's play *Pebbles in the Hand.*

tion, among them. There were complaints that the former Georgian NKVD officer Nadaraya, a "specialist in shooting wives and daughters," only received ten years after Beria's death and was now at liberty; that Colonel Monakhov, who had shot several hundred foreign Communists in the Solovetsk camps at the beginning of the Finnish War, was living in a villa near Leningrad, an attempt to have him expelled from the Party having been prevented by Tolstikov, then First Secretary of the Leningrad province; that the leading interrogator of the Jewish doctors in 1952, A. G. Sugak, had a job as Assistant Director of a museum, and a villa near Moscow; and so on.

In September 1966, new articles were added to the Criminal Code, providing for the imprisonment of those given to uttering or writing material "discrediting the Soviet State" or participating in "group activities" involving "disobedience in the face of the lawful demands of the authorities." [117] Such laws led to those increasing repressions against writers and dissidents which were such a mark of the period.

Further, in 1966 pressure from Party traditionalists grew for a "partial or indirect" rehabilitation of Stalin at the XXIIIrd Party Congress that year. It was laid down that the concept "the period of the personality cult"—the mildest of all hostile descriptions of the Stalin period—was "mistaken and un-Marxist." [118] Strong resistance to this neo-Stalinism was aroused, being expressed in particular in a letter by the leading members of the Soviet intelligentsia, and for the moment no more was said. But in 1969, the neo-Stalinists had consolidated, and a further determined attempt was made, in connection with Stalin's ninetieth birthday. A statue was planned; special lectures at the Institute of Marxism-Leninism were to take place; orders for busts and portraits were made; an edition of Stalin's *Works* was prepared. A set-piece article in *Kommunist* wrote of Stalin's malpractices that "these were mistakes in practical work which was essentially correct in fulfilling the scientifically based general line of the Party." [119] A pro-Stalin novel by Kochetov appeared in *Oktyabr'*. By the birth date in December, a long *Pravda* article was ready. But by now, foreign Communist leaders started to put pressure on the Soviet leadership. Finally, the Politburo decided "by a small majority" to cancel most of the celebrations. [120] Nevertheless, the trend remained regression, not progress.

It may be argued that the élan of the regime was now dead and that only momentum, habit, and institutions remained. If this view is taken, the system might appear like the legitimist monarchies of the early nineteenth century—impressive, powerful, but dead at heart, and remaining only as an integument which eventually broke.

The argument of the Communist heroine and martyr Rosa Luxemburg against the suppression of hostile opinion, and against the closed society, was not a moral one. It was simply that

> without general elections, without unrestricted freedom of press and assembly, without a free struggle of opinion, life dies out in every public institution, becomes a mere semblance of life, in which only the bureaucracy remains as the active element. . . .
> Yes, we can go even further: such conditions must cause a brutalization of public life. . . . [121]

This was a sound prediction of developments in Russia. Until its recommendations were complied with, the Soviet Union could best be described as not fully cured, but still suffering from a milder and more chronic form of the affliction which had reached its crisis in the Yezhov years.

The Khrushchev period, in spite of its inconsistencies, had to some extent shown the way forward. And it had made the major falsifications of the Terror period untenable. In the two decades which followed Khrushchev's fall, the regime was in the intellectually scandalous position of having no official story at all, true or false, about the trials.

But the twenty-year "period of stagnation," as it is now officially designated, saw ubiquitous falsification eating away at the intellectual, the social, the economic, and the political structure until little was left but a hollow shell. The command economy—"barracks socialism," as it is now called—drove the country deeper and deeper into unacknowledged crisis. By the mid-1980s, this had become so profound that, first, all serious economic and social observers had seen the imminent danger, and second, there had been time for this knowledge to percolate to an important section of the political leadership.

The decisions taken to attempt a radical reconstruction and abandonment of the false socio-economic principles which had led to this crisis involved freeing the forces of intellectual criticism, repudiating the heritage of Stalinism, and releasing the truth.

# THE TERROR TODAY

*Whoever knew Truth put to the worse, in a free and open encounter?*
Milton

As the world knows, from 1986, and much more so in the ensuing years, the USSR entered the period of *glasnost*. Among the first products of *glasnost* was truth about current economic and social disasters. Its sponsors made it plain, moreover, that the command-economy system of Stalinism, based on endless coercion, was in itself a dead end and needed dismantling. Thus the horrors of Stalinism were at first often attacked less on humanitarian grounds than as economically counterproductive: the Soviet economist Nikolai Shmelyov, in a crucial (though in theory confidential) speech in June 1987, told for the first time of 5 million peasant families having been deported, of 17 million souls having passed through the Gulag. But his theme was that this was economically worthless. What had the prisoners contributed—three canals, one of which was useless (a reference to the Baltic–White Sea Canal) and a quantity of lumber which could have been better produced by free labor.[1]

But the new *glasnost* about the past was never solely economic. From the start, it became clear that Stalinism had to be tackled as a whole—if only because the dug-in Stalinist *apparat* could be discredited only by a full-scale and continued campaign. It was also clear that a great pressure had built up among the better elements of the intelligentsia. The lies which they had been forced to accept had already been shaken in Khrushchev's time. In the meanwhile, the sacrifices of *samizdat* writers, the contributions of Western scholars, the output of Western radios, had left the lies intellectually nonviable. And when the opportunity was given, a number of editors went ahead with the continued publication of facts about the Terror.

I ended *The Great Terror* with the comment that one sign of a recovery from Stalinism "would be a frank confrontation with the past; so that Russians could freely and fully investigate the events of which some account has meanwhile been given in these pages." And in the Russian edition of *The Great Terror,* published in Florence in 1972, I deplored the fact that a history of the Terror could, at that time, only be written and researched abroad.

This is no longer true. Readers will have seen how often in these pages the facts are drawn from Soviet publications of the past two or three years. Not only have certain historical points been clarified and added to, but also the very nature of the Terror has been confirmed. Fearful stories of labor-camp life, of torture, of denunciation and falsification have appeared. And, just as important, massive confirmation of the huge impact of the Terror and of the numbers of dead, deported, and imprisoned have been made public.

It had been clear since the 1940s, from a variety of testimonies, that the victims numbered millions. By the late 1960s, when *The Great Terror* appeared, it was possible to go further. Over the years since then, additional evidence accumulated, in particular from Soviet *samizdat* writers like Roy Medvedev, Anton Antonov-Ovseenko, Peter Yakir, and others, though also from a variety of émigré and Western sources—and even from occasional Soviet material. Khrushchev himself told us in his memoirs that "ten million or more of our citizens paid with their lives in Stalin's jails and camps"!

In *The Great Terror,* I gave estimates of approximate casualty figures for 1937–1938. My rough totals, arrived at through the examination of a number of separate trains of evidence, were

| | |
|---:|:---|
| Arrests, 1937–1938 | about 7 million |
| Executed | about 1 million |
| Died in camps | about 2 million |
| In prison, late 1938 | about 1 million |
| In camps, late 1938 (assuming 5 million in camp at the end of 1936) | about 8 million |

I also concluded, from much Soviet and other testimony, that not more than 10 percent of those then in camp survived.

My estimates were based on thirty-odd sources, mostly unofficial—though including considerations of the 1959 census and of the secret NKVD section of the 1941 State plan. A number of further unofficial testimonies of some value have meanwhile emerged, confirming the earlier. But they, and the fifteen pages of calculations and considerations in *The Great Terror,* have been made superfluous by Soviet figures given in 1987–1989. However, we may look briefly at the categories:

1. Arrests. My approximately 7 million was derived from (among several solid sources) analyses by Alexander Weissberg and other ex-prisoners of the numbers arrested in the catchment areas of various prisons, and based on prison documents warranting high confidence. Full Soviet figures have not been given. But those provided for the Kursk province[2] imply a total of about 8 million for the USSR as a whole.

2. Executed: approximately 1 million. This would be the result for the USSR as a whole for those shot by Troikas alone, if figures now given for Uzbekistan are taken as typical.[3] Figures from Irkutsk imply over 1.5 million.[4] The evidence of the Kuropaty mass graves in Minsk and the Bukovnya mass graves near Kiev suggest higher figures still. My estimate was based in part on relatives' reports of the proportion of death sentences to other sentences. But while realizing that "10

years without the right of correspondence" was often a euphemism for the death sentence, we did not then know that it *always* was.[5] I, and Roy Medvedev (who also gives the 1 million figure), will probably turn out to have underestimated this.

3. Died in camps, 1937 and 1938: approximately 2 million. This was based on prisoners' reports of the death rate and (taken together with the execution figures) on Yugoslav sources. It would include those executed in camps, who do not figure in the execution estimate above (on the evidence of Kolyma and Bamlag, this may be approximately 600,000 to 700,000).

4. In prison, late 1938: 1 million. This rough estimate was based on the known prison accommodation and many reports of the level of overcrowding, together with figures of inmates for particular prisons. These last are now confirmed in Soviet accounts.[6]

5. In camps, late 1938: approximately 8 million. This is based in the main on multifarious reports from ex-prisoners. The assumption that 5 million were already in camps at the beginning of 1937 was derived merely from the estimates by other students of the matter, and may be too high. I should be inclined to reduce the 8 million at the end of 1938 to 7 million, or even a little less. Such a figure is consonant with the 12 million now given in Moscow for the camp population in 1952.[7]

The above are, in any case, only approximations.

*The Great Terror* was only peripherally concerned with the total casualties of the Stalin epoch. But it reckoned the dead as no fewer than 20 million. This figure is now given in the USSR. And the general total of "repressed" is now stated (e.g., in the new high-school textbooks) as around 40 million, about half of them in the peasant terror of 1929 to 1933 and the other half from 1937 to 1953.[8]

Thus it would now be accepted almost everywhere that the estimates given above cannot be far wrong. But it is just worth recording that, though it has long been clear that the victims ran into the millions or tens of millions, Western misconceptions of the sort we discussed in Chapter 15 recently had a brief revival. Over the years, a vast amount of true information had established itself in the Western consciousness. But by an inexplicable development, when such notions no longer seemed possible, a few Western Sovietologists began to assert that the Terror had claimed far fewer victims, and that ordinary life was not affected. The writer of a Western Sovietological textbook concerned to reduce the estimates to, as he put it, a few hundred thousand or even a few tens of thousands, wrote, "Surely we don't want to hypothesise 3 million executions or prison deaths in 1937–1938 or anything like this figure, or we are assuming most improbable percentages of men dying."[9] The key word here is "improbable." The Stalin epoch is replete with what appear as improbabilities to minds unfitted to deal with the phenomena. Similarly with the argument that Stalin could not have killed millions of peasants, since that would have been "economically counterproductive." Following such leads, a new group of Westerners came forward, with singularly bad timing, in the mid-1980s and told us (in the words of one of them) that the terror had only killed "thousands" and imprisoned "many thousands."[10] Such views could only be formed by ignoring, or actively rejecting, the earlier evidence. This was accomplished by saying that those who produced it were opposed to Stalin and Stalinism, and therefore prejudiced, and that some of the material was second-hand. Thus it was not merely a matter of mistaken assessment of the evidence. It was, contrary to the duties of a historian, a refusal to face it.

There were even demographers who, among other errors, accepted the faked census of 1939. A Soviet demographer, deploring this, explains that that census was unacceptable on three grounds. First (as I had already registered in Chapter 16 of *The Harvest of Sorrow*), the earlier 1937 census had been suppressed and the Census Board shot as spies who had "exerted themselves to diminish the population," thus providing a certain incentive to their successors to find higher figures than were justified. Second, the 1939 totals were announced by Stalin before the new Census Board had examined the material. Third, censuses of the period omitted the deaths of those who had "died in custody." [11] It is unfortunate that implausibly benign assessments should have appeared in one or two Western textbooks and periodicals and that students should thus have been methodically misinformed. Soviet professionals with whom I have discussed this are, naturally, especially outraged. And, indeed, it is worth noting of *glasnost* that it has produced a number of articles attacking Western apologists for the regime, from the Webbs on.

Anything like complete accuracy on the casualty figures is probably unattainable. As a Soviet analysis puts it, some records were lost, or never existed. In addition, when it comes to the terror-famine of 1932–1933, it will be almost impossible to sort out the infant deaths from those unborn owing to the decline in birth rate, since registration of births and deaths ceased in the affected areas over the critical period (moreover, under the then procedures, infants dying within a few days of birth were counted as unborn). Nevertheless, it now seems that further examination of the data will not go far from the estimates we now have except, perhaps, to show them to be understated. For example, Sergo Mikoyan, son of the Politburo member, has recently given from his father's unpublished memoirs a figure reported to the Politburo by the KGB on Khrushchev's orders in the 1960s: of, between 1 January 1935 and 22 June 1941, just under 20 million arrests and 7 million deaths. [12] The respected A. Adamovich has lately criticized me in a historians' "round table" in *Literaturnaya gazeta:* "always lowering the numbers of the repressed, he is simply unable to understand the true size of these fearful figures, to understand that one's own government could so torment the people." It is true that I always described my figures as conservative; but hitherto, I have been more used to objectors finding them unbelievably large.

In any case, the sheer magnitudes of the Stalin holocaust are now beyond doubt.

In *Voprosy istorii,* in December 1988, a group of Soviet historians which included the long-rejected Roy Medvedev discussed the Stalin regime; Medvedev argued that once such fearful numbers were reached, it was also a question of the "quality" as well as the "quantity." It was a matter of

the most cruel tortures, interrogations, the fearful abuse of human dignity, when in connection with the repressed anything was permitted, when right and legality were destroyed . . . if it was necessary to cut you to pieces, they cut you to pieces; if it was necessary to whip you, they whipped you. . . .

He continues with even more horrible particulars.

To the Western view we have deplored above, the Terror—not in any case very great in extent—was little more than a rough-and-ready means of replacing the old officialdom with new and younger cadres. But the nature of the new cadres was, of course, determined by the Terror! We are often told in current Soviet publications of this "negative selection"[13] in such terms as

> Stalin's people and 'new cadres' started coming to power in an avalanche. The cadres only required to lack 'suspect' connections, independent political thinking and even the potential for such thinking and to be ready to fulfil any order from above without question. . . . The finest peasants, intellectuals and Communists were killed, broken or corrupted. . . . Mercy and dignity became hindrances to survival. A civil stand, a critical rational attitude to political developments meant definite destruction.[14]

And time and time again, one reads of the enormous blow dealt to the consciousness of the population. For example, "the fear which it instilled in our minds and souls still puts people's consciousness in chains and paralyses it. . . . All of this generated constant fear of authority, alienated the human being from the state and made relations between them abnormal."[15] Or, in the words of the writer Chingiz Aitmatov, "it is terrible to imagine just how profoundly our society has been paralyzed by Stalinist repression, and Stalin's authoritarian regime!" In fact, Soviet writers are now frequently and movingly telling of the fearful long-term effects of Stalinism, which, as Joseph Berger earlier remarked, left the Soviet Union in the condition of "a country devastated by nuclear warfare."[16]

As to the continuing effect of Stalinism on society and on the economy, Aitmatov also speaks typically of "the absurd Stalinist obsession of having a wealthy state but a poor population, which has never been achieved or will be."[17] Scores of assessments by Soviet economists have made clear the negative results. And this includes condemnation of collectivization and what is now openly described as the "terror-famine" of 1932 to 1933, concluding that the most efficient elements of the peasantry were liquidated, the habit of work was destroyed among the others, and rural production was ruined to this day. Everyone agrees that the Stalinist command economy was, and remains, a disaster.

The struggle to publish the truth was not an easy one. But over the past three years, not just once, but continually, every falsehood about the period has been ripped to pieces. The accused in the great trials have all, with the exception of Yagoda, been rehabilitated. The mass graves of victims are being dug up, and the bodies given decent burial. More difficult, the effects on the consciousness of the Soviet peoples of a whole epoch of great fear and false indoctrination are being faced. Recovery cannot be instantaneous, and there may even be relapses. But the strongest and most effective medicine is, and is seen to be, the truth.

Terror and falsehood have been repudiated. As the organ of the Soviet Government lately wrote, "Not only did they annihilate people physically, but they also hoped to destroy even the memory of them."[18] They succeeded in the first, but not in the second. And the restoration of the truth is not the concern merely of historians, but of Soviet society as a whole, and emerges not only in the journals, but also in the activities of a great public movement—Memorial—which works to discover the fates of the mass of victims, long-mourned relatives of so many living citizens.

If *The Great Terror* had a virtue, it was in giving a full, consistent, and evidential account of that critical period, at a time when only incidental and individual records otherwise existed. The present book's fuller and sounder record of these events is above all bound up with the fact that the suppression and falsification which for so long prevented the emergence of truth in the USSR itself have now collapsed. The world, whatever its other problems, is a better place without them.

# NOTES

**Preface**

1. *Moscow News,* no. 13 (1989).
2. *Leningradskiy rabochiy,* 7 April 1989.


**Introduction: The Roots of Terror**

1. See Boris Souvarine, *Stalin* (London, 1949), p. 316.
2. See Isaac Deutscher, *Stalin* (London, 1949), p. 234.
3. See Souvarine, *Stalin,* p. 302.
4. Ibid., p. 303.
5. See Leonard Schapiro, *The Communist Party of the Soviet Union* (London, 1960), p. 215.
6. Souvarine, *Stalin,* p. 329.
7. V. I. Lenin, "The Deception of the People" (speech of 19 May 1919).
8. *Kommunist,* no. 5 (1957), p. 21, quoted in Schapiro, *Communist Party of the Soviet Union,* p. 207.
9. See Louis Fischer, *The Life of Lenin* (London, 1965), p. 589.
10. Alexander Barmine, *One Who Survived* (New York, 1945), p. 94.
11. Sapronov, speech to the IXth Party Congress.
12. Victor Serge, *Memoirs of a Revolutionary, 1901–1941* (London, 1963), p. 190.
13. Anton Ciliga, *The Russian Enigma* (London, 1940), p. 86.
14. E. H. Carr, *Socialism in One Country* (London, 1958), vol. 1, p. 151.
15. Barmine, *One Who Survived,* pp. 93–94.
16. Milovan Djilas, *The New Class* (London, 1957), p. 50.
17. *Pravda,* 18 December 1923.
18. See Souvarine, *Stalin,* p. 249.
19. Ibid.
20. Ibid.
21. See Robert V. Daniels, *The Conscience of the Revolution* (Oxford, 1960), p. 28.
22. *XIV s"ezd Vsesoyuznoy kommunisticheskoy partii (b) 18–31 dekabrya 1925 g. Stenograficheskiy otchet* (Moscow, 1926).

23. Souvarine, *Stalin,* p. 418.

24. *Pravda,* 17 October 1926.

25. Souvarine, *Stalin,* pp. 489–90.

26. See Isaac Deutscher, *The Prophet Unarmed* (London, 1959), pp. 388–89.

27. Ibid., p. 351.

28. Ciliga, *Russian Enigma,* p. 74.

29. Alexander Weissberg, *Conspiracy of Silence* (London, 1952), p. 501.

30. Victor Kravchenko, *I Chose Freedom* (London, 1947), p. 275.

31. Nikita Khrushchev, " 'Confidential Report' to the XXth Party Congress," in *The Crimes of the Stalin Era* (New York, 1956) (henceforward referred to as Secret Speech).

32. See Deutscher, *Prophet Unarmed,* p. 548.

33. "Letter of an Old Bolshevik," in Boris I. Nicolaevsky, *Power and the Soviet Elite* (New York, 1965), p. 48.

34. *Komsomolskaya pravda,* 2 April 1988.

35. *Report of the Court Proceedings in the Case of the Anti-Soviet Trotskyite Centre,* English ed. (Moscow, 1937), p. 482 (henceforward referred to as *Pyatakov Trial*).

36. V. I. Lenin, *Sobranie sochineniy,* 3rd ed. (Moscow, 1926–37), vol. 29, p. 229.

37. See Souvarine, *Stalin,* p. 246.

38. Deutscher, *The Prophet Unarmed,* p. 82.

39. Leon Trotsky, *My Life* (London, 1930), vol. 2, p. 207.

40. See Souvarine, *Stalin,* p. 424.

41. D. J. Dallin and B. I. Nicolaevsky, *Forced Labour in the Soviet Union* (London, 1948), p. 116.

42. Rudzutak, speech to the XVIth Party Congress.

43. Abdurakhman Avtorkhanov, *Stalin and the Soviet Communist Party* (London, 1959), p. 124.

44. Kaganovich, speech to the XVIth Party Congress.

45. *Pravda,* 6 January 1930.

46. *Report of the Court Proceedings in the Case of the Anti-Soviet 'Bloc of Rights and Trotskyites,'* English ed. (Moscow, 1938), p. 708 (henceforward referred to as *Bukharin Trial*).

47. *Leningradskaya pravda,* 2 December 1962.

48. See Ciliga, *Russian Enigma,* p. 96.

49. G. A. Tokaev, *Betrayal of an Ideal* (London, 1954), pp. 167–68.

50. Deutscher, *Stalin,* p. 349.

51. *Sovetskaya kul'tura,* 1 October 1988; *Sobesednik,* no. 49 (1988).

52. Kravchenko, *I Chose Freedom,* p. 130.

53. Raphael R. Abramovitch, *The Soviet Revolution* (London, 1962), pp. 346–47.

54. Nicolaevsky, *Power and the Soviet Elite,* p. 18.

55. Ibid., pp. 18–19.

### Chapter 1: Stalin Prepares

1. *Deviatyi s''ezd professional'nykh soyuzov. Stenograficheskiy otchet* (Moscow, 1933), pp. 205, 253.

2. *Pravda,* 2 December 1930.

3. *Vsesoyuznaya kommunisticheskaya partiya (b) v rezolyutsyakh i resheniyakh s''ezdov, konferentsii i plenumov TsK,* 5th ed. (Moscow, 1936), vol. 1, p. 668.

4. *Yunost'*, no. 11 (1988); *Literaturnaya gazeta*, 29 June 1988; *Izvestiya TsK KPSS*, no. 6 (1989).

5. Anton Ciliga, *The Russian Enigma* (London, 1940), p. 279.

6. "Letter of an Old Bolshevik," in Boris I. Nicolaevsky, *Power and the Soviet Elite* (New York, 1965), p. 29.

7. *Yunost'*, no. 11 (1988); *Literaturnaya gazeta*, 29 June 1988.

8. *Yunost'*, no. 11 (1988).

9. *Bukharin Trial*, p. 390.

10. "Letter of an Old Bolshevik," p. 30.

11. Raphael R. Abramovitch, *The Soviet Revolution* (London, 1962), pp. 353, 355.

12. *Pravda*, 17 November 1964.

13. *Druzhba narodov*, no. 6 (1987), p. 52; *Literaturnaya gazeta*, 29 June 1988.

14. Ciliga, *Russian Enigma*, p. 279.

15. *Vsesoyuznaya kommunisticheskaya partiya*, vol. 2, p. 669.

16. *Oktyabr'*, no. 12 (1988); *Izvestiya TsK KPSS*, no. 6 (1989).

17. *Yunost'*, no. 11 (1988); *Literaturnaya gazeta*, 29 June 1988.

18. *Vsesoyuznoe soveshchanie o merakh uluchsheniya podgotovki nauchnopedagogicheskikh kadrov po istoricheskim naukam* (Moscow, 1964), p. 291 (henceforward referred to as *Conference of Historians*, 1962).

19. Ibid.

20. Boris Nicolaevsky, in *Sotsialisticheskiy vestnik*, June 1956; and see *Druzhba narodov*, no. 6 (1987), p. 52.

21. *Bukharin Trial*, p. 644.

22. Karl Radek, *Portraits and Pamphlets* (London, 1935), p. 31.

23. Alexander Barmine, *One Who Survived* (New York, 1945), pp. 101–2.

24. *Byuletten oppozitsii*, no. 34, quoted in Isaac Deutscher, *Stalin* (London, 1949), p. 352.

25. *Report of the Court Proceedings: The Case of the Trotskyite–Zinovievite Terrorist Centre*, English ed. (Moscow, 1936), p. 14 (henceforward referred to as *Zinoviev Trial*).

26. Abramovitch, *Soviet Revolution*, p. 343; see also Merle Fainsod, *How Russia Is Ruled*, 2nd ed. (London, 1963), p. 263.

27. *Pravda*, 25 May 1933.

28. Rakovsky, declaration of April 1930.

29. "Letter of an Old Bolshevik," p. 56.

30. Radek, *Portraits and Pamphlets*, p. 31.

31. *Byuletten oppozitsii*, no. 33 (1932).

32. See Ciliga, *Russian Enigma*, chaps. 5, 7.

33. Nikita Khrushchev, Secret Speech.

34. Stalin, report to the XVIIth Party Congress.

35. *XVII s''ezd Vsesoyuznoy kommunisticheskoy partii (b) 26 yanvarya–10 fevralya 1934. Stenograficheskiy otchet* (Moscow, 1934).

36. See "Letter of an Old Bolshevik"; Barmine, *One Who Survived*.

37. L. Shaumyan, in *Pravda*, 7 February 1964.

38. S. Sinelnikov, *Sergei Mironovich Kirov: Zhizn' i deyatel'nost'* (Moscow, 1964), pp. 194–95.

39. *Ogonek*, 13 December 1987. For a fuller account and documentation of these episodes see Robert Conquest, *Stalin and the Kirov Murder* (New York, 1989), chap. 4. See also *Izvestiya TsK KPSS*, no. 7 (1989); *Ogonek*, no. 28 (1989).

40. *Izvestiya TsK KPSS*, no. 7 (1989).

41. G. A. Tokaev, *Betrayal of an Ideal* (London, 1954), p. 166.

42. Nicolaevsky, *Power and the Soviet Elite*, p. 100.

43. Resolution of the XVIIth Party Congress; Party Constitution of 1934.

44. N. Ruslanov, in *Sotsialisticheskiy vestnik*, nos. 7–8 (1953).

45. Nicolaevsky, *Power and the Soviet Elite*, pp. 94–95.

46. *Bol'shaya sovetskaya entsyklopediya*, 1st ed. (Moscow, 1926–47), s.v. ''Shkiryatov.''

47. Fadeyev, speech to the First Soviet Writers' Congress, August 1934.

48. Nikita Khrushchev, *Khrushchev Remembers* (New York, 1970), p. 61.

49. Sinelnikov, *Sergei Mironovich Kirov*, p. 196.

## Chapter 2: The Kirov Murder

1. *Pravda*, 4 December 1934.

2. *Zinoviev Trial*, pp. 31, 32, 34.

3. S. V. Krasnikov, *S. M. Kirov v Leningrade* (Leningrad, 1966), p. 200.

4. Alexander Orlov, *The Secret History of Stalin's Crimes* (New York, 1953), p. 28.

5. Ibid., pp. 259–60.

6. *Bukharin Trial*, p. 572.

7. Ibid., p. 376.

8. Orlov, *Secret History of Stalin's Crimes*, pp. 29–30.

9. Krasnikov, *S. M. Kirov v Leningrade*, p. 196.

10. Z. T. Serdyuk, speech to the XXIInd Party Congress (*Pravda*, 31 October 1961).

11. Krasnikov, *S. M. Kirov v Leningrade*, p. 196.

12. Nikita Khrushchev, Secret Speech.

13. Ibid.

14. A. N. Shelepin, speech to the XXIInd Party Congress (*Pravda*, 27 October 1961).

15. N. S. Khrushchev, speech to the XXIInd Party Congress (*Pravda*, 29 October 1961).

16. *Bukharin Trial*, p. 558.

17. Svetlana Alliluyeva, *Twenty Letters to a Friend* (London, 1967), p. 150.

18. *Argumenty i fakty*, 11 February 1989; *Ogonek*, no. 28 (1989).

19. Elizabeth Lermolo, *Face of a Victim* (New York, 1955), p. 17.

20. ''Letter of an Old Bolshevik,'' in Boris I. Nicolaevsky, *Power and the Soviet Elite* (New York, 1965), p. 40.

21. *Pravda*, 21 December 1934.

22. *Zinoviev Trial*, p. 136.

23. *Pravda*, 6 December 1934.

24. *Pravda*, 18 December 1934.

25. Hrihory Kostiuk, *Stalinist Rule in the Ukraine* (Munich, 1960), pp. 98–100. See also *Ukrains'ka Radians'kii Entsiklopedichnii Slovnik* (Kiev, 1966), vol. 1, s.v. ''Vlyzko.''

26. *Pravda*, 10 June 1935.

27. Merle Fainsod, *How Russia Is Ruled*, 2nd ed. (London, 1963), pp. 56–57.

28. Anton Ciliga, *The Russian Enigma* (London, 1940), p. 71.

29. *Vechernyy Leningrad*, 30 December 1964.

30. *VII s''ezd vsesoyuzogo Leninskogo kommunisticheskogo soyuza molodezhi* (Moscow and Leningrad, 1926), p. 108.

31. *Pravda,* 27 December 1934.

32. Ibid.

33. "Letter of an Old Bolshevik," p. 51.

34. Ibid.

35. Ibid., pp. 51–52.

36. *Zinoviev Trial,* p. 74.

37. *Bukharin Trial,* pp. 556–57.

38. Ibid., p. 557.

39. *Pravda,* 17 December 1934.

40. *Pravda,* 22 December 1934.

41. *Pravda,* 23 December 1934.

42. Lermolo, *Face of a Victim,* p. 245.

43. *Pravda,* 27 December 1934.

44. "The Crime of the Zinoviev Trial Opposition," p. 19, quoted in Pierre Broué, *Le Parti bolchevique* (Paris, 1963), p. 351.

45. *Pravda,* 27 December 1934.

46. Lermolo, *Face of a Victim,* pp. 46–48.

47. Ibid., pp. 45–46.

48. *Pravda,* 30 December 1934.

49. *Pravda,* 17 January 1935.

50. Isaac Deutscher, *Stalin* (London, 1949), p. 357.

51. *Zinoviev Trial,* p. 142.

52. Ibid., pp. 147–48.

53. Ibid., p. 143.

54. Ibid., p. 145.

55. *Pravda,* 29 March 1937.

56. *Bukharin Trial,* p. 480.

57. Orlov, *Secret History of Stalin's Crimes,* pp. 23–24.

58. Ibid., p. 22.

59. Victor Kravchenko, *I Chose Justice* (London, 1951), p. 260.

60. Vladimir Petrov, *Soviet Gold* (New York, 1949), p. 185.

61. Khrushchev, Secret Speech.

62. *Oktyabr',* no. 12 (1988).

63. *Moscow News,* no. 48 (1988).

64. *Leningradskaya pravda,* 1 December 1988.

65. Fainsod, *How Russia Is Ruled,* p. 422.

## Chapter 3: Architect of Terror

1. Alexander Weissberg, *Conspiracy of Silence* (London, 1952), p. 507.

2. Arthur Koestler, *Darkness at Noon* (London, 1940), pp. 23–24.

3. Milovan Djilas, *Conversations with Stalin* (London, 1962), pp. 57–58.

4. Bukharin, conversation with Theodore Dan and Lydia Dan, 1935 (Raphael R. Abramovitch, *The Soviet Revolution* [London, 1962], p. 416).

5. F. Beck and W. Godin, *Russian Purge and the Extraction of Confession* (London, 1951), p. 227.

6. Bernhard Roeder, *Katorga: An Aspect of Modern Slavery* (London, 1958), p. 196.

7. The problem is clearly and wittily unravelled in Bertram D. Wolfe, *Three Who Made a Revolution* (London, 1966).

8. Boris Souvarine, *Stalin* (London, 1949), p. 287.

9. Ibid., p. 485.

10. Nikita Khrushchev, Secret Speech.

11. G. A. Tokaev, *Stalin Means War* (London, 1951), p. 115.

12. Ilya Ehrenburg, in *Novyy mir*, no. 4 (1964).

13. Djilas, *Conversations with Stalin*, p. 172.

14. Iremashvili, *Memoirs*, quoted in Wolfe, *Three Who Made a Revolution*, p. 508.

15. Svetlana Alliluyeva, *Twenty Letters to a Friend* (London, 1967), p. 117; Alexander Barmine, *One Who Survived* (New York, 1945), pp. 263–64; Alexander Orlov, *The Secret History of Stalin's Crimes* (New York, 1953), pp. 316–18.

16. Alliluyeva, *Twenty Letters to a Friend*, p. 122.

17. Ibid., p. 116.

18. Orlov, *Secret History of Stalin's Crimes*, 314–25.

19. Alliluyeva, *Twenty Letters to a Friend*, p. 62.

20. Tokaev, *Stalin Means War*, p. 128.

21. Ibid., p. 120; and see Alliluyeva, *Twenty Letters to a Friend*, chap. 19.

22. H. G. Wells, *The Outline of History* (New York, 1971).

23. Barmine, *One Who Survived*, p. 267; and see Alliluyeva, *Twenty Letters to a Friend*, pp. 54–55.

24. Souvarine, *Stalin*, p. 244.

25. Khrushchev, Secret Speech.

26. Barmine, *One Who Survived*, p. 305.

27. Leon Trotsky, *My Life* (London, 1930), vol. 2, p. 255.

28. Isaac Deutscher, *Stalin* (London, 1949), p. 291.

29. *Nuovi Argomenti* [Special issue on the XXIInd Party Congress], October 1961.

30. Milovan Djilas, *The New Class* (London, 1957), p. 128.

31. Deutscher, *Stalin*, chap. 1.

32. Djilas, *New Class*, p. 128.

33. Barmine, *One Who Survived*, p. 161.

34. Djilas, *Conversations with Stalin*, p. 60.

35. Robert V. Daniels, *The Conscience of the Revolution* (Oxford, 1960), p. 182.

36. Professor Tibor Szamuely.

37. *Novyy mir*, no. 5 (1962).

38. *Izvestiya*, 6 February 1963.

39. *Mikhail Koltsov kakim on byl* (Moscow, 1965), p. 71.

40. B. Bazhanov, *Stalin der Rote Diktator* (Berlin, 1931), p. 21.

41. Barmine, *One Who Survived*, p. 257.

42. Konstantin Simonov, in *Znamya*, May 1964.

43. Trotsky, *My Life*, vol. 2, p. 184.

44. Stalin, Speech at the First Anniversary of Lenin's Death, 1925.

45. Djilas, *Conversations with Stalin*, p. 63.

46. Adolf Hitler, *Mein Kampf*, trans. James Murphy (London, 1939), p. 110.

47. Joseph Stalin, *Notes of a Delegate* (London, 1941), p. 13.

48. *Novyy mir*, no. 4 (1964).

49. Stalin, official criticism of Academician Orbeli at a joint session of the Academy of Sciences and the Academy of Medical Sciences (*Pravda*, 1 July 1950).

50. Souvarine, *Stalin*, p. 267.

51. Khrushchev, Secret Speech.

52. George Kennan, Introduction to Boris I. Nicolaevsky, *Power and the Soviet Elite* (New York, 1965), p. xvii.

53. Alliluyeva, *Twenty Letters to a Friend*, p. 65.

54. *Novyy mir,* no. 4 (1962).

55. Humphrey Slater, *The Heretics* (New York, 1947).

56. *Znamya,* May 1964.

57. Khrushchev, speech to the XXIInd Party Congress (*Pravda,* 29 October 1961).

58. Vladimir Petrov, *Soviet Gold* (New York, 1949), pp. 122ff.

59. For example, *Bol'shaya sovetskaya entsyklopediya,* 2nd ed. (Moscow, 1949–58), s.v. "Kavtaradze."

60. See Lavrentiy Beria, *Questions of the History of the Bolshevik Organizations in Transcaucasia* (Moscow, 1935); *Bol'shaya sovetskaya entsyklopediya,* vol. 26.

61. Barmine, *One Who Survived,* p. 257.

62. Bukharin, conversation with Kamenev, July 1928.

## Chapter 4: Old Bolsheviks Confess

1. See, for example, Boris I. Nicolaevsky, *Power and the Soviet Elite* (New York, 1965), p. 66; Leonard Schapiro, *The Communist Party of the Soviet Union* (London, 1960), p. 402; G. A. Tokaev, *Betrayal of an Ideal* (London, 1954), p. 248.

2. *Pravda,* 16 January 1935.

3. *Pravda,* 23 January 1935.

4. *Bukharin Trial,* pp. 536–37.

5. Ibid., p. 537.

6. Ibid., p. 536.

7. "Letter of an Old Bolshevik," in Nicolaevsky, *Power and the Soviet Elite,* p. 46.

8. Alexander Orlov, *The Secret History of Stalin's Crimes* (New York, 1953), p. 216.

9. Nikita Khrushchev, *Khrushchev Remembers* (New York, 1970), p. 46.

10. *Pravda,* 1 March 1935.

11. *Pravda,* 9 March 1935.

12. Merle Fainsod, *How Russia Is Ruled,* 2nd ed. (London, 1963), p. 58.

13. *Sovetskaya molodezh,* 15 October 1988.

14. *Sotsialisticheskaya industriya,* 2 November 1988; *Moscow News,* no. 50 (1987).

15. *Znamya,* no. 12 (1988).

16. Fainsod, *How Russia Is Ruled,* p. 374.

17. Ibid., p. 223.

18. Ibid., pp. 223ff.

19. Ibid., pp. 56–57.

20. A. A. Piontkovskiy and V. D. Menshagin, *Kurs sovetskogo ugolovnogo prava* (Moscow, 1955).

21. *Izvestiya,* 8 April 1935.

22. Orlov, *Secret History of Stalin's Crimes,* p. 53.

23. For example, Nicolaevsky, *Power and the Soviet Elite,* p. 224; Elizabeth Lermolo, *Face of a Victim* (New York, 1955), pp. 206–7; George Saunders, ed., *Samizdat: Voices of the Soviet Opposition* (New York, 1974).

24. *Izvestiya TsK KPSS,* no. 7 (1989).

25. *Politicheskoe obrazovanie,* no. 15 (1988); *Izvestiya TsK KPSS,* no. 7 (1989).

26. *Bukharin Trial,* p. 419.

27. V. I. Lenin, *Polnoe sobranie sochineniy,* 5th ed., vol. 53 (Moscow, 1965); *Eesti Noukogude Entsüklopeedia.*

28. *Bukharin Trial,* p. 396.

29. "Letter of an Old Bolshevik," p. 56.

30. *Pravda*, 26 May 1935.

31. *Pravda*, 19 May 1962.

32. *Znamya*, June 1964.

33. *Pravda*, 8 June 1935.

34. *Pravda*, 16 June 1935, 19 June 1935.

35. Orlov, *Secret History of Stalin's Crimes*, pp. 310–11.

36. Nicolaevsky, *Power and the Soviet Elite*, p. 224.

37. Orlov, *Secret History of Stalin's Crimes*, p. 312.

38. *Pravda*, 28 June 1935.

39. *Zinoviev Trial*, p. 174.

40. *Izvestiya TsK KPSS*, no. 7 (1989).

41. *Pravda*, 8 February 1935.

42. Nicolaevsky, *Power and the Soviet Elite*, p. 22.

43. Ibid., pp. 14–16.

44. *SSSR: Vnutrenie protivorechiya*, no. 22 (1988).

45. "Letter of an Old Bolshevik," p. 62.

46. Orlov, *Secret History of Stalin's Crimes*, p. 73.

47. Ibid., p. 89.

48. *Zinoviev Trial*, p. 24.

49. Orlov, *Secret History of Stalin's Crimes*, p. 73; and see *Neva*, no. 6 (1988), p. 19.

50. See *Soviet Affairs*, no. 1 (1956) (St. Anthony's Papers), p. 13.

51. Orlov, *Secret History of Stalin's Crimes*, p. 123.

52. Ibid., pp. 338–51.

53. Andrei Vyshinskiy, *Sudostroitel'stvo v SSSR*, 3rd ed. (Moscow, 1936), p. 24.

54. *Izvestiya TsK KPSS*, no. 8 (1989).

55. Orlov, *Secret History of Stalin's Crimes*, pp. 82–84.

56. Ibid., p. 73.

57. Ibid., p. 119.

58. *Zinoviev Trial*, p. 97; *Izvestiya TsK KPSS*, no. 8 (1989).

59. "Ivan Ivanov," in *Sotsialisticheskiy vestnik*, March 1951.

60. *Izvestiya TsK KPSS*, no. 8 (1989).

61. *Pyatakov Trial*, p. 40.

62. Orlov, *Secret History of Stalin's Crimes*, pp. 110–11.

63. See Robert V. Daniels, *The Conscience of the Revolution* (Oxford, 1960), p. 170.

64. Orlov, *Secret History of Stalin's Crimes*, p. 109.

65. *Zinoviev Trial*, p. 158; *Izvestiya TsK KPSS*, no. 9 (1989).

66. Raphael R. Abramovitch, *The Soviet Revolution* (London, 1962), p. 414.

67. *Izvestiya TsK KPSS*, no. 8 (1989); Orlov, *Secret History of Stalin's Crimes*, pp. 82–84.

68. *Izvestiya TsK KPSS*, no. 8 (1989).

69. *Zinoviev Trial*, pp. 13, 31.

70. Ibid., p. 33.

71. Orlov, *Secret History of Stalin's Crimes*, p. 86.

72. Ibid., p. 130.

73. "Ivan Ivanov," in *Sotsialisticheskiy vestnik*.

74. Orlov, *Secret History of Stalin's Crimes*, pp. 129–30.

75. Ibid., pp. 124ff.

76. "Letter of an Old Bolshevik," p. 62.

77. *Bukharin Trial*, p. 510.

78. Orlov, *Secret History of Stalin's Crimes*, p. 131.

79. Nikita Khrushchev, Secret Speech.

80. Walter G. Krivitsky, *In Stalin's Secret Service* (London, 1939), p. 204.

81. *SSSR: Vnutrenie protivorechiya*, no. 22 (1988).

82. Orlov, *Secret History of Stalin's Crimes;* Krivitsky, *In Stalin's Secret Service.*

83. *Zinoviev Trial*, p. 159.

84. *SSSR: Vnutrenie protivorechiya*, no. 22 (1988).

85. *Pravda*, 24 March 1937; Fainsod, *How Russia Is Ruled*, pp. 56–57.

86. Fainsod, *How Russia Is Ruled*, p. 234.

87. *Nedelya*, no. 41 (1988).

88. Orlov, *Secret History of Stalin's Crimes*, p. 117.

89. *Nedelya*, no. 41 (1988).

90. "Ivan Ivanov," in *Sotsialisticheskiy vestnik.*

91. Ibid.; Saunders, *Samizat*, pp. 170ff.; Hrihory Kostiuk, *Okayanni Roki* (Toronto, 1978), p. 156; Nicolaevsky Archive, serial 1701, Hoover Institution Archives; *Nedelya*, no. 41 (1988).

92. *Bukharin Trial*, p. 556.

93. *Izvestiya TsK KPSS*, no. 8 (1989); G. A. Tokaev, *Comrade X* (London, 1956), pp. 56–57.

94. Krivitsky, *In Stalin's Secret Service*, pp. 207–8, 230; Alexander Barmine, *One Who Survived* (New York, 1945), pp. 294–95; *Politicheskoe obrazovanie*, no. 15 (1988).

95. Orlov, *Secret History of Stalin's Crimes*, p. 149.

96. "Letter of an Old Bolshevik," p. 63.

97. Ibid.

98. Orlov, *Secret History of Stalin's Crimes*, p. 162.

99. Ibid., chap. 13.

100. N. Ulyanovskaya and M. Ulyanovskaya, *Istoriia odnoy sem'i* (New York, 1982), p. 136.

101. Ibid., pp. 167–68.

102. Roy Medvedev, *Nikolai Bukharin* (New York, 1980), p. 151.

103. Ibid., p. 150.

104. Ibid.

105. Orlov, *Secret History of Stalin's Crimes*, p. 174; and see V. Petrov and E. Petrov, *Empire of Fear* (London, 1956), p. 45.

106. Khrushchev, Secret Speech.

107. Shelepin, speech to the XXInd Party Congress.

108. *Pravda*, 3 April 1964.

109. Orlov, *Secret History of Stalin's Crimes*, pp. 168–69.

110. *Zinoviev Trial*, p. 16.

111. Ibid., p. 37.

112. Ibid., p. 34.

113. Ibid., p. 39.

114. Victor Serge, *From Lenin to Stalin* (London, 1937), p. 82.

115. *Zinoviev Trial*, p. 151.

116. Ibid., p. 51.

117. Ibid., p. 61.

118. Ibid.

119. Ibid., p. 145.

120. Ibid., pp. 63–64.

121. Ibid., p. 66.

122. Ibid., p. 54.

123. Ibid., p. 68.

124. Ibid., p. 70.

125. Ibid., p. 81.

126. Ibid., p. 72.

127. Ibid., pp. 77–78.

128. Ibid., pp. 84–85.

129. Ibid., p. 81.

130. Ibid., p. 154.

131. Ibid., p. 153.

132. *Rundschau*, September 1936, p. 1630.

133. Isaac Don Levine, *The Mind of an Assassin* (New York, 1959), p. 26.

134. *Pravda*, 21 August 1936.

135. *Socialdemocraten*, 1 September 1936.

136. Dewey Commission, *Not Guilty* (New York, 1937), p. 85.

137. Orlov, *Secret History of Stalin's Crimes*, pp. 70–71.

138. See especially Pierre Broué Manuscripts, Hoover Institution Archives.

139. *Zinoviev Trial*, p. 103.

140. Ibid.

141. Ibid., p. 105.

142. Ibid., p. 147.

143. Ibid., p. 116.

144. *Izvestiya TsK KPSS*, no. 5 (1989).

145. *Zinoviev Trial*, p. 119.

146. Ibid., p. 120.

147. Ibid., p. 128.

148. Ibid., pp. 152–53.

149. Ibid., p. 163.

150. Orlov, *Secret History of Stalin's Crimes*, p. 174.

151. *Zinoviev Trial*, p. 166.

152. Ibid.

153. Orlov, *Secret History of Stalin's Crimes*, pp. 175–76.

154. *Zinoviev Trial*, p. 171.

155. Ibid.

156. Serge, *From Lenin to Stalin*, pp. 146–47; Nina Murray, *I Spied for Stalin* (New York, 1951); and see *Neva*, no. 6 (1988).

157. Serge, *From Lenin to Stalin*, p. 145; Emmanuel d'Astier de la Vigerie, *Staline* (Paris 1936), quoted in *Sotsialisticheskaya industriya*, 11 January 1989.

158. Orlov, *Secret History of Stalin's Crimes*, pp. 104, 116.

159. Roy Medvedev, *Let History Judge* (New York, 1971), p. 273.

160. *Leningradskaya pravda*, 13 November 1988.

161. Peter Yakir, "Letter to the Editor of *Kommunist*," 2 March 1969, translated in *Survey*, nos. 70–71 (1969).

162. *Nedelya*, no. 25 (1988); *Sotsialisticheskaya industriya*, 11 January 1989.

163. Kostiuk, *Okayanni Roki*, pp. 150, 156; A. Ryabov, *Tridsat' pyatyi i drugye gody* (Moscow, 1989), pp. 246–47; *Izvestiya TsK KPSS*, no. 8 (1989); "Rodsvenniki G. E. Zinovieva postradalshie ot repressiy" (*samizdat* manuscript).

164. Kostiuk, *Okayanni Roki*, p. 154.

165. Margarete [Buber] Neumann, *Under Two Dictators* (London, 1949), pp. 151ff.

166. "Letter of an Old Bolshevik," p. 63.

167. *Zinoviev Trial*, p. 19.

168. Ibid., p. 20.

169. Ibid., p. 31.

170. Ibid., p. 33.

171. Ibid., p. 59.

172. Ibid., p. 67.

173. Orlov, *Secret History of Stalin's Crimes*, p. 179.

174. Joseph Berger, *Shipwreck of a Generation* (London, 1971), pp. 96–97.

175. Isaac Deutscher, *The Prophet Outcast* (London, 1963), pp. 416–18.

176. D. J. Dallin and B. I. Nicolaevsky, *Forced Labour in the Soviet Union* (London, 1948), p. 39.

177. Roy Medvedev, *On Stalin and Stalinism* (Oxford, 1979), p. 117.


**Chapter 5: The Problem of Confession**

1. F. Beck and W. Godin, *Russian Purge and the Extraction of Confession* (London, 1951), p. 38.

2. Abdurakhman Avtorkhanov, *Stalin and the Soviet Communist Party* (London, 1959), p. 138.

3. Raphael R. Abramovitch, *The Soviet Revolution* (London, 1962), p. 416.

4. Boris I. Nicolaevsky, *Power and the Soviet Elite* (New York, 1965), p. 25.

5. Boris Souvarine, *Stalin* (London, 1949), pp. 362–63.

6. *Pravda,* 29 February 1928.

7. N. Valentinov [N. V. Volsky], quoted in Leonard Schapiro, *The Communist Party of the Soviet Union* (London, 1960), p. 381.

8. Valentinov, unpublished manuscript, quoted in Abramovitch, *Soviet Revolution,* p. 415.

9. Valentinov, quoted in Schapiro, *Communist Party of the Soviet Union,* p. 381.

10. Anton Ciliga, *The Russian Enigma* (London, 1940), p. 75.

11. Ibid., p. 85.

12. Arthur Koestler, *Arrow in the Blue* (London, 1945), vol. 2, p. 155.

13. Ciliga, *Russian Enigma,* p. 255.

14. *Pravda,* 15 December 1923.

15. *Pravda,* 18 January 1924.

16. Abramovitch, *Soviet Revolution,* p. 288.

17. *XIV s''ezd Vsesoyuznoy kommunisticheskoy partii (b). Stenograficheskii otchet* (Moscow, 1926).

18. See Souvarine, *Stalin,* p. 459.

19. Ibid., p. 440.

20. See Schapiro, *Communist Party of the Soviet Union,* pp. 294–95.

21. Angelica Balabanoff, *Impressions of Lenin* (Ann Arbor, Mich., 1964).

22. *Zinoviev Trial,* p. 133.

23. *Pravda,* 16 June 1933.

24. "Letter of an Old Bolshevik," in Nicolaevsky, *Power and the Soviet Elite,* pp. 54–55.

25. Eugenia Ginzburg, *Journey into the Whirlwind* (New York, 1967), pp. 105–6.

26. *Nedelya,* 11–17 July 1988.

27. Arthur Koestler, *Darkness at Noon* (London, 1940), p. 242.

28. Beck and Godin, *Russian Purge and the Extraction of Confession,* p. 86.

29. Ibid.

30. A. Tairov, before the French "Commission Rogatoire," cited in Dewey Commission, *Not Guilty* (New York, 1937), p. 370.

31. Koestler, *Darkness at Noon*, p. 183.

32. *Bukharin Trial*, pp. 777–78.

33. Alexander Orlov, *The Secret History of Stalin's Crimes* (New York, 1953), pp. 117–118.

34. Victor Serge, *From Lenin to Stalin* (London, 1937), p. 145.

35. Orlov, *Secret History of Stalin's Crimes*, pp. 145–46.

36. Ibid., p. 149.

37. Ciliga, *Russian Enigma*, p. 283.

38. *Nedelya*, 11–17 July 1988.

39. *Pyatakov Trial*, p. 204.

40. Nikita Khrushchev, concluding remarks to the XXIInd Party Congress.

41. *Neva*, no. 10 (1988).

42. Nikita Khrushchev, Secret Speech.

43. *Podem*, December 1988.

44. *Trud*, 26 May 1988.

45. Victor Kravchenko, *I Chose Justice* (London, 1951), pp. 252–54.

46. Ibid., p. 169.

47. Ibid., p. 154.

48. Elizabeth Lermolo, *Face of a Victim* (New York, 1955), p. 44.

49. Kravchenko, *I Chose Justice*, pp. 169–70.

50. G. A. Tokaev, *Betrayal of an Ideal* (London, 1954), pp. 264–66.

51. For example, Margarete [Buber] Neumann, *Under Two Dictators* (London, 1949), p. 41; R. V. Ivanov-Razumnik, *Memoirs* (London, 1965), p. 222; *The Dark Side of the Moon* (London, 1946); Ginzburg, *Journey into the Whirlwind*, p. 97.

52. Ivanov-Razumnik, *Memoirs*, p. 240.

53. Ibid., p. 253.

54. Ibid., p. 246; Ginzburg, *Journey into the Whirlwind*, pp. 118, 122; Kravchenko, *I Chose Justice*, pp. 274–75.

55. Ibid., p. 253.

56. *Moscow News*, 19 June 1988.

57. Khrushchev, Secret Speech.

58. *Izvestiya TsK KPSS*, no. 5 (1989).

59. A. V. Gorbatov, *Years Off My Life* (New York, 1964), p. 113.

60. Roy Medvedev, *Let History Judge*, rev. ed. (New York, 1989), p. 493; Ivanov-Razumnik, *Memoirs*, p. 250.

61. Ivanov-Razumnik, *Memoirs*, pp. 248–49.

62. Medvedev, *Let History Judge*, rev. ed., p. 187.

63. *Izvestiya TsK KPSS*, no. 4 (1989).

64. *Literaturnaya gazeta*, 23 November 1988.

65. *Sovetskoe gosudarstvo i pravo*, no. 3 (March 1965).

66. Alexander Weissberg, *Conspiracy of Silence* (London, 1952), p. 236.

67. Antoni Ekart, *Vanished Without a Trace* (London, 1954), p. 175.

68. Ginzburg, *Journey into the Whirlwind*, pp. 69–72.

69. *Moscow News*, no. 19 (1988).

70. Beck and Godin, *Russian Purge and the Extraction of Confession*, pp. 53–54.

71. Weissberg, *Conspiracy of Silence*, pp. 163–64.

72. Ibid., p. 297.

73. Ibid., pp. 386–87.

74. Beck and Godin, *Russian Purge and the Extraction of Confession*, p. 71.

75. El Campesino, *Listen, Comrades* (London, 1952), p. 132; and see Aleksandr Solzhenitsyn, *The First Circle* (London, 1968), p. 150.

76. Z. Stypulkowski, *Invitation to Moscow* (London, 1951), chaps. 12–14.

77. Artur London, *L'Aveu* (Paris, 1969).

78. Evzen [Eugen] Loebl and Dusan Pokorny, *Die Revolution Rehabilitiert Ihre Kinder* (Vienna, 1968); and see Michael Charlton, *The Eagle and the Small Birds* (Chicago, 1984), pp. 82–83.

79. *Moscow News,* no. 18 (1988).

80. Charlton, *Eagle and the Small Birds*, p. 84.

81. Ciliga, *Russian Enigma*, p. 154.

82. Orlov, *Secret History of Stalin's Crimes*, p. 54.

83. Stypulkowski, *Invitation to Moscow*, p. 242.

84. Medvedev, *Let History Judge*, rev. ed., pp. 15, 490.

85. *Izvestiya TsK KPSS*, no. 4 (1989).

86. Arthur Koestler, Introduction to Weissberg, *Conspiracy of Silence*, pp. xi–xii.

87. Kravchenko, *I Chose Freedom*, pp. 284–90.

88. Ivanov-Razumnik, *Memoirs*, p. 250; Medvedev, *Let History Judge*, rev. ed., p. 493.

89. *Nova mysl*, no. 7 (10 July 1968).

90. Weissberg, *Conspiracy of Silence*, p. 415.

91. Ibid., pp. 352–55.

92. *Novaya zhizn'*, 8 June 1918, cited in J. E. Scott, "The Cheka," *Soviet Affairs*, no. 1 (1956), p. 8.

93. *Sovetskoe gosudarstvo i pravo*, no. 3 (March 1965).

94. Kravchenko, *I Chose Justice*, pp. 169–72.

## Chapter 6: Last Stand

1. "Letter of an Old Bolshevik," in Boris I. Nicolaevsky, *Power and the Soviet Elite* (New York, 1965), p. 26.

2. *Pyatakov Trial*, pp. 202, 214.

3. Ibid., p. 561.

4. *Sovetskaya industriya*, 10 June 1988; *Izvestiya TsK KPSS*, no. 9 (1989).

5. *Pyatakov Trial*, p. 167.

6. *Pravda*, 1 September 1936.

7. *Oktyabr'*, no. 12 (1988).

8. *Znamya*, no. 12 (1988); *Izvestiya TsK KPSS*, no. 5 (1989).

9. "Letter of an Old Bolshevik," p. 63.

10. *Pyatakov Trial*, p. 17.

11. *Bukharin Trial*, p. 125.

12. Roy Medvedev, *Nikolai Bukharin* (New York, 1980), p. 131.

13. Ibid.

14. *Pravda*, 9 October 1988; *Voprosy istorii*, no. 10 (1988).

15. Nikita Khrushchev, Secret Speech; *Izvestiya TsK KPSS*, no. 9 (1989).

16. "Letter of an Old Bolshevik," p. 64.

17. Alexander Orlov, *The Secret History of Stalin's Crimes* (New York, 1953), p. 143.

18. *Bukharin Trial*, p. 556.

19. Simon Wolin and Robert M. Slusser, *The Soviet Secret Police* (New York, 1957), p. 45.

20. *Bukharin Trial*, p. 553.

21. G. A. Tokaev, *Betrayal of an Ideal* (London, 1954), pp. 249–50.

22. "Letter of an Old Bolshevik," p. 63.
23. Khrushchev, Secret Speech.
24. *Literaturnaya gazeta,* 29 June 1988.
25. *Bukharin Trial,* p. 281.
26. *Izvestiya TsK KPSS,* nos. 5–6 (1989).
27. *Sotsialisticheskaya industriya,* 10 June 1988.
28. Orlov, *Secret History of Stalin's Crimes,* p. 180.
29. *Znamya,* no. 12 (1988).
30. Orlov, *Secret History of Stalin's Crimes,* p. 206.
31. *Pyatakov Trial,* p. 134.
32. Orlov, *Secret History of Stalin's Crimes,* p. 205.
33. Pierre Broué, *Le Procès de Moscou* (Paris, 1964), p. 276.
34. Alexander Weissberg, *Conspiracy of Silence* (London, 1952), p. 56.
35. *Izvestiya TsK KPSS,* no. 9 (1989).
36. *Sovetskoe gosudarstvo i pravo,* no. 3 (March 1965).
37. *Pyatakov Trial,* p. 287.
38. Orlov, *Secret History of Stalin's Crimes,* p. 182.
39. Victor Kravchenko, *I Chose Freedom* (London, 1947), p. 331.
40. Weissberg, *Conspiracy of Silence,* p. 232.
41. Kravchenko, *I Chose Freedom,* pp. 329–330.
42. *Pyatakov Trial,* p. 257.
43. Ibid., p. 537.
44. Orlov, *Secret History of Stalin's Crimes,* p. 183.
45. Aleksandr Solzhenitsyn, *The Gulag Archipelago* (New York, 1973), vol. 1, p. 415.
46. Medvedev, *Nikolai Bukharin,* p. 130.
47. Stalin, speech to the February–March plenum of the Central Committee, 5 March 1937.
48. *Pravda,* 29 May 1937.
49. G. Maryagin, *Postyshev* (Moscow, 1965), p. 291.
50. Veljko Micunović, *Moscow Diary* (New York, 1986), p. 28.
51. *Izvestiya TsK KPSS,* no. 5 (1989).
52. *Znamya,* no. 12 (1988).
53. Solzhenitsyn, *Gulag Archipelago,* vol. 1, p. 416; Anton Antonov-Ovseenko, *The Time of Stalin* (New York, 1981), p. 618; Medvedev, *Nikolai Bukharin,* pp. 131–32; *Izvestiya TsK KPSS,* no. 5 (1989).
54. *Izvestiya TsK KPSS,* no. 9 (1989).
55. Orlov, *Secret History of Stalin's Crimes,* p. 207.
56. Ibid., p. 350.
57. *Znamya,* no. 12 (1988); *Izvestiya TsK KPSS,* no. 5 (1989).
58. *Znamya,* no. 12 (1988).
59. Ibid.
60. Ibid.
61. Ibid.
62. *Teatr,* no. 7 (1988).
63. Resolutions of the Congress of the Communist Party of the Ukraine (*Pravda,* 13 June 1937).
64. *Visti,* 1 June 1937.
65. *Moscow News,* no. 26 (1988); *Mazoji Lietuviskoji Tarybine Enciklpedija; Bol'shaya sovetskaya entsyklopediya,* 3rd ed. (Moscow, 1970–78).
66. *Pyatakov Trial,* p. 40.

67. Alexander Barmine, *One Who Survived* (New York, 1945), p. 295.

68. For example, *Pravda,* 12 September 1936.

69. Stalin, speech to the February–March plenum of the Central Committee, 3 March 1937.

70. *Pyatakov Trial,* p. 7.

71. Ibid., p. 14.

72. Ibid., p. 43.

73. Ibid., p. 48.

74. Ibid., p. 49.

75. Ibid.

76. Ibid., p. 25.

77. Ibid., p. 413.

78. Ibid., p. 69.

79. Ibid., pp. 58ff.

80. Orlov, *Secret History of Stalin's Crimes,* p. 191.

81. *Pyatakov Trial,* p. 443.

82. Ibid., p. 85.

83. Ibid., p. 125.

84. Ibid.

85. Ibid., p. 127.

86. Ibid., p. 129.

87. Ibid., p. 135.

88. Ibid., p. 105.

89. Ibid., p. 160.

90. *Sotsialisticheskaya industriya,* 10 June 1988.

91. *Pyatakov Trial,* p. 209.

92. Ibid., p. 210.

93. Ibid., p. 245.

94. Ibid., p. 257.

95. Ibid., p. 258.

96. Ibid., p. 283.

97. Ibid., p. 280.

98. Ibid., p. 288.

99. Ibid., p. 248.

100. Ibid., p. 271.

101. Ibid., p. 272.

102. Ibid., p. 229.

103. Ibid., p. 226.

104. Ibid., p. 222.

105. N. M. Shvernik, speech to the XXIInd Party Congress (*Pravda,* 26 October 1961).

106. *Pyatakov Trial,* p. 222.

107. Ibid., p. 511.

108. Ibid., p. 475.

109. Ibid., pp. 303–33.

110. Ibid., pp. 566–67.

111. Ibid., p. 569.

112. Ibid., p. 367.

113. Ibid., p. 368.

114. Ibid., p. 365.

115. Ibid., pp. 371–72, 378.

116. Ibid., p. 412.
117. Ibid., p. 463.
118. Ibid., p. 466.
119. Ibid., p. 480.
120. Ibid., p. 494.
121. Ibid., p. 474.
122. Ibid., p. 468.
123. Ibid., p. 514.
124. Ibid., p. 476–77.
125. Ibid., p. 489.
126. Ibid., p. 207.
127. Ibid., p. 170.
128. Ibid., p. 502.
129. Ibid., p. 512.
130. Ibid., p. 517.
131. Ibid., p. 481.
132. Ibid., p. 516.
133. Ibid., p. 517.
134. Ibid., p. 541.
135. Ibid., p. 548.
136. Ibid., p. 543.
137. Elisabeth K. Poretsky, *Our Own People* (London, 1969), p. 198.
138. Orlov, *Secret History of Stalin's Crimes*, p. 212.
139. *Izvestiya TsK KPSS*, no. 7 (1989); V. Petrov and E. Petrov, *Empire of Fear* (London, 1956), p. 69; Gustaw Herling, *A World Apart* (London, 1951).
140. *Izvestiya TsK KPSS*, no. 9 (1989).
141. Wolin and Slusser, *Soviet Secret Police*, p. 194.
142. Elizabeth Lermolo, *Face of a Victim* (New York, 1955), pp. 134–35.
143. *Knizhnoe obozrenie*, 4 November 1988.
144. Khrushchev, speech of 8 March 1963.
145. *Pyatakov Trial*, p. 545.
146. Ibid., p. 514.
147. Ibid., p. 353.
148. *Pravda*, 29 January 1937.
149. *Pravda*, 31 January 1937.
150. *Neva*, no. 6 (1988), p. 69.
151. Kravchenko, *I Chose Freedom*, p. 239.
152. *Pyatakov Trial*, p. 510.
153. *Izvestiya*, 22 November 1963; *samizdat* manuscript; *Literaturnaya Rossiya*, May 1989.
154. Robert Conquest, *Power and Policy in the U.S.S.R.* (London, 1961), pp. 449–53.
155. *Izvestiya*, 22 November 1963; I. M. Dubinsky-Mukhadze, *Ordzhonikidze* (Moscow, 1963), p. 6.
156. *Literaturnaya gazeta*, 7 September 1988.
157. *Izvestiya*, 22 November 1963; Dubinsky-Mukhadze, *Ordzhonikidze*, p. 6.
158. *Literaturnaya gazeta*, 7 September 1988.
159. *Izvestiya*, 22 November 1963; Dubinsky-Mukhadze, *Ordzhonikidze*, p. 6.
160. *Pravda*, 19 February 1937.
161. Dubinsky-Mukhadze, *Ordzhonikidze*, p. 7.
162. *Pravda*, 19 February 1937.

163. *Bol'shaya sovetskaya entsyklopediya,* 2nd ed. (Moscow, 1949–58), s.v. "Ordzhonikidze."

164. Roy Medvedev, *Let History Judge* (New York, 1971), p. 194.

165. *Na rubezhe,* nos. 3–4 (1952).

166. Kravchenko, *I Chose Freedom,* p. 240.

167. Khrushchev, speech to the XXIInd Party Congress.

168. *Bakinskiy rabochiy,* 17 June 1962.

169. Eugenia Ginzburg, *Journey into the Whirlwind* (New York, 1967), p. 73.

170. *Pravda,* 17 November 1964.

171. For example, Orlov, *Secret History of Stalin's Crimes,* pp. 196–98.

172. Khrushchev, speech to the XXIInd Party Congress.

173. Private interview with author.

174. Abdurakhman Avtorkhanov, *Stalin and the Soviet Communist Party* (London, 1959), p. 229.

175. *Neva,* no. 6 (1988).

176. *Izvestiya,* 22 November 1963.

177. Medvedev, *Nikolai Bukharin,* p. 134; *Nedelya,* no. 12 (1988).

178. *Komsomolskaya pravda,* 2 April 1988.

179. *Neva,* no. 6 (1988), p. 69.

180. *Komsomolskaya pravda,* 2 April 1988.

181. *Zinoviev Trial,* p. 162.

182. *Gorizont,* no. 5 (1988), p. 36.

183. *Pravda,* 19 February 1937.

184. *Bol'shaya sovetskaya entsyklopediya,* 2nd ed., vol. 31.

185. *Samizdat* manuscript.

186. *Znamya,* no. 12 (1988).

187. P. I. Yakir and Ya. A. Geller, *Komandarm Yakir* (Moscow, 1963), p. 211.

188. Khrushchev, Secret Speech.

189. Satyukov, speech to the XXIInd Party Congress.

190. *Sovetskaya kul'tura,* 13 September 1988; *Znamya,* no. 12 (1988).

191. *Znamya,* no. 12 (1988).

192. *Voprosy istorii KPSS,* no. 2 (1989).

193. Khrushchev, in *Pravda,* 17 March 1937.

194. Ikramov, quoted in *Bukharin Trial,* p. 349.

195. Avtorkhanov, *Stalin and the Soviet Communist Party,* p. 118.

196. *Kommunist,* no. 13 (1988).

197. Walter G. Krivitsky, *In Stalin's Secret Service* (London, 1939), p. 228.

198. *Yunost',* no. 3 (1988), p. 60.

199. *Kommunist,* no. 13 (1988).

200. Ibid.

201. *Oktyabr',* no. 12 (1988); *Izvestiya TsK KPSS,* no. 5 (1989).

202. *Znamya,* no. 12 (1988).

203. *Pravda,* 6 March 1937.

204. *Visti,* 1 February 1937.

205. *Pravda,* 8 February 1937.

206. *Pravda,* 9 February 1937.

207. Khrushchev, Secret Speech.

208. Ibid.

209. Ibid.

210. Hrihory Kostiuk, "The Fall of Postyshev," *Research Program on the U.S.S.R.,* no. 6a (1954), in *Stalinist Rule in the Ukraine* (Munich, 1960), pp. 118–22.

211. *Oktyabr'*, no. 12 (1988).

212. Khrushchev, Secret Speech.

213. Krivitsky, *In Stalin's Secret Service*, p. 228.

214. *Znamya*, no. 12 (1988).

215. *Oktyabr'*, no. 12 (1988).

216. Shvernik, speech to the XXIInd Party Congress (*Pravda*, 26 October 1961).

217. W. P. Coates and Zelda K. Coates, comps., *The Moscow Trial* (London, 1937), p. 249.

218. Ibid., p. 253.

219. Ibid., p. 205.

220. Quoted by Vyshinsky, in *Bukharin Trial*, p. 626.

221. Coates and Coates, *Moscow Trial*, pp. 275–76.

222. Ibid., p. 277.

223. Ibid., p. 279.

224. *Visti*, 17 March 1937.

225. Report of the January plenum of the Central Committee (*Pravda*, 19 January 1938).

226. *Pravda*, 23 March 1937.

227. *Pravda*, 29 May 1937.

228. *Pravda*, 30 May 1987.

229. *Visti*, 2 June 1937.

230. Orlov, *Secret History of Stalin's Crimes*, p. 221.

231. Ibid.

232. Krivitsky, *In Stalin's Secret Service*, p. 167.

233. Orlov, *Secret History of Stalin's Crimes*, p. 222.

234. *Bukharin Trial*, p. 482.

235. Orlov, *Secret History of Stalin's Crimes*, p. 225.

236. *Literaturnaya gazeta*, no. 4 (1987).

237. *Bukharin Trial*, p. 569.

238. Ibid., p. 571.

239. Ibid., p. 556.

240. *Pravda*, 4 April 1937.

241. *Pravda*, 5 April 1937.

242. *Znamya*, no. 12 (1988).

243. Zbigniew Brzezinski, *The Permanent Purge* (Cambridge, Mass., 1956), p. 229.

244. Svetlana Alliluyeva, *Only One Year* (New York, 1969), p. 388.

245. *Sovetskoye gosudarstvo i pravo*, no. 3 (March 1965).

246. *Sotsialisticheskaya zakonnost'*, no. 1 (1938).

247. *Pravda*, 20 January 1937.

248. *Pravda*, 9 April 1937.

249. *Voprosy istorii KPSS*, no. 9 (1965).

## Chapter 7: Assault on the Army

1. *Pravda*, 11 June 1937.

2. *Pravda*, 15 June 1937.

3. John Erickson, *The Soviet High Command* (London, 1962), p. 58.

4. Robert S. Sullivant, *Soviet Politics and the Ukraine, 1917–1957* (New York, 1963), p. 342.

5. Erickson, *Soviet High Command*, p. 51.

6. Ibid., p. 99.

7. Isaac Deutscher, *The Prophet Unarmed* (London, 1959), p. 350.

8. *Izvestiya*, 24–30 January 1963; N. I. Koritskiy et al., *Marshal Tukhachevskiy* (Moscow, 1965).

9. *Bukharin Trial*, p. 188.

10. P. Deriabin and F. Gibney, *The Secret World* (London, 1960), pp. 110–11.

11. Isaac Deutscher, *Stalin* (London, 1949), p. 379.

12. F. Beck and W. Godin, *Russian Purge and the Extraction of Confession* (London, 1951), p. 95.

13. Ibid., p. 253.

14. Ibid., p. 256.

15. Ibid., p. 71.

16. Alexander Orlov, *The Secret History of Stalin's Crimes* (New York, 1953), p. 242.

17. Walter G. Krivitsky, *In Stalin's Secret Service* (London, 1939), p. 7.

18. I. V. Dubinskiy, *Naperekor vetram* (Moscow, 1964), pp. 243ff.

19. *Zinoviev Trial*, pp. 34, 41.

20. Vassili Grossman, *In the Town of Berdichev*.

21. Alexander Barmine, *One Who Survived* (New York, 1945), pp. 89–90.

22. *Zinoviev Trial*, p. 36.

23. Dubinskiy, *Naperekor vetram*.

24. *Pravda*, 23 August 1936.

25. *Pyatakov Trial*, p. 181.

26. Ibid., p. 94.

27. Dubinskiy, *Naperekor vetram; Voenno-istoricheskiy zhurnal*, no. 6 (1965).

28. Dubinskiy, *Naperekor vetram*.

29. *Zinoviev Trial*, p. 116.

30. *Izvestiya TsK KPSS*, no. 5 (1989).

31. Barmine, *One Who Survived*, p. 311.

32. *Izvestiya TsK KPSS*, no. 4 (1989).

33. Ibid.

34. Erickson, *Soviet High Command*, pp. 376–77.

35. *Izvestiya TsK KPSS*, no. 4 (1989).

36. *Zinoviev Trial*, p. 22.

37. Dubinskiy, *Naperekor vetram*.

38. Erickson, *Soviet High Command*, p. 427; *Znamya*, no. 12 (1988).

39. Abdurakhman Avtorkhanov, *Stalin and the Soviet Communist Party* (London, 1959), p. 48.

40. *Pyatakov Trial*, p. 146.

41. Krivitsky, *In Stalin's Secret Service*, p. 239.

42. P. I. Yakir and Ya. A. Geller, *Komandarm Yakir* (Moscow, 1963), pp. 207ff.

43. Ibid., p. 212.

44. Yu. P. Petrov, *Partiynoe stroitel'stvo v sovetskoy armii i flote (1918–1961)* (Moscow, 1964), p. 299.

45. Ibid.

46. Yakir and Geller, *Komandarm Yakir*, p. 212.

47. Krivitsky, *In Stalin's Secret Service*, pp. 250–51; Barmine, *One Who Survived*, p. 7.

48. *Izvestiya TsK KPSS*, no. 4 (1989).

49. Koritskiy et al., *Marshal Tukhachevskiy*, pp. 219ff.

50. Petrov, *Partiynoe stroitel'stvo v sovetskoy armii i flote*, p. 303.

51. Dubinskiy, *Naperekor vetram.*

52. *Izvestiya TsK KPSS*, no. 4 (1989).

53. *Izvestiya TsK KPSS*, no. 6 (1989).

54. Ibid.

55. *Izvestiya TsK KPSS*, no. 4 (1989).

56. Ibid.

57. *Pravda*, 29 April 1988.

58. *Izvestiya TsK KPSS*, no. 6 (1989).

59. *Izvestiya TsK KPSS*, no. 4 (1989).

60. *Pravda*, 29 April 1988.

61. W. Schellenberg, *The Schellenberg Memoirs* (London, 1956), p. 49.

62. See O. Pyatnitsky, speech to the XIIth plenum of the Executive Committee of the Comintern.

63. *Novyy mir*, no. 4 (1964).

64. Beck and Godin, *Russian Purge and the Extraction of Confession,* p. 198.

65. *XVII s''ezd Vsesoyuznoy kommunisticheskoy partii (b) 26 yanvarya–10 fevralya 1934 g. Stenograficheskii otchet* (Moscow, 1934).

66. Krivitsky, *In Stalin's Secret Service,* p. 31.

67. Major V. Dapishev of the Soviet General Staff, at a session of the Department for the History of the Great Patriotic War at the Institute of Marxism-Leninism, 18 February 1966 (*Posev*, 13 January 1967); see also Ernst Genri [S. N. Rostovsky] (*Grani*, no. 63 [1967]).

68. Erickson, *Soviet High Command*, pp. 433–34.

69. *Izvestiya TsK KPSS*, no. 6 (1989).

70. *Oktyabr'*, no. 12 (1988).

71. *Politicheskoe obrazovanie*, no. 5 (1989).

72. Wilhelm Hoettl, *The Secret Front* (London, 1954); and see *Nedelya*, 13 February 1989.

73. W. Gomulka, report to the IXth plenum of the Central Committee of the Polish Workers' Party (*Trybuna Ludu*, 23 November 1961).

74. For example, Lev Nikulin, *Marshal Tukhachevskiy* (Moscow, 1964); Khrushchev, speech to the XXIInd Party Congress; Winston Churchill, *The Second World War*, vol. 1, *The Gathering Storm* (London, 1948), p. 224; and see *Voenno-istoricheskiy zhurnal*, no. 10 (1988).

75. Léon Blum, quoted in Erickson, *Soviet High Command*, p. 433; *Novaya i noveyshaya istoriya*, no. 1 (1989).

76. *Trybuna Ludu*, 23 November 1961.

77. Private information from John Erickson.

78. Nikulin, *Marshal Tukhachevskiy*, pp. 189–94.

79. *Novaya i noveyshaya istoriia*, no. 1 (1989) (accepting the testimony of Schellenberg, *Schellenberg Memoirs*, and Hoettl, *Secret Front*); *Sovetskaya Rossiya*, 18 September 1988; *Politicheskoe obrazovanie*, no. 5 (1989).

80. *Ukrains'ka Radians'ka Entsiklopediia* (Kiev, 1959–65).

81. Krivitsky, *In Stalin's Secret Service*, p. 27.

82. D. V. Pankov, *Komkor Eideman* (Moscow, 1965), p. 103.

83. *Voprosy istorii KPSS*, no. 12 (1964).

84. Koritskiy et al., *Marshal Tukhachevskiy*, p. 134.

85. Nikulin, *Marshal Tukhachevskiy.*

86. *Oktyabr'*, no. 12 (1988).

87. Koritskiy et al., *Marshal Tukhachevskiy*, pp. 128–29.

88. Ibid.; *Voenno-istoricheskiy zhurnal*, no. 10 (1965).

89. Nikulin, *Marshal Tukhachevskiy*.

90. Yakir and Geller, *Komandarm Yakir*, pp. 227ff.

91. *Izvestiya TsK KPSS*, no. 6 (1989).

92. P. N. Aleksandrov et al., *Komandarm Uborevich* (Moscow, 1964), pp. 230ff.

93. *Izvestiya TsK KPSS*, no. 6 (1989).

94. A. V. Gorbatov, *Years Off My Life* (New York, 1964), p. 103.

95. Yakir and Geller, *Komandarm Yakir*.

96. Dubinskiy, *Naperekor vetram;* Nikulin, *Marshal Tukhachevskiy;* Yakir and Geller, *Komandarm Yakir*.

97. *Pravda*, 1 June 1937.

98. *Oktyabr'*, no. 12 (1988).

99. *Krasnaya zvezda*, 6 June 1937.

100. A. N. Shelepin, speech to the XXIInd Party Congress (*Pravda*, 27 October 1961).

101. Yakir and Geller, *Komandarm Yakir*, pp. 230–32.

102. Dubinskiy, *Naperekor vetram*, chap. 14.

103. *Pravda*, 29 April 1988.

104. Petrov, *Partiynoe stroitel'stvo v sovetskoy armii i flote*, pp. 299–300.

105. *Izvestiya TsK KPSS*, no. 4 (1989).

106. Ibid.

107. Anton Antonov-Ovseenko, *The Time of Stalin* (New York, 1981), p. 185.

108. Nikulin, *Marshal Tukhachevskiy*, pp. 189–94.

109. Peter Yakir, at a session of the Department for the History of the Great Patriotic War at the Institute of Marxism-Leninism, 18 February 1966 (*Posev*, 13 January 1967).

110. *Bukharin Trial*, p. 5.

111. *Pravda*, 29 April 1988.

112. *Izvestiya TsK KPSS*, no. 4, 1989.

113. Ibid.

114. Ibid.

115. Ibid.

116. Dubinskiy, *Naperekor vetram*, p. 267; *Izvestiya TsK KPSS*, no. 4 (1989).

117. Lev Nikulin, in *Ogonek*, no. 13 (March 1963).

118. *Izvestiya TsK KPSS*, no. 4 (1989).

119. Dubinskiy, *Naperekor vetram*, p. 268.

120. *Oktyabr'*, no. 12 (1988).

121. Khrushchev, speech to the XXIInd Party Congress.

122. Shelepin, speech to the XXIInd Party Congress.

123. Yakir and Geller, *Komandarm Yakir*, pp. 230–32.

124. *Kazakhstanskaya pravda*, 15 October 1963.

125. Margarete [Buber] Neumann, *Under Two Dictators* (London, 1949), p. 56.

126. Yakir and Geller, *Komandarm Yakir*, p. 232.

127. Khrushchev, speech to the XXIInd Party Congress.

128. *Bilshovik Ukrainy*, no. 6 (1938).

129. Aleksandrov et al., *Komandarm Uborevich*, pp. 265ff.

130. Lev Nikulin, in *Oktyabr'*, nos. 2–5 (1965).

131. Antoni Ekart, *Vanished Without a Trace* (London, 1954), p. 244.

132. *Ogonek*, no. 13 (1963).

133. Barmine, *One Who Survived*, p. 8.

134. Simon Wolin and Robert M. Slusser, *The Soviet Secret Police* (New York, 1957), p. 194.

135. Peter Yakir, "Letter to the Editor of *Kommunist*," 2 March 1969, translated in *Survey,* nos. 70–71 (1969).

136. *Pravda,* 29 April 1988.

137. *Izvestiya TsK KPSS,* no. 4 (1989).

138. Yakir, "Letter to the Editor of *Kommunist*," pp. 72, 75.

139. Barmine, *One Who Survived,* p. 8.

140. G. A. Tokaev, *Betrayal of an Ideal* (London, 1954), p. 244.

141. Marshal S. T. Biryuzov, *Sovetskii soldat na Balkanakh* (Moscow, 1963), p. 141.

142. A. T. Stuchenko, *Zavidnaya nasha sudba* (Moscow, 1964), p. 63.

143. Ibid., p. 64.

144. Barmine, *One Who Survived,* pp. 6–8.

145. Gorbatov, *Years Off My Life,* p. 104.

146. L. T. Starinov, *Miny zhdut svoego chasa* (Moscow, 1964), pp. 149–66.

147. *Moscow News,* no. 14 (1988).

148. Biriuzov, *Sovetskii soldat,* pp. 137, 143.

149. Gorbatov, *Years Off My Life,* p. 104.

150. Alexander Weissberg, *Conspiracy of Silence* (London, 1952), pp. 422–23.

151. *Ogonek,* no. 46 (1988).

152. Stuchenko, *Zavidnaya nasha sudba.*

153. *Byelarus,* no. 7 (1965).

154. Petrov, *Partiynoe stroitel'stvo v sovetskoy armii i flote,* pp. 299–300.

155. *Krasnaya zvezda,* 2 June 1937.

156. L. Gaglov and I. Selishchev, *Komissary* (Moscow, 1961).

157. Petrov, *Partiynoe stroitel'stvo v sovetskoy armii i flote,* p. 302; *Kommunist,* 27 September 1988.

158. *Krasnaya zvezda,* 1 June 1937.

159. Genri, in *Grani.*

160. Petrov, *Partiynoe stroitel'stvo v sovetskoy armii i flote,* pp. 299–300.

161. Ibid., p. 302.

162. Ibid., pp. 301–2.

163. Ibid., p. 302.

164. Ibid., p. 304.

165. Ibid., p. 312.

166. Ibid., p. 303n.

167. Ibid., pp. 299–300.

168. V. I. Lenin, *Polnoe sobranie sochineniy,* 5th ed., vol. 51 (Moscow, 1965).

169. A. Dyakov, in *Oktyabr',* no. 7 (1964).

170. Gorbatov, *Years Off My Life,* p. 107.

171. Ibid., pp. 108ff.

172. Beck and Godin, *Russian Purge and the Extraction of Confession,* pp. 96–97.

173. Khrushchev, speech to the XXIInd Party Congress.

174. Beck and Godin, *Russian Purge and the Extraction of Confession,* p. 48.

175. *Oktyabr',* no. 12 (1988).

176. Weissberg, *Conspiracy of Silence,* p. 27.

177. *Krasnaya zvezda,* 2 March 1965.

178. *Komsomolskaya pravda,* 13 November 1964.

179. Blagoy Popov, *Ot Layptsigskiya protses v Sibirskie lageri* (Paris, 1979), p. 41.

180. *Sovetskaya Bukovina,* 10 February 1965.

181. Ilya Ehrenburg, in *Novyy mir,* no. 5 (1962).

182. Orlov, *Secret History of Stalin's Crimes,* p. 241.

183. Ilya Ehrenburg, *Men, Years, Life* (New York, 1961), vol. 4, pp. 152, 146.

184. *Pod znamenam Ispanskoy respubliki* (Moscow, 1965), p. 190.

185. Milovan Djilas, *Conversations with Stalin* (London, 1962), p. 13.

186. Genri, in *Grani*.

187. Erickson, *Soviet High Command*, p. 475.

188. Tevosyan, speech to the XVIIIth Party Congress.

189. Ibid.

190. R. V. Ivanov-Razumnik, *Memoirs* (London, 1965), p. 246.

191. Ibid.; S. E. Zakharov et al., *Tikhookeanskiy flot* (Moscow, 1966).

192. *Novyy mir*, no. 8 (1961), pp. 160–83.

193. Petrov, *Partiynoe stroitel'stvo v sovetskoy armii i flote*, p. 301.

194. *Voenno-istoricheskiy zhurnal*, no. 6 (1963).

195. Orlov, *Secret History of Stalin's Crimes*, p. 246.

196. *Oktyabr'*, no. 12 (1988).

197. *Pravda*, 17 February 1964.

198. Boris Souvarine, *Stalin* (London, 1949), p. 258.

199. *Geroi grazhdanskoy voyny* (Moscow, 1963), p. 330.

200. Barmine, *One Who Survived*, p. 95.

201. *Oktyabr'*, no. 12 (1988).

202. *Pravda*, 3 April 1964.

203. Erickson, *Soviet High Command*, pp. 66–67.

204. *Pravda*, 7 October 1988.

205. *Nedelya*, 6 February 1989.

206. G. Lyushkov, in *Kaizo*, April 1939.

207. Nikita Khrushchev, *Khrushchev Remembers* (New York, 1970), p. 88.

## Chapter 8: The Party Crushed

1. *Pravda*, 14 April 1937.

2. I. V. Spiridonov, speech to the XXIInd Party Congress.

3. *Pravda*, 21 March 1937.

4. D. A. Lazurkina, speech to the XXIInd Party Congress.

5. *Pravda*, 30 May 1937.

6. *Pravda*, 5 June 1938.

7. Anton Ciliga, *The Russian Enigma* (London, 1940), p. 48.

8. Ibid., p. 160.

9. *Bukharin Trial*, p. 160.

10. Nikita Khrushchev, Secret Speech.

11. Ibid.

12. *Zinoviev Trial*, p. 34.

13. *Ocherki po istorii Leningrada* (Moscow and Leningrad, 1964), vol. 4, p. 381.

14. Zbigniew Brzezinski, *The Permanent Purge* (Cambridge, Mass., 1956), p. 226.

15. Lazurkina, speech to the XXIInd Party Congress.

16. Khrushchev, Secret Speech.

17. Ibid.

18. Serdyuk, speech to the XXIInd Party Congress.

19. Yu. M. Vecherova, speech to the XXIInd Party Congress.

20. Roy Medvedev, *Let History Judge* (New York, 1971), p. 347.

21. *Moscow News*, no. 48 (1988); *Ocherki istorii Ivanovskoy organizatsii KPSS* (Moscow, 1967).

22. A. N. Vasilev, "Are There Any More Questions?" *Moskva,* June 1964.

23. Merle Fainsod, *Smolensk under Soviet Rule* (Cambridge, 1958), p. 59.

24. Ibid., pp. 134–37.

25. *Bakinskiy rabochiy,* 17 June 1962.

26. Khrushchev, Secret Speech.

27. *Ural'skiy sledoput',* no. 8 (1988).

28. *Ocherki istorii partiynoy organizatsii Tatarii* (Kazan, 1962).

29. Arvo Tuominen, *The Bells of the Kremlin* (London, 1983), pp. 299ff.

30. *Voprosy istorii,* no. 9 (1988); *Ogonek,* no. 19 (1988).

31. *Literaturnaya Rossiya,* 25 March 1988.

32. Radio Moscow, 18 September 1964.

33. *Bukharin Trial,* p. 76.

34. K. T. Mazurov, speech to the XXIInd Party Congress.

35. Ibid.

36. *Sovetskaya Byelorossiya,* 11 October 1988.

37. *Rabochiy,* 8 June 1937.

38. *Izvestiya,* 23 May 1964.

39. Mazurov, speech to the XXIInd Party Congress.

40. *Rabochiy,* 12 August 1937.

41. F. Beck and W. Godin, *Russian Purge and the Extraction of Confession* (London, 1951), p. 92.

42. See Brzezinski, *Permanent Purge,* pp. 180–84.

43. See Robert Conquest, *Inside Stalin's Secret Police* (London, 1985), p. 54.

44. *Kommunist* (Yerevan), 28 November 1963.

45. Boris I. Nicolaevsky, Notes to *The Crimes of the Stalin Era* (New York, 1956).

46. *Pravda,* 23 June 1929.

47. *Pyatakov Trial,* p. 74.

48. *Bukharin Trial,* p. 304.

49. Alexander Orlov, *The Secret History of Stalin's Crimes* (New York, 1953), p. 249.

50. *Zarya vostoka,* 3 March 1989.

51. *Byuletten oppozitsii,* nos. 56–57 (1937).

52. *Voprosy istorii KPSS,* no. 5 (1963).

53. Boris Souvarine, *Stalin* (London, 1949), p. 638.

54. Medvedev, *Let History Judge,* p. 269.

55. Dzhashi, speech to the XVIIIth Party Congress.

56. *Pravda,* 17 May 1937.

57. *Ocherki istorii kommunisticheskoy partii Armenii* (Yerevan, 1967), pp. 386–87.

58. *Kommunist* (Yerevan), 15 November 1963.

59. Ibid.; Shelepin, speech to the XXIInd Party Congress.

60. Mary Matossian, *The Impact of Soviet Politics in Armenia* (Leiden, 1962); *Ocherki istorii kommunisticheskoy partii Armenii,* pp. 386–87.

61. *Kommunist* (Yerevan), 15 November 1961.

62. *Zarya vostoka,* 31 December 1937.

63. Eugenia Ginzburg, *Journey into the Whirlwind* (New York, 1967), p. 100.

64. Robert S. Sullivant, *Soviet Politics and the Ukraine, 1917–1957* (New York, 1963), p. 194.

65. S. Kossior, speech to the XIIIth Congress of the Communist Party of the Ukraine, 27 May 1937.

66. *Pravda,* 26 May 1937.

67. *Pravda,* 29 May 1937.

68. *Partiynoe stroitel'stvo,* no. 15 (1937).

69. I. V. Stalin, *Sobranie sochinenii* (Moscow, 1946–54), vol. 8, pp. 149–50.

70. Bukharin, conversation with Kamenev, July 1928.

71. G. A. Tokaev, *Comrade X* (London, 1956), p. 57.

72. Pyatakov, speech to the VIIIth Party Congress (Sullivant, *Soviet Politics and the Ukraine,* p. 32a).

73. See Robert Conquest, *The Harvest of Sorrow* (New York, 1986).

74. Sullivant, *Soviet Politics and the Ukraine,* p. 193.

75. G. Petrovsky, speech to the XVIIth Party Congress.

76. *Komsomolskoe znamya,* 22 November 1988, 23 November 1988.

77. *Posev,* vol. 6, nos. 45 and 50 (1950); Vladimir Dedijer, *Tito Speaks* (London, 1953), p. 201.

78. *Komsomolskoe znamya,* 23 November 1988.

79. Ibid.

80. Ibid.

81. *Komsomolskoe znamya,* 27 November 1988.

82. *Pravda,* 21 July 1937.

83. *Pravda,* 22 July 1937.

84. *Pravda,* 25 July 1937.

85. *Komsomolskoe znamya,* 27 November 1988.

86. Ibid.

87. *Komsomolskoe znamya,* 29 November 1988.

88. Ibid.

89. *Pravda,* 18 September 1937.

90. *Pravda,* 1 October 1937, 29 December 1937.

91. *Pravda,* 25 September 1937.

92. *Pravda,* 4 October 1937.

93. *Pravda,* 18 September 1937.

94. *Volodimir Petrovich Zatonsky* (in Ukrainian) (Kiev, 1964), p. 132.

95. *Pravda,* 19 January 1938.

96. Z. T. Serdyuk, speech to the XVIIIth Party Congress.

97. Brzezinski, *Permanent Purge,* p. 78.

98. *Pravda,* 22 February 1938.

99. Alexander Weissberg, *Conspiracy of Silence* (London, 1952), pp. 461–62.

100. *Visti,* 28 January 1938.

101. Sullivant, *Soviet Politics and the Ukraine,* p. 223.

102. Burmistenko, speech to the XVIIIth Party Congress.

103. Edward R. Stettinius, Jr., *Roosevelt and the Russians: The Yalta Conference* (Garden City, N.Y., 1949).

104. Khrushchev, Secret Speech.

105. Ibid.

106. Medvedev, *Let History Judge,* p. 43.

107. *Moskovskaya pravda,* 10 January 1989.

108. For example, *Moskovskaya pravda,* 10 February 1989.

109. Z. T. Serdyuk, speech to the XXIInd Party Congress (*Pravda,* 31 October 1961); *Moscow News,* no. 18 (1988).

110. *Oktyabr',* no. 12 (1988); *Moskovskaya pravda,* 6 April 1989.

111. *Moscow News,* no. 18 (1988).

112. R. V. Ivanov-Razumnik, *Memoirs* (London, 1965), p. 307; Orlov, *Secret History of Stalin's Crimes,* p. 241.

113. Weissberg, *Conspiracy of Silence,* p. 168.

114. *Voprosy istorii KPSS,* no. 2 (1964), p. 19.

115. *Literaturnaya gazeta,* no. 9 (1987).

116. *Sovetskaya Byelorossiya,* 22 January 1988.

117. Fitzroy Maclean, *Eastern Approaches* (London, 1949), p. 28.

118. *Československy Časopis Historicky,* no. 4 (1964).

119. Ginzburg, *Journey into the Whirlwind,* p. 115; and see German Trukans, *Yan Rudzutak* (Moscow, 1963).

120. Svetlana Alliluyeva, *Only One Year* (New York, 1969), p. 388.

121. *Bukharin Trial,* p. 277.

122. Louis Fischer, *Men and Politics* (London, 1941), p. 414.

123. Alexander Barmine, *One Who Survived* (New York, 1945), p. 307.

124. *Bukharin Trial,* p. 252.

125. Ibid., p. 55.

126. *Trud,* 26 May 1988.

127. *Bukharin Trial,* p. 777.

128. A. N. Shelepin, speech to the XXIInd Party Congress (*Pravda,* 27 October 1961).

129. *Bukharin Trial,* pp. 459–67.

130. *Pravda,* 17 November 1964.

131. Ginzburg, *Journey into the Whirlwind,* pp. 118, 139.

132. *Bukharin Trial,* p. 78.

133. Anton Antonov-Ovseenko, *The Time of Stalin* (New York, 1981), p. 127.

134. *Moscow News,* no. 15 (1988); Pavel Gol'dshtein, *Tochka opory* (Jerusalem, n.d.).

135. *Moscow News,* no. 15 (1988).

136. Khrushchev, Secret Speech.

137. *Voprosy istorii KPSS,* no. 11 (1965).

138. Nikita Khrushchev, *Khrushchev Remembers: The Last Testament* (Boston, 1974), p. 88.

139. A. S. Yakovlev, *Tsel' zhizni* (Moscow, 1966), p. 177.

140. *Izvestiya,* 19 December 1964.

141. Maroosha Fischer, *My Lives in Russia* (New York, 1944), p. 186.

142. Beck and Godin, *Russian Purge and the Extraction of Confession,* p. 80.

143. Victor Kravchenko, *I Chose Justice* (London, 1951), p. 235.

144. *Pravda,* 22 July 1937.

145. *Pravda,* 17 March 1937.

146. *Pravda,* 20 August 1937.

147. *Pravda,* 29 August 1937.

148. *Pravda,* 30 October 1937.

149. *Pravda,* 8 September 1937.

150. V. I. Lenin, *Polnoe sobranie sochineniy,* 5th ed., vol. 50 (Moscow, 1965).

151. *Bukharin Trial,* p. 764.

152. Fischer, *Men and Politics,* p. 409.

153. *Bukharin Trial,* p. 796.

154. Barmine, *One Who Survived,* p. 245.

155. *Bukharin Trial,* p. 623.

156. *Sovetskoe gosudarstvo i pravo,* no. 3 (March 1965); see also Kravchenko, *I Chose Justice,* p. 157.

157. See *Bukharin Trial,* p. 696.

158. *Oktyabr',* no. 12 (1988).

159. A. Binevich and Z. Serebryanskiy, *Andrei Bubnov* (Moscow, 1964), pp. 78–79.

160. *Voprosy istorii KPSS,* no. 4 (1963).

161. Shelepin, speech to the XXIInd Party Congress.

162. Beck and Godin, *Russian Purge and the Extraction of Confession,* p. 97.

163. Margarete [Buber] Neumann, *Under Two Dictators* (London, 1949), p. 26.

164. For example, *Pravda,* 2 May 1937, 15 June 1937, 29 October 1937.

165. *Voprosy istorii KPSS,* no. 2 (1963).

166. *Pravda,* 25 December 1964; *Voprosy istorii KPSS,* no. 7 (1964).

167. G. Maryagin, *Postyshev* (Moscow, 1965), p. 247.

168. *Voprosy istorii KPSS,* no. 7 (1965).

169. *Sovetskoe gosudarstvo i pravo,* no. 3 (March 1965).

170. *Pravda,* 7 November 1937.

171. *Pravda,* 20 December 1937.

172. *Bukharin Trial,* p. 22.

173. Ibid., p. 23.

174. Lidiya Shatunovskaya, *Zhizn' v Kremle* (New York, 1982), pp. 105–7.

175. Antonov-Ovseenko, *Time of Stalin,* p. 178.

176. *Samizdat* manuscript.

177. *Politicheskiy dnevnik,* no. 55 (1969).

178. *Pravda,* 21 December 1937.

179. *Oktyabr',* no. 12 (1988).

180. *Pamyat',* no. 3 (1980), p. 404.

181. *Pravda,* 19 January 1938.

182. *Kommunisticheskaya partiya Sovetskogo soyuza v rezolyutsiyakh i resheniyakh s''ezdov konferentsii i plenumov TsK,* 7th ed. (Moscow, 1953), vol. 2.

183. Maryagin, *Postyshev,* p. 298.

184. *Oktyabr',* no. 12 (1988).

185. Radio Moscow, 8 February 1964.

186. Peter Yakir, "Letter to the Editor of *Kommunist,*" 2 March 1969, translated in *Survey,* nos. 70–71 (1969).

187. *Pyatakov Trial,* p. 207.

188. *Stanislav Vinkentiyovich Kossior* (in Ukrainian) (Kiev, 1963), p. 173.

189. *Pravda,* 28 January 1938.

190. *Pervaya sessiia Verkhovnogo soveta SSSR* (Moscow, 1938).

191. Yu. P. Petrov, *Partiynoe stroitel'stvo v Sovetskoy armii i flote (1918–1961)* (Moscow, 1964), pp. 299–300.

192. *Kommunisticheskaya partiya Sovetskogo soyuza v rezolyutsiyakh i resheniyakh s''ezdov konferentsii i plenumov TsK,* 7th ed. (Moscow, 1954–60), vol. 2, p. 851.

193. *Trud,* 6 July 1988.

194. Roy Medvedev, *On Stalin and Stalinism* (Oxford, 1979), p. 217; *Izvestiya,* 11 August 1987.

195. Ivanov-Razumnik, *Memoirs,* p. 313.

196. See Souvarine, *Stalin,* p. 575.

197. Ivanov-Razumnik, *Memoirs,* p. 313.

198. *Izvestiya,* 11 August 1987.

## Chapter 9: Nations in Torment

1. *Nedelya,* no. 5 (1988).

2. *Argumenty i fakty,* 13–19 February 1988.

3. *Daily Mail,* 24 October 1958.

4. Ilya Ehrenburg, in *Novyy mir,* no. 5 (1962).

5. Victor Kravchenko, *I Chose Freedom* (London, 1947), p. 211.

6. *Novyy mir,* no. 9 (1961).

7. *Moskva,* no. 4 (1965).

8. *Bilshovik Ukrainy,* no. 1 (1938), p. 53.

9. *Visti,* 23 May 1938.

10. *Visti,* 17 June 1938.

11. *Visti,* 14 February 1938.

12. *XVIII s''ezd, 10–21 marta 1939 g. Stenograficheskiy otchet* (Moscow, 1939).

13. F. Beck and W. Godin, *Russian Purge and the Extraction of Confession* (London, 1951), pp. 166–71.

14. Ibid., p. 143.

15. Ibid., pp. 174–79.

16. *Ogonek,* no. 20 (1988).

17. *Sovetskaya Byelorossiya,* 3 March 1989.

18. Kravchenko, *I Chose Freedom,* p. 448.

19. Alexander Weissberg, *Conspiracy of Silence* (London, 1952), p. 364.

20. *Moscow News,* no. 42 (1988).

21. Ilya Ehrenburg, *Men, Years, Life* (New York, 1961), vol. 4, p. 45.

22. *Krug,* no. 574, p. 45.

23. Ilya Ehrenburg, in *Novyy mir,* no. 4 (1962).

24. Nikita Khrushchev, Secret Speech.

25. Zbigniew Brzezinski, *The Permanent Purge* (Cambridge, Mass., 1956), p. 205.

26. *Bukharin Trial,* p. 335.

27. See, for example, *Lithuanian Bulletin* (New York, 1945–50), vols. 3–8.

28. Report of the Credentials Commission to the XIXth Party Congress (*Pravda,* 9 October 1952).

29. Order no. 001233, quoted in *Lithuanian Bulletin;* see also Order no. 0054 of Lithuanian NKVD Commissar Gusevitius, in *The Dark Side of the Moon* (London, 1946), pp. 50–51.

30. Kravchenko, *I Chose Freedom,* p. 213.

31. *Yunost',* no. 3 (1988).

32. Eugenia Ginzburg, *Journey into the Whirlwind* (New York, 1967), p. 137.

33. Roy Medvedev, *Let History Judge* (New York, 1971), p. 234.

34. *Trud,* 7 January 1989.

35. *Sovetskaya Moldaviya,* 20 April 1989.

36. *Argumenty i fakty,* no. 18 (September 1988).

37. *Nedelya,* 1 February 1988.

38. Ehrenburg, *Men, Years, Life,* vol. 4, pp. 193ff.

39. Louis Fischer, *Men and Politics* (London, 1941), p. 409.

40. Beck and Godin, *Russian Purge and the Extraction of Confession,* pp. 88–89.

41. John A. Armstrong, *Ukrainian Nationalism* (New York, 1963), p. 274.

42. A. T. Stuchenko, *Zavidnaya nasha sudba* (Moscow, 1964), p. 65.

43. Ginzburg, *Journey into the Whirlwind,* p. 387.

44. Beck and Godin, *Russian Purge and the Extraction of Confession,* p. 88; and see Ginzburg, *Journey into the Whirlwind,* p. 25.

45. Antoni Ekart, *Vanished Without a Trace* (London, 1954), p. 283.

46. Ivan Stadniuk, "People Are Not Angels," *Neva,* no. 12 (1962).

47. *Sovetskoe gosudarstvo i pravo,* no. 3 (March 1965).

48. Nicholas Prychodko, *One of the Fifteen Million* (Boston, 1952), p. 83.

49. Anton Antonov-Ovseenko, *The Time of Stalin* (New York, 1981), p. 164–66.

50. *Tikhookeanskaya zvezda,* 9 May 1937.

51. *Sotsialistik Kazakhstan,* 23 November 1937.

52. *Kizil Uzbekistan,* 11 November 1937.

53. *Sovetskaya Kirghizia,* 11 January 1938.

54. *Kizil Uzbekistan,* 17 January 1938.

55. Abudurakhman Avtorkhanov, *The Reign of Stalin* (London, 1953), pp. 140ff, and *Narodoubistvo v SSSR* (Munich, 1952), passim.

56. A. V. Gorbatov, *Years Off My Life* (New York, 1964), p. 108.

57. Harijs Heislers, "The Unfinished Story," *Zvaigzne,* no. 23 (December 1956).

58. *Bol'shaya sovetskaya entsyklopediya,* 2nd ed. (Moscow, 1949–58).

59. Victor Kravchenko, *I Chose Justice* (London, 1951), p. 175.

60. Beck and Godin, *Russian Purge and the Extraction of Confession,* p. 132.

61. *Moscow News,* no. 39 (1988).

62. *Sovetskaya Byelorossiya,* 12 October 1988.

63. Margarete [Buber] Neumann, *Under Two Dictators* (London, 1949), p. 10.

64. *Novyy mir,* no. 12 (1961).

65. Kravchenko, *I Chose Freedom,* p. 192.

66. Ibid., pp. 192–94.

67. Gorbatov, *Years Off My Life,* p. 113.

68. See, for example, Aleksandr Solzhenitsyn, *The First Circle* (London, 1968), pp. 155, 215–16.

69. R. V. Ivanov-Razumnik, *Memoirs* (London, 1965), p. 209.

70. For example, Neumann, *Under Two Dictators,* p. 32.

71. Eleanor Lipper, *Eleven Years in Soviet Prison Camps* (London, 1951), p. 57.

72. *Prostor,* no. 1 (1989).

73. Ivanov-Razumnik, *Memoirs,* p. 349.

74. Kravchenko, *I Chose Freedom,* p. 291.

75. Weissberg, *Conspiracy of Silence,* p. 89.

76. Roy Medvedev, *Let History Judge,* rev. ed. (New York, 1989), p. 503.

77. *Radians'ka Ukraina,* 26 October 1988.

78. Beck and Godin, *Russian Purge and the Extraction of Confession,* p. 66.

79. Neumann, *Under Two Dictators,* p. 36.

80. Ibid., p. 39.

81. Ibid., p. 33.

82. Ivanov-Razumnik, *Memoirs,* p. 212.

83. Beck and Godin, *Russian Purge and the Extraction of Confession,* p. 59.

84. Ibid., p. 65.

85. Kravchenko, *I Chose Freedom,* pp. 155–56.

86. Jozsef Lengyel, *From Beginning to End* (London, 1966), p. 15.

87. Gustaw Herling, *A World Apart* (London, 1951), p. 9.

88. *Bukharin Trial,* p. 256.

89. Ivanov-Razumnik, *Memoirs,* p. 348.

90. Neumann, *Under Two Dictators,* p. 38.

91. Weissberg, *Conspiracy of Silence,* p. 469.

92. Ivanov-Razumnik, *Memoirs,* pp. 74, 116.

93. Ginzburg, *Journey into the Whirlwind,* chap. 41.

94. Beck and Godin, *Russian Purge and the Extraction of Confession,* p. 62; and see Ivanov-Razumnik, *Memoirs,* p. 314.

95. Ginzburg, *Journey into the Whirlwind,* p. 185; and see Kravchenko, *I Chose Freedom,* p. 253; Ivanov-Razumnik, *Memoirs,* p. 327.

96. See, for example, Elizabeth Lermolo, *Face of a Victim* (New York, 1955), pp. 163ff.

97. Weissberg, *Conspiracy of Silence*, p. 421.

98. Ibid., p. 432.

99. Beck and Godin, *Russian Purge and the Extraction of Confession*, p. 60.

100. See Ginzburg, *Journey into the Whirlwind*, pp. 60ff.

101. Lermolo, *Face of a Victim*, pp. 191–92.

102. Ginzburg, *Journey into the Whirlwind*, p. 149.

103. Beck and Godin, *Russian Purge and the Extraction of Confession*, p. 65.

104. For example, Ivanov-Razumnik, *Memoirs*, p. 311.

105. Lipper, *Eleven Years in Soviet Prison Camps*, p. 7.

106. A. V. Gorbatov, in *Novyy mir*, April 1964.

107. Neumann, *Under Two Dictators*, p. 39.

108. Ibid., p. 57; and see *Moscow News*, no. 47 (1988).

109. Lipper, *Eleven Years in Soviet Prison Camps*, pp. 25–29; Ginzburg, *Journey into the Whirlwind*, p. 124.

110. Ivanov-Razumnik, *Memoirs*, pp. 342ff.

111. Personal information; and see Solzhenitsyn, *First Circle*, p. 150.

112. Herling, *World Apart*, p. 9.

113. Vladimir Petrov, *Soviet Gold* (New York, 1949), passim.

114. Weissberg, *Conspiracy of Silence*, p. 89.

115. Ginzburg, *Journey into the Whirlwind*, p. 83.

116. *Trybuna Ludu*, 23 November 1961.

117. Herling, *World Apart*, p. 105.

118. Weissberg, *Conspiracy of Silence*, pp. 447–51.

119. For example, Beck and Godin, *Russian Purge and the Extraction of Confession*, p. 45.

120. Ibid., p. 87.

121. Weissberg, *Conspiracy of Silence*, p. 285.

122. Ekart, *Vanished Without a Trace*, p. 204.

123. Henry W. Morton, *Soviet Sport* (New York, 1963), pp. 186–93.

124. Medvedev, *Let History Judge*, p. 353.

125. Ivanov-Razumnik, *Memoirs*, pp. 305–6.

126. Beck and Godin, *Russian Purge and the Extraction of Confession*, p. 118.

127. Ibid., p. 119.

128. Ibid., p. 46.

129. Neumann, *Under Two Dictators*, p. 37.

130. Kravchenko, *I Chose Justice*, pp. 189–91.

131. Beck and Godin, *Russian Purge and the Extraction of Confession*, p. 46.

132. Ibid., pp. 122–23.

133. Ibid., p. 110.

134. Weissberg, *Conspiracy of Silence*, p. 326.

135. Beck and Godin, *Russian Purge and the Extraction of Confession*, p. 114.

136. Ibid., p. 154.

137. Kravchenko, *I Chose Justice*, p. 161–62.

138. Weissberg, *Conspiracy of Silence*, pp. 350–51.

139. *Pamyat'*, no. 3 (1978), p. 221.

140. Neumann, *Under Two Dictators*, p. 133.

141. *Bezbozhnik*, no. 7 (1937).

142. F. O. Oleshchuk, *Bor'ba tserkvi protiv naroda* (Moscow, 1939), pp. 85–86.

143. Ibid., p. 65.

144. Ibid., p. 87.

145. *Bolshevik*, no. 30 (1938).

146. Joseph Berger, *Shipwreck of a Generation* (London, 1971), p. 147.

147. Oleshchuk, *Bor'ba tserkvi protiv naroda*, p. 55.

148. Serdyuk, speech to the XXIInd Party Congress (*Pravda*, 31 October 1961).

149. Brzezinski, *Permanent Purge*, p. 229.

150. Neumann, *Under Two Dictators*, pp. 42–43.

151. Lermolo, *Face of a Victim*, p. 202.

152. Ibid., chap. 18; Neumann, *Under Two Dictators*, pp. 40–41.

153. Alexander Orlov, *The Secret History of Stalin's Crimes* (New York, 1953), pp. 226–27.

154. Ibid., pp. 227–28.

155. Weissberg, *Conspiracy of Silence*, pp. 407–8; and see Ivanov-Razumnik, *Memoirs*, p. 316.

156. Orlov, *Secret History of Stalin's Crimes*, p. 251; *Sovetskaya Sibir'*, 17 February 1939, 21–24 February 1939.

157. L. P. Petrovsky, "Letter to the Central Committee of the CPSU," in *For Human Rights* (Frankfurt, 1969).

158. Lipper, *Eleven Years in Soviet Prison Camps*, p. 72.

159. I. V. Spiridonov, speech to the XXIInd Party Congress.

160. Stalin, speech to the February–March plenum of the Central Committee, 3 March 1937.

161. *Itogi vsesoyuznoy perepisi naseleniya 1959 g.* (Moscow, 1962), vol. 1, pp. 161–64.

162. Ekart, *Vanished Without a Trace*, p. 156.

163. Kravchenko, *I Chose Justice*, p. 288.

164. *Sovetskoe gosudarstvo i pravo*, no. 2 (1988).

165. *Gorizont*, no. 5 (1988), p. 36.

166. B. P. Beshchev, speech to the XXIInd Party Congress.

167. N. M. Shvernik, speech to the XXIInd Party Congress.

168. Ibid.

169. Kravchenko, *I Chose Justice*, chap. 9.

170. Beck and Godin, *Russian Purge and the Extraction of Confession*, p. 99.

171. Lengyel, *From Beginning to End*, p. 14.

172. Neumann, *Under Two Dictators*, p. 49.

173. Ivanov-Razumnik, *Memoirs*, pp. 291–97.

174. Ginzburg, *Journey into the Whirlwind*, pp. 65–66.

175. For example, Gorbatov, *Years Off My Life*, p. 111.

176. Anton Ciliga, *The Russian Enigma* (London, 1940), p. 141.

177. For example, Beck and Godin, *Russian Purge and the Extraction of Confession*, p. 47.

178. Weissberg, *Conspiracy of Silence*, p. 238.

179. Beck and Godin, *Russian Purge and the Extraction of Confession*, p. 57.

180. Antonov-Ovseenko, *Time of Stalin*, p. 156.

181. *Literaturnaya gazeta*, 9 December 1987.

182. Beck and Godin, *Russian Purge and the Extraction of Confession*, p. 145.

183. *Moscow News*, no. 28 (1988).

184. Ibid., p. 147.

185. Neumann, *Under Two Dictators*, pp. 63–64.

186. N. Mandelshtam, *Hope Against Hope* (New York, 1970), p. 356.

187. Weissberg, *Conspiracy of Silence*, p. 281.

188. Ginzburg, *Journey into the Whirlwind*, p. 97.

189. Ibid., p. 122.

190. Khrushchev, Secret Speech.
191. Weissberg, *Conspiracy of Silence*, p. 238.
192. *Sovetskoe gosudarstvo i pravo*, no. 3 (1965).
193. Kravchenko, *I Chose Justice*, pp. 177–79.
194. Beck and Godin, *Russian Purge and the Extraction of Confession*, p. 102.
195. Arthur Koestler, Introduction to Weissberg, *Conspiracy of Silence*.
196. Beck and Godin, *Russian Purge and the Extraction of Confession*, p. 102.
197. Ibid.
198. Arthur Koestler, in *The God That Failed*, ed. Richard E. Crossman (London, 1950), p. 77.
199. Beck and Godin, *Russian Purge and the Extraction of Confession*, p. 46.
200. Ibid.
201. Ginzburg, *Journey into the Whirlwind*, p. 122.
202. A. Dyakov, in *Oktyabr'*, no. 7 (1964).
203. Weissberg, *Conspiracy of Silence*, p. 231.
204. Ibid., pp. 368–69.
205. Beck and Godin, *Russian Purge and the Extraction of Confession*, p. 47.
206. Ibid.
207. Lengyel, *From Beginning to End*, pp. 92–93.
208. Ivanov-Razumnik, *Memoirs*, p. 248.
209. Neumann, *Under Two Dictators*, p. 183.
210. *Izvestiya*, 6 September 1964.
211. Ginzburg, *Journey into the Whirlwind*, p. 52.
212. Ibid., pp. 130–31.
213. *Krasnaya zvezda*, 8 April 1989.
214. *Sorok let Sovetskogo prava* (Leningrad, 1957), p. 486.
215. A. A. Piontkovskiy and V. D. Menshagin, *Kurs sovetskogo ugolovnogo pravda* (Moscow, 1955), p. 187.
216. *Sorok let Sovetskogo prava*, pp. 485–504.
217. Piontkovskiy and Menshagin, *Kurs sovetskogo ugolovnogo pravda*, p. 187.
218. Kravchenko, *I Chose Justice*, p. 91.
219. *Sovetskoe gosudarstvo i pravo*, no. 3 (1965).
220. Ibid.
221. Ibid.
222. Ibid.
223. Lipper, *Eleven Years in Soviet Prison Camps*, p. 48.
224. Simon Wolin and Robert M. Slusser, *The Soviet Secret Police* (New York, 1957), p. 186.
225. Petrov, *Soviet Gold*, p. 64.
226. Wolin and Slusser, *Soviet Secret Police*, p. 188.
227. Ginzburg, *Journey into the Whirlwind*, p. 105.
228. Ibid., p. 88.
229. Blagoy Popov, *Ot Layptsigskiya protses v Sibirskie lageri* (Paris, 1979), p. 36.
230. X. Kulski, *The Soviet Regime* (Syracuse, N.Y., 1954), pp. 233–34.
231. Wolin and Slusser, *Soviet Secret Police*, passim.
232. *Sovetskoe gosudarstvo i pravo*, no. 3 (1965).
233. Ibid.
234. See Wolin and Slusser, *Soviet Secret Police*, passim; Lipper, *Eleven Years in Soviet Prison Camps*, pp. 33–34.
235. Wolin and Slusser, *Soviet Secret Police*, p. 191.
236. Ivanov-Razumnik, *Memoirs*, p. 313.

237. Ibid., p. 312.

238. Antonov-Ovseenko, *Time of Stalin*, p. 59.

239. V. Petrov and E. Petrov, *Empire of Fear* (London, 1956), p. 89.

240. Wolin and Slusser, *Soviet Secret Police*, p. 134.

241. *U.S.S.R. Laws 1937*, vol. 61, p. 266.

242. Ginzburg, *Journey into the Whirlwind*, p. 62.

243. Kravchenko, *I Chose Freedom*, p. 207.

244. Avtorkhanov, *Reign of Stalin*, p. 147.

245. I. I. Evtikhiev and V. A. Vlasov, *Administrativnoe pravo SSSR* (Moscow, 1946), p. 191; *Izvestiya TsK KPSS*, no. 10 (1989).

246. Ivanov-Razumnik, *Memoirs*, pp. 305–6; *Sovetskoe gosudarstvo i pravo*, no. 2 (1988); *Moscow News*, nos. 18 and 48 (1988).

247. Petrov and Petrov, *Empire of Fear*, 73–75.

248. *Pravda Ukrainy*, 4 May 1989.

249. Beck and Godin, *Russian Purge and the Extraction of Confession*, p. 72.

250. Spiridonov, speech to the XXIInd Party Congress.

251. *Sovetskoe gosudarstvo i pravo*, no. 3 (1965).

252. Petrov and Petrov, *Empire of Fear*, p. 71.

253. *Amtliches Material zum Massenmord von Winniza* (Berlin, 1944), p. 73; *Izvestiya*, 12 September 1988.

254. *Soviet Analyst*, 12 October 1988.

255. *Literaturnaya gazeta*, 2 November 1988.

256. *Izvestiya*, 12 November 1988; *Izvestiya TsK KPSS*, no. 4 (1989); Khrushchev, Secret Speech.

257. Kravchenko, *I Chose Justice*, pp. 281–82.

258. *Daugava*, no. 10 (1988).

259. Ibid.

260. Beck and Godin, *Russian Purge and the Extraction of Confession*, p. 46.

261. Weissberg, *Conspiracy of Silence*, p. 286.

262. Ibid., pp. 288–89.

263. Fitzroy Maclean, *Eastern Approaches* (London, 1949), pp. 40–41.

264. Ginzburg, *Journey into the Whirlwind*, p. 109.

265. Weissberg, *Conspiracy of Silence*, p. 414.

266. Beck and Godin, *Russian Purge and the Extraction of Confession*, p. 49.

267. Weissberg, *Conspiracy of Silence*, p. 414.

### Chapter 10: On the Cultural Front

1. N. M. Shvernik, speech to the XXIInd Party Congress (*Pravda*, 26 October 1961).

2. *Pravda*, 21 April 1937.

3. *Pyatakov Trial*, p. 163.

4. Ibid., p. 94.

5. Ibid., p. 217.

6. Victor Kravchenko, *I Chose Justice* (London, 1951), chap. 2.

7. F. Beck and W. Godin, *Russian Purge and the Extraction of Confession* (London, 1951), p. 154.

8. Ibid., pp. 149–65.

9. *Voprosy istorii KPSS*, no. 1 (1965).

10. Victor Kravchenko, *I Chose Freedom* (London, 1947), p. 304.

11. *Oktyabr'*, no. 12 (1988).

12. Beck and Godin, *Russian Purge and the Extraction of Confession*, p. 29.

13. Ibid., p. 37.

14. *Sovetskaya Byelorossiya*, 11 October 1988.

15. Alexander Weissberg, *Conspiracy of Silence* (London, 1952), pp. 359–60.

16. *Moscow News*, no. 17 (1988).

17. *Nedelya*, 3–9 November 1963.

18. *Moscow News*, no. 48 (1987).

19. Ibid.

20. R. V. Ivanov-Razumnik, *Memoirs* (London, 1965), p. 246.

21. Markoosha Fischer, *My Lives in Russia* (New York, 1944), p. 196.

22. A. Kuusinen, *The Rings of Destiny* (New York, 1974), p. 133; *Nedelya*, no. 45 (1988).

23. *Literaturnaya gazeta*, 9 November 1988.

24. Kuusinen, *Rings of Destiny*, p. 133.

25. *Literaturnaya gazeta*, 9 November 1988.

26. Joseph Berger, *Shipwreck of a Generation* (London, 1971), p. 23.

27. *Politicheskiy dnevnik 1965–1970* (Amsterdam, 1972), p. 726.

28. See Robert E. McCutchen, "The 1936–1937 Purge of Soviet Astronomers" (Paper presented at the 173th Meeting of the American Astronomical Society, 9 January 1989).

29. *New York Times*, 27 December 1936.

30. *Ukrains'ka Radians'ka Entsiklopediya* (Kiev, 1959–65), vol. 16, p. 600.

31. A. Nekrich, *Otreshis ot strakha* (London, 1979), p. 19.

32. For the biologist Vavilov in particular, see especially Zhores A. Medvedev, *The Rise and Fall of T. D. Lysenko* (New York, 1969); and see *Nauka i zhizn'*, no. 11 (1988); *Moscow News*, no. 46 (1987); *Ogonek*, no. 47 (1987); *Knizhnoe obozrenie*, 10 February 1989. Much of this information was also given in a book published in the USSR in the late 1960s—S. Reznik, *Nikolai Vavilov*—which, however, was later withdrawn (*Khronika*, no. 10).

33. *Pravda vostoka*, 5 September 1988; *Knizhnoe obozrenie*, 4 November 1988.

34. N. Mandelshtam, *Hope Against Hope* (New York, 1970), p. 364.

35. Ilya Ehrenburg, in *Novyy mir*, no. 4 (1962).

36. *Literaturnaya gazeta*, 28 December 1988.

37. Aleksandr Solzhenitsyn, letter to the IVth Congress of Soviet Writers (*Survey*, no. 64 [July 1967]).

38. *Moscow News*, no. 48 (1988).

39. *Literaturnaya gazeta*, 28 December 1988.

40. *Literaturnaya gazeta*, 15 August 1936, 27 August 1936; *Pravda*, 27 August 1937.

41. *Literaturnaya gazeta*, 20 April 1937; Lazar Fleishman, *Boris Pasternak v tridsatye godi* (Jerusalem, 1984), p. 407.

42. *Literaturnaya gazeta*, 15 May 1937.

43. *Literaturnaya gazeta*, 26 April 1937.

44. Pavel Gol'dshtein, *Tochka opory* (Jerusalem, n.d.), vol. 1, p. 38.

45. *Wielka Encyklopedia Powszechna PWN* (Warsaw, 1962–70); and see *Zeszyty Historycne*, no. 69 (1984); *Pamir*, no. 11 (1988).

46. Ilya Ehrenburg, *Men, Years, Life* (New York, 1961), vol. 4, p. 197.

47. *Ogonek*, no. 39 (1989).

48. F. N. Petrov, *M. V. Frunze* (Moscow, 1962).

49. *Malaya sovetskaya entsyklopediya* (Moscow, 1933–47), vol. 5.

50. See *Survey*, April–June 1961, p. 89.

51. Victor Serge, *Memoirs of a Revolutionary, 1901–1941* (London, 1963), p. 269.

52. *Pravda*, 17 May 1937.

53. Vera T. Reck, *Boris Pilnyak* (Montreal, 1975), p. 2.

54. *Moscow News*, no. 48 (1988).

55. Ivanov-Razumnik, *Memoirs*, pp. 220, 308; Ehrenburg, *Men, Years, Life*, vol. 4, pp. 185–86.

56. Reck, *Boris Pilnyak*, p. 2.

57. Alexander Orlov, *The Secret History of Stalin's Crimes* (New York, 1953), p. 196.

58. *Mikhail Koltsov kakim on byl* (Moscow, 1965), p. 75.

59. Simon Wolin and Robert M. Slusser, *The Soviet Secret Police* (New York, 1957), p. 187.

60. Margarete [Buber] Neumann, *Under Two Dictators* (London, 1949), p. 115.

61. Ivanov-Razumnik, *Memoirs*, p. 237.

62. Nikolai Klyuev, *Sochineniya* (n.p., 1969), vol. 1, pp. 148–50.

63. *Na rubezhe*, nos. 3–4 (1952).

64. *Literaturnaya gazeta*, 11 December 1964.

65. Ehrenburg, *Men, Years, Life*, vol. 4, p. 191.

66. *Bol' shaya sovetskaya entsyklopediya*, 2nd ed. (Moscow, 1949–58), vol. 2.

67. *Voprosy literatury*, November 1964.

68. Robert Conquest, *The Harvest of Sorrow* (New York, 1986), passim.

69. Hrihory Kostiuk, *Stalinist Rule in the Ukraine* (Munich, 1960), pp. 101–2.

70. *Pisateli Kazakhstana* (Alma-Ata, 1969).

71. *Revolyutsiya i natsional'nosti*, no. 8 (1937).

72. N. A. Zabolotskiy, *Stikhotvoreniya i poemy* (Moscow and Leningrad, 1965), p. 37.

73. *Times Literary Supplement*, 9 October 1981; *Pamyat'*, no. 5 (1981), pp. 336–53; *Kazakhstanskaya pravda*, 26 August 1988.

74. Pavel Antolkolsky, in *Novyy mir*, no. 4 (1966).

75. Marina Tsvetaeva, *Izbrannye proizvedeniya*, intro. V. Orlov (Moscow and Leningrad, 1964).

76. Aleksandr Solzhenitsyn, quoted in *Survey*, no. 64 (July 1967).

77. Mandelshtam, *Hope Against Hope*, pp. 3, 372, 377, 380–81, 385, 391; *Literaturnaya gazeta*, 15 June 1988.

78. Ehrenburg, *Men, Years, Life*, vol. 4, p. 190.

79. *Kazakhstanskaya pravda*, 26 August 1988.

80. Priscilla Johnson, *Khrushchev and the Arts* (Cambridge, Mass., 1965), pp. 13–14.

81. *Mladost*, 2 October 1957.

82. Mandelshtam, *Hope Against Hope*, p. 364.

83. Dmitri Shostakovich, *Testimony: The Memoirs of Dmitry Shostakovich* (New York, 1979), p. 121.

84. *Zarya vostoka*, 28 June 1963.

85. D. J. Dallin and B. I. Nicolaevsky, *Forced Labour in the Soviet Union* (London, 1948), p. 22.

86. Nikolai A. Gorchakov, *The Theater in Soviet Russia* (New York, 1957).

87. Eugenia Ginzburg, *Journey into the Whirlwind* (New York, 1967), p. 267.

88. *Pravda*, 8 January 1938.

89. Yuri [George] Annenkov, *Dnevnik moikh vstrech* (New York, 1966), vol. 2, p. 97.

90. Gorchakov, *Theater in Soviet Russia; Literaturnaya gazeta*, 27 June 1988.
91. *Sovetskaya Rossiya*, 15 February 1989.
92. *Teatral'naya entsyklopediya* (Moscow, 1961).
93. Annenkov, *Dnevnik moikh vstrech*, p. 98; see also Dallin and Nicolaevsky, *Forced Labour in the Soviet Union*, p. 123.
94. E. A. Gnedin, *Vykhod iz labarinta* (New York, 1982), p. 194.
95. Beck and Godin, *Russian Purge and the Extraction of Confession*, p. 33.
96. *Zarya vostoka*, 19 November 1961.
97. *Kazakhstanskaya pravda*, 26 August 1988.

### Chapter 11: In the Labor Camps

1. Bertrand Russell, Introduction to Gustaw Herling, *A World Apart* (London, 1951).
2. M. Z. Nikonov Smorodin, *Krasnaya katorga* (Sofia, 1938).
3. Sylvestre Mora and Pierre Zwierniak, *La Justice soviétique* (Rome, 1945).
4. D. J. Dallin and B. I. Nicolaevsky, *Forced Labour in the Soviet Union* (London, 1948).
5. Victor Kravchenko, *I Chose Justice* (London, 1951), passim.
6. *Dekrety Sovetskoy vlasti* (Moscow, 1964), vol. 3, pp. 291–92.
7. See Simon Wolin and Robert M. Slusser, *The Soviet Secret Police* (New York, 1957), p. 42.
8. *Vsya Rossiya* (Moscow, 1923), pt. 3, col. 55.
9. Kravchenko, *I Chose Justice*, p. 225.
10. Anton Ciliga, *The Russian Enigma* (London, 1940), p. 180.
11. Ibid., p. 250.
12. Ibid., p. 180.
13. *Izvestiya*, 21 December 1988.
14. V. Tikhonov, in *Literaturnaya gazeta*, 3 August 1988, p. 10.
15. S. Swianiewicz, *Forced Labour and Economic Development* (London, 1965), p. 123.
16. Dallin and Nicolaevsky, *Forced Labour in the Soviet Union*, p. 54.
17. *Tyur'ma kapitalisticheskikh stran* (Moscow, 1937), pp. 54, 61, 143.
18. Antoni Ekart, *Vanished Without a Trace* (London, 1954), p. 71.
19. Eleanor Lipper, *Eleven Years in Soviet Prison Camps* (London, 1951), p. 76.
20. Gurgen Maari, in *Voprosy literatury*, November 1964; Roy Medvedev, *Let History Judge*, rev. ed. (New York, 1989), p. 504.
21. Vladimir Petrov, *Soviet Gold* (New York, 1949).
22. Jozsef Lengyel, *From Beginning to End* (London, 1966), p. 15.
23. Margarete [Buber] Neumann, *Under Two Dictators* (London, 1949), pp. 62–63.
24. Eugenia Ginzburg, *Journey into the Whirlwind* (New York, 1967), pp. 212ff.
25. *The Dark Side of the Moon* (London, 1946), p. 666.
26. Ibid., p. 57.
27. Ibid., p. 67.
28. Ginzburg, *Journey into the Whirlwind*, p. 263.
29. A. V. Gorbatov, *Years Off My Life* (New York, 1964), pp. 125–26.
30. Ibid., p. 133.
31. Ibid., p. 129.
32. Ibid., pp. 140–41.

33. Lipper, *Eleven Years in Soviet Prison Camps*, p. 95.

34. *Dark Side of the Moon*, p. 158.

35. Neumann, *Under Two Dictators*, p. 122.

36. Lipper, *Eleven Years in Soviet Prison Camps*, p. 149.

37. Dallin and Nicolaevsky, *Forced Labour in the Soviet Union*, p. 17.

38. Kravchenko, *I Chose Justice*, p. 258.

39. Andrée Sentaurens, *L'Air du temps* (Paris, 1963).

40. Victor Kravchenko, *I Chose Freedom* (London, 1947), p. 339.

41. Sentaurens, *L'Air du temps*, passim.

42. Kravchenko, *I Chose Justice*, p. 240.

43. Dallin and Nicolaevsky, *Forced Labour in the Soviet Union*, p. 28.

44. Wolin and Slusser, *Soviet Secret Police*, p. 194.

45. *Moscow News*, no. 48 (1988).

46. *Kazakhstanskaya pravda*, 25 October 1987.

47. *Komsomolets Tadzhikistana*, 11 November 1988.

48. *Molodezh' Gruzii*, 17 November 1988; *Turkmenskaya iskra*, 24 September 1988.

49. *Kazakhstanskaya pravda*, 26 June 1989.

50. Herling, *World Apart*, pp. 21–22.

51. Boris Pasternak, *Doctor Zhivago* (New York, 1958), p. 452.

52. Dallin and Nicolaevsky, *Forced Labour in the Soviet Union*, pp. 35–36.

53. Ibid., pp. 34–35.

54. Neumann, *Under Two Dictators*, p. 72.

55. Ginzburg, *Journey into the Whirlwind*, p. 254.

56. Aleksandr Solzhenitsyn, *One Day in the Life of Ivan Denisovich*, trans. Max Hayward and Ronald Hingley (New York, 1963), p. 7.

57. Kravchenko, *I Chose Freedom*, pp. 336–41.

58. Solzhenitsyn, *One Day in the Life of Ivan Denisovich*, p. 136.

59. Ibid., p. 3.

60. *Nedelya*, no. 19 (1988).

61. Peter Yakir, "Letter to the Editor of *Kommunist*," 2 March 1969, translated in *Survey*, nos. 70–71 (1969), p. 83.

62. A. Dyakov, in *Oktyabr'*, no. 7 (1964).

63. Solzhenitsyn, *One Day in the Life of Ivan Denisovich*, p. 203.

64. Lipper, *Eleven Years in Soviet Prison Camps*, p. 144.

65. Ekart, *Vanished Without a Trace*, p. 105.

66. Julia de Beausobre [Lady Namier], *The Woman Who Could Not Die* (London, 1948).

67. *Nauka i religiya*, November 1965.

68. Solzhenitsyn, *One Day in the Life of Ivan Denisovich*, p. 203.

69. Ibid., p. 185.

70. For example, Herling, *World Apart*, p. 45.

71. Solzhenitsyn, *One Day in the Life of Ivan Denisovich*, p. 8.

72. For example, Lengyel, *From Beginning to End*, p. 31.

73. Yakir, "Letter to the Editor of *Kommunist*," p. 64.

74. Solzhenitsyn, *One Day in the Life of Ivan Denisovich*, pp. 43–44.

75. Ibid., p. 28.

76. Ibid., p. 198.

77. Ibid., p. 12; and see Ekart, *Vanished Without a Trace*, p. 57; Lipper, *Eleven Years in Soviet Prison Camps*, p. 138.

78. Solzhenitsyn, *One Day in the Life of Ivan Denisovich*, pp. 26–27.

79. Ibid., pp. 23–24.

80. Dallin and Nicolaevsky, *Forced Labour in the Soviet Union*, p. 12; see also Varlam Shalamov, "In the Bathhouse," in *Kolyma Tales*, trans. John Glad (New York, 1980), pp. 39–45.

81. Solzhenitsyn, *One Day in the Life of Ivan Denisovich*, p. 22; see also Petrov, *Soviet Gold*, p. 185.

82. Ginzburg, *Journey into the Whirlwind*, p. 264.

83. Dallin and Nicolaevsky, *Forced Labour in the Soviet Union*, p. 36.

84. Solzhenitsyn, *One Day in the Life of Ivan Denisovich*, p. 146.

85. Ibid., pp. 150ff.

86. Dallin and Nicolaevsky, *Forced Labour in the Soviet Union*, p. 18.

87. *Nedelya*, no. 19 (1988).

88. *Literaturnaya gazeta*, 4 April 1964.

89. Joseph Berger, *Shipwreck of a Generation* (London, 1971), p. 209.

90. *Nedelya*, no. 19 (1988).

91. Herling, *World Apart*, p. 41.

92. Swianiewicz, *Forced Labour and Economic Development*, pp. 21–22.

93. V. Lashkin, in *Novyy mir*, no. 1 (1964).

94. Solzhenitsyn, *One Day in the Life of Ivan Denisovich*, p. 20.

95. Ibid., p. 142.

96. For example, ibid., pp. 36–37, 166–67.

97. For example, Ginzburg, *Journey into the Whirlwind*, pp. 240, 279; Kravchenko, *I Chose Justice*, p. 237.

98. Neumann, *Under Two Dictators*, p. 124.

99. Kravchenko, *I Chose Justice*, p. 341.

100. Raphael R. Abramovitch, *The Soviet Revolution* (London, 1962), pp. 418–20.

101. *Sotsialisticheskiy vestnik*, nos. 1–3 (1951).

102. A. Kuusinen, *The Rings of Destiny* (New York, 1974), p. 160.

103. N. Mandelshtam, *Hope Against Hope* (New York, 1970), p. 387.

104. *Komsomolskaya znamya*, 14 October 1988.

105. Solzhenitsyn, *One Day in the Life of Ivan Denisovich*, pp. 193–94.

106. Ibid., p. 14.

107. Dallin and Nicolaevsky, *Forced Labour in the Soviet Union*, p. 13.

108. Ibid., p. 24.

109. Ibid., p. 37.

110. El Campesino, *Listen, Comrades* (London, 1952), p. 162.

111. Aleksandr Solzhenitsyn, *The First Circle* (London, 1968), p. 175.

112. Solzhenitsyn, *One Day in the Life of Ivan Denisovich*, p. 137.

113. Ibid., p. 41.

114. Ibid., p. 128.

115. Ekart, *Vanished Without a Trace*, p. 42.

116. Neumann, *Under Two Dictators*, p. 111.

117. Robert Conquest, *Kolyma: The Arctic Death Camps* (London, 1978), chap. 9.

118. For Kolyma, see especially Gorbatov, *Years Off My Life;* Lipper, *Eleven Years in Soviet Prison Camps;* Kravchenko, *I Chose Justice*, pp. 268–70; Wolin and Slusser, *Soviet Secret Police*, pp. 180–238; *Dark Side of the Moon*, pp. 266–315; G. Shelest, "Kolyma Notes," *Znamya*, no. 9 (1963); Shalamov, *Kolyma Tales;* Conquest, *Kolyma*.

119. Kravchenko, *I Chose Justice*, p. 269.

120. Dallin and Nicolaevsky, *Forced Labour in the Soviet Union*, p. 130.

121. Lipper, *Eleven Years in Soviet Prison Camps*, passim.

122. Dallin and Nicolaevsky, *Forced Labour in the Soviet Union*, p. 128–29.

123. Andrei D. Sakharov, *Progress, Coexistence and Intellectual Freedom* (London, 1969), p. 53.

124. Lipper, *Eleven Years in Soviet Prison Camps,* p. 93.

125. Ginzburg, *Journey into the Whirlwind,* p. 270.

126. Lipper, *Eleven Years in Soviet Prison Camps,* p. 94.

127. Ginzburg, *Journey into the Whirlwind,* p. 272.

128. Lipper, *Eleven Years in Soviet Prison Camps,* p. 90.

129. Ibid., p. 208.

130. Ibid., chap. 9.

131. Ibid., p. 108.

132. Ibid., p. 197.

133. Ibid., pp. 169–70.

134. *Dark Side of the Moon,* p. 120.

135. Ibid., p. 121.

136. *Radians'ka Ukraina,* 26 October 1988.

137. Shelest, "Kolyma Notes."

138. Ginzburg, *Journey into the Whirlwind,* chap. 55.

139. Lipper, *Eleven Years in Soviet Prison Camps,* pp. 125–33.

140. Shelest, "Kolyma Notes."

141. Ibid.

142. Kravchenko, *I Chose Justice,* p. 270.

143. Henry A. Wallace, *Soviet Asia Mission* (New York, 1945).

144. Lipper, *Eleven Years in Soviet Prison Camps,* p. 113.

145. Solzhenitsyn, *One Day in the Life of Ivan Denisovich,* p. 33.

146. *National Geographic,* December 1944.

147. Lipper, *Eleven Years in Soviet Prison Camps,* p. 253.

148. Ibid., p. 268.

149. *National Geographic,* December 1944.

150. Dallin and Nicolaevsky, *Forced Labour in the Soviet Union,* p. 38.

151. *Izvestiya,* 9 September 1988.

152. Kravchenko, *I Chose Freedom,* pp. 405–6.

153. Swianiewicz, *Forced Labour and Economic Development,* p. 39.

154. Karl Marx manuscript (*Bolshevik,* nos. 5–6 [1932]).

155. Sidney Webb and Beatrice Webb, *Soviet Communism: A New Civilization,* 2nd ed. (London, 1937), p. 585.

156. Alexander Weissberg, *Conspiracy of Silence* (London, 1952), p. 321.

157. Engineer Pobozhy, in *Novyy mir,* August 1964; *Komsomolskaya pravda,* 17 May 1988, 18 January 1989.

158. Ekart, *Vanished Without a Trace,* p. 259.

159. Swianiewicz, *Forced Labour and Economic Development,* passim.

160. Pobozhy, in *Novyy mir,* August 1964.

161. Naum Jasny, cited in Swianiewicz, *Forced Labour and Economic Development,* pp. 193–94.

162. Kravchenko, *I Chose Justice,* p. 250.

163. Lipper, *Eleven Years in Soviet Prison Camps,* p. 198.

164. Shelest, "Kolyma Notes."

165. *Dark Side of the Moon,* p. 161.

166. Dallin and Nicolaevsky, *Forced Labour in the Soviet Union,* p. 10.

167. *Dark Side of the Moon,* p. 97.

168. Christopher Hill, ed., *Rights and Wrongs* (London, 1969).

169. L. Gouré, *The Siege of Leningrad* (Oxford, 1962). More detail is given in Dmitri V. Pavlov, *Leningrad and the Blockade* (Chicago, 1965).

170. Solzhenitsyn, *One Day in the Life of Ivan Denisovich*, p. 28.

171. Ibid., pp. 84–85.

172. Ibid., p. 86.

173. Ibid., p. 69.

174. Dallin and Nicolaevsky, *Forced Labour in the Soviet Union*, p. 7.

175. Solzhenitsyn, *One Day in the Life of Ivan Denisovich*, p. 71.

176. Ibid., p. 99.

177. Ibid., p. 140.

178. Ibid., pp. 18–19.

179. Kravchenko, *I Chose Justice*, p. 235.

180. Ekart, *Vanished Without a Trace*, p. 227.

181. Lengyel, *From Beginning to End*, p. 37.

182. Ibid., pp. 37–38.

183. Solzhenitsyn, *One Day in the Life of Ivan Denisovich*, p. 81.

184. For example, Lipper, *Eleven Years in Soviet Prison Camps*, pp. 168–69.

185. Dallin and Nicolaevsky, *Forced Labour in the Soviet Union*, p. 72.

186. Herling, *World Apart*, pp. 56–57.

187. Swianiewicz, *Forced Labour and Economic Development*, p. 296.

188. Ibid., p. 297.

189. Ibid., p. 224.

190. Dallin and Nicolaevsky, *Forced Labour in the Soviet Union*, p. 38.

191. Herling, *World Apart*, p. 41.

192. Gorbatov, *Years Off My Life*, p. 130.

193. Lengyel, *From Beginning to End*, p. 15.

194. Ibid., p. 17; see also Herling, *World Apart*, p. 150.

195. F. Beck and W. Godin, *Russian Purge and the Extraction of Confession* (London, 1951), p. 76.

196. *Livre blanc sur les camps de concentration soviétiques* (Paris, 1952), p. 144.

197. Kravchenko, *I Chose Justice*, p. 259.

198. P. J. de la F. Wiles, quoted in Swianiewicz, *Forced Labour and Economic Development*, p. 17.

199. Lipper, *Eleven Years in Soviet Prison Camps*, p. 232.

200. Solzhenitsyn, *One Day in the Life of Ivan Denisovich*, p. 78.

201. Roy Medvedev, *Let History Judge* (New York, 1971), p. 45; Sakharov, *Progress, Coexistence and Intellectual Freedom*, p. 55.

202. Mosa Pijade (Yugoslav Politburo member), speech of 1 August 1951 (Vladimir Dedijer, *Tito Speaks* [London, 1953], p. 201).

203. *Nedelya*, no. 41 (1988).

204. *Moscow News*, no. 44 (1988).

205. Aleksandr Tvardovsky, "Tyorkin in the Other World," *Izvestiya*, 18 August 1963.

## Chapter 12: The Great Trial

1. V. I. Lenin, *Polnoe sobranie sochineniy*, 5th ed. (Moscow, 1964), vol. 53, Biographical Notes.

2. Ibid.

3. Peter Yakir, "Letter to the Editor of *Kommunist*," 2 March 1969, translated in *Survey*, nos. 70–71 (1969).

4. Alexander Orlov, *The Secret History of Stalin's Crimes* (New York, 1953), pp. 264, 302; Pavel Gol'dshtein, *Tochka opory* (Jerusalem, n.d.).

5. Orlov, *Secret History of Stalin's Crimes*, p. 119.

6. Vladimir Voinovich, *The Ivankiad* (New York, 1977), p. 57.

7. Fitzroy Maclean, *Eastern Approaches* (London, 1949), p. 86.

8. *Nedelya*, no. 7 (1988).

9. *Oktyabr'*, no. 12 (1988); *Izvestiya TsK KPSS*, no. 1 (1989).

10. Maclean, *Eastern Approaches*, p. 86.

11. *Bukharin Trial*, p. 36.

12. Maclean, *Eastern Approaches*, p. 86.

13. Roy Medvedev, in *New Left Review*, no. 109 (May–June 1978).

14. *Bukharin Trial*, p. 716.

15. Ibid., p. 49.

16. Ibid., p. 716.

17. Ibid., pp. 49–50.

18. Ibid., p. 51.

19. Ibid., p. 52.

20. Ibid., p. 53.

21. Ibid.

22. Ibid., p. 54.

23. Ibid., pp. 58–59.

24. Maclean, *Eastern Approaches*, p. 87.

25. *Bukharin Trial*, p. 59.

26. Ibid., p. 18.

27. Ibid., p. 81.

28. Maclean, *Eastern Approaches*, p. 98.

29. *Bukharin Trial*, p. 76.

30. Ibid., p. 83.

31. G. A. Tokaev, *Stalin Means War* (London, 1951), p. 7.

32. *Bukharin Trial*, p. 724.

33. *Pravda*, 30 October 1937.

34. *Bukharin Trial*, p. 104.

35. Ibid.

36. Ibid., p. 91.

37. Ibid., pp. 96–97.

38. Ibid., p. 109.

39. Ibid., p. 123.

40. Ibid., p. 124.

41. Ibid., pp. 131–33.

42. Ibid., p. 137.

43. Ibid., pp. 143–44.

44. Maclean, *Eastern Approaches*, pp. 92–93.

45. Ibid., p. 87.

46. G. A. Tokaev, *Comrade X* (London, 1956), p. 91.

47. *Bukharin Trial*, p. 157–58.

48. Alexander Weissberg, *Conspiracy of Silence* (London, 1952), p. 425; *Oktyabr'*, no. 12 (1988).

49. Weissberg, *Conspiracy of Silence*, p. 425; Robert Payne, *The Rise and Fall of Stalin* (London, 1966), p. 520.

50. Orlov, *Secret History of Stalin's Crimes*, pp. 291–92.

51. *Bukharin Trial*, p. 252.

52. *Chelovek i zakon*, November 1988.
53. Medvedev, in *New Left Review*.
54. *Nedelya*, no. 18 (1988).
55. *Bukharin Trial*, p. 163.
56. Ibid., p. 164.
57. Ibid., p. 210.
58. Ibid., p. 206.
59. Ibid., p. 207.
60. Ibid.
61. Ibid., p. 208.
62. Ibid., p. 217.
63. *Pravda vostoka*, 27 June 1937.
64. *Zarya vostoka*, 10 June 1937.
65. *Pravda*, 8 September 1937.
66. *Pravda*, 10 September 1937.
67. *Znamya*, no. 6 (1989); *Bukharin Trial*, p. 757.
68. *Pravda*, 12 September 1937.
69. *Pravda*, 9 April 1964.
70. *Pravda vostoka*, 10 September 1937, 11 September 1937, 12 September 1937.
71. *Pravda*, 9 April 1964.
72. *Pravda*, 27 September 1937.
73. *Bukharin Trial*, p. 348.
74. Ibid., p. 757.
75. *Pravda*, 13 September 1937.
76. *Pravda*, 20 September 1937.
77. *Pravda*, 10 September 1937, 12 September 1937.
78. *Pravda*, 23 May 1938.
79. *Bukharin Trial*, p. 234.
80. Ibid., p. 225.
81. Ibid., p. 223.
82. Ibid., p. 348.
83. Ibid., p. 351.
84. Ibid., p. 361.
85. Ibid., p. 250.
86. Alexander Barmine, *One Who Survived* (New York, 1945), pp. 228–29.
87. For example, *Pyatakov Trial*, p. 207; *Izvestiya TsK KPSS*, no. 5 (1989).
88. *Bukharin Trial*, p. 312.
89. Ibid., p. 288.
90. Ibid., p. 302.
91. Ibid., p. 248.
92. Ibid., p. 313.
93. Ibid., p. 328.
94. Ibid., p. 332.
95. Ibid., p. 333.
96. Ibid., p. 335.
97. Ibid., p. 330.
98. Ibid., p. 430.
99. Orlov, *Secret History of Stalin's Crimes*, p. 283.
100. Louis Fischer, *Russia Revisited* (London, 1957), p. 64.
101. *Podem*, December 1988.
102. *Oktyabr'*, no. 12 (1988).

103. *Yunost'*, no. 11 (1988).

104. Ibid., pp. 284–85.

105. *Bukharin Trial*, p. 424.

106. Ibid., p. 370.

107. Ibid., p. 372.

108. Ibid., p. 374.

109. Ibid., p. 376.

110. Ibid., p. 381.

111. Ibid., p. 383.

112. Ibid., p. 384.

113. Ibid., p. 407.

114. Ibid., p. 413.

115. Ibid., p. 415.

116. Ibid.

117. Ibid., p. 417.

118. Ibid., p. 419.

119. Ibid., p. 424.

120. Ibid., p. 437.

121. *Pravda*, 3 January 1924.

122. *Bukharin Trial*, p. 470.

123. Ibid., p. 474.

124. Maclean, *Eastern Approaches*, p. 99.

125. *Bukharin Trial*, p. 492.

126. *Politicheskiy dnevnik 1965–1970* (Amsterdam, 1972); Abdurakhman Avtorkhanov, *Narodoubistvo v SSSR* (Munich, 1952), pp. 707, 712; *Pamyat'*, no. 2 (1977), p. 80.

127. Anton Ciliga, *The Russian Enigma* (London, 1940), p. 292.

128. *Bukharin Trial*, p. 491.

129. Ibid., p. 504.

130. Ibid., p. 508–9.

131. *XI s''ezd RKP(b) mart–aprel' 1922 g. Stenograficheskiy otchet* (Moscow, 1961).

132. V. I. Lenin, *Polnoe sobranie sochineniy*, 5th ed. (Moscow, 1965), vol. 50.

133. *Sovetskaya istoricheskaya entsyklopediya* (Moscow, 1967), vol. 10.

134. *Pravda*, 12 September 1966, and *Voprosy istorii*, no. 6 (1967), give 1944, but in recent accounts 1941 is the date.

135. *Pravda*, 8 June 1937.

136. *Pravda*, 17 May 1937; *Izvestiya TsK KPSS*, nos. 1 and 5 (1989).

137. *Bukharin Trial*, p. 590.

138. Ibid., p. 544.

139. Ibid., p. 516.

140. Ibid., p. 546.

141. Ibid., p. 549.

142. Ibid., p. 548.

143. Ibid., p. 518.

144. Ibid., p. 519.

145. Ibid., p. 527.

146. Maclean, *Eastern Approaches*, p. 102.

147. *Bukharin Trial*, p. 525–26.

148. Ibid., p. 529.

149. Ibid., p. 530.

150. Walter Duranty, *The Kremlin and the People* (London, 1942), pp. 84–85.
151. Maclean, *Eastern Approaches,* pp. 119–20.
152. Orlov, *Secret History of Stalin's Crimes,* p. 264.
153. *Bukharin Trial,* pp. 535, 539.
154. Ibid., p. 546.
155. Ibid., p. 551.
156. Ibid., p. 511.
157. *Ogonek,* no. 7 (1988).
158. *Bukharin Trial,* p. 562.
159. Ibid., p. 564.
160. *Neva,* no. 6 (1988).
161. Maclean, *Eastern Approaches,* p. 105.
162. *Bukharin Trial,* p. 576.
163. Ibid., pp. 578–79.
164. Ibid., p. 573.
165. Ibid., pp. 577–78.
166. Orlov, *Secret History of Stalin's Crimes,* pp. 267–68.
167. *Pravda,* 8 June 1937.
168. I. M. Dubinsky-Mukhadze, *Ordzhonikidze* (Moscow, 1963), p. 5.
169. *Pravda,* 8 June 1937.
170. Gol'dshtein, *Tochka opory.*
171. Orlov, *Secret History of Stalin's Crimes,* p. 268.
172. Gol'dshtein, *Tochka opory,* p. 71.
173. *Bukharin Trial,* p. 590.
174. Ibid., p. 591.
175. Ibid., pp. 596–97.
176. Ibid., p. 608.
177. Ibid., p. 609.
178. Anton Antonov-Ovseenko, *The Time of Stalin* (New York, 1981), p. 330.
179. Gustaw Herling, *A World Apart* (London, 1951), appendix.
180. *Voprosy istorii KPSS,* no. 6 (1988).
181. *Znamya,* no. 11 (1988).
182. *Bukharin Trial,* p. 684.
183. *Sotsialisticheskiy vestnik,* no. 6 (June 1954).
184. Isaac Don Levine, *I Rediscover Russia* (New York, 1964), p. 175.
185. *Bukharin Trial,* pp. 622–23.
186. Maclean, *Eastern Approaches,* p. 107.
187. *Bukharin Trial,* p. 625.
188. Ibid., p. 626.
189. Ibid., p. 631.
190. Ibid., p. 676.
191. Ibid., p. 664.
192. Ibid., p. 679.
193. Ibid., p. 694.
194. Ibid., p. 697.
195. Ibid., p. 728.
196. Ibid., p. 734.
197. Ibid., p. 736.
198. Ibid., p. 737–38.
199. Ibid., p. 738.
200. Ibid., p. 739.

201. Ibid., pp. 740–41.

202. Ibid., p. 758.

203. Medvedev, in *New Left Review*.

204. V. Petrov and E. Petrov, *Empire of Fear* (London, 1956), p. 46.

205. *Bukharin Trial*, p. 786.

206. Ibid., p. 782.

207. Ibid., p. 769.

208. Maclean, *Eastern Approaches*, p. 110.

209. *Bukharin Trial*, p. 769.

210. Ibid., p. 770.

211. Ibid., p. 771.

212. Ibid., p. 774.

213. Ibid., p. 778.

214. Ibid., p. 779.

215. *Literaturnaya gazeta*, 15 June 1988.

216. Victor Kravchenko, *I Chose Freedom* (London, 1947), p. 283.

217. *Politika*, 21 May 1965.

218. *Conference of Historians*, 1962, p. 298.

219. Roy Medvedev, *Nikolai Bukharin* (New York, 1980), p. 164.

220. *Literaturnaya gazeta*, 23 November 1988; *Znamya*, no. 11 (1988).

221. *Moscow News*, no. 40 (1988).

222. *Moscow News*, no. 11 (1988).

223. *Znamya*, no. 10 (1988).

224. Zbigniew Brzezinski, *The Permanent Purge* (Cambridge, Mass., 1956), p. 229; Elizabeth Lermolo, *Face of a Victim* (New York, 1955), p. 207.

225. Eleanor Lipper, *Eleven Years in Soviet Prison Camps* (London, 1951), p. 15.

226. Eugenia Ginzburg, *Journey into the Whirlwind* (New York, 1967), pp. 114–15; Maroosha Fischer, *My Lives in Russia* (New York, 1944), p. 237; *Voprosy istorii*, no. 9 (1988).

227. *Teatr*, no. 7 (1988).

228. Kravchenko, *I Chose Freedom*, p. 283.

229. *Znamya*, no. 11 (1988).

230. *XVIII s''ezd, 10–21 marta 1939 g. Stenograficheskiy otchet* (Moscow, 1939), p. 26.

231. *Bukharin Trial*, p. 87.

232. For example, ibid., pp. 80, 185–86, 235.

233. For example, ibid., pp. 182–83, 201, 293–94, 303, 314, 318–19.

234. For example, ibid., pp. 71, 80.

## Chapter 13: The Foreign Element

1. Ignazio Silone, in *The God That Failed*, ed. Richard H. Crossman (London, 1950), pp. 109ff.

2. Anton Ciliga, *The Russian Enigma* (London, 1940), p. 61.

3. *Conference of Historians*, 1962, p. 69; *Kommunist*, no. 10 (1963).

4. *Conference of Historians*, 1962, p. 286.

5. *Osteuropa*, no. 8 (1958), p. 33.

6. Arvo Tuominen (former Secretary-General of the Finnish Communist Party), *Kremls Klockor* (Helsinki, 1958), p. 210 (quoted in Milorad M. Drachkovitch and Branko Lazitch, eds., *The Comintern—Historical Highlights* [New York, 1966], p. 161).

7. Margarete [Buber] Neumann, *Under Two Dictators* (London, 1949), p. 8.

8. Arthur Koestler, *Arrow in the Blue* (London, 1945), vol. 2, p. 209.

9. Neumann, *Under Two Dictators*, p. 5.

10. Ibid., p. 23.

11. Ibid., p. 168.

12. Ibid., p. 143.

13. Herbert Wehner, *Erinnerungen* (Bonn, 1957), p. 160.

14. Elisabeth K. Poretsky, *Our Own People* (London, 1969), p. 181.

15. Neumann, *Under Two Dictators*, p. 171.

16. F. Beck and W. Godin, *Russian Purge and the Extraction of Confession* (London, 1951), p. 108; *Beiträge zur Geschichte der Arbeiterbewegung* 1 (1969).

17. A. Kuusinen, *The Rings of Destiny* (New York, 1974), pp. 156–57.

18. Neumann, *Under Two Dictators*, p. 55.

19. Ibid., p. 53.

20. Eugenia Ginzburg, *Journey into the Whirlwind* (New York, 1967), p. 118.

21. Beck and Godin, *Russian Purge and the Extraction of Confession*, p. 109.

22. Ibid.

23. R. V. Ivanov-Razumnik, *Memoirs* (London, 1965), p. 307.

24. Koestler, *Arrow in the Blue*, vol. 2, p. 407; Ruth Fischer, *Stalin and German Communism* (London, 1948).

25. Gustaw Herling, *A World Apart* (London, 1951), p. 62.

26. Alexander Weissberg, *Conspiracy of Silence* (London, 1952), pp. 487–89.

27. *Moscow News*, no. 48 (1988).

28. Beck and Godin, *Russian Purge and the Extraction of Confession*, p. 76.

29. Victor Serge, *Memoirs of a Revolutionary, 1901–1941* (London, 1963), p. 187.

30. Arvo Tuominen, in *Uusi Kavalehti*, nos. 10–13 (22 June 1956), and *The Bells of the Kremlin* (London, 1983), pp. 221–23; *Ogonek*, no. 45 (1988).

31. Kun Béláné, *Kun Béla* (Budapest, 1966), pp. 489–90. (The date of his arrest is here given as the end of June, which conflicts with other accounts.)

32. Ciliga, *Russian Enigma*, p. 253.

33. Walter G. Krivitsky, *In Stalin's Secret Service* (London, 1939), p. 217.

34. Ibid., p. 219; *Voprosy istorii KPSS*, no. 3 (1989).

35. Ivanov-Razumnik, *Memoirs*, p. 315.

36. Hungarian News Agency, 10 February 1989.

37. *Small Polish Encyclopedia* (Warsaw, 1958).

38. Kun Béláné, *Kun Béla*.

39. Eleanor Lipper, *Eleven Years in Soviet Prison Camps* (London, 1951), p. 16.

40. Ivanov-Razumnik, *Memoirs*, p. 315.

41. Renato Mieli, *Togliatti 1937* (Milan, 1964); Guelfa Zaccaria, *200 Communiste Italiani tra le vittime dello Stalinismo* (Milan, 1964).

42. Paoli Robotti, speech to the Central Committee of the Italian Communist Party, December 1961.

43. Ginzburg, *Journey into the Whirlwind*, pp. 169–70.

44. Tito, speech to the Central Committee of the Yugoslav Communist League, 19 April 1954 (*Borba*, 20 April 1969); speech to the IXth Party Congress, 11 March 1969; and see *Kommunist* (Belgrade), 3 April 1969.

45. Fitzroy Maclean, *Disputed Barricade* (London, 1957), pp. 103–4.

46. Tuominen, in *Uusi Kavalehti*.

47. Kuusinen, *Rings of Destiny*, pp. 146, 158.

48. Ivan Karaivanov, *Liudi i Pigmeji* (Belgrade, 1953), p. 112.

49. Ivanov-Razumnik, *Memoirs*, p. 308.

50. Victor Kravchenko, *I Chose Justice* (London, 1951), p. 279.

51. *Zarya na Komunizma*, 22 September–3 October 1988; and see Blagoy Popov, *Ot Layptsigskiya protses v Sibirskie lageri* (Paris, 1979), p. 23.

52. John D. Bell, *The Bulgarian Communist Party from Blagoev to Zhivkov* (Stanford, Calif., 1986), pp. 49–51.

53. Popov, *Ot Layptsigskiya protses v Sibirskie lageri*, p. 12.

54. Jerzy Morawski (Secretary of the Polish Central Committee), speech of 27 March 1956; and see *Voprosy istorii KPSS*, no. 12 (1988).

55. *Wielka Encyklopedia Powszechna PWN* (Warsaw, 1962–70).

56. Wehner, *Erinnerungen*, pp. 141–42.

57. Neumann, *Under Two Dictators*, p. 6.

58. *Voprosy istorii KPSS*, no. 12, 1988.

59. Ibid.

60. *Kommunist International*, nos. 1–3 (1938).

61. *Voprosy istorii KPSS*, no. 12 (1988).

62. Neumann, *Under Two Dictators*, pp. 8–9.

63. Ibid., p. 19.

64. *Survey*, no. 32 (1960).

65. Ibid.

66. *Voprosy istorii KPSS*, no. 8 (1965).

67. Roy Medvedev, *Let History Judge* (New York, 1971), p. 46.

68. Alfred Burmeister, *Dissolution and Aftermath of the Comintern* (New York, 1955), pp. 1–4; Kuusinen, *Rings of Destiny*, pp. 40–46; *Sotsialisticheskiy vestnik*, 18 March 1938.

69. Neumann, *Under Two Dictators*, p. 34.

70. *Bukharin Trial*, p. 575.

71. Alexander Orlov, *The Secret History of Stalin's Crimes* (New York, 1953), p. 229.

72. Ibid., pp. 230–31.

73. Ibid., p. 232.

74. Ibid., p. 233.

75. Ibid., p. 238; *Sovetskiy voin*, no. 4 (1989).

76. For example, *Pravda*, 17 December 1936.

77. Jesús Hernández, *Yo fui un ministro de Stalin* (Mexico City, 1953).

78. Julián Gorkin, "L'Assassinat d'Andrés Nin," Commission pour la Vérité sur les Crimes de Staline, *Bullétin d'information*, no. 1 (May 1962).

79. Ibid.

80. *Novyy mir*, no. 5 (1962).

81. El Campesino, *Listen, Comrades* (London, 1952), p. 35.

82. *Materiaux pour l'histoire de notre temps*, nos. 3–4 (1985).

83. Beck and Godin, *Russian Purge and the Extraction of Confession*, p. 108.

84. *Materiaux pour l'histoire de notre temps*, nos. 3–4 (1985).

85. *Observer*, 10 October 1965.

86. See Isaac Deutscher, *The Prophet Outcast* (London, 1963), p. 175.

87. *Byuletten oppozitsii*, no. 33 (1932).

88. See Bertram D. Wolfe, *Three Who Made a Revolution* (London, 1966), p. 520.

89. Adam B. Ulam, *The Bolsheviks* (New York, 1965), pp. 573–75.

90. Ciliga, *Russian Enigma*, p. 85.

91. Isaac Don Levine, *The Mind of an Assassin* (London, 1959), p. 27.

92. D. J. Dallin, in *New Leader*, 19–26 March 1956.

93. Levine, *Mind of an Assassin*, p. 41; see also Commission pour la Vérité sur les Crimes de Staline, *Bullétin d'information*, no. 1 (May 1962).

94. V. Petrov and E. Petrov, quoted in Levine, *Mind of an Assassin*, p. 50.

95. Ibid., p. 188.

96. E. Castro Delgado, *J'ai perdu la foi à Moscou* (Paris, 1950).

## Chapter 14: Climax

1. Yu. P. Petrov, *Partiynoe stroitel'stvo v Sovetskoy armii i flote (1918–1961)* (Moscow, 1964), p. 301.

2. *Voprosy istorii KPSS*, no. 1 (1965).

3. *Stanislav Vinkentiyovich Kossior* (Kiev, 1963), p. 174.

4. Nikita Khrushchev, Secret Speech.

5. Ibid.

6. V. Drobizhev and N. Dumova, *V. Ya. Chubar: Biograficheskiy ocherk* (Moscow, 1963), pp. 65–71.

7. Khrushchev, Secret Speech.

8. *Bukharin Trial*, p. 107.

9. Khrushchev, Secret Speech.

10. *Izvestiya TsK KPSS*, no. 4 (1989).

11. *Nedelya*, 6 February 1989; *Voenno-istoricheskiy zhurnal*, no. 6 (1989).

12. Khruschev, Secret Speech.

13. *Ogonek*, no. 36 (1987); and see *Moscow News*, no. 44 (1988).

14. *Izvestiya*, 11 August 1987.

15. *Literaturnaya gazeta*, 1 June 1988.

16. Anton Antonov-Ovseenko, *The Time of Stalin* (New York, 1981), p. 127.

17. *Moscow News*, no. 15 (1988).

18. Zbigniew Brzezinski, *The Permanent Purge* (Cambridge, Mass., 1956), p. 229.

19. A. Kuusinen, *The Rings of Destiny* (New York, 1974), p. 167.

20. Ibid., pp. 136–37.

21. *Moscow News*, 3 January 1988.

22. Margarete [Buber] Neuman, *Under Two Dictators* (London, 1949), p. 55.

23. Eleanor Lipper, *Eleven Years in Soviet Prison Camps* (London, 1951), p. 15.

24. For example, Boris Nicolaevsky, in *New Leader*, 16 January 1956.

25. Boris I. Nicolaevsky, *Power and the Soviet Elite* (New York, 1965), p. 122.

26. Abdurakhman Avtorkhanov, *The Reign of Stalin* (London, 1953), p. 80.

27. Svetlana Alliluyeva, *Only One Year* (New York, 1969), p. 388.

28. Alexander Weissberg, *Conspiracy of Silence* (London, 1952), p. 39; see also NKVD Lieutenant A. Zhigunov, quoted in John A. Armstrong, *The Politics of Totalitarianism* (New York, 1961).

29. Abdurakhman Avtorkhanov, *Narodoubistvo v SSSR* (Munich, 1952), p. 223.

30. *Bukharin Trial*, p. 426.

31. Ibid., pp. 290–91.

32. Alexander Barmine, *One Who Survived* (New York, 1945), p. 8.

33. Nina Murray, *I Spied for Stalin* (New York, 1951), chap. 6.

34. *Molodoy kommunist*, no. 1 (January 1962).

35. Ilya Ehrenburg, in *Novyy mir*, no. 4 (1964).

36. E. A. Gnedin, *Vykhod iz labarinta* (New York, 1982).

37. Ehrenburg, in *Novyy mir*.

38. *Sovetskaya istoricheskaya entsyklopediya* (Moscow, 1961–76).

39. *Novyy mir,* no. 11 (1964); and see *Sotsialisticheskaya zakonnost',* no. 10 (1988).

40. See Robert Conquest, *Inside Stalin's Secret Police* (London, 1985), p. 134.

41. Barmine, *One Who Survived,* p. 21.

42. Blagoy Popov, *Ot Layptsigskiya protses v Sibirskie lageri* (Paris, 1979), p. 62.

43. Jonathan Haslam, *The Soviet Union and the Struggle for Collective Security* (London, 1984), p. 149.

44. Raskolnikov, open letter to Stalin, 17 August 1939 (*Samizdat I* [Paris, 1969], p. 97).

45. S. Pavlov, speech to the November 1962 plenum of the Central Committee of the CPSU.

46. *Izvestiya,* 14 November 1963.

47. Popov, *Ot Layptsigskiya protses v Sibirskie lageri,* p. 3.

48. *Komsomolskaya znamya,* 21 October 1988.

49. Merle Fainsod, *How Russia Is Ruled,* 2nd ed. (London, 1963), pp. 423–25.

50. Shkiryatov and Poskrebyshev, speeches to the XVIIIth Party Congress; *Isvestiya,* 14 November 1963; *Pravda,* 14 November 1963; *Aleksandr Kosarev* (Moscow, 1963), pp. 111–12.

51. See Armstrong, *Politics of Totalitarianism,* p. 75.

52. Dr. S. Ploss, in *Problems of Communism,* September–October 1958.

53. *Moskovskii komsomolets,* 8 June 1988; *Komsomolskaya znamya,* 21 October 1988.

54. *Moskovskii komsomolets,* 8 June 1988.

55. Admiral N. G. Kuznetsov, in *Oktyabr',* no. 11 (1964).

56. See E. Wollenberg, *The Red Army* (London, 1938); Edgar O'Ballance, *The Red Army* (London, 1964), p. 121.

57. Geoffrey Bailey, *The Conspirators* (London, 1961), p. 229.

58. *Na rubezhe,* March 1952.

59. Bailey, *Conspirators,* p. 229.

60. R. V. Ivanov-Razumnik, *Memoirs* (London, 1965), p. 311.

61. Kuznetsov, in *Oktyabr'.*

62. Marshal Rokossovsky, in *Krasnaya zvezda,* 13 December 1964.

63. *Voenno-istoricheskiy zhurnal,* no. 12 (1965); *Kommunist vooruzhenykh sil,* no. 16 (1989).

64. Mekhlis, speech to the XVIIIth Party Congress.

65. On Lyushkov, see Alvin D. Coox, in *Soviet Studies,* January 1968.

66. John Erickson, *The Soviet High Command* (London, 1962), p. 494; A. Svetlanin, *Dalnevostochniy zagovor* (Frankfurt, 1953), pp. 103ff.

67. *V. K. Blyukher* (Moscow, 1963).

68. *Biographical Directory of the USSR* (New York, 1958).

69. N. Kondryatsev, *Marshal Blyukher* (Moscow, 1965).

70. Roy Medvedev, *All Stalin's Men* (Garden City, N.Y., 1984), pp. 14–15.

71. Tass, 22 February 1964.

72. Kondryatsev, *Marshal Blyukher,* p. 292.

73. This account is based on those given in Kondryatsev, *Marshal Blyukher,* and V. Dushenkin, *Ot Soldata do marshala* (Moscow, 1961).

74. *Voprosy istorii KPSS,* no. 11 (1964).

75. Dushenkin, *Ot Soldata do marshala,* p. 223.

76. *Oktyabr',* no. 12 (1988).

77. *Nedelya,* 22–28 February 1988.

78. Antonov-Ovseenko, *Time of Stalin,* p. 190.

79. F. W. Deakin and G. R. Storry, *The Case of Richard Sorge* (London, 1966).

80. *Pravda,* 2 November 1938.

81. *Pravda,* 16 December 1938.

82. Conquest, *Inside Stalin's Secret Police,* pp. 81–84.

83. *Pravda,* 22 January 1939.

84. Roy Medvedev, *On Stalin and Stalinism* (Oxford, 1979), pp. 109–16; Alinger Manuscript, Nicolaevsky Archive, Hoover Institution Archives.

85. Roy Medvedev, *Let History Judge* (New York, 1971), pp. 240–41.

86. Zhigunov interrogation (captured German documents [National Archives, microfilm, T84, roll 287]).

87. *Ogonek,* no. 7 (1988).

88. *Ogonek,* no. 18 (1988).

89. See their sponsoring organizations at the XVIIIth Party Congress.

90. A. V. Gorbatov, *Years Off My Life* (New York, 1964), p. 110.

91. *Oktyabr',* no. 12 (1988).

92. Weissberg, *Conspiracy of Silence,* pp. 311–12.

93. Ivanov-Razumnik, *Memoirs,* p. 323; Joseph Berger, *Shipwreck of a Generation* (London, 1971), p. 37.

94. *Oktyabr',* no. 12 (1988).

95. *Pravda,* 22 October 1938.

96. F. Beck and W. Godin, *Russian Purge and the Extraction of Confession* (London, 1951), p. 146.

97. Weissberg, *Conspiracy of Silence,* p. 12; *Visti,* 29–31 December 1938.

98. Weissberg, *Conspiracy of Silence,* pp. 411–12.

99. Khrushchev, Secret Speech.

100. Ibid.

101. Ibid.

102. *Oktyabr',* no. 12 (1988).

103. *Sovetskaya molodezh,* 13 February 1988.

104. Medvedev, *Let History Judge,* p. 295.

105. Kuusinen, Rings of Destiny, p. 139.

106. *SSSR: Vnutrenie protivorechiya,* no. 3 (1982).

107. *Kommunist Kazakhstana,* no. 8 (1938).

108. *Izvestiya,* 27 November 1988; *Sovetskaya Byelorossiya,* 22 January 1989.

109. See Conquest, *Inside Stalin's Secret Police,* p. 70.

110. *Izvestiya,* 12 November 1988.

111. *Stanislav Vinkentiyovich Kossior,* p. 174; *Pravda,* 3 April 1964.

112. Lipper, *Eleven Years in Soviet Prison Camps,* p. 16.

113. Peter Yakir, "Letter to the Editor of *Kommunist,*" 2 March 1969, translated in *Survey,* nos. 70–71 (1969).

114. Kuusinen, *Rings of Destiny,* p. 139.

115. *Pravda,* 3 April 1964.

116. *Sovetskaya molodezh,* 18 February 1988; *Ogonek,* no. 7 (1988).

117. F. Bega and V. Aleksandrov, *Petrovskiy* (Moscow, 1963), p. 315.

118. *Izvestiya,* 15 September 1966; L. P. Petrovsky, "Letter to the Central Committee of the CPSU," in *For Human Rights* (Frankfurt, 1969).

119. *Voprosy istorii KPSS,* no. 2 (1963).

120. *Ukrains'ka Radians'ka Entsyklopediya* (Kiev, 1959–65).

121. Bega and Aleksandrov, *Petrovskiy,* p. 304.

122. L. Davydov, comp., *U istokov partii* (Moscow, 1963).

123. Beck and Godin, *Russian Purge and the Extraction of Confession,* p. 132.

124. Ivanov-Razumnik, *Memoirs,* p. 316.

125. Bega and Aleksandrov, *Petrovskiy,* pp. 304–5.

126. Ibid., pp. 305–6.

127. Compiled by Professor Tibor Szamuely.

128. Medvedev, *Let History Judge,* p. 295.

129. *Pravda,* 6 May 1953.

130. *Izvestiya,* 4 September 1918.

131. *Conference of Historians,* 1962, p. 260.

132. Jerzy Walenczyk, "Meditations," *Po Prostu,* 23 December 1956.

133. *Conference of Historians,* 1962, p. 260.

134. Antonov-Ovseenko, *Time of Stalin,* p. 140.

135. Khrushchev, Secret Speech.

136. Roy Medvedev, *Fau-il rehabiliter Staline?* (Paris, 1969), p. 42; *Izvestiya TsK KPSS,* no. 12 (1989).

137. J. Stalin, *Problems of Leninism* (Moscow, 1947), p. 625.

138. Khrushchev, Secret Speech.

139. Boris Nicolaevsky, Notes to *The Crimes of the Stalin Era* (New York, 1956).

140. *Pravda,* 3 April 1964.

141. *Sovetskaya istoricheskaya entsyklopediya;* and see I. A. Kozlov et al., *Severny flot* (Moscow, 1966); *Voenno-istoricheskiy zhurnal,* no. 7 (1965).

142. *Sovetskaya kul'tura,* 26 November 1988; *Izvestiya TsK KPSS,* nos. 1 and 3 (1989); *Nedelya,* no. 27 (1989); *Pravda Ukrainy,* 6 May 1989.

143. Brzezinski, *Permanent Purge,* p. 229.

## Chapter 15: Heritage of Terror

1. Ilya Ehrenburg, *Men, Years, Life* (New York, 1961), vol. 4, p. 196.

2. R. V. Ivanov-Razumnik, *Memoirs* (London, 1965), pp. 304–7.

3. F. Beck and W. Godin, *Russian Purge and the Extraction of Confession* (London, 1951), pp. 182–83.

4. Ibid., pp. 93, 203.

5. Adolf Hitler, *Mein Kampf,* trans. James Murphy (London, 1939), p. 171.

6. Beck and Godin, *Russian Purge and the Extraction of Confession,* p. 194.

7. George Lukács, in *Nuovi Argomenti,* October 1962.

8. See Boris Souvarine, *Stalin* (London, 1949), p. 661.

9. Zhores A. Medvedev, *The Rise and Fall of T. D. Lysenko* (New York, 1961), p. 267.

10. Commission pour la Vérité sur les Crimes de Staline, *Bullétin d'information,* no. 3 (January 1964).

11. Ibid.

12. See Robert Conquest, *The Nation Killers* (London, 1970).

13. *Ogonek,* no. 28 (1987).

14. *Ogonek,* no. 25 (1989); *Politicheskoe obrazovanie,* no. 5 (1989); *Kommunist vooruzhenykh sil,* no. 12 (1989).

15. Nikita Khrushchev, Secret Speech.

16. *Izvestiya TsK KPSS,* no. 4 (1989).

17. *Znamya,* May 1964.

18. V. A. Anfilov, *Nachalo velikoy otechestvennoy voiny* (Moscow, 1962), p. 28.

19. A. V. Gorbatov, *Years Off My Life* (New York, 1964), p. 134.

20. Yu. P. Petrov, *Partiynoe stroitel'stov v Sovetskoy armii i flote (1918–1961)* Moscow, 1964), p. 304.

21. Khrushchev, Secret Speech.

22. Ibid.

23. Mekhlis, speech to the XVIIIth Party Congress *(XVIII s''ed, 10–12 marta 1939 g. Stenograficheskiy otchet* [Moscow, 1939], p. 276).

24. John Erickson, *The Soviet High Command* (London, 1962), p. 583.

25. Ibid.

26. Ibid., p. 552.

27. See *Nazi Conspiracy and Aggression* (Washington, D.C., 1946), vol. 6, p. 981.

28. See Erickson, *Soviet High Command*, p. 566.

29. Petrov, *Partiynoe stroitel'stvo v Sovetskoy armii i flote*, p. 332.

30. Erickson, *Soviet High Command*, p. 583.

31. Ibid., p. 578.

32. Ehrenburg, *Men, Years, Life*, vol. 4, p. 256.

33. Ilya Ehrenburg, in *Novyy mir*, no. 4 (1964).

34. *Voprosy istorii*, no. 9 (1988).

35. *Nauka i zhizn'*, no. 2 (1989).

36. Ibid.

37. *Voprosy istorii*, no. 8 (1988).

38. See Erickson, *Soviet High Command*, chap. 17.

39. Isaac Deutscher, *Stalin* (London, 1949), p. 486.

40. *Ogonek*, no. 25 (1989).

41. Konstantin Simonov, in *Znamya*, May 1964; *Sovetskiy voin*, no 1 (1989).

42. S. T. Biryuzov, *Sovetskii soldat na Balkanakh* (Moscow, 1963), pp. 140–41.

43. *Novyy mir*, no. 1 (1965).

44. Gustaw Herling, *A World Apart* (London, 1951), pp. 175–76.

45. Ibid., pp. 221–24.

46. Beck and Godin, *Russian Purge and the Extraction of Confession*, pp. 189–90.

47. Victor Kravchenko, *I Chose Justice* (London, 1951), p. 405.

48. Ibid., p. 282.

49. Joseph Berger, *Shipwreck of a Generation* (London, 1971), p. 204.

50. Boris Pasternak, *Doctor Zhivago* (New York, 1958).

51. *Pravda*, 27 June 1945.

52. *Komsomolskaya pravda*, 15 November 1964.

53. See Khrushchev, speech of 9 December 1963.

54. Personal information; see also Aleksandr Solzhenitsyn, *One Day in the Life of Ivan Denisovich*, trans. Max Hayward and Ronald Hingley (New York, 1963).

55. V. I. Lenin, *The Development of Capitalism in Russia* (1899).

56. *Kommunist*, no. 17 (November 1962).

57. V. Frolov, in *Voprosy filosofii*, no. 3 (1967).

58. See Souvarine, *Stalin*, pp. 578–79.

59. *Voprosy istorii*, no. 1 (1964).

60. V. V. Parin, in *Literaturnaya gazeta*, 24 February 1962.

61. K. N. Plotnikov, in *Conference of Historians*, 1962.

62. D. G. Sturua, speech to the All-Union Conference on Ideological Work, 25–28 December 1961.

63. A. Sumbat-Zade, in *Conference of Historians*, 1962, p. 338.

64. *Oktyabr'*, no. 2 (1949).

65. *Pravda*, 1 August 1951.

66. *John Cornford: A Memoir*, ed. Pat Sloan (London, 1938), p. 178.

67. "Letter of an Old Bolshevik," in Boris I. Nicolaevsky, *Power and the Soviet*

*Elite* (New York, 1965), p. 64; Walter G. Krivitsky, *In Stalin's Secret Service* (London, 1939), p. 207.

68. Victor Serge, *Memoirs of a Revolutionary, 1901–1941* (London, 1963), p. 318.

69. Julian Symons, *The Thirties* (London, 1960), p. 142.

70. *New Leader,* 10 October 1964.

71. Bertolt Brecht, "The Informer," in *New Writing,* n.s., vol. 2 (London, 1939).

72. *Bol'shaya sovetskaya entsyklopediya,* 2nd ed. (Moscow, 1954), vol. 28.

73. *Komsomolskaya pravda,* 2 September 1962.

74. *Preuves,* March 1953.

75. Arthur Koestler, *Arrow in the Blue* (London, 1945), vol. 2, p. 208.

76. Symons, *Thirties,* p. 143.

77. Sidney Webb and Beatrice Webb, *Soviet Communism: A New Civilization,* 2nd ed. (London, 1937), pp. 586–88.

78. Jerzy Gliksman, *Tell the West* (New York, 1948).

79. Herling, *World Apart,* p. 11.

80. D. N. Pritt, *From Right to Left* (London, 1966), pp. 109–11.

81. Walter Duranty, *The Kremlin and the People* (London, 1942), p. 37.

82. Ibid., p. 59.

83. Owen Lattimore, in *Pacific Affairs,* September 1938.

84. Joseph Davies, dispatch of 7 March 1938; see also Joseph Davies, *Mission to Moscow* (London, 1942), vol. 1, p. 39.

85. Webb and Webb, *Soviet Communism,* p. 1156.

86. Ibid., p. 1145.

87. Ibid., p. 114.

88. Ibid. p. 1153.

89. Harold J. Laski, *Law and Justice in Soviet Russia* (London, 1935), p. 21.

90. John Maynard, *The Russian Peasant and Other Studies* (London, 1942), p. 252.

91. Bernard Pares, *A History of Russia* (London, 1962), p. 584.

92. Bernard Pares, *Russia* (London, 1940), p. 33.

93. Introduction to Bernard Pares, *History of Russia.*

94. Bernard Shaw, letter to the Secretary of the British Committee for the Defence of Leon Trotsky, 21 July 1937 (quoted in Isaac Deutscher, *The Prophet Outcast* [London, 1963], p. 369).

95. J. Dallin and B. I. Nicolaevsky, *Forced Labour in the Soviet Union* (London, 1948).

96. Kravchenko, *I Chose Justice,* p. 134–35.

97. Ibid.

98. Stephen Spender, in *The God That Failed,* ed. Richard H. Crossman (London, 1950), p. 256.

99. Pat Sloan, *Soviet Democracy* (London, 1937), p. 111.

100. Pat Sloan, *Russia Without Illusions,* preface by B. Webb (London, 1938), p. 246.

101. *Spectator,* 3 June 1966.

102. Dallin and Nicolaevsky, *Forced Labour in the Soviet Union,* p. 33.

103. *Yunost',* no. 1 (1965).

104. Decision of a Joint Meeting of the Central Committee of the CPSU, the Council of Ministers of the USSR, and the Presidium of the Supreme Soviet (*Pravda,* 7 March 1953).

105. Resolution of the Central Committee of the Communist Party of the Soviet Union (*Pravda*, 2 July 1956).

106. Palmiro Togliatti, "Nine Questions on Stalinism," *Nuovi Argomenti*, 16 June 1956.

107. Tass, 1 February 1963.

108. *Program of the C.P.S.U.* (Moscow, 1961), pt. 1, sec. 3.

109. *Sovetskoe gosudarstvo i pravo*, no. 1 (1956).

110. *Pravda*, 26 December 1958.

111. *Moscow News*, no. 18 (1988).

112. *Politika*, 16 October 1962.

113. *Conference of Historians*, 1962, p. 298.

114. *History of the U.S.S.R.* (Moscow, 1968), book 2, vol. 3, pp. 103, 523.

115. *Kommunist*, no. 3 (February 1969); and see L. P. Petrovsky, "Letter to the Central Committee of the CPSU," in *For Human Rights* (Frankfurt, 1969).

116. *Kazakhstanskaya pravda*, 17 January 1965.

117. *Pravda*, 30 January 1966.

118. *Kommunist*, no. 3 (February 1969).

119. Ibid.

120. Roy Medvedev, *On Stalin and Stalinism* (Oxford, 1979), p. 180–81.

121. Rosa Luxemburg, *The Russian Revolution* (Ann Arbor, Mich., 1961), p. 71.

### Epilogue: The Terror Today

1. *Christian Science Monitor*, 16 January 1987.

2. *Agitator*, no. 18 (1988).

3. *Moscow News*, no. 18 (1988).

4. *Sotsialisticheskaya industriya*, 29 January 1989.

5. For example, *Yunost'*, no. 3 (1988).

6. For example, *Radians'ka Ukraina*, 26 October 1988.

7. For example, *Moskovskii komsomolets*, 24 February 1988.

8. For example, *Nedelya*, no. 15 (1988).

9. Jerry Hough, *How the Soviet Union Is Governed* (London, 1979), p. 176.

10. J. Arch Getty, *Origins of the Great Purge* (New York, 1985), p. 8.

11. *Sovetskaya Byelorossiya*, 14 July 1988; *Ogonek*, no. 51 (1987).

12. *Literaturnaya gazeta*, 9 August 1989.

13. *Moscow News*, no. 42 (1988).

14. *Moscow News*, no. 48 (1988).

15. Ibid.

16. Joseph Berger, *Shipwreck of a Generation* (London, 1971), p. 266.

17. *Izvestiya*, 4 May 1989.

18. *Izvestiya*, 12 March 1988.

# BIBLIOGRAPHY

## Books and Articles

Abramovitch, Raphael R. *The Soviet Revolution*. London, 1962.
Adler, Frederick. *The Witchcraft Trial in Moscow*. London, 1936.
*Aleksandr Kosarev*. Moscow, 1963.
Aleksandrov, P. N., et al. *Komandarm Uborevich*. Moscow, 1964.
Alliluyeva, Svetlana. *Only One Year*. New York, 1969.
———. *Twenty Letters to a Friend*. London, 1967.
*Amtliches Material zum Massenmord von Winniza*. Berlin, 1944.
Anfilov, V. A. *Nachalo velikoy otechestvennoy voiny*. Moscow, 1962.
Annenkov, Yuri [George]. *Dnevnik moikh vstrech*. 2 vols. New York, 1966.
Antonov-Ovseenko, Anton. *The Time of Stalin*. New York, 1981.
Armstrong, John A. *The Politics of Totalitarianism*. New York, 1961.
———. *Ukrainian Nationalism*. New York, 1963.
d'Astier de la Vigerie, Emmanuel. *Staline*. Paris, 1936.
Avtorkhanov, Abdurakhman. *Narodoubistvo v SSSR*. Munich, 1952.
———. *The Reign of Stalin*. London, 1953.
———. *Stalin and the Soviet Communist Party*. London, 1959.
Bailey, Geoffrey. *The Conspirators*. London, 1961.
Balabanoff, Angelica. *Impressions of Lenin*. Ann Arbor, Mich., 1964.
Barmine, Alexander. *One Who Survived*. New York, 1945.
Bazhanov, B. *Stalin der Rote Diktator*. Berlin, 1931.
Beausobre, Julia de [Lady Namier]. *The Woman Who Could Not Die*. London, 1948.
Beck, F., and W. Godin. *Russian Purge and the Extraction of Confession*. London, 1951.
Bega, F., and V. Alkesandrov. *Petrovskiy*. Moscow, 1963.
Bell, John D. *The Bulgarian Communist Party from Blagoev to Zhivkov*. Stanford, Calif., 1986.
Berger, Joseph. *Shipwreck of a Generation*. London, 1971.
Beria, Lavrentiy. *Questions of the History of the Bolshevik Organizations in Transcaucasia*. Moscow, 1935.
Binevich, A., and Z. Serebryanskiy. *Andrei Bubnov*. Moscow, 1964.
*Biographical Directory of the USSR*. New York, 1958.

Biryuzov, Marshal S. T. *Sovetskii soldat na Balkanakh*. Moscow, 1963.

*Bol'shaya sovetskaya entsyklopediya*. 1st ed. Moscow, 1926–47.

*Bol'shaya sovetskaya entsyklopediya*. 2nd ed. Moscow, 1949–58.

*Bol'shaya sovetskaya entsyklopediya*. 3rd ed. Moscow, 1970–78.

Brecht, Bertolt. "The Informer." In *New Writing*, n.s., vol. 2. London, 1939.

Broué, Pierre. *Le Parti bolchevique*. Paris, 1963.

———. *Le Procès de Moscou*. Paris, 1964.

Burmeister, Alfred. *Dissolution and Aftermath of the Comintern*. New York, 1955.

Brzezinski, Zbigniew. *The Permanent Purge*. Cambridge, Mass., 1956.

El Campesino. *Listen, Comrades*. London, 1952.

Carr, E. H. *Socialism in One Country*. 3 vols. London, 1958.

Castro Delgado, E. *J'ai perdu la foi à Moscou*. Paris, 1950.

Charlton, Michael. *The Eagle and the Small Birds*. Chicago, 1984.

Churchill, Winston. *The Second World War*. 6 vols. London, 1948–50.

Ciliga, Anton. *The Russian Enigma*. London, 1940.

Coates, W. P., and Zelda K. Coates, comps. *The Moscow Trial*. London, 1937.

Conquest, Robert. *The Harvest of Sorrow*. New York, 1986.

———. *Inside Stalin's Secret Police*. London, 1985.

———. *Kolyma: The Arctic Death Camps*. London, 1978.

———. *The Nation Killers*. London, 1970.

———. *Power and Policy in the U.S.S.R.* London, 1961.

———. *Stalin and the Kirov Murder*. New York, 1989.

Crossman, Richard H., ed. *The God That Failed*. London, 1950.

Dallin, D. J., and B. I. Nicolaevsky. *Forced Labour in the Soviet Union*. London, 1948.

Daniels, Robert V. *The Conscience of the Revolution*. Oxford, 1960.

*The Dark Side of the Moon*. London, 1946.

Davies, Joseph. *Mission to Moscow*. 2 vols. London, 1942.

Davydov, L., comp. *U istokov partii*. Moscow, 1963.

Deakin, F. W., and G. R. Storry. *The Case of Richard Sorge*. London, 1966.

Dedijer, Vladimir. *Tito Speaks*. London, 1953.

*Dekrety Sovetskoy vlasti*. Vol. 3. Moscow, 1964.

Deriabin, P., and F. Gibney. *The Secret World*. London, 1960.

Deutscher, Isaac. *The Prophet Outcast*. London, 1963.

———. *The Prophet Unarmed*. London, 1959.

———. *Stalin*. London, 1949.

*Deviatyi s''ezd professional'nykh soyuzov. Stenograficheskiy otchet*. Moscow, 1933.

Dewey Commission. *Not Guilty*. New York, 1937.

Dimitrov, Georgi. *Selected Articles*. London, 1951.

Djilas, Milovan. *Conversations with Stalin*. London, 1962.

———. *The New Class*. London, 1957.

Drachkovitch, Milorad M., and Branko Lazitch, eds. *The Comintern—Historical Highlights*. New York, 1966.

Drobizhev, V., and N. Dumova. *V. Ya. Chubar: Biograficheskiy ocherk*. Moscow, 1963.

Dubinskiy, I. V. *Naperekor vetram*. Moscow, 1964.

Dubinskiy-Mukhadze, I. M. *Ordzhonikidze*. Moscow, 1963.

Duranty, Walter. *The Kremlin and the People*. London, 1942.

Dushenkin, V. *Ot Soldata do marshala*. Moscow, 1961.

*Eesti Noukogude Entsüklopeedia* (Estonian Soviet encyclopedia).

Ehrenburg, Ilya. *Men, Years, Life*. 4 vols. New York, 1961.

*XVIII s''ezd, 10–21 marta 1939 g. Stenograficheskiy otchet*. Moscow, 1939.

Ekart, Antoni. *Vanished Without a Trace*. London, 1954.

*XI s"ezd RKP (b) mart–aprel' 1922 g. Stenograficheskiy otchet*. Moscow, 1961.

Erickson, John. *The Soviet High Command*. London, 1962.

Evtikhiev, I. I., and V. A. Vlasov. *Administrativnoe pravo SSSR*. Moscow, 1946.

Fainsod, Merle. *How Russia Is Ruled*. 2nd ed. London, 1963.

———. *Smolensk under Soviet Rule*. Cambridge, 1958.

Fischer, Louis. *The Life of Lenin*. London, 1965.

———. *Men and Politics*. London, 1941.

———. *Russia Revisited*. London, 1957.

Fischer, Maroosha. *My Lives in Russia*. New York, 1944.

Fischer, Ruth. *Stalin and German Communism*. London, 1948.

Fleishman, Lazar. *Boris Pasternak v tridsatye gody*. Jerusalem, 1984.

*XIV s"ezd Vsesoyuznoy kommunisticheskoy partii (b) 18–31 dekabrya 1925 g. Stenograficheskiy otchet*. Moscow and Leningrad, 1926.

Gaglov, L., and I. Selishchev. *Komissary*. Moscow, 1961.

*Geroi grazhdanskoy voyny*. Moscow, 1963.

Getty, J. Arch. *Origins of the Great Purge*. New York, 1985.

Ginzburg, Eugenia. *Journey into the Whirlwind*. New York, 1967.

Gliksman, Jerzy. *Tell the West*. New York, 1948.

Gnedin, E. A. *Vykhod iz labarinta*. New York, 1982.

Gol'dshtein, Pavel. *Tochka opory*. Jerusalem, n.d.

Gorbatov, A. V. *Years Off My Life*. New York, 1964.

Gorchakov, Nikolai A. *The Theater in Soviet Russia*. New York, 1957.

Gorkin, Julián. "L'Assassinat d'Andrés Nin." Commission pour la Vérité sur les Crimes de Staline. *Bullétin d'information*, no. 1 (May 1962).

Gouré, L. *The Siege of Leningrad*. Oxford, 1962.

Grossman, Vassili. *In the Town of Berdichev*.

Haslam, Jonathan. *The Soviet Union and the Struggle for Collective Security*. London, 1984.

Herling, Gustaw. *A World Apart*. London, 1951.

Hernández, Jesús. *Yo fui un ministro de Stalin*. Mexico City, 1953.

Hill, Christopher. ed. *Rights and Wrongs*. London, 1969.

*History of the U.S.S.R.* Moscow, 1968.

Hitler, Adolf. *Mein Kampf*. Translated by James Murphy. London, 1939.

Hoettl, Wilhelm. *The Secret Front*. London, 1954.

Hough, Jerry. *How the Soviet Union Is Governed*. London, 1979.

*Itogi vsesoyuznoy perepisi naseleniya 1959 g.* Moscow, 1962.

Ivanov-Razumnik, R. V. *Memoirs* London, 1965.

Johnson, Priscilla. *Khrushchev and the Arts*. Cambridge, Mass., 1965.

Karaivanov, Ivan. *Liudi i Pigmeji*. Belgrade, 1953.

Khrushchev, Nikita. " 'Confidential Report' to the XXth Party Congress." In *The Crimes of the Stalin Era*. New York, 1956.

———. *Khrushchev Remembers*. New York, 1970.

———. *Khrushchev Remembers: The Last Testament*. Boston, 1974.

Klyuev, Nikolai. *Sochineniya*. N.p., 1969.

Koestler, Arthur. *Arrow in the Blue*. 2 vols. London, 1945.

———. *Darkness at Noon*. London, 1940.

*Kommunisticheskaya partiya Sovetskogo soyuza v rezolyutsiyakh i resheniyakh s"ezdov konferentsii i plenumov TsK* (The Communist Party of the Soviet Union in resolutions, etc.) 7th ed. 2 vols. Moscow, 1953.

*Kommunisticheskaya partiya Sovetskogo soyuza v rezolyutsiyakh i resheniyakh s''ezdov konferentsii i plenumov TsK* (The Communist Party of the Soviet Union in resolutions, etc.) 7th ed. 3 vols. Moscow, 1954–60.

Kondrayatsev, N. *Marshal Blyukher*. Moscow, 1965.

Koritskiy, N. I., et al. *Marshal Tukhachevskiy*. Moscow, 1965.

Kostiuk, Hrihory. *Okayanni Roki*. Toronto, 1978.

———. *Stalinist Rule in the Ukraine*. Munich, 1960.

Kozlov, I. A., et al. *Severny flot*. Moscow, 1966.

Krasnikov, S. V. *S. M. Kirov v Leningrade*. Leningrad, 1966.

*Kratkaya Literaturnaya Entsyklopediya*. 9 vols. Moscow, 1962–78.

Kravchenko, Victor. *I Chose Freedom*. London, 1947.

———. *I Chose Justice*. London, 1951.

Krivitsky, Walter G. *In Stalin's Secret Service*. London, 1939.

Kulski, X. *The Soviet Regime*. Syracuse, N.Y., 1954.

Kun Béláné. *Kun Béla*. Budapest, 1966.

Kuusinen, A. *The Rings of Destiny*. New York, 1974.

Laski, Harold J. *Law and Justice in Soviet Russia*. London, 1935.

Lengyel, Jozsef. *From Beginning to End*. London, 1966.

Lenin, V. I. *Polnoe sobranie sochineniy*. 5th ed. 55 vols. Moscow, 1958–65.

———. *Sobranie sochineniy*. 3rd ed. 30 vols. Moscow, 1926–37.

Lermolo, Elizabeth. *Face of a Victim*. New York, 1955.

Levine, Isaac Don. *I Rediscover Russia*. New York, 1964.

———. *The Mind of an Assassin*. New York, 1959.

Lipper, Eleanor. *Eleven Years in Soviet Prison Camps*. London, 1951.

*Livre blanc sur les camps de concentration soviétiques*. Paris, 1952.

Loebl, Evzen [Eugen], and Dusan Pokorny. *Die Revolution Rehabilitiert Ihre Kinder*. Vienna, 1968.

London, Artur. *L'Aveu*. Paris, 1969.

Luxemburg, Rosa. *The Russian Revolution*. Ann Arbor, Mich., 1961.

Maclean, Fitzroy. *Disputed Barricade*. London, 1957.

———. *Eastern Approaches*. London, 1949.

*Malaya sovetskaya entsyklopediya*. Moscow, 1933–47.

Mandelshtam, N. *Hope Abandoned*. New York, 1974.

———. *Hope Against Hope*. New York, 1970.

Maryagin, G. *Postyshev*. Moscow, 1965.

Matossian, Mary. *The Impact of Soviet Politics in Armenia*. Leiden, 1962.

Maynard, John. *The Russian Peasant and Other Studies*. London, 1942.

*Mazoji Lietuviskoji Tarybine Enciklopedija* (Latvian Soviet encyclopedia).

McCutchen, Robert E. "The 1936–1937 Purge of Soviet Astronomers." Paper presented at the 173th Meeting of the American Astronomical Society, 9 January 1989.

Medvedev, Roy. *All Stalin's Men*. Garden City, N.Y., 1984.

———. *Faut-il rehabiliter Staline?* Paris, 1969.

———. *Let History Judge*. New York, 1971.

———. *Let History Judge*. Rev. ed. New York, 1989.

———. *Nikolai Bukharin*. New York, 1980.

———. *On Stalin and Stalinism*. Oxford, 1979.

Medvedev, Zhores. *The Rise and Fall of T. D. Lysenko*. New York, 1969.

Micunović, Veljko. *Moscow Diary*. New York, 1986.

Mieli, Renato. *Togliatti 1937*. Milan, 1964.

*Mikhail Koltsov kakim on byl*. Moscow, 1965.

Mora, Sylvestre, and Pierre Zwierniak. *La Justice soviétique*. Rome, 1945.

Morton, Henry W. *Soviet Sport*. New York, 1963.

Murray, Nina. *I Spied for Stalin*. New York, 1951.

*Nazi Conspiracy and Aggression*. 16 vols. Washington, D.C., 1946.

Nekrich, A. *Otreshis ot strakha*. London, 1979.

Neumann, Margarete [Buber]. *Under Two Dictators*. London, 1949.

Nicolaevsky, Boris I. *Power and the Soviet Elite*. New York, 1965.

Nikonov-Smorodin, M. Z. *Krasnaya katorga*. Sofia, 1938.

Nikulin, Lev. *Marshal Tukhachevskiy*. Moscow, 1964.

O'Ballance, Edgar. *The Red Army*. London, 1964.

*Ocherki istorii Ivanovskoy organizatsii KPSS*. Moscow, 1967.

*Ocherki istorii kommunisticheskoy partii Armenii*. Yerevan, 1967.

*Ocherki istorii partiynoy organizatsii Tatarii*. Kazan, 1962.

*Ocherki po istorii Leningrada*. 4 vols. Moscow and Leningrad, 1964.

Oleshchuk, F. O. *Bor'ba tserkvi protiv naroda*. Moscow, 1939.

Orlov, Alexander. *The Secret History of Stalin's Crimes*. New York, 1953.

Pankov, D. V. *Komkor Eideman*. Moscow, 1965.

Pares, Bernard. *A History of Russia*. London, 1962.

―――. *Russia*. London, 1940.

Pasternak, Boris. *Doctor Zhivago*. New York, 1958.

Pavlov, Dmitri V. *Leningrad and the Blockade*. Chicago, 1965.

Payne, Robert. *The Rise and Fall of Stalin*. London, 1966.

*Pervaya sessiia Verkhovnogo soveta SSSR*. Moscow, 1938.

Petrov, F. N. *M. V. Frunze*. Moscow, 1962.

Petrov, V., and E. Petrov. *Empire of Fear*. London, 1956.

Petrov, Vladimir. *Soviet Gold*. New York, 1949.

Petrov, Yu. P. *Partiynoe stroitel'stvo v Sovetskoy armii i flote (1918–1961)*. Moscow, 1964.

Petrovsky, L. P. "Letter to the Central Committee of the CPSU." In *For Human Rights*. Frankfurt, 1969.

Piontkovskiy, A. A., and V. D. Menshagin. *Kurs sovetskogo ugolovnogo prava*. Moscow, 1955.

*Pisateli Kazakhstana*. Alma-Ata, 1969.

*Pod znamenam Ispanskoy respubliki*. Moscow, 1965.

Popov, Blagoy. *Ot Layptsigskiya protses v Sibirskie lageri*. Paris, 1979.

Poretsky, Elisabeth K. *Our Own People*. London, 1969.

Pritt, D. N. *From Right to Left*. London, 1966.

*Program of the C.P.S.U.* Moscow, 1961.

Prychodko, Nicholas. *One of the Fifteen Million*. Boston, 1952.

Radek, Karl. *Portraits and Pamphlets*. London, 1935.

Rauschning, Herman. *Hitler Speaks*. New York, 1940.

Reck, Vera T. *Boris Pilnyak*. Montreal, 1975.

*Report of the Court Proceedings in the Case of the Anti-Soviet "Bloc of Rights and Trotskyites."* Moscow, 1938. *[Bukharin Trial]*

*Report of the Court Proceedings in the Case of the Anti-Soviet Trotskyite Centre*. Moscow, 1937. *[Pyatakov Trial]*

*Report of the Court Proceedings: The Case of the Trotskyite–Zinovievite Terrorist Centre*. Moscow, 1936. *[Zinoviev Trial]*

Roeder, Bernhard. *Katorga: An Aspect of Modern Slavery*. London, 1958.

Rybakov, A. *Tridsat' pyatyi i drugye gody*. Moscow, 1989.

Sakharov, Andrei D. *Progress, Coexistence and Intellectual Freedom*. London, 1969.

*Samizdat I*. Paris, 1969.

Saunders, George, ed. *Samizdat: Voices of the Soviet Opposition.* New York, 1974.

Schapiro, Leonard. *The Communist Party of the Soviet Union.* London, 1960.

Schellenberg, W. *The Schellenberg Memoirs.* London, 1956.

Sentaurens, Andrée. *L'Air du temps.* Paris, 1963.

Serge, Victor. *From Lenin to Stalin.* London, 1937.

———. *Memoirs of a Revolutionary, 1901–1941.* London, 1963.

*VII s''ezd Vsesoyuznogo Leninskogo kommunisticheskogo soyuza molodezhi.* Moscow and Leningrad, 1926.

*XVII s''ezd Vsesoyuznoy kommunisticheskoy partii (b) 26 yanvarya–10 fevralya 1934 g. Stenograficheskiy otchet* (The XVIIth Party Congress). Moscow, 1934.

Shalamov, Varlam. *Kolyma Tales.* New York, 1980.

Shatunovskaya, Lidiya. *Zhizn' v Kremle.* New York, 1982.

Shostakovich, Dmitri. *Testimony: The Memoirs of Dmitry Shostakovich.* New York, 1979.

Sinelnikov, S. *Sergei Mironovich Kirov: Zhizn' i deyatel'nost'.* Moscow, 1964.

*XVI s''ezd Vsesoyuznoy kommunisticheskoy partii (bol'sheviki). Stenograficheskiy otchet* (Report of the XVIth Party Congress). Moscow, 1930.

Slater, Humphrey. *The Heretics.* New York, 1947.

Sloan, Pat. *Russia Without Illusions.* London, 1938.

———. *Soviet Democracy.* London, 1937.

———, ed. *John Cornford: A Memoir.* London, 1938.

*Small Polish Encyclopedia.* (Warsaw, 1958).

Solzhenitsyn, Aleksandr. *The First Circle.* London, 1968.

———. *The Gulag Archipelago.* 3 vols. New York, 1973.

———. *One Day in the Life of Ivan Denisovich.* Translated by Max Hayward and Ronald Hingley. New York, 1963.

*Sorok let sovetskogo prava.* Leningrad, 1957.

Souvarine, Boris. *Stalin.* London, 1949.

*Sovetskaya istoricheskaya entsyklopediya.* 16 vols. Moscow, 1961–76.

Stalin, Joseph. *Notes of a Delegate.* London, 1941.

———. *Problems of Leninism.* Moscow, 1947.

———. *Sobranie sochinenii.* 13 vols. Moscow, 1946–54.

*Stanislav Vinkentiyovich Kossior.* (In Ukrainian) Kiev, 1963.

Starinkov, L. T. *Miny zhdut svoego chasa.* Moscow, 1964.

Stettinius, Edward R., Jr. *Roosevelt and the Russians: The Yalta Conference.* Garden City, N.Y., 1949.

Stuchenko, A. T. *Zavidnaya nasha sudba.* Moscow, 1964.

Stypulkowski, Z. *Invitation to Moscow.* London, 1951.

Sullivant, Robert S. *Soviet Politics and the Ukraine, 1917–1957.* New York, 1963.

Svetlanin, A. *Dalnevostochniy zagovor.* Frankfurt, 1953.

Swianiewicz, S. *Forced Labour and Economic Development.* London, 1965.

Symons, Julian. *The Thirties.* London, 1960.

*Teatral'naya entsyklopediya.* Moscow, 1961.

Tokaev, G. A. *Betrayal of an Ideal.* London, 1954.

———. *Comrade X.* London, 1956.

———. *Stalin Means War.* London, 1951.

Trotsky, Leon. *My Life.* 2 vols. London, 1930.

Trukans, German. *Yan Rudzutak.* Moscow, 1963.

Tsvetaeva, Marina. *Izbrannye proizvedeniya.* Moscow and Leningrad, 1965.

Tuominen, Arvo. *The Bells of the Kremlin.* London, 1983.

*Tyur'ma kapitalisticheskikh stran.* Moscow, 1937.

*Ukrains'ka Radians'ka Entsiklopediya.* Kiev, 1959–65.

*Ukrains'ka Radians'kii Entsiklopedichnii Slovnik.* Kiev, 1966.

Ulam, Adam B. *The Bolsheviks.* New York, 1965.

Ulyanovskaya, N., and M. Ulyanovskaya. *Istoriia odnoy sem'i.* New York, 1982.

*U.S.S.R. Laws 1937.*

*V. K. Blyukher.* Moscow, 1963.

Voinovich, Vladimir. *The Ivankiad.* New York, 1977.

*Volodimir Petrovich Zatonsky* (in Ukrainian). Kiev, 1964.

*Vsesoyuznaya kommunisticheskaya partiya (b) v rezolyutsyakh i resheniyakh s''ezdov, konferentsii i plenumov TsK* (The All-Union Communist Party [Bolsheviks] in resolutions, etc.) 5th ed. 2 vols. Moscow, 1936.

*Vsesoyuznoe soveschchanie o merakh uluchsheniya podgotovki nauchno-pedagogicheskikh kadrov po istoricheskim naukam.* (The All-Union Conference on Measures to Improve the Training of Scientific-Pedagogic Cadres in the Historical Sciences [18–21 December 1962]). Moscow, 1964. [*Conference of Historians,* 1962]

*Vsya Rossiya.* Moscow, 1923.

Vyshinskiy, Andrei. *Sudostroitel'stvo v SSSRR.* 3rd ed. Moscow, 1936.

Wallace, Henry A. *Soviet Asia Mission.* New York, 1945.

Webb, Sidney, and Beatrice Webb. *Soviet Communism: A New Civilization.* 2nd ed. London, 1937.

Wehner, Herbert. *Erinnerungen.* Bonn, 1957.

Weissberg, Alexander. *Conspiracy of Silence.* London, 1952.

Wells, H. G. *The Outline of History.* New York, 1971.

*Wielka Encyklopedia Powszechna PWN.* Warsaw, 1962–70.

Wolfe, Bertram D. *Three Who Made a Revolution.* London, 1966.

Wolin, Simon, and Robert M. Slusser. *The Soviet Secret Police.* New York, 1957.

Wollenberg, E. *The Red Army.* London, 1938.

Yakir, P. I., and Ya. A. Geller. *Komandarm Yakir.* Moscow, 1963.

Yakovlev, A. S. *Tsel' zhizni.* Moscow, 1966.

Zabolotskiy, N. A. *Stikhotvoreniya i poemy.* Leningrad and Moscow, 1965.

Zaccaria, Guelfa. *200 Communiste Italiani tra le vittime dello Stalinismo.* Milan, 1964.

Zakharov, S. E., et al. *Tikhookeanskiy flot.* Moscow, 1966.

### Periodicals

*Agitator*

*Argumenty i fakty*

*Bakinskiy rabochiy*

*Beiträge zur Geschichte der Arbeiterbewegung*

*Bezbozhnik*

*Bilshovik Ukrainy*

*Bolshevik*

*Borba* (Belgrade)

*Byelarus*

*Byuletten oppozitsii*

*Československy Časopis Historicky*

*Chelovek i zakon*

*Christian Science Monitor*

*Daily Mail*

*Daugava* (Riga)
*Druzhba narodov*
*Gorizont*
*Grani*
*Izvestiya*
*Izvestiya TsK KPSS*
*Kaizo*
*Kazakhstanskaya pravda*
*Khronika*
*Kizil Uzbekistan*
*Knizhnoe obozrenie*
*Kommunist*
*Kommunist* (Belgrade)
*Kommunist* (Yerevan)
*Kommunist International*
*Kommunist Kazakhstana*
*Kommunist vooruzhenykh sil*
*Komsomolets Tadzhikistana*
*Komsomolskaya pravda*
*Komsomolskoe znamya*
*Krasnaya zvezda*
*Krug*
*Leningradskaya pravda*
*Leningradskiy rabochiy*
*Literaturnaya gazeta*
*Literaturnaya Rossiya*
*Materiaux pour l'histoire de notre temps*
*Mladost* (Belgrade)
*Molodezh' Gruzii*
*Molodoy kommunist*
*Moscow News*
*Moskovskaya pravda*
*Moskovskii komsomolets*
*Moskva*
*Na rubezhe* (Paris)
*National Geographic*
*Nauka i religiya*
*Nauka i zhizn'*
*Nedelya* (*Izvestiya* weekly supplement)
*Neva*
*New Leader*
*New Left Review*
*Nova mysl*
*Novaya i noveyshaya istoriya*
*Novyy mir*
*Nuovi Argomenti*
*Observer*
*Ogonek*
*Oktyabr'*
*Osteuropa*
*Pacific Affairs*

*Pamir*
*Pamyat'*
*Partiynoe stroitel'stvo*
*Podem*
*Politicheskiy dnevnik*
*Politicheskoe obrazovanie*
*Politika*
*Po Prostu* (Warsaw)
*Posev*
*Pravda*
*Pravda Ukrainy*
*Pravda vostoka*
*Preuves*
*Problems of Communism*
*Prostor*
*Rabochiy* (Minsk)
*Radians'ka Ukraina*
*Revolyutsiya i natsional'nosti*
*Rundschau*
*Sobesednik*
*Socialdemocraten*
*Sotsialisticheskaya industriya*
*Sotsialisticheskiy vestnik*
*Sotsialisticheskaya zakonnost'*
*Sotsialistik Kazakhstan*
*Sovetskaya Bukovina*
*Sovetskaya Byelorossiya*
*Sovetskaya Kirghizia*
*Sovetskaya kul'tura*
*Sovetskaya Moldaviya*
*Sovetskaya molodezh*
*Sovetskaya Rossiya*
*Sovetskaya Sibir'*
*Sovetskiy voin*
*Sovetskoe gosudarstvo i pravo*
*Soviet Affairs*
*Soviet Analyst*
*Soviet Studies*
*Spectator*
*SSSR: Vnutrenie protivorechiya*
*Survey*
*Teatr*
*Tikhookeanskaya zvezda*
*Trud*
*Trybuna Ludu* (Warsaw)
*Turkmenskaya iskra*
*Ural'skiy sledoput'*
*Uusi Kavalehti* (Helsinki)
*Vechernyy Leningrad*
*Visti* (Kiev)
*Voenno-istoricheskiy zhurnal*

*Voprosy filosofii*
*Voprosy istorii*
*Voprosy istorii KPSS*
*Voprosy literatury*
*Yunost'*
*Zarya na Komunizma* (Lovech)
*Zarya vostoka*
*Zeszyty Historycne*
*Znamya*
*Zvaigzne* (Riga)

# INDEX